The Jews in Soviet Russia since 1917

Alice Nakhimovsky

The Jews in Soviet Russia since 1917

Edited by
LIONEL KOCHAN

Bearsted Reader in Jewish History, University of Warwick

Third Edition

Published for the
Institute of Jewish Affairs, London
OXFORD UNIVERSITY PRESS
OXFORD LONDON NEW YORK
1978

Oxford University Press, Walton Street, Oxford OX2 6DP

OXFORD LONDON GLASGOW
NEW YORK TORONTO MELBOURNE WELLINGTON
IBADAN NAIROBI DAR ES SALAAM LUSAKA CAPE TOWN
KUALA LUMPUR SINGAPORE JAKARTA HONG KONG TOKYO
DELHI BOMBAY CALCUTTA MADRAS KARACHI

© Oxford University Press, 1970, 1972, and 1978

First published 1970
Second edition 1972
Third edition 1978

British Library Cataloguing in Publication Data
The Jews in Soviet Russia since 1917.—3rd ed.
  1. Jews in Russia—History
  I. Kochan, Lionel   II. Institute of Jewish Affairs
947'.004'924   DS135.R92   77–30424
ISBN 0–19–281199–1

Printed in Great Britain by
The Camelot Press Ltd, Southampton

Contents

         R. AINSZTEIN

14   Antisemitism in Soviet Russia   300
         B. D. WEINRYB

15   After the Six-Day War   333
         ZEV KATZ

16   The 'Jewish Question' in the Open: 1968–71   349
         PHILIPPA LEWIS

17   The Soviet-Jewish Problem: Internal and International Developments
         1972–1976   366
         LUKASZ HIRSZOWICZ

     Epilogue   410
         L. KOCHAN

     Index   413

Notes on Contributors

C. ABRAMSKY Born Minsk, 1916. Studied history and philosophy at the Hebrew University, Jerusalem. Goldsmid Professor of Jewish history at University College, London; formerly Senior Research Fellow, St. Antony's College, Oxford. Joint author with Dr. Henry Collins of *Karl Marx and the British Labour Movement, 1860–1874* (1965). Author of numerous articles on modern Jewish art. At present working on a book on the political and philosophical ideas of Karl Marx.

R. AINSZTEIN Born Wilno, 1917. Educated at Wilno and Université Libre, Brussels. Has contributed to *Midstream, Jewish Social Studies, Jewish Quarterly, The Twentieth Century, International Affairs, The Times Literary Supplement,* the B.B.C. Third Programme. Has made a special study of Soviet wartime history and literature, and the destruction of Polish Jewry. Author of *Jewish Resistance in Nazi-occupied Eastern Europe* (1974). At present engaged in writing a history of the Jewish presence in modern Europe.

S. ETTINGER Associate Professor in modern Jewish history, Hebrew University, Jerusalem; editor, *Zion*, quarterly for research in Jewish history (in Hebrew).

M. FRIEDBERG Professor and Head of the Department of Slavic Languages and Literatures, University of Illinois at Urbana-Champaign, U.S.A. Taught at Indiana University, Columbia University, New York University, held a Fulbright Visiting Professorship at the Hebrew University; a former associate of the Russian Research Center at Harvard. Guggenheim Fellow. Departmental editor for Russian Literature, *Encyclopedia Judaica* (1971–2). Publications: *Russian Classics in Soviet Jackets* (1962), *The Party and the Poet in the USSR* (1963), *The Jew in Post-Stalin Soviet Literature* (1970) and editor of *A Bi-Lingual Collection of Russian Short Stories* (vol. I, 1964; vol. II, 1965). Has written widely on Russian literature, particularly its modern period, for various scholarly journals and reference works as well as for *Commentary, Midstream, Saturday Review,* etc.

Y. A. GILBOA Israeli author and journalist. Publications: *Gehalim Lohashot* (Glowing Embers, 1954)—an anthology of Hebrew and Yiddish literature in the Soviet Union, with a review of their history and development; *Al Horvot Hatarbut Hayehudit Bivrit Hamoatzot* (On the Ruins of Jewish culture in the Soviet Union, 1959); *The Black Years of Soviet Jewry 1939–53* (1971). 1965–7— Senior Research Associate in the Institute of East European Jewish Affairs, Brandeis University; 1969—Research Associate, Diaspora Research Institute, University of Tel Aviv.

L. HIRSZOWICZ Born Grodno 1920. Educated at the Hebrew University, Jerusalem, St. Antony's College, Oxford, and Warsaw. Presently edits *Soviet Jewish Affairs*, and lectures on the Middle East in international politics at the London School of Economics. Publications include *Iran 1951–1953, Oil—Nationalism—Imperialism* (1958); *The Third Reich and the Arab East* (1966).

Z. KATZ Born Jaroslav (Poland), 1924. Educated at the Pedagogical Institute, University of Kazakhstan; Hebrew University, Jerusalem; and London School of Economics. Senior Lecturer/Research Fellow, Department of Russian Studies and School for Overseas Students, The Hebrew University, Jerusalem. Formerly Research Fellow and Visiting Lecturer, Russian Research Center, Harvard, and lecturer in Department of Politics and Sociology at University of Glasgow and in Department of Government at University of Essex. Author of numerous specialist and general articles on Soviet politics.

L. KOCHAN Born London, 1922. Educated Cambridge and London School of Economics. Bearsted Reader in Jewish history, University of Warwick. Publications: *Russia and the Weimar Republic* (1951); *Acton on History* (1954); *Pogrom—November 10 1938* (1954); *The Making of Modern Russia* (1962); *The Struggle for Germany 1914–1945* (1963); *Russia in Revolution 1890–1918* (1966); *The Jew and his History* (1977).

W. KOREY Director of the B'nai B'rith United Nations Office and of research on international affairs for the B'nai B'rith International Council. Educated University of Chicago and Columbia University (Russian Institute). Previously on the faculties of Columbia University, City College of New York and Long Island University as Assistant Professor of History and Social Science. Former Ford Foundation Fellow, and author of numerous articles for scholarly and popular journals including: *American Slavic and East European Review*; *Slavic Review*; the *Annals* of the American Academy of Political Science; *Problems of Communism*; *Survey*, a Journal of Soviet and East European Studies; *The New Republic*; *Saturday Review*; *Midstream*; *Commentary*; and *The Progressive*.

S. LEVENBERG Born Kursk, 1907. Studied law and economics at University of Riga. Member, Bureau of the Socialist International; Treasurer of the British and Overseas Socialist Fellowship; Chairman, International Affairs Committee, World Jewish Congress. Publications include *The Problem of Minority Rights*, (1934), *Dubnow—The Historian of Russian Jewry* (1963), *European Jewry Today* (1967).

PHILIPPA LEWIS Educated University of Cambridge and London School of Economics. Assistant Editor of the *Slavic and Soviet Series*, Russian and East European Research Centre, Tel-Aviv University.

J. MILLER Senior Lecturer, Institute of Soviet and East European Studies, University of Glasgow. Studied economic planning in Moscow, 1936–7. An editor of *Soviet Studies* since 1949. Editor of *Soviet Jewish Affairs*, 1971–2.

J. A. NEWTH　Lecturer, Institute of Soviet and East European studies, University of Glasgow.

A. NOVE　Professor of Economics and Director of the Institute of Soviet and East European Studies, University of Glasgow. Previously employed in the Board of Trade and British Embassy, Moscow. Publications include *The Soviet Economy* (1961); *Was Stalin Really Necessary?* (1964), *An Economic History of the U.S.S.R.* (1969), and numerous articles in specialist and popular journals.

J. ROTHENBERG　Research Associate at the Institute of East European Jewish Studies, Brandeis University. Author of *The Jewish Religion in the Soviet Union* (1971).

L. SCHAPIRO　Professor of Political Science, London School of Economics. Publications include *The Origin of the Communist Autocracy* (1955); *The Communist Party of the Soviet Union* (1960); *Rationalism and Nationalism in Russian Nineteenth Century Political Thought* (1967).

J. SCHECHTMAN　Born Odessa, 1891; died New York, 1970. Educated Universities of Berlin and Novorossiysk. Active in Zionist work from early youth, and member of All-Russian Jewish Congress (Petrograd, 1917) and Ukrainian National Assembly (Kiev, 1918). Co-founder with Jabotinsky of Zionist-Revisionist movement. Leading member of Jewish Agency and World Jewish Congress. Author of several major studies of Jewish, Zionist and population problems, including *Les Pogromes en Ukraine sous les gouvernements ukrainiens* (1927); a two-volume biography of Jabotinsky, *Rebel and Statesman*, and *Fighter and Prophet* (1956, 1961); *European Population Transfers 1939–1945* (1946); and *Star in Eclipse: Russian Jewry Revisited* (1961).

CH. SHMERUK　Professor of Yiddish Literature, Hebrew University of Jerusalem.

B. D. WEINRYB　Professor of History, The Dropsie College, Philadelphia, Pa. Taught formerly at Yeshiva University, Columbia University, and Brooklyn College. Served also as Area Specialist and Communications Officer in the U.S. Department of State. Author of twelve volumes and over 300 studies dealing, for the most part, with the history of the Jews of central and eastern Europe.

Introduction

LEONARD SCHAPIRO

It would not be far wrong to regard Russia as the classical home of antisemitism. Its vast Jewish population—some five to six million on the eve of the First World War—was kept legally, and for the most part socially, herded away from the rest of the inhabitants of the country. The emperors of Russia were easily persuaded that the simple, pious Orthodox Russian peasant had to be protected from exploitation by alien infidels, and steadfastly resisted the arguments in favour of emancipation of the Jews which their more liberal-minded advisers from time to time urged upon them. Even Alexander II, the most enlightened of the Russian emperors, whose reign, after his death, was (rightly) looked back on by the Jews as a golden age, never went further than giving the 'better' Jews a chance of working towards their emancipation and assimilation. In his own words of 1856, his policy was 'to revise all existing legislation regarding the Jews so as to bring it into harmony with the general policy of merging this people with the native population, so far as the moral status of the Jews will allow it'.

There is no doubt that a large element in Russian antisemitism, both official and popular, arose from the fact that the Jew followed a faith alien to the national Russian Orthodox Christianity. Dostoevsky openly voiced the view that the Jew was a harmful and alien element in the Orthodox community. (Some of the antisemitic comments in his private letters are so sharp that they embarrassed the Soviet editors of his correspondence sufficiently for them to excise them.) At the other end of the spectrum lay the fact that the Jew who adopted Christianity, however formally, immediately became free of all legal restrictions and limitations. But in my view this religious antisemitism was as often as not an aspect of nationalism, a sense that the Jew did not belong to the Russian way of life, that the aims and ideals associated with him—such as capitalism, or a progressive philosophy—made him a creature apart in the traditional Russian world, less than human, even. Even some enlightened and liberal Russian nineteenth-century writers, who rejected the intolerant policy of their government, often had no inhibitions against expressing antisemitic views in private.

It is only fair to add that the attitude of Dostoyevsky and others to Jews belongs to the period before the emergence of official Russian anti-semitism in the form in which it was to shock so much of the civilized world—such as the pogroms after 1881, the Beilis Case, and the Protocols of the Elders of Zion. Of course, the long period of the policy of restriction and discrimination against the Jews created the basis on which the bar-barous edifice of violent antisemitism could be erected. There was also, no doubt, some latent, indigenous or natural antisemitism in the areas of the Jewish Pale of Settlement, based on primitive prejudice. The evidence often adduced to explain this 'folk antisemitism'—that the Jew was seen as a merciless exploiter of his innocent Christian victim in the towns and villages of the Jewish Pale, and thus bred hatred, as was so often urged in the past by official apologists of antisemitism in Russia—will not, however, stand up to any rigorous examination. Indeed, Jews and Russians often lived side by side in amity. The great pogroms were organized in the sense that the hooligan ringleaders were brought in by the authorities from other areas to start them, and in that the local authorities encouraged the inclinations of local hooligans to plunder, by making it plain that violence against Jews could be carried out with impunity. The most that can be said is that a distinctive and alien minority will always be at the risk of the lowest elements among the majority, unless and until it is made manifest to all that the forces of law and order will not tolerate dis-crimination against, or oppression of, any of the citizens of the country.

The results of imperial Russian policy towards the Jews, which con-tinued right up to the Revolution of 1917, were varied and momentous —for the Jews, for Russia, and for the whole world. One of them is the presence of most of British and American Jewry in their respective coun-tries: between 1870 and 1914 the vast Jewish emigration from Russia and Poland (which formed an integral part of Russia) virtually created, or at any rate enlarged beyond recognition, the Jewish communities of Britain and the United States. Another result was the birth of the dream of found-ing a Jewish state in Palestine, of Zionism. The dream became a reality after the First World War, though its full realization did not come about until after the Second World War, under the impact of the Holocaust. The readers of this volume, however, will be more concerned with the effects of official policy on those Jews who remained in Russia, since in many respects they lie at the root of the Jewish problem in Soviet Russia today.

In spite of the impetus towards assimilation and some form of emancipation which the reforms of Alexander II gave to quite large numbers of Russian Jews, the great majority remained alien and apart. According to the census of 1897 fewer than a quarter of Russian Jews could read and write in Russian. It was on this soil, among a minority aware of its national separateness, yet lacking the territory which characterizes a nation, and drawing much of its national consciousness from a religious tradition, that the great Yiddish and to a lesser extent Hebrew culture of Russian Jewry grew. The Soviet authorities and their apologists always contend that this 'ghetto' culture has now become irrelevant, since the ghetto which gave rise to it no longer exists. Even if this were true, which I very much doubt, it is not easy, or indeed right or desirable, to wipe out of the consciousness of any people the rich and varied linguistic and literary heritage of its past.

Another direct result of official policy on the Russian Jews in the nineteenth century was that many of them threw themselves into revolutionary activity. If we look at the first main wave of revolutionary activity in Russia, up to the assassination of Alexander II on 1 March 1881, the number of Jewish revolutionaries (according to official police returns) was not disproportionate to the relative size of the Jewish population. The position changed markedly during the second phase of the Russian revolutionary movement, which was characterized by the rise of social democracy. Count Witte told Theodor Herzl in 1903 that fifty per cent of all Russian revolutionaries were Jews, and attributed this to the unjust way in which the Jews were treated. He may have been right on both scores. Certainly, there can be no doubt of the fact that Russian Jews thronged into the revolutionary movement in great numbers. If one recalls that the specifically Jewish Bund, operating within the Jewish Pale, was in 1903 the only mass workers' party as yet in existence in Russia, Witte's estimate may well have been correct. Moreover, the treatment to which the Jews were subject no doubt provided the immediate impetus for young Jews to embrace revolution as the way out of their humiliating predicament.

It would, however, be quite wrong to see the motives of the Jewish revolutionary in Russia in joining one of the parties as primarily Jewish emancipation, or indeed as exclusively or even mainly related to the fate of the Jews at all. For a Jew to join a revolutionary party was consciously and deliberately to break with Jewish tradition, religion, and culture, and to embrace something which, as he saw it, offered for Russia, and the world, a future in which nationality would become totally irrelevant. It was not an accident that Jews so much more readily joined the Menshevik than the Bolshevik faction of the Social Democrats, rightly discerning in it the more western, more internationalist, more universal wing of the movement. Even the Bolsheviks, among whom, with the benefit of hindsight, we can now discern very significant nationalist characteristics, did not appear in this light in the climate of 1903, or 1912, or 1917, when the Marxist origins were still so much stronger and so much less diluted and distorted than they are now. For the Jewish social democrat—and I include the Jewish Bundist in this context—the advent of the socialist revolution meant not so much a better way of life for the Jew as a Jew, but a better life for all, or at any rate for all the inhabitants of the Russian empire, in a world in which, as it were, there would be 'neither Jew nor Greek'.

Thus the Jewish revolutionary usually broke decisively with his Jewish past—a fact which was to have important consequences for Soviet Jewry. When so many Jews came to power in the wake of the Bolshevik victory of November 1917 their aim, so far as the Jews were concerned, was to achieve their total assimilation, in an atheist society. For the most part they showed even less sympathy than did the non-Jewish Bolsheviks for the national, cultural or religious aspirations of their former co-religionists. This is one of the many factors in the complex kaleidoscope of the history of the Jews in the Soviet state which makes it so difficult to speak of Soviet Jewry as a homogeneous and readily identifiable and definable community; and this lack of conformity of aims and aspirations in a variegated body of citizens in turn complicates the problem of examining the status of what is comprehensively called 'the Soviet Jew'. In fact 'Soviet-Jewry' denotes men or women whose aims and hopes can vary from a desire for complete assimilation with their Russian neighbours to the other extreme of national, cultural or religious separateness—with many stages intermediate between the two extremes.

The only form of society which can cater for this variety of aspirations of a minority in its midst is one in which the liberal tolerance of opinions, faiths and mores prevails within the framework of equality under law. It is obvious that this framework is quite inconsistent with the 'totalitarian' society into which the Soviet state has evolved. The part played by Russian Jews in the revolutionary and radical movements has been much publicized. Antisemitic anticommunists have argued from the fact of this participation that the Russian Jews were out to destroy the foundations of Christian Russian society. While this was true of most Jewish Bolsheviks —as it was true of most non-Jewish Bolsheviks and of some Mensheviks— it was far from true of the Jewish radicals as a whole. For the fact is that a great number of them joined the ranks of Russian liberalism, where they found a rapturous welcome. The emancipation of the Jews almost became a rallying cry of the non-Jewish Russian liberal—in the Zemstvo movement, before the parties emerged in 1905, and then in the liberal party programme. To be pro-semitic in Russian radical-liberal circles was as morally obligatory as, say, to oppose discrimination on racial grounds would be in enlightened political circles in Britain today. The great advocates who gave their services free in the defence of Mendal Beilis were for the most part not Jews. This alliance between Russian and Jew was founded on the closest identity of principle, not on self-interest; both Jew and non-Jew realized that there could be no civilized future for Russia unless the future political order was founded on the principles of tolerance, non-discrimination and equality for all before the law. The pro-semitism of the non-Jewish liberal stemmed not from any particular love for the Jew, but from his realization of the elementary principle that unless *all* are free under the law *none* will be free. A number of more enlightened bureaucrats under the imperial regime had urged this very view, without result, on successive emperors. As the Chairman of the Committee of Ministers, Reutern, said in 1882: 'Everyone must be protected against every form of illegal attack. Today it is the Jews who are being incited against and plundered, tomorrow it will be the turn of the so-called kulaks. Then it will be the turn of the merchants and landowners.' Looking further into the future, he could have then added that the day after tomorrow it would be the turn of the commissars. But this was an argument that neither the last two emperors nor the communist rulers were ever able to grasp. Indeed, this basic liberal principle is even less consistent with the views of the rulers of a 'totalitarian' state than it was with the views of the Russian autocrats, because the 'totalitarian' state claims as of right to do what it will with every individual in the interests of some higher principle, be it the community or the future of the community.

The Provisional Government, weak and ineffectual as it proved to be, enacted the emancipation of the Jews as one of its first legal acts. Russian Jews welcomed the fall of tsarism in March 1917—it would have been very strange if they had formed an exception among the overwhelming majority in the country. Many Russian Jews did indeed also welcome the triumph of Bolshevism, but, as I have already suggested, they welcomed it more as internationalists than as Jews, for they were Jews who for the most part had already renounced their Jewish consciousness. For those Jews who wished to be both Jews and Russians, who were loyal to Russia yet conscious of a difference of religion, of cultural history, of language, and anxious to preserve that difference, or who wished either for themselves or for their children to further the Jewish national cause in Palestine—for those Jews the collapse of liberalism and its principles after November 1917 was the greatest blow which they ever suffered.

The story of the disappointment which the Revolution has brought to Soviet Jewry is told in the several essays of which this volume is composed. The present plight of the Soviet Jew is also analysed in detail. The story is not uniformly black. No serious scholar, no scholars of the standing of those whose contributions appear in the pages which follow, would go so far as to equate the position of the Jew in the Soviet Union today with the oppression of the Jew in the Russia of 1881 or 1903.

Countless Soviet Jews suffer not as Jews but as Soviet citizens, along with many other Soviet citizens of Russian and other nationalities, from the nature of the Soviet regime: its intolerance, its excessive paternalism, its arbitrariness, its flouting of its own laws, its policy of cultural *Gleichschaltung*. Even so, the Jew, in the Soviet Union as elsewhere, is a special case. Like all Jews living in the Diaspora, his peculiar historical and cultural predicament calls for a special and complex kind of tolerance, if he is to fulfil himself both as a Jew and as a citizen of the Soviet Union. The Soviet regime is intolerant of all minorities and of all non-conformists, but the Jew is more vulnerable than most to this intolerance.

The Soviet Union is a multinational state, and incorporates minority communities of non-Russian nationality, both willing and unwilling, both long-conquered and newly conquered, both concentrated in one territory and more dispersed. In spite of repeated boasts to the contrary, it is very far from being the case that the 'nationalities problem' has been solved in the U.S.S.R. The Ukrainians, for example, have good cause to complain of discrimination, and of restrictions on their national aspirations, culture, and consciousness. Indeed, Soviet theory makes no secret of the fact that the ultimate aim is the forging of an all-Soviet nationality in which national peculiarities will not disappear, but will be, as it were, merged in the greater Soviet nationality. To many of the national minorities 'all-Soviet' must seem little more than a euphemism for 'Russian'. At the same time the communist authorities make a twofold attempt to sweeten the pill. In the first place, by offering full assimilation to members of backward and underdeveloped national minorities they bring to them the benefits of modern material culture, which always seem to exercise such a powerful attraction on primitive peoples—at any rate, in the first instance. Second, they combine party (and police) discipline with concessions to national susceptibilities which are of little political significance—folk-dancing, the encouragement of literary efforts in the most outlandish tongues, however small the number of people who speak them, the translation into such recondite languages of the works of Pushkin, and the like.

The complex nature of the Jewish community in the Soviet Union makes all this of very little relevance to the Jew. In the first place the Jew, unlike the Mordvin or the Yakut, is, as often as not, not a foreigner living in Russia, but a Russian—in language, in culture, and in outlook. Second, the Jew has no territory—the fiction of Biro-Bidzhan, the far eastern Jewish autonomous region notwithstanding. Biro-Bidzhan (described in one of the essays in this volume) was set up in 1928 as a somewhat grotesque attempt to create a national Jewish home on the waste borders of China: the extent of the failure of the scheme is evident in the fact that in 1959 its Jewish population of some 14,000 formed under 9 per cent of its total population. Third, the national consciousness of the Jew, where it exists, revolves around two points among others which are alien and repugnant to the Soviet regime—religion and Zionism.

The Soviet regime is, of course, intolerant, oppressive, arbitrary, paternalistic, and indifferent to the individual in the case of Jew and non-Jew alike. As I have already suggested, the predicament of the Soviet Jew must in large measure be explained in terms of the collapse of the liberal ideals which followed on the victory of the Bolsheviks, and which alone could infuse the tolerance of diversity which the Jew in the Diaspora everywhere needs if he is to lead a civilized life. Yet there are certain respects in which the Soviet Jew is often liable to be in a worse position as a consequence of general communist policy than most other Soviet citizens.

First, the impact of anti-religious propaganda: the Jewish religious community (as one essay in this volume shows) is in fact worse off than most. But quite apart from this circumstance, the Jew suffers from anti-religious propaganda not only as a believer, but as a Jew. If you publish articles listing the iniquities of Orthodox priests, this no doubt offends the feelings of the Orthodox believers, and conceivably makes priests unpopular and hated—conceivably, because nothing has proved such a dismal failure as Soviet atheist propaganda. But propaganda against priests does not have the effect of arousing hostile feelings against Armenians or Georgians, let alone against Russians. In contrast if you publish lurid stories about the alleged immorality and dishonesty of a particular rabbi—a very popular form of Soviet propaganda—and if, moreover, the rabbi is suitably caricatured with a hooked nose and other distinctive

Jewish features, the effect is to stimulate hostility against the Jew as such and, what is even worse, to create a sense among non-Jews that the Soviet authorities treat the Jews as second-class citizens, and that the Jews are therefore 'fair game'.

Exactly the same line of reasoning applies to anti-Zionism or to anti-Israeli propaganda. Apologists of the Soviet authorities often assert that all apparent manifestations of antisemitism in the Soviet Union are really anti-Zionism, and that there is no quarrel with the non-Zionist 'loyal' Jew. One may incidentally well ask what disloyalty there is in a Jew supporting a national Jewish home for those Jews who cannot lead a full life in the Diaspora. But apart from that, one wonders if Soviet apologists outside the Soviet Union have ever read any of the so-called anti-Zionist articles, or seen the cartoons which often accompany them. They are couched in the language of bitter hatred of the Jew which is completely indistinguishable from the language of classical antisemitism. The same applies even more forcibly to the outpourings against Israel which have been appearing in the Soviet press and radio since the end of the June war of 1967—no doubt partly to console the Arabs for the Soviet failure to give them any aid in the course of the war. It may well be that the primary aim of this propaganda is to further Soviet policy in the Middle East in support of the Arabs against Israel. But again, the nature of the immoderate language and drawings used can only have one effect at home—that of stimulating hatred and contempt for the Jew: not the Zionist, not the Israeli, but the ordinary, probably assimilated, Jew who lives next door. Indeed, some recent commentators have, with justice in my view, pointed to the similarity between the language used in Soviet anti-Israel propaganda dealing with what is described as the world Zionist conspiracy, and that of the Protocols of the Elders of Zion.

The third respect in which the Jew often differs from other non-Russian nationals (accepting, for the moment, which I personally do not accept, that a Soviet Jew can be properly described as non-Russian) is in his intellectualism, his drive to acquire education, and indeed his greater aptitude for it in language and tradition than can be the case where some of the more undeveloped Soviet national minorities are concerned. As appears from some of the studies in this volume, the university is probably the one place where discrimination against the Jew is most serious. Here we are up against a form of pure Russian chauvinism, which reveals how imperfectly, for all the fine speeches, the dominant Russian in the communist hierarchy of the Soviet Union has accepted the Jew as one of his own. Since Jews formed a very disproportionate part of the total body of intellectual workers after the Revolution (especially after the communist inroads on the old intelligentsia) and, since in view of Jewish disposition, the disproportion was likely to be perpetuated in the next generation, the Russians in effect had to choose between a *numerus clausus*, however unofficial, and complete acceptance of a disproportionate Jewish presence in the white-collar sphere. There are some areas where such a presence has been accepted—the theatre, for example, or the legal profession. But in many other areas this is not so, which suggests that deliberate steps are taken to make sure that Jews are kept down or excluded. As a high Soviet Minister once frankly told a visiting socialist delegation: 'Formerly we did not have our own intelligentsia, so we had to rely on Jews. But now that we have our own intelligentsia . . .'. What a world of significance there is in those three words, 'our own intelligentsia'! And, one may add, our 'own' intelligentsia from the point of view of officials like this one usually includes the non-Russian minorities of the Soviet Union, since to those of them who became assimilated to Russian culture and language every opportunity of promotion is offered.

There is a further peculiar circumstance which applies to the Jews, and to the Jews alone in the Soviet Union: the way in which throughout the history of Russian communism antisemitism has been woven into the fabric of political conflicts. To a slight extent, very slight perhaps, antisemitism was an element in the original conflict between Bolshevism and Menshevism—the Jews were distinctly more numerous among the Mensheviks; there was also the Bund, whose political orientation was closest to that of the Mensheviks. After the Revolution, the prevalence up to the mid-thirties of Jews at all levels of the dominant, often unpopular, communist machine, and particularly in the police—the Cheka, the G.P.U., and the N.K.V.D.—often led to an identification of anti-communism with antisemitism. It was probably in large measure owing to this circumstance that the Soviet regime until the thirties was very active in repressing manifestations of antisemitism—in fact, in enforcing the laws against antisemitism which, though still in force, have now virtually become a dead letter. When the conflict with Trotsky was at its height—as we know from the Trotsky and the Smolensk party archives which fell into Allied hands in the last war—clandestine fostering of antisemitic motifs as part of the campaign against Trotsky and his supporters played quite a significant role. And then, of course, came the era of the great purges, in which the Jewish element in the communist party probably suffered more heavily than any other single national element. I am not suggesting that antisemitism was Stalin's main motive. One of the objects of the purges was to destroy the old Bolshevik element in the party, to eliminate those whose loyalty was to Lenin and to the mystique of 1917 in favour of the new men whom Stalin was anxious to promote in order to create a basis of support for himself. But it was precisely among the older generation of Bolsheviks that Jews were so numerous. Stalin is no more, and many features of his regime have been reversed or modified. But the Russian nationalism which was a part of it was a deeply rooted element of Bolshevism, even if it was kept in check by Lenin, who was singularly devoid of any trace of chauvinism in his character. It has, I believe, come to stay.

The last peculiar factor in the predicament of Soviet Jews, not shared with any other national minority, is the trauma resulting from the Nazi Holocaust. There are many difficulties in assessing exactly the extent of the devastation caused to the Jews on the territory of the Soviet Union by the German invasion. But the best estimate, based on all information available (according to the essay by Nove and Newth in this volume) is that, taking total Soviet wartime losses of population as thirty millions, the Jewish share of these losses was two and a half millions. This reduced the Jews from $2\frac{1}{2}$ per cent of the population in 1941 to around 1 per cent at present; and meant that Jewish losses were proportionately four times as severe as those of the Soviet population as a whole. In addition, the Soviet Jew, like Jews throughout the Diaspora, suffered the moral impact of the annihilation of several more million co-religionists in neighbouring Poland, in Germany and elsewhere. This traumatic experience, which has been hard enough to bear for those Jews who have remained unscathed, has been made infinitely harder to bear for the Soviet Jew by the policy of the Soviet authorities. Because of their hostility to Zionism and to the new State of Israel (after a short initial period of support) the Soviet rulers have deprived Soviet Jews of the consolation of pride in the new Jewish state and contacts with it. Because of their fear of encouraging any kind of national consciousness among their Jewish population, the Soviet authorities have imposed a blanket of silence on the terrible facts which I have just quoted: Jewish losses have invariably been merged in all publications on the war in general Soviet losses, without any specific mention of the Jewish element, and the particular tragedy of the Jews passed over in silence. Many are no doubt familiar with the protest by the poet Yevtushenko on the cynical obliteration, by building a recreation ground, on the scene of one of the worst massacres of Jews at Babi Yar. It is indeed some consolation that non-Jewish Russian intellectuals quite often find the courage now to protest against the policy of their government towards the Jews. This reminds one of the great alliance between the Jewish and non-Jewish Russian liberals in the decades before the Revolution, and raises some faint hope for the future.

The essays contained in this volume deal in detail, and in what seems to me a scholarly, balanced and fair manner, with the position of the Soviet Jew. They describe the restrictions on the practice of Jewish religion, which are probably more severe than those applied to any other religious community in the Soviet Union—if one excepts certain sects which are banned altogether. They show the quite marked extent to which the Jew—in contrast to members of other nationalities (and to be a Jew in the Soviet Union means technically to be a member of a non-Russian nationality)—is denied any substantial facilities for maintaining alive, let alone furthering, the great Yiddish culture of the past. They examine carefully the evidence of discriminatory practices which exist in some—not all— spheres of life, and especially in entry to the university, and in public and political life. The reader of this volume is not going to derive a very comforting impression so far as the plight of the Soviet Jew is concerned. Even if there is no deliberate and coherent policy of oppression of the Jews, as there was before 1917, the fact remains that the Jew suffers more than other Soviet citizens from the circumstance that he lives in a totalitarian state, in which the principles of tolerance and equality before an independent law are not observed. Because the plight of the Jew is less the result of deliberate antisemitism, and more a consequence of general Soviet arbitrariness, it is difficult to be very optimistic about the immediate future. Real improvement in the situation of the Soviet Jew will only come when—and if—the Soviet Union begins to evolve along the path upon which Yugoslavia seems to have embarked, and on which Czechoslovakia tried unsuccessfully to embark, in other words the path of legal order. So long as the U.S.S.R. remains in essence a police state, the Jew will remain an object of suspicion and distaste to the communist party rulers.

But while it would be foolhardy to be optimistic about the future of Soviet Jewry, there are two facts to be discerned in the situation which are on the positive side. One is the evidence that to a limited but notable extent the Soviet authorities react to publicity and pressure from abroad and are prepared (while stoutly denying it) to modify their policy in the face of them. This is not due either to altruism or even to embarrassment, but rather to the material calculation that if they offend the Western 'capitalist' powers too much they will endanger the 'détente' from which they hope to gain credits, trade, and technology. Between the date of the completion of the manuscript of this book and the appearance of the first edition in print in 1970 a remarkable change had taken place in Soviet Jewry: some of the hitherto 'silent minority' (as they were called) had become the most vocal and the best publicized of all the protesters and dissenters who had been active for some years previously in the U.S.S.R.

Details of this new Jewish protest movement will be found elsewhere in this volume. Agitation began on a significant scale in 1969, and has continued ever since. A considerable number of protests, petitions, and other writings have been circulated by Jews inside the U.S.S.R., have reached the West and have been published—much in the manner of all that Russian *samizdat* material with which we are becoming increasingly familiar. But the Jewish protesters enjoy an advantage over the non-Jewish protesters whose example they strove to follow: they can immediately command wide publicity from co-religionists in non-communist countries, and they have indeed attracted publicity and support on a very wide, and sometimes dramatic, scale. Support from outside has, in turn, given them the courage to intensify their protests and their pressure inside the U.S.S.R.

The reaction of the communist authorities to this new phase of the Soviet human rights movement has been predictably inconsistent, alternating between repression and concession. On the one hand there have been several big trials, followed by heavy sentences, and many cases of cruel and arbitrary persecution of those who apply to emigrate; on the other hand the protest has undoubtedly had its effect. Although exact figures are not available, it is generally accepted that no fewer than 13,000 Soviet Jews were allowed to emigrate to Israel in 1971. (The total for all the previous nine years had been only around 7,000.) By the end of 1976 nearly 130,000 Soviet Jews had been allowed to emigrate, about 100,000 in 1972 and 1973 alone: since then there has been a drastic falling off in numbers. This is not solely due to harassment by the Soviet authorities: reports of disappointment of expectations by some immigrants to Israel getting back to the Soviet Union may also have had their effect. Even so, there are still believed to be over 180,000 Soviet Jews who have in the past requested affidavits from relatives in Israel and who have not yet succeeded in getting out. There has also been a change in the pattern of emigration: in 1973 the proportion of those arriving in Vienna who announced their intention to settle in the U.S.A. or other Western countries was 4·2 per cent. In 1976, it had grown to 49·1 per cent of the very much smaller total number of Jews who reached Vienna. It was very usual before 1970 for those of us who urged publicity for the plight of Soviet Jewry to be met with the argument (in Israel as well as elsewhere) that foreign agitation could only make the position of Soviet Jews worse: the view is seldom voiced today.

But emigration of Soviet Jews to Israel, however satisfactory it may be to those Soviet-Jewish citizens who wish to emigrate (and to Israel), is not a solution of the problems which Soviet Jews face. At best, emigration can only solve the problems of a small minority of the Soviet-Jewish population—for the difficulties faced by those who stay behind will remain as acute as before, if not worse, and it is with these difficulties that this book is concerned. The Soviet Jew who does not feel sufficiently alienated from Soviet society to want to abandon it for ever, will still suffer if he is prevented from assimilating as fully as he desires, from practising his religion freely, or from keeping alive traditional Russian-Jewish culture. There is also a risk that in the glare of publicity that the nationalistic protesters have attracted, those Soviet Jews who suffer from the effects of Soviet antisemitism in education, in their professions, or in their religious and cultural activities, will be quietly forgotten by the outside world. Israel in particular will not, it must be hoped, in its zeal to acquire new immigrants, forget the plight of those Soviet Jews who do not wish to emigrate; or, worse still, suppress information which reaches them on the general life of Soviet Jewry today for fear of offending the Soviet authorities. For in police states those who are forgotten, those whose plight never reaches the public notice of the outside world, are left at the mercy of arbitrary persecutors with unlimited power. In the case of Soviet Jews there is the further risk that the K.G.B. will exact its vengeance for those who have escaped on those who have stayed behind, for example by encouraging, or not discouraging, latent popular antisemitism. It is therefore to be hoped that the publicity reaped by the Zionist minority of Soviet Jews (rightly, if only for their courage and their persistence) will not put an end to interest outside the Soviet Union in what is happening to the rest of Soviet Jewry. This new edition of a book of which the moderation and accuracy have been widely acclaimed is therefore welcome and timely. If protest and publicity abroad about the position of Soviet Jewry is to be effective, it must be based on accurate and balanced information. And where a question can so easily become charged with emotion, exaggerated allegations easily obtain currency. The sober and fully documented studies which make up this volume should enable those who wish to do so to obtain an assessment of the position of the Soviet Jew which is the best that current scholarship can provide.

The second encouraging fact is that there are some signs inside the Soviet Union that the pressure for legal order and for the observance of the constitution is growing in many sections of Soviet society. The cause of legal order in the Soviet Union is the cause of the Jew—today, exactly as it was before 1917, when Jewish and non-Jewish liberals formed a close union, and perished together under the onslaught of the Bolsheviks. In 1917 many Russian Jews helped the Bolsheviks to seize and to hold power, and to destroy the liberals and the principles for which they stood. The liberals and their policies belong to the past: their principles do not. In the Churches, among the intellectuals, among the scientists and the lawyers, a movement is growing in the Soviet Union for the basic notions of legality, human dignity, and tolerance. It cannot be emphasized too strongly that this is not an 'anti-Soviet' movement, as the Soviet policemen assure us—just as the tsarist police assured us that all opposition to the regime was exclusively the work of Jews and aliens. The new Soviet movement of protest is acting in the name of Soviet legality, Soviet justice, Soviet humanity—all these values, little different from the basic values of the radical liberals, which once formed an essential part of the ideals of Bolshevism. It was for the sake of these ideals that many Russian Jews joined non-Jewish Russians in 1917. Their destruction has struck Jews and non-Jews alike. For over a century enlightened Russians have known that tolerance and justice for the Jews are an integral part of tolerance and justice for all. Now at last some of them are finding the courage to say so. Let us hope that history will give the Soviet Jews another chance to work side by side with non-Jewish Soviet churchmen, intellectuals, and scientists for a return to the ideals of 1917.

I

The Jews in Russia at the Outbreak of the Revolution

S. ETTINGER

When tsarism fell in March 1917 one of the first acts of its successor, the Provisional Government, was to abolish all legal restrictions on the Jews. 'All the limitations on the rights of Russian citizens imposed by hitherto existing laws on the basis of religion, creed or nationality are hereby revoked', the government's decree stated. This was followed by an extraordinary political and cultural efflorescence amongst the millions of Russian Jews. It was unprecedented, but very short-lived, two years at most.[1]

As soon as the Revolution broke out, the mutual aid societies (which had grown in the years of wartime hardship) began to take soundings with a view to summoning a national congress of Russian Jews. The Jewish political parties, too, awoke to new life, after years of weakness in the years preceding the war and during the war itself. The socialist parties (the Bund, the 'United', Poale Zion), the Zionists and even the religious camp were flooded with new members. These parties re-drafted their programmes, established new branches and new institutions, and embarked on a wide range of activities. Most of the Jewish bodies saw that the first essential was to summon a nation-wide Russian-Jewish congress. This should create autonomous institutions for Russian Jewry and frame Jewish demands from the state, in anticipation of the meeting of that constituent assembly dreamt of by most of Russia's liberal and revolutionary parties. At the local level, communities were soon set up in towns and villages, their institutions democratically elected by the local Jews. The same period

[1] It is impossible to give a precise estimate of the number of Jews under tsarist rule at the outbreak of the Revolution. According to the 1897 census 5¼ million Jews resided in the Russian empire. According to an estimate of the Jewish Statistical Society (*Yevreiskoe Naselenie Rossii*, Petrograd, 1917), 3,837,000 Jews lived in European Russia (excluding the kingdom of Poland, which until the war formed part of the Russian empire), in the areas not conquered by the Germans. In the Caucasus, Siberia, and central Asia, the 1897 census recorded a population of 105,000 Jews. Jews constituted slightly over 50 per cent of the combined urban population of Lithuania and White Russia. The census of 1897 also showed that in the Ukraine the Russians formed 35·5 per cent of the urban population, followed by the Jews (30 per cent) and the Ukrainians (27 per cent).

saw the awakening and flourishing of journalism and publishing in Russian, Hebrew, and Yiddish, and the establishment of a comprehensive system of Jewish education, from kindergarten to teachers' seminary. All the while, in the political developments of that turbulent period, and in the leadership of the main political parties, Jews played a prominent part.[1]

How could this development be accounted for? There had been no preparation among the Jewish public in earlier years. The very legal existence of Jewish communities had ceased to be recognized by the authorities in 1844. In a memorandum presented to the government by a committee for Jewish affairs at the time it was stated that the Jews did not co-operate with the authorities. They lived according to the Talmud, regarded their residence in Russia as exile, and awaited the coming of the Messiah.[2] In the 1840s the Jews of Russia had no cultural or public organization or any periodical of their own. Only a few individual Jews of that day attended schools and universities. Even in the last years of the century, only 1 per cent of the Jews in the country gave Russian as their mother tongue; for 97 per cent it was Yiddish. The same census, in 1897, revealed that only 24·6 per cent of the Jewish population could read and write in Russian.[3]

What, then, were the factors that led to the extraordinary, unexpected activity of Russian Jews in 1917? It is clear that one factor was the sudden end to long-continued oppression, combined with the immediate release of hitherto suppressed economic and social forces. Other factors were the attitude of the Russian Government and Russian society to the Jews, the demographic and economic changes among the Jews themselves since the beginning of the nineteenth century, and their own social and ideological development.

Russian antisemitism, the heritage of generations, played no small part in determining the attitude of Russian society and the Russian authorities towards the Jews.[4] The religious and social ferment of fifteenth-century Russia, known as 'the heresy of the Judaizers', had combined with other

---

[1] This period in the history of Russian Jewry has not yet been properly investigated and described. The introductions by Y. Slutski and Ch. Shmeruk to *Jewish Publications in the U.S.S.R.,1917–1960*, issued by the Historical Society of Israel, Jerusalem, 1961, give some idea of the range of publications; see also M. Altschuler, 'The Attempt to organize an All-Russian Jewish Congress' in *Heavar* (Quarterly of Russian Jewish History), Tel Aviv, 1965, no. 12, pp. 75–89. *Heavar*, no. 15 (1968), is a special issue devoted to the period between February and October 1917.

[2] S. Dubnov, Istoricheskie soobshcheniya, *Knizhki Voskhoda*, April 1904, pp. 30–1.

[3] B. Brutskus, *Statistika Yevreiskogo Naseleniya*, St. Petersburg, 1909, pp. 35, 48.

[4] See my article, 'Eredita antisemita in Russia e sua influenza nei tempi', *Gli ebrei nell' U.R.S.S.*, Milan, 1966, pp. 77–98.

factors to ingrain extreme hostility towards the Jews, and a determination not to let one single Jew settle on the soil of 'Holy Russia'. Russian military actions outside the borders of the state were accompanied by attacks on Jews and sometimes even by their extermination. After the three partitions of Poland, however, at the end of the eighteenth century, Russia acquired large territories populated by hundreds of thousands of Jews. The government had to seek means of ruling this population. The refusal to allow Jews to leave the annexed territories and to settle in inner Russia, the creation of that 'Pale of Settlement' which afflicted the Jews of Russia until the Russian Revolution—all this was the fruit of traditional Jew-hatred. From the beginning of the nineteenth century, government policy towards the Jews took definite shape: the authorities wished to oust the Jews from all village occupations. They had accepted the hate-inspired claim of the Polish landowners that the Jews exploited the peasant (as though the villages were in the hands of the Jews and not in those of the landowners themselves). On the other hand, they tried to settle Jews on the land in parts of New Russia (i.e. near the Black Sea) and took steps to encourage crafts and industry among them. They even hoped to bring the Jews nearer to Russian society, and ultimately to merge them in it by education in Russian schools and conversion to Christianity. Tsar Alexander I had already offered a series of concessions to Jewish converts, and Nicholas I made conversion one of the basic aims of his policy towards the Jews. By imposing compulsory military service upon them, by kidnapping boys and even small children into the army, he hoped to create a large group of Jews who would adopt Christianity and serve as an example to the rest. The instructions of the Holy Synod (the supreme Church authority in Russia) to army chaplains from 1843 emphasized the importance of converting young Jews serving in the army.[1] All these efforts brought no significant result; on the contrary, there were many cases of extraordinary self-sacrifice by Jewish lads under ruthless pressure. An equal lack of success attended Nicholas I's other measures, such as the compulsory education of Jewish boys in government schools and (at the other extreme) the severest persecution, such as the withdrawal of the legal recognition of the Jewish communities, mentioned above, and the proposal to declare 80 per cent of the Jews a body of outlaws.

The reign of Nicholas was to be remembered by Russian Jewry as a time of the harshest decrees. Yet it failed to change Jewish society, either in action, organization, or consciousness. This failure caused the government of Alexander II to try gentler methods of bringing the Jews closer to

[1] S. Ginsburg, *Historische Werk* (Yiddish), vol. iii, New York, 1937, pp. 351–69.

their environment and altering their lives. This was in general the period
of 'the great reforms' in Russian life—the abolition of serfdom, the establishment of an independent judiciary, the introduction of press freedom.
The Jews, too, gained from the spirit of change. Rich and educated Jews
were allowed to leave the Pale of Settlement, to study and even to enter
government service. Jewish newspapers were founded and a Jewish intelligentsia began to grow up, whose mother tongue was Russian.[1] Artisans'
and soldiers' sons were also granted concessions. But after a very few
years, from the mid-sixties onwards, various sectors of Russian society
began to show signs of displeasure at this increasing integration. The
government also tended to become more reactionary in the second half of
Alexander's reign. The attitude to the Jews was one of the crucial points in
the political and social polemics of the time. Opposing social trends spoke
with the same voice. The Slavophiles saw the Jews as a foreign element
introducing destructive western influences into Russia, while the revolutionary *Narodniki* (Populists) saw them as agents of capitalism, exploiting
the people. The authorities were worried by the growing Jewish part in
the rising revolutionary ferment in Russia, especially among secondary
school pupils, and rabbinical and university students. The slogan appeared:
'*Zhid idyot*' ('the Jew is upon you').

The result of this development became clear in the decisive change that
came over the Russian Government and most of the Russian people in
their attitude to the Jews at the beginning of the 1880s, after the assassination of Alexander II by revolutionaries.

The accession of Alexander III in 1881 ushered in a period of reaction
in Russia that lasted in effect until 1917. The Jews were identified in the
eyes of the Russian public (and eventually in their own eyes) with everything 'western', i.e. every aspiration to personal and social rights, to
rational thought, to any trend considered by the theorists of Russian
'originality' (*samobytnost*) contrary to the 'nature' of Russia and its political
and social traditions. A wave of pogroms swept over Ukrainian Jewry
after the murder of Alexander II. Not one element in Russian society—
not even the revolutionaries—stood up for them. The government
embarked upon a virulent and open anti-Jewish policy. It closed the civil
service to the Jews, forbade them to take academic posts, and made it
difficult for them to enter the liberal professions. The *numerus clausus* was
introduced in secondary schools and universities. The regulations governing the Pale of Settlement were made more stringent and obstacles were

---

[1] See Y. Slutski's article, 'The rise of the Russian-Jewish intelligentsia', in *Zion* (Hebrew),
XXV (1960), pp. 212–37.

put in the way of Jewish economic activity. Jews living in Moscow, according to the existing regulations, were expelled from the city in 1891. The corrupt Russian police continually increased its pressure on the Jews. Following the Russian failure in the war against Japan in 1905, when the whole autocratic political structure began to tremble, the government sought to win public favour by militant anti-Jewish propaganda. It arranged pogroms in hundreds of Jewish settlements in October 1905[1] (the mobs were organized by the police under army protection), supported antisemitic right-wing political parties, and organized gangs, such as the Union of the Russian People and the 'Black Hundreds'[2] in order to attack Jews and opponents of the regime.

This policy of violent aggression had many results. One of the most significant was to make all opponents of the autocracy in Russia into opponents of official antisemitism and the government's persecution of the Jews. This attitude developed despite a certain ambivalence in the assessment of the Jewish problem found earlier, among liberal and revolutionary circles opposed to tsarism. Even when confronted with the Kishinev pogrom (1903) the liberal leaders Struve and Yuzhakov, whilst expressing their sympathy with the suffering of the Jews and their repugnance at the instigators of the pogrom, violently attacked Jewish nationalism and the 'not too attractive character of the Jews'.[3]

Both in the debates of the Duma and in the public debate that surrounded the government's attempt to invent a blood libel in Kiev in 1911–13—the infamous 'Beilis Case'[4]—a running battle was fought between the government and its opponents.

The Jewish question thus became one of the central political questions of Russia in the twentieth century—the touchstone of difference between reactionary and progressive. The struggle sharpened and the situation of the Jews worsened when the First World War broke out, particularly after the defeats suffered by the Russian army on the eastern front. The tsarist government sought to explain away these defeats by blaming 'traitors' disloyal to Russia—chief among them the Jews.[5] Violent attacks

---

[1] L. Motzkin (ed.): *Die Judenpogrome in Russland*, vols. i, ii, Cologne and Leipzig, 1910.

[2] Some of the material gathered by the special investigating committee of the Russian Provisional Government in 1917 on the activities of these organizations was published by A. Chernovsky, *Soyuz Russkogo Naroda*, Moscow–Leningrad, 1929.

[3] See Itzhak Maor, *The Jewish Question in the Russian Liberal and Revolutionary Movement, 1890–1914* (Hebrew), Jerusalem, 1964, pp. 53–7 for the polemic aroused by these remarks.

[4] See A. B. Tager, *The Decay of Czarism—the Beilis Trial*, Philadelphia, 1935; M. Samuel, *Blood Accusation*, London, 1967.

[5] There are known to have been acts of treachery in the Russian army but they were perpetrated by high-ranking officers belonging to the pro-German party in the government.

were made on the Jewish population, almost all of whom lived in areas affected by military operations; hundreds of thousands of Jews were expelled from their homes to inner Russia at 24 or 48 hours' notice; Jewish leaders were seized as hostages for the political loyalty of the Jewish population; false charges were trumped up alleging Jewish aid to the enemy and innocent Jews were even sentenced by court martial to be shot.[1] The situation of the Jews was desperate; clearly, only the fall of the tsarist regime could save them. The feelings of relief with which they greeted the February (March) Revolution, the fall of the tsar, and the assumption of power by liberal leaders can be easily understood. The Jews of Russia were in a state of terror and Messianic expectation, and the deliverance from oppression that came with the Revolution burst all bounds and gave impetus to a huge and independent Jewish activity.

Those demographic and economic processes that had affected the Jews of Russia before the Revolution also played their part. One formative factor that characterized the Russian Jews was their high rate of natural increase. Russia as a whole had a high rate of natural increase in the nineteenth century, but that of the Jews was roughly double.[2] Only towards the end of the century did the pace slacken and approximate to that of the rest of the population, i.e. about 2 per cent per annum.[3]

The congestion in the enclosed Pale of Settlement, together with administrative pressure from the authorities, gave rise to a Jewish population surplus and to a feeling among the Jews that they were being throttled. All this took place against a background of rapid capitalist development which began in Russia after the defeats of the Crimean War and the emancipation of the serfs in 1861. This new departure affected the sources of livelihood of many Jews connected with feudal estates who had served as intermediaries between town and country on the basis of economic relations that went back for centuries. As a result, economic differentiation increased within Jewish society, and a growing number of Jews turned to manual labour, most of them as craftsmen and artisans (in

[1] See *The Jewish Question in the Duma, Speeches by Deputies*, London, 1915. Anti-Jewish government and army publications were reprinted in a pamphlet of the foreign committee of the Bund in January 1916. This was the second publication in the series *Razgrom Yevreev v Rossii*. There is also much material in *The Jews and the War, Memorandum of the Jewish Socialist Labour Confederation Poale Zion*, The Hague, 1916. The allegation that Jews had hidden German soldiers in the small town of Kuzhi in Lithuania and that these soldiers had afterwards set fire to the place, created special alarm. The incident was investigated by Kerensky, a member of the Duma (afterwards Prime Minister in the Provisional Government of Russia), and shown to be a complete fabrication.

[2] J. Lestschinsky, *The Jewish People in Numbers* (Yiddish), Berlin, 1922, p. 29.

[3] M. Klintsin, in the publication of the Jewish Statistical Society (see note 1, p. 14).

the last decade of the nineteenth century the number of skilled craftsmen, with their labourers and apprentices, reached half a million); the minority became hired workmen (about 150,000).[1] At that time more Jews were occupied in craft and industry than in trade—a radical change from the position at the beginning of the century.[2] The numbers of those in need of charity rose. A sizable proportion of the Jewish population of Russia lived in conditions that shocked the objective observer.[3] Since heavy industry was concentrated in those areas outside the Jewish Pale of Settlement, it was axiomatic that it employed no Jewish workers. But even the textile industry, the sugar and food products industry, all of which were relatively well developed in the Pale (and some of which were even in Jewish hands) did not open their gates to the Jewish worker. Most of the labour needed in these industries was unskilled, and it was more convenient for the employer to take on primitive villagers or peasants who would come to town for seasonal work. Not only did the Jewish workman still abstain from working on the sabbath, but he was also better educated and better organized. Given the abundant labour force available to industry in Russia, employers had no need to hire Jews. There were, however, a few isolated places where the power of Jewish hired labour was felt—among the dockers of Odessa, for example.

Most of those making their living by manual labour were therefore artisans. But even here there were many callings into which Jews could not enter. A Jewish apprentice could not live with a Christian master, so Jewish artisans as a rule stuck to a few trades traditional among the Jews. The census of 1897 showed that almost half (43·6 per cent) of those Jews making a living in craft and industry were garment manufacturers. Jews also turned to this branch because of the small investment needed to open a workshop and because women were able to work in it. As compared with the huge number of tailors and seamstresses, shoemakers comprised 14·4 per cent of all Jewish craftsmen, carpenters 6 per cent, locksmiths 3·1 per cent, etc.[4]

The multiplication of Jewish tradesmen in a restricted number of callings led to stiff competition among them, to price-cutting and to a consequent deterioration in quality. The main customers for the products

---

[1] *Sbornik Materialov ob Ekonomicheskom Polozhenii Yevreiskogo Naseleniya v Rossii*, vol. i, St. Petersburg, 1904, p. 201.

[2] According to the 1897 census 36·3 per cent of all Jewish breadwinners made their living in manufacturing and industry, and 31 per cent in trade and business.

[3] See, for example, impressions of a journey through the Pale of Settlement by the economist A. Subbotin, *V Cherte Yevreiskoi Osedlosti*, St. Petersburg, 1888, 1890.

[4] *Sbornik Materialov . . .*, vol. i., p. 198.

of Jewish tradesmen were the peasants and townsmen of western Russia, and they certainly did not need first-class goods. But other factors worked against the Jewish artisan. Cut-throat competition harmed him, as did his dependence on loans for current credit, a dependence that endangered the very existence of Jewish trades in the Pale of Settlement. One attempt to improve the condition of Jewish tradesmen was the foundation of credit co-operatives, which enabled tradesmen to buy raw materials on easy terms when they were cheapest, and also to accumulate a stock of ready-made goods for festive seasons or fairs. The tradesman thus escaped the network of middlemen. Fifty such Jewish co-operatives were founded between 1898 and 1902, but in the latter years the Russian Ministry of Finance demanded that two-thirds of the directors of every such co-operative should be Christians, and this arrested their development. After the 1905 Revolution this condition was no longer enforced. The co-operatives once again began to develop rapidly and became the symbol of Jewish mutual aid. On 1 January 1913 there were 632 Jewish credit co-operatives in the Pale of Settlement; their membership ran into hundreds of thousands and their annual turnover was 30 million roubles.[1]

Yet despite the rapid development of mutual-aid institutions, Jewish tradesmen were the first to emigrate. Emigration became one of the characteristic phenomena of Russian Jewry.[2]

In the years 1898–1914 about one and a quarter million Jews left Russia, thus removing the Jewish population surplus that resulted from the high rate of natural increase. The percentage of emigrants among the Jews of Russia was three times or more that amongst other peoples leaving Russia at that time—the Finns and Poles, for example. About 40 per cent of Jewish emigrant breadwinners made their living by the needle; two-thirds owed their livelihood to trade in general. Jewish emigration was also characterized by the relatively very small number of those who returned (5 to 7 per cent, as against one-third of the general emigration), by the large number of women and children leaving, and by the fact that so many emigrants had their fares paid by relatives.[3] The Jews of Russia, in short, left for good, not in order to make money abroad, not in order to return, but in order to settle permanently elsewhere.

Jewish emigration from Russia was also peculiar in that it contained so many diverse elements. It was not only the population surplus from the

[1] I. Blum and L. Zak, *Kooperatsiya Sredy Yevreev*, St. Petersburg, 1913, pp. 16–17.

[2] Cf. *Yevreiskoe Naselenie Rossii*, pp. v–vi.

[3] L. Hersch, 'The International Migration of the Jews', in *International Migrations* (ed. by W. E. Wilcox), vol. ii, New York, 1931, pp. 471–590.

Pale of Settlement that left, but all those seeking escape from persecution and government discrimination. The number of emigrants always rose suddenly in years of persecution and pogroms, e.g. after the expulsion of the Jews from Moscow in 1891 or after the wave of pogroms in October 1905. One may say, therefore, that very many Russian Jews, despairing of ever attaining their rights within that country, 'voted with their legs' (to use Lenin's phrase) for Jewish emancipation. Moreover, the dimensions of the mass migration were taken in various Jewish political circles as symbol and proof of the need to solve the Jewish problem either by finding some territory where Jews could settle or by creating a separate territorial-political framework for them.

Differentiation amongst Russian Jewry was sharply accentuated in this period. At the same time as masses of Jews were painfully turning to manual labour, becoming proletarianized, pauperized, and forced to emigrate, at the same time as mutual aid and internal solidarity were growing, the small number of rich and educated Jews continued to devise plans for their assimilation into Russian life and were taking an active part in Russia's economic development.

It is a fact that when it was proposed to plan the emigration of Russian Jewry in the 1880s and 1890s, or to try to organize and direct the flow, wealthy Jews objected, on the grounds that any such activity would strengthen the hands of those people in Russia who claimed that the Jews were not natives of the country and did not belong there.[1] Wealthy Jews played a very large part in Russian railway construction, especially in the sixties and seventies (from the eighties onwards the Russian Government began to build railways on its own account, and hastened to take the existing lines out of Jewish hands). Equally great was the Jewish share in the development of banking, especially commercial and mortgage banks. According to a Russian government source, the brothers Poliakoff 'played a prominent role in introducing land credit'.[2] We have already mentioned Jewish interests in the textile and food industries in the Pale of Settlement. Jews were also active in river transport and the extraction of precious metals. Jewish capitalists were affected by the economic crisis that struck

[1] A conference of Jewish notables held in St. Petersburg in April 1882 adopted the following resolution: 'First, to reject completely the thought of organizing emigration, as being subversive of the dignity of the Russian body politic and of the historic rights of the Jews to their present fatherland. . . .' The conference was summoned and led by Baron Horace Günzburg, and was attended, amongst others, by the railroad magnate Poliakoff, Professor Bakst, and the famous rabbi of Kovno, Rabbi Yitzhak Elhanan Spector. (Cf. S. Dubnow, *The History of the Jews in Russia and Poland*, vol. ii, Philadelphia, 1946, pp. 304–8).

[2] K. Kh. Spassky, *Istoriya Torgovli i Promyshlennosti v Rossii*, 4th issue, St. Petersburg, 1911, p. 37.

Russia in the last years of the nineteenth century and continued throughout the Russo-Japanese war and the 1905 Revolution. But in 1908 a revival began and Jewish capitalists strengthened their interests in the coal production of southern Russia, in the refining and marketing of oil in the Caucasus.[1] They even entered heavy industry, in partnership with capitalists from western Europe. They took part increasingly in light industries too, despite stringent government regulations that demanded a Christian majority on the boards of enterprises (as in the case of the credit co-operatives) and despite government encouragement of banks and companies whose declared aim was to 'rid the Russian economy of Jewish influence'.

These demographic developments and economic changes had a decisive influence on Russian Jewry. The Jewish masses lost faith not only in the government but also in that whole class of Jewish notables whose efforts and feelings were devoted to ends so removed from those of the majority. The masses began to put their faith more in independent Jewish organization, in mutual aid and in long-term political plans which to some extent turned their attention outside Russia. All this led to extensive political and social activity that embraced very wide sections of the Jewish public—far more so than in the case of any other national group. All the while the rich and educated became more and more distant in their language, ideas, and way of life, from the Jewish masses. Yet even they felt that their position in Russian society, particularly in the state, was far from consonant with their real weight and the dimensions of their economic activity, not to speak of their contribution to social and political thought. The two sections of the Jewish people in Russia awaited political changes with bated breath, and were ready for them.

What forms did the political and social activity of Russian Jewry take at that time? We shall not be able to judge the peculiar nature of that action unless we try to uncover its deeper roots. Jewish political thought took shape mainly in medieval Europe, when the Jews were allotted the place of a religious-social corporation within general society. The Jewish community in Europe developed from co-operation between a Jewish leadership that was concerned with maintaining internal discipline in the Jewish society, and the authorities who saw that leadership as a means of achieving fiscal objectives and as a tool for administrative control of the Jews. This co-operation between the Jewish leaders and the authorities became the distinguishing mark of the Jews' legal status in the eyes of the surrounding people and sometimes caused great suffering to the Jews in times

---

[1] F. D. Henry, *Baku: An Eventful History*, London, 1905, p. 113.

of outbreaks and bitterness. Within Jewish society also, reliance on the government and loyalty to it became a clear and established trend.

The change came with the appearance of the Hassidic movement in the second half of the eighteenth century, and with the increased support given by the governments of Russia and Austria to the plans of the Jewish *maskilim* (followers of the Enlightenment) to weaken internal Jewish autonomy. The Jewish public reacted with great hostility to these trends and to the intervention of the government in its internal affairs. The Hassidic communities and the courts of the Hassidic *zaddikim* became cells of opposition. In fact, the whole of Jewish society, apart from a few intellectuals, began in eastern Europe to pass from unity in support of the authorities to a more fervent unity without the authorities or even against them. It was this rebellious spirit in the Jews (who had traditionally always been loyal to the government, and usually inert), that moved Nicholas I to the step mentioned above, i.e. to withdraw in 1844 the legal recognition hitherto extended to the Jewish communities. By this means the government hoped to split the internal unity of the Jews.

The *Haskalah* (Enlightenment) movement among eastern European Jewry was confined to a small section of the rich and part of the youth, and did not reach the mass of Jewry. In the 1870s and 1880s enlightened young Jews were already devoting themselves to political and social movements utterly opposed to that co-operation with the authorities preached by the *maskilim* of the previous generation. Some of these young people turned to the Russian revolutionary movement and became an important element in it; others became leaders of the Jewish national movement; still others began to work for socialism among the Jews, in their own language, emphasizing their specific problems.[1]

A deep ideological gulf divided the holders of these opinions. No reconciliation was possible between those who sought a revolutionary change in the existing political order of Russia and those who despaired of Russia entirely and saw redemption in the establishment of a special Jewish state. There was, however, one similarity between the opposing groups. The common factor was that both distrusted the government's intentions towards the Jews and saw it as a hostile element without which—or against which—the solution of the 'Jewish problem' would have to come. In this they gave expression to trends which, as we have said, were already

[1] Cf. L. G. Deitsch, *Rol Yevreev v Russkom Revolyutsionnom Dvizhenie*, Berlin, 1923; Yivo, *Historische Schriften* (Yiddish), vol. iii, Paris, 1939. N. A. Buchbinder, *Istoriya Yevreevskovo Rabochevo Dvizheniya v Rossii*, Leningrad, 1926. A comprehensive bibliography of the history of the national movement is given in I. Gruenbaum, *The Development of the Zionist Movement* (Hebrew), vols. 1–4, Jerusalem, 1942.

implanted in the Jewish public as a whole, and accounted for the great popularity of national and revolutionary circles. When the first Zionist congress met in Basle in 1897 and in the same year the first all-Russian congress of the Bund (the Jewish Social Democratic Union) took place, giving expression to both national and social radicalism, the enthusiasm aroused among the Jews of Russia was vast and overwhelming. It was as though, overnight almost, this great mass of people had awoken from its political slumber and had begun to develop ideologies, examine political programmes, and even establish political groups and parties, workers' funds, trade unions, and mutual-aid societies. It was not long before the first efforts were made to merge national and social radicalism into the one movement of Zionist-socialist ideology.

The Kishinev pogrom of March 1903 marked another turning-point in this process. It then became clear to the Jews that not only was the government indifferent to the preservation of public order and Jewish lives, but was actively aiding the murderous mobs. At this time there originated that heroic chapter in the secret organization of fighting units for self-defence, to preserve Jewish lives and honour. The Revolution of 1905–7 gave sharp and far-reaching expression to this movement.

This was a period of revival and ferment in the political life of Russia; councils, unions, and political parties arose; strikes multiplied; demonstrations were held; armed rebellions struck. In all these events the Jews played a leading part. The non-socialist elements among them combined into the Union for the Attainment of Equal Rights for Russian Jewry. Their aim was to prepare a plan for the national organization of all Russian Jews; they also wished to establish a 'club' of Jewish representatives within the Duma, or at least to instruct these representatives in questions affecting the Jews. (The Jewish members of the Duma were chosen from all-Russian lists, and it was necessary to reach an agreed position on Jewish matters.)

The socialist forces among the Jewish public organized strikes and demonstrations, and set up fighting squads to repel the pogrom-maddened mobs and to resist the police and soldiers protecting the mobs. The years of the first Russian Revolution thus served as a new stage in the public awakening of the Jews of Russia; they began to organize for action in the political sphere, and through their strength came to realize that they must take their fate into their own hands.[1]

The political coup of June 1907, that limited yet further the powers of the Duma, dealt revolutionary and liberal forces in Russia a bitter blow.

[1] L. Greenberg, *The Jews in Russia*, vol. ii, New Haven, 1945.

It also silenced the political activity of the Jewish parties as well. The outbreak of the First World War intensified their despair. The government, as we have seen, sought a scapegoat for its military and political failures, and tried by all means in its power to present the Jews as enemy agents, disloyal to Russia. Correspondence in Yiddish was prohibited, and on 5 July 1915 a ban was imposed on all publications printed in Hebrew characters.[1] This affected a population of millions, the vast majority of whom used no other language. But the Jewish public soon shook off its despair. The persecutions and expulsions of the war years stimulated an immediate renewal of activity among the Jews, as they went out to help the hundreds of thousands of Jewish refugees expelled or in flight from the battle zones. Even the authorities were forced to take account of this new situation, and by a decision of the Council of Ministers of 4 August 1915, the ban on the settlement of Jews outside the Pale was temporarily lifted and Jews were permitted to enter educational institutions and to establish their own institutions in inner Russia.[2] The Jewish Association for the Relief of War Victims (E.K.O.P.O.) organized large-scale activities in conjunction with the Jewish Colonization Association and with the aid of the Joint Distribution Committee. This 'awakening' stimulated all types of Jewish bodies into attempting to revive their activities in other fields. The pent-up forces within Russian Jewry were only waiting for a political change in order to renew their social and political activity with greater vigour. The change came, of course, when the Revolution broke out in February 1917.

The renewed activity in conditions of freedom derived from the experience gained in the Revolution of 1905. It was clear to all sections of the Jewish public that the Jewish people of Russia was a separate national unit whose rights must be secured. All the spokesmen of the Jewish parties saw the future of Russia as a federation of free nations, enjoying autonomy within the wider political framework. As we have seen, they first planned to summon a congress of elected representatives of the whole of Russian Jewry (the all-Russian Jewish congress) which would draw up the political programme. The main debates centred on the precise form and limits of national autonomy, on the links with other sections of the Jewish people, outside the borders of Russia, and on the attitude to the Zionist idea, i.e. the effort to establish an independent Jewish state in the land of Israel. In

[1] Cf. *Iz Nedavnego Proshlogo. Ryechi Yevreiskikh Deputatov v Gosudarstvennoi Dume za Gody Voiny*, Petrograd, 1917, pp. 67–9.

[2] Ya. I. Gimpelson, L. M. Bramson, *Zakony o Yevreiakh. Dobavlenie: Rasshirenie Cherty Yevreiskoi Osedlosti*, Petrograd, 1916.

the elections to the congress (in which, for various reasons, only a small section of Russian Jewry took part) the Zionists and the religious groups won a decisive majority. The elections to democratic communities set up in many places produced similar results. The Zionist influence grew even stronger when the Balfour Declaration was published in November 1917. It swept Russian Jewry to a peak of enthusiasm. On the other hand, the work of the socialist parties was greatly appreciated. Although they constituted only a minority of the total Jewish public, they were outstanding in their dynamism and in their close connections with Russian political parties and those of other national groups inhabiting the empire.

Two powerful forces opposed the vision of a federal Russia granting autonomy to all its peoples. The separatist ambitions of some nations, notably the Ukrainian, within whose borders lived most of Russia's Jews, formed one source of opposition. The second was the centralizing tendency of the Bolshevik party, which, though it gradually (and in theory only) recognized the right of peoples to national autonomy,[1] in fact restricted this right to peoples who inhabited definite territories. They thus excluded the Jews from the right to national autonomy. The Jewish parties in 1917 went some of the way with the Ukrainian parties, in the hope that the latter would not finally sever their connections with Russia. Their hopes were in vain: Ukrainian separatists not only cut themselves off from Russia and took up arms against Russia; in the process they perpetrated mass murders of Ukrainian Jews.[2] Only the utter failure of the Ukrainian attempt at independence restored the Jews to security and, for the most part, to the boundaries of Russia. But most crucial for the fate of Russian Jewry was the policy of the Bolsheviks, who within a short time dealt a mortal blow to the political awakening and cultural efflorescence of the Jews.

To sum up, for the space of a year or two the forces of Russian Jewry were released by the democratic revolution, and then just as quickly quenched.

The communist revolution put an end to the social, cultural, and national hopes of the Russian Jews. The stupendous activity of 1917–18 arose from the complex processes of earlier years, when the Jewish public learnt to rely on itself. Developments in Jewish autonomy, its trends and the deficiencies imposed on it; the experiences of the Jewish intelligentsia,

[1] Cf. E. H. Carr, *The Bolshevik Revolution*, vol. i, London, 1950, pp. 286–379.

[2] For these trends cf. J. S. Reshetar, *The Ukrainian Revolution*, Princeton, 1952; for the condition and activity of the Jews in the Ukraine, see I. E. Tscherikover, *Antisemitizm i Pogromy na Ukraine, 1917–1918*, Berlin, 1923.

their participation and then loss of hope, in the all-Russian struggle; the organization of cultural institutions and the development of a Jewish press; national and socialist activity and the means whereby both might be merged—all this prepared the way for the great upsurge of that short period. The brevity of the efflorescence reflects the weakness of Russian democracy.

2
Soviet Jewry:
Some Problems and Perspectives

S. LEVENBERG

During the festivities arranged to commemorate the fiftieth anniversary of the October Revolution considerable satisfaction was expressed at the success of the Soviet nationalities policy. 'The whole world knows of the success of the Leninist nationalities policy', L. I. Brezhnev told the joint jubilee meeting of the Central Committee of the C.P.S.U., the Supreme Soviet of the U.S.S.R. and the Supreme Soviet of the R.S.F.S.R.

All the nations and nationalities of the Soviet Union are flourishing and have achieved colossal progress in the promotion of industry, agriculture, science and culture. . . . The unity of the multinational Soviet people is as solid as a diamond. As a diamond sparkles with multi-coloured facets, so does the unity of our people scintillate with the diversity of nations, each of which lives a rich, full-blooded, free and happy life.[1]

J. E. Paletskis, the chairman of the Supreme Soviet of Nationalities, expressed an identical view. The 'great October' had put an end to the discrimination practised by the tsarist regime and given all the peoples of Russia equal opportunity, he asserted.[2]

Neither Brezhnev nor Paletskis—in their survey of the history of the past fifty years—mentioned the Jews: their sufferings under the tsarist regime, their great contribution to the revolutionary movement, the outstanding part that they played among the leaders of the 'great October', their contribution to Soviet society, their part in the war, the extermination of the Jewish population by the Nazi invaders, the anti-Jewish campaign during the last period of Stalin's life. Not one single reference was made to any of these facts during the official gatherings to commemorate fifty years of Soviet rule.

But before considering the position of the Jews in more detail, it is

[1] *Great October: 1917–67*, report by L. I. Brezhnev, Moscow, 1967, pp. 34–5.
[2] 'The Great Friendship of Nations.' Talk with the Chairman of the Supreme Soviet of the Council of Nationalities, J. E. Paletskis, *Novy Mir*, no. 10, October 1967, pp. 11–16.

important to locate them in the context of the Soviet Union as a multi-national state.

The U.S.S.R. contains fifteen Soviet Socialist Republics which vary greatly in total area and number of inhabitants. Each of these republics has as a major sector of the population one particular national group:

Area and Population of the Union of Soviet Socialist Republics

	Area* ('ooo sq. km.)	Population† ('ooo)	Number of people per square kilometre
Total U.S.S.R.	22,402	241,720	10·8
R.S.F.S.R.	17,075	130,079	7·6
Ukrainian S.S.R.	603	47,127	78·2
Byelorussian S.S.R.	208	9,002	43·3
Uzbek S.S.R.	450	11,799	26·2
Kazakh S.S.R.	2,715	13,009	4·8
Georgian S.S.R.	70	4,686	66·9
Azerbaijan S.S.R.	87	5,117	58·8
Lithuanian S.S.R.	65	3,128	48·1
Moldavian S.S.R.	34	3,569	105·0
Latvian S.S.R.	64	2,364	36·9
Kirghiz S.S.R.	143	2,933	20·5
Tajik S.S.R.	143	2,900	20·3
Armenian S.S.R.	30	2,492	83·1
Turkmen S.S.R.	488	2,159	4·4
Estonian S.S.R.	45	1,356	30·1

* On 1 July 1971. *SSSR. Administrativno-territorialnoe delenie soiuznykh respublik*, Supreme Soviet Presidium, Moscow, 1971.

† 'Tsentralnoe statisticheskoe upravlenie pri Soviete ministrov SSSR', *Itogi vsesoiuznoi perepisi naseleniya 1970 goda*, vol. i, Moscow, 1972, p. 7.

The Russians form the majority of the population of the U.S.S.R. True, this majority is not large but together with two other Slav nationalities—the Ukrainians and the Byelorussians—it constitutes the most powerful element in the country. If we bear in mind the economic strength and the cultural influence of the Russians, their great impact on Soviet affairs becomes undeniably obvious. Their position is strengthened by the number of Russians in the various union Republics as shown on page 32.[1]

Among the most important reasons for the settlement of Russians throughout the entire Soviet Union have been the industrialization of the

[1] Ibid., vol. iv, pp. 12–15.

country, the establishment of new economic centres, and the movement of population during the Second World War. Another reason is the tendency in favour of maintaining Russian influence in the smaller republics.

Number of Russians in the Union Republics

	('000)	Percentage
R.S.F.S.R.	107,748	82·8
Ukrainian S.S.R.	9,126	19·4
Kazakh S.S.R.	5,521	42·4
Uzbek S.S.R.	1,473	12·5
Byelorussian S.S.R.	938	10·4
Kirghiz S.S.R.	856	29·2
Azerbaijan S.S.R.	510	10·0
Latvian S.S.R.	705	29·8
Georgian S.S.R.	397	8·5
Moldavian S.S.R.	414	11·6
Turkmen S.S.R.	313	14·5
Tajik S.S.R.	344	11·9
Estonian S.S.R.	335	24·7
Lithuanian S.S.R.	268	8·6
Armenian S.S.R.	66	2·7

According to the 1970 census, of the 241·7 million persons living in the U.S.S.R., 142 million or almost 60 per cent of the population gave Russian as their native language; this exceeded the number of Russians in the U.S.S.R. by 13 million.[1] (In 1926 there were 6·6 million persons of non-Russian nationality who considered Russian their native language.)

Officially there is no single state language in the U.S.S.R., but Russian serves as the link between the various nationalities. Russian is the second language in the educational system of the smaller Soviet republics. Russian culture is spread throughout the country by the media of radio, television, and the press. Thus the younger generation in all the republics is encouraged to speak, read, and exchange ideas in Russian. There are only 135,324 out of 9,126,331 Russians living in the Ukraine who consider Ukrainian their native tongue,[2] and 203,769 out of 129,015,140 Russians who gave as their native tongue the language of other nationalities.[3]

The progress of the Russian language has made considerable headway in the Soviet Union. Whereas the advance made by the various national

---

[1] Ibid., vol. iv, p. 20.   [2] Ibid., vol. iv, p. 152.   [3] Ibid.

groups in the U.S.S.R. during the last half century is undeniable, the process of ethnic assimilation is a fact of life.

Let us now turn to the Jews. Numerically, they are not a negligible factor. According to the census of 1959 there were 2,268,000 Jews in the U.S.S.R. Two years later, in 1961, according to the Soviet Institute of Ethnography, the Jewish population totalled 2,468,000. In another official publication it was estimated that in 1966 there were some 3 million Jews in the U.S.S.R.[1] Some experts consider this figure an underestimate. According to the 1970 census there were 2,151,000 Jews in the U.S.S.R.

The Jewish population is roughly similar to the total number of inhabitants in eight of the fifteen Soviet Socialist republics: Lithuania, Moldavia, Latvia, Kirghisia, Tajikistan, Armenia, Turkmenia, and Estonia. But this does not yet convey the full picture. The Jews are an urban element. The total number of people residing in Soviet towns is 136 million;[2] among them live the Jews, representing almost 2 per cent. The importance of the Jewish element is in fact greater, because it is largely concentrated in a number of the major Soviet urban centres such as Moscow, Leningrad, Kiev, Odessa, Kharkov, Minsk, Kishinev, Vilna, Riga, Lvov, Tashkent, Baku, Tbilisi, Novosibirsk.

According to the 1970 census there were 808,000 Jews in the R.S.F.S.R. (0·6 per cent of the total population); 777,000 in the Ukraine (1·6 per cent); 148,000 in Byelorussia (1·6 per cent); 103,000 in Uzbekistan (0·9 per cent); 55,000 in Georgia (1·2 per cent); 24,000 in Lithuania (0·8 per cent); 98,000 in Moldavia (2·7 per cent); 37,000 in Latvia (1·6 per cent); 5,000 in Estonia (0·4 per cent). The same census also gave a total of 252,000 Jews living in Moscow (3·6 per cent of the total population of the city); 163,000 in Leningrad (4·1 per cent); 152,000 in Kiev (9·3 per cent); 47,000 in Minsk (5·1 per cent); 50,000 in Kishinev (14·0 per cent); 31,000 in Riga (4·2 per cent); 20,000 in Tbilisi (2·2 per cent), and 16,000 in Vilnius (4·4 per cent).[3]

These figures are considered by some Jewish sociologists outside the U.S.S.R. as a gross underestimate of the number of Jews in Soviet cities. According to one such estimate of 1963, over one and a quarter million Jews resided in seven cities, as follows: Moscow, 500,000; Leningrad, 325,000; Kiev, 154,000; Odessa, 118,000; Kharkov, 80,000; Kishinev, 42,000; and Minsk, 38,000. This makes the total Jewish population of these cities 1,257,000.[4]

[1] Solomon Rabinovich, *Jews in the Soviet Union*, Moscow, 1967, p. 45.
[2] *Itogi*, vol. i, p. 8.
[3] Ibid., vol. iv.   [4] *American Jewish Year Book*, vol. 63, 1963, p. 350.

One thing is clear. The number of Jews in some Soviet cities is considerable. Of special importance is their increase in the territory occupied by the Russian republic. In 1897, 11·9 per cent of the total Jewish population of the country resided there; today the proportion is 37·6 per cent.[1]

Qualitatively, the Jews are an important element in the Soviet Union. According to official statistics, they account for 14·7 per cent of all Soviet doctors, 8·5 per cent of writers and journalists, 10·4 per cent of all judges and lawyers, and 7·7 per cent of actors, musicians, and artists,[2] while the number of scientific workers is given as 927,709, this latter total including 64,392 Jews.[3] Jewish scientists take third place after Russians and Ukrainians. The number of Jewish specialist workers with a higher or specialized secondary education was about half a million in 1964.[4]

In spite of their comparatively large numbers and the important positions which they occupy in certain fields, the Jews as a group are at a great disadvantage. They do not form a majority of the population in any of the republics of the Soviet Union, the autonomous republics, autonomous regions, or national areas. They are dispersed all over the country and constitute a minority in all those territories which together form the Soviet Union. Thus, according to the theories of Lenin and Stalin on the nationality problem—which still influence Russian policy—the Jews are not a nation in spite of their official designation as a nationality.

During the first decade after the Revolution, certain Soviet leaders realized the great disadvantage in which the Jewish community was placed. The problem was aggravated by the economic disaster which overtook many Jews in the Ukraine and Byelorussia—their main places of concentration—as a result of the First World War, and the social policies practised by the new communist government. The idea that the Jews should take up agriculture and enjoy a measure of territorial concentration was actively encouraged by Mikhail Kalinin, the then President of the U.S.S.R. Kalinin was convinced that the Jews could never develop into a fully-fledged nation in the U.S.S.R. as long as they were concentrated in towns—least of all the Moscow Jews living in an international city where national peculiarities were bound to be effaced. Above all, he was conscious of the importance of Jewish public opinion abroad. For him the Jews constituted 'one of the most lively and politically most influential nations'.[5] A special committee was established to give assistance to those

[1] *Itogi*, vol. iv.
[2] *Soviet Weekly*, London, 4 June 1966.
[3] See M. Checinski, *Soviet Jewish Affairs*, vol. 3, no. 2, 1973.
[4] *Soviet Weekly*, London, 28 May 1966; see also Rabinovich, op. cit., p. 56.
[5] W. Kolarz, *Russia and her Colonies*, London, 1952, pp. 174-5.

Jews who were prepared to go back to the land. Another mass voluntary organization—Ozet—was formed to assist Jews who wished to become farmers. Special areas in the southern Ukraine were designated for this purpose. Three Jewish national districts were established in the Kherson and Dnepropetrovsk regions and two in the Crimea.[1]

Jewish agricultural colonies had already existed under the tsarist regime but the number of Jews living in them was at no time higher than 90,000 and considerably below that figure on the eve of the First World War. The total number of Jewish collective farms in the U.S.S.R. in the mid-1930s amounted to 500, and there were 225,000 Jews engaged in agriculture of whom 90 per cent lived in Byelorussia, the Crimea, and various parts of the Ukrainian republic. This figure diminished, however, in the years before the Second World War.[2] The Nazi invasion destroyed the work carried out over many years by the Jewish farmers.

Settlement of the Jews in Biro-Bidzhan was another project to 'normalize' the Jewish position in the U.S.S.R. through territorial concentration. Three major reasons guided an experiment whose purpose was the establishment of a Jewish autonomous region in the Soviet far east. One was to bring about a solution of Russia's Jewish problem by giving the Jews a homeland and creating a Jewish nation. The second reason was to arouse sympathy among Jewish communities abroad for the project of a 'Soviet-Jewish state'. The third was to increase the defence potential of the U.S.S.R., by recruiting settlers for an exposed far eastern border area.

The Biro-Bidzhan project was received with greater enthusiasm in certain Jewish circles abroad than in Moscow or Kiev. In the light of growing antisemitism in Europe and the increasing restriction on Jewish immigration into Palestine, the new project was looked upon as a chance for a national life in the Soviet Union, a new hope for Jewry in the U.S.S.R., where Jewish life was on the decline since the communist revolution. Dr. Chaim Weizmann—the President of the World Zionist Organization—greeted the Biro-Bidzhan plan as a 'station' on the road to the Jewish homeland in Palestine. But subsequent events have proved that life in the far east had little national appeal for Soviet Jewry.[3]

In 1942 Biro-Bidzhan had a population of 100,000 due to the influx during the war of people of whom less than a half were Jews.[4] But the area

[1] Rabinovich, op. cit., pp. 46–7.
[2] Kolarz, op. cit., p. 172.
[3] B. Z. Goldberg, *The Jewish Problem in the Soviet Union*, New York, 1961, p. 174.
[4] Kolarz, op. cit., p. 178.

never became an important centre of Jewish agricultural settlement because urbanization proceeded at a quick pace; more than a quarter of its population lived in the capital. The 1959 census indicated that the total population of Biro-Bidzhan was 162,856—of these the Russians formed a large majority: 127,281 (78·2 per cent); the Ukrainians came next with a population of 14,425 (8·9 per cent). The Jews occupied third place (8·8 per cent).[1] According to the 1970 census, the total population of Biro-Bidzhan was 172,449, the Jews occupying second place with a population of 11,452 (6·64 per cent).[2]

Why are there so few Jews in Biro-Bidzhan? The following reply was given by a Jewish contributor to the official Soviet Novosti agency:

by the end of the thirties, especially in the war years, there was no longer any need for Jews with jobs to move. Why should a person living in Vinnitsa, Kiev or Sverdlovsk, leave a place where he has lived for a long time, give up his permanent job, and acquaintances? There may have been other reasons. And, of course, Soviet power is not to blame for the fact that tens of thousands and not hundreds of thousands went to Biro-Bidzhan.[3]

Who, then, is to blame? Whatever the answer, the fact is that the attempts at Jewish territorial concentration in the Soviet Union ended in failure.

This lack of a Jewish national centre puts the large Jewish community in the U.S.S.R. into a category of its own. Its situation cannot be compared with any of the national groups which form a majority in one of the territorial units of the Soviet Union.

Another factor which has an important impact on the position of the Jewish population—apart from the lack of a territorial centre—is its special socio-economic structure. Whereas 44 per cent of the inhabitants of the U.S.S.R. live in rural areas[4] nearly 98 per cent of the Jews reside in urban centres.[5] In the mid-1930s over 10 per cent of the Jewish working population was engaged in agriculture,[6] but today there are few Jews working on the land.

As to Jewish urban occupations there are no reliable data available. But there is no doubt that the Soviet regime has accomplished a

[1] Rabinovich, op. cit., p. 28.

[2] See L. Hirszowicz, 'Birobidzhan After Forty Years', *Soviet Jewish Affairs*, vol. 4, no. 2, 1974.

[3] Ibid., p. 29   [4] *Itogi*, vol. i, p. 9.

[5] *Studies in Jewish Demography*, The Hebrew University, Institute of Contemporary Jewry and the Institute of Jewish Affairs, 1975, p. 195.

[6] Rabinovich, op. cit., pp. 57–8.

socio-economic transformation of the Jewish population in the U.S.S.R. by comparison with tsarist times.

In 1939, Soviet Jewry included 30 per cent manual workers, 41 per cent employees and members of the liberal professions, 20 per cent artisans, 6 per cent farmers, and 3 per cent people of miscellaneous professions.[1] The Jewish 'declassed' element—poor and without any definite occupation—had almost disappeared. But the disasters of the Nazi period, the advance of industrialization, the anti-Jewish campaign of the Stalin period, the considerable growth of the educated Jewish element—all this has had a considerable effect on the socio-economic structure of the Jewish population. A tendency developed in favour of administrative posts, white-collar jobs, teaching and similar occupations, and positions in the service and distribution industries. With the premium placed on managerial, operative, and supervisory qualifications young Jews have shown an inclination for these particular jobs.[2]

André Blumel, a leader of the Franco-Soviet Friendship League, was informed during one of his frequent visits to the U.S.S.R. that about 50 per cent of the lawyers in Leningrad and Kharkov were Jews; that of the 1,190 lawyers in Moscow 405 were Jews. Madame Furtseva, Soviet Minister of Culture, also told Blumel that 10 per cent of the members of the Soviet Academy of Science and 34 per cent of the personnel in the Soviet film industry were Jews.

Thus Soviet Jews are prominent in certain spheres of the Soviet economy. This is partly due to the fact that they are town-dwellers, partly to their high educational standards. Other factors are the traditional Jewish characteristic of hard work and special ability in some managerial, administrative, and professional jobs. This does not mean that there are no Jewish workers in the Soviet Union; quite the contrary. They are to be found in many enterprises and construction projects—in the Urals, Donbas, Kharkov, Moscow, Leningrad, Riga, Vilnius, and elsewhere.[3]

On the other hand, there is no doubt that the socio-economic structure of the Jewish population is different from that of other nationalities in the Soviet Union. In a way, the present Jewish occupational structure is due to the fact that Jews play either a minor part, or no part at all, in those spheres where they were prominent during the first period of the Revolution: in government, the leadership of the communist party, the diplomatic

[1] 'Jewish Agricultural Colonization in Russia and the U.S.S.R.' (Hebrew), *Gesher*, Jerusalem, September 1966, p. 38.

[2] N. Barou, *The Jews in Work and Trade*, London, 1945, p. 30.

[3] Goldberg, op. cit., pp. 317–33; see also Rabinovich, op. cit., p. 58.

service, the higher echelons of the army and elsewhere in the Soviet 'establishment'.

Whereas the *de facto* exclusion of Jews from certain areas of public life, as introduced by Stalin, has never been revoked, their prominence in other fields creates problems in the various republics and encourages antisemitism.

'Antisemitic sentiments still exist here', Khrushchev explained to an official delegation of the French socialist party, in May 1956.

They are remnants of a reactionary past. This is a complicated problem because of the position of the Jews and their relations with other peoples. At the outset of the Revolution, we had many Jews in the leadership of the party and of the state. They were educated, maybe more revolutionary than the average Russian. In due course we have created new cadres. Should the Jews want to occupy the foremost positions in our republics now, it would naturally be taken amiss by the indigenous inhabitants. The latter would ill receive their pretensions, especially as they don't consider themselves less intelligent or less capable than the Jews. Or, for instance, when a Jew in the Ukraine is appointed to an important post and he surrounds himself with Jewish collaborators, it is understandable that this should create jealousy and hostility towards the Jews. But we are not antisemites. . . .

It is clear that there exists a Jewish socio-economic problem in the Soviet Union. It is not likely to become easier when 'new cadres'— to use Khrushchev's expression—are created and higher educational standards emerge among the majority groups in the various Soviet republics.

Sixty years of communist rule have made a great impact on the economic structure of the Jewish population, but there still remain certain 'peculiarities'. These are characteristic of many minorities and, especially, of Jewish life in the Diaspora. This fact influences the position of the Jewish population in Soviet society. But this lack of territorial concentration and a specific socio-economic structure are not the only reasons for the special position of the Jewish minority in the Soviet Union. Another aspect of the problem is the great discrepancy between its official status as one of the nationalities of the U.S.S.R. and the realities of the situation.

The highest organ of state power in the U.S.S.R. is the Supreme Soviet, which consists of two chambers: the Council of the Union and the Council of Nationalities. The latter is intended to represent the specific interests of the various peoples of the U.S.S.R., as determined by the particular characteristics of their economy, culture, language, and way of life.[1] But the Jewish nationality as such is not represented on the Council of Nationalities which—according to Article 35 of the Soviet constitution —is elected by the citizens of the U.S.S.R. voting by Union republics, autonomous republics, autonomous regions and national areas. Of the five deputies elected in Biro-Bidzhan in 1970 only two were Jews.[2] According to the Soviet statistical abstract of 1959 there was one Jewish deputy among the 457 in the Ukraine; two out of 407 in Byelorussia; three out of 209 in Lithuania. These are all areas with a large Jewish population. Of the 5,312 members elected to the Supreme Soviet in the republics only 14 were Jews.[3] They were selected in their individual capacity only. Thus the Jewish population as a collective entity has no voice on the Council of Nationalities. This makes the Jewish minority 'a group apart', without any possibility of expressing its views on matters of specific interest to the Jewish population.

This special position of the Jewish nationality is not confined to external matters. There is no internal Jewish communal structure in the U.S.S.R. Individually, Jews are described in their internal passports as of Jewish nationality but as a group their nationality is barely recognized. Three million Jewish individuals exist but there is no elected or appointed organ to represent them. Such large Jewish communities as those of the Ukraine and White Russia, with their long tradition of Jewish creative activity, have no educational or cultural institutions.[4]

It was not always so. During the first period of the communist regime Jewish cultural life was encouraged. In 1925 there were 250 Jewish schools in the Ukraine. There was an institute of Jewish culture in the Ukrainian Academy of Sciences. A number of Jewish theatrical companies existed. In 1935 there were ten Yiddish newspapers in the Ukraine. Jewish scholars, writers, and poets enjoyed facilities for creative activity.[5] When the best Jewish writers of the Soviet Union were executed on 12 August 1952, seven of these were sons of Ukrainian Jewry; Dovid Bergelson, Der Nister, Dovid Hofstein, Aaron Kushnirov, Leyb Kvitko, Perets Markish, Itzik Fefer. They embodied the intellectual strength and vitality of

---

[1] I. P. Tsamerian and S. L. Ronin, *Nationalities in the U.S.S.R.*, Unesco, Paris, 1962, p. 49.

[2] L. Hirszowicz, op. cit.

[3] *Socialist International Report of Working Party on the situation of the Jewish Community in the U.S.S.R.*, London, October, 1967, p. 5.

[4] Dr. S. Levenberg, 'Soviet Jewry—Fact and Fiction', *Jewish Vanguard*, London, 17 June 1966.

[5] Dr. S. Levenberg, 'Ukrainian Jewry—Community without a voice', *Jewish Vanguard*, London, 17 December 1965. See also Dr. S. Levenberg, 'Byelorussia—Tragedy of a great community', *Jewish Vanguard*, London, 31 December 1965.

Ukrainian Jewry. But during the years 1948–59 not one Jewish book was published in the Soviet Union. Between 1959 and 1965 thirteen Yiddish books were issued. There has been no fundamental change in the situation since then.[1]

Today, there are no Jewish schools, no Jewish literary societies, and no Jewish newspapers, even in the Ukraine. No organized Jewish life exists. There is no contact between Jews in one city and Jews in another city on matters of common concern. This situation characterizes the general situation of Soviet Jewry.

In December 1966 the Warsaw Yiddish newspaper, *Folkshtimme*, published a survey which revealed that in recent years fifty-six Yiddish books had been published in Poland, eight in Rumania, and only seven in the U.S.S.R. The latter has proportionately the largest Yiddish-speaking population in the world. In the whole of the U.S.S.R. there are only two Jewish publications: the monthly *Sovietish Heymland* with a circulation at home and abroad of 25,000 and a small newspaper in Biro-Bidzhan that appears five times a week.

It is the official policy of the U.S.S.R. to provide children with instruction in the native language, but not a single school in the Soviet Union teaches Hebrew, Yiddish, or any other Jewish dialect, whereas the R.S.F.S.R. alone has forty-five different languages of instruction and a total of fifty-nine languages is used in the schools of the U.S.S.R. Jewish history and literature are also not taught in Russian or any other language. The Jewish minority has had no state theatre ever since the forcible closure of the famous Moscow Yiddish State Theatre during the last period of Stalin's life, together with all Jewish publishing houses, magazines, schools and other educational and cultural institutions. It is significant that much smaller Jewish communities in communist countries such as Poland (less than 10,000 Jews) and Rumania (45,000 Jews) have their own state theatre, newspaper, and some other institutions.[2] This lack of Jewish cultural activity must be judged in the light of the fact that in 1959 487,786 Russian Jews gave Yiddish, or one of the other Jewish dialects, as their mother tongue.[3] In Lithuania the proportion was 75 per cent; in Moldavia, 50 per cent; in the Kiev region, 32 per cent; in Gomel and Mogilev, 26 per cent. Altogether, about one-quarter of all those Jews who gave Yiddish as their mother tongue were concentrated in areas where they comprised about half of the total Jewish population. But there are

[1] Leon Schapiro, 'Yiddish books in the Soviet Union after Stalin', *Jewish Book Annual*, vol. 24, New York, 1966.
[2] *Socialist International Report*, pp. 2–3.   [3] Ibid., p. 2.

still neither Jewish educational nor cultural institutions in those areas of the U.S.S.R.[1] This contradicts Article 121 of the Soviet constitution which promises 'instruction in schools in the native language'.

What, then, are the cultural facilities of the Jew in the U.S.S.R.? In reply to this question from a member of a French socialist delegation, Khrushchev replied:

I would like to give you the example of Moldavia. The intellectuals in that republic don't like to send their children to Moldavian schools. They prefer the Russian ones. Similarly in the Ukraine they prefer Russian schools. The Ukrainian writers are displeased about it. This is explained by practical motives and by the interest of the populations themselves. The Russian school is being preferred because, coming from a school in Moldavia, it is more difficult later on to continue studies at a university elsewhere, while all universities of the Soviet Union are open to a student with a certificate from a Russian school.

As far as the Jews are concerned, even if Jewish schools were established, very few volunteers would be found willing to attend them. The Jews are dispersed over the entire Union. One could never establish a university in the Jewish language. There would not be a sufficient number of students. On the other hand, with regard to the Yiddish or Hebrew languages, there exists no demand for them in the administration and the Soviet institutions. If Jews were compelled to attend Jewish schools, there would certainly be a revolt. It would be considered as a kind of ghetto. The Jewish theatre pined away for lack of audiences in spite of subventions and subscriptions. However, the theatre is open to Jews. Thus in Lvov, there is a Russian theatre, yet the majority, if not all, of the actors are Jews.[2]

Khrushchev clearly favoured the assimilation of Soviet nationalities to Russian culture. But his facts were not accurate. Compulsory attendance at Jewish schools has never been suggested. The success or failure of a Jewish education effort, whether in Yiddish, Hebrew, or Russian can only be judged if the Jewish nationality be granted the same facilities as those enjoyed by the other nationalities in the U.S.S.R.

The claim that Soviet Jews themselves desire to 'assimilate' and are indifferent to Jewish culture has been contradicted by the immense popularity of Jewish concerts. In 1957 alone, 3,000 such concerts took place; each attracted an average paying audience of 1,000, according to the Soviet Press Agency Novosti.[3] Many foreign visitors have noted that Soviet Jews will turn any occasion, even an evening of Jewish songs, into

[1] Joshua Rotenberg, *Yiddisher Kampfer*, New York, 6 May 1966.

[2] Report on the talks conducted between the members of the Praesidium of the communist party of the U.S.S.R. and the members of the delegation of the French socialist party, *Réalités*. Paris, May 1967.

[3] Isi Leibler, *Soviet Jewry and Human Rights*, Melbourne, 1956, p. 26.

a demonstration of national pride.[1] Further, Khrushchev's statement that the Jewish theatre disappeared for lack of an audience is belied by its tremendous success prior to its arbitrary liquidation and by the considerable interest that the Jewish population has displayed in the occasional performances by Jewish amateur groups.[2]

What lies behind Soviet policy towards the Jewish minority in the sphere of education and culture? If the Jews are not to be a nation, centred in some special area, then they must become ordinary simple Soviet citizens, Professor Hyman Levy, formerly a leading member of the British Communist Party, has explained. If they cannot be induced to become the former, then they must be canalized into complete identification with their Soviet neighbours. According to Professor Levy, however, such an *either–or* attitude, if followed with ruthless logic, must necessarily mean that all avenues of Jewish cultural expression would be shut down and the voices of those who sought to develop it, or spoke on its behalf, would be closed. Professor Levy concludes: 'the *either–or* attitude was itself of course un-Marxist. Moreover it showed a lack of understanding of the nature and strength—the quality and quantity—of the cultural background of Jewry, and its present-day attachment to old national feelings.'[3]

These old national feelings of the Jewish population of the U.S.S.R. were greatly strengthened by their tragic experience during the Nazi period and the Second World War. The situation of Soviet Jews was unique, one observer commented, in that they suffered losses 'approaching total extermination' in the German-occupied regions of the Soviet Union.[4] The shock to the Jewish population was all the greater because they lacked sufficient information about the cruelties of the Nazi armies during the years 1939–41 (when the Stalin–Hitler agreement was in force).[5]

Memories of the Nazi period are still very strong in the Soviet Union—especially among the Jewish survivors of the Holocaust who had made the younger generation familiar with their experiences. But official Soviet publications rarely mention the traumatic experience of the Jewish population and its great contribution to victory. This is why Yevtu-

[1] *Socialist International Report*, p. 3.

[2] S. Schwarz, *Evrei v Sovetskom Soiuze s nachala vtoroi mirovoi voiny* (Jews in the Soviet Union, from the beginning of the Second World War), New York, 1966, pp. 283–7.

[3] Professor Hyman Levy, *Jews and the National Question*, London, 1958, p. 77.

[4] Michael K. Roof, 'Soviet Population Trends', *Survey*, London, July–September 1961, p. 37.

[5] Solomon M. Schwarz, *The Jews in the Soviet Union*, Syracuse University Press, New York, 1951, pp. 283–7.

shenko's poem 'Babi Yar' made a deep impression in Soviet Jewish circles:

> I am each old man that was slaughtered here
> I am each small child that was slaughtered here
> Nothing in me can forget this. . . . [1]

The inability to forget their sufferings as Jews is one of the factors which have kept alive Jewish consciousness among the Jewish population of the U.S.S.R. The loss of many close relatives is deeply felt and this makes the problem of reunion with members of families residing outside the U.S.S.R. so acute. It has to be realized that during the years 1880–1930, over 2 million Jews emigrated from Russia.[2] Thus many Soviet Jews have relatives abroad—especially in Western countries and Israel, where pioneers from Russia have played an outstanding part in the building up of the country.

It is difficult for a Soviet citizen to secure permission to travel outside the U.S.S.R. on trips of limited duration; it is even more difficult to emigrate to another country. In practice, however, some persons, mainly of foreign origin, have been able to emigrate legally. But their number is not large.[3] The number of Jews allowed to leave the U.S.S.R. was small, owing to considerations of internal Soviet policy, i.e. to the cold war and to Soviet pro-Arab policy in the Middle East. After the Six-Day War immigration to Israel was suspended for over a year.

But the number of Jews allowed to leave increased in 1969, decreased in 1970, and reached nearly 14,000 in 1971; 31,000 in 1972; 35,000 in 1973; over 20,000 in 1974; less that 12,000 in 1975.

Another factor which keeps Jewish consciousness alive in the Soviet Union are the sad memories of the anti-Jewish campaign of the Stalin period. These memories are especially strong among the older and middle-aged people of Jewish origin. 'It was not surprising that while so much crude national arrogance was being fostered, the old and only half-hidden prejudices of antisemitism also surged up', wrote the late Isaac Deutscher, in referring to the years 1948–53.

Despite all that the Bolshevik governments have done, in their better years, to combat these prejudices, enmity towards Jews was almost unabated. Antisemitism drew nourishment from many sources; from Greek Orthodoxy and the native tradition of pogroms; from the population's wartime contacts with Nazism; from

---

[1] Quoted Salo W. Baron, *The Russian Jew under Tsars and Soviets*, New York, 1964, pp. 335–6.

[2] Arthur Ruppin, *Jewish Fate and Future*, 1940, pp. 44–5.

[3] Mary Jane Moody, 'Tourists in Russia and Russians Abroad', *Problems of Communism*, Washington, November–December 1964.

the fact that Jewish traders and artisans, unadjusted to a publicly-owned economy, were conspicuous in the illicit and semi-illicit commerce flourishing amid a scarcity of goods; from the great number of Jews among the early Bolshevik leaders and from their relative importance, even after the extermination of those leaders, in the middle layers of the Stalinist bureaucracy. The simple-minded communist often looked upon the Jews as the last surviving element of urban capitalism; while the anti-communist saw them as influential members of the ruling hierarchy.[1]

Though the Soviet Union could not dispense with their services, the Jews found themselves under a cloud during the last period of Stalin's life, distrusted by superiors, envied by subordinates, uncertain of the future, stigmatized as 'cosmopolitans', and incriminated in the 'Doctor's Plot'. Before that period finally ended, the cloud hanging over the Jewish minority in the U.S.S.R. grew darker still and more menacing.[2] The subsequent period of liberalization in the Soviet Union has brought great relief to the Jewish population but the threats have not disappeared altogether. Two factors have aggravated the situation: first, the campaign against the Jewish religion—as part of the general communist belief in atheism—has been transformed into a campaign against Judaism, Zionism, and Israel, which are presented as tools of imperialism and reaction. Whereas the Soviet attitude towards the Jewish religion is based on its general ideological principles, it often has undertones of antisemitism. Since the Jewish religion is associated exclusively with the Jewish people, attacks on Jewish traditional beliefs are easily taken by some non-Jews as attacks on the Jews. The average Soviet reader of publications hostile to the Jewish religion would require to make a special effort to differentiate between anti-Judaism and antisemitism. Some writers, such as the notorious Trofim Kichko (the author of *Judaism without Embellishment*), have not borne this distinction in mind. Second, the violent attacks in the Soviet press on the Zionist movement and Israel following the Middle East developments of 1967 and 1973 have also exacerbated the situation. Again, it must be difficult for the average Soviet reader to distinguish between Zionism, Israel, and the Jews in the U.S.S.R. To quote, at random, an article which was published in *Izvestiya* on 15 June 1967 and was broadcast over Moscow radio:

having treacherously attacked the Arab countries and capitalized on the advantages of their sudden blow, the Israeli forces seized territory almost four times as large as the entire size of Israel. The invaders are killing prisoners of war and defenceless peasants, driving the inhabitants from their homes and publicly executing men, women, and children. Even Western correspondents compare these crimes with what the Nazis did in the occupied countries during World War II.[1]

The long-term repercussions of the Middle East situation on the position of the Jewish nationality in the U.S.S.R. are fairly obvious; there is cause for concern. The fact that there are 26 million Moslems in the U.S.S.R. (13 per cent of the total population)[2] has added a new dimension and a new complication to the many-sided 'Jewish problem' in the Soviet Union.[3] It is impossible to predict the future but it is important to appreciate the essentials of a most complex situation.

[1] 'The U.S.S.R. and the Middle East War', *Jews in Eastern Europe*, November 1967, p. 77.
[2] *A Study in Discrimination and Abuse of Power*, U.S. Government Printing Office, Washington, 1965, p. 12.
[3] The new results of the 1970 census which are available do not change the arguments in this paper based on the 1959 census data.

3

Soviet Theory on the Jews

Among those features of the Soviet mental world which have influenced
thought on the Jews, perhaps the most decisive is the traditional Russian
sense of cultural identity, expressed before the Soviet period in the form
of Russian Orthodox Christianity and for the past fifty years, at least at the
official and conventional levels, in the form of Soviet Marxism. The common ground of these two ideologies is their deep-rooted assumption of
mental homogeneity. All Russians in both periods are deemed to partake
of it, at the intellectual level appropriate to their education and status. If
they do not, this is because they have, in some more or less vicious sense,
cut themselves off. The extent to which this assumption has included
nations other than the Russians has varied with historical circumstances.
Until the expansion of the state into non-Slav areas it held good, in
principle, for all subjects of the state. From the eighteenth century, however, when large bodies of people (including the Polish-Lithuanian Jews)
were brought within the expanding state, the assumption was modified,
only to become universal once again under the Bolshevik state: all citizens
of the U.S.S.R. must, at the level proper to their education and function,
have Marxist ideas and communist attitudes. The assumption itself, of
homogeneity under the state, is of more deep-seated relevance to Soviet
thought on the Jews than is the content, whether Christian or communist,
of the particular homogeneity of the epoch. Both the official and the
popular mind, in a country where the assumption of homogeneity is so
strong, will tend to be especially sensitive to anything culturally or
ethnically alien which exists amongst them. This historical psychology is
sometimes seen in favoured treatment of foreigners, beyond what is
normal elsewhere. A Russian Jew encountering official or popular discrimination is a victim of the same psychology. He is not a visitor from
another world, but an insider who is also an outsider.

Another point, of similar generality but perhaps more controversial,
may be relevant to the Soviet state of mind on the Jews. In the late fifteenth
century a certain danger to the state was seen in terms of the spread of

'Judaizing' ideas at the highest levels of society. The movement was suppressed, but with some difficulty because of its extent and strength. Subsequent antisemitism and the exclusion of Jews may have had one of its roots in this real or supposed threat to the national identity. In early communist Russia the state may again have appeared to be in danger of becoming Jewish, this time because of the number of actual Jews in positions of power, locally as well as centrally, and this again may have influenced both official and popular thought throughout the Soviet period.[1]

Soviet theory on the Jews proceeds from the theories of nationality and of religion. These are logical and simple in principle but the more they are pursued in detail the more complex and self-contradictory they become. So far as the theory of national minorities is concerned, this

[1] While the proportion of Jews in the revolutionary movement, and in the senior ranks of the ruling party until the purge of 1937, was certainly high, there is a tendency at all periods and from a wide range of viewpoints to equate either the movement as a whole or selected parts of it with Jews. Thus Plehve, when Minister of the Interior, told Mackenzie Wallace that 70 per cent of all political delinquents known to the police were Jews (D. M. Wallace, *Russia*, 1912 edn., p. 716. Wallace, a careful observer, mentions the figure with reserve and suggests that Plehve may have been thinking of the western and southern provinces). Stalin, describing the fifth congress of the R.S.D.L.P. in London (1907), which he had attended, said the majority of the Menshevik delegates were Jews (and incidentally reported a dubious joke that the Bolsheviks, as real Russians, could have made a pogrom: Stalin, *Sochineniya*, vol. 2, p. 50). According to the Soviet record of this congress, however (*Pyatyi s"ezd R.S.D.R.P.*, pp. 656–9), of the 96 Menshevik delegates 22 were Jews and of the 105 Bolsheviks 12 were Jews (Stalin explicitly excluded the 57 Bundist delegates from his quantitative statement). Nicholas II shared Stalin's illusion: '. . . nine-tenths of the troublemakers are Jews', but uses it without joking to justify pogroms: '. . . the people's whole anger turned against them' (letter to the tsarina, quoted in L. Kochan, *Russia in Revolution 1890–1918*, p. 50). The Bolshevik historian M. N. Pokrovsky is quoted as observing that Jews comprised from a quarter to a third of the organizer-stratum of all the revolutionary movements (*Large Soviet Enyclopaedia*, 1st edn., vol. 24, col. 74: this may well be a fair estimate).

The popular post-revolutionary mythology of the Bolsheviks as Jews arose from two sources: the high proportion of Jews amongst prominent senior members, and the influx of Jews into the party from the left wings of the Bund and other revolutionary or extremist groups. Many of the Jewish communists, old and new, had in their youth made a sharp and emotionally difficult break with a peculiarly narrow and concentrated mode of the past in the social and religious tradition of their upbringing, and tended to go further in administering the new order than their gentile colleagues. The Jewish masses probably suffered more from this than did the gentiles, since such revolutionaries staffed the state and party organizations administering Jewish affairs, but the idea of Jewish communist bosses went wide and deep. A recent re-statement of this feeling may be found in the novel by the Soviet Ukrainian author Anatoly Dimarov, *Shlyakhami zhittya*, first published in 1963 (in the magazine *Dnipro*, nos. 9 and 10): the Jewish communist Lyanders takes the opportunity of local power given to him by the Revolution to oppress the honest ordinary Ukrainians, whom he holds in contempt. Trotsky is cited as his model and the author gives a historically unscrupulous account of how each former generation of Lyanders oppressed and despised the Ukrainian masses in accordance with the opportunities of their times.

problem has been solved by the construction of socialism, which ends the exploitation of minor nationalities by abolishing the exploiting classes of all Soviet nationalities, which now consist of state industrial workers, kolkhoz peasants, and intellectuals, working harmoniously, irrespective of nationality, in the common aim of constructing communist society. Socialism encourages, for strictly socialist purposes, the flowering of national cultures, but in mature communist society the national cultures will be absorbed in a common culture to which all will have contributed. In the meantime, each nation has its own state (a Union or autonomous republic within the U.S.S.R.). Before the Revolution, the struggle for national equality of rights must subserve the class struggle which is the engine of revolution; after, the legal and practical granting of national equality by the revolutionary state must subserve the construction of socialism, and subsequently of full communism, which is the *raison d'être* of the revolutionary state.

As for religion, this is a set of irrational beliefs and practices deriving from the need to make life tolerable in the conditions of alienation and exploitation of class society. Religion in the U.S.S.R. is thus a survival from earlier periods which must disappear in the conditions of the rational society which will provide fully for the needs of the human personality. The Jews satisfy the theory of religion, but not that of nationality, since they live scattered throughout Soviet territory and thus cannot have their own state. In any case, for that same reason they are undergoing rapid assimilation and therefore do not need a national state within the U.S.S.R. It has been, and is, open to the Soviet Jews to dwell in a compact territory of their own within the U.S.S.R., namely the autonomous region of Biro-Bidzhan, but they have not so far chosen to do so. (The existence of the State of Israel is irrelevant, except that as an arm of American and British imperialism it seeks to subvert Soviet Jews. Its language, the traditional religious vehicle of Jewry, is also reactionary.)

Systematic theoretical treatments of the Jewish Question

A fuller treatment of the theory on the Jews meets the difficulty that there are few systematic expositions in classical Marxism, pre-revolutionary Bolshevism, or in the Soviet period. The most systematic classical treatment was a review written by the young Marx in 1843, well before the main features of Marxism as a system were formulated.[1] This docu-

---

[1] A long review, 'Zur Judenfrage', of some writings by Bruno Bauer. The review was written when Marx was 25 years old and appeared in his *Deutsch-Französische Jahrbücher* in 1844. (The review is translated and annotated by T. B. Bottomore in his *Karl Marx: Early Writings*, London, 1963.) The quotations below are from Professor Bottomore's translation.

ment has been and remains something of an embarrassment to Marxists because of its apparent extreme antisemitism. Marx identifies Judaism or Jewry as the embodiment of huckstering (*Schacherei*, translated in Russian by *torgashestvo*) and the power of money generally; the Jews thus represent that which has destroyed the cohesion of society, replacing the proper relation of the human personality to other people and to things by the mediating factor of the market and of money, which atomizes society. In this (second) part of the review, Marx is dealing with an article by Bauer on 'The capacity of present-day Jews and Christians to become Free'. His solution is a return to social cohesion. This involves the elimination of *Judentum*, which has conquered Christendom. The document bristles with statements pithily and strikingly expressed, which at their face value are oddly similar to the most extreme antisemitic views and could provide excellent slogans in the service of antisemitism.[1] (The use of these passages from Marx in books on Judaism by T. Kichko, published in the Ukraine in 1963 and 1968, constitutes a step towards incorporation of anti-semitism in the official ideology or even—the authority being Marx—in the theory.) The young Marx was already concentrating his social analysis on the concept of alienation and the necessity of a return to social cohesion, which became the key to his entire mature system. In this sense, his analysis of the Jewish problem in 1843 remains valid within subsequent Marxism, including Soviet Marxism. Much depends, in the interpretation of his review of Bauer, on the extent to which his style of work at the time and his use of words and concepts are taken into account. He used *Judentum* deliberately, at some points at least, in its dual meaning of Jewry or Judaism and of commerce.[2] His Hegelian style of thought and writing, with its inordinate use in his earlier years of analysis by paradox, lends itself

[1] E.g. 'What is the worldly cult of the Jew? *Huckstering*. What is his worldly god? *Money*.'
'In the final analysis the *emancipation* of the Jews is the emancipation of mankind from *Judaism*.'
'Money is the jealous god of Israel, beside which no other god may exist. . . . The god of the Jews has been secularized and has become the god of this world. The bill of exchange is the real god of the Jew.'
'The *chimerical* nationality of the Jew is the nationality of the trader, and above all of the financier.'
'It was only then [when Christianity had made the alienation of man from himself and from nature theoretically possible] that Judaism could attain universal domination and could turn alienated man and alienated nature into *alienable*, saleable objects in thrall to egoistic need and huckstering.'
'The tenacity of the Jew is to be explained, not by his religion, but rather by the human basis of his religion—practical need and egoism.'

[2] Bottomore, p. 36, note 3.

to extreme statements. Marx was, in the second part of his review, criticizing Bauer for taking religion at its face value and not going behind it to the destruction of social cohesion by the market; his thesis is that the Jews, like the gentiles, can become fully human again only by the restoration of social cohesion. This is, in effect, the Soviet thesis that socialism is the only way of solving the Jewish problem (though we may guess what Marx would have said of the Soviet view that the problem is now solved in the U.S.S.R.).

The main document in Bolshevik thought on the Jews before 1917 is Stalin's essay of 1913, *Marxism and the National Question.*[1] This represented the authoritative Bolshevik view in that it was consistent with Lenin's occasional observations on the subject, it received Lenin's *cachet* and was in fact written under his guidance when the Bolsheviks were clarifying their basic policy on national minorities. Subsequently the authority of this document derived from the fact that it was written by Stalin. Since the ending of Stalin's infallibility in 1956 the theory embodied in this essay has not been altered authoritatively (though problems of definition concerning national identity have recently been discussed). In it Stalin firmly denies the status of nationhood to the Jews since they lack certain elements of his formula: 'A nation is a historically evolved, stable community of language, territory, economic life, and psychological make-up manifested in a community of culture'.[2] In his reference to the Jews, Stalin was arguing against the Bund, the specifically Jewish section of the revolutionary Marxist movement in Russia which, like Bolshevism, was one of the components of the Russian social democratic movement and indeed its oldest, and for some years its most active and effective element. The Bund insisted on the monopoly of agitation amongst Jewish workers, within the movement, for fear that the movement as a whole might sacrifice the specific interests of the Jewish workers. Until the First World War Yiddish was virtually the universal language of the Jewish workers and petty traders within the Pale of Settlement, which effectively ruled out non-Jewish agitators and organizers. Criticism of the Bund by other members of the movement, in particular that by Stalin, turned on its tendency to subordinate the class struggle to the needs of the struggle for national rights, whereas Marxist theory demanded the opposite.

Ignoring the fact that the activities of the Bund were entirely concerned

---

[1] In English translation in the collection from Stalin, *Marxism and the National and Colonial Question* (London, Martin Lawrence, no date). Page references and quotations are from this volume.

[2] Ibid., p. 8.

with a linguistically homogeneous population of Jews concentrated in the area of the Pale, in parts of which they were a majority of the urban population, Stalin asks:

... what ... national cohesion can there be ... between the Georgian, Daghestanian, Russian and American Jews? ... if there is anything common to them left it is their religion, their common origin and certain relics of national character.... But how can it be seriously maintained that petrified religious rites and fading psychological relics affect the 'fate' of these Jews more powerfully than the living social, economic and cultural environment that surrounds them? And it is only on this assumption that it is generally possible to speak of the Jews as a single nation.[1]

The Jews in Russia are heading for inevitable assimilation. Not only do they possess no integral territory but

the fact of the matter is primarily that among the Jews there is no large and stable stratum associated with the soil, which would naturally rivet the nation, serving not only as its 'framework' but also as a 'national' market. Of the five or six million Russian Jews, only three to four per cent are connected with agriculture in any way. The remaining 96 per cent are employed in trade, industry, town institutions, and in general they live in towns; moreover they are spread all over Russia and do not constitute a majority in a single province.

Thus, interspersed as national minorities in areas inhabited by other nationalities, the Jews as a rule serve 'foreign' nations as manufacturers and traders and as members of the free professions, naturally adapting themselves to the 'foreign nations' in respect to language and so forth. All this, taken together with the increasing reshuffling of nationalities characteristic of developed forms of capitalism, leads to the assimilation of the Jews. The abolition of the Pale would only serve to hasten this process.[2]

It is the process of inevitable assimilation which creates a struggle against it, reflected in the policy of the Bund for Jewish national autonomy. But

if there is no democracy in the country there can be no guarantee of 'the complete freedom of cultural development of nationalities'. One may say with certainty that the more democratic a country is, the fewer are the 'attempts' made on the 'freedom of nationalities', and the greater are the guarantees against such 'attempts'. Russia is a semi-Asiatic country and therefore in Russia the policy of 'attempts' not infrequently assumes the grossest form, the form of pogroms.

The Bund's aim of securing special Jewish rights, such as Saturday as the day of rest, is retrogressive:

[1] Ibid., p. 10.   [2] Ibid., p. 36.

It is to be expected that the Bund will take another 'forward step' and demand the right to observe all the ancient Hebrew holidays. . . . The maintenance of everything Jewish, the preservation of *all* the national peculiarities of the Jews, even those that are patently noxious to the proletariat, the isolation of the Jews from everything non-Jewish, even the establishment of special hospitals—that is the level to which the Bund has sunk.[1]

Stalin freely accepts the principle of cultural rights: 'There can be no possibility of a full development of the intellectual faculties of the Tatar or Jewish worker if he is not allowed to use his native language at meetings and lectures, and if his schools are closed down.'[2] But this point is made within a warning that the struggle for minority rights is 'under the conditions of *rising* capitalism', always a struggle of the bourgeoisie of the minority nation against that of the dominant nation, a struggle into which the proletariat of the minority is drawn by its bourgeoisie. 'And this creates a favourable soil for the lying propaganda regarding "harmony of interests", for glossing over the class interests of the proletariat and for the intellectual enslavement of the workers. This creates a serious obstacle to the work of uniting the workers of all nationalities.'[3] However, Stalin does not go quite so far as the by then traditional social democratic attitude on the question of national cultures.

The Russian social democratic view, which the Bund contradicted by its tendencies to preserve and stimulate Jewish culture, amounted to the abolition of all ethnic restrictions and inequalities but without stimulating or endeavouring to preserve national cultures, because their existence hindered international working-class solidarity. This view reflected the cosmopolitan education of the more articulate Bolshevik leaders and their impatience with any obstacles to the unity of the proletariat throughout the Russian empire, and indeed the world. Lenin's statements of this position with reference to the Jews are particularly pungent, not only because they are made in the struggle against Bundist particularism as a betrayal of Marxism. He and his type saw the Jewish traditional ethos as the extreme embodiment of backward exclusiveness. Assimilation meant more than the emancipation of the Jews. It symbolized the emancipation of mankind for which he fought. Something of this sharpness and passion may have been carried over into Soviet popular thought on the Jews through the vulgarizing medium of the communist party in power, making in the upshot some contribution to antisemitism in a way that Stalin's rather ponderous and less urgently felt treatise could not do. With such statements as 'Jewish national culture—the slogan of the rabbis and the

[1] *Marxism and the National and Colonial Question*, p. 42.   [2] Ibid., p. 17.   [3] Ibid., p. 17.

bourgeois, the slogan of our enemies',[1] Lenin would be no less useful a source of quotations than Marx, should Soviet politicians ever wish to use him unscrupulously in promoting antisemitism, or even in admitting and justifying their present discriminatory treatment.

The only systematic treatment of the 'Jewish Question' which I have been able to find in the Soviet period is the substantial article under that title in the first edition of the *Large Soviet Encyclopaedia*, in a volume published in 1932.[2] The Jewish Sections of the communist party, around whose work there had been a fairly wide range of discussion about the nature and future of Soviet Jewry, had been abolished in 1930, with the increasing centralization of political and ideological life. But the 'socialized' cultural Jewish life of the 1920s had basically survived the collectivization of agriculture and the first Five Year Plan. Serious treatment of the Jewish question was still in order in 1932, but the function of the author, M. Volfson, could only be to attempt a comprehensive analysis and statement of the solution within the framework of Marx and of the traditional Bolshevik and Soviet official views so far as these existed.

Volfson distinguishes three approaches: the religious, originating in feudal society; the national struggle for equality, reflecting the interests of the Jewish bourgeoisie of the capitalist period; and the proletarian or Marxist-Leninist, based on the class struggle and providing the solution in the classless and eventually stateless society to be constructed.

In the feudal period, writes Volfson, the Jews displayed a prototype of the future bourgeois society, producing capitalists, traders, craftsmen, workers, and scholars, but not the feudal classes of landlords and peasants. This discrepancy between the commodity-money economy of Jewry and the feudal-natural economy of the gentile environment was one of the main obstacles to assimilation. The gentile masses identified all classes of Jews with the Jewish exploiters, and their hostility took a religious form because religion was the ideology of the epoch. The religious approach

[1] Lenin, *Sochineniya*, 4th edn., vol. 20, p. 9 (written 1913).

[2] Vol. 24. The treatment of Jewish matters in the first edition of the *Encyclopaedia*, which appeared in the 1920s and 1930s, is detailed and solid, but of course within the Marxist framework on other than technical topics such as language, music, theatre, art. The twenty articles whose titles begin with the word 'Jews' or 'Jewish' in this edition, occupying seventy-six pages, contrast strikingly with the single article, entitled 'Jews', occupying two pages in the second edition (vol. 15, published in 1952); there is also a highly propagandist article on the Jewish autonomous region of Biro-Bidzhan in the second edition. A similar contrast may be found between the second edition of the *Small Soviet Encyclopaedia* (twelve informative articles with a total of twelve pages in vol. 4, issued in 1936) and its third edition, with four articles in vol. 3 (1959), totalling one and a half pages which, however, on the smaller scale of this encyclopaedia does show, in space and treatment, some recovery from the low point of 1952.

survived in countries where elements of feudalism remained: Jews were forcibly baptized, the Talmud 'exposed', etc., until the nineteenth century. Racial theory (apparently regarded by Volfson as a variant of the religious view) emerged in the period of finance capital, the way being paved by the Jewish and gentile view of some absolute unchanging Jewish spirit.

The rise of capitalism and its associated national states stimulated civil equality, but of bourgeois Jews with bourgeois gentiles. These Jewish assimilationists spoke of a common human culture but in practice associated themselves with their national culture, or rather its bourgeois part. They were not fully accepted, and tended to join the Jewish petty bourgeoisie, to which the gentile petty bourgeoisie was hostile, and drift with it towards Zionism. At this point Volfson critically surveys various non-proletarian approaches to the problem, in particular those in late-tsarist Russia, and then deals with Marx's analysis as follows:

The working-class movement and Marxist-Leninist theory puts the Jewish question and solves it in the spirit of the class struggle of the proletariat and the achievement of socialism. As early as 1844 Marx gave in his answer to Bauer ('The Jewish Question') the first economic treatment of the Jewish question . . . Marx concludes that emancipation from *Schacherei* and money, from the practical reality of Jewishness, would be the self-emancipation of our time. Such an organization of society as would break with the very roots of *Schacherei* and would make such activity impossible, would make it impossible for Jews to exist.

Jewish nationalists and some critics of Marx see in Marx's treatment of the Jewish question: (1) antisemitism; (2) mechanical transference of the characteristics of German bourgeois Jewry, as if Marx knew only them, to the whole of Europe; (3) replacement of the capitalist spirit by *Schacherei*. In fact, there is absolutely nothing of antisemitism in it, not only because Marx wrote it in defence of Jewish equality of rights but also because he gave a true conception of Christian–Jewish historico-economic reality: the Jewish economy was evoked by the needs of Christian (feudal) society. And this is true not only of German bourgeois Jewry but also all Jewry of that time, since at determinate historical stages (as the same Marx established) the ideology of the dominant classes becomes the ideology of the whole of society, and in the closed Jewish community the dominant class consisted of the capitalist traders and moneylenders. Finally, in so far as Jewish capital played an insignificant part in the developing capitalist industry, and played its main role in trade and moneylending (trading in money), it is clear that *Schacherei* (not capitalist production) and money (not the means of production) could become the cult and god of 'the Jew' as a particular historico-economic type. Here it is that we find in Marx the proletarian solution of the Jewish question, in that Jewry (as a determinate social group placed in exceptionally burdensome conditions) can disappear only when capitalist society disappears; the Jewish question is insoluble in capitalist society. Marx and Engels, and later Lenin and Stalin, showed that in general the national question is insoluble under capitalism....

Volfson then criticizes the Austrian Marxists for denying that the Jews are a nation, whereas, by virtue of their 'idealist' criteria of language, like-thinking and national character the Jews would qualify: e.g. 7 million Jews, two-thirds of their total number in the world, speak Yiddish. (It is possible that here he is questioning Stalin's denial of national status, in a devious way.)

There follows a survey of Russian socialist thought on the Jewish question, from the Populists' shock at the pogroms which followed the assassination of Alexander II in 1881 and the tendency amongst some of them to accept pogroms as being 'of the people'. A sympathetic account is given of the Bund's origin and history, though with the obligatory criticism that it came to put the national struggle above the class struggle. The Bolshevik solution of the Jewish question was to transform society. National self-determination in the U.S.S.R. is made feasible for the Jews by their being drawn into a higher form of economic life: 'True to the nationality policy of Bolshevism, the Soviet power does not, of course, restrict itself to the mere proclamation of the right to self-determination, but does everything to make this right effective. . . .' (Here Volfson specifies the higher forms of economic life but does not show how they facilitate national self-determination.) Thus, the existence of a large number of Jewish industrial workers and 'significant masses' of Jewish farmers in the U.S.S.R. has exploded the view that Jews are of a special economic nature. Jewish agriculture has big possibilities in the U.S.S.R. because collectivization has eliminated the land-hunger which prevents successful Jewish settlement in capitalist countries. (Volfson must have known that Jewish settlers in the U.S.S.R. had in fact encountered this problem.) There are more Jewish schools, courts, and local governments in the U.S.S.R. than anywhere else in the world. The Soviet state has effectively combated antisemitism since the Revolution, a survival from tsarism. The Jews, like all other nationalities in the U.S.S.R., are creating their culture, 'socialist in content and national in form', in Stalin's words.

The contribution to theory of the short article issued in 1952 in the *Large Soviet Encyclopaedia*, second edition, on 'The Jews' is as follows: '. . . the Lenin–Stalin national policy of equality of rights and friendship of the peoples has led to a situation in which "the Jewish question" does not exist in the U.S.S.R.'[1] This reflected the official view, which has not

---

[1] *Large Soviet Encyclopaedia*, 2nd edn., vol. 15, 1952, p. 378.

changed since. The same article makes the generalization that in capitalist countries Jewish capitalists and workers fuse with their gentile classes, but the Jewish petty bourgeoisie remains distinct, preserving religious rituals, dietary laws, etc.

Theory and reality

Although Stalin's 1913 article remained (and still remains) the official theory, for lack of anything to supplant it, some adaptations of the theory had to be made when the Bolsheviks found themselves in power and faced the practical problems of administering many ethnic minorities. The right of minority nations to form independent states was accepted in the full sense of the right of such states to secede from the Russian-dominated area. A distinction was, however, made between bourgeois and socialist nations, the interest of the latter being self-evidently to remain united with socialist Russia. This position is still embodied in the 1936 constitution, which recognizes the right of Union republics to secede but at the same time recognizes, by a general statement on the function of the communist party, the local section of the party as the controlling factor within each republic. The resulting complete centralization of final authority is in fact fully in line with the Bolshevik traditional outlook and general theory on what had come to be called 'democratic centralism' since the party first emerged in 1903. On the question of the existence of national cultures, which Lenin denied (except in the sense of Disraeli's two nations) the Bolsheviks in power took the obvious course of recognizing the national culture of the working masses as distinct from that of the exploiters. Each socialist nation could thus have its own culture, but the difficulty remained that in theory national culture must not be allowed to keep the working masses apart. Stalin overcame this difficulty in 1925 through the formula, 'socialist in content and national in form', which meant, in effect, that all the national cultures of the U.S.S.R. were the same, or were going to be made the same, in economic life, education, beliefs, aspirations, etc., but used their own languages for this purpose and such other national characteristics as did not hinder the common achievement of socialism.

The first adaptation of theory, on the question of secession, is not relevant to the Jews since they were not a nation and thus could not have a state (though in the mid-1920s their possible achievement of nationhood by mass settlement on the land did come to be openly and officially canvassed). The question of national culture was of direct concern to the Jews. The language of the Jewish masses was Yiddish, and the Bolsheviks (whose Jewish members included few with an adequate knowledge of the

language or interest in Jewish matters) lost no time inviting or manœuv-
ring other Jewish revolutionaries, mainly from the left wing of the Bund,
into their ranks for this work. It was these newcomers who staffed the
'Jewish Commissariat' offices and the Jewish Sections of local party organizations in the Jewish towns and who, in the main, destroyed Jewish communal organization, although they were unable to put anything adequate
in its place, and uprooted religion, the Hebrew language and the Jewish
educational system. The Jewish Commissariat was closed in the early 1920s
but the Jewish Sections of the party operated throughout the decade.
Working always as agents of the local party organizations, not as elective
Jewish party groups, they certainly did much to make Jewish culture
more socialist and less Jewish in content. However, as the Bund itself had
done, they also tended to become identified with the Jewish nationality,
and their discussions of policy and principle reflect the national hopes and
fears as well as the party line to which they worked. They were excited at
the prospect of their assistance in the land settlement schemes contributing
to the establishment of a Jewish republic, which was first publicly posed
by one of their leaders in 1925. A sufficient number of Jewish settlers
would provide not only an ethnic territory but the common economic
life, including roots in the soil, that Stalin had noted in 1913 as a condition
of nationhood. In November 1926 M. I. Kalinin, a senior member of the
Politburo and head of state of the U.S.S.R., but not a policy-maker,
who took a personal interest in Jewish affairs, recommended this possibility to the Jewish Land Settlement Society in a remarkable speech. The
tsars, he said, had forced assimilation on small nationalities but this had
had the opposite effect on the Jews. The Soviet state 'had no reason whatever to extinguish, assimilate, or destroy this or that nationality'—nor to
preserve them. The government was concerned with practical problems.
The Revolution had caused economic ruin to the Jewish masses, and the
solution to this problem offered a great opportunity for the Jewish people
to 'preserve its nationality' by establishing a compact population numbering at least some hundreds of thousands. The government could provide
limited means, and foreign Jewish capitalists would help; the Jewish poor
and part of the Jewish intelligentsia were willing. So success was quite
feasible. Antisemitism had increased since the Revolution owing to the
high proportion of Jews in the administration, which in turn was due to
the Russian bourgeoisie's rejection of the Revolution. Land settlement
would draw the Jews away from the big cities, where their arrival
increased antisemitism and where they formed mixed marriages and lost
interest in Jewish matters. (Kalinin expressed the same opinion on Jewish

movement to the big cities and the effect of this on Jewish ethnic identity on several other occasions, and also during the 1930s although there was at that time an urgent need for more industrial workers.)

In theoretical terms, the special difficulty facing the Jews was that only a small proportion of them were industrial workers and virtually none peasants: there were not enough Jews in productive occupations to be the bearers of a class socialist culture. Land settlement on a sufficient scale, together with industrial recruitment, would solve this problem as well as the problem of nationhood. Kalinin's speech showed a fatherly interest in the future of Jewry and appeared to open all doors. Reaction to the speech at a conference of the Jewish Sections in the following month, December 1926, was, however, mixed.[1]

Both nationalist and assimilationist trends had appeared in the Sections. The leaders were undecided and unwilling to commit themselves without a specific party directive. Kalinin's remarks, however, were stated by the platform to lack the authority of such a directive. The platform opposed 'idle talk about the dictatorship of the Jewish proletariat in the Jewish street'—i.e. autonomous local administration (which would probably have been the solution if the Provisional Government of 1917 had not been overthrown). Dictatorship could be exercised only by the entire Soviet proletariat. Similarly, a demand to make the Jewish Sections 'the representative of the [Jewish] people', as distinct from agencies of the party, was firmly rejected as dangerous nationalist ideology. Statehood following successful land settlement could well be accompanied by assimilation of those Jews who became industrial workers elsewhere. Both the assimilationists, who wanted to drop Yiddish, and the nationalists, who wanted to preserve the Jewish people, must be opposed, the latter with the greater energy because they strengthened nationalist leanings amongst the Jewish masses. However, the establishment of a Jewish state would be important for Jews elsewhere in the U.S.S.R. also. The Jewish intelligentsia should be attracted, if necessary, by their national sense, but the motive inspiring the Sections could only be the building of socialism as such. However desirable an autonomous agricultural territory might be, the building of socialism now needed industrial workers more than farmers, and industrialization must have 'elemental assimilatory effects'. The construction of socialism takes precedence over the national ideal,

[1] See Solomon Schwarz, *The Jews in the Soviet Union* (Syracuse U.P., New York, 1951), pp. 122–8, for an account of the platform speeches and resolution and inferences on the views expressed from the floor. Schwarz, especially chaps. II and III, also gives a good historical account of Bolshevik nationality theory in relation to the Jews.

even if it leads to complete assimilation. The overriding task is to *assist the Jewish masses to take part in the building of socialism*.

(A year before, in 1925, Stalin had spoken of assimilation, in reply to a letter from some Buryats requesting information on such 'for us very serious and difficult questions'. His answer was that 'in the process of the formation of a universal proletarian culture, undoubtedly certain nationalities may, and even certainly will, undergo a process of assimilation'. Stalin was already important enough for his words to hang over the conference. But he had specified no nationalities by name.)

This was the last gathering of the Jewish Sections. They were disbanded in 1930 with the beginning of the industrialization drive, the elemental effects of which brought the Jewish *shtetl* to its end. Like the more influential party leaders of other minority nationalities, they perished in the great purge. Since they were mere instruments of the party, their views are not of historical importance, but they have been noted here as relevant to ideas concerned with the Jewish future in the U.S.S.R.

The period from 1930 to the 1960s, which saw the status accorded to the Yiddish language sink to a pariah condition and then recover slightly, also saw a certain modification in some aspects of the general theory of national culture. In 1930 Stalin clarified the apparent contradiction between the aims of promoting national cultures and the communist goal of the destruction of all barriers by invoking a standard dialectical concept:

It may seem strange that we, who are in favour of the *fusion* of national cultures in the future into one common culture (both in form and in content), with a single common language, are at the same time in favour of the *blossoming* of national cultures at the present time. . . . But there is nothing strange in this. The national cultures must be permitted to develop and expand and to reveal all their potential qualities, in order to create the conditions necessary for their fusion into a single common culture with a single, common language.[1]

At that time the period of full communism, in which a culture world-wide in both form and content would emerge, was relegated to a very distant future, when the single language would be 'neither Great Russian nor German, but something new'.[2] The time scale was foreshortened in 1939, when Stalin put forward the thesis that full communism could be achieved within the U.S.S.R. alone in a still capitalist world, though the state would have to be retained to organize defence. A further and somewhat ambiguous modification was made in his contribution to the discussion on

[1] Stalin, *Marxism and the National and Colonial Question*, p. 261.   [2] Ibid., p. 264.

linguistics in 1950, when he noted the durability of languages in relation to the rate of social change, and made of this fact a canon of Marxist social theory. At the same time, he pointed out the ability of the Russian language to survive in competition with other languages and to incorporate them without much alteration in itself, but he soon after dissociated this observation from his 1930 statement that the future single world language would be a new one. In 1961 the communist party, in adopting a new party programme, declared the transition to full communism to have begun, and that its threshold would be reached by about 1980. These theoretical propositions relevant to the establishment of a single culture within the U.S.S.R. have not been formally drawn together, but there is probably some connection between the official current stage of rapid transition to communism and impatience with the continued existence of the Jewish anomaly in the sphere of nationality and secularized-socialized culture. The intensification of the attack on religion and on 'economic crime', which occurred with the decision to reach the condition of full communism in the near future, has had particularly severe effects on the Jews, and this may be in part due to their anomalous nature in relation to theory as well as at a less abstract level of ideas.

Questions and doubts concerning certain aspects of this anomaly began to appear occasionally in the early 1960s, in connection with discussions of social theory following the proclamation of 1961 that the transition to communism had begun. Unpublished discussions were held on nationality theory and throughout 1966 *Voprosy Istorii* (the journal of general history) began an open discussion on the subject. The discussion is highly relevant to Soviet thinking on the Jews, but not directly so, as Soviet Jewry has so far been specifically referred to by one participant only. It was then firmly assigned to its traditional non-national status on the grounds that it lacked common economic life, territory, or language. It is more important, however, that the discussion is taking place at all, and in a manner which tends increasingly to question for the present and future the validity of the traditional theory.

The most relevant factor in the discussion so far is a general consensus of opinion that ethnic self-awareness or self-identification, the desire of a community to become or remain a nation, is a key to nationhood. (In Soviet official practice, the dependence of ethnic identity on the wishes of those concerned has been recognized to a decreasing extent, now that the urban population have internal passports in which nationality is inscribed and the only choice normally open to them is between the two nationalities of the parents in a mixed marriage.)

However, the importance of the new emphasis on mass national self-identification should be seen in its effect upon the Lenin–Stalin insistence on the territorial qualification, which has hitherto been the prime theoretical obstacle to Jewish national status in the U.S.S.R. If, as several participants in the discussion point out, the desire to remain a nation survives political partition (the Poles, contemporary Germans, etc.) or dispersal (the Armenians, Tatars, etc.) or exists despite lack of a common language (the Bashkirs, etc.) or a common economy (e.g. economically advanced and backward areas of the Ukraine), then a temporary or even prolonged absence of one or more of these territorial, linguistic or economic factors is not necessarily a bar to nationhood. In the large number of examples given of peoples both in the U.S.S.R. and elsewhere on this point in the discussion, the Jews are conspicuous by their absence.

Another question dealt with that is directly relevant to the status of the Jews is the somewhat sterile one of terminology, which dominates the discussion. The terms in question are the singular nouns: nation (*natsiya*), nationality (*natsionalnost*), people (*narod*), and *narodnost*, the ending *nost* indicating here a smaller or minor variety. These terms have traditionally been used fairly loosely in Soviet practical and theoretical classification, with the important exception that a *natsiya* is normally associated with statehood in capitalism and always with full constitutional statehood as a Union republic in the U.S.S.R. (which is theoretically a voluntary union of fifteen equal nations, each having its Union republic). The relevance of the terminological discussion is in its tendency to play down or abandon differences of connotation between the terms other than in matters of mere size. Several of the authors include in Soviet statehood not only the secondary level of autonomous republic (which involves possession of a government and a Supreme Soviet) but also the very much lower level of autonomous region (which involves, in all cases other than the Jewish autonomous region of Biro-Bidzhan, certain linguistic and other cultural rights). More important than this inclusive view of ethnic Soviet statehood, which is not new, is the idea that all ethnic groups are in some basic sense equal and that the different levels of statehood or political importance should not be taken as affecting this principle. This idea is expressed in various ways, and again the Jews are all the more conspicuous for lack of reference to them. A. G. Agaev, for example, points out[1] that every Soviet *narodnost* with over 300,000–400,000 population has become in effect a nation. He implicitly excludes the Jews by invoking the qualification of a definite territory, but other participants note (in a slightly different

[1] *Voprosy Filosofii*, no. 11, 1965.

connection) instances of the majority of a *natsiya* living outside the territory of its republic, such as 73 per cent of the Tatars.

A good deal of emphasis is in fact placed by various contributors on the ethnic effect of population movements in the U.S.S.R., which is seen as likely to increase considerably and which has already seriously reduced the validity of the 'definite territory' qualification. ('One has only to look at the ethnic map to see dozens of similar [to the Tatars] ethno-territorial problems'—Kozlov in *Voprosy Istorii*.[1] This circumstance, and associated changes in the direction of supra-ethnic (i.e. common Soviet) cultural and economic identity are noted to such an extent in the discussion that it would be logical (though politically impossible) to refer to the Jews as having the same claims as various Soviet ethnic groups of similar size to substantial constitutional recognition, to say nothing of the linguistic, religious, and general cultural rights normally granted.

In fact, the only specific reference to the Soviet Jews, at least in the *Voprosy Istorii* discussion up to its issue of January 1967, is made in such a manner as to exclude them from nationhood on any conceivable grounds. M. S. Dzhunusov[2] writes:

Some *narodnosti*, represented by urban or only by rural population, do not find it possible to use the Soviet economy as the material basis of becoming a nation. Dwelling in groups that are not large in various republics and provinces, they cannot attain mature intranational economic relations. Thus, of the 2·3 million Jewish population of the U.S.S.R., 2·2 million persons (i.e. 96 per cent) live in towns. Due to its historically formed dispersal and social composition the Jewish *natsionalnost* cannot (*ne mozhet*) develop into a nation. These same factors influence also the fact of two languages among the Jewish population.

There are references elsewhere in the discussion to connections with the soil as a feature of nationhood, but these are general historical references to the emergence of nations. Agriculture has no *Boden* status in the U.S.S.R. It is not the lack of an agricultural economy as such which Dzhunusov ascribes to the Jews, so much as some imbalance due to dependence on industry alone. Other writers in the discussion select industrial employment as the feature of a modern Soviet nation and make no mention of the presence or absence of agriculture. This is a modern adaptation of Stalin's 'community of economic life'; his inclusion of roots in the soil as a characteristic of nationhood is virtually ignored.

Development of the discussion in the pages of *Voprosy Istorii* from January 1966 to January 1967 shows a distinct tendency to greater freedom

---

[1] *Voprosy Istorii*, no. 1, 1967.
[2] 'The Nation as a Social-Ethical Community of People', in *Voprosy Istorii*, no. 4, 1966.

and realism, with perhaps half the contributors demanding serious study of the facts; the other half is more inclined to be content with re-interpretation of terms and definitions. It is difficult to see how the discussion can continue much longer without the case of the Jews receiving a more serious consideration as distinct from its mere dismissal by Dzhunusov.

A quite new approach to the Jewish question, as a problem of racial or ethnic prejudice to be treated with the aid of psychological rather than political theory, appeared in 1966. The relatively progressive and courageous literary magazine *Novy Mir* carried an article by the young Jewish philosopher I. Kon entitled 'The Psychology of Prejudice', with the sub-title 'On the social-psychological roots of ethnic preconceptions'.[1] This article is in substance a sympathetic, respectful and informative survey of American investigations and theories concerning prejudice against Jews and Negroes. Kon considers the work of the social psychologists in this field as offering a greater contribution than that of individual psychology or psychiatry, but sees no easy solution. He mentions socialism as providing a framework within which a solution may become possible in the future, but makes it clear by inference that the problem of antisemitism is becoming increasingly urgent in the U.S.S.R. The article is, in essence, a plea for similar research to be conducted in the U.S.S.R. and for the party not to be carried into antisemitism by the mood of the masses but to do everything possible against this psychologically and historically deep-seated evil.[2]

[1] *Novy Mir*, no. 9 (September), 1966. For a summary see *Patterns of Prejudice* (London, Institute of Jewish Affairs), vol. i, no. 2 (March–April), 1957. The article concludes as follows: '. . . as V. I. Lenin instructed us, it is precisely in the sphere of national relations that the survivals of the past are especially tenacious. The social psyche is not immediately liberated from the historical traditions of international conflict and the prejudices to which they give rise. It would seem that they have entirely disappeared and been forgotten—but quite the contrary, at a sharp turn in history, when certain difficulties arise, they again make themselves felt, carrying with them backward sections of the population. This is why well-planned systematic internationalist training of the working people is one of the most important ideological tasks of the Marxist–Leninist parties, a necessary condition for the construction of communism.'

[2] The relevant Soviet publications since 1967 have not been examined for developments in the theory.

4

The Biro-Bidzhan Project, 1927–1959

CHIMEN ABRAMSKY

After the October Revolution the Jews of Russia found themselves in a highly complicated and paradoxical situation, which resulted, through its contradictions, partly in tragedy. Under the tsars the Jews suffered from constant persecutions, frequent pogroms, disenfranchisement, and the majority were banned from living in Russia proper, where the main industrial and cultural centres were situated, and were confined to the area of the Pale of Settlement, the poorest part of Russia. The persecution caused many Jews to join the revolutionary movement, but the majority were petty traders, small artisans, and shopkeepers, and as such were classified by the Soviet authorities as members of the bourgeoisie. For the first eleven years of Soviet power they were treated, if not as enemies, then as second-class citizens. In addition to this contradiction the Whites and the Ukrainians during their struggle against the communists regarded the Jews as their principal enemy, and declared that the Bolsheviks were acting on behalf of world Jewry aiming to dominate Russia. This paradoxical position needs a brief elaboration to clarify the picture.

The antisemitic policy of tsarism placed the Jews in the eyes of the radicals and revolutionaries amongst the exploited and oppressed, and they felt it their bounden duty to take up the defence of the Jews. Pogroms and restrictions on the Jews were viewed by them as attempts by tsarism to divert the anger of the masses against the ruling classes, and to make the Jews the scapegoat for the tsarist misdeeds. Many Jews saw in the revolutionaries allies in their fight for emancipation and human rights. No wonder that large numbers of Jews, mainly intellectuals and semi-intellectuals flocked to swell the revolutionary ranks.[1]

A few figures will illustrate this. Between 1884 and 1890, 4,307 people were arrested for revolutionary activities; of them, 579 were Jews (13·4 per cent). The proportion of Jews rose even higher in the next decade.

---

[1] On Jewish disabilities in Russia, see S. Dubnow, *History of the Jews in Russia and Poland*, vol. 3, Philadelphia, 1920; Louis Greenberg, *The Jews in Russia: The Struggle for Emancipation*, Yale University, 1967.

Arrests for revolutionary activities:

	Number of arrested	Jews	Percentage of the total
1898	1,140	213	18·7
1899	1,414	351	24·8[1]

The number of Jews arrested was nearly double that of the previous decade.

The Bund claimed that in 1903–4, in conditions of illegality, it had a membership of 30,000, an astonishing figure for the time. The Bund probably commanded a larger following than the Russian Social Democratic Party (R.S.D.R.P.). The Zionist-Socialists (the Z.S.) stated in its report to the Stuttgart congress of the Second International in 1907 that it had a membership of 27,000. A Jewish historian estimated that the Jewish labour movement numbered about 70,000 members.[2]

Both the police authorities and the revolutionary leaders were impressed by the large number of Jews in the revolutionary movement, the first for antisemitic reasons, and the latter from genuine sympathy, and even admiration. On the eve of the February Revolution, Lenin delivered in Geneva a lecture on the 1905 Revolution, in which he stated publicly:

The hatred of the tsars was particularly directed against the Jews. On one side, the Jews provided an extremely high percentage (compared to the total of the Jewish population) of leaders of the revolutionary movement. In passing, it should be said to their credit that today the Jews provide a relatively high percentage of representatives of internationalism compared with other nations.[3]

When the February Revolution broke out the Jews welcomed it with immense enthusiasm. They were fully confident that all their disabilities and sufferings had ended, that they had been delivered 'from bondage unto freedom, from darkness unto great light'. The enthusiasm mounted even higher when the Bolsheviks, led by Lenin, captured power in November 1917, and many Jews were prominent in the first Council of Commissars. Trotsky, Zinoviev, and Kamenev became household words for Jews in power. They were doubly symbolic: as a sign of full Jewish

---

[1] Cf. E. Tscherikover, 'Yidn Revolutsionern in Russland', in *Historische Schriften*, vol. 3, p. 129, Wilno–Paris, 1939, and B. Dinur, 'Demutah hahistorit shel hayahadut harusit ubaayot hakheker ba', in *Zion*, vol. xxii, p. 114, Jerusalem, 1957. There is no detailed study of the Jews in the Russian revolutionary movement in the twentieth century.

[2] See for the Bund, *Doklad Internatsionalnovo Sotsialisticheskovo Kongressa v Amsterdame*, Geneva, 1904, p. 14, and for the S.S. *Unser Weg*, 19 August 1907, p. 12, and Dinur, op. cit.

[3] Cf. Lenin, *Sochineniya*, 2nd edn., vol. 19, p. 354–5, Moscow, 1929. Stalin in 1907 was rather cynical about the Jews amongst the Mensheviks. See Stalin, *Sochineniya*, vol. 2, *Notes of a Delegate*.

emancipation, and as a pretext for the counter-revolutionaries to whip up a campaign against the Jews.

The first Soviet Government appointed a special Commissar of Nationalities to deal specifically with the multitudinous problems of the many nationalities inhabiting the Russian empire. The Commissar himself, was, symbolically, a member of a national minority, the Georgian, Joseph Stalin. This was the first time in history that such a Ministry was created. The Commissariat appointed a special Jewish Section—the Yevsektsia— to help the Jews and deal with the many problems relating to them.[1]

It is of considerable interest to note that though there were many Jews in the revolutionary movement, there were few amongst the Bolsheviks who still had roots amongst the Jews, or had Jewish knowledge. The communist party had to bring in Jews from outside its ranks. Of the six men who formed the leadership of the Yevsektsia there was only one old Bolshevik, Shimon Dimanshtein, who in his youth had been a Yeshivah student. The rest were either members of the Bund or Poale Zion (Workers of Zion) or ex-members who had recently joined the Bolsheviks. The composition of this body was of decisive importance for policy towards the Jews. A contradictory line developed, one tendency being influenced by the Bund concept of cultural autonomy, while another sought a solution to the Jewish problem along the lines of a territorial-state unit. Needless to say, this conflicting policy caused much suffering to large numbers of Jews.

The October Revolution was accompanied, as is well known, by a bloody civil war, and a wave of mass pogroms by Ukrainians and the Whites. It has been reliably estimated that over 200,000 Jews were massacred in the Ukraine alone, over 300,000 children left orphans and over 700,000 rendered homeless.[2] Apart from the Nazi atrocities, this was the most gruesome tragedy in Jewish history since the massacres in 1648–9 by the bands of Bogdan Khmielnitsky.

[1] The foundation of the Yevsektsia is variously given as January 1918 and as 15 February 1918. On the Yevsektsia as a whole there is no good book, although much has been written about it. On the early period only, cf. the important study by Mordecai Altshuler, *Reishit Ha'Yevsektsia, 1918–1921*, Jerusalem, 1966, p. 210. On the formation of the People's Commissariats, see M. P. Iroshnikov, *Sozdanie Sovietskogo Tsentralnogo Gosudarstvennogo Apparata*, Leningrad, 1966, p. 296.

[2] On the pogroms in the Ukraine, the figures are sometimes contradictory, and the figures quoted perhaps conservative. Cf S. Dimanshtein, 'Fun Tsarishn "Techum" bis Sovietisher avtonomie', in *Yidn in F.S.S.R.*, Moscow, 1935, p. 19; J. Lestchinsky, *Tswishn Lebn un Toit*, vol. i, Wilno, 1930, pp. 19–53. Salo Baron, *The Russian Jew*, New York, 1964, pp. 220–1, gives much lower figures, which run counter to those given by E. Tscherikover, S. Dubnow, and Krasny Admoni, and also to those quoted above.

The end of the civil war witnessed the enormous tragedy of the Russian-Jewish population, mortally wounded and materially destitute. In addition to the pogroms, the period of war communism played havoc with the Jews, particularly in Byelorussia, where many Jewish businessmen lost all their property through government requisitioning measures.

Lenin's New Economic Policy (N.E.P.) of 1921 improved matters slightly, and helped, to a certain degree, to restore partially the Jewish economy, though even in this sector contradictory trends manifested themselves quite early on. On the one hand, the Soviet Government badly needed the goods which only the Nepmen could provide. These were required to pacify the peasantry. On the other hand, the government was continually short of money, and as a result it squeezed the traders hard, frequently putting them out of business. The main beneficiaries of the N.E.P. were probably Jews, as they also turned out to be the majority of the sufferers, that is, up to collectivization in 1928.

The economic situation in Russia between 1921 and 1928 was extremely mixed. An impoverished peasantry complained of the shortage of goods and credit; in the towns there was growing mass unemployment. Large numbers of Jews found themselves treated by the Soviet authorities as petty-bourgeois elements, members of the exploiting class, and as such to be treated as representatives of the class enemy, and considered second-class citizens.

The Yevsektsia at first wooed the relatively small Jewish working class, artisan rather than proletarian, and concentrated its fire on the bulk of the Jews, the shopkeepers, clergy and those people generally known as '*luft-menschen*'. It has been calculated on reliable evidence, that by 1925, 1,120,000 Jews had been forced to close down their small businesses. They therefore added to the growing number of unemployed.[1] This compelled the Jews either to deal on the black market, at considerable risks to themselves, or to emigrate *en masse* to the interior of Russia, particularly to Moscow, Leningrad, Kiev, Kharkov, etc., and to seek their fortunes there, by entering the new industrial enterprises just beginning to emerge, or by enrolling in the various government offices, in the *apparat*. Over half a million left the traditional *shtetlach*, the townships, and migrated to the big cities. It was the biggest internal wave of emigration since the Jewish exodus to America at the end of the last century. The mass of the remaining Jews clamoured for some improvement in their impoverished position. The leaders of the Yevsektsia busied themselves with attacking the Jewish clergy and religion rather than seeking the help of the Soviet authorities to

[1] See Lestschinsky, op. cit., pp. 137-8.

put the Jews on their feet again. A number of Jews who discussed this problem with Lev Kamenev, then one of the leaders of the Soviet Government and communist party, and himself an assimilated Jew, told him that the biggest enemy of the Jew was the Yevsektsia.[1] Something drastic had to be done, and to be done quickly, to prevent a complete catastrophe.

The large influx of Jews into the big industrial centres attracted at the same time considerable numbers into the communist party. In 1927 they formed the third largest national group in the party, i.e. 45,342, and also the third largest group in the young communist league, i.e. 98,323 members. Since then, it seems, their numbers dwindled, as no exact figures are available.[2] These groups were set on an assimilationist process, and were lost to the influence of the Jewish communist leaders.

For the bulk of the Jews remaining in the former Pale of Settlement, in the *shtetlach*, a solution to their economic hardships was offered through settling them on the land. This was not a new idea. Before the First World War there were in the Ukraine about 52,000 Jewish farmers, or 'colonists', as they were called. Because of the pogroms most of them fled to the towns in search of security and safety. By 1923, 76,000 Jews were earning their living as farmers.[3]

In January 1925 the Soviet Government set up a new body, *Geselschaft far ainordenung af erd Arbetndike Yidn in F.S.S.R.* (Society to settle working Jews on the land in the U.S.S.R.), known as 'Geserd', or in the Russian abbreviation, 'Ozet', composed of leading members of the Yevsektsia, and leading personalities of the Soviet state. A chairman was appointed, the well-known economist, Yuri Larin (Lurye, the son of a 'government-rabbi'). Amongst the leading people delegated to it were the Soviet President, Mikhail Kalinin, the Commissar for Foreign Affairs, Chicherin, the Commissar for Foreign Trade, Leonid Krassin, the Vice-President of the Supreme Soviet, Peter Smidovich, all non-Jews and old Bolsheviks, and also the well-known diplomat, the Jew Maxim Litvinov (Wallach), later to become famous as the Soviet Commissar for Foreign Affairs. The original plan was to settle about half a million Jews by the end of 1926, and 100,000 hectares were allocated for that purpose in the Ukraine and Crimea. Over 40,000 families applied immediately for registration. The Soviet Government was desperately short of money, and the leaders of Geserd resorted to the traditional Jewish method of appealing to world Jewry to help raise the necessary funds, and an agreement was signed with the American 'Joint Distribution Committee'.

Soviet leaders who propounded the idea that Jews were not a nation,

[1] See Lestschinsky, op. cit., pp. 137-8.   [2] Dimanshtein, op. cit., p. 24.   [3] Ibid., p. 20.

and as a group were destined for total assimilation, underlined the differences between their form of settling Jews on land, and the Zionist method in Palestine. Yet at the same time they adopted similar means to those of the Zionists and appealed to world Jewry both to help financially, and, later on, even to come and settle in Biro-Bidzhan.[1]

At that time the former Zionist-Socialist leaders, Merezhin, Chemerisky, Litvakov, Novakovsky, and Bragin, came to the fore in the leadership of Geserd and Yevsektsia, and the former Bundists, Weinstein, Rafes, and Esther Frumkina were reduced in influence. The fact that leading diplomats such as Chicherin, Litvinov, and Krassin were involved, revealed the importance attached by the Soviet authorities to the appeal made to world Jewry.

Some of the Soviet leaders, such as President Kalinin, understood fully that the idea of having entire Jewish settlements, with a judiciary, educational, and political institutions conducting their affairs in Yiddish would awaken national sentiments. Indeed, in spite of the fact that the official slogan was 'socialist in content and national in form', it did appeal to Jewish national sentiments. Hence came the many attempts by Soviet writers to stress the immense difference between themselves and Zionism. Later it will be shown that even some of the Yevsektsia leaders consciously or subconsciously, paraphrased well-known Zionist phrases.

Kalinin, the most pro-Jewish of Soviet leaders, in his famous speech of 17 November 1926 at the Congress of Geserd, declared:

To me this trend appears as one of the forms of national self-preservation. As a reaction to assimilation and national erosion which threaten all small peoples deprived of the opportunities for national evolution, the Jewish people has developed the instinct of self-preservation, of the struggle to maintain its national identity. . . . The Jewish people now faces the great task of preserving its nationality. For this purpose a large segment of the Jewish population must transform itself into a compact farming population, numbering at least several hundred thousand souls.[2]

In 1934, Kalinin introduced an important additional nuance, which will be examined later.

[1] Ibid., pp. 20–4. On Jewish colonization in the Ukraine in the nineteenth century there is a considerable amount of literature in Russian and Hebrew. The idea stemmed originally from the Court poet, Gabriel Derzhavin who in 1800 submitted to Tsar Paul a memorandum in which he outlined the idea. The two best studies of this subject are Victor Nikitin, *Yevrei Zemledeltsy 1807–1887*, St. Petersburg, 1887, and S. I. Borovoi, *Yevreiskaya Zemledelcheskaya Kolonisatsia v Staroi Rossii*, Moscow, 1928.

[2] *Emes*, Moscow, 11 July 1927. First published in the stenographic report of the Congress of Geserd, or, as it was known in Russian, 'Ozet'.

An additional factor why relatively so few Jews could be absorbed on the land in the Ukraine and in the Crimea was the acute competition for land in these areas. Moreover the native Ukrainian and Tatar populations were hostile to the invading Jews. Antisemitic propaganda was widespread amongst the peasantry, which the Soviet authorities combated with great vigour.[1]

The leaders of Geserd and the Yevsektsia realized the urgency of solving the problem of Jewish poverty. On their advice, therefore, the Soviet authorities were looking for another territory, free, or barely populated, so that the hostility of the native population would not be aroused. The commission which was appointed at first looked in the Azov Sea area, north of the Caucasus, and the steppes of northern Kazakhstan.[2] The expedition consisted of 180 people, including eighty-five scientific workers. It finished its investigation in the spring of 1928, and produced a multi-volume report, which, it seems, was never discussed, and was only mentioned after the Biro-Bidzhan plan had been approved of.[3]

The Biro-Bidzhan project was not the product of Jewish initiative. It stemmed from the People's Commissariat of Agriculture, and was strongly supported by the Commissariat for Defence and the Agricultural Academy. Actually some of the leading members of Geserd, such as the agronomist Abraham Bragin, and the economist mentioned above, Yuri Larin, and a few others strongly opposed the scheme, on the grounds that the climate was harsh, and the soil unsuitable for cultivation. The opposition to the Biro-Bidzhan project argued in favour of creating a Jewish republic in the Crimea.[4]

It seems that the Soviet Government was primarily prompted by strategic considerations: i.e. to safeguard its far eastern frontier with Japan. The area was sparsely populated, and covered a large underdeveloped region at the confluence of the rivers Bira and Bidzhan. It lay in the southern part of the Soviet far east, on the left bank of the river Amur, and extended over 36,000 kilometres. Before the territory was offered to the Jews in 1927, the inhabitants in the area numbered 1,192, consisting of

[1] See Yuri Larin, *Yevrei i Antisemitizm v S.S.S.R.*, Moscow, 1929, for a full survey of this campaign and the counter-measures undertaken by the Soviet Government.

[2] Merezhin's statement to the full meeting of Ozet of 23–5 December 1927, in *Tribuna*, nos. 1–2, Moscow, 1928, quoted in Jacob Levavi (Babitzki) *Hahityashvut Hayehudit Bebiro-Bidzan*, Jerusalem, 1965, p. 43, n. 10. I have used this important study on many points in this article and I would like to express my thanks to the author.   [3] Ibid.

[4] S. Dimanshtein, 'Sovietishe Yidishe Melukhishkeit' in *Forpost*, Biro-Bidzhan–Moscow, no. 1, 1936, p. 124. The title of the article is essentially permeated with Jewish national ideas of statehood. The famous leader of the Yevsektsia and former right-hand man of Stalin was liquidated soon after this article appeared. It contains important admissions.

Koreans, Kazakhs, and members of a primitive tribe—the Tungus. Their numbers dwindled, according to Professor B. Bruk, because of climatic conditions.[1]

The periodical *Tribuna*, the organ of Geserd, more or less admitted to this political motivation: 'the masses of the Jewish toilers, who are permeated with loyalty and devotion to the Soviet regime, are going to Biro-Bidzhan . . . they are not only fighting for their country, not for a new fatherland, as the U.S.S.R. is already for them, but for strengthening the Soviet Union in the Far East.'[2] One has the impression that the decision might have been taken in a hurry, for fear of a clash with Japan, which did not occur until late 1931.[3] Later on Kalinin claimed that he was responsible for suggesting Biro-Bidzhan.

The Soviet authorities, by creating a Jewish territorial unit, which was later to be transformed into a state unit, hoped to receive the moral and financial support of the Jews, mainly from America. The state would also, it was hoped, turn the attention, both of Soviet and foreign Jews, away from Zionism.[4]

Alexander Chemerisky, secretary of the Yevsektsia, boasted that 'the autonomous Jewish territory will be the heaviest blow to the Zionist and religious ideology'.[5] Though propaganda among Soviet Jews in favour of settling in Biro-Bidzhan was accompanied by the constant denunciation of Zionism, the ex-Zionist-socialist and neophyte communists, out of their great enthusiasm for the project, themselves fell under Zionist influence. They proclaimed the aim: '*Tsu a Yiddish Land*' ('towards a Jewish State'). Another, forgetting that he was paraphrasing Herzl, stated: '*Oib ir wet dos weln—wet dos sein*' ('if you want it—then you will achieve it').[6] These remarks were sharply criticized at the time, and their authors had to recant.

[1] B. Bruk, 'Birsko-Bidjhanski rai'on i evo Zaselenie', in *Tikho-Oke'anskaya Zvezda* of 17 and 26 June 1928, quoted Levavi, op. cit, p. 24. Professor Bruk was a well-known agronomist, and member of the executive of Geserd; also a member of the expedition which was sent to investigate Biro-Bidzhan.

[2] Issue no. 9, 1932. A similar hint was contained in Kalinin's famous speech delivered on 28 May 1934 at a reception for Moscow factory workers, in *Yidn in F.S.S.R.*, p. 36.

[3] This is the meaning of Michael Rashkes's remarks at the executive of Geserd, quoted *Tribuna*, no. 3, 1929.

[4] Kalinin's speech at the second congress of Geserd, held in Moscow in December 1930, in *Tribuna*, no. 36, 1930.

[5] Alexander Chemerisky, 'Biro-Bidzhan—der grosser onzog', in *Oktiabr*, 30 March 1928, quoted Levavi, op. cit., p. 46.

[6] Ibid., p. 50. The statements were made by Merezhin, the chairman of Geserd, and Chemerisky, the secretary of Yevsektsia, respectively. Both were later liquidated during the purges.

Considerable propagandist energies were devoted to popularizing Biro-Bidzhan amongst large sections of Soviet Jewry, and also amongst Jews abroad. The Jews responded by giving verbal approval, but refraining from migrating there. 'The Jews raise their hands easily for Biro-Bidzhan, but not their feet', complained a correspondent of *Emes* in April 1928.

In March 1928 the executive committee of the Supreme Soviet (V.T.I.K.) approved the request of Komzet (the committee to settle Jews on the land) for the development of Biro-Bidzhan, with the aim of making it 'a national Jewish unit, administratively and territorially'. Some of those who opposed this scheme were accused of left deviations, others of nationalism. Opposition soon disappeared altogether, although Larin made his hostility public. Biro-Bidzhan, he argued, consisted of swamps, 'gnus' (a kind of Siberian tsetse fly), floods, a long winter in which the temperatures dropped to minus 40°C. and lay over 1,000 kilometres from the sea. Those Jews who did favour it were the victim of hasty judgements, created a noise and aimed to turn it into a kind of Zionism, replacing Israel by Biro-Bidzhan.[1]

Amongst the Bolsheviks, the first person who argued that it would be necessary to create in the future territorial state units for nations which were deprived of them, was Lenin. In October–December 1913, in his well-known article, *Critical Remarks on the National Question*, he wrote as follows, and this view, as far as I know, occurs only once in Lenin's writings:

It is beyond doubt that in order to abolish all national oppression it is extremely important to create autonomous areas even of the smallest dimensions, each with an integral uniform national composition of population, towards which the members of the given nationality, scattered in different parts of the country, or even of the world, could 'gravitate' and with which they could enter into relations and free association of every kind.[2]

It is not clear whether Lenin had Jews in mind for his scheme, though the article is primarily a polemic against the Bundists Liebman Hersch and Vladimir Medem. It is of some interest to note that though Lenin was quoted constantly, for every political occasion, this idea was not mentioned by the planners of Biro-Bidzhan.

[1] *Na Agrarnom Fronte*, Moscow, 1929, no. 3, and also in his book *Yevrei i Antisemitizm v S.S.S.R.*, pp. 183–90, and 306–7.

[2] Lenin, *Sochineniya*, vol. xvii, p. 158, 2nd edn. The first European to have toyed with the idea of offering a territory to Jews, was the English seventeenth-century political thinker and friend of Cromwell, James Harrington, in his *Oceana* (published 1655). He visualized the Jews as the colonizers and subjugators of Ireland (Panopea). (See *Oceana*, preface.) It is very doubtful whether Lenin, or any other Soviet politician had even heard of him.

The first group of immigrants received free passage and a very little pocket money. In the first year, 1928, 600 permits were granted; of these, 450 went to representatives of families and 150 to individuals. In all 654 people actually arrived in Biro-Bidzhan.

The number of Jews who migrated between 1928 and 1933 was as follows:

1928	1929	1930	1931	1932	1933
654	555	860	3,231	14,000	3,005

In 1929, it was planned to settle 3,000 families (2,500 families on the land) or approximately 15,000 people. Actually about 1,000 people arrived and a large number left. In 1930 the number of Jews reached nearly 1,500 out of a population of 37,000, i.e. 8 per cent.[1] That year was extremely difficult for the absorption of immigrants, probably because of the general difficulties stemming from collectivization, and the leaders of Geserd, Rashkes, Robinson, and Stolov recommended that only individuals and not families should be sent. In 1931 an appeal was made to Jewish ex-servicemen. The Soviet authorities were clearly concerned over the military position in the Far East. This explains the higher number of immigrants for that year, which included 995 people over 18 years of age. The other interesting feature is that the majority of the immigrants came from the Ukraine, the most poverty-stricken Jewish area. The number of people who left was estimated at between 20 per cent and 30 per cent of the immigrants. Some consider this to be on the conservative side.[2] The year 1932 saw a very sharp rise in the number of immigrants; again the vast majority, 6,200, of 44·3 per cent of the total, came from the Ukraine. That year also saw a sharp rise in the number who left, and a well-known worker of Geserd, B. Trotsky, estimated that 80 per cent left. The communist party secretary of Biro-Bidzhan, Khavkin, admitted to 66 per cent.

The plan for 1933 was that 25,000 Jews should migrate; but less than one-eighth actually did so. That year more people left Biro-Bidzhan than arrived.

This process also showed itself between 1934 and 1939. For 1934 the plan was to absorb about 10,000 people; actually 5,267 arrived, including teachers, doctors, accountants, students and technical graduates. In 1935, 8,344 arrived in Biro-Bidzhan, including 820 non-Jews. The Jews complained of the lack of housing and other facilities. Again the Jews from the

[1] The figures published in the Soviet Union at the time are often contradictory. This is discussed fully by Levavi, op. cit., pp. 81–93.

[2] J. Bregman in *Tribuna*, no. 7, 1932. Levavi, op. cit., p. 86, thinks that those who left were more numerous.

Ukraine formed 70 per cent of the immigrants. There were 962 building workers (26·6 per cent), 223 tailors and shoemakers (6·1 per cent), 171 fitters and blacksmiths (4·7 per cent), 159 wood-workers (4·4 per cent). The number who left dropped as low as 170. At the end of 1935, the number of Jews in Biro-Bidzhan reached 14,000 (23 per cent) of the total population. This was the highest percentage ever to be reached by the Jewish immigrants.

During 1936, 6,758 immigrants arrived, but a large number left again. The leaders of Biro-Bidzhan tried to hide these ugly facts from the population, as Dimanshtein himself later admitted.

In 1937 the Soviet Government (Prime Minister Molotov himself was on this occasion involved in the actual decree) planned to absorb 17,000 immigrants in Biro-Bidzhan. In fact, only just over 3,000 arrived. That year saw a new feature. The N.K.V.D. (the secret police) became responsible for the transportation of the Jews. This took place at the climax of the famous Yezhov purges, which deeply affected the whole of Biro-Bidzhan. From 1938 to the end of the war, immigration drastically declined, and both the Komzet and Geserd were closed down.[1] Almost all the leaders of the former Yevsektsia and Geserd fell victim during that period and were liquidated.[2]

To make the Biro-Bidzhan project more attractive to Jews, the Soviet Government, in May 1934, proclaimed the area a Jewish autonomous region. The President of the Soviet Union, Mikhail Kalinin, made an important speech on this occasion, which requires a brief analysis. He elaborated his earlier thesis of 1926, quoted above, on preserving the Jewish nationality. Now, however, he added nuances of very great importance. 'You ask', he said, 'why the Jewish autonomous region was formed. The reason is that we have three million Jews, and they do not have a state system of their own, being the only nationality in the Soviet Union in this situation. The creation of such a region is the only means of a normal development for this nationality. The Jews in Moscow will have to assimilate. . . . In ten years' time Biro-Bidzhan will become the most important guardian of the Jewish-national culture and those who cherish

[1] The figures given by Gregor Aronson, in his *The Jews in Soviet Russia*, in *The Jewish People Past and Present*, vol. xi, New York, 1948, p. 65, and in his pamphlet *Soviet Russia and the Jews*, New York, 1949, p. 6, are not fully accurate, as Levavi's figures show conclusively, see op. cit., pp. 80–98.

[2] Amongst those arrested and shot were Merezhin, chairman of Geserd, and Moyshe Litvakov, editor of *Emes*, A. Chemerisky, formerly secretary of the Yevsektsia, Simon Dimanshtein, J. Liberberg, chairman of the Biro-Bidzhan Soviet and formerly the head of the Jewish Scientific Institute of Kiev, and many others.

a national Jewish culture', he stated explicitly, 'must link up with Biro-Bidzhan. . . . We already consider Biro-Bidzhan a Jewish national state.' He admitted that immigration had not been very successful, as many more Jews returned rather than stayed. He expressed the hope that if only 4,000 Jews would immigrate yearly, then within ten years a great deal would have been achieved. When 100,000 Jews had settled there, the Soviet Government would consider creating a Soviet Jewish republic. He stressed the significance of defending the Soviet far east. He attacked Zionism, and acknowledged the help received from the Joint Distribution Committee.[1]

None other than Stalin himself, on 25 November 1936, two and a half years later, gave a very diplomatic and subtle reply to these optimistic hopes of Kalinin and the Geserd people. Stalin, the acknowledged expert on nationalities, had kept silent on the Jews since writing his celebrated essay, *Marxism and the National Question* in 1913. But at the end of 1936 he delivered his well-known speech 'On the Draft Constitution of the U.S.S.R.'. Without mentioning either the Jews or Biro-Bidzhan, he declared that three conditions must be fulfilled were autonomous regions to become constituent Soviet republics. 'First, the republic must be a border republic, not surrounded on all sides by U.S.S.R. territory.' 'Second, the nationality which gives its name to a given Soviet republic must constitute a more or less compact majority within that republic.' Third and most important: 'the republic must not have too small a population; it should have a population of, say, not less, but more than a million.'[2]

Taking Kalinin's figure of 4,000 Jewish immigrants a year and assuming that this process were to continue without interruption, then it would have taken between 200 and 250 years for Biro-Bidzhan to attain the distinction of becoming a Soviet Jewish republic. Stalin thereby declared that Biro-Bidzhan project bankrupt from the outset. By that time most of the Soviet-Jewish leaders were either already imprisoned, or in decline, and could not comment on this statement.

After the war, the Moscow Jewish Anti-Fascist Committee tried to revive immigration to Biro-Bidzhan. Within three years (1946-8) 6,326 Jews arrived there. But when all Jewish institutions were closed down in November 1948 immigration virtually ceased.

The 1959 census showed that there were 14,269 Jews, out of a total population of 162,856 (8·8 per cent). Of these, 6,313 were men and 7,956

[1] The whole speech is in *Yidn in F.S.S.R.*, Moscow, 1935, pp. 31-8. It is the most 'Zionist' declaration ever made by a Soviet statesman. It recalls 'down with Zionism, long live Soviet "Zionism" '.   [2] J. Stalin, *Leninism*, London, 1940, p. 584.

women. Those who gave Yiddish as their mother tongue totalled 5,597 (39·2 per cent).[1]

Finally, a few remarks on Yiddish culture: before the war of 1939–45, a group of Yiddish writers settled in Biro-Bidzhan. The most prominent were Kazakevitch, Dobin, Falikman, Rabinkov, Olievsky, Gen, Wasserman and Aron Vergelis. Of all these, only one writer remained, Lyuba Wasserman. Between 1932 and 1948 less than a dozen Yiddish booklets appeared. The journal *Forpost* which was founded in 1936 and ceased publication in 1938, was actually published in Moscow.[2] Now only a small tabloid, *Biro-Bidzhaner Shtern*, appears and has a circulation of 1,000 a day. Until November 1948 a Yiddish theatre was active and performed plays by Sholom Aleichem and Soviet Yiddish playwrights.

One of the most astonishing phenomena is the re-appearance of some mild form of religious activity amongst the Jews. In spite of a strong anti-religious campaign, even the early settlers organized, at first *secretly*, prayer-houses and refrained from working on the Jewish New Year and Day of Atonement. In 1947 a synagogue was erected which was burnt down in 1956. It has since been reported that there is a regular *Minyan* (a quorum for prayer) in the town of Biro-Bidzhan, and on Saturdays about twenty Jews assemble for prayer. The community has a *chazan* and *schochet* (cantor and ritual slaughterer).[3]

In April 1958 Khrushchev gave an interview to the correspondent of the French newspaper *Figaro*, in which he stated that the Biro-Bidzhan project failed because Jews were incapable of collective work; they were individualists and not inclined to do agricultural work.

Few people will agree with Salo Baron that 'the conception of a Biro-Bidzhan settlement was highly imaginative and by far transcended the mere scheme of agricultural colonization, such as had long been under way in the European parts of the Union.'[4] Larin's opposition and his arguments of 1928 were sound. The outcome was as he foresaw. The project, born of contradictory trends in policy, executed haphazardly, and without due

[1] See *Itogi Vsesoyuznoi perepisi naselenia 1959 goda*, Moscow, 1962–3, pp. 334–5; 360–1; 384–5. For a compact analysis of the Jewish population in the Soviet Union based on the 1959 census, see Mordchaj Altshuler, *The Jews in the Soviet Union Census, 1959* (Hebrew and English), Jerusalem, 1963. (Stencilled.)

[2] See Levavi, op. cit., pp. 309–33.

[3] See ibid., pp. 250–2. Jack Miller, 'A Sociological Survey of Judaism in Biro-Bidzhan', in *Bulletin on Soviet Jewish Affairs*, London, no. 1, January 1968 (published by Institute of Jewish Affairs of the World Jewish Congress), pp. 61–3, quotes a Soviet survey, which gives the members of the congregation as forty-three with eight 'firm believers', aged between 63 and 84.

[4] See Salo W. Baron, *The Russian Jew under Tsars and Soviets*, New York, 1964, pp. 230–1.

consideration for Jewish feelings and sentiments, was doomed to failure and tragic collapse.

SELECTED BIBLIOGRAPHY
(In addition to the references in the footnotes)

IN YIDDISH

Oif Naie Wegn. Almanakh. Dreisig Yohr Sovietish Yiddish shafn, New York, Ikuf, 1949.

Alberton, M., *Biro-Bidzhan. Wegn aindrukn*, Kharkov, Tsentrfarlag, 1939.

Alamazov, S., *Tsen Yohr Biro-Bidzhan* (1923–38), New York, Ikor, 1938.

Nadel, B. and Rubin, A. (eds.), *Birobidzhan. Literarishe Zamlung*, Moscow, Der Emes, 1936.

Bergelson, D., *Birobidzhaner*, Moscow, Der Emes, 1934.

Bergelson, D. and Kazakevitch, E. M., *Birobidjhan*, Moscow, Der Emes, 1939.

Dimanshtein, S., *Di Yiddishe avtonome gegnt*, Moscow, Der Emes, 1934.

Lestschinsky, J., *Di Yidn in Soviet Russland*, New York, 1941.

Singer, L., *Dos Banaite Folk*, Moscow, Der Emes, 1941.

Singer, L., *Dos Ufgerichte Folk*, Moscow, Der Emes, 1948.

Trotsky, B., *Biro-Bidzhan in 1935 un in 1936*, Moscow, Der Emes, 1936.

Dimanshtein, S. (ed.), *Yidn in F.S.S.R. Zamlbuch*, Moscow, Der Emes, 1935.

IN HEBREW

Goldelman, Shalom, *Goral Hayahadut Bivrit Hamoatzot 1917–57*, Jerusalem, 1958.

Shmeruk, Ch., *Hakibutz Hayehudi Vehahityashvut Hahaklait Hayehudit Bebyelo-Russia Hasovietit (1918–32)*, Jerusalem, 1961.

IN RUSSIAN

Bragin, A. and Koltsov, Michael, *Sud'ba Yevreiskikh mass v Sovietskom Souze*, Moscow, Gosizdat, 1924.

Kantor, Y., *Natsionalnoye Stroitel'stvo Sredi Yevreyev v S.S.S.R.*, Moscow, Vlast Sovietov, 1935.

Kirzhnits, A., *Yevreiskaya Avtonomnaya Oblast*, Moscow, Der Emes, 1936.

Merezhin, A., *O Biro-Bedzhane*, Moscow, Komzet, 1929.

IN ENGLISH

Bergelson, D., *The Jewish Autonomous Region*, Moscow, 1939.

Marley, Lord, *Biro-Bidzhan*, London, n.d. (1935).

Schwarz, Solomon M., *The Jews in the Soviet Union*, Syracuse University Press, New York, 1951.

5

The Legal Position of Soviet Jewry: A Historical Enquiry[1]

WILLIAM KOREY

Bolshevik ideologists, prior to the October Revolution, denied that the Jewish community had those specific characteristics which they considered essential for nationhood, particularly a 'closed territory of settlement' and an agricultural base. None the less, they recognized, Jews have a 'common "national character"'.[2] V. I. Lenin, as early as March 1914, drafted for the Bolshevik delegation in the Duma a bill on nationality which clearly defined the future legal status of the Jewish community as a distinct nationality entity in the communist state. The bill provided for 'the repeal of all restrictions upon the rights of Jews, and, in general of all restrictions based on a person's descent or nationality'. After noting that the 'citizens of all nationalities of Russia' were to be equal before the law, Lenin's draft went on to specify the removal of barriers against Jews.[3] Following the Bolshevik seizure of power, Lenin once again identified Jews as a distinct nationality.[4] A communist party resolution, adopted at its tenth congress in March 1921, specifically mentioned Jews among a very small list of examples of nationalities and national minorities.[5]

Political expression to the legal status of a Jewish nationality was formally extended in January 1918, when a Commissariat for Jewish National Affairs was established as a special section of the Peoples' Commissariat for Nationality Affairs. The latter body was created one day after the Bolshevik seizure of power. Under the leadership of Stalin, the Commissariat was to function as 'the initiator of the entire Soviet legislation on the national question . . . measures regarding the economic and cultural uplifting of the nationalities, etc.' Its special Section dealing with

---

[1] The author has published an article on a similar subject in E. Goldhagen, *Ethnic Minorities in the Soviet Union* (New York: Praeger, 1968).

[2] See particularly J. Stalin, *Marksizm i natsionalno-kolonial'nyi vopros*, Moscow, 1937, pp. 6, 8.

[3] V. I. Lenin, *Sochineniya*, vol. xvii, 3rd edn., Moscow, 1937, p. 292.

[4] V. I. Lenin, *Sochineniya*, vol. xxiv, 3rd edn., Moscow, 1937, p. 96.

[5] Stalin, op. cit., p. 209.

Jewish national affairs was assigned the task of establishing 'the dictatorship of the proletariat in the Jewish streets'.[1] Aside from propagandizing the Jewish masses with the ideas of Bolshevism, the Commissariat for Jewish National Affairs brought about the abolition of the existing autonomous institutions of the Jewish community and the transfer of their funds and property to itself. A decree of 5 August 1919 formalized the dissolution.

As distinct from the state apparatus, the communist party in 1918 created within its own structure Jewish Sections (Yevsektsii). They had the task of carrying out party policy among Jewish workers and of conducting propaganda in the Yiddish language so 'that the Jewish masses [would] have a chance to satisfy all their intellectual needs in that language. . . .'[2] The Commissariat for Jewish National Affairs ceased to exist in early 1924 but the Jewish Sections continued a checkered existence until January 1930. In that year they, too, were liquidated. Yet the category of Jewish nationality remained and finds expression today in all official publications that deal with nationalities or that indicate nationality categories.

The use of the native language or mother tongue was integral to the functions of the Jewish Sections. Indeed, Yiddish was formally recognized as a fundamental component of the Jewish nationality. Thus, the Byelorussian republic decreed in law that Yiddish was among the four official languages of the government.[3] That republic contained the largest number of compact Jewish communities in Soviet Russia. 90·7 per cent of the Jews there expressly stated, in the 1926 census, that Yiddish was their mother tongue. (The 1897 census had indicated that 97 per cent of the Jewish population of tsarist Russia identified Yiddish as its 'mother tongue', and the 1926 census showed that, notwithstanding the assimilatory process of the intervening decades, 70·4 per cent of the 'Jewish nationality' of Soviet Russia declared Yiddish to be their mother tongue.)

While, on the one hand, the Jewish community, *qua* community, acquired a fixed legal status as a nationality so, on the other hand, did the individual born of Jewish parents. A Jew in Soviet Russia is not someone who desires to be so or chooses to identify himself as such. He is, in fact, a juridically defined person who unavoidably is a part of the Jewish nationality. The determining legal factor in fixing the designation is not the

---

[1] S. Schwarz, *The Jews in the Soviet Union*, New York, 1951, p. 97.

[2] Ibid., and B. Z. Goldberg, *The Jewish Problem in the Soviet Union*, New York, 1961, p. 360. In contrast, the Hebrew language was conceived of as 'reactionary' and an instrument of Zionism. After being permitted a shadowy existence, for a few years, Hebrew schools were suppressed or taken over by local officials.

[3] *Prakticheskoe reshenie natsionalnovo voprosa v Byelorusskoi S.S.R.*, part I, Minsk, 1927, p. 120.

distinctive attributes, whether supposed or real, of the ethnic group; rather it is the simple biological fact of being born of Jewish parents.

The establishment of a legal category that permanently fixed the identity of a person who descended from Jewish parents as being a Jew by nationality did not come until late 1932. The circumstances under which the category was introduced, oddly enough, bore no direct relationship to the national question. A decree was adopted on 27 December 1932 by the Central Executive Committee and the Council of Peoples' Commissars that created the 'single passport system' for the U.S.S.R.[1] (This system continues to prevail today.) According to the government edict, passports which were to be issued in 1933 would contain reference to the 'nationality' of the bearer. Urban residents, 16 years of age and over, were to acquire passports. The principal reason for the introduction of the passports was the severe housing shortage in the major urban areas, a consequence of the enormous influx of new workers into cities resulting from the intensified industrialization effort of the Five Year Plan. The passport became the basic means for regulating the distribution of apartments.

Nationality ranked high among the items which the decree listed for specification in the passport. Thus, it was listed immediately after name, date, and place of birth. Only after nationality did there appear such categories as social position, permanent residence, and place of work. The passport was also to specify documents which offered proof of both nationality and of the other designated categories. The types of required documents were to be spelled out in 'instructions'. While such 'instructions' were not published, it is known that among the documents required was the birth certificate which carried, among other types of 'proof', the nationality of the person involved.

Specification of nationality is, virtually, an automatic process.[2] A Soviet citizen is required to register with governmental authorities when he reaches the age of 16. Upon registration, he is obliged to produce papers which indicate the nationality of each of his parents. If both are of the same nationality—which has been the characteristic phenomenon— then that nationality is the one inserted in 'Point 5' of the passport. No voluntary choice is permitted: if both parents are Jewish, the youngster is listed as 'Yevrei'—Jewish. The only option that exists for the 16-year-old

---

[1] *Pravda*, 28 December 1932. For a discussion of the important current statistical uses of the passport system, see *Vestnik statistiki*, July 1965, pp. 16–21. The article indicates that in various rural areas the passport system has not yet been introduced.

[2] See the *New York Times*, 18 February 1963, and the findings of André Blumel as reported in a Paris press conference and published in the *Jerusalem Post*, 23 October 1960.

is when the parents are each of different nationality. In this case, he selects one of the two nationalities as his own.

The question might be raised as to the permanence of the legal category in the light of the fact that the passport decree came into existence under a set of special circumstances. That the passport itself will remain can hardly be doubted since it serves a myriad of uses besides coping with the continuing housing shortage. It is not to be excluded, however, that the specifying of nationality on the passport could be declared to be a voluntary act. A 1963 Soviet Government report submitted to the U.N. is pertinent in this respect. The government went out of its way to insert a special footnote in the report declaring that the 'data on nationality' in the 1959 census were 'the result of self-determination; that is, the nationality recorded in the census was that stated by the respondent himself'.[1] As the term 'self-determination' carries in current Soviet usage, a favourable normative judgement, it is possible that it could be extended to the declaration on nationality in the passport itself. However, there are as yet no indications that such action is contemplated for the immediate future.

Special problems relating to the fixed personal category of Jews emerge when cognizance is taken of the fact that, unlike most other Soviet nationalities, Jews have no distinct geographical national base. It is true that the so-called Jewish autonomous region of Biro-Bidzhan was established by decree of the Presidium of the Central Executive Committee of the U.S.S.R. on 7 May 1934. Despite government statements that followed recommending Biro-Bidzhan as a 'homeland' for Soviet Jews, the area, lacking any historical sentiment, attracted relatively few Jews as permanent residents. Today only 14,270 persons or 8·8 per cent of the region's population are of the Jewish nationality.[2] The region has five representatives in the Soviet of Nationalities of the Supreme Soviet and only one is identified as Jewish. Thus, to refer to the geographical unit as a Jewish autonomous region is an anomaly. It would be meaningless, for example, to apply to the region Article 110 of the U.S.S.R. constitution which requires 'juridical proceedings' to be 'conducted in the language' of the region. Certainly that language could not be Yiddish.

[1] United Nations General Assembly, *Manifestations of Racial Prejudice and National and Religious Intolerance*, Doc. A/5473/Add.1, 25 September 1963, p. 42, Hereafter referred to as *Manifestations*. The footnote, besides being the only clarifying one in the report (the only other footnote was directed to a source), was unusual in that it served no particular purpose except to indicate a normative judgement. The observation about the census is, of course, correct.

[2] Tsentral'noe staticheskoye upravlenie pri Sovete Ministrov S.S.S.R., *Itogi Vsesoiuznoi perepisi naseleniia 1959 goda*, S.S.S.R., Moscow, 1962, p. 204. For information on the region's representatives see *Deputy Verkhovnovo Soveta S.S.S.R.*, Moscow, 1962.

Jews are dispersed throughout all of the fifteen Union republics. This is one of their distinguishing demographic features. According to the census of 1959, which indicated 2,268,000 persons who identified themselves as Jews, the following figures define the geographical dispersal of the Jewish community: 38 per cent in the Russian Republic; 37 per cent in the Ukraine; 7 per cent in Byelorussia; 15 per cent in Uzbekistan, Georgia, Lithuania, Moldavia, Latvia, and Estonia; and the balance of 95,000 in the remaining six republics. In each Union republic, Jews constitute a small minority, their highest percentage of the republic population being in Moldavia—3·3 per cent—and in the Ukraine—2 per cent. Their percentage of the total population on a national level is equally small: 1·09.[1]

Due to their dispersal the normal Soviet trend of linguistic assimilation has particularly affected them. The trend is further accelerated by the fact that 95 per cent of the Jews live in urban areas, making them one of the most highly urbanized nationalities in the U.S.S.R. The data on the use by Jews of their native language or 'mother tongue' in the 1959 census highlights this point. If the census of 1926 showed that over 70 per cent of the Jews specified Yiddish as their native language, the 1959 census showed, in contrast, that approximately 18 per cent, or a little more than 400,000 Jews designated Yiddish as their native language.[2] The figure of 20·8 per cent or 472,000 persons, often cited by both western and Soviet analysts, is an error resulting from a misreading of the data. The data was broken down to indicate whether the respondents declared their native language was that of their nationality or whether it was Russian or another language, other than that of their nationality. While 20·8 per cent of the Jews were reported as saying that their native language was that of their nationality, the native language or 'mother tongue' of the Jews of Georgia, Bokhara, and Daghestan is *not* Yiddish. The figures concerning the language declarations of these groups of Jews have erroneously been added to that of the other Soviet Jews to arrive at a mistaken total.

The 1959 census demonstrated that Jews ranked far and away the

[1] The data are in *Pravda*, 4 February 1960. Since respondents were not required to produce proof of nationality, it is quite possible that a considerable number of Jews, especially those involved in mixed marriages, may have declared a nationality other than that indicated on their passport. In this connection, it is to be noted that parents were given the right of specifying the nationality of their children. See *Manifestations*, Doc. A/5473/Add. 1, p. 42. Parents in a mixed marriage relationship could have chosen the non-Jewish designation for their children.

[2] Tsentral'noe staticheskoe upravlenie pri Sovete Ministrov S.S.S.R., *Chislennost' sostav razmeshchenie naseleniia S.S.S.R.*, Moscow, 1961, p. 25; and *Itogi Vsesoiuznoi perepisi naseleniia 1959 goda, S.S.S.R.* op. cit., pp. 184–202. 35,700 Jews indicated Georgian; 20,800 indicated Tadzhik; and 25,400 indicated Tatar. The adjusted figure for the total number of Jews who declared their native language to be that of their nationality is 487,800.

lowest among the nationalities in declaring that their native language was the language of the nationality to which they belonged. But, as one Soviet Jewish specialist, Yakov Kantor, has shown, the formulation of the census questions distorted and exaggerated the extent of linguistic assimilation. In his analysis which was published by the Warsaw Jewish Historical Institute, Kantor observed that the census instructions did not define 'native language'. Many Jews, in consequence, thought it meant 'language spoken'.[1] Kantor commented: 'many people who speak and read Yiddish, enjoy Yiddish books and appreciate Yiddish plays nevertheless gave Russian as their language because they speak Russian at work, in the street, and even to an extent at home.'

Attention must also be drawn to the data concerning Jews inhabiting the territories incorporated into the Soviet state in 1939–41. Here the percentage of Jews specifying Yiddish as their native tongue is fairly high —69 per cent in Lithuania, 48 per cent in Latvia, and 50 per cent in Moldavia. Significantly, official interpretations of the extent of linguistic assimilation among Jews have been seriously questioned in scholarly circles. Thus M. Friedberg, a Soviet linguistic researcher at the University of Leningrad, has criticized as 'wholly incorrect' the assertion in the *Large Soviet Encyclopaedia* that the Soviet Jewish community is on the road to 'complete linguistic assimilation'.[2] He pointed to the extensive use of Yiddish among compact Jewish populations in areas of the Ukraine and Byelorussia in order to demonstrate his thesis.

The Jewish community, as a distinctive nationality in the U.S.S.R., was and is entitled to enjoy a complex of national rights which have been inscribed in laws that go back to the early days of the Soviet regime. A week after the seizure of power, on 15 November, the government issued a formal Declaration of Rights of Peoples which proclaimed the 'free development of national minorities and ethnic groups inhabiting Russian territory'.[3] The first Soviet constitution of 1918[4] stipulated, in Article 22, that 'to oppress national minorities or impose any limitations whatsoever on their rights' is 'contrary to the fundamental laws' of the regime. After the formation of the U.S.S.R. in 1922 and the introduction of the new

[1] Y. Kantor, 'Aynike Bamerkungen un Oisfiren tsu di Fareffentlichte Sakh'haklen fun der Folks-Tselung in Ratenverband dem 15 Yanuar, 1959', *Bleter Far Geshichte*, Warsaw, xv, 1962–3, pp. 146–7. This work did not appear until early 1964.

[2] The author has examined a section of the article by M. Friedberg, 'Slozhnopodchinennoe predlozhenie v Idish-Taitch, XVI–XVIII vv.,' *Voprosy sintaksisa Romano-Germanskikh iazikov*, Leningrad, 1961.

[3] *Sobranie uzakonenii i rasporiazhenii*, no. 51, Moscow, 1918, pp. 599–609.

[4] *Sistematicheskoe sobranie deistvuiushchikh zakonov Soiuza Sovetskikh Sotsialisticheskikh Respublik*, Moscow, 1927.

federal constitution in 1924, the principle of equality of rights for nation-alities was re-stated in the constitutions of individual republics. Thus the 1925 constitution of the R.S.F.S.R., in Article 13, declared that 'oppression of national minorities in whatsoever form, [and] any restriction of their rights . . . are wholly incompatible with the fundamental laws of the Republic'.

The same Article 13 filled the general principle of equality with linguis-tic content by stipulating that R.S.F.S.R. citizens 'have the right to use their native language freely in meetings, in the courts, in administrative bodies and in public affairs'. The Article went on to state that the national minorities 'have the right to receive education in their native tongue'.

Where sizeable compact Jewish communities existed, as, for example, in the Ukraine and Byelorussia, statutes were enacted to give expression to linguistic rights.[1] The Ukrainian Code of Criminal Procedure of 1922 provided for court proceedings 'in the language of the majority of the population concerned'. A decree adopted in the Ukraine on 1 August 1923 spelled out 'measures to ensure the legal equality of languages' and emphasized that in localities where one of the minority nationalities con-stituted the majority of the population, the authorities were to use the language of that nationality. This right was re-stated in a subsequent decree of July 1927. It required the teaching of the native language together with both Russian and Ukrainian in minority schools.

In Byelorussia, the Declaration of Independence of 1 August 1920 recognized Yiddish as being one of the four 'legal' languages—enjoying 'equality' with Byelorussian, Russian, and Polish. The Declaration was reiterated in a formal act of the Byelorussian Central Executive Com-mittee in February 1921 and in a decree of 15 July 1924 'concerning practical measures to implement the policy on nationalities'. That decree guaranteed both the maintenance of native schools and the use of the 'mother tongue in dealing with any kind of organ and institution of the republic'. The Byelorussian constitution of 1927 again recognized Yiddish as an official language.[2]

The decrees in the Ukraine and Byelorussia led to the establishment in the twenties of a complex of Jewish administrative and judicial institutions in those areas where the Jews constituted a numerically significant and

---

[1] See *Sobranie uzakonenii i rasporiazhenii Rabochevo i Krest'ianskovo Pravitel'stva Ukrainskoi S.S.R.*, Kiev, 1922, no. 41; and *Prakticheskoe reshenie natsional'novo voprosa Byelorusskoi S.S.R.*, part I, op. cit.

[2] Cited in Schwarz, op. cit., p. 137.

cohesive group. With the intensified industrialization campaign of the thirties, however, the compactness of old Jewish communities broke up and a dispersion of their population to new industrial areas followed. The result was the crumbling of Jewish institutions. The process of disintegration was deepened by both administrative pressures and the voluntary actions of assimilationists. The school apparatus, however, was far from destroyed. As late as 1940, a sizeable segment of the apparatus remained intact. In that year, according to Jacob Lestchinsky, there were some 85,000 to 90,000 Jewish children studying in schools where Yiddish was the language of instruction. This constituted 20 per cent of the Jewish student population.

The Stalin constitution of the U.S.S.R., adopted in 1936, no longer made reference to the right of use of the native language in meetings, courts, and administrative bodies. However, it reaffirmed in Article 121 the right of 'instruction in schools . . . in the native language'.[1] Similar provisions were inserted in the constitutions of all the union and autonomous republics. In August 1962, the U.S.S.R. ratified the UNESCO Convention against Discrimination in Education which obliged it, according to Article 5 (1c), 'to recognize the right of members of national minorities to carry on their own educational activities, including the maintenance of schools and . . . the use or the teaching of their own language . . .'.[2]

But even before the U.S.S.R. ratified the UNESCO Convention, a decisive statute was enacted to give effect to constitutional requirements. Entitled 'Concerning the Strengthening of the Connection of the Schools with Life and the Furthest Development of the System of Peoples' Education in the R.S.F.S.R.', the statute adopted by the Russian republic on 16 April 1959, declared in Article 15: '. . . the education in schools will be conducted in the native language of the students. The right is given to parents to decide with what language in schools to register their children.'[3] The Deputy Minister of Education of the Russian republic, A. Arsenyev, indicated, in a letter written in 1956, that Soviet law provided that, should ten parents request that their children receive an education in their mother

[1] *Konstitutsiia S.S.S.R. Konstitutsii soiuznikh i avtonomnykh Sovetskikh Sotsialisticheskikh Respublik*, Moscow, 1960.
[2] Commission on Human Rights, *Study on Discrimination in Education*, Doc. E/CN.4/Sub. 2/210, 5 January 1961, p. 6. See also the statement made by the Soviet Government to UNESCO: 'The Union of Soviet Socialist Republics reports that every Soviet citizen may have his children taught in any language he wishes. . . .' See Commission on Human Rights, *Periodic Reports on Human Rights covering the period 1960–1962*, Doc. E/CN.4/861/Add.2, 20 December 1963, p. 42.
[3] *Novaia sistema narodnovo obrazovaniia v S.S.S.R.*, Moscow, 1960, p. 79.

tongue, the authorities are required to arrange 'the organization of such a class in any school'.[1]

In 1961, the twenty-second party congress adopted a historic programme which, among other assurances, emphasized the Soviet commitment to the teaching of the native language. The programme assured 'the complete freedom of each citizen in the U.S.S.R. to speak and to rear and educate his children in any language, ruling out all privileges, restrictions and compulsion in the use of this or that language'.[2]

Yet, in spite of the various, far-reaching laws covering education in the native tongue, there does not exist anywhere in the Soviet Union today either a Yiddish school or a Yiddish class. Those Jewish schools in the Ukraine and Byelorussia which had lasted until 1941 and were destroyed by the Nazis were not reopened by the Soviets. Post-war efforts to restore a Yiddish school system in Lithuania, after this republic had been freed of the German army, were unsuccessful.[3] Even the few Jewish schools that had remained open in Biro-Bidzhan until 1946 were shut down.

Soviet authorities have offered two types of arguments to explain the absence of Jewish schools. One argument is based upon the burdensome costs involved in establishing schools for a widely dispersed nationality. N. Khrushchev told Professor Jerome Davis in 1956 that since 'Jews are dispersed', 'to set up separate schools all over Russia would be expensive'.[4] But the validity of this argument becomes questionable when examination is made of recent school privileges granted Soviet Germans, who are also a dispersed ethnic group. The German population in the U.S.S.R. totals 1,600,000, considerably smaller than the Jewish population. They are spread out over a wide area embracing eastern parts of the R.S.F.S.R. and almost a dozen other Union republics, their autonomous republic having been abolished early in the Second World War. A 1964 decree of the Presidium of the U.S.S.R. Supreme Soviet partially restored their national rights. The decree disclosed that 'in districts of a number of provinces, territories, and republics that have a German population, there are secondary and elementary schools where teaching is conducted in German or German is taught to children of school age . . .'.[5]

---

[1] A photostat of the Russian letter is in J. B. Schechtman, *Star in Eclipse: Russian Jewry Revisited*, New York, 1961, p. 151.   [2] *Pravda*, 2 November 1961.

[3] Concerning these efforts and their failure, as well as the school closures in Biro-Bidzhan, see E. Schulman, 'The Jewish School System in the Soviet Union, 1918–48', an unpublished doctoral dissertation at Dropsie College, 1965.

[4] *Report of the American-European Seminar on the U.S.S.R.*, West Haven, n.d. (1957).

[5] *Vedomosti Verkhovnovo Soveta S.S.S.R.*, no. 52 (1293), p. 931. The decree was published on 28 December 1964, but it was signed earlier on 29 August 1964.

The second argument which is advanced by Soviet leaders to explain the absence of a Jewish school system is the presumed extent of assimilation of Jews. Nikita Khrushchev in 1956 told a parliamentary delegation of French socialists that assimilation is so advanced that 'even if Jewish schools were established very few would attend them voluntarily'.[1] The then Soviet Premier added that 'if the Jews were compelled to attend Jewish schools there would certainly be a revolt. It would be considered some kind of ghetto.' This explanation raises more questions than it answers. If it be assumed that there is an insufficient number of Jews desiring a school conducted in Yiddish, why are there no special Jewish classes? Merely the request of ten parents is required to provide such classes. Is it conceivable that in areas of large Yiddish-speaking populations, such as in Vilna, Kovno, and Riga or in various cities in Moldavia and the western parts of the Ukraine and Byelorussia, no such request would be forthcoming? Just posing this question is to suggest the determination of school administrators to discourage requests, or to avoid informing parents of their rights to make such requests.

There is yet a more fundamental question: is not the assimilation of Jews a product, at least in part, of the absence of specific Jewish institutions to teach Yiddish and Jewish culture? Kantor, who had written in the thirties an authoritative work on Jewish institutions, noted in 1964:

... such things as schools of all kinds, museums, theatres, libraries, even sections of academies and so on, all work towards the consolidation, the support, and the strengthening of minority cultures.

Unhappily, the Jews belong to that group of national minorities where such supporting and strengthening factors for their culture do not exist. They have not existed for a number of years, since the time of the reinforced cult of the personality.[2]

The word 'unhappily' indicates the author's conviction and judgement that the absence of schools and other cultural institutions is not a reflex of the assimilation process but is rather the decisive factor in causing assimilation.

The complete destruction of the complex of Jewish cultural institutions followed by just a few years the elimination of the last Jewish schools in the U.S.S.R. During 1946–7 much of the remaining but, none the less, extensive pre-war publishing structure of the Jewish community was uprooted. In November 1948, the Yiddish publishing firm Der Emes was shut down. It had published in Moscow the thrice-weekly *Aynikayt*, and a total of 110 books and studies during the post-war period. The same month saw the dissolution of the Jewish Anti-Fascist Committee. Its chairman, the actor Solomon Mikhoels, had been murdered by the secret police in January 1948, and most of the other officials were later liquidated. Finally, in 1949 the doors of the famed Jewish State Theatre in Moscow were locked.

A cultural desert characterized the Jewish national scene in the U.S.S.R. for the following eleven years. Except for the *Biro-Bidzhaner Shtern*, a small partly Yiddish periodical that appeared three times weekly and had a 1,000 circulation, produced locally in Biro-Bidzhan, there were no Yiddish theatres, no Yiddish books, and no Yiddish publication. The popular Yiddish concerts given by troupes of travelling singers were the only national source of linguistic nourishment. A slight change began in 1959 with the publication of a tiny number of books in Yiddish. The first to appear in that year was a book by Sholom Aleichem, followed during the next three years by four other Yiddish books written by Jewish authors long deceased. But then came a halt with no further books published between 1962 and 1964. Since 1965, in response to sharp criticism from western sources, including numerous leftists, the Soviet have published several more Yiddish books. The most important development, however, was the establishment in August 1961 of a bi-monthly Yiddish literary review, *Sovietish Heymland*, with a press run of 25,000. In January 1965 it was turned into a monthly with a larger number of pages per issue. In addition to publishing the writings of over 100 Jewish authors, the journal has organized a number of literary conferences some of which have been attended by audiences running into the hundreds. The Yiddish theatre, in contrast, has not been restored. In its place a token substitute was extended. In 1962 a touring Yiddish repertory company was launched under Veniamin Schwartser, a former member of the Jewish State Theatre of Moscow.

In contradistinction to the question of Soviet Jewish schools, there exist no laws or statutes in the U.S.S.R. which would guarantee the cultural rights of minorities. These rights, however, had been implicit in the party policy on the nationality problem elaborated in the twenties. The tenth party congress in March 1921 decided formally that it would assist the nationalities 'to set up a press, schools, theatres, community centres, and cultural and educational institutions generally, using the native language'.[1] Stalin, in his famous speech at the Communist University of the Toilers of the East in May 1925, provided an elaborate dialectical

[1] Stalin, op. cit., p. 207.

rationale for party support of 'national culture'. National cultures, he said, 'must be given an opportunity to develop, expand and reveal all their potentialities in order to establish the conditions for their fusion into a single common culture with a single common language'.[1]

The early years of the post-war period were marked by a decisive reversal of this policy so far as the Jewish national culture was concerned. And arbitrary administrative actions implemented the new policy. The new policy has been continued by Stalin's successors, with the exception, already noted, of the minor changes introduced in the field of publications in 1959.

Future developments involving the Jews can properly be understood in the context of party decisions taken at the congress in 1961. The eventual objective of a 'single common culture' as formulated by Stalin, has been underscored by the party which, in its new programme, calls for 'the effacement of national distinctions . . . including language distinctions'.[2] Ridicule was poured on those 'who complain about the effacement of national distinctions', and the party was advised that it must not 'freeze and perpetuate national distinctions'.[3] The implication of an activist programme dedicated to achieving the 'voluntary' adoption of Russian as 'the common medium of intercourse and co-operation'—in the language of the programme—is clear. Also clear was the determination to accelerate the process of assimilation, of the 'drawing even closer together' of the nationalities of the U.S.S.R.

M. S. Dzhunusov, a prominent Soviet expert on the national question, emphasized the process of 'drawing closer' by calling attention to statistics on the changing ethnic composition of the Union republics, the more extensive use of the Russian language by non-Russian nationalities, and the frequency of intermarriage. He noted the presence of large numbers of Russian and Ukrainians in the various non-Slavic Union republics and pointed to figures showing that over 10 million Soviet citizens of non-Russian nationality consider Russian their native language.[4] A Soviet report to the U.N. reveals that there are in urban areas, 151 mixed families per 1,000 families in the U.S.S.R. as a whole, 108 in the R.S.F.S.R., 263 in the Ukraine, and 237 in Byelorussia.[5] Whether and to what extent intermarriage affects the highly urbanized Jewish community has not been ascertained.

[1] Ibid., p. 194.   [2] *Pravda*, 2 November 1961.
[3] *Materialy XXII syezda K.P.S.S.*, Moscow, 1961, p. 192.
[4] The article from *Istoriia S.S.S.R.*, no. 3 (1962) is translated in *Soviet Sociology*, vol. i, no. 2, pp. 10–28.   [5] *Manifestations*, Doc. A/5473/Add.1, p. 48.

At the party congress, it was also emphasized, however, that besides the 'drawing together' of nationalities, there was simultaneously taking place a contrary development of 'tempestuous all-round national development'.[1] For a number of nationalities this is clearly the case. R. Pipes has shown that major Soviet national groups, in areas where they enjoy a numerical and administrative preponderance, are acquiring a 'linguistic hegemony', counterposed to the Russian hegemony elsewhere, and that such hegemony is an indication of their 'national viability'.[2]

Kantor also took note of the two opposing tendencies, assimilation and the strengthening of minority cultures and languages, but emphasized the fact that the decisive factor is the presence or absence of vital institutions among the minority nationalities. It is precisely because of the dismantling of such institutions of the Jewish nationality, in violation of rights inscribed in Soviet law and expressed in party policy, that the victory of the first tendency has been facilitated.

The nature of the political structure of the U.S.S.R. makes necessary a certain distinction between the Jew as part of a specific national entity in a multi-national state and as an individual in Soviet society as a whole. *National-communal* rights embracing linguistic and cultural attributes are something quite different from *civil* rights—the political, economic, and social rights of a citizen in the Soviet state.

Under the tsars, there had existed a host of severe limitations on the civil rights of Jews—residence, military service, participation in government or in elections, schooling, and related spheres. The very first decree of the Provisional Government that had taken power following the overthrow of the tsar, in March 1917, abolished all discrimination based upon ethnic, religious, and social grounds.[3] Two weeks later the Ministry of Defence removed all discrimination against Jews in the army (where they had been permitted to serve only as soldiers) and in the navy (where they could not serve at all). And on 5 April, the Provisional Government issued a number of decrees that specified the areas where restrictions on the rights of citizens on grounds of race or creed were to be eradicated: residence and movement, ownership and use of property, employment, and schooling.

---

[1] *Materialy XXII s'ezda K.P.S.S.*, p. 192.

[2] R. Pipes, 'The Forces of Nationalism', *Problems of Communism*, January–February 1964, p. 6.

[3] For a listing of tsarist legal restrictions, see I. P. Tsamerian and S. L. Ronin, *Equality of Rights Between Races and Nationalities in the U.S.S.R.*, Nijmegen, 1962, pp. 17–21. The Provisional Government's acts are in *Sbornik ukazov i postanovlenii Vremennovo Pravitel'stva*, 12 March–18 May 1917, Petrograd, 1917, pp. 8, 46.

The Bolshevik seizure of power in November 1917 was accompanied almost immediately by assurances concerning hard-won civil rights. On 15 November 1917, the Declaration of Rights of Peoples, signed jointly by Lenin as head of the government and by Stalin as Commissar of Nationalities, formally abolished 'all national and national-religious privileges and restrictions'. The first Soviet constitution reaffirmed the Declaration at least as far as non-discrimination on ethnic grounds was concerned. The anti-religious campaign already launched by the Bolsheviks precluded guarantees of non-discrimination on creedal grounds. Article 22 of the 1918 constitution of the R.S.F.S.R. recognized 'that all citizens enjoy equal rights without distinction of race or nationality [and] . . . it is contrary to the fundamental laws of the Republic to grant or tolerate any privileges or advantages based on race or nationality . . .'. Similar civil rights provisions were inserted in the constitutions of other Soviet republics—Article 15 of the Byelorussian constitution (1919); Article 32 of the Ukrainian constitution (1919); Article 13 of the Azerbaizhanian constitution (1921); and Article 7 of the Georgian constitution (1922).

Following the formation of the U.S.S.R. in the early twenties, the new republic constitutions repeated with slight variations the earlier formulation on civil rights. Thus the Constitution of the R.S.F.S.R., adopted in 1925, stated in Article 13 that 'the principle of the equality of rights of all citizens without distinction of race or nationality' is fundamental and 'any restriction' of these rights and 'still more, the granting or toleration of any national privilege whatsoever, whether direct or indirect, are wholly incompatible with the fundamental laws . . .'.

The 1936 constitution of the U.S.S.R. gave expression to the historic emphasis upon civil rights of all Soviet citizens and spelled out the areas to be covered. Article 123 reads:

Equality of rights of citizens of the U.S.S.R., irrespective of their nationality or race, in all spheres of economic, government, cultural, political and other public activity is an indefeasible law.

Any direct or indirect restriction of the rights of, or conversely, the establishment of any direct or indirect privileges for citizens on account of their race or nationality . . . is punishable by law.

Article 135 applied the guarantees on civil rights to all Soviet elections. Soviet citizens 'irrespective of race or nationality' are eligible to vote and to be elected. In the constitutions of each of the Soviet republics there are to be found formulations similar to those of Article 123 and Article 135. Provisions of the various criminal codes give additional support to constitutional laws on civil rights. Article 8 of the law on the Fundamentals of Criminal Jurisprudence of the U.S.S.R. and the Union republics emphasizes that all citizens are equal before the law and the courts. The latest Criminal Code of the R.S.F.S.R. (1 January 1961) is especially pertinent.[1] Article 74 of the Code carries the title 'Infringement of National and Racial Equal Rights', and specifies that 'any direct or indirect limitation of rights or the establishment of direct or indirect privileges' on grounds of race or nationality will be punished by either deprivation of freedom for a period of from six months to three years or by exile from two to five years.

With reference to certain fields, Jews enjoy civil rights described in constitutional statutes. Housing restrictions do not exist; nor are there barriers to entrance into the party, trade unions, army, and the social services. Opportunities in such fields as science, medicine, law, and the arts are widespread, as available data indicates.[2] On the other hand, there is considerable evidence that discrimination against Jews in a number of vital and decision-making fields occurs despite the numerous constitutional provisions and criminal statutes. With respect to certain fields, for example, unpublished governmental regulations appear to have been issued, whether in written or oral form, which establish quotas limiting educational or employment opportunities for Jews. No evidence is available as to whether the criminal codes have been used against anyone for discrimination against Jews on racial or national grounds.

Employment in administrative and in various governmental bureaus, it is clear, has been subject to discriminatory quota regulations. Certainly this was not the case in the twenties. In December 1927 at the fifteenth congress of the communist party, S. Ordzhonikidze, Commissar for Workers' and Peasants' Inspection, reported that Jews held 10·3 per cent of the administrative offices in Moscow, 22·6 per cent of the civil service posts in the Ukraine, and 30·6 per cent of the posts in Byelorussia.[3] At the time Jews constituted 1·8 per cent of the total population, 5.4 per cent of the population in the Ukraine and 8·2 per cent of the population in Byelorussia.

But the thirties and forties were characterized by a sharp drop in these

---

[1] *Ugolovnyi kodeks R.S.F.S.R.*, Moscow, 1964, p. 39. The Ukrainian Criminal Code provides for imprisonment from six months to three years. The Codes of other republics specify similar penalties.

[2] See, for example, Tsentral'noe staticheskoe upravlenie pri Sovete Ministrov, S.S.S.R., *Vysshee obrazovanie v S.S.S.R.*, Moscow, 1961, p. 49; and 'Jews in The Soviet Union', Novosti Press Agency (n.d. [1963]).

[3] *XV s'ezd Vsesoiuznoi Kommunisticheskoi Partii (b)*, Moscow, 1928, pp. 400–1.

percentages. And three separate interviews in 1956 with top Soviet officials demonstrated that the Central Government had consciously established quota systems to restrict Jewish employment, and that even sharper quota devices were established in the various Union republics.

The first interview was conducted with Khrushchev and other high officials by a visiting parliamentary delegation of the French socialist party.[1] At a third meeting of the delegation with the Russians held on 12 May, Khrushchev said:

Our heterogeneous populations have their republics. . . . Each of them has an autonomous government. Formerly backward and illiterate, these peoples now have their engineers and professionals. . . .

Antisemitic sentiments still exist there. They are remnants of a reactionary past. This is a complicated problem because of the position of the Jews and their relations with the other peoples. At the outset of the Revolution, we had many Jews in the leadership of the party and state. They were more educated, maybe more revolutionary than the average Russian. In due course we have created new cadres. . . .

Khrushchev was then interrupted by Pervukhin who attempted to clarify the phrase, 'new cadres'. He explained: 'Our own intelligentsia.' Khrushchev then resumed his comments with a particularly vulgar rationalization for a set of quota devices:

Should the Jews want to occupy the foremost positions in our republics now, it would naturally be taken amiss by the indigenous inhabitants. The latter would ill receive these pretensions, especially as they do not consider themselves less intelligent nor less capable than the Jews. Or, for instance, when a Jew in the Ukraine is appointed to an important post and he surrounds himself with Jewish collaborators, it is understandable that this should create jealousy and hostility towards Jews.

The following month, the Minister of Culture, Yekaterina Furtseva made these remarks in an interview with a correspondent of the *National Guardian*:[2]

The Government has found in some of its departments a heavy concentration of Jewish people, upwards of 50 per cent of the staff. Steps were taken to transfer them to other enterprises giving them equally good positions and without jeopardizing their rights.

The final interview took place in August. J. B. Salsberg, a former

[1] *Réalités*, May 1957.
[2] *National Guardian*, 25 June 1956.

Canadian communist leader, met a number of prominent Soviet officials,[1] one of whom validated Furtseva's observation:

He tried terribly hard to prove to me with examples that the transfer or dismissal of Jewish employees in once-backward republics, that now have 'their own' intelligentsia and professional people capable of occupying posts previously held by Jews or Russians, has nothing to do with antisemitism.

Khrushchev was to return to this argument in an unpublished speech given to a meeting of artists on 17 December 1962.[2] He declared that anti-semitism would grow if Jews were to occupy too many top positions.

If the interviews and the Khrushchev speech were hidden from the Russian public and appeared only in the western press, the facts about restrictions and the use of the quotas were none the less known to many in the Soviet population. In March 1962, at a meeting of the Central Committee, Academician Konstantin Skriabin, speaking on the importance of appointing competent cadres in the scientific field, critically commented, in an indirect manner, upon the misuse of the passport. 'From my point of view, a scientist should not be evaluated by his passport but by his head, from the point of view of his ability and social usefulness.'[3]

Another oblique disclosure of the preferential uses of the quota was made in the party theoretical journal *Kommunist* in June 1962: 'The less developed nations of the U.S.S.R. were granted various privileges and advantages . . . in the preparation of cadres. Only under these circumstances could the actual equality of nations be achieved.'[4]

That the discriminatory employment devices used against Jews may have deleteriously affected efforts to maximize production in a more rational manner and may have interrupted the initiative to make government machinery a more efficient and flexible instrument in order to further economic objectives are suggested in an editorial that appeared in *Pravda* on 5 September 1965. It first noted that Lenin had 'wrathfully assailed any manifestations of nationalism whatsoever, and in particular demanded an unceasing "struggle against antisemitism, that malicious exaggeration of racial separateness and national enmity"'. The editorial then firmly asserted:

[1] Salsberg's visit is reported in *Vochenblatt* and in *Morgen Freiheit*. The series of articles appeared on an irregular basis from 25 October to 20 December 1956. The quoted section is translated in J. Salsberg, 'Anti-Semitism in the U.S.S.R.?', *Jewish Life*, February 1957, p. 38.

[2] Its contents were revealed by the London *Observer*, 13 January 1963.

[3] *Pravda*, 8 March 1962. The stenographic report states that a voice called out 'Correct' after Skriabin made this observation, and that applause followed.

[4] P. Rogachev and M. Sverdlin, 'Sovetskii narod-novaia istoricheskaia obshchnost liudei', *Kommunist*, June 1963, p. 13.

It is necessary to remember that the growing scale of communist construction requires a constant exchange of cadres among the peoples. Therefore any manifestations of national separateness in the *training and employment* of personnel of various nationalities in the Soviet republics are intolerable. (Emphasis added.)

The significance of the editorial lay in the fact that it was the first time in at least two decades that the principal organ of the party had editorially attacked antisemitism, giving emphasis to the condemnation by quoting Lenin. Whether the editorial led to the issue of policy directives to reverse earlier instructions on both a national and local level cannot be determined.

Discrimination against Jews in political life since the forties is also apparent. The composition of various Soviet bodies provides one example. On the level of the Supreme Soviet, a drastic decline in the number and percentage of Jews has set in since 1937.[1] Though the Jews constitute over 1 per cent of the population they have, since the forties, numbered at the most but 0·5 per cent of the highest legislative organ. In view of the fact that the selection of candidates to run for deputy to the Supreme Soviet is a party-controlled affair, it is difficult to resist the conclusion that some understanding exists to avoid placing more than a token number of Jews on the ballot. Article 135 of the constitution is thus emptied of content so far as Jews are concerned.

The discriminatory pattern is even more obvious in the selection of deputies to the Supreme Soviets of the 15 Union republics.[2] 5,312 deputies were elected for these bodies in 1959 and only 14 were Jewish—0·26 per cent. Only one Jewish deputy was to be found among the 835 deputies in the Russian republic; a single Jew among the 457 deputies in the Ukraine (0·22 per cent of a Jewish population constituting 2 per cent of the total); and but two Jews among the 407 deputies in Byelorussia (0·45 per cent of a Jewish population constituting 1·9 per cent of the total). Similar percentages are to be found in various non-Slavic republics. For example, of the 281 deputies in Moldavia where Jews constitute 3·3 per cent of the population, there was not a single Jew; of the 200 deputies in Latvia where Jews number 1·7 per cent of the population, no Jew was chosen. Lithuania was an exception; Jewish representation in the Supreme Soviet here paralleled its percentage in the population with three out of 209 deputies or 1·44 per cent.

The significant decline in the number and percentage of Jews serving in

[1] Schwarz, op. cit., pp. 355, 364. Further information is extracted from *Deputaty Verkhovnovo S.S.S.R.*, Moscow, 1962.

[2] *Sostav Deputatov Verkhovnykh Sovetov Soiuznykh Avtonomnykh Respublik i Mestnykh Sovetov Trudiashchikhsia, 1959*, Moscow, 1959. Data on the composition of later republic Supreme Soviets have not been published.

the Supreme Soviet was accompanied by an extraordinary decrease of Jews in the élitist Central Committee of the communist party.[1] The percentage of Jews in this organ, in 1939, had been 10·8, higher than the combined percentage of both Ukrainians and Byelorussians. But by 1952 this percentage dropped to three, then to two in 1956. In 1961, the percentage fell to a mere 0·3. Of the current 330-member Central Committee, only one person is a Jew, Veniamin Dymshits. The data enabled a specialist studying Soviet élitism to observe: 'The Jews are the only nationality whose relative weight and absolute numbers in élite representation declined consistently in both the Stalinist and post-Stalin eras.'

Party membership is, however, another matter. Here restrictions upon Jews do not appear to obtain. Data on party membership[2] shows that of 11,758,200 members and candidates, 1,035,300 are listed (in a breakdown by nationality) as belonging to the category 'other nationalities and peoples'. Precise figures were given for the principal nationality of each of the fifteen republics. The sizeable figure of the residual category points to the likelihood of a considerable number of Jews. The new rules adopted by the party at its twenty-second congress demand adherence to a 'moral code' that includes 'intolerance of national and racial hostility'.[3] But, if this code is applicable to the lower levels of the party, none the less a pattern of exclusion is clearly apparent in its upper reaches.

The most disturbing discriminatory pattern is to be found in the admission practices of universities, the key to promotion in Soviet society. In 1959, the Minister of Higher Education, V. P. Yeliutin, vehemently denied the existence of quotas directed against Jews.[4] And three years later the U.S.S.R. ratified the UNESCO Convention against Discrimination in Education which obligates contracting states 'to abrogate statutory provisions and any administrative practices which involve discrimination in education'. But two Soviet journals published in 1963 point to contrary evidence. *Kommunist*, by implication, and the *Bulletin of Higher Education*[5] explicitly, acknowledged the existence of 'annually planned preferential admission quotas'. N. DeWitt, an American specialist on Soviet education, has explained that the quota system operates 'to the particularly severe disadvantage of the Jewish population'. Noting that the quota system operates on the principle of 'equivalent-balance' (i.e. 'The representation

[1] S. Bialer, 'How Russians Rule Russia', *Problems of Communism*, September–October 1964, pp. 46, 48.

[2] *Partiinaia Zhizn*, no. 10, May 1965, pp. 8–17.   [3] *Pravda*, 3 November 1961.

[4] *The New York Times*, 29 September 1959.

[5] See V. Komarov and V. Artamoshkina, 'Takova ikh nauchnaia ob'ektivnost'!', *Vestnik vysshei shkoly*, December 1963, p. 78.

of any national or ethnic grouping in overall higher education enrolment should be as the relation of the size of that group to total U.S.S.R. population.') DeWitt presented data showing that between 1935 and 1958 'the index of representation rose for most nationalities, but fell for Georgians and all national minorities, with a very drastic decline for the Jews'.[1]

Soviet statutes extend beyond discrimination on national and racial grounds, to cover the banning of overt expressions of antisemitism. The first effort to make antisemitism a state crime came in July 1918 when the Council of People's Commissars issued an order which called for destruction of 'the antisemitic movement at its roots' by outlawing 'pogromists and persons inciting to pogroms'.[2] The R.S.F.S.R. Criminal Code of 1922 banned 'agitation and propaganda arousing national enmities and dissensions',[3] and specified a minimum of one year's solitary confinement and death in time of war for those perpetrating such an offence. The R.S.F.S.R. Criminal Code of 1927 established the penalty of loss of freedom of 'no less than two years' for 'propaganda or agitation aimed at arousing national or religious enmities and dissension'. Similar punishment was to be inflicted for the dissemination, manufacture, or possession of literature which stirs national and religious hostility.[4] The present R.S.F.S.R. Criminal Code which went into effect in 1961 reads:[5] 'Propaganda or agitation aimed at inciting racial or national enmity or discord ... is punishable by loss of personal freedom for a period of six months to three years, or exile from two to five years.' (Article 74.) Article 11 of the Fundamentals of Criminal Jurisprudence of the U.S.S.R. which was adopted by the Supreme Soviet in December 1958 provided the basis for this section of the Criminal Code.

During the twenties the Soviet press frequently reported instances of antisemitic activity as well as the legal proceedings taken against offenders.[6] At the same time, party organs expressed a strong condemnation of antisemitism and demanded vigilant action against it and its various manifestations. During the thirties the number of reported antisemitic occurrences declined sharply and press attention to the subject became infrequent. But it was made clear that antisemitism would not be countenanced by the party. A speech by V. M. Molotov, Chairman of the Council of People's

[1] N. DeWitt, *Education and Professional Employment in the U.S.S.R.*, Washington, 1961, pp. 358–60.
[2] *Izvestiya*, 27 July 1918.
[3] *Ugolovnyi kodeks R.S.F.S.R.*, Moscow, 1922, Sec. 83, p. 18.
[4] *Ugolovnyi kodeks R.S.F.S.R.*, Moscow, 1953, Sec. 59–7, p. 23.
[5] *Ugolovnyi kodeks R.S.F.S.R.*, Moscow, 1964, Article 74, p. 39.
[6] The subject is treated at length in Schwarz, op. cit., pp. 241–99.

Commissars, to the eighth Soviet congress in November 1936 and carried in *Pravda*[1] was particularly pertinent. He read the text of a statement by Stalin given to the Jewish Telegraphic Agency in January 1931 (but which had not, at that time, appeared in the Soviet press) which declared that antisemitism was a 'phenomenon profoundly hostile to the Soviet regime. . . .'

The immediate post-war period, in contrast, was marked not only by the absence of condemnatory references to antisemitism but, instead, beginning in 1948–9, with the campaign against 'cosmopolitanism', an open public incitement against Jews. The climax was reached with the hoax of the 'Doctors' Plot' of early 1953 which generated a dangerously anti-Jewish atmosphere. Stalin's death and the subsequent exposure of the plot as a fraud, fabricated by the organs of state security, ended the threatening antisemitic currents. *Pravda* hinted at the antisemitic character of the plot,[2] but neither it nor any other major organ nor, indeed, any top Soviet official took the occasion then or later to identify the plot as a specifically antisemitic one, or to use it for a public educational campaign directed against antisemitism. Even in Khrushchev's secret speech at the twentieth party congress in 1956, which disclosed some shocking details of the episode, no reference was made to its antisemitic character. Khrushchev was later to imply that the plot, in his judgement, did not involve an antisemitic policy. He wrote to Bertrand Russell in February 1963, saying:[3] '*There never has been* and there is not any policy of antisemitism in the Soviet Union, since the very nature of our multi-national socialist state precludes the possibility of such a policy. (Emphasis added.)

Since the 'Doctors' Plot' and until recently, the principal organs of the U.S.S.R. have avoided inveighing against manifestations of antisemitism. No specific court cases involving Article 74, if they have taken place, have been reported in the press. And, with one exception, the Soviets have not publicly dealt with charges about incidents or propaganda of an anti-semitic nature which have been reported in the press of the west.

That exception involved a book entitled *Judaism without Embellishment* and written by T. Kichko. Published in October 1963, by the Ukrainian Academy of Sciences, the supposed study depicted Judaism as fostering hypocrisy, bribery, greed, and usury. Judaism was, in turn, linked with Zionism, Israel, Jewish bankers, and western capitalists in a crudely con-cocted world-wide conspiracy. A series of viciously antisemitic caricatures matched the vulgarities of the text. After world-wide protests, including

---

[1] *Pravda*, 30 November 1936.   [2] *Pravda*, 6 April 1953.
[3] *Pravda*, 28 February 1963. The letter was dated 21 February 1963.

sharp criticism by leading western communist parties, Soviet party authorities began reacting with concern. In April 1964, the Ideological Commission of the Party's Central Committee denounced the book for 'erroneous statements and illustrations likely to offend believers and [which] might be interpreted in a spirit of antisemitism'.[1] The resolution was worded in a somewhat vague manner: the book itself was not charged specifically with being antisemitic and the author was not accused of violating Article 66 of the Criminal Code of the Ukraine (which is similar to Article 74 of the R.S.F.S.R. Code).

During 1961-4 Soviet authorities engaged in a vigorous campaign against economic crimes in which antisemitism made its appearance. Emphasis was given in the press on various occasions to the Jewish national origin of those charged with and executed for economic crimes.[2] But no prosecutor or newspaper was criticized for indulging in racism or bigotry. Indeed, Khrushchev publicly rejected world-wide charges of antisemitism, terming them 'a crude concoction, a vicious slander on the Soviet people, on our country'.[3]

Only in 1965 were some positive steps taken. The *Pravda* editorial of 5 September 1965 was preceded in July 1965 by a published speech of Premier A. N. Kosygin. Addressing a large rally in Riga, Latvia,[4] the Premier denounced 'the manifestation of nationalism, great-power chauvinism, racism, antisemitism' as 'absolutely alien to and in contradiction to our world view'. These statements did not, however, signal an educational effort to eliminate antisemitic manifestations, using the full force of Soviet law to do so. For the present, the implementation of laws on antisemitism, like the application of various statutes affecting the linguistic-cultural rights of Jews, leaves something to be desired.

But if the deprivations in the field of linguistic-cultural rights have the anticipated consequence of satisfying the higher party goal of assimilation, deprivations in the field of civil rights have the latent unanticipated consequence of heightening the sense of self-identity. For, inevitably, the question arises for individuals: what is unique or distinctive in one's ethnic origin that causes personal discrimination? Thus, the separate discrimination patterns, though running parallel with each other, in fact,

---

[1] *Pravda*, 4 April 1964. Initially, the Soviets avoided response to the criticism by observing that Kichko was merely engaged in anti-religious propaganda, protected by the constitution. See the statement of Novosti Press Agency, 24 March 1964.

[2] For a detailed and carefully evaluated examination of the antisemitic facets of the economic crimes campaign see 'Economic Crimes in the Soviet Union', *Journal of the International Commission of Jurists*, Summer 1964, pp. 3–47.

[3] *Pravda*, 28 February 1963.   [4] *Pravda*, 19 July 1965.

have the effect of contradicting one another. A striking feature of the current Jewish scene in Soviet Russia, to many independent observers, is not the decline in national self-consciousness, but rather the very opposite.

The growth of Jewish national self-consciousness, which manifested itself in a powerful drive for exodus to Israel, was profoundly intensified by a new Soviet ideological line that made its appearance in 1967–8. The line drew upon two separate perceptions of Jews: Jews as Zionists, and Jews as troublesome dissenters. These were integrated into a single view which identified the Jew, racially, as an endemically anti-Soviet element. Soviet antisemitism, in the form both of an articulated rationalization and of sharper restrictions upon admission to universities, now became apparent.

Some time during late July 1967, a high-level decision was taken in Moscow to launch a massive internal and external propaganda campaign depicting Zionism as a major threat to the Communist world, the newly independent states, and the national-liberation movements. In the first week of August 1967, an article entitled 'What is Zionism?' appeared simultaneously in the principal provincial organs of the U.S.S.R. Its opening paragraph struck the dominant note of the campaign: 'A wide network of Zionist organizations with a common centre, a common programme, and funds exceeding by far the funds of the Mafia "Cosa Nostra" is active behind the scene of the international theatre.'

Stereotypic images of the Jew abound in the paranoid portrait sketched by the author. The global 'Zionist Corporation' is composed of 'smart dealers in politics and finance, religion and trade' whose 'well-camouflaged aim' is the 'enrichment by any means of the "international Zionist network"'. Exercising control over more than a thousand newspapers and magazines in 'very many countries of the world' with an 'unlimited budget', the world Zionist 'machine' services the vast monopolies of the West in their attempt 'to establish control over the whole world'.

While the campaign had its psychological roots in the dark phantasmagoric past, roots which had been nourished in the climate of Stalin's last years, it also served a pragmatic political purpose. With the Soviet Union's client Arab states suffering a major débâcle in the Six-Day War and the Communist regime itself badly thwarted in its diplomatic endeavour at the United Nations to compel an Israeli withdrawal from occupied territory, a convenient scapegoat was needed to rationalize severe setbacks. Tiny Israel and public opinion were surely not the factors behind these failures. The enemy must rather be presented as a hidden, all-powerful, and perfidious international force, linked somehow with Israel. 'World Zionism' was the ideological cloth that could be cut to fit the designated adversary. During the months following the Six-Day War, the citizenry of Communist states as well as those of the Arab and Afro-Asian world were literally saturated with this theme. Foreign radio broadcasts beamed from Moscow chattered away endlessly about Zionism as if this mysterious ghost would take on flesh by repeated incantation.

The campaign reached a climax on 18 February 1971, when an authoritative and lengthy article in *Pravda* written by V. Bolshakov dusted off the infamous and provocatory phrase of the Great Purge—'an enemy of the Soviet people'—and applied it to all Jews everywhere, including those in the U.S.S.R., who sympathized with 'Zionism'. If, initially, a certain meticulousness in language avoided the specific identification of 'Jew' with 'Zionist', in time the distinction disappeared. By mid-1974, Bolshakov, writing in *Za Rubezhom*, used the terms interchangeably. The same journal carried several articles in 1974, including a particularly vulgar one in the issue for 6–12 December 1974, which virtually equated Jew and Zionist.

The second perception—the Jew as troublesome dissenter—sprang from the fact that Jews played a significant role, far greater than their percentage in the population would warrant, in the incipient dissent movement in the U.S.S.R. (which found an echo in Poland and Czechoslovakia). The Dubcek phenomenon in Czechoslovakia and the 'Spring' developments in Poland reinforced such trends. An extraordinary ideological formulation of the perception, totally unprecedented in Marxist history, surfaced in Poland. Significantly, the formulation also took account of and incorporated the perception of Jews as Zionists.

In June 1968, the journal *Miesieczik Literacki* carried a 10,000-word article written by Andrzej Werblan, the Polish Communist Party's leading ideologist, who, at the time, was director of the Central Committee's Education Department. Entitled 'On the Genesis of the Conflict', it addressed itself to the origin of the 'March Events'—the student uprisings which were to be crushed by the state organs. Werblan traced the 'March Events' to 'a large group of people of Jewish origin' who played 'a considerable role' among 'revisionists, academic workers at Warsaw University and students involved in the hostile activity'. Despite the fact that the total number of Jews at the time in Poland constituted but an infinitesimal percentage of the population—25,000 out of 30 million—Werblan was convinced that their influence was 'larger than one might expect on the basis of the percentage of the Jewish population in our society'.

A long disquisition on the history of Jews in the Communist Party followed. Werblan's analysis led him to conclude that Jews have 'a particular susceptibility to revisionism'—by which he meant reformism or liberalism—and to 'Jewish nationalism in general and Zionism in particular'. The overtly racist formulation, which attributed to Jews as a group inherent qualities antithetical to orthodox Communism, necessarily required that surgical treatment be applied to excise the disease from the body politic. Werblan specifically mentioned universities and publishing houses among those 'institutions in which there was a concentration . . . of people of Jewish origin' and which, inevitably, produced a 'bad political atmosphere'. The solution to the problem was clear: 'the correction of the irregular ethnic composition'. Ultimately, it found expression in the veritable expulsion of most of the country's tiny remnant of Jews.

It is not unlikely that the Werblan essay was supported, if not prompted by, circles of the Soviet ideological apparatus. Were not Soviet Jews excessively represented (in proportion to their number in the population) in the burgeoning dissent movement (the equivalent of 'revisionism' in Poland) in the U.S.S.R.? And had not the Six-Day War evoked among sectors of Soviet Jews, including some of the most assimilated, a certain sense of kinship with the Israeli?

By 1970, the Werblan thesis obtained, although in much less vulgar fashion, a Soviet reformulation. A book, *Social Progress*, published by the Soviet ideologist V. Mishin, emphasized that admission to universities must be governed by the principle of 'proletarian internationalism', by which a *numerus clausus* is justified to limit the number of students of each nationality to the percentage the nationality constitutes of the total population. From Mishin's viewpoint, the relatively higher number of Jewish students is contrary to the principle of 'proletarian international-ism'. As early as November 1971, the brilliant Soviet literary critic Grigory Svirsky, in an important *samizdat* essay, recognized the significance of the Mishin book as a critical indicator of the new ideology aimed at restricting the enlargement of the Jewish intelligentsia.

Significantly, at the very moment when Werblan's article appeared in Poland, Academician Andrei D. Sakharov in the U.S.S.R. called attention to a speech made at a Moscow Communist Party Conference by no less an authority than Mstislav V. Keldysh, President of the Soviet Academy of Sciences, which justified discrimination against Jews. Sakharov asked: 'Is it not disgraceful to allow another backsliding into antisemitism in our appointments policy . . . ?'

On the heels of the formulation of the blatantly racist ideology in 1967–8 there would unfold a host of discriminatory practices against Jews which concentrated, appropriately enough, upon higher education. Quotas were so severely tightened that, for the first time in Soviet history, the number of Jews in higher education began to decline. Between 1968–9 and 1970–1, the absolute figures fell from 111,900 to 105,800. By 1972–3, they drastically plummeted to 88,500. The geometric rate of decline was portentous.

Even more dramatic was the drop in the number of Jews admitted to postgraduate work. Between 1970 and the beginning of 1974, it fell by 30 per cent—from 4,945 to 3,456. At the same time—as if to mock the principle of 'proletarian internationalism'—the number of Russian postgraduate students increased by over 1,000. The impact of the current trend in university admission policy is already being felt in the career opportunities for Jews, since higher education in the U.S.S.R., as in any advanced industrial society, is the key to personal advancement in economic and social life. Especially is this the case when the political-security area is almost totally closed to Jews.

The number of Jews who entered the ranks of 'scientific workers' during 1972–3 was minimal—about 1,000 as compared to 2,000–3,000 per annum between 1955 and 1971. Within the near future, when the impact of the drastic drop in Jewish university students will have made itself felt, a marked absolute decline of Jewish 'scientific workers' will set in. Indeed, the absolute decline had already begun in one of the most 'popular' of Jewish professions—medicine—at least in the biggest union-republic, the Russian Republic.

If Jews continue to constitute a sizeable percentage of 'scientific workers', it is because many are hold-overs from earlier periods when access to this category was easier. A striking feature of Jewish 'scientific workers' is the fact that their average age is higher by ten years than the general average age of 'scientific workers'.

Limitations upon access to the category of 'scientific workers' through the admission policy of universities is but one aspect of the problem. Drastic restrictions were introduced into the policy of appointment of Jews to most institutions of higher learning and specialized research institutes. The policy did not ordinarily strike at older Jews who already occupied senior and administrative positions. It was the middle and younger generation of gifted scientists and academics who were, in the main, affected. The result is the statistical fact that the percentage of Jews on the teaching staff of higher universities (5·5) is about half of the percentage of Jews among research institute workers (9·1).

If the number of Jews was sharply restricted in administrative positions and in higher institutions, one area was apparently made *Judenrein*. A secret Government circular, distributed in 1970 to sensitive scientific agencies, specified the undesirability of employing Jews at 'responsible levels' in institutions connected with defence, rocketry, atomic weaponry, and 'other secret work'. A euphemism was used instead of the word 'Jews' ('persons belonging to a nationality the state organization of which pursues an unfriendly policy in relation to the U.S.S.R.').

Roy Medvedev, in his very perceptive analysis of the Soviet Jewish question, has called the new antisemitism in the U.S.S.R. 'especially refined and subtle'. But if refined, it is hardly subtle. Even those who are identified in their internal passports as 'Great Russian' but who may have either a Jewish father or a Jewish mother —as Medvedev himself documents—will not be hired for sensitive positions. Racism, based upon blood-lines, and in violation of both classical Marxism and Soviet law, had clearly entered the Soviet scene. The result was a deepening of Jewish self-consciousness that propelled the initially incipient exodus movement to significantly greater heights.

SELECTED BIBLIOGRAPHY
(In addition to the references in the footnotes)

Commission on Human Rights. *Study of Discrimination in the Matter of Religious Rights and Practices, Conference Room Paper, No. 35*, 30 January 1959.

Goldberg, B. Z., *The Jewish Problem in the Soviet Union*, New York, 1961,.

Iakubovich, M. I. and Vladimirov, V. A. (ed.), *Gosudarstvennye prestuplenia uchebnoe posobie sovetskomu ugolovnomu pravu*, Moscow, 1960.

Kantor, Y., 'Aynike Bamerkungen un Oisfiren tsu di Fareffentlichte Sakhhakalen fun der Folks-tselung in Ratenverband dem Yanuar, 1959', *Bleter far Geshichte*, (xv), Warsaw, 1962–3.

Konstitutsiia S.S.S.R. Konstitutsii soiuznikh i avtonomnykh Sovetskikh Sotsialisticheskikh Respublik, Moscow, 1960.

Korey, W., *The Soviet Cage: Anti-Semitism in Russia*, New York, 1973.

Korey, W., 'Quotas and Soviet Jewry', *Commentary*, May 1974.

Korey, W., 'The Soviet Jewish Future: Some Observations on the Recent Census', *Midstream*, November 1974.

Lenin, V. I., *Sochineniya*, vols. xvii and xxiv, 3rd edn., Moscow, 1937.

Men'shagin, V. D. and Kurinov, B. A., *Nauchno-prakticheskii kommentarii k zakonu ob ugolovnoi otvetsvennoi za gosudarstvennye prestupleniia*, Moscow, 1960.

Novaia sistema narodnovo obrazovaniia v S.S.S.R., Moscow, 1960.

Prakticheskoe reshenie natsionalnovo voprosa v Belorusskoi S.S.R., part I, Minsk, 1927.

Schwarz, S., *The Jews in the Soviet Union*, New York, 1951.

Sistematicheskoe sobranie deistvuiushchikh zakonov Soiuza Sovetskikh Sotsialisticheskikh Respublik, Moscow, 1927.

Sobranie uzakonenii i rasporiazhenii, no. 51, Moscow, 1918.

Sobranie uzakonenii i rasporiazhenii Rabochevo i Krestianskovo Pravitelstva Ukrainskoi S.S.R., no. 41, Kiev, 1922.

Stalin, J., *Marksizm i natsionalno-kolonialnyi vopros*, Moscow, 1937.

Tsamerian, I. P. and Ronin, S. L., *Equality of Rights Between Races and Nationalities in the U.S.S.R.*, Nijmegen, 1962.

Tsentralnoe staticheskoye upravlenie pri Sovete Ministrov S.S.S.R., *Itogi Vsesoiuznoi perepisi naseleniia 1959 goda*, Moscow, 1962.

Ugolovnyi kodeks R.S.F.S.R., Moscow, 1922.

Ugolovnyi kodeks R.S.F.S.R., Moscow, 1953.

Ugolovnyi kodeks R.S.F.S.R., Moscow, 1964.

United Nations General Assembly, *Manifestations of Racial Prejudice and National and Religious Intolerance*, Doc. A/5473/Add.1, 25 September 1963.

XV syezd Vsesoiuznoi Kommunisticheskoi Partii (b), Moscow, 1928.

6

The U.S.S.R., Zionism, and Israel

J. B. SCHECHTMAN

When, after a successful *coup d'état* in October 1917, the Bolshevik party came to power, the new regime found in its domain a powerful, dynamic, deeply rooted Zionist mass movement.

In Russian Jewry, Zionism as an idea and as a movement predates Herzl's *Judenstaat* and the emergence of the World Zionist Organization. The early writings of Peretz Smolenskin, Moshe-Leib Lilienblum, and Leon Pinsker, contained nearly all the basic elements of the classical Zionist concept. The first conference of *Hovevei Zion* (Lovers of Zion) met at Katowicz in 1884, thirteen years before the first Zionist congress in Basle, and practical colonization work in Palestine started even before that date. There were in Russia at that time some 80 *Hovevei Zion* groups in 50 towns.[1] The precursors of the idealistic *Aliyoth* were the *Biluim*, the fourteen Jewish students from Kharkov who landed at Jaffa in 1882. The second *Aliyah* (1903–15) was predominantly Russian. The majority of the forty settlements that existed in Palestine before the First World War were created by Russian Jews.[2]

Russian Jewry's response to Herzl's call was overwhelming. Of the 197 participants in the first Zionist congress (1897), 66 were from Russia. Next year, the movement counted 373 local groups. At the fourth congress (1900) Russian Zionists were represented by more than 200 delegates, and at the fifth (1901) they played a leading part in the formation of the Democratic Faction, which demanded that more attention be given to Jewish national education and culture.[3] The first all-Russian Zionist conference met in 1902 at Minsk, with the participation of 500 delegates, representing some 75,000 *shekel*-holders.[4] At the sixth Zionist congress (1903), the Russian delegation constituted the bulk of the 177 *Neinsagers* who opposed Herzl's proposal to appoint a commission to investigate the British Government's Uganda offer and walked out after the proposal had been accepted. By that time, Russian Zionism with its 1,572 local groups was a major force in the World Zionist Organization.

[1] *Kniga o Russkom Yevreistve* (Book on Russian Jewry), New York, 1960, p. 318.
[2] Ibid., pp. 321, 242, 246.   [3] Ibid., pp. 253–5.   [4] Ibid., pp. 255, 259–60.

Russian Zionists were an ideologically alert and diversified movement. After Herzl's death, the majority of the seventh Zionist congress (1905) decisively rejected the Uganda project. The dissenting minority created a world-wide Jewish Territorialist Organization, but this failed to capture the imagination of the Zionist masses in Russia. It found considerable and active support in labour Zionist circles. The Zionist-Socialist Party (Z.S.) founded in 1904–5, branded the Palestine solution as utopian, and devoted its main attention to problems of Jewish migration which, it believed, would automatically develop into a movement of colonization, and thereby solve the Jewish problem. Another socialist group with a Zionist background emerged in 1905–6. It opposed both the Palestinian and other territorialist solutions of the Jewish problem, and advocated Jewish national autonomy in Russia, based on an elected Jewish national assembly; they were called 'Sejmists', from the Polish term *Sejm* (Diet). Both groups later merged in a United Socialist Party, known as the Fareinikte. By the spring of 1917, their combined membership was estimated at 13,000.[1]

Palestine-oriented labour Zionism has been represented since 1900 by Poale Zion, whose Zionist concept was strictly materialistic, expressed in Marxist terms. For a time they worked within the general framework of the Zionist organization; later, emphasis was increasingly put on proletarian class consciousness, which barred continued co-operation with the middle-class Zionist movement. Since 1903 an intermediate position had been occupied by the Tzeirei Zion groups. Their orientation was socialist, non-Marxist, and with no stress on the class struggle. Tzeirei Zion constituted the backbone of the *Halutz* (pioneer) movement in Russia, and were prominently represented in the second *Aliyah*. From 1901 the religious wing in Zionism was represented by Mizrachi.

Prior to the 1905 Revolution, the Russian Zionists consistently abstained from active participation in the country's general political life. The all-Russian Zionist convention in Helsingfors, Finland (November 1906) reversed this stand. A comprehensive and imaginative 'Helsingfors Programme' encompassed all aspects of Jewish interest in Russia. It offered, on the one hand, an organic synthesis between the struggle for Jewish civic and national rights in the country, and the upbuilding of the Jewish homeland in Palestine, on the other.[2]

In tsarist Russia, Zionism was an illegal movement and like all other

---

[1] Oscar I. Janowsky, *The Jews and Minority Rights*, New York, 1933, pp. 218–19; *Der Yiddisher Proletarier* (The Jewish Proletarian), Kiev, August 1917.

[2] Janowsky, op. cit., pp. 107–8; *Yevreiskaya Mysl* (Jewish Thought), Odessa, 7 December 1906.

political parties was largely handicapped in its expansion. The Revolution of February 1917 removed the shackles and led to an unprecedented growth.

In the wake of a series of district conferences, an all-Russian Zionist convention met at Petrograd in May 1917; its 552 delegates represented 140,000 *shekel*-holders (as against 26,000 in 1913) in 700 Jewish communities.[1] The Balfour Declaration of 2 November 1917 gave powerful impetus to the movement and made the Zionists the dominant party in Russian Jewry. In the 1917–18 elections to the all-Russian Jewish congress, the Zionist slate was far ahead; in the Ukraine, Zionist slates out-polled all the four opposing parties combined (Bund, Fareinikte, Poale Zion, and Dubnov's Folkspartei). The Zionists also controlled the conference of the 149 representatives from forty Jewish communities of central Russia, held in Moscow in July 1918. The Zionist-sponsored educational society, *Tarbut* (Culture) maintained over 250 Hebrew educational institutions throughout the country. By September 1917 there were thirty-nine Yiddish Zionist periodicals, ten in Hebrew, and three in Russian.[2]

The Soviet regime thus confronted a strong, well-organized, truly popular Zionist movement. With some 1,200 local groups and a membership of 300,000,[3] it enjoyed virtual hegemony in Russia's Jewish community.

The Zionist cause could expect little understanding, let alone sympathy, from Russia's new rulers. As early as 1903, Lenin wrote in the party's central organ, *Iskra* (The Spark), that the very idea of a Jewish nationality was 'manifestly reactionary', and 'in conflict with the interests of the Jewish proletariat'. Ten years later, the verdict was reasserted by Stalin in the pamphlet *Marxism and the National Question*.

Nevertheless, in its early stages, the new regime did not noticeably affect Zionist activities. A 'Palestine Week', proclaimed in the spring of 1918, was successfully conducted in hundreds of Jewish communities. Palestine emigration offices, established in Petrograd, Minsk, and several Jewish centres in the Ukraine, with a central office in Odessa, functioned freely. A concerted effort was made to mobilize private initiative and capital for the upbuilding of Palestine. Within a year of the overthrow of the tsarist regime, Zionist activities were thus in full operation throughout Russia. In the London *Zionist Review* of October 1918, Isaak A. Naiditch, a leading Zionist and vice-chairman of the Moscow Jewish Council, was able to

[1] *Yevreiskaya Mysl*, 25 May 1917.

[2] *The Zionist Review*, London, July and November 1918; Aryeh Leib Tsentsiper, *Eser Sh'not R'difot* (Ten Years of Persecution), Tel Aviv, 1930, p. 27; A. Kishnits, *Di Yiddishe Presse in Ratnfarband* (The Jewish Press in the Soviet Union), Minsk, 1928, p. 68.

[3] Tsentsiper, op. cit., p. 39.

relate that the Jewish Commissariat (Yevkom), established in January 1918 as a subdivision of the People's Commissariat for National Affairs, 'which at first proclaimed the combating of Zionism . . . as one of its chief tasks, has up to now accomplished nothing of any consequence'.

Yevkom's early absence of a noticeably anti-Zionist record was primarily the result of its personal composition. It was staffed in the main by men who had virtually no specifically Jewish national background, who had no axe to grind and who lacked any strong motivation for militant anti-Zionist action. They saw their principal mission in winning the Jewish masses for the communist cause through appeals in Yiddish, and in liquidating the existing Jewish community councils. The Yevkom had neither time nor incentive or particular inclination to indulge in a sustained anti-Zionist crusade.

Nevertheless, by way of precaution, also through its awareness of the new regime's built-in suspicion of any non-communist political formation, the Zionist leadership decided to disregard the domestic aspects of the Helsingfors programme. A Zionist conference, attended by sixty delegates, met in Moscow on 5–8 May 1918, and hailed the Balfour Declaration as the first step to international recognition of a Jewish Palestine, but passed a resolution calling for strict neutrality in Russia's internal political affairs.[1]

The year 1918 passed in relative tranquillity. But the Jewish Sections of the communist party (known as the Yevsektsia), established simultaneously with the Yevkom and composed of virulently anti-Zionist former militants of the Bund and the Fareinikte, turned communist, had by the summer of 1918 begun to denounce 'the counter-revolutionary essence' of Zionism. Early in 1919, they made their first attempt to convert verbal thrusts into anti-Zionist deeds. In February Zionist headquarters in Petrograd reported that throughout the Soviet domain Zionist offices were being requisitioned and Zionist periodicals banned.

Yet at that time anti-Zionist harassment was in the main still the result of Yevsektsia's 'private initiative'. At the Zionist conference in Petrograd (March 1919) delegates from the provincial groups complained of frequent administrative interference in their activities, but made the point that local Jewish communist officials rather than government institutions were usually responsible for such measures.[2] Isolated cases of direct government interference were, however, also not lacking; two months later, the Yiddish daily *Petrograder Togblatt*, the official organ of the Zionist Central Committee, was suspended.

<hr />

[1] *The Zionist Review*, September 1918.   [2] Ibid., May 1919.

Meanwhile, a full-scale anti-Zionist crusade had been unleashed in the Ukraine (occupied by the Soviet troops in February 1919). Hitherto, under the various Ukrainian regimes, the Zionist movement in all its ramifications was able to develop unimpeded. Though fiercely assailed by the socialist Bund and the Fareinikte, it succeeded in establishing a dominant position in Ukrainian Jewry. In the elections to the so-called Temporary Jewish National Assembly (November 1918) the three Zionist slates (General Zionists, Tzeirei Zion, and Poale Zion) emerged with an absolute majority; 112,851 votes out of a total of 209,128. In the elections to the Jewish community councils, the same three slates received 54·4 per cent of the votes; 59 per cent of the membership of the newly elected councils were Zionists.[1]

The initiative for an official anti-Zionist course belonged to the former leaders of the Fareinikte and the Bund. Large sections of the two parties had joined the communist front. In May 1919 they formed the Komfarband (*Kommunistische Farband*), which on 4 July addressed a memorandum to the Ukrainian Commissariat of Internal Affairs, insisting that it was 'absolutely necessary to liquidate the activities of the Zionist party and all its factions'. The Commissariat responded quickly and vigorously: two days later, the homes of scores of prominent Zionists in Kiev were searched by the Cheka (Soviet secret police), accompanied by Komfarbandists. On 12 July decree no. 325/625 ordered fifteen Zionist organizations, as well as the *Tarbut* and the *Kehilah*, to cease functioning forthwith. The Kiev pattern was later repeated in Odessa, Kharkov, and other Jewish centres where the Komfarband carried weight.[2]

Anti-Zionist repression had no time to assume a systematic and wholesale character because in the second part of 1919 Denikin's Volunteer Army conquered most of the Ukraine. Repression was resumed early in 1920, after the final defeat of Denikin's forces, which had marked their rule by bloody Jewish pogroms.

In the R.S.F.S.R. proper, in the second half of 1919, the Yevsektsia sternly condemned the government's failure to act vigorously and speedily against Zionism and Zionists. Composed mostly of recent converts from the traditionally anti-Zionist socialist parties (Bund and Fareinikte), the Yevsektsia's leadership was eager to square old accounts with the Zionists, whose political hegemony in Russian Jewry they had been unable to

---

[1] *Der Yiddisher Natzionaler Sekretariat un die Yiddishe Nationale Autonomie in Ukraine* (The Jewish National Secretariat and the Jewish National Autonomy in the Ukraine), Kiev, 1920, *passim*.

[2] *Yevreiskaya Mysl*, 1 and 14 September 1919.

overcome within the framework of the normal democratic process; they also were anxious to prove to the communist regime that they had purged themselves of all vestiges of Jewish nationalism. The second conference of Yevsektsia and Yevkom groups in Moscow (June 1919) urged the dissolution of the 'counter-revolutionary . . . clerical and nationalistic Zionist organization . . .', an 'instrument in the hands of entente imperialism in its war against the proletarian revolution'.[1]

At that early date, the central Soviet authorities showed no inclination to yield to Yevsektsia's prodding. The year 1919 was the most critical in the life of the new regime. Fully absorbed by the desperate struggle against the advancing anti-Soviet armies, it was not inclined to pay attention to such a relatively innocuous movement as Zionism.

Yet apparently alarmed by the attack of the Yevsektsia conference, the Central Committee of the Zionist Organization, in July 1919, submitted to the All-Russian Central Executive Committee of Soviets (VTsIK) a memorandum, requesting a certification of legality for the Zionist movement; the memorandum avoided any mention of the essence of Zionist ideology, maintaining that Zionist activities were merely directed at transforming Jewish small merchants into farmers and artisans in Palestine. In reply to this request, the VTsIK on 21 July resolved that since no decree of the VTsIK or the Council of People's Commissars had declared the Zionist party counter-revolutionary, and since the cultural and educational activities of the Zionist organization did not contradict the decisions of the communist party, the Presidium of the VTsIK instructed all Soviet organizations not to hamper the Zionist party in its activities.[2]

The Zionist Central Committee rather optimistically interpreted this resolution as an implicit legalization of Zionism in the Soviet Union. Actually, it was but an equivocal and negatively-phrased expression of official tolerance; it remained valid as long as no other Soviet body declared Zionism and Zionists to be counter-revolutionary. In practice, the regime played a cat-and-mouse game with Zionist activities.

On 1 September 1919, the Cheka invaded and sealed the headquarters of the Zionist Central Committee in Leningrad, confiscated all documents and 120,000 roubles in cash, arrested several Committee members, and closed the Zionist weekly *Khronika Yevreiskoy Zhizny* (Chronicle of Jewish Life). The next day, several Zionist leaders were arrested in Moscow, where the Hebrew Zionist periodical *Ha'Am* (The People) was

---

[1] A. Agursky (ed.), *Die Yiddishe Kommisariatn un di Yiddishe Kommunistishe Sektzies* (The Jewish Commissariats and the Jewish Communist Sections), Minsk, 1928, p. 288.
[2] Tsentsiper, op. cit., pp. 50, 51.

suspended on 13 September, allegedly for refusing to print government decrees; next month, the Russian-language Zionist weekly *Rassviet* (The Dawn) was suppressed as an 'organ of the bourgeoisie'. Similar harassment took place in many other Russian towns.

But these activities did not assume the character and dimension of a massive and consistent anti-Zionist drive. Repression was intermittent and was more often than not followed by relaxation. Zionists arrested in Moscow were released after a brief internment, and in Leningrad the Cheka on 6 November reopened the Zionist headquarters, returning sequestered funds and some of the documents. The ban on the publication of Zionist periodicals, however, remained in force.[1] The authorities apparently felt that by silencing the Zionist press, they would obstruct the main channel of Zionist influence among Soviet Jewry.

Undaunted by sporadic harassment, the Zionist Central Committee, in the spring of 1920, called an all-Russian Zionist convention. One hundred and nine delegates and guests gathered on 20 April in Moscow's *Tarbut* Hall; out-of-town delegates arrived on the strength of special travel permits issued by the local Soviet authorities. For two days, the convention functioned normally. Then, on 23 April, a Cheka squad appeared, led by a Jewish girl, and arrested seventy-five participants. On the way to the Cheka building, the prisoners demonstratively marched singing the Zionist anthem 'Hatiqva'.[2]

In compliance with the VTsIK resolution, the official charges against the arrested Zionists were based not on the illegality of Zionism as such, but rather on staging an unlicensed conference and on alleged counter-revolutionary activities and contacts abroad. They were also accused of possessing some unidentified 'compromising documents', of expressing pro-British sympathies, of collaboration with American Zionists, of giving financial aid to Admiral Kolchak, head of the White Guards, and of supporting anti-Soviet forces elsewhere. In addition, the official organ of the Soviet Government, *Izvestiya*, on 16 May 1920, reported that peroxylin slabs of guncotton had been found in the offices of the Zionist Central Committee. The journal added that 'a thorough investigation is in progress, in which Jewish communists are actively participating'. In an unprecedented

---

[1] Tsentsiper, *Ba-Ma'avak li-Geulah* (In the Struggle for Redemption), Tel Aviv, 1956, p. 34, 54; *The American Jewish Yearbook*, vol. 21, pp. 280–1.

[2] Tsentsiper. *Esser Sh'not R'difot*, pp. 58ff.; Benjamin West (ed.), *Struggle of a Generation*; *the Jews under Soviet Rule*. Tel Aviv, 1959 (later referred to as 'West'), pp. 144–5. (This book is an English edition of *Naftule Dor*, a two-volume anthology of personal accounts and essays, published in Tel Aviv in 1945.) Also: Léon Lénéman, *La Tragédie des Juifs en U.R.S.S.*, Paris, 1959, pp. 250–2.

gesture of political fair-play, never to be repeated, *Izvestiya*, on 20 May, published a refutation by the arrested Zionists; the promised 'investigation' was then quietly dropped.

The seventy-five imprisoned Zionists were held in the notorious Butirki gaol for three months without formal legal proceedings being initiated against them. Sixty-eight were released in mid-July following intervention by two representatives of the American Joint Distribution Committee, Harry Fisher and Max Pine, who were at that time on a mission to Moscow to inspect the J.D.C.'s relief work in the Soviet Union. The remaining seven were sentenced to hard labour for periods ranging from 6 months to 5 years; they were later released, after pledging themselves to refrain from any further Zionist activities. The Zionist Central Committee then decided to move underground. Until the end of the 1920s a clandestine Central Bureau continued to co-ordinate the work of these local Zionist groups in the R.S.F.S.R.[1] that remained in existence.

The Yevsektsia was increasingly dismayed by the apparent semi-tolerance of the Soviet authorities and urged total proscription and liquidation of Zionism. In July 1920, its third conference declared that there was

no longer any ground for a cautious attack on Zionism. It is necessary to put an end to the vacillation of the official attitude towards the general Zionist party and to all its cultural and economic organizations. It is essential that a total liquidation be carried out, notwithstanding the socialist phraseology of the Tzeirei Zion and Zionist socialists.[2]

There was no uniformity in the Soviet Government's response to Yevsektsia's pressure. In Odessa, local authorities resorted to mass arrests among the Zionists, and throughout 1920 similar harassments took place in other Jewish centres, usually in the wake of Yevsektsia-inspired newspaper articles and denunciations; Zionist students were frequently expelled from the universities as 'ideologically alien elements'. On the other hand, there were communities where Zionist activities continued unhampered.

In the early stages of the New Economic Policy (N.E.P.), inaugurated by Lenin in 1921, the general relaxation of the regime's administrative pressure made life easier for the Zionist groups as well. For some eight months they enjoyed a measure of respite from extensive harassment. Yevsektsia angrily protested at the government's 'leniency'. Their daily *Emes* (The Truth) of 13 January 1922 called for 'a campaign to exterminate Zionism in the U.S.S.R. forever'.

[1] Tsentsiper, *Ba-Ma'avak li-Geulah*, pp. 123–214.
[2] Agursky, *Die Yiddishe Komissariatn*, p. 352.

Repressions were resumed by mid-1922. Their main target was the Tzeirei Zion party. This dynamic Zionist formation underwent a split at its May 1920 conference in Kharkov. The left wing, outspokenly pro-Marxist and pro-Soviet, seceded and organized an independent, Zionist-Socialist party; the right wing maintained its non-Marxist programme, refused to give any overt support to the Bolshevik regime, remained within the Zionist Organization, moved underground with it, and assumed the name of the Zionist Labour party.[1] It constituted the mainstay of the underground Zionist movement, and was particularly strong in the Ukraine.

Two illegal Tzeirei Zion conferences, called with consummate conspiratorial precautions, went undetected. But the third conference, in a Kiev synagogue on 30 April 1922, was raided by the Cheka on the fourth day of its deliberations; fifty-one persons were arrested, and thirty-seven of them appeared on 26 August before the Soviet military court. The indictment read:

The Tzeirei Zion is a popular wing of the Zionist party, which, under the mask of democracy, seeks to corrupt the Jewish youth and to throw them into the arms of the counter-revolutionary bourgeoisie in the interests of Anglo-French capitalism. To restore the Palestine state, these representatives of the Jewish bourgeoisie rely on reactionary forces, ranging from Tiutiunik and Petliura to such rapacious imperialists as Poincaré, Lloyd George, and the Pope.

The court unanimously pronounced the defendants guilty as charged: twelve were sentenced to two years' hard labour, and fifteen to one year. Ten were released. After thirteen months those sentenced to two years were permitted to leave the Soviet Union.[2]

Arrests continued on a massive scale throughout the next two years. In September 1922 more than 1,000 Zionists were arrested in Odessa, Kiev, Berdichev, and several other Ukrainian urban centres. In 1923 and 1924 arrests and trials multiplied. Some 3,000 Zionists were simultaneously arrested in 150 localities on the night of 2 September 1924, and arrests continued through October.[3] Both interrogation and trial were conducted in camera. The defendants were charged with, and convicted of, often unspecified 'criminal offences'. These usually involved sentences of three to ten years in prison or hard labour in 'isolation camps', at first in central

[1] Tsentsiper, *Ba-Ma'avak li-Geulah*, p. 131; Guido G. Goldman, *Zionism Under Soviet Rule 1917–28*, New York, 1960, p. 74.

[2] Tsentsiper, *Esser Sh'not R'difot*, pp. 99–103; Goldman, op. cit., pp. 75–6; West, op. cit., pp. 169–70.

[3] Lénéman, op. cit., p. 262; *Emes*, 8 September 1924.

Russia, later in Siberia, in the Ural Mountains, on the Solovki Islands, in Kirgizia, and central Asia.

In certain cases, the convicted Zionists were offered the tantalizing alternative of deportation to Palestine in return for a full recantation. This included an admission that the goals of Zionism were indeed anti-Soviet and/or counter-revolutionary. Those who signed such a statement were permitted to apply for the conversion of their sentence into a deportation order; they could then obtain an exit passport, valid only for travel to Palestine.[1]

The rationale for this opening of a tiny loophole was apparently twofold: the Soviet authorities might have been eager to get rid of hundreds of Zionist devotees; and they also wanted to impress world Jewish opinion favourably by showing that Zionists were persecuted not because of the immigrationary aspect of their programme, but only for their 'counter-revolutionary' sympathies and activities within the Soviet Union.

This latter consideration also seems to have accounted for the government's benevolent gesture towards the Histadruth (General Labour Federation in Palestine), which was invited to participate in the International Agricultural Exhibition in Moscow in the summer of 1924.[2] The Palestine pavilion attracted tens of thousands of enthusiastic Jewish visitors from all parts of the Soviet Union; special excursions came from four large cities. Emboldened by this impressive demonstration, Zionist youths in Odessa marched in formation in the streets singing the 'Hatiqva'; they were dispersed by mounted police, and thirty-two were arrested; they declared a five-day hunger strike as a protest against their treatment by the prison authorities.[3]

By the end of 1924, thousands of Zionists were languishing in Soviet prisons and detention camps. Julius Margolin, a noted writer, who was himself an inmate in Soviet places of detention, relates that as late as 1941 he met in the deportation camps of the Soviet far north Zionist leaders who had spent 16–17 years there.

Zionists were strongly represented among the tens of thousands of political prisoners. In 1928, L. Steinberg related in *Kuntres* that he had in his possession a list containing 775 names of Zionist-Socialists (including women and children) languishing in Soviet gaols and camps. They were often scattered in tiny, isolated groups in the most remote areas. Life was extremely hard. Available accounts of their treatment tell a grim and

---

[1] Tsentsiper, *Esser Sh'not R'difot*, p. 181–2; West, op. cit., p. 150.
[2] Judd L. Teller, *The Kremlin, the Jews, and the Middle East*, New York, 1957, p.45.
[3] Teller, op. cit., pp. 50–1.

ghastly tale of undernourishment bordering on starvation; of hunger strikes, savage beatings, torture, solitary confinement, forced marches; of illness, compounded by totally inadequate medical care; of suicides and arbitrary killings by the guards.[1]

Defying the swelling wave of harassment, arrests, and deportations, the Zionist youth movement held its ground—and continued to grow in all its branches: Tzeirei Zion, Zionist Socialist party, *Hechalutz*, *Hitachdut*, United Zionist Youth, various unaffiliated local Zionist groups. They overwhelmingly outnumbered the Jewish communists. Yevsektsia's Moscow daily, *Emes*, complained on 16 June 1922, that in certain areas 'there are scarcely any Jewish communists . . . while the Zionists are strongly organized'. On 27 October 1925, the same paper lamented 'the development of Zionism, whose influence on the petty-bourgeois-elements of the Jewish youth is very large'. The number of those who in one way or another were at that time involved in Zionist activities is estimated at 30,000.[2]

On 25 August 1925 two Zionist leaders, Professor David Shor and Itzhak Rabinovich, submitted to Peter Smidovich, acting head of the VTsIK, a memorandum outlining Zionist aims and activities and asking for the release of all Zionist prisoners, cessation of further arrests, and authorization of emigration to Palestine. A special session of the VTsIK discussed the request at considerable length, but inconclusively. The Zionists were advised to submit a project for a legalized emigrationary society. This was done. But the Yevsektsia immediately intervened and urged the Politburo of the communist party to reject any concession to the Zionists; a few days later Smidovich meaningfully told Rabinovich: 'Your own people are advancing all kinds of hindrances.' The attempt to establish agreement with the regime petered out.[3]

The very fact that the highest echelons of the Soviet regime were prepared to negotiate with the Zionists at that time, the repeated assertions that the Soviet Government was actually 'not against Zionism', and that all the harassment of the Zionists was the work of the Yevsektsia only, may appear puzzling. Why did a mighty authoritarian regime resort to all these subterfuges in dealing with a movement which it could formally outlaw and crush without much ado—just as it had done, ruthlessly and effectively, in regard to much more powerful Russian

[1] *Sotsialisticheskii Vestnik* (Socialist Herald), 7 April and 3 May 1928.

[2] Nahum Gergel, *Di Lage fun di Yidn in Russland*, Warsaw, 1926, p. 174, Tsentsiper, *Ba-Ma'avak li-Geulah*, p. 186.

[3] Tsentsiper, *Esser Sh'not R'difot*, p. 234ff.; Itzhak Rabinovitch, *M'Moskva v'ad Yerusholaim* (From Moscow to Jerusalem), Jerusalem, 1957, pp. 68ff.

political parties, such as the Social Revolutionaries and the Mensheviks?

A partial answer to this query is, of course, that the Soviet rulers saw no real 'danger' in the existence of a Zionist movement. It did not belong to the mainstream of Russia's political life struggle, was in no way a challenge to their power, and could be treated as a mere 'exotic' sideline in the country's motley set-up. Yielding to the Yevsektsia's pressure, the regime was willing to permit its Jewish communist henchmen to abuse Zionism and intermittently persecute Zionists. But during the first decade of communist rule the Soviet Government was not prepared to make Yevsektsia's words and deeds the regime's official policy.

The rationale for this restraint has to be sought, in the first place, in the government's vague apprehension lest an outright, clearly enunciated anti-Zionist policy unfavourably affect Soviet Russia's image in the Jewish communities of the western world. Contrary to the widespread notion, Soviet Russia was at that time very sensitive to world public opinion and was loath to experience the vigour and effectiveness of any eventual adverse Jewish reaction to the clear-cut official persecution of Zionism. It was in this spirit that communist leaders did not refuse to discuss some *modus vivendi* with the non-legalized but also not outlawed Zionists. Negotiations to this effect proceeded intermittently and inconclusively for more than half a year. They ended abruptly on 16 March 1926, when more than 100 Zionists, including the chief negotiator, Rabinovich, were arrested and subsequently sentenced to three years' exile in Kazakhstan.[1]

Somewhat different in character and timing was the liquidation of the *Hechalutz* movement. At an early stage, its programme of intensive training for settlement in Palestine on collective agricultural farms offered a certain appeal to the Soviet regime's ideology, and the *Hechalutz* was permitted to grow. The number of local groups throughout the U.S.S.R. increased from seventy-five in 1922 to more than a hundred with some 3,000 members by the end of 1923.[2] In August of that year, the Commissariat on Internal Affairs, disregarding Yevsektsia's strenuous objections, issued a charter to the 'Labour Federation *Hechalutz*'.[3]

But a large segment, about one-third, of the Russian Hechalutz was apprehensive of the regime's intentions. They refused to accept the offered legal status as conducive to the infiltration of communist agents into their ranks and to undermining the movement's Zionist content. The dissidents

[1] Goldman, op. cit., p. 87.

[2] *Emes*, Moscow, 5 February 1922; Dan Pines, *Hechalutz B'kur Hamahapecha* (The Hechalutz in the Crucible of the Revolution), Tel Aviv, 1938, p. 234.

[3] *Jewish Telegraphic Agency, Daily News Bulletin*, 30 October 1923.

formed an independent (and illegal) *Hechalutz HaLeumi HaAmlani* (National Pioneer Labour Organization).[1]

Both wings of the movement had their troubles with the Soviet authorities, particularly in the Ukraine and the Crimea. Arrests started in 1924 and were intensified in 1926. In March 1926 the Hechalutz House in Moscow was raided, and many *Halutzim* arrested. Further arrests followed in Odessa in April, and, during the summer, in Leningrad, Nezhin, Poltava, Simferopol, and Moscow, as well as the colonies in the Kherson province and in the Krivoi Rog region of the Crimea. In May 1928 the World Union of *Hashomer Hatzair* reported that 148 members of the *Hechalutz* colonies of *Shomria* and *Zofim* were imprisoned, awaiting trial, and that 39 more were deported.[2]

The arrests continued throughout 1927. In 1928 and 1929 the total liquidation of all existing *Hechalutz* colonies was achieved. The backbone of the movement was broken; its leaders languished in gaols and labour camps.

Some of the Halutzim succeeded in reaching Palestine. During the years 1924–30, their number totalled 1,034. This represented a considerable proportion of the steadily declining flow of immigrants from Soviet Russia which was still considerable (21,157) in 1925–6. But in the next four years (1927–30) the number of immigrants fell to 1,197; in the six years between 1931 and 1936, only 1,848 immigrants were able to arrive from the Soviet Union.[3]

In the latter part of the 1920s, Yevsektsia's position in the Soviet regime's general structure started to deteriorate. The total liquidation of all Jewish national institutions (*Kehiloth*, *Tarbut*, O.R.T., O.S.E., etc.), the actual disappearance of the Bund, the Fareinikte and the Poale Zion, as well as the increasingly efficacious persecution of all forms of Zionist activities throughout the U.S.S.R., for which the Yevsektsia claimed full credit, undermined its usefulness to the regime. By the end of the decade, the authorities apparently came to the conclusion that the Yevsektsia had outlived its usefulness: 'The Moor has done his duty—the Moor can go.' Yevsektsia's last conference was held in December 1926; throughout the following four years it shrank in size and importance, and in January 1930, it was abolished as a distinctive collective body within the framework of the communist party. It may be assumed that neither Yevsektsia nor the Yevkom (which was dissolved early in 1924, together with the People's Commissariat for Nationality Affairs, of which it was a subdivision),

---

[1] Dan Pines, op. cit., pp. 222–54.   [2] *The American Jewish Yearbook*, vol. 29, p. 97.
[3] *Hechalutz in Russia*, Tel Aviv, 1932; Leneman, op. cit., p. 260.

were ever devised as permanent institutions to handle Jewish affairs in the communist spirit. The communist party and the governmental machinery took over.

Though no longer able to function collectively as a body, Yevsektsia's stalwarts continued their vicious activity individually, from long-established positions of influence in the communist party and the governmental apparatus. Their task was considerably facilitated by the fact that by that time a consistently anti-Zionist course, aimed at total destruction of the 'Zionist hydra' had become the declared policy of both the party and the government. Years of Yevsektsia's persistent indoctrination, coupled with the traditional anti-nationalist outlook of Leninist communism, were bearing fruit.

Hostility towards Zionism and persecution of Zionists continued unabated, even increased. Zionists deported to the farthest confines of the U.S.S.R. were not permitted to return. Many who had already served their full sentence were simply 'forgotten' in Siberia and central Asia.

Zionist activities were effectively crippled. The last citadel of organized underground Zionism—the Moscow Central Executive Committee of Tzeirei Zion and the Union of Zionist Youth—was liquidated in September 1934; its members received long-term sentences.[1] In the years 1936-9, the government mounted an intensive, large-scale campaign against 'Zionist imperialist oppression of the Palestinian Arabs'. The Zionists were denounced on the radio, in the communist press, and in the resolutions passed at factory meetings. Zionism, officially pronounced dead and buried,[2] still occupied a prominent place in the regime's propaganda effort.

By the end of the thirties the last visible vestiges of organized Zionism had been ruthlessly and efficaciously eradicated in the U.S.S.R. Whatever Zionist beliefs had survived the pressure of the authoritarian apparatus of the state, remained deeply embedded in the minds and souls of the then three-million-strong Soviet Jewish community. The regime considered 'the Zionist chapter' fully and irretrievably closed.

It was dramatically reopened in the early stages of the Second World War. In September 1939 the Soviet Union annexed Poland's eastern and south-eastern provinces, with a Jewish population of about 1,200,000–1,250,000 (some 300,000 Jews came in later as refugees from the German-

---

[1] Teller, op. cit., p. 55; West, op. cit., pp. 178-9.

[2] In volume 51 of the first edition of the *Large Soviet Encyclopaedia*, 1944, Zionism was summarily dismissed as 'moribund': the final 'ideological rout of Zionism came with the victory of the Great Soviet Revolution of October 1917'.

occupied areas). In June 1940 the Rumanian provinces of Bessarabia and Northern Bukovina were incorporated in the U.S.S.R. According to the Rumanian census of 1930, these had a Jewish population of 277,949. The almost simultaneous annexation of Latvia, Estonia, and Lithuania added a further 265,000 Jews. Within nine months, the Jewish community of the Soviet Union increased by some two million.

Zionists constituted a high percentage of this influx. Polish Jewry, says Professor Bernard D. Weinryb in the authoritative study, *The Jews in the Soviet Satellites*, was 'the backbone' of the World Zionist Organization. Forty-three per cent of Jewish councilmen, elected by 374,398 Jewish voters in the 1934 municipal elections, belonged to various Zionist groups. The two Zionist-sponsored Hebrew school systems (*Yabneh* and *Tarbut*) comprised 403 institutions with 59,241 pupils. In the 1931 census, 243,339 Jews listed Hebrew as their mother tongue. Four weeklies and twenty-four other periodicals appeared in Hebrew.[1] A similar pattern, in varying degrees, prevailed in other annexed areas. The Soviet Union found itself saddled with a two-million-strong, predominantly Zionist, 'new' Jewish minority.

The Soviet repressive machinery went into action to remedy efficiently and ruthlessly a state of affairs that was intolerable to the regime. What had been done to 'indigenous' Soviet Zionists during more than two decades was now inflicted on those from the newly acquired areas within a far shorter period. Jewish newcomers constituted a sizeable percentage of the estimated 400,000 newly acquired Soviet subjects who were sent to concentration and forced labour camps in the forests of Arkhangelsk, the Komi district, the Siberian tundra, or to the mines of the Don Basin in south-east Russia.[2]

In June 1941 Hitler's armies invaded Soviet territory. The Jews became the main target of Nazi savagery. Hundreds of thousands were murdered. Throughout the war years, the German terror was simultaneously accompanied by the continued, often intensified, Soviet persecution of Zionism and Zionists.[3]

Simultaneously with its persistent anti-Zionist policy on the home front, the Soviet Government made a sustained effort to enlist the sympathy and support of world Jewry for its war effort by an appeal to Jewish solidarity.

[1] Bernard D. Weinryb, 'Poland', in *The Jews in the Soviet Satellites*, Syracuse, 1953, pp. 218–21, 224.

[2] West, op. cit., pp. 16, 70–1, 84–5, 102–29.

[3] David Grodner, 'In Soviet Poland and Lithuania', *Contemporary Jewish Record*, IV 1948, p. 14.

On 24 August 1941 Jews the world over heard for the first time over the radio a voice from Moscow, addressing them as *Brider Yiden* (Brother Jews). In this broadcast the poet Perets Markish said that all Jews were now one people and one army and that no longer would the ocean divide them.

In April 1942 came the announcement of the formation in Moscow of a Jewish Anti-Fascist Committee. The Committee's main purpose was to build up pro-Soviet public opinion among the Jews in the western countries. It was an obvious Soviet command performance, headed by Solomon M. Mikhoels, the renowned actor, and Itzik Feffer, Red Army colonel, communist poet laureate, and past glorifier in verse of the Mufti's terror against the Jews of Palestine. But the very fact of the Committee's emergence was in itself an assertion of Jewish national solidarity. Feffer's wartime poem, 'I am a Jew', had the ring of Zionist anthems, evoking the Maccabeans, heroes and symbols of the Jewish national revolt.

In 1943, Mikhoels and Feffer went with Stalin's personal blessing to the United States and England, to plead for active Jewish support of the Soviet war effort. They were understandably eager to secure Zionist understanding and sympathy for their mission. In London, Mikhoels declared that Zionism was 'a great idea', though it was inapplicable to Soviet Jewry with its deep roots in Russia. On his return to Moscow, he and Feffer, in December 1944, sent greetings on Dr. Weizmann's seventieth birthday.[1] Interest in Palestine and Zionism was also shown by Ivan Maisky, the former Soviet envoy to London, who visited Palestine in October 1943 and sent to Moscow a glowing account. In November 1944, Shachna Epstein, secretary of the Jewish Anti-Fascist Committee, wrote in the Committee's organ, *Aynikayt*, that 'the Jewish people has a right to political independence in Palestine', and that 'no sensible and freedom-loving person can have any objection to the Jews there continuing to develop in freedom the home that they had set up through hard, constructive work, on the basis of self-government'. In January of that year, permission was granted for a display in Moscow of farm produce from the Jewish agricultural settlements in Palestine. The following April, the Palestine communist party, which during the bloody anti-Jewish riots of 1929 and 1936 observed the Kremlin's directives and glorified the 'national-revolutionary nature' of the Mufti's henchmen, received new instructions and announced its readiness to co-operate with the Histadrut in combating the infamous British White Paper. At the World Trade Union Conference (W.T.U.C.) in London (February 1945) the Soviet delegation endorsed a resolution

[1] West, op. cit., p. 24.

stating that 'the Jewish people must be enabled to continue the rebuilding of Palestine as their National Home'. It was also noted with satisfaction that the Moscow paper *Red Star*, organ of the Red Army, published an article highly critical of the Arab League on 13 July 1945. Two days later its content was broadcast by Radio Moscow in Arabic.

The Soviet Government welcomed Great Britain's submission, in the spring of 1947, of the Palestine issue to the United Nations as signifying the end of British rule in Palestine and converting the country's future into an international problem. At the early stage of the U.N. deliberations, the Soviet delegation was officially non-committal *vis-à-vis* Zionist aspirations for statehood. But the Soviet deputy Foreign Minister, Andrei A. Gromyko voted, together with the United States delegation, for the granting of a hearing to the Jewish Agency which, he well knew, was identical with the Executive of the World Zionist Organization. David Horowitz, a member of the Jewish Agency team at the United Nations, together with Moshe Shertok (Sharett) and Eliahu Epstein (Elath)—all of whom spoke Russian fluently and maintained contact with the Soviet representatives—recalls that the latter—Semyon K. Tsarapkin and Boris Stein—'showed keen sympathy and understanding of our efforts and interests'. On one occasion, Tsarapkin brought a bottle of wine, filled the five glasses and, raising his own, gave the toast: 'The future Jewish state.'[1]

On 13 October 1947 Tsarapkin officially announced Soviet Russia's support for the partition of Palestine into a Jewish and an Arab State.[2] The entire Soviet bloc (except Yugoslavia, which abstained) voted for partition on 29 November 1947.

When commandos of the Mufti-led Arab Higher Committee, reinforced by contingents from neighbouring Arab countries, launched a series of bloody attacks against the Jews that met with fierce resistance, the American U.N. delegation, on 30 March 1948, introduced into the Security Council a resolution calling 'upon Arab and Jewish armed groups in Palestine to cease acts of violence immediately'. On behalf of the Soviet delegation, Gromyko denounced the U.S. proposal as 'inequitable and unjust', and unfair to the Jews, and submitted an amendment that insisted on the 'immediate withdrawal of all armed groups which have invaded Palestine from the outside' and called for the 'prevention of the invasion of such groups into Palestine in the future'. When the U.S.

[1] David Horowitz, *The State in the Making*, New York, 1953, p. 27.
[2] U.N. Ad Hoc Committee on Palestine: Summary Records of Meetings, 25 September–25 November 1947, pp. 69–70.

delegation reneged on the partition decision and tried to substitute for it a 'temporary trusteeship', Gromyko gave determined support to several other amendments proposed by Moshe Shertok in the name of the Jewish Agency. When he addressed the U.N. Security Council on 30 March, Gromyko accused the United States of 'burying' the partition of Palestine and demanded the full implementation of the United Nations' decision of 29 November 1947[1]

It is significant, however, that in their addresses, both Gromyko and Tsarapkin did not once give the slightest inkling of the existence and effort of the Zionist movement as the background of the *Yishuv*'s struggle against British rule and Arab aggression.

When the State of Israel was proclaimed on 14 May 1948, the Kremlin granted *de jure* recognition within two days (Washington's *de facto* recognition preceded it by 48 hours). During Israel's struggle against the invading Arab armies, desperately needed arms came from Czechoslovakia with Moscow's tacit approval and in defiance of the United Nations' embargo on the introduction of arms and fighting men into the Middle East. Arms deliveries were paid for in cash, so that there was no 'philanthropy' in this action. But at that time, arms—from whatever source and at any price—were a matter of life or death for Israel. In 1965, seventeen years later, when Katriel Katz, Israel's newly appointed ambassador to Moscow, presented his credentials to the Soviet head of state, Anastas Mikoyan, he stressed that the Jewish people in Israel would never forget the deep understanding which the Soviet Union had revealed during the struggle for its establishment as a sovereign state; the Soviet Union occupied a special place in the history of Israel.

When Dr. Chaim Weizmann was elected President of Israel's Provisional Council, he received the congratulations of the Chief Rabbi of Moscow. The Jewish Anti-Fascist Committee was also permitted to dispatch a congratulatory cable. While praising the policy of the Soviet Government, which 'ceaselessly fought for a just solution of the Palestine problem', the Committee conveyed to Dr. Weizmann and the Jews of Eretz Israel its

hearty good wishes on the establishment of the Jewish state. This event is regarded as one of the most important in the history of the Jewish people. . . . With all our hearts we wish you and the working people in the State of Israel a victory over the aggressors, quiet and fruitful work for all freedom-loving peoples and for the Jewish people itself.[2]

[1] Security Council: Official Record, Third Year, nos. 16–19, p. 247; nos. 36–51, pp. 248–53; *The New York Times*, 31 March 1948.   [2] *Davar*, Tel Aviv, 22 June 1948.

The advocacy of Jewish statehood by the Soviet U.N. delegation was widely publicized in the entire Soviet press, reawakening long-suppressed Zionist feelings and expectations. The Kremlin apparently became apprehensive lest things go 'too far', and felt that a halt must be called to any display of Soviet Jewry's involvement in the renascence of Jewish statehood. Ilya Ehrenburg published in *Pravda* a four-column article (21 September 1948) which condemned the Zionists as 'mystics', and denied that there was any affinity between Jews in different countries: while the Soviet Union was sympathetic to Jewish aspirations for statehood, it had no sympathy for Israel's 'bourgeois' government; the workers in Israel 'must fight not only against the invaders, but against the bourgeoisie for whom war, as for all bourgeoisie, above all, means profits'.

Ehrenburg's obviously officially inspired article was intended as a stern warning to Soviet Jews to dampen their enthusiasm for everything connoted by Israel and Zionism. It was certainly no coincidence that it appeared almost simultaneously with the arrival in Moscow of the first Israeli legation, headed by Mrs. Golda Meyerson (Meir). When Mrs. Meir and members of her legation attended the Jewish New Year service at Moscow's central synagogue, on 16 October, they were received with unprecedented enthusiasm by tens of thousands of fervent worshippers; crowds accompanied them on the return walk to the hotel, shouting *'Am Yisroel Hai'* ('the Jewish People Lives'). A similar demonstration took place a week later, after a Day of Atonement service. The news of the inspiring encounter between the Israel legation members and the Jews of Moscow spread with lightning speed throughout provincial Jewish communities. Very soon, Jews started applying to the legation for visas and asking for assistance in obtaining exit permits from the Soviet authorities.[1] Administrative counter-action was swift and ruthless. Arrests and deportations of all those who, in one way or another, gave vent to their pro-Zionist or pro-Israel sentiments, assumed ever-widening dimensions. Emigration to Israel was barred: from 15 May 1948, till the end of 1951, only four old women and one disabled ex-serviceman were permitted to leave for Israel.

Soviet support in the United Nations for the creation of a Jewish state was motivated primarily by the desire to eliminate Great Britain from Palestine, to weaken the British position in the Middle East, and to facilitate Soviet penetration into this strategically important area. As Israel showed no inclination to become a Soviet satellite, Moscow became increasingly disappointed and angry. But in the early years hostility to

[1] West, op. cit., p. 44; Lénéman, op. cit., p. 279.

Zionism rather than to the State of Israel appears to have been the dominant feature of the Kremlin's policies. In the years 1948–53, the Soviet Government on the whole refrained from active interference in Middle Eastern affairs: there was for some twenty months no Soviet reaction to the tripartite Anglo-French-American declaration of 25 May 1950, guaranteeing the integrity of the existing frontiers and the 'balance of armaments' between the Middle Eastern states. The attitude towards Israel during this five-year period could be best defined as 'unfriendly indifference', the element of 'unfriendliness' being largely motivated by considerations of an internal political nature. The Jewish minority in the U.S.S.R., with its deep-seated sentiment for Israel, its weakened but still potent Zionist background, and its strong sympathies for the west with its numerous Jewish communities, was viewed as inherently 'unreliable', and Israel was regarded as a major 'diversionary' source of this alleged unreliability. Anti-Jewish, anti-Zionist and anti-Israel tendencies of the Soviet regime were organically interconnected. When *Pravda* unrolled the infamous 'Doctors' Plot' on 13 January 1953, the six Jews among the nine accused physicians were charged with being in league not only with American and British agents, but also with 'Zionist spies'. The same day, *Izvestiya*, berated 'the dirty face of Zionist espionage'. This piece of anti-Zionist demagogy provoked an angry reaction in Israel. On 9 February, 'unknown persons' planted a bomb in the Soviet embassy in Tel Aviv. Accusing the Israel police of complicity, Moscow three days later broke off diplomatic relations with Israel.

On 4 April, four weeks after Stalin's death, Moscow radio announced that the 'Doctors' Plot' was a provocation and that the charges against the physicians were false. During the short-lived post-Stalin regime of Malenkov, the tension subsided somewhat. Diplomatic relations were resumed on 20 July 1953; the Soviet mission in Tel Aviv and the Israel legation in Moscow were converted into embassies. There was also a more co-operative response to individual pleas for emigration permits: between July 1953 and September 1955 some 125 immigrants from the U.S.S.R. (almost exclusively from the areas annexed in 1938–45) reached Israel and were reunited with their families. These immigrants were all old people; the average age of the twelve who arrived up to September 1954 was 65.

In mid-1954, Malenkov was replaced by Nikita S. Khrushchev, under whose regime the Soviet Middle East policy became more aggressive and pro-Arab, more anti-Israel and more anti-Zionist. It reached a climax in the wake of the Sinai Operation (1956). The Soviet envoy in Tel Aviv was recalled to Moscow as a 'warning that should be properly assessed', and returned only in April 1957; in February 1957 the delivery of Soviet oil to Israel was stopped.

Nevertheless, a 200-member Israel delegation was permitted in July 1957 to participate in the International Youth Festival in Moscow. And, just as in 1948, huge and enthusiastic Jewish crowds—both local Muscovites and thousands of guests from the provinces—were bold enough to give an overt and passionate expression to their attachment to the reborn Jewish state. They ardently applauded the Israelis, accosted them in the streets, asked for Israeli postcards, match-boxes, stamps, pins as keepsakes; invited them to their homes.[1]

A high price was paid for this emotional outburst. During the festival, the police did not interfere. But shortly after the foreign delegations had left, retaliation began. Hundreds—some estimates speak of thousands—of Jews guilty of the offence of 'fraternization' were removed on various pretexts from their jobs. Many were arrested, some were sent to the Vorkuta hard-labour camp in Siberia.

In recent years, Soviet propaganda has increasingly linked its crusade against Judaism and Jewish national identity, with Zionism and Israel.

'Judaic sermons are the sermons of bourgeois Zionists' declared a Ukrainian-language broadcast from Kirovograd (9 December 1959). The Kuibishev daily *Volszhskaya Kommuna* wrote on 30 September 1961: 'The character of the Jewish religion serves the political aims of the Zionists—the awakening of a nationalistic frame of mind.' A pamphlet by A. Edelman, *In the Name of the Lord Jehovah*, published in 1963, is devoted to the 'debunking of Jewish bourgeois nationalism, Zionism, the spiritual source of which is Judaism . . . Zionism and Judaism concluded an alliance . . . to isolate the Jewish working masses and distract them from the class struggle'. The same year there appeared in *Kommunist Moldavia* (no. 12) an article by N. Shilintzev whose main thesis is that 'inseparably linked with Judaism is Zionism—a bourgeois-nationalist movement which arose at the end of the nineteenth century; this reactionary trend is rooted in the idea of the exclusiveness of the Jewish people'.

Sentiment for Israel and latent interest in immigration to the Jewish state—both highly unpalatable to the regime—are invariably ascribed to 'Zionist propaganda'—propaganda of a movement long declared defunct.

'Believing the Zionist lies', Nekhama Fogel decided to go to Israel, reported *Radianska Ukraina* on 10 January 1960. The trade union daily *Trud*, of 17 July 1960, published a letter by a 'group of Jews', who, 'deceived by Zionist propaganda, had left the Soviet Union for Israel'.

[1] Léneman, op. cit., pp. 295–7.

The popular magazine *Ogonek* (August 1960) sadly told the story of two members of the Gershuni family who, 'succumbing to Zionist propaganda, emigrated to Israel'. *Sovetskaya Byelorussia* (26 February 1961) assailed 'deceitful propaganda of the bourgeois Zionists'. *Sovetskaya Moldavia* (27 May 1961) upbraided the Zionists for 'kindling nationalist feelings'.

The Soviet propaganda machinery is busily tracing a 'Zionist hand' in every manifestation of Jewish national identity and self-assertion. Almost two full generations of Soviet Jews have grown up without ever having read a Zionist article or book or heard a word of Zionist indoctrination. Yet the Soviet regime still hunts Zionism with nearly obsessive persistence:[1] 'Why whip a dead horse?' asked B. Z. Goldberg, a noted pro-Soviet, non-Zionist author, after his visit to the U.S.S.R. in 1959.[2]

Apparently, deep in their hearts, the Soviet authorities are not sure that the horse is dead. Zionism is the most active national Jewish spiritual force, the living idea of the common origin, culture and destiny of the Jewish people. Branding it as an enemy and coupling it with 'Jewish bourgeois nationalists', which might include most Jews in the capitalist world, warns Soviet Jews to hold themselves aloof from things Jewish abroad.

The same motive accounts for anti-Israel propaganda within the Soviet Union. Israel is a small country indeed in the global scheme of Soviet foreign policy. Do the Soviet Jews have such sympathy for Israel that a strong antidote is necessary to rid them of it?

This seems, indeed, to be the case, according to a recent (December 1965) special issue, *Israel in the Soviet Mirror* of the authoritative series 'Jews in Eastern Europe'.[3] The study and analysis of a rich assortment of articles, drawn from a wide variety of Soviet papers, shows that these are replete with 'monotonous and obtrusive repetition of charges that Zionist and Israel leaders are accomplices of the Nazis, practise an odious racialism, are cynical confederates of neo-Nazism, and act as instruments of imperialist repression against former colonial peoples'. The amount of newspaper space and the intensity of abuse allocated to Israel and Zionism is clearly out of all proportion to their intrinsic importance to Soviet foreign policies:[4]

[1] At the October 1965 session of the United Nations Third (Social, Humanitarian and Cultural) Committee, dealing with the draft Convention for the Elimination of All Forms of Racial Discrimination, the Soviet delegation offered an amendment equating Nazism with Zionism. (*Israel Horizons*, New York, November 1965; *The Jewish Chronicle*, London, 22 October 1965.)

[2] B. Z. Goldberg, *The Jewish Problem in Soviet Russia*, New York, 1961, p. 272.

[3] Published by European Jewish Publications Ltd., London.

[4] *The New York Times*, 4 and 5 December 1966.

The Soviet reader could easily get the impression that Israel was a powerful country; that she played a key role in the aggressive policies of the imperialists, conducting far-reaching subversion in Africa, Asia and even in the Soviet Union itself.

There is undoubtedly a pronounced ambivalence in the Soviet attitude towards Israel. On the positive side, there has been in the past two years a certain expansion of cultural exchange between the U.S.S.R. and Israel, chiefly in the musical field. Artists and other cultural representatives of each country have been enthusiastically received in the host country. This is, of course, arranged through Soviet Government channels, which means that the authorities knowingly permit the Soviet public, and in particular the Soviet Jewish audience, to warm itself in the glow of these expanded contacts.

It was also considered significant that the Moscow weekly, *New Times* (which appears in English and other European languages, as well as in Russian), published a lengthy paraphrase of a letter to the editor on 15 November 1965, from one Mordechai Kaspi, then the Moscow correspondent for the Israeli communist paper, *Kol Ha'Am*. The letter took strong exception to an article attacking Israel which had appeared in an earlier issue of the paper and pointed out that it was wrong and unjust to portray Israel in black colours only, for Israel also has a proletariat, a communist party and other 'progressive' forces. The letter also insisted that Israel had as much right to the waters of the river Jordan as the Arab states. What seems to be most remarkable about this publication is not only that Kaspi's pro-Israel views were published, but that the editor concluded with the following unprecedented remark: 'We publish these comments of an Israeli communist journalist in the belief that they will give our readers a more rounded and objective picture of Arab–Israel relations.'

These modest positive developments are more than balanced by hostile moves.

In the Arab–Israel conflict, particularly in regard to Syria, Soviet propaganda invariably takes a pronounced anti-Israel stand. For a time the Soviet press had eliminated extreme anti-Israel passages from reports of speeches by Arab leaders. But *Izvestiya* on 4 April 1966 reproduced in full the Syrian Premier's statement that 'Israel continues to be the major imperialist bastion in this region and a bridgehead which imperialism and neo-colonialism use to rob the markets of Asia and of Africa.' And on 8 May, the official Soviet journal wrote that Israel's Prime Minister was seeking to inflame anti-Syrian sentiments by alleging Syrian responsibility for the activity of 'mythical diversionary groups' and for the existence in

Syria of a terrorist centre directed against Israel. When the majority of the U.N. Security Council voted on 4 November 1966 in favour of a resolution condemning the Syrian Government for terrorist raids on Israel by Syria-based El Fatah commandos, a Soviet veto blocked its formal acceptance. The Soviet Union continues its policy of making massive arms deliveries to Egypt, in full knowledge that these arms are intended for use against Israel. At the same time, *Pravda* wrote on 4 December 1966 that 'the Soviet Union is interested in lessening tension and securing peace in the Middle East. . . . It is not on the battlefield but on construction sites that people build their future.' The article contained an apparent hint to the Soviet-backed regime in Syria to tone down its calls for a 'war of liberation' against Israel.

Israel's concern for the plight of the three million Jews in the U.S.S.R. was branded in a Moscow French-language transmission of 6 July 1966 as 'an orchestrated and officially sanctioned campaign' to slander the Soviet Union by suggesting that Soviet Jews feel attached to Israel and by alleging that 'danger threatens the Jews in the U.S.S.R.': Jews of the Soviet Union, said the radio commentator, have a country of their own, and 'they have not felt, they cannot feel, any particular attraction to Israel'. The comment ended on a threatening note addressed to the 'instigators' of the 'campaign'.

In an abrupt departure from a long-established policy, the Soviet Premier, Aleksei Kosygin announced on 3 December 1966 that 'as far as the reunification of families is concerned, if some families wish to meet or if they want to leave the Soviet Union, the road is open to them and there is no problem in this ...'. This statement, distributed by the Soviet embassy in Paris, assumes additional significance because of its publication, on 5 December, on the front page of *Izvestiya*, the official organ of the Soviet Government: for the first time a major announcement on a matter of Jewish interest was publicized not only 'for export' but also for domestic information.

Kosygin's announcement stimulated a large number of applications for permits to leave for Israel. The latest information indicates, however, that applicants are being strongly discouraged by Soviet officials and press. The latter is publishing articles and letters to the editor, which paint life in Israel in the blackest possible colours and call on Jews not to leave their Soviet motherland for capitalist Israel.

The Israeli Government spares no efforts to improve relations with the Soviet Union. In the spring of 1967, Gideon Rafael, Israel's new chief delegate to the United Nations, made a detour of a thousand miles to Moscow on his way to New York and spent a week in the Soviet capital, establishing personal contact with the moulders of Soviet policies in the Middle East. Another approach in the same direction was made by Yigal Allon, Israel's Labour Minister, who went to Leningrad ostensibly as the head of a delegation to the international conference on social insurance. The Soviet attitude, however, remained implacably hostile. Egypt and Syria became the beneficiaries of a most generous Soviet economic and military aid, amounting to 2 (U.S.) billion dollars. Moscow has also given unconditional political support to militant Arab nationalism directed against Israel. Soviet representatives in the United Nations steadfastly opposed and vetoed several U.N. votes on numberless acts of Syrian aggression during recent years. When Egypt's President Nasser closed the Straits of Tiran to Israel shipping, the U.S.S.R. not only approved of this move, but also threatened military intervention against any outside power or group of powers that might take action to restore freedom of movement through the Straits.

Relying largely on Soviet backing and on abundant and modern military hardware supplied by the U.S.S.R., Egypt and Syria, reinforced by a last-minute alliance with Jordan, encircled Israel with a ring of steel. On 5–11 June, Israel's defence army and airforce inflicted a smashing defeat on the armies of the three Arab countries, destroying hundreds of Russian-made MIGs and tanks.

While deeply disappointed by the poor performance of the Arab forces it had so lavishly equipped, the Soviet Government continued, and intensified, its political support to the Arab states. On 10 June 1967 it broke off diplomatic relations with Israel; other countries of the Soviet bloc (Poland, Czechoslovakia, Hungary, Bulgaria, and Yugoslavia) followed suit; only Rumania refused to do so. In the U.N. Security Council, Soviet delegate Nikolai Federenko branded Israel as 'aggressor' and out-harangued the Arab representatives in invective and incitement against Israel. Subsequently, so did Premier Kosygin in the General Assembly. Simultaneously, the Soviet authorities withdrew permission from forty Soviet Jews to leave for Israel to rejoin relatives. They had already obtained exit visas, had purchased tickets for the trip, had given up their homes and sold their belongings.

An intensified radio and press campaign was also launched in which, characteristically, Zionism and Zionists, rather than the State and people of Israel, were pictured as the real villain: a pointed distinction was made between 'criminal' Zionism and the ordinary Israeli citizen. A broadcast by Moscow Radio in Hungarian on 6 July insisted that propagators of Zionism were not to be confused with the people of Israel. The theme that

Zionism was evil and the Israeli people merely one of its victims, was picked up on 13 July by *Komsomolskaya Pravda* which reaches an estimated 15 million readers, and *Za Rubezhom* (4 August). In an article 'What is Zionism?', *Sovietskaya Latvia* (5 August) described Zionism as a kind of international 'Cosa Nostra'—the Sicilian criminal Mafia organization—which was active behind the international scenes through the 'wide network of Zionist organizations, with a common centre, a common programme and funds'. This new version of the Protocols of the Elders of Zion claimed that 'the latest aggression of Israeli militarism against the Arab states' was 'a classical example of the practices of the Zionist corporation', so powerful that Israel's ruling circles were only its junior partners. In a broadcast in Czech and Slovak, on 7 September, Moscow Radio argued that Zionism had no justification for identifying itself with the State of Israel, where there were exploited and exploiters, working people and racialists and reactionaries: Zionism, 'the enemy of all working people', was, in the first place, the enemy of the Jews.

SELECTED BIBLIOGRAPHY[1]

(In addition to the references in the footnotes)

Goldberg, B. Z., *The Jewish Problem in Soviet Russia*, New York, 1961.

Goldman, Guido G., *Zionism under Soviet Rule, 1917–28*, New York, 1960.

Horowitz, David, *The State in the Making*, New York, 1953.

Lénéman, Léon, *La Tragédie des Juifs en U.R.S.S.*, Paris, 1959.

Pines, Dan, *Hechalutz B'kur Hamahapecha* (The Hechalutz in the Crucible of the Revolution), Tel Aviv, 1938.

Schechtman, Joseph B., *Star in Eclipse: Russian Jewry Revisited*, New York, 1961.

Schechtman, Joseph B., *Zionism and Zionists in Soviet Russia. Greatness and Drama*, New York, 1966.

Tsentsiper, Aryeh Leib, *Esser Sh'not R'difot* (Ten Years of Persecution), Tel Aviv, 1930.

Tsentsiper, Aryeh Leib, *Ba-Ma'avak li-Geulah* (In the Struggle for Redemption), Tel Aviv, 1956.

West, Benjamin (ed.), *Struggle of a Generation; the Jews under Soviet rule*, Tel Aviv, 1959.

[1] See also chapters 16 and 17.

7

The Jewish Population: Demographic Trends and Occupational Patterns

ALEC NOVE AND J. A. NEWTH

A. *What information is there?*

The present chapter has a dual aim: to examine in outline the demographic development of Soviet Jewry over the first fifty years of Soviet power; and in the light of our findings to attempt to construct a picture of the current sociological scene, as it affects the Jews. Little will be said—for little is known—about the specifically oriental Jews of the Caucasus or Turkestan; the geographical centre of our attention will be the traditional Pale of Settlement, the western fringe of the present-day territory of the U.S.S.R., plus Moscow and Leningrad.

At the very outset, we must offer a few brief comments on the nature of the statistical materials with which we have to deal. There have been five published censuses of population since the Revolution; in 1920, 1923, 1926, 1939, and 1959. The first and second of these were very incomplete; the census of 1920 was carried out before the dust of the civil war had settled, while that of 1923 was confined to urban areas. In fact, however, in 1923 the term 'urban' was construed in a wider sense than in later administrative practice, and included many of the small 'market towns' (*mestechko, shtetl*) of the former Pale with their dense Jewish communities; soon after 1923 most of these places were down-graded to the status of villages, and tended to wither away for reasons which will be mentioned below. The census of 1926 is both comprehensive and fully detailed, and it remains our main source of information for the early Soviet period. The census of 1939 was never published in full—its findings were of course rendered to a major extent obsolete by the onset of the war, and we are here limited to the few scraps of information published before the war, one book by a Jewish author on the situation of the Jews in the U.S.S.R. which was published in Moscow within a few weeks of the German invasion, and to a rather meagre selection of items as at 1939 included in the report of the 1959 census. This last gives us a very considerable body of organized information, but again has many gaps which can be filled only by informed guesswork.

As to the quality of the analysis to which these materials and the results of other *ad hoc* investigations have been subjected, we should note that in the twenties and for most of the thirties a body of Jewish Soviet scholars, receiving official support and access to official materials, were concerned with research into the situation of Soviet Jews in all its aspects, and with drafting proposals for such remedial measures as seemed desirable; since the war—if we except the 1948 study by Lev Zinger, which is a revised version of his 1941 work, with a new but virtually useless chapter on the war and immediate post-war period—no such work has been undertaken in the U.S.S.R.; or at least none has been published; and we are at the mercy of the formal official attitude. The normal practice at the present time (i.e. since the mid-fifties, when the publication of any kind of really usable statistical material was resumed) is to classify material concerning national (ethnic) groups under the headings of the titular nationalities of the fifteen Union republics (Russians, Ukrainians, Byelorussians . . . Turkmens, Estonians) in a stereotyped order; sometimes followed by the nationalities of the autonomous republics (Bashkirs, Tatars, and so forth), leaving all groups which are not associated with a first or second grade territorial unit in an undifferentiated residual. The categories of information which are not subject to this rule will be noted below.

Next, the question of the consistency of the data, i.e. the stability of the category 'Jewish'. It has been the practice in all Soviet censuses that the data should be collected by enumerators, who interview each member of the population and record on the appropriate forms the verbal replies given to the census questionnaire. For the enumerators' guidance (and perhaps the respondents' also) lists of nationalities, languages, occupations, and so on are drawn up; and the respondent is technically free to answer questions as to his nationality or native tongue, etc., in any way he pleases; the enumerator's duty is simply to record the response in the form in which it is given. The onus then rests on the citizen to decide to which national group he belongs, or what language he considers to be his mother-tongue; and it is on him, rather than on the officials responsible for carrying out the census, that the social pressures discussed below will operate. As to the question of infants, a difficulty only arises if the parents belong to different national groups; and here it appears to be the practice to record the infant under the nationality of its *mother* for the purposes of the census.

There exists at the present time, however, a completely separate system of nationality recording which is by no means necessarily compatible with census data; urban residents at the age of 16 have, since the introduction of the system in 1934, received an internal passport in which is recorded *inter alia* their nationality. Since the passport document has to be produced, e.g. on application for admission to a university or when applying for a job, it is always possible for the personnel department of an establishment to specify quite readily the national composition of its staff. Nevertheless, while Soviet manpower planning and recording is extremely detailed and precise for all qualified personnel, it is extremely imprecise at the lower levels of manpower, and so no central index may exist which would enable the authorities to determine rapidly the number of persons of a given nationality currently employed in the Soviet economy as a whole. The cost of procuring such information would be very great, and it would impose an intolerable burden on the overworked statistical services; nor is it easy to think of any practical benefit to the operation of the economy which could ensue from such an exercise. It is quite another matter when we look at the case of, say, the medical profession, for which we may reasonably suppose the Health Ministry keeps a central registry to assist in its task of ensuring the appropriate distribution of the medical services.

B. *What, then, is a Jew?*

Has the definition in fact been constant? Has the pressure of opinion or the methods by which the census has been taken been such as to distort the figure at different dates, or more at some dates than others? It is the nature of these kinds of questions that they admit of no definite answer. In tsarist days there were no statistics of Jewish nationality, only of Jewish religion. Any Jew who chose to become Greek Orthodox or Catholic ceased to be categorized as a Jew. It is only in Soviet times that an official Jewish nationality appeared in the census and in documents and statistics. The entering of a Jewish nationality on papers was not in itself a reflection of any intention to identify Jews as such, and certainly had nothing to do with antisemitism. The Soviet Union is a multinational state, and many of its nationalities are highly self-conscious and would resent the omission of their nationality from their identity papers and passports. For example a Georgian is very proud of being a Georgian and would like always to be considered such. The Soviet authorities themselves liked to produce statistics showing the relative backwardness and rate of advance of various nationalities within the Union. It is true that the Jewish nationality did not fit into the usual Marxist definitions of what constitutes a separate nation, since it lacked a definite territory. None the less, since the large majority of Jews felt themselves to be such, and the vast majority of the other nationalities of the U.S.S.R. regarded the Jews as being members of a nationality other than their own, legal and documentary recognition was given to this.

As already pointed out, until 1934 there was no compulsory carrying of documents on which the nationality of the citizen was marked, and consequently a man who might have answered a nationality question in one way in the 1926 census might well have declared a different nationality when these documents were issued eight years later. However, in 1934 there seemed no particular reason to alter or conceal one's nationality. Once documented as a Jew (or a Georgian, or Ukrainian, or Uzbek) the citizen could not change his nationality of his own volition. Children would be registered in the nationality of their parents. It was virtually impossible to change one's surname, and this too added to the practical difficulties of adopting a different nationality.

In any country the concept of Jewish nationality is hard to define. There have been some remarkable court cases involving this question in Israel. Elsewhere it is often said that a Jew is a person who says that he is a Jew. In religious times one could opt out by adopting a different religion. In Nazi times it was impossible to opt out at all. The point is by no means an insignificant one. If, as happened in January 1959, 2,267,814 persons (or in the case of children, their parents) answered the question concerning nationality by saying 'Jew', this represents one possible measure of the number of Jews in the Soviet Union. The figure could be understated, however, if anyone who was desirous to conceal his nationality chose to make a false statement. Thus a man who was and felt himself to be a Jew but who lived somewhere in the depths of Siberia, among neighbours who did not know he was a Jew, might well prefer to claim Russian nationality to the census taker, since the census taker might well be a local inhabitant. In this instance the person in question makes an incorrect statement with regard to what he really feels. It is another matter, or can be said to be another matter, if the individual actually wishes to forget that his parents were Jewish and is using the census to establish a genuinely held claim to be a Russian. No one who knows the drive towards assimilation which was characteristic of a portion of the Jewish intellectuals in Russia can doubt that such persons also exist.

Here one must introduce a complication. It is highly probable that some of both the last-named categories of individuals are recorded as Jews on their internal passports. This means that there is another, legal, definition of Jews: all persons recorded as such on their passports. Since these documents have to be produced whenever one applies for a job, it follows that statistics of Jewish doctors, scientific workers, graduates or students are based not on what the persons in question said to the census enumerator, but on the entry in their documents. Unfortunately it does not follow that the Soviet authorities have before them an accurate total of so-called 'passport Jews'. The reason is simple: passports are issued only to adults and only to residents in urban areas, with some exceptions. Therefore nationality statistics based solely on passport data are meaningless and are quite possibly not collected at all. It is none the less possible that perhaps several hundreds of thousands of individuals, who are entered as Jews on their passports, did not describe themselves as such to the census enumerator, and there was no need at this point to produce documents, so that their mis-statement could not have been identified. It must be emphasized, however, that this is the merest surmise, which is based on no firm proof in the very nature of things.

The situation is still further complicated by the large number of mixed marriages. Statistics have already been quoted showing that mixed marriages were very prevalent in the Russian republic (R.S.F.S.R.) as early as 1926. This reflected the relatively weak sense of Jewish nationality, and the marked tendency towards assimilation, in Moscow and Leningrad in particular. Mixed marriages were far fewer in the predominantly Yiddish-speaking areas of the west. However, it is these areas that suffered grievously from the Nazi massacres. The combined effects of the destruction of much of Jewish community life, and the relatively much greater weight among the survivors of the more assimilated and non-Yiddish-speaking Jews, inevitably increased the general rate of mixed marriages.[1] Small children are generally registered as having the nationality of their mother, but they have the right at the age of 16 to opt for either nationality. But of course in answering census questions the nationality given could be that of the father. We have no means of telling, and neither have the

---

[1] As everywhere, the U.S.S.R. has long maintained a system of birth registration, and in this case also it appears to be the practice to register the infant's nationality as that of its mother in the case of mixed marriages. It would then appear that the proper interpretation of statistics (available only for the twenties) on birth- and death-rates for specific national groups is some- what uncertain for births, although obviously unambiguous for deaths; in the case of the birth-rates, there are three individuals concerned (father, mother, and child), and unless the parents state when registering the birth that all three belong to the same group, it is hard to see what sort of rate is being measured. If then, as seems reasonable, the children of mixed marriages are not recorded as contributing to the birth-rate of the national groups of either parent, the effect will be to diminish the apparent national birth-rates concerned. If for example there are in a certain place 10,000 Jews; in a given year 400 married couples (in each case Jewish husband and wife) have a child, while a further 100 couples (let us say, in 50 cases Jewish husband and Russian wife, and in the other 50 cases Russian husband and Jewish wife) also each have a child, the recorded births for Jews will be 400, although the local registry office records will show the birth of 450 children registered as Jewish.

census takers. The available evidence suggests that more Jewish men marry non-Jewish wives than vice versa. This would suggest that more of the children of mixed marriages under the age of 16 would be registered as non-Jews. On the other hand, it seems inherently more probable that children of a Jewish father, bearing an obviously Jewish surname, are likely at the age of 16 to write down their nationality as Jewish. It might otherwise seem odd that an individual whose surname is Finkelstein and who is living in Kiev should claim Ukrainian nationality. But this too is the purest surmise. It may be significant that there are two women deputies to the Supreme Soviet, named respectively Resnik and Spivak, neither of whom is stated to be Jewish. They might well be daughters of mixed marriages, with a Jewish father.

In view of all the above complications, it seems to us extraordinary that various sources continue not only to claim that the official Soviet census figure is a vast understatement, but even to substitute accurate-looking figures of their own. Thus a newspaper in Israel boldly cited a figure of 3,437,000 as the right one. We can agree that a correction for the difference between passport entries and census claims could well be significant. However, we see no grounds for claiming any precise figure, and can only re-emphasize the uncertainties both of definition and of enumeration. It would be another matter if we could see evidence of political pressure designed to persuade either the Jews or the census takers so to act as to understate the number of Jews in Russia. This does not seem to be the case.

It may be that the relatively high figures quoted by critics in Israel and elsewhere are based on an underestimate of wartime losses and above all on an overestimate of the natural growth of population. It should not be forgotten that fertility among the Jews has been consistently well below the All-Union average, and the effect of mixed marriages has been still further to depress the rate of growth of the Jewish population, and perhaps to turn it in some years into a minus figure.

C. *Changes in numbers, locations, age composition*

With the caveats indicated above, we proceed to the first part of our analysis: the total number and territorial distribution of Soviet Jews over the last half-century.

Over the twenty years preceding the Revolution, the number of Jews in the area which was to become the U.S.S.R. (the territory of the twenties and thirties) remained virtually constant, with perhaps a small reduction in numbers. The prime cause of this stability was heavy emigration particularly to the United States, which received during these two decades about half a million Jews originating from future Soviet territory. Until the very end of the imperial period Jews were, of course, denied the opportunity of free migration to the east of (broadly) the future borders of the R.S.F.S.R., so that at the beginning of this century only about one Jew in seven lived to the east of the Pale. The great majority of the Jews were urban: but at this time the term covers a very wide spectrum, from the Jewish communities in large cities—Odessa, for example, had about 150,000 Jews before the Revolution—down to the often minuscule *shtetls* with a Jewish population of a couple of hundred. The overwhelming majority of the non-Jewish inhabitants of the Pale were Ukrainian or Byelorussian peasants, whose birth- and death-rates (and natural increase rates) were significantly higher than those of the Jews. During the First World War and the civil war the Jews of the Pale (now legally abolished) were in the zone of the front; their birth-rate fell off sharply, infant mortality was high, and on top of the inevitable hardships and the mass deportations of wartime came a wave of pogroms which claimed a large number of Jewish victims (possibly as many as 100,000), particularly in the exposed small towns.

The effect of the Bolshevik Revolution on the way of life of the Jewish communities was disastrous economically. During the war-communism period, when private trade was banned, and even small workshops 'nationalized', Jewish traders and craftsmen were left destitute in the areas under Soviet control, as well as being adversely affected by fighting in the civil war. In 1921 trading and private workshops were once again legalized, but their scope was restricted by lack of materials and things to sell, and these restrictions were intensified after 1926 as part of the government's effort to squeeze out private enterprise, culminating in virtually total nationalization at the end of the decade. This made it appallingly hard to earn a living by traditional means in the towns (and especially the *shtetls*) of the old Pale of Settlement. The Revolution provided new opportunities, which the young seized eagerly, but there was a painful process of adjustment, and the Jewish Section of the party was active at this time proposing various schemes of retraining and resettlement, to cope with a very acute problem.

In consequence, there was extensive Jewish migration into the big cities (the Jewish population of Odessa shot up to 190,000 in 1920) and the tide of migration over the eastern border set in. By 1923 Moscow (with 86,000 Jews) and Petrograd (52,000) had become the largest Jewish towns after Kiev and Odessa: the Jewish population of Odessa had now shrunk to

130,000 as the refugees of the civil war period returned to their home or migrated from the district; Kiev had shown a steadily increasing Jewish population throughout the period: 1897, 27,000; 1910, 51,000; 1920, 111,000; 1923, 129,000. Odessa was now a frontier city on the Rumanian border; Kiev, although not yet the capital of the Ukrainian S.S.R. (up to 1934 Kharkov held this rank), was already a major administrative, industrial and cultural centre.

In the interval between the end of the civil war and the end of 1926, when the New Economic Policy was at its height, the Jewish population expanded at a steady rate *pari passu* with the population as a whole, while the process of migration from west to east continued. In 1923 and 1926 the Jewish population of the three main sectors was as follows:

	1923 (ʼ000)	1926 (ʼ000)
Ukraine	1,483	1,574
Byelorussia	423	407
R.S.F.S.R. and rest of U.S.S.R.	525	620
Total	2,431	2,601

The 1926 total given here omits the approximately 80,000 Asiatic Jews, many of whom (in Khiva and Bukhara) would not have been Soviet citizens in 1923.

Natural increase tended, as we shall see, to be higher in the western areas than in the R.S.F.S.R., so that we can suppose that these figures reflect a migration of something over 60,000 persons to the east in this interval— perhaps about 20,000 per annum.[1] We shall see that the tempo of migration appears to accelerate during the years 1927 to 1939. Meanwhile, this migration process involved the growth of the Jewish population of large towns at the expense of the rural areas and small towns, not only across the former Pale boundary, but also within it. As to the first point, the growth of the Jewish population of Moscow and Leningrad between 1923 and 1926 was 72,000, while the growth of the rest of the R.S.F.S.R. and all other areas east of the Pale was only 23,000 (excluding Asiatic Jews in both cases). In the Ukraine, the total Jewish population of the thirty-seven *okrug* (district) centres increased in this interval from 765,000 to 849,000, i.e. by 11 per cent, while the rest of the Jewish population of the Ukraine

[1] The 1923 estimate refers to the beginning of the year; the 1926 one, to December 1926. Assuming even growth from 2,431,000 to 2,601,000 (i.e. about 7 per cent) was paralleled in each region, we should have for 1926: Ukraine, 1,587,000; Byelorussia, 453,000; R.S.F.S.R., 561,000. The difference between this 561,000 and the observed 620,000 indicates an eastward movement of at least 60,000, overwhelmingly from Byelorussia.

increased by only 1 per cent. In spite of heavy migration out of Byelo-russia, the same phenomenon was observed: the *okrug* towns gained 3 per cent while the rest of the republic lost 9 per cent of its population. At this stage the main industrial centres of the Ukraine had not begun to attract large numbers of Jews; the basic tendency seems to have been to shift from small places to larger within the same area rather than to migrate over longer distances, unless one was going right out of the region.

At this stage we should pause to examine the age and sex composition of the Jewish population of the U.S.S.R. as at 1926. As we would expect, the Jews of both Byelorussia and the Ukraine had a higher proportion of women than the total population of these areas:

		Women per Thousand Men, 1926
Byelorussia:	Jews	1,122
	total population	1,042
Ukraine:	Jews	1,140
	total population	1,058

Numerous factors contribute to the explanation of this: the greater tendency of Jews to migrate—men being more likely to migrate than women; the more favourable Jewish death-rate—women tend to survive longer than men, especially if they bear fewer children, and the lower the total death-rate, the more pronounced this effect becomes; men were in general more susceptible to the risks of pogroms Conversely—as a demonstration of the migration effect—the Jews in the R.S.F.S.R. had a lower proportion of women than the general population (1,040 Jewish women per thousand men; general population, 1,094 women per thousand men). For similar reasons, there were considerable differences in the age-structure of R.S.F.S.R. Jews compared with the inhabitants of the former Pale.

The most striking disparity emerging from the table on p. 134 is the extreme difference in fertility between east and west; a crude, but for the present purpose effective, measure is to compare the number of children under 5 with the number of adults between 20 and 39. For the R.S.F.S.R., we find about one child per six such adults; for the western regions, about one child per three adults—fertility was twice as high. Even allowing for the obvious point that very many of the 'easterners' were recent immigrants who had not yet had time to settle down and found a family, while the 'westerners' were to a much larger extent permanent residents, the disparity is very great.

Age-structure of Jewish Population, 1926 (in per cent)
(west = Ukraine and Byelorussia; east = R.S.F.S.R. and other republics)

	east	west
0–4	7·0	11·7
5–9	6·2	8·3
10–14	6·8	10·3
15–19	10·3	12·5
20–24	13·7	10·8
25–29	13·5	9·7
30–34	10·1	7·0
35–39	7·2	5·7
40–44	5·4	4·8
45–49	4·6	4·3
50 and over	15·2	14·9

This low fertility was associated with a low birth-rate (as indicated by the published figures, which may have tended to understate the position, for the reasons indicated above) and with the low death-rate which one would expect in a population with such a high proportion of young adults. The net result was that the Jewish population of the R.S.F.S.R. had a very much lower rate of natural increase than the Russian population of that republic (10 per thousand, as against 30 per thousand). In the Ukraine and Byelorussia, the gap was considerably less:

Natural Increase Rates, 1926–7

Ukraine:	Ukrainians	25 per thousand
	Jews	16
Byelorussia:	Byelorussians	27
	Jews	18

The high rates for the population at large, which was at this date over-whelmingly rural, were bound to fall as urbanization proceeded (and were of course much reduced in the event by collectivization); but it was already clear by 1926 that the Jewish communities of the R.S.F.S.R. were approaching the point at which their numbers could only be sustained by a stream of new immigrants from less sophisticated areas. The net repro-duction rate would seem to have already fallen to a point at which in the long run without this immigration the Jewish population would have begun to dwindle; and in addition we must take account of the pheno-menon of mixed marriages. Already by 1926, the proportion of Jewish marriages was:

Jewish husband, Jewish wife	75 per cent
Jewish husband, non-Jewish wife	25 per cent

Jewish wife, Jewish husband   83 per cent
Jewish wife, non-Jewish husband   17 per cent

These figures refer to the R.S.F.S.R.; the corresponding figures for the Ukraine and Byelorussia were much lower. We note two points: first, more Jewish men than Jewish women were getting married (the figures quoted suggest ten men to nine women), and second, men were more likely to marry outside their minority community than women. If we confine our attention for the moment to 'legal' or 'registration' assimilation, as distinct from the social realities, it is evident that there would be more cases of children with Jewish fathers and non-Jewish mothers (hence recorded as non-Jewish children) than the reverse; and that this would lead with accelerating intensity to absorption. We must not, however, exaggerate the speed at which this process would operate; if the situation indicated here continued unchanged for an indefinite period, the rate of absorption would be 10 per cent per generation.

Such an absorption rate, applying only to the most 'advanced' section of the country, whose population was continually being replenished by immigration, would have hardly any perceptible effect in a mere half-century; the main form taken by assimilation—if indeed statistically measurable assimilation has taken place—would be social assimilation: that a man or woman registered at birth as a Jew should cease to consider himself or herself as Jewish in the conditions of daily life and also when the time came to stand up and be counted. The total number of Jews at any moment of time is therefore a vague and uncertain quantity, and must inevitably become more and more so as time goes on.

Although the period 1926–39 includes many investigations of Jewish working conditions and so on, we have a chasm in our sources of information as to total numbers and location until the census of 1939. As indicated above, little of the results of this census appeared in print at the time; we have, however, enough to give us a tentative picture of the developments of the intervening period. As to the territorial distribution in 1939 of the Jewish population—and indeed of the Soviet population as a whole—we are perhaps entitled to look at the official figures with some reserve; it is quite certain that at that date a substantial number of persons, running into several million adults, had been obliged to leave their homes and were engaged in one of the various forms of forced labour, often in remote areas; and we have reason to suspect that in some at least of these cases the deportees were recorded in the census under the district from which they came, rather than the district in which they happened to be at the time. Since deportation into Byelorussia or the Ukraine was virtually unknown, whereas deportation to the thinly populated eastern areas of the R.S.F.S.R. or of the Asiatic republics was common enough, it is possible that the alleged number of Jews in Byelorussia and the Ukraine in 1939 is in fact somewhat exaggerated. One can only speculate on the categories of the Jewish population who might have been deported: the dual impact of collectivization and the destruction of local handicraft industries might have led to the denunciation of some small-town and rural Jews in the western region as kulaks; and the series of purges of officials and intellectuals (Jews being strongly represented in both categories) certainly involved many Jews.

But taking the figures as given, we are informed that the Jewish population of the then U.S.S.R. rose between 1926 and 1939 from 2,680,000 to 3,020,000: both figures include Asiatic Jews, who numbered 80,000 in 1926. If we assume that this last group—who had in fact (and still have) little contact with European Jews—increased at the same average rate as their non-Jewish neighbours (Uzbeks, Georgians, Dagestanis), i.e. by about 25 per cent, we should have the European Jewish population of 2·6 millions increasing in twelve years to about 2,920,000; or about 11·2 per cent over the period, about 0·9 per cent per annum. This compares with an increase in the total Soviet population of 15·9 per cent over the same period (1·2 per cent per annum), including several years in the early thirties when the increase was negligible.

The pre-1926 trends in Jewish internal migration continued in the interval 1926–39; the Jewish population of the Ukraine fell from 1,574,000 to 1,533,000; and of Byelorussia from 407,000 to 375,000; consequently, the rest of the country rose from 699,000 to 1,112,000. If we assume again that natural increase was uniform overall, this would imply a migration of some 324,000 persons from west to east, or about 30,000 per annum. In broad terms, the rate of migration out of the former Pale area into the interior during the pre-war Soviet period was of the same order of magnitude as the migration westward out of the tsarist empire in the twenty years before the Revolution; but since fertility had now fallen, the Jewish population of the former Pale was now slowly shrinking.

In this connection, we may at this point review the changing age and sex structure of the Soviet Jewish population. Comparing 1939 with 1926, we see that both males and females increased by the same amount:

	1926 ('000)	1939 ('000)	Changes ('000)
Males	1,267	1,437	+ 170
Females	1,413	1,583	+ 170

In other words, since boys and girls are born in approximately equal numbers, the number of male deaths during the period was about equal to the number of female deaths.

The collectivization crisis (1930–4) hit the peasantry much more severely than the urban population; and since we know that in the twenties the Jewish population had a rather favourable death-rate, that they were predominantly and increasingly urbanized, and tended as time wore on to move into 'middle class' occupations, we can hardly be wrong in supposing that the Jewish death-rates (specific for age and sex) were more favourable during the period 1926–39 than the population as a whole.

Anticipating the march of events to a slight extent, we note that the age-distribution of Polish Jews (many of whom entered the U.S.S.R. in 1939) as at the last Polish census of 1931, was:[1]

	0–14	15–49	50–64		65 and over (per cent)	
Polish Jews	29·6	53·8	11·3		5·3	
U.S.S.R. Jews, 1926	29·0	56·3	——	14·7		——
U.S.S.R. Jews, 1939	29·1	55·3	——	15·6		——

This close similarity seems to entitle us to suppose that the incorporation of the Jews of the so-called 'western Byelorussia' and 'western Ukraine' in 1939 made virtually no difference to the demographic structure of the Soviet Jewish population.

At each of the census dates (1926 and 1939) the Jewish age-distribution clearly appears as a much more 'advanced' one than that for Soviet citizens at large; the general Jewish age distribution is in fact rather more like that of the U.S.S.R. in the late fifties (after the colossal losses of 1941–5) than that of the U.S.S.R. in the thirties. Nor is this surprising; for a relatively long period the Jews had had a much lower birth-rate and a more favourable death-rate; fewer Jews were born, but they tended to live longer. The most striking change in the Jewish age-distribution indicated by our figures, however, is the rapid decline, both in absolute numbers and per-centagewise, in the age-groups which would have provided the students of the twenties and thirties: about 900,000 Jews aged between 15 and 29 in 1926, and only about 750,000 in 1939. This fall is matched by a rise in the group which would be at the height of its working powers (aged 30 to 44): an increase from 490,000 in 1926 to 760,000 in 1939. The calculations on which these conclusions are based are relatively unsophisticated, and

[1] Szyja Bronsztejn; *Ludnosc zydowska w Polsce w okresie miedzywojennym*, Wroclaw, 1963, p. 138. The writers are obliged to Mr. R. Jenkins of Glasgow University for this reference. The 1939 figures are calculated estimates.

the margin of error substantial; but it seems very improbable that they are seriously at fault.

Our figures also give us a glimpse of what might have been, had there been no war and no massacre: in 1926, the proportion of children was lower among the Jewish community than among the population as a whole; at all ages above about 15, the Jewish proportion was relatively higher. By 1939, the percentage of Jews in all age groups up to about 30 was relatively lower—the 'turnover point', so to speak, had moved up with the passing of time. Even if we allow for the reduction in the general birth-rate and the improvement in death-rates concomitant upon urbanization, it was virtually inevitable that the Jewish population should become relatively older (compared with the general population) as time went on; and by the present day, we would expect a 'turnover point' around the age of 50. The effect of mixed marriages upon this process would have been slight (from a 'biological' point of view); the social pressures that might have operated in a situation which did not in fact take place are a subject for rather unprofitable speculation.

D. *War losses*

The annexations of 1939–40 had the effect of increasing the Jewish population of the U.S.S.R. by some 50 to 70 per cent. In very round numbers, we may suppose that the 1931 Jewish population of Poland—no census had been taken there since that date—of 3·1 millions (including about 100,000 in Wilno and district) had increased by 1939 to about 3·3 millions, of whom about 1·3 millions resided in the eastern half of the country; the speed of the German advance was such that flight eastwards into the Soviet zone was surely on a very small scale. The Jewish population of the Baltic states was of the order of a quarter of a million; and of the area recovered from Rumania (Bessarabia and Bukovina), a little more. During the course of 1940 and the early part of 1941 some spontaneous movement towards the east, and some deportation by the Soviet authorities, undoubtedly took place, but in view of the very approximate data with which we have to operate, it would seem of little value to try to give a quantitative estimate. Let us then suppose that at the middle of 1941 the total Soviet Jewish population amounted to approximately as shown on page 139.

The newly acquired territories of western Byelorussia and western Ukraine had the highest proportion of Jews: about 13–14 per cent. The Baltic states, together with the 'old' Ukraine and Byelorussia, averaged about 5 per cent, while the R.S.F.S.R. and the east had less than 1 per cent

	Jews	Total pop.	Jewish
		('000,000)	per cent
All U.S.S.R.	4·8	198	2·4
R.S.F.S.R. and all eastern republics	1·1	139	0·8
Byelorussia, 'old'	0·4	6	7
'new'	0·4	3	13
Ukraine/Moldavia, 'old'	1·5	36	4
'new'	1·1	8	14
Baltic states	0·3	6	5

of Jews among the population. When the German attack came in 1941, the advance like that into Poland two years previously came so quickly that relatively few inhabitants of Byelorussia, much of the Ukraine, or the Baltic states would have had the opportunity to move eastwards; the principal categories of exception to this rule being young men who had been called up for military service (from the new territories equally with the old)—many, of course, were captured in the earliest phase of the war, and of these very few Jews would have survived—*plus* those men and women who held positions of sufficient importance in the economy or administration to justify their systematic evacuation. The surprise effected by the Germans was, however, such that hardly any Jews from the new territories could have escaped under this heading; such areas as the Donbas were a little more fortunate, although even there the chaos of the early weeks precluded any systematic evacuation. In order to profit from planned measures of evacuation, it was necessary to live as far behind the original frontiers as Moscow or Leningrad, which in any case the Germans failed to capture. In the face of this, one is inclined to suggest that the surprising fact is not that there were so few Jews surviving the war, but that there were so many. In addition to the possibility of migration, freely or under official duress, to the unoccupied eastern regions of the U.S.S.R., there were two avenues of escape for Jews from former Polish territories: membership of the Polish army which was reconstituted on Soviet soil during the war, and allowed to move to the west, and participation in the post-war transfer of population from the U.S.S.R. to Poland. Under a series of agreements, citizens of pre-war Poland who were of Polish or Jewish nationality were allowed to return to Poland (most of the Jews naturally regarded this as the first step to further movement), and in the first wave of transfers (up to 1948) something of the order of 175,000 Polish Jews left the U.S.S.R. The second wave of movement, beginning in 1957, involved a much smaller number of Jews: about 10,000 in 1957, and apparently much smaller numbers in later years. The overwhelming majority of these migrants originally resided in the western areas of the Ukraine and Byelorussia, but had been scattered all over the U.S.S.R. in the years before their departure; it seems very probable that the western areas have never had a dense Jewish population since the war.

It is as yet impossible to give a coherent picture of total Soviet war losses, let alone their territorial or national distribution; we have, it is true, annual population estimates for each year after 1950, which indicate that the principal reduction in the Soviet population took place in the west—which is, after all, what one would suppose—and that the losses were on such a scale that, coupled with the secular drift to the towns and the removal of large numbers of rural population to the new lands of the east in the fifties, the population of large parts of the western half of the U.S.S.R. has been unable to recover, and will in all probability never do so again. It is in fact obvious that the post-war period has continued the pre-war trends of eastward movement (accelerated by the war, and only temporarily interrupted by the need to re-colonize and re-construct the devastated west). The picture which we can form, therefore, of the territorial distribution of Soviet Jews fourteen years after the end of the war in Europe does not necessarily accurately reflect the immediate post-war situation.

With this reservation, we proceed to outline the situation as at 1959: the total Jewish population recorded by the census (2,268,000) comprises approximately 2,047,000 in the pre-1939 area of the country (ignoring such territorial changes as the acquisition of Tuva and Southern Sakhalin), and 221,000 in the western regions, acquired in 1939–40 and after the war. These figures are approximate, since in the absence of a breakdown of the 1959 census at less than *oblast* (province) level, we cannot adjust exactly for the boundary changes involved; but the figures given above are sufficiently precise. We infer that the 1939 population of 3,020,000 Jews has been reduced by about one-third; while the losses of the western territories (perhaps 1·8 million Jews at the time that the territories were taken over) have amounted to about 90 per cent of their Jewish population.

The losses in the 'old' Soviet territory are unevenly distributed; whereas Byelorussia had 375,000 Jews at the 1939 census, the same area had only about 135,000 twenty years later—a drop of two-thirds. Even if we assume that emigration from Byelorussia towards the east has been taking place since the war (or at any rate during the interval since the 1939 census), we cannot avoid the conclusion that the overwhelming majority of these losses were directly due to the German invasion. The 'old' Ukraine (including an estimate for pre-war Moldavia) has fallen from

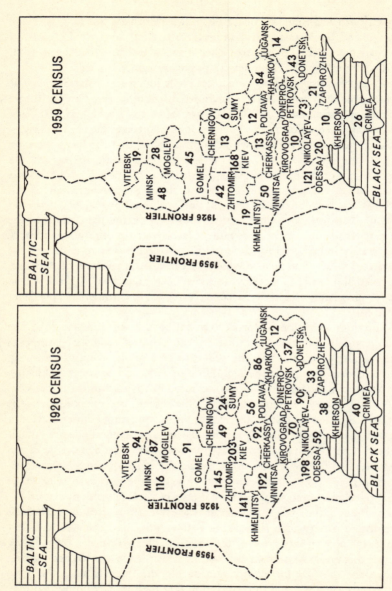

Jewish inhabitants of the Ukraine and Byelorussia in 1926 and 1959 (thousands)

1,533,000 Jews in 1939 to 770,000 Jews in 1959: a drop of one-half. Again some small migration, perhaps, but again, losses due to the war must dominate. The rest of the U.S.S.R. (R.S.F.S.R. including the Crimea, which was part of the R.S.F.S.R. in 1939, Transcaucasia, central Asia) shows a slight increase over the pre-war Jewish population: 1939, 1,112,000; 1959, 1,142,000. The Jewish population of the R.S.F.S.R. has fallen from 948,000 to 902,000; and it is noteworthy that the 1959 census indicates only 14,000 Jews in Bryansk *oblast*, and none are mentioned for Smolensk *oblast*, both of which certainly had substantial Jewish populations in 1939.[1]

To offset these losses, we note rises in Transcaucasia (from 84,000 to 93,000); in Kazakhstan (from 19,000 to 28,000) and in central Asia (a substantial increase, from 61,000 to 119,000). These figures indicate Jewish participation in the movement of Europeans into these developing areas, particularly in the fifties; and also the fact that many wartime evacuees to such centres as Tashkent or Alma Ata have preferred to remain.

The Jewish population of the 1939–40 annexations was, in 1959: Baltic states 66,000, about one-fifth of the pre-war figure; western Byelorussia, about 15,000, compared with a pre-war figure of the order of 400,000. Even allowing for the possibility of emigration (as mentioned above) and of movement to the interior, it is clear that the Jewish population of this area was the hardest hit of all. Even the western Ukraine fared a little better, with about 140,000 Jewish survivors out of 1·1 million.

To sum up, we may say that if the total extent of Soviet wartime losses of population were of the order of 30 millions, the Jewish share of these losses amounted to more than two and a half millions; the Jews, who comprised 2½ per cent of the Soviet population at the beginning of the war, had losses which reduced them to about 1 per cent of the present population. The Jewish losses were, percentagewise, about four times as severe as those of the Soviet population as a whole.

With this pattern of losses, what can we say about the effects on age-composition and social structure? We have indicated above that throughout the Soviet period there seems to have been a distinct difference between the Jews who moved eastwards and those who remained in the Pale area. With the destruction of the Jews of the western border regions, and the severe losses of those in the eastern parts of the old Pale, we should expect the trend towards an ageing and ultimately vanishing Jewish population to be much accentuated. The massacres took no regard of age and sex; those who were perhaps most likely to escape—the young able-

---

[1] The ethnographical atlas published in 1964 does, however, mark Jews in both places.

bodied of both sexes, but chiefly men—were most likely to emigrate in the post-war period, which failing, to remain in the eastern parts of the country rather than return to their native district. This consideration may help to illuminate the very sketchy information which we can elicit from the published results of the 1959 census as to the age-composition of the current Soviet Jewish population.

E. *1959 census data on mixed marriages and age-composition*

This information falls under two categories: (*a*) tables giving the percentage of persons of various nationalities who are married; and (*b*) some information as to educational levels. This first set of figures gives us some light on the question of mixed marriages. The proportion of Jews (aged 16 and over) who were married at the time of the census was:

	Byelorussia (per cent)	Moldavia (per cent)	R.S.F.S.R. (per cent)	Ukraine (per cent)
Men	76·4	81·8	75·8	78·1
Women	56·9	63·6	51·1	55·6

The proportion of Jews who were under the age of 16 is not explicitly stated.

If we assume that the Jewish figure is the same as their fellow citizens, it then emerges that the number of married Jewish men and women in these republics is:

	Men ('000)	Women ('000)	Minimum *number of Jewish* men with non-Jewish wives ('000)
Byelorussia	35·3	34·4	0·9
Moldavia	24·9	24·0	0·9
R.S.F.S.R.	216·0	180·4	35·6
Ukraine	208·6	201·4	7·2

In the R.S.F.S.R., therefore, at least one Jewish husband in seven has a non-Jewish wife (and the proportion would only be as low as this if every Jewish wife had a Jewish husband). If we were to assume a 2:1 ratio between male and female mixed marriages,[1] then about a quarter of all male Jews in the R.S.F.S.R. must have married non-Jewish wives. In the other republics considered the extent of mixed marriages is very considerably less. On this point we can adduce the evidence of a Soviet study on mixed marriages (such things are decidedly rare):[2] in the course of an

[1] This is the proportion, for instance, in Australia (see *Jewish Journal of Sociology*, June 1966, tables on pp. 115–16).

[2] *Sovetskaya etnografiya*, 1966, no. 3, pp. 109–18.

investigation concerning mixed marriages in one ward of Vilnius (Vilna) it transpired that over the run of years from 1945 to 1964 the number of marriages in which a Jewish husband was concerned regularly exceeded the number of marriages in which a Jewish wife was concerned—the same situation as that in the R.S.F.S.R. in 1926; and what is perhaps more surprising, the proportions were of the same order of magnitude: only about 80 per cent of the Jewish men who married took Jewish wives. This is in an area where the population, which includes only a small number of Jews, is probably composed of recent immigrants; and it would be rash to generalize it too far.

Given, however, that the foregoing discussion is correct in its interpretation of the evidence: that in fact there is a rather low proportion of mixed marriages-in-being in the old Pale area, and quite a high proportion in the areas to which movement really began after 1917, this seems to represent the logical conclusion of the process beginning in the twenties, and that the rate of assimilation automatically produced by intermarriage is likely to be more or less stable (once again we stress that we speak here of *formal*, documented, legal, assimilation, and that social assimilation may run a different course).

The proportion of children can be estimated indirectly from the education statistics: only in the case of the R.S.F.S.R. can we demonstrate conclusively that the proportion of Jewish children is significantly lower than that among the population as a whole (of the order of 19 per cent—Jewish children under 16—as against the general proportion of about 30 per cent); the obvious implication is that the proportion of adults is correspondingly higher. In independent support of this proposition, we find a very curious situation in the statistics concerning marriages. In the R.S.F.S.R., for example, the proportion of Jewish men (aged 16 and over) who were married as at 1959 was 76 per cent; among the population at large, the figure was 69 per cent. Nevertheless, at every age up to 60 years, the Jewish proportion of married men was *lower*: e.g. between ages 25 and 29, 66 per cent of R.S.F.S.R. Jews were married; in the population as a whole, 80 per cent of the men were married. Over the age of 60, relatively more Jewish men were married. This seems to lead inescapably to the conclusion that the average age of Jewish men is higher than among the general population; possibly that the kind of 'skewness' which we have found as at 1926 and 1939 now operates with the turnover point at a higher age (i.e. that up to some age the proportion of Jews is lower than among the population at large, and above that age, the Jewish proportion is higher; and that that age is now perhaps of the order of 50 years). But it must be stressed that this is a hypothesis, which however plausible, is not directly open to conclusive proof.

To sum up, then, at this stage: the scattered information which we have at our disposal indicates that the Jewish population of the U.S.S.R. early divided into two streams, one of which exhibits the characteristics of an immigrant population which might easily dissolve away into the surrounding population (high frequency of mixed marriage), while the other group, remaining at home, were much more conservative. The addition of a great increment to the latter group in 1939–40 was almost immediately offset by the war; and the destruction of Jewry in the west of the U.S.S.R. has tilted the balance in favour of the 'R.S.F.S.R.' pattern of demographic characteristics.[1]

F. Education

The most recent information is given in tables A–E, pp. 154–6. It can be and has been used by Soviet propagandists to document the non-existence of any anti-Jewish discrimination. On the face of it the figures would seem to bear out this proposition. The proportion of Jews attending higher educational institutions is far and away the highest of any nationality in the Union.

Yet the official answer is still unsatisfactory and does not disprove discrimination or *numerus clausus*. There are several reasons for this.

First, the available statistics include every higher educational institution, from Moscow University to the Metallurgical Institute of Tomsk. The fact that a large number of Jews obtain higher education does not mean that they are able to get into universities of their choice on equal terms with competitors of other nationalities. A parallel could be drawn with the situation in London. It is notorious that some of the most famous public schools in the London area operate a strict *numerus clausus* so far as the Jews are concerned. However, if we were to have only the figures of persons attending secondary schools of all kinds in the London area, it could no doubt be demonstrated that more Jews attend than do English children in proportion to their numbers. From this it does not in the least follow that it is equally easy for the child of Mr. Smith and of Mr. Cohen to get into the same London public school. The same logic can apply to Russia too.

---

[1] The latest available datum indicates a growth in the Jewish population of the U.S.S.R. (European Jews only) from 2,186,100 in 1959 to 2,300,000 in 1962 (at 1 January). If one were certain that this last figure means 'between 2,295,000 and 2,305,000' we could assert a percentage increase of 5·2 in the three years—higher than the increase rate of the Russians. But it is uncertain precisely what this rounded figure means. (*Atlas narodov mira*, 1964, p. 158.)

Secondly, the demand for higher education among children of Jews is abnormally high. This is due partly to the high level of urbanization (a much greater proportion of children of townsmen have higher education than do children of villagers), but their social composition must also be taken into account. The Nazi invasion had the effect of wiping out the majority of the Jewish proletariat, concentrated as it was in the west. The Jews are predominantly white-collar workers, professional men, engineers, and scientists, or in retail trade. Unfortunately no systematic analysis of the occupational composition of Russian Jewry is possible. The only available statistics will be quoted in the pages that follow, and these only cover a relatively small proportion of the total. None the less, enough is known to make it clear that, both because of their present occupations and because of the high standing of learning among Jews in general, a much larger proportion of Jews than of other nationalities endeavours to obtain higher education. It is this fact that may well give rise to discrimination. Some officials may feel that it is wrong for Jews to be so overwhelmingly non-proletarian in their composition. Others, particularly in the national republics, are concerned to provide special educational advantages for the relatively backward peoples of their own nationality. All this could well make special difficulties for Jews, and the statistics quoted in our table in no way prove the contrary.

Thirdly, statistics for a number of national areas do in fact show systematic preference for the nationality of the area, so that, for example, the number of Uzbek day-students as a proportion of total Uzbek students considerably exceeds the number of Jewish day-students as a proportion of all Jewish students in Uzbekistan. Since it may be assumed that virtually all applicants desire to be full-time day-students, this suggests discrimination, though the discrimination appears to be pro-Uzbek rather than anti-Jewish. There being no Uzbek tradition of antisemitism, this may seem a reasonable instance of special care being taken of a backward nationality within the borders of their own republic. However, it so happens that within the borders of this republic Jews have lived as compact communities for thousands of years. Yet they do not seem to be treated as if they were natives of the area in which they live. In the Ukraine too the proportion of Jewish day-students is markedly lower than that of Ukrainians, and since this is an area of traditional antisemitism we may surmise that this reflects the motivation of local officials, who decide on eligibility for full-time study.

There is also the question of comparison with pre-war figures. Readers are referred to tables B and C, p. 155. The total for all students seems

quite 'creditable'. Numbers are very slightly up, it is true, and the percentage heavily down, but, after all, numbers of Jews fell substantially between
1935 and 1965, and total numbers of students multiplied. But this table (B)
includes external (correspondence) students, whom we would not consider to be students at all. If attention is confined to 'real' students, the
Jewish figures show a very sharp drop, from nearly 75,000 to 45,000.
(Before 1940, the external student was practically a non-existent category.)
Is *this* evidence of discrimination, of a downward trend in educational
opportunity? The more so as the change in social composition of Jewry
would cause a relative rise in demand for higher education.

The answer is not as clear as it might seem at first sight. It can be *very*
roughly deduced from figures quoted earlier that, around 1935, there were
something like 250,000 young people aged between 18 and 23 (i.e. of
student age), so that of this group about 30 per cent had higher education,
a remarkably high percentage. In 1965, not only is the total Jewish population far below the 1935 level, but, for reasons explored at length, the
younger age-groups are relatively small. There may, in fact, be only somewhere between 125,000 and 150,000 in the relevant age-group. If this is so,
then this *could* mean that a higher percentage was attending college in
1965 than in 1935, despite appearances to the contrary. However, demand
has gone up, and we can be sure that some of the roughly 32,000 young
Jews who are registered as external students have done their utmost to
secure entry to full-time higher education, in the face of stiff competition,
and that some of them were better qualified than those who did secure
admittance. (The problem of entry into universities, in Russia as in Britain,
has been accentuated by the fact that the increase in secondary education
has greatly exceeded the growth in the available places in higher
education.)

Circumstances have naturally varied at different dates. There seems to
have been no effort to keep Jewish numbers down in the twenties and
thirties. In the last four years of Stalin's life, during the campaign against
homeless cosmopolitans, educational discrimination became very noticeable indeed. One of the authors was told about it shamefacedly by a
Russian student who had got into a medical school ahead of a much better
qualified Jewish friend. Conditions improved after Stalin's death, but
worsened again when Khrushchev tried to reform higher education and
to give special preference for children of workers. It may be that conditions have again got better since his removal. There also appear to be
some rather surprising differences between different departments of the
same university. Thus we have been told by a recent student that a

considerable number of Jews may be seen studying mathematics and physics, but very few are accepted for the humanities.

Naturally these are impressions which cannot be supported by any systematic statistical analysis. However, we must not be surprised that, given the traditional attitudes of people, in the vigorous competition that exists for scarce university places the Jews suffer by reason of their nationality, which can always be identified since the passport must be produced as part of the documentation involved in an application for admission. All other major national groups in the Soviet Union can give preference to their own nationality in universities located in their own national republican territories. For obvious reasons this cannot be done for the Jews, save in Biro-Bidzhan where their numbers are insignificant and the educational opportunities insignificant also.

Employed graduates

The largest category of Jews for whom occupational statistics are available is that comprised by those known as 'specialists in the national economy'. This represents every employed graduate. This is not a total of all graduates, since some are now old-age pensioners and others (for instance housewives) may not be working. The available figures are given in the table. Once again the *proportion* of Jewish graduates among the total number of employed graduates has been falling, and is well below the pre-war figure. This is the natural consequence of the falling proportion of Jews among the rapidly rising total of the graduating population, i.e. of those attending higher educational institutions. In this instance, however, there is ample evidence to show that the proportion of graduates among the total Jewish population has been rising, and is certainly very much higher than it was before the war, though one reason for this has been the destruction of so many of the less educated sections of Jewry by the Nazis in the western areas. The figure of over 322,000 for November 1964 represents a remarkably high percentage of the total Jewish population: about $13\frac{1}{2}$ per cent, of a total which includes children and old people. One has only to compare this with the figure for the Russians, which at the same date was only 2·4 per cent. Some superficial critics maintain that there is something wrong about the relationship between the proportion of Jewish working graduates and the proportion of Jewish students. The former is 7·1 per cent, the latter only slightly over $2\frac{1}{2}$ per cent. They seem to imagine that this must show that the absolute numbers of Jewish working graduates must be falling. Obviously, a glance at the statistics shows that this is not the case. The contrast between the two percentages is a reflection of the much higher proportion of Jewish students in the pre-war years. In the four years 1960 to 1964 the proportion of Jewish working graduates in the total number of working graduates had indeed somewhat fallen, but the absolute numbers have risen, by 32,000 or by about 11 per cent. The many difficulties which face Jews in Russia today are not to be resolved by incorrect deductions from the available statistics.

Scientific workers

This is the usual translation of the Russian term *nauchnye rabotniki*. A better translation would be 'learned persons'. It covers all persons, regardless of speciality, employed by universities, research institutes, the Academy of Sciences and its various organs, and so forth. Since almost all these persons must be graduates, the figures given in the table largely overlap those already included under the heading 'specialists in the national economy'. As the table shows, absolute numbers have been growing, and growing fairly rapidly at that, more than doubling in the period 1955 to 1964. However, since the total increased much faster than this, the share of Jews among the total of scientific workers has been falling, and particularly so if comparison is made with pre-war years. None the less the role of Jews in this field immensely exceeds their proportion in the population. It is even more pronounced than in the case of 'specialists in the national economy'. Thus out of every thousand Jews of all ages, no less than 22·5 are scientific workers. For the Russians the figure is 4, for the Ukrainians considerably less than 2. Such disproportions are so striking that the fact of a steadily falling percentage share of the Jews in the rapidly rising total can give no grounds for reasonable criticism.

It is sometimes asserted that the large number of Jews that are still prominent among scientific workers reflect the past, when the Jewish share was high and a number of very eminent specialists were trained. If by this is meant that the further recruitment of Jewish scientific workers no longer takes place, this is plainly disproved by the figures in the table. It is quite another matter if one is considering promotion. One finds few Jews in the position of directors of institutes or chief editors of journals, though there are exceptions to this.

A long list of names can be readily assembled to show how important the role of Jews still is in various branches of knowledge. There are physicists, technologists, economists, and many others. Thus among economists very prominent in recent debates, and with significant achievements to their credit, one finds such names as Kantorovich, Lourie, Liberman, Finkelstein, Katzenelenboigen, Kronrod, and quite a few others. The press recently published a list of 110 persons in all branches of knowledge whose names were submitted for consideration for the highest scientific and technical awards in 1966 (the Lenin Prizes). Nineteen of them had plainly Jewish names. Needless to say it does not follow that they necessarily either feel Jewish or in any way are intending to continue the Jewish tradition. A number of them are known to have non-Jewish wives, and perhaps their children will be registered in future as Russians. However, that is another question altogether.

Other 'professional' data

For the late thirties there exist data published in Yiddish in Moscow, by Zinger, also cited by S. Schwarz in his *The Jews in the Soviet Union* (the date is given as 1939, but could be 1937):

	Total of given professions ('000)	Jews	Per cent Jews
Doctors	132	21	16
Art and theatre	159	17	11
Engineers, technologists, architects	250	25	10
Culture (journalism, librarians, etc.)	297	30	10
University staffs, etc.	80	7	9
Nurses, etc.	382	31	8
Accountants, bookkeepers	1617	125	8
Technical staffs	810	60	7
Schoolteachers	969	46	5
Agronomists and agricultural specialists	180	2	1

The total of 364,000 Jews probably represents the equivalent of the sum of graduate and non-graduate specialists, given for 1964 in tables F1 and F2, p. 156, which amount to 483,000. This reflects the increasing share in the total of what might be called professional and quasi-middle-class occupations.

The only analogous data for recent years were published in *Soviet Weekly* (London) for 4 June 1966. They gave Jewish doctors as 14·7 per cent of all Soviet doctors at an unspecified date, 8·5 per cent of all writers and journalists, 10·4 per cent of all judges and lawyers, 7·7 per cent of actors, musicians, and artists. Since there are about 365,000 doctors in the U.S.S.R., the total number of Jews must be 54,000, a big increase over the late thirties. But systematic analysis is rendered impossible by lack of recent figures.

This contrasts with the situation in the early years of Soviet power. For example, the reader may like to note the figures contained in tables I, J and K, pp. 157–8. This shows the occupational composition, for example in the Ukraine, in some detail. The table on the army shows that while, as is natural in a conscript army, the number of private soldiers was about equal to the proportion of Jews in the population, their numbers were significant among the higher ranks, and particularly among political officers. At the same time accusations to the effect that the majority of political officers were Jewish were plainly false, since they numbered 9 per cent of the total. It is virtually certain that the number of Jewish political officers today is exceedingly small, but on this, as on so much else, there are no figures.

Communist party membership is not now analysed in terms of nationality. This applies to central publications. However, some republican communist parties have published such analyses, and figures have already been quoted for Jewish members of the party in the republic of Uzbekistan. It is interesting that they show the highest party membership, in proportion to population, of any national group in Uzbekistan. There is absolutely no evidence to suggest that this is also the case in such republics as the R.S.F.S.R. or the Ukraine. However, there is no particular reason to suppose that Jews as such are excluded from membership of the party, and it seems reasonably probable that the number of Jewish party members would be either proportionate to their numbers in the total population or proportionate to their numbers in the urban population. (The Jews being predominantly urban, and the party also.) However, since the war there has been a marked lack of Jews in the higher councils of the party and very few are ever given posts in the regional party organizations or in the Central Committee machine. It is extremely rare to encounter a single Jewish name among long lists of provincial and district party secretaries or second secretaries. We have yet to see a single one, but cannot pretend that we have perused all the names. The last Jew on the Politburo of the party was Kaganovich, and he was removed in 1957. There are roughly 300 members of the Central Committee, if one includes alternate members. Of these exactly one, Dymshits, is a Jew, representing 0·3 per cent of the total. In 1939 there were 139 members of the Central Committee, including alternates. The number of Jews was then 15, or 10·8 per cent. Yet this was after the great purge, in which numerous prominent party leaders of Jewish origin had been killed or imprisoned.

It seems to follow that the quite numerous Jewish members of the party either hold relatively subordinate political positions, or they are prominent, if at all, outside of strictly party activities.

The same pattern emerges if one analyses the Supreme Soviet. Names are not always a sure guide to nationality, and we have already quoted the names of two deputies which suggested that they might be Jewish but in fact were respectively Russian and Ukrainian. Such identification has been facilitated by the appearance of an illustrated handbook to the Supreme Soviet, which includes potted biographies and photographs of every deputy as at 1962, together with his or her nationality. There were 1,443 deputies of the Soviet of the Union and the Soviet of Nationalities, the two chambers into which the Supreme Soviet is divided. Five of these deputies were Jews, being 0·35 per cent of the total number of deputies, very far below the proportion of Jews in the total population. Of these, one was a representative of the 'Jewish autonomous province', i.e. Biro-Bidzhan, there being four other representatives of this province in the Soviet of Nationalities (these were Russians and Ukrainians, as was perfectly proper in view of the fact that Jews form a small minority of the population of this province). In 1966 a new Supreme Soviet was elected, and it would appear that the number of Jewish deputies has been again fixed at five. The total number of deputies is now 1,517, bringing the proportion of Jews down to 0·30 per cent. Of course, if the selection or election of deputies was a matter in which the mass of the membership of the party or of the total population had a say, one could regard it as a by-product of folk antisemitism. People might simply be unwilling to elect Jews. However, this would be a most unreasonable interpretation. The deputies of the Supreme Soviet are 'elected' after they have been chosen by senior levels of the party machine, and there is never a contested election. The choice is deliberate. The Jewish proportion is prearranged, just as the proportions of peasants, writers, generals, Tatars, Armenians, and steel workers are prearranged. Of course, favourable treatment is given, especially in the Soviet of Nationalities, to individuals who are natives of various national republics and regions. Here again the Jews are handicapped by not having any compact territorial area of their own, though one deputy still represents, if represents is the word, the Jews of Biro-Bidzhan. None the less, one might well expect the adoption of some Jewish candidates for important centres of culture and science, centres like Leningrad and Moscow in which there are many Jews who play a significant part in the life of these great cities. Yet in fact there is not a single Jewish Supreme Soviet deputy for either Moscow or Leningrad, or for any constituency in the Ukraine or Byelorussia or Lithuania or Moldavia.

Furthermore, exactly the same pattern may be seen in a recent analysis which one of the authors found in a Soviet publication and reproduced in the *Jewish Journal of Sociology*. The figures relate to 1959 and are as follows for the republics in which Jews form a significant part of the population (0·7 per cent or over):

	Total no. of deputies	Of which Jews	Per cent Jews	Per cent of Jews in population
R.S.F.S.R.	835	1	0·12	0·70
Ukraine	457	1	0·22	2·00
Byelorussia	407	2	0·45	1·90
Uzbekistan	444	2	0·44	1·20
Lithuania	209	3	1·44	0·90
Moldavia	281	0	0	3·30
Georgia	368	0	0	1·30
Latvia	200	0	0	1·70
Azerbaijan	325	1	0·31	1·09

With one relatively minor exception the number of Jewish deputies in these Soviets is invariably and substantially below the proportion of Jews in the population of the respective republics.

The total absence of Jews both from diplomacy and from foreign trade, which has been frequently noted by commentators, is all the more striking if one considers how important they were in just these branches of activity during the first twenty years of Soviet power. It may be objected that one does not meet many Jews in the British Foreign Office or in the Quai d'Orsay. However, it might not be irrelevant to point out that the vast majority of British Jews arrived in this country relatively recently, and nearly all have foreign-born parents or grandparents. Most of these were in fact born within the borders of the Russian empire. So were the parents and great-grandparents of the vast majority of Russian Jews. In any event, the Soviet Foreign Office was not supposed to be functioning according to the principles of selection of western career diplomats.

Conclusion

It seems clear that Jews remain disproportionately prominent in science, many of the arts, journalism, medicine, and a wide range of technological and cultural occupations, and considerably more Jews are highly educated than the Russians or the other nationalities of the U.S.S.R. Their lead in these respects was diminishing and continues to diminish, though this must be explained above all by the relatively rapid progress of the other nationalities and not by any diminution of the number of Jews taking part in these activities, though there is a sizeable decrease in the numbers of full-time students since the middle thirties, explained perhaps by a sharp drop in relative numbers of Jewish youth. However, Jews have practically disappeared from politics and from foreign affairs generally. Discrimination in various forms undoubtedly makes life difficult for many Jews in many walks of life, but its existence cannot be proved by any of the official statistics to which we have access. Endeavours to use these statistics for this purpose would expose the users to devastating and deserved counter-attack. The Jewish population is very heavily 'tilted' towards the professions, and its age-composition suggests that its total numbers must diminish statistically, whatever may be the trend in the strength (or absence) of Jewish national consciousness among those who are regarded by Soviet officials as being of Jewish nationality.

TABLE A

Students at Higher Educational Institutions, 1960–1
(including external students)

	Total students	Of which, Jews	Percentage of Jews in no. of students	Percentage of Jews in total population	Percentage of Jews in urban population
Russian Federal Republic	1,496,097	46,555	3·1	0·7	1·3
Ukraine	417,748	18,673	4·4	2·0	4·2
Byelorussia	59,296	3,020	5·1	1·9	5·8
Uzbekistan	101,271	2,902	2·9	1·2	3·3
Kazakhstan	77,135	837	1·1	0·3	0·6
Georgia	56,322	910	1·6	1·3	2·6
Azerbaijan	36,017	906	2·5	1·1	2·2
Lithuania	26,713	413	1·6	0·9	2·3
Moldavia	19,217	1,225	6·4	3·3	13·8
Latvia	21,568	800	3·7	1·7	3·1
Kirghizia	17,379	263	1·6	0·4	1·1
Tadzhikistan	19,519	391	2·0	0·6	1·9
Armenia	20,165	52	0·2	0·06	0·1
Turkmenistan	13,151	104	0·8	0·3	0·6
Estonia	13,507	126	0·9	0·5	0·8
Total, U.S.S.R.	2,395,545	77,177	3·2	1·1	2·2

Source: *Vyssheye obrazovanie v S.S.S.R.*

TABLE B

Total Students, U.S.S.R.
(including evening and external students)
('000)

	1928–9	1935	1960–1	1962–3	1963–4	1965–6	1970–1	1972–3
Total	162·8	563·5	2395·5	2943·7	3260·7	3860·5	4580·6	4630·2
Of which:								
Russians	95·0	306·5	1479·5	1803·8	1987·9	2362·0	2729·0	2774·1
Ukrainians	16·4	80·6	343·6	426·9	476·4	588·6	621·2	618·8
Jews	23·4	74·9	77·2	79·3	82·6	94·6	105·8	88·5
Per cent Jews	14·4	13·3	3·2	2·7	2·5	2·45	2·3	1·9

Sources: 1928–9; *Natsionalnaya politika VPK(b) v tsifrakh;* 1935: *Sotsialisticheskoe stroitelstvo* (1936); post-war figures: *Nar. Khoz.,* 1963, 1965.

TABLE C

Total Students, Excluding External (correspondence) Students

		1928–9	1935	1963–4
Total		162·8	563·5	1400·4
Of which:	Russians	95·0	306·5	870·5
	Ukrainians	16·4	80·6	168·8
	Jews	23·4	74·9	45·0
	Per cent Jews	14·4	13·3	3·2

Source: As above. Figure for Jews in 1963–4 is an estimate based on data for 1960–1.

TABLE D

Students of Technical Institutes
('secondary specialist education')

	1962–3	1963–4	1965–6	1970–1	1972–3
Total	2667·7	2982·8	3659·3	4388·0	4437·9
Of which:					
Jews	47·2	51·3	52·0	40·0	37·1
Per cent Jews	1·77	1·72	1·42	0·9	0·8

Source: Nar. Khoz., 1963, 1964, 1965.

TABLE E

Day, Evening and Correspondence Students in some Republics, 1960–1
(percentage of total of given nationality)

	Day	Evening	Correspondence
R.S.F.S.R., Total	46·7	11·2	42·1
Russians	46·9	11·8	41·3
Jews	46·4	12·9	40·6

TABLE E *(continued)*

	Day	Evening	Correspondence
Ukraine, Total	47·6	10·5	41·9
Russians	48·6	13·1	38·2
Ukrainians	47·6	8·8	43·7
Jews	37·8	18·9	43·2
Uzbekistan, Total	50·7	6·9	42·4
Russians	40·5	12·2	47·3
Uzbeks	58·1	4·6	37·3
Jews	42·9	10·7	46·4
Moldavia, Total	54·2	2·6	43·2
Russians	48·8	4·7	46·5
Moldavians	61·9	1·0	37·1
Jews	47·5	8·3	45·0

Source: *Vyssheye obrazovanie v S.S.S.R.*

TABLE FI

Specialists in National Economy—Graduates

	1941 (Jan.)	1957 (Dec.)	1960 (Dec.)	1962 (Dec.)	1964 (Nov.)
Total, U.S.S.R.	909,000	2,805,000	3,545,234	4,409,700	4,547,600
Of which: Russians	493,900	1,627,200	2,070,333	2,376,800	2,679,900
Ukrainians	128,800	401,000	517,729	595,700	667,200
Jews	154,000	260,900	290,707	310,600	322,700
Per cent Jews	17	9·3	8·2	7·06	7·1

Source: *Vyssheye obrazovanie v S.S.S.R.*, 1961, pp. 70–1 and *Nar. Khoz.*, 1963 and 1964. The 1941 total for Jews is a rough calculation 'by remainder'.

TABLE F2

'Non-graduate Specialists'
('000)

	1957	1964
Total U.S.S.R.	4016·1	6702·1
Of which: Jews	108·0	159·7
Per cent Jews	2·7	2·4

Source: *Nar. Khoz.*, 1965.

TABLE G
Scientific Workers

	1955	1958	1959	1960	1961	1963	1965	1970
Total: All nationalities	223,893	264,038	310,022	354,158	404,126	565,958	664,584	927,709
Of which:								
Russians	144,285	182,567	199,987	229,547	263,838	373,498	440,976	611,883
Ukrainians	21,762	27,803	30,252	35,426	40,950	59,221;	70,797	100,215
Jews	24,620	28,966	30,633	33,529	36,173	48,012	53,067	64,392
Per cent Jews	11.0	10·2	9·8	9·5	8·9	8·5	8·0	7·1

Sources: *Kulturnoe stroitelstvo S.S.S.R.*, 1957; *Narodnoe khozyaistvo S.S.R. v 1962 godu*, and *Nar. Khoz.*, 1963 and 1964.

TABLE H
Intellectual Occupations, per thousand of Given Nationality, 1963–4

	Students (higher education)*	Specialists in national economy	Scientific workers
Russians	15·9	21·4	3·2
Ukrainians	11·6	16·3	1·6
Georgians	21·7	36·8	4·2
Jews	34·4	134·5	21·2
All Soviet average	14·4	20·0	2·7

* Including external (correspondence) students. Calculated from above tables.

TABLE I
Jews in Ukraine, 1929

Per cent of total in given occupation:

Agricultural workers	1·06
Industrial workers	7·89
Craftsmen	38·42
Railwaymen	1·1

Per cent of trade union members:

Total		24·7
Of which:	clothing	66·8
	printing	42·2
	leather work	48·0
	medical workers	26·7
	woodworkers	29·3
	arts	37·2
	miners	0·9
	railwaymen	0·8

TABLE J
U.S.S.R.: Jews in the Army, 1929

	Per cent
Total, all ranks	2·09
Private soldiers	1·78
N.C.O.s	1·61
Administration	3·44
Political officers	8·62
Officers	4·28
Senior officers	3·44
(Jews in total population	1·7)

TABLE K
Communist Party Members, 1929 (U.S.S.R.)
('000)

	Full members	Candidate members
Total	720·2	341·6
Of which: Jews	34·4	10·9
Per cent Jews	4·8	3·2

Source (of all 1929 figures): *Natsionalnaya politika VKP(b) v tsifrakh*, 1930.

SUPPLEMENTARY NOTE

The Jewish population of the U.S.S.R. declined between the censuses of 1959 and 1970 from 2,268,000 to 2,151,000 (by 5·2 per cent), compared with a total population increase of 15·7 per cent. Migration during this period was nearly insignificant. The regional distribution of Jews changed as follows:

('000)

	1959	1970	Per cent change
R.S.F.S.R.	875	808	− 7·7
Ukraine	840	777	− 7·5
Lithuania	25	24	− 4·0
Estonia	5·4	5·3	− 1·9
Byelorussia	150	148	− 1·3
Latvia	37	37	nil
Moldavia	95	98	+ 3·2
Georgia	52	55	+ 5·8
Uzbekistan	95	103	+ 8·4
All other republics	94	96	+ 2·1

These percentage changes correspond pretty exactly to the evidence earlier available as to the age-distribution of Jews in the various parts of the U.S.S.R.; and we may note that the greatest increases occur in those areas (Georgia and Uzbekistan) where a substantial part of the Jewish population are indigenous, rather than immigrants from European Russia. Even here, though, the increase is small compared with that of the titular nationality of the republic (Georgians, +20 per cent; Uzbeks, +53 per cent.)

On the question of *native tongue*: the proportion of Jews with a 'Jewish' native tongue (mostly Yiddish, but including also about 100,000 Oriental Jews in 1959) has fallen from 21·5 per cent to 17·7 per cent, i.e. from 488,000 to 381,000; this fall of 107,000 is close to, but somewhat smaller than, the overall fall of 117,000. We may interpret this at this point by supposing that some of the Jewish children born between the censuses have a 'Jewish' native tongue, and that among those who have died, a preponderance were 'Jewish' (i.e. Yiddish speakers, rather than Russian speakers, who may well tend to be younger than Yiddish speakers). We may examine the somewhat analogous cases of other national groups which have declined between 1959 and 1970 both in national and in linguistic terms. The number of Poles fell from 1,380,000 to 1,167,000 (by 213,000), while Polish speakers fell from 624,000 to 379,000 (by 245,000). The corresponding falls for the Karelians were 21,000 for the nationality and 27,000 for the language; and for the Finns, a fall of 8,000 for the nationality and 12,000 for the language. All these groups are heavily susceptible to assimilation, but each had in 1959 about one-half of its members speaking the national tongue, whereas only about one Jew in five spoke a 'Jewish' language. In each of these three cases the decline in total numbers is far in excess of what could be attributed to natural causes, and we must assume that individuals switched nationality and also claimed a new native language. This is by no means the necessary explanation for the figures concerning the Jews.

There is some evidence strongly pointing to a very high proportion of Jews of the older age groups, and relatively few children. It is certainly clear that the numbers of young people of Jewish nationality are very far below those of the Russians, and yet the Russians are worried about the consequences of *their* low birth rate! Precise statistical evidence is available only for the Russian Republic (R.S.F.S.R.), for which the figures are as follows in the 1970 census: 35·5 per cent of the inhabitants of Russian nationality were under 20, but only 15·1 per cent of the Jewish inhabitants. 12 per cent of the Russians were over 60, but no less than 26·4 per cent of the Jews were over 60. It is, of course, possible that the figures are affected by concealment of nationality on the part of those who wished to assimilate. However, it is abundantly clear that the Jewish population of the U.S.S.R. is a very much more elderly population than the generality, and that it is not producing nearly enough children to maintain itself. It therefore follows that even without emigration there was bound to be an accelerated decline in the number of Jews in the U.S.S.R. With emigration the decline must accelerate still further.

8

Jewish Religion in the Soviet Union

JOSHUA ROTHENBERG

Despite the turbulence and flux characteristic of Jewish history, there is no precedent for the rapidity and extensive changes sustained by the Jews during the first half-century of their existence in the Soviet Union. Perhaps no aspect of Jewish life in the Soviet Union has undergone a more radical transformation than the religious. Of the thousands upon thousands of synagogues and prayer houses, only several dozen still remain after the ravages of fifty years. Of the many thousands of religious schools, both elementary and advanced, practically none has survived. The thousands of rabbis have been reduced to a mere handful who still function in a religious capacity.

Are these profound changes merely the result of the natural processes of secularization and communization of the country—as the apologists of the system maintain? Or have they been brought about by persecution and administrative measures—as the critics claim? As it is more likely that the changes were due to a combination of both factors, it would be useful to ascertain which of the two is dominant. In an attempt to shed some light on these questions, we will consider the factors and processes which have directly or indirectly affected Jewish religion during the past fifty years under the Soviet regime.

For several hundred years, the Jews living in the territories now included in the Soviet Union had formed their own religious institutions, customs, and modes of religious observance. They enjoyed a long history of national and religious semi-autonomy, organized principally within the framework of the Kehilah (Jewish communal council) and its affiliated organizations. These activities and distinctive religious practices survived well past the revolution of October 1917.

Although the tsarist regime confined the Jews to the overcrowded hamlets and towns of the Pale of Settlement, stifling their talents and energies by discrimination and exclusion from many occupations, it did not, as a rule, interfere too deeply in the *inner affairs* of the Jewish community. This particular situation allowed the Jewish community of tsarist Russia to make use of its own resources, and to develop, in spite of discrimination and persecution, a meaningful Jewish life and Jewish culture.

The rhythm and character of Jewish life within this semi-autonomous framework, the economic activities, communal procedures, and personal attitudes of the people were largely influenced by Jewish religious precepts and concepts. Jews submitted their pecuniary disputes to rabbinical courts; kosher slaughtering, administered by the Kehilah, provided meat for the whole community and furnished funds for the Kehilah. Many synagogues were organized by craft unions. Burial societies extracted large funds from rich estates for the needs of the community (a *sui generis* form of death duties). A hostelry (*hekdesh*), free of charge, was provided for indigent transients, and the communal ritual bath (*miqveh*) served the whole Jewish community as the only accessible bath. During centuries the synagogue, and the communal institutions affiliated with it, constituted the focal point of every Jewish community.

At the end of the nineteenth and the beginning of the twentieth centuries, the established order within the Jewish community was strongly challenged by new political and social movements—primarily, Zionism and socialism. Yet though these new ideologies, forceful and vibrant, weakened the established Jewish religious and communal organizations, they by no means destroyed them. Indeed, the new forces which came to the fore of Jewish life even tried to adapt the old institutions to their own purposes: they attempted to foster secular Jewish activities through the Kehilahs. The attempt to organize a new, comprehensive form of Jewish *secular-religious* autonomy manifested itself with particular force in the years of the civil war (1918–21) in the Ukraine and in Lithuania.[1]

The February Revolution of 1917, which abolished the tsarist regime and promised to establish a western-type democracy, was joyfully welcomed by the Russian Jews. On 2 April 1917 the Provisional Government issued a decree lifting all restrictions upon the rights of citizens based on race or religion. For the first time, Russian Jews acquired equal civil rights.

The new freedom also activated religious leaders and rabbis. On 16 April 1917 the constituent assembly of *Mesoret ve-Herut* (Tradition and Freedom), a group akin to the *Mizrachi* movement, was convened in Moscow. The assembly demanded 'national autonomy' for the Jews,

---

[1] For a short time 'Ministries for Jewish Affairs' with Jews as ministers functioned in (initially non-communist) Ukraine and Lithuania.

based on religious and democratic principles. Another religious conference made up of groups supporting the orthodox *Agudat Israel*, took place in Moscow three months later, and a similar conference was also held in Kiev.

The Bolshevik Revolution of October 1917 altered the situation of the Russian Jews perhaps more radically than that of other national groups in the Russian empire. As compared with other groups, the Jews had the smallest representation among the workers and the peasants, the two classes which benefited the most—or lost the least—from the October Revolution. The majority of the Jewish population were merchants and self-employed artisans; and in addition, the proportion of paupers, unemployed, and refugees was larger than in any other population group in the country.[1]

The first act of the Soviet Government that directly affected the religious and national rights of the Jews was the Declaration of the Rights of the Peoples of Russia. This rescinded all 'national-religious privileges and restrictions' and promised to promote the free development of the national groups living within the confines of Russia.

For several of those minority groups of the Russian empire, including Armenians and Jews, who had suffered both national and religious persecution, the restrictions on nationality and religion were sometimes identical or overlapping. The use of the hyphenated term 'national-religious' in the Declaration indicates that the Soviet leaders were, at that time at least, aware of the close relationship between the 'national' and the 'religious' elements in the character of some of the minority groups inhabiting Russia.

The effects of the religious element on Jewish national identity were acknowledged by the communists themselves. For instance, in a resolution adopted at the conference of workers in the field of education, held in September 1921 in Minsk, the difficulty of secularizing Jewish education was explained by the fact that 'Jewish religion has penetrated into all aspects of the Jewish way of life'.[2]

The first legal act *directly regulating religious life* in the country was the decree of the Council of People's Commissars (under the signature and

---

[1] Hundreds of thousands of Jews were uprooted following the pogroms in the civil war of 1918–22 and the deportation of Jews from border territories ordered by the Russian high command during the First World War, as a punishment for allegedly helping the enemy.

[2] A. A. Gershuni, *Yahadut be-Russia ha-Sovietit*, Jerusalem, 1961, pp. 48–9.

co-authorship of Lenin) of 23 January 1918, entitled 'On separation of Church from State and School from Church'.[1]

The most important enactments of this decree (which is still in effect) are:

(1) the complete secularization of the state;
(2) the confiscation of all religious property and funds;
(3) the withdrawal of the status of legal entity from churches and church organizations;
(4) the prohibition of religious instruction in schools.

The January 1918 decree dealt a particularly damaging blow to the Russian Orthodox Church, the state church of tsarist Russia. The provision which most affected the *Jewish religion* was that prohibiting religious education for the young.

The position of the Jews in the Soviet Union, as a distinct group, had been uncertain from the inception of Soviet rule. As a *religious entity*, the Jewish people were under constant attack, as were members of other religious cults in the country. As a *national entity*, they did not benefit from the clearly established nationality status of other ethnic groups which were territorially concentrated. Thus, the Jews suffered as a 'religious group' and did not reap the full benefits which should have accrued to them as a 'Soviet nationality'.

The problem as to whether Jews constitute, in terms of communist doctrine, a 'nationality', has remained essentially unresolved, and this fact lies at the root of many of the continuous fluctuations and contradictions in Soviet policy towards the Soviet Jews, even up to the present day.

The next act of the Soviet Government directly affecting Jewish religion was the dissolution of the Kehilahs; this measure was adopted at the first conference of the newly established Jewish Commissariat and the Jewish Section of the communist party (Yevsektsia) in October 1918, and formally promulgated, under the signature of the Commissar for Nationality Affairs, Joseph Stalin, in June 1919.

The dissolution of the Kehilahs created many immediate hardships for the Jewish population, as the new governmental agencies were unable to assume quickly and effectively the ramified functions of the Kehilah institutions in social welfare and education.

In its initial period, the Soviet regime had shown some reluctance in

---

[1] 'Ob otdelenii tserkvi ot gosudarstva i shkoly ot tserkvi', Dekret Sovieta Narodnykh Komissarov, in *Sobranie Uzakonenii i Razporiazhenii Rabochevo i Krestianskovo Pravitelstva*, no. 18, 26 January 1918.

attacking the Jewish religion. After all, harassment of Judaism had been a favourite activity of the despised tsarist regime. Moreover, only four years earlier the liberal world had been stunned by the 'Beilis trial', engineered by the tsarist government to discredit the Jewish religion and the Jews, by charging that Jewish ritual prescribed the use of Christian blood in the preparation of unleavened bread for the Passover.

After a short respite, however, attacks on the Jewish religion were resumed in the Soviet Union. The 'mission' was entrusted to Jewish communists, who could not be accused of antisemitism or adherence to tsarist anti-Jewish policies. The Jewish communists did not hesitate to indict Jewish religious functionaries for their alleged former collaboration with the tsarist regime and for their 'opposition' to the new regime. In fact, however, Jewish religious leaders had not made any attempts to oppose the new government. It was hardly conceivable that they would have done so by supporting the enemies of the Soviet regime who had instigated or at least tolerated the anti-Jewish pogroms of the civil war. While it is true that large sectors of the Jewish population resented many of the policies and actions of the new regime, they did not seek to translate their resentment into active opposition.

Yet Jewish clergymen and religious organizations were often penalized, if for no other reason than because action was taken against other religious leaders. The communists, especially the Jewish communists, feared that dissimilar treatment of the Jews would provoke antisemitic feelings. Thus, if a Russian clergyman was deported, more often than not a Jewish clergyman had to be deported as well. In addition Jewish communists craved 'action' and distinction, which could best be gained by the discovery, and denunciation, of the 'enemies' in their own midst.

During the civil war, and immediately afterwards, the Soviet Government, desperately in need of the support of the millions of peasants and workers who were religious adherents, sought and achieved a compromise with the Russian Orthodox Church. The Soviet rulers never even entertained a similar concord with the Jewish 'synagogue', because they never really feared it or considered it a power to be reckoned with in the syndrome of the political struggle.

The Yevsektsia (Jewish communist Sections in charge of Jewish affairs) had a double purpose: to enforce government policies on the Jewish *milieu*, and to 'enlighten the Jewish masses in the materialistic world outlook'.

In its first years of existence, the Yevsektsia employed a peculiar form of persuasion drawn from its arsenal of anti-religious propaganda—

namely, the 'community trials'. These trials were conducted against the Jewish religion in general, against the Cheder (religious school) and Yeshivah (secondary school), and against particular Jewish holidays and observances. The trials were highly publicized, supposedly impartial, and allowed the accused the right of self-defence.[1] Yet they were not always successful, and those who dared to take up the defence of the accused often had the sympathies of the audience. The number of trials consequently decreased with each year, as administrative enforcement increased. The latest known trial, which was on circumcision, took place in Kharkov in 1928.[2]

The local authorities, with the help of the Yevsektsia, now embarked on the forceful liquidation of the primary and secondary Jewish schools, even in those localities where public schools were not yet available for all children. In contrast to these actions, which had a legal basis in the Decree of 23 January 1918 (par. 9), other measures aimed at closing synagogues and prayer houses in blatant disregard of existing Soviet law.

In most of those cases that involved the closure and confiscation of synagogues, legality was supplanted by an appeal to public exigency: an ordinance based on the decision of a mass meeting to use the synagogue premises for other 'pressing needs' of the community. Sometimes not even the pretence of a mass meeting was offered.

The 'pressing needs' for housing quarters were, nevertheless, real. Hundreds of thousands of orphaned or abandoned children roamed the countryside, since no housing was available. Demands that some of the existing prayer houses be converted into emergency housing for orphans and sick people often evoked sympathetic responses even among believers. Soviet officials adroitly used this situation to reduce the number of prayer houses so that they would be able to concentrate their efforts at some later date on *a diminished number of targets*.

In many towns, religious Jews vigorously opposed the closing of syna-

[1] The 'Trial of the Cheder', staged in 1921 in Vitebsk has become famous. The communists widely publicized the 'Trial of the Yeshivah', which took place in the winter of 1921 in Rostov. A 'Trial of Rosh Hashana' was conducted in Kiev in 1921.

[2] Characteristic of the mood of the period was the following parable told by a *mohel* (ritual circumciser) in place of a defence speech at one of the 'Trials': The lion once said to the rooster: I shall devour you. Why have I deserved it? asked the rooster.—Because, said the lion, after the floor is swept, you scratch up the garbage again.—But, objected the rooster, because of my scratching, valuable things are sometimes found in the garbage.—I shall devour you, insisted the lion.—Why? wondered the rooster.—Because you wake up people in the morning.—But my crowing makes people get up and go to work, protested the rooster.—I shall devour you, the lion said again.—Why now? wondered the rooster.—Because I am strong and you are weak, explained the lion.—This time the rooster was quiet; he could not find any more questions to ask. (Gershuni, op. cit., p. 45.)

gogues *on any pretext*. For instance, in Vitebsk in 1921, worshippers openly refused to vacate a synagogue requisitioned for a children's dormitory; a large group of Jews assembled in the yard, donned prayer shawls, and refused to move. Force had to be used to take over the synagogue. Ironically, it turned out that instead of a children's dormitory, a school for adults was opened on the premises.

Concurrently, a fierce campaign was initiated against clergymen of all faiths. A series of measures of increasing degrees of harshness was implemented: (1) deprivation of civil rights; (2) restrictions on rights of habitation in publicly owned buildings; (3) discrimination in the provision of rationed foods, medical aid, and educational opportunities for the children of clergymen; (4) heavy taxation of the clergymen's income, which was arbitrarily appraised by state officials; (5) public defamation; and (6) the ultimate penalty: charges of 'counter-revolutionary activities', entailing arrest, prison, deportation and sometimes execution.

The arrests and deportations of Jewish clergymen, especially rabbis, *shokhtim* (ritual slaughterers), and *mohalim* (ritual circumcisers) increased considerably in the late 1920s. Jewish clergymen, together with clergymen of other faiths, were also accused of supporting Trotsky and his followers, and of agitating against the forced collectivization of agriculture (1928–32). These charges were obviously unfounded, since both the political involvement of Jewish clergymen, and the number of Jewish peasants subject to collectivization were negligible. Furthermore, rabbis who were too successful in their work had ultimately to pay for their success. For instance, Rabbi Lazarov of Leningrad, who secured permission to obtain unleavened bread for the Passover from abroad when ration cards for flour were withdrawn in 1929 and the baking of such bread had become impossible, was later sentenced, on a flimsy charge, to three years of deportation. He returned from exile a sick and broken man. Jewish religious rites, especially circumcision and ritual slaughter, were attacked with particular fierceness, both by propaganda and administrative measures, although the performance of both rites was permissible under Soviet law.

Before the arrival of each important Jewish holiday, the Yevsektsia, the Yiddish press, and the Yiddish organ of the 'Fighting atheists', the 'Apikoires', instituted anti-religious campaigns. The most violent seasonal campaigns were those conducted before the High Holidays and before Passover. Especially irritating to religious Jews were the street parades and meetings staged in a most offensive manner in front of prayer houses on Yom Kippur (the Day of Atonement) and Passover.

Many Jews still managed, for a number of years after the Revolution, to observe the day of rest on Saturdays and not to work on Jewish holidays. Such an arrangement was possible in those manufacturing co-operatives (*artels*) and *kolkhozes* where all or almost all of the members were Jews. In the co-operatives, members had a formal right to decide which day of the week to adopt as a day of rest. A prolonged fight for the observance of the sabbath and particularly of the High Holidays was waged in the Jewish *artels* and *kolkhozes* until resolutions at 'workers' meetings' were everywhere manoeuvred through, making Sunday the obligatory day of rest.[1]

The religious ceremonies conducted in homes were not exempt from official scrutiny. Those known to have taken part in such rites as the Passover *Seder* lived in fear of reprisals. It was a tenet of Soviet policy to keep citizens in the dark as to the exact consequences they might incur by engaging in actions distasteful to the government. A person participating in religious ritual was labelled a 'reactionary' or an 'untrustworthy element'. Of course, no one holding a position of any significance, and particularly no younger person, could run the risk of being marked in such fashion.

Securing unleavened bread for Passover was, from the very beginning of Soviet rule, a perennial problem. Government policy has varied from year to year, and from place to place. Obstacles have been placed at every step along the way—in the securing of flour, in the baking of the bread, and in its distribution. Imports which might have alleviated the shortage were not allowed. An exception was made in 1929, when the Soviet Government, faced with the great food shortages of that year, and the impossibility of providing a flour ration for the entire population, granted permission for the import of a large shipment of unleavened bread donated by Jews in the western countries.

Not only were synagogues requisitioned, but ritual objects and religious books were often confiscated, in defiance of the existing law, which provided that such objects should be entrusted to believers for use in other houses of prayer.[2] In those instances where people were aware of the law and dared to resist, books and religious objects were sometimes salvaged.

Hebrew, the language of the Bible and the prayer book, and the language of the Jewish community in Palestine was declared to be intrinsi-

---

[1] Walter Kolarz notes in his book (*Religion in the Soviet Union*, New York, 1961) that 'Jewish communists infiltrated into the artels and bullied them into deciding by majority vote that Saturday should be made an ordinary working day mandatory for all members' (p. 378).

[2] This provision is included in the 'Law on Religious Associations' of 8 April 1929 (par. 40c), *Sobranie Uzakonenii i Rasporiazhenii Rabochekrestianskovo Pravitelstva R.S.F.S.R.*, no. 35, 1929, text no. 353.

cally reactionary, irrespective of content. Even communist slogans in Hebrew would have been considered counter-revolutionary and would have been subject to repression. Hebrew was ultimately outlawed in the late 1920s—the only language *condemned unconditionally* in the Soviet Union.

Placing Hebrew outside the law and making it legally impossible for children to study the language, dealt the intended blow not only to Zionism but to the Jewish religion as well. It made the study of religious subjects and Hebrew prayers that much more difficult and perilous.

A campaign was launched in the late 1920s by the Yevsektsia to force Jewish houses of prayer to donate ritual objects to provide funds for the first Five Year Plan (1928–33). The amount of funds realized from the sale of Jewish religious objects was, however, negligible, since most Jewish houses of prayer of the tsarist Pale of Settlement were not endowed with many ritual objects of pecuniary value. Nevertheless, the campaign served as a useful pretext for the elimination of a large number of devotional objects and religious books.

The Soviet authorities were always careful to persecute on a basis of equality. Thus, if a richly endowed church had to 'donate' its golden ritual objects, then the poor Jewish synagogue in the hamlet was forced 'to make a gift' of its copper candlesticks. If one of the numerous Russian Orthodox churches in town was closed, then one of the few synagogues had to share the same fate.[1]

Some other, more devious schemes were implemented by the Soviet regime in an attempt to debilitate the Jewish religion. One abortive example of such schemes was the attempt to organize an apostatic 'Living Synagogue' modelled after the 'Living Russian Orthodox Church' which introduced drastic innovations into the Church dogmas and ritual, and which was fiercely opposed to the established Church. While the 'Living Church' of the Russian Orthodox faith, organized in the 1920s, succeeded, initially, in shaking the Church to its very foundations, the 'Living Synagogue' was soon abandoned by its founders; it was regarded by all Jews, believers and non-believers alike, as an absurd parody of Jewish religion. This abortive venture proved, if proof were necessary, that an 'opposition' to the existing 'Synagogue' was totally unwarranted, since—in contrast to the Christian ecclesiastical establishments—Jewish religion was not organized hierarchically and was not in opposition to the existing regime.

---

[1] Kolarz writes that 'Soviet anti-Jewish practice has always had a slightly different character from the rest of the communist anti-religious offensive . . . a good deal of the day-to-day agitation has been aimed less at wiping out religious Judaism, although this is of course a communist objective, than of depriving the Russian and Ukrainian antisemites of a favourite argument', op. cit., p. 373.

In 1929, local authorities imposed additional restrictions on those clergy-men who were still functioning in official capacities. These new strictures proved to be so inhuman that the government finally called a halt to the 'expulsion of clergymen from their homes and their towns, wholesale deprivation of medical aid, prohibition of building, expulsion of their children from schools, etc.'[1]

In the period following the collectivization of agriculture (the early 1930s), the Soviet political police (G.P.U., later O.G.P.U.) assumed un-limited powers in dealing with 'enemies of the people', which included both real and arbitrarily designated opponents of the regime. The political police enjoyed the right to arrest any persons considered dangerous and to deport them without trial to prisons and labour camps. These powers were applied quite extensively in regard to clergymen of all faiths.

The central bureau of the Jewish Sections (Yevsektsia) was dissolved in 1930, and all its local sections shortly thereafter. In the short period of its existence the Yevsektsia had become notorious for its efforts to outdo even official Soviet policy in uprooting Jewish religion, Jewish conscious-ness, and Jewish feelings.

It is true that in a number of cases, those acts of the Yevsektsia which were flagrantly illegal were overruled by the higher authorities who sus-tained appeals from the local Jewish citizens. However, as we gain more historical perspective, we are inclined to conclude that these 'excesses' of the Yevsektsia were instigated, or at least welcomed by the same authori-ties, who later rescinded some of the 'excessive acts' in a fraudulent demonstration of magnanimity. If the Yevsektsia had not existed, its acts would have been executed by some other agency of the regime.

It is by now obvious that the liquidation of the Yevsektsia did not bring about an amelioration of the condition of Soviet Jewry, and did not diminish the scope of the 'excesses'. Intemperance in anti-religious measures became even more rampant in later years. In respect to secular Jewish culture and education, the results of the Yevsektsia's disappearance were even more manifest; it ushered in the gradual liquidation of secular Jewish culture. The absence of a distinct Jewish body or organization has been an added handicap to the preservation of Jewish identity in the Soviet Union. Here any central organization would have been preferable to no organization at all.

The machiavellian policy of the Soviet Government during the early years of Soviet rule cannot, however, absolve the sins of the Yevsektsia;

---

[1] *Izvestiya*, 23 March 1930, quoted J. S. Curtiss, *The Russian Church and the Soviet State*, Boston, 1953, p. 233.

the transgressions of the master do not absolve the guilt of the henchman.

The onslaught on Jewish religion could not claim total victory. In an attempt to perpetuate the traditional values of learning, many people disregarded the injunction against religious instruction, in spite of the severe penalties which they incurred in case of detection. Particularly prolonged and stubborn was the heroic struggle of those groups which belonged to the Chasidic movements of *Braslav* and *Chabad*, the latter headed by the *Lubavicher Rebe*, Yosef Ytschok Schneurson.[1] Rabbi Schneurson was finally arrested and threatened with the death sentence. However, following world-wide protests, he was allowed to leave the country at the end of 1928. His followers remained undaunted, nevertheless, and continued their underground religious activities for many years after his departure.

In the early 1930s, the hard 'Stalinist line' became the rule in the regime's handling of religious matters. Most of the rabbis still living in the smaller communities were forced to resign, often submitting a letter of resignation that was revised by the authority at will and published in the government-controlled Yiddish press. The two most frequent reasons for resignation adduced in the letters were: (1) 'There is no further need of our services'; and (2) 'Our eyes have opened and we see now the stupidity and harm of religious superstitions.' Some of the 'retired' rabbis continued to function clandestinely, receiving secret financial support from their followers.

Some degree of relaxation in the harassment of religion took place in the period between 1934 and 1937. This reflected the economic and political consolidation of the country under the now undisputed leadership of Stalin. The period of relative quiet was, however, short-lived. A new orgy of savagery swept the country with the bloody purges of 1937-8.

The reverberation of the purges also reached the clergymen, although to a lesser degree than might have been expected. They probably fared better than other sectors of Soviet society, including members of the communist party. A number of Jewish clergymen was none the less charged with espionage and participation in the 'Trotskyist plots', and received punishments commensurate with the charges.[2]

---

[1] The initials of the word 'Chabad' stand for Chochmo (wisdom), Bina (understanding) and Daas (knowledge).

[2] For instance, Rabbi Medalia of the Moscow Central Synagogue was accused in Pravda (1 October 1938) of being a Polish intelligence agent and of assorted other crimes. He disappeared shortly thereafter. In April 1964, the wife of Rabbi Medalia was informed by the authorities that her husband had been sent to Siberia and executed during the purges of the 'personality cult', and that he was now found to have been innocent of the charges brought against him (Jews in Eastern Europe, November 1964, p. 22).

Concurrently with the assault on Jewish religion, fundamental changes took place *within Soviet Jewry* itself. These changes were to have a great impact on the future fate of Judaism in the country, and to contribute to the success of the regime in eradicating religious observances among the Jewish population.

Following the adoption of the first Five Year Plan in 1928, tens of thousands of Jews, particularly of the younger generation, were absorbed into the economic, social and cultural mainstream of the country, and were recruited into industry and the government and party apparatus. Large numbers left the Jewish hamlets of the Ukraine and Byelorussia and moved to Moscow, Leningrad, and to the new industrial centres which were being developed all over the country.

The younger generation was exhilarated by new vistas and prospects offered by their great country. Indoctrinated in Soviet schools and in the Pioneers and Komsomol organizations, the majority of young Jews became alienated not only from religion and religious practices, but to a large extent from their national origins as well. For a time it seemed to them that not only religion but 'national distinctions' as well would soon disappear. All Soviet citizens would then become members of the great 'Soviet people', which would not know distinctions of nationality, origin, or religion.

Intermarriage, a relatively infrequent phenomenon in the early days of Soviet rule, became very widespread with the increase of contact between Jews and non-Jews following the internal migration of Jews and their absorption into the economy of the country. Reliable statistics on the rate of intermarriage in the Soviet Union are not available. It is known, however, that the rate fluctuated; it reached its zenith in the 1930s, and fell again after the outbreak of the German–Soviet war in 1941.

Concurrently, many religious Jews of the older generation became resigned and reluctantly began to adjust themselves to the new conditions of life. 'Life has changed', they would say with a sigh, and then proceed to conform to what they did not like. Religious observance was regarded with derision by the authorities and could bring nothing but unpleasantness. In addition, facilities for religious observance as well as persons qualified to officiate at religious ceremonies became scarcer, and in many cases practically inaccessible.

Nevertheless, an adamant and dedicated minority devoted to the perpetuation of the Jewish religion and tradition persisted through the 1930s, and continued to preserve Jewish religious life, to the extent that this was at all possible in the new circumstances. There was hardly a town or hamlet, in which a group of religious Jews, large or small, would not keep their faith alive. The places of worship of these groups, overt or clandestine, were sometimes the only quarter where a needy Jew could find sympathy and assistance, and an itinerant Jew refuge. For religious Jews the house of prayer remained the only 'Jewish address' in a Soviet town.

Jewish religious life, particularly in the European sectors of the country, had less opportunity to perpetuate itself than had other religious faiths. An observer who, after some interval, revisited the Soviet Union in 1934, made the following remarks:

The truth was that Jews to a greater extent than followers of other faiths, were deprived of the opportunity to implant their religion into the hearts of the new generation, to raise a clergy for the future, and even to obtain the minimal objects of worship, such as phylacteries, prayer shawls, prayer books. It was deplorable to find religious Jews in socialist Russia bereft of the means of self-expression they had been free to use under the tsars.[1]

The Stalin constitution of 1936 restored civil rights to the *Lishentsy* (those deprived of their rights), which included also the clergy. The heavy income taxes previously imposed on clergymen were substantially reduced. It seemed to many, friends and foe alike, that religion had been beaten; the remnants could thus be left to wither away in peace. This seemed to be particularly true with regard to Jewish religion.

But the future did not evolve in the way that Soviet ideologists and more impartial observers had predicted.

The acquisition of new territories after the outbreak of the Second World War, with a Jewish population of nearly two million, reinforced both secular and religious Judaism in the Soviet Union. Although the former borders between the old and the newly-acquired territories were not removed, and special permits were required for inter-territorial travel, some communication between west and east was maintained.

At the outset, the Soviet authorities did not interfere excessively in the religious life of the population in the new territories; this applied to the Jewish as well as to the other religions. Thus the disparity between west and east in this respect was substantial during this period.

The German–Soviet war changed the situation of Soviet Jewry brutally and irrevocably. In the wake of the rapid German penetration into the conquered territories, more than a million Jewish men, women, and children were machine-gunned by the Einstzkommandos (special German

[1] B. Z. Goldberg, *The Jewish Problem in the Soviet Union*, New York, 1961, p. 26.

units given the task of carrying out the mass execution of the Jewish population). Much of the Jewish population of the conquered territories escaped annihilation by fleeing before the invading armies arrived. Within a few months, the great majority of the surviving Soviet Jews had become uprooted refugees, and the historic centres of Jewish life and culture in the western parts of the Soviet Union had ceased to exist.

Within the Soviet Union, the Fatherland War brought an abrupt end to all anti-religious campaigns; many religious properties previously requisitioned by the authorities 'at the wishes of the populace' were restored to the believers.

In 1943 a council for the affairs of the Russian Orthodox Church and a council for all other religious cults, including the Jewish, were established. The councils were to be 'the liaisons between the government and the leaders of the corresponding cults on questions affecting those cults and requiring action by the government of the U.S.S.R.'[1] A formal, although not publicly announced, agreement had been reached between the state and the Russian Orthodox Church, which granted this church many liberties not accorded to other religious cults, thus restoring to the Russian Orthodox Church the privileged position it had lost in October 1917, *mutatis mutandis*.

Most Jews who were evacuated from the occupied or war-ravaged territories settled in central Asia. Consequently, large Jewish communities arose in several towns, particularly in Tashkent and Samarkand, where followers of the *Chabad* and *Braslav* Chasidic movements established illegal Yeshivahs. Houses of prayer and *minyanim* were organized in many places, especially for the High Holidays. Although they were for the most part unregistered, and therefore illegal, the new houses of prayer were tolerated by the authorities, in keeping with the new official policy of benevolence toward religious observances.

In the post-war period Soviet Jewry consisted of a mass of people in search of physical and mental rehabilitation. Jews were still bewildered by the unforeseen growth of antisemitism and were horror-stricken at the enormous extent of the mass murders of the Jewish population. But Nazi genocide and the upsurge of antisemitism simultaneously evoked a substantial increase in Jewish loyalties and Jewish cohesiveness.

[1] See Conference Room paper no. 35, 30 January 1959, U.N. Commission on Human Rights, Sub-Commission on prevention of discrimination and protection of minorities: *Study of discrimination in the matter of religious rights and practices.* Summary of information relating to the U.S.S.R., p. 18.

Although the Jewish religion, like other religions, enjoyed a greater measure of tolerance during and immediately after the war, the advantages procured during these lenient years did not prove of lasting value.

Several factors helped to prevent a more durable accommodation. Most Jews were refugees who considered their places of residence as temporary and were not inclined to make long-range commitments; the Jewish religion had no representative body capable of issuing demands and of providing organizational assistance to realize available opportunities; unlike most other Churches, the Jewish religious establishment had apparently very little to offer to the Soviet Government in its foreign policy stratagems. The Jewish establishment was, therefore, treated with a measure of disdain: it could not be of much help, and it did not present much of a threat either.

It is not surprising then, that after the end of the war, Jewish religious leaders were not always asked to join other religious representatives in ecumenical undertakings organized by the Soviet Government. For instance, they were not invited to join, with clergymen of other faiths, the Committee for the Defence of Peace organized in 1951. On other occasions, when they were asked to participate, as in the Zagorsk conference of religious leaders in May 1952, only two individual synagogues (in Moscow and Kiev) were authorized to send representatives. The absence of a central Jewish religious body continued to be a great handicap, both in the conduct of internal Jewish affairs and in relations with the government.

Also, Jewish religious leaders, sensing the inequity of treatment dared not be as bold in their demands as were leaders of other religious cults. They probably concluded that their efforts would not have been of much avail.

The division of Soviet policy towards religion into periods of varying lenience and severity—as appears in most studies on the subject—does not always apply to the Jewish religion. The Soviet attitude towards Judaism is not accurately reflected in the generally accepted delineations of Soviet policy into three periods: (1) persecution till 1941, (2) tolerance from 1941 to 1948 and (3) after 1948 renewed persecution.[1]

Walter Kolarz notes, in his study of religion in the Soviet Union, that Judaism was singled out for special treatment:

Stalin anticipated that religious Judaism would disappear much more quickly than other religions which had preserved their sociological roots, and he was determined

[1] Nikita Struve, in *Les Chrétiens en U.R.S.S.*, Paris, 1963, notes, however, that 'Judaism under Soviet rule is a subject in itself'.

to hasten this natural process as effectively as possible. It became clear that Stalin would not extend to the Jews the concessions he was prepared to grant to other religious communities.[1]

The discriminatory policy of the Soviet Government towards Jews as a Soviet *nationality*, and the policy of the government towards the *State of Israel*, which emerged in 1948, have no doubt exerted some influence on Soviet policy towards the Jewish religion, but the extent of the influence and the time intervals between cause and effect are hard to identify.

However, a turning point in Soviet policy towards the Jewish minority occurred in 1948. At the end of that year, all remaining Jewish organizations and Yiddish publications were shut down, including the Jewish Anti-Fascist Committee and its organ, *Aynikayt*, which had been established at the beginning of the war with Germany. In the ensuing period, referred to by the Jews as the 'Black Years', almost all persons active in Yiddish culture and literature were either executed or imprisoned. Russian intellectuals of Jewish descent were reprimanded as 'cosmopolitans', and in a dramatic climax with medieval undertones, a group of Jewish doctors was formally charged with organizing a plot to poison the Soviet leaders at the instigation of Jewish organizations abroad. The inescapable result of all these actions and accusations was a new wave of popular antisemitism, unprecedented in its overtness.

Strangely enough, the suppression of secular Jewish culture, together with the liquidation of the people working in this field, was not accompanied by a comparable assault on Jewish religion and on Jewish clergymen. (Only a few rabbis were arrested, and most of them were released soon thereafter.) None the less, the 'Black Years' had a profound effect upon Soviet Jewry, religious and non-religious alike, the repercussions of which are still felt. No action, *or inaction*, on the part of Soviet Jews can be understood without taking into account the traumatic impact of this period, when Jews were treated as 'a foreign element', and every Jew was unsure of his future.

The less stringent policy in respect to Jewish religion during this period may well have been dictated by the Soviet assumption that Jewish religion was anyway on the verge of extinction, and that stern measures would be superfluous. By contrast, Jewish 'nationalism' was viewed as a dormant force, potentially dangerous to both communist ideology and to the regime itself.

In relation to the policy of total annihilation of Jewish secular culture,

[1] Op. cit., p. 388.

the regime's attitude towards the Jewish religion seemed at that time almost benevolent. In reality, however, it had continued to remain under relentless pressure and harassment. As before, rights granted to other religions, such as the pursuit of religious education, the maintenance of sectarian publications, and the procurement of ritual articles were consistently denied to religious Jewry.

We may assume with certainty that in the early 1950s the expectation of the Soviet Government was that Soviet conditions of life and persistent governmental pressures would inevitably, and in a short time, lead to the dissolution of both the Jewish religion and the Jewish nationality. Consistent with this expectation a policy was evolved whereby public references to Jewry, both in terms of 'nationality' and religion, past or present, were deleted, effaced, or glossed over. The intention was to 'silence to death' a living organism by *creating the illusion that it did not exist—until such time as it would in fact cease to exist.* This policy may be deduced not only from what was printed about the Jews, but even more from what was left out in the new editions of Soviet encyclopedias, and in textbooks published during that period. It was also evident from the fact that, for the first time, Jews as a separate group were omitted from newly revised lists of 'Heroes of the Soviet Union'. (Jews had been the fifth largest group to bear this highest Soviet military distinction.)

Even the unspeakable tragedy of the Jews under the Nazis was expunged from public mention. Jewish victims of Nazi atrocities were rarely identified as Jews, even where Jews were the only victims of the crimes. Several monuments erected at the sites of mass executions of Jews were removed by the Soviet authorities, and other memorials erected in their place; former inscriptions in Yiddish or Hebrew and the word 'Jewish' were omitted from the texts of the new inscriptions. In Lithuania, for example, such operations were performed on the memorials erected at the mass graves of the Nazi victims at the 'Ninth Fort' in Kovno and at Ponary in Vilno, among others. The monuments which now stand at both places do not even mention that Jews were murdered there.[1]

Babi Yar in Kiev, the place where the number of Jews killed probably reached 50,000, has become the symbol of Soviet attitudes towards the

---

[1] As reported by an eyewitness in the *Day-Morning Journal*, New York (29 December 1966). See also: S. Schwarz, *Evrei v Sovetskom Soiuze s nachala vtoroi mirovoi voini* (Jews in the Soviet Union, from the beginning of the Second World War), New York, 1966, footnote 16, pp. 252-3. It was also reported that in Baranovichi, Byelorussian S.S.R., a monument was erected in 1945 to the memory of 4,000 Jews killed by the Nazis, and that the monument was later destroyed and in its place a public latrine constructed (*Jews in Eastern Europe*, mid-September 1959, p. 3).

Jewish tragedy in the Nazi period. 'There is no monument in Babi Yar', protests the embittered Soviet poet Yevgenii Yevtushenko in his famous poem, 'Babi Yar'. Indeed, there was no monument at all at Babi Yar, not even a monument from which the word 'Jew' is omitted. But memorials were erected all over the Soviet Union on sites where non-Jewish Soviet citizens were killed by the German invaders, and where the number of victims was far less than 50,000.

In keeping with these attitudes, the Jewish religion was not listed among the important religious faiths in the very important Edict (*Postanovlenie*) issued by the communist party on 7 July 1954, entitled 'On the strengthening of anti-religious activities'.[1] This seems to this writer to have been not in the nature of an oversight at all, but rather in line with general policy.

A vigorous campaign against the Jewish religion was initiated again in 1957, apparently at the anti-religious conference held in that year in Moscow. Soon thereafter, a large number of the remaining synagogues was forced to close. At the same time, some concessions were granted, probably to confuse and to offset the anticipated protests from abroad. The concessions, which seemed important at that time, did not usher in a new era in Soviet relations to Jewish religion, as many Soviet Jews had hoped. Indeed, they turned out to be of short duration.

In 1957, a photostat edition of a Hebrew prayer book in 3,000 copies was published, and a seminary for the training of religious personnel established. The prayer books were sold out so quickly that many Jewish communities outside Moscow did not receive a single copy.[2] The seminary dwindled into a fictitious institution, after only a few years' existence.

The oriental communities of Bukharan Jews in central Asia, Mountain Jews and Georgian Jews in the Caucasus, with a total population of around 150,000, always enjoyed a greater measure of religious freedom than the western (Ashkenazic) Jews, greater even than those western Jews who lived in the same areas as the oriental Jews. Thus the privileged religious status enjoyed by the oriental Jews cannot be solely attributed to geographical location and local discretion. Rather, the main reasons for

---

[1] 'O krupnykh nedostatkakh v nauchno-ateisticheskoi propagande i merakh ee uluchsheniia', Postanovlenie TsK KPSS, 7 July 1954; 'O Religii i Tserkvi, sbornik dokumentov', Moscow, 1965, pp. 71–7.

[2] Joseph Schechtman, the Jewish writer who visited the Soviet Union in 1959, was told by a Jew in Kiev, 'I have heard that 3,000 prayer books were published by the State Publishing House for the Moscow religious community, but not a single copy has reached us. Nobody cares for a provincial Jewish community which very few foreign tourists visit.' (Joseph Schechtman, *Star in Eclipse*, New York, 1961, p. 126.)

the preferred treatment of oriental Jews lie elsewhere: first, in the greater extent of religious devotion manifested by the majority of oriental Jews, and the correspondingly greater measure of defiance that could be expected from them in case of encroachments on their basic religious rights; second, in the general policy of the Soviet state to 'go easy' in combating the religious beliefs among the less developed segments of the Soviet population; third, in the smaller degree of Jewish 'nationalistic' consciousness prevalent among oriental Jews, in contrast to the western Jews among whom the religious currents were believed to fan the fires of nationalism. The Soviet regime feared Jewish nationalism more than it feared the Jewish religion. One illustration of this attitude is the statement of an 'Old Bolshevik' made to the Jewish-American journalist Joseph Schechtman, in the editorial offices of the central organ of the Soviet communist party, *Pravda*, in Moscow:

Why should we bother combating Jewish religion actively? It will croak by itself (*sama sdokhnet*). . . . If we sometimes close Jewish houses of prayer it is not because we are aiming at the synagogues as religious strongholds—they are in themselves of no consequence. But they serve as the last assembly for our Jews, often even for those who are no longer religious. They help to maintain cohesion, to nurture the feeling of belonging to a distinctive Jewish entity. And this is exactly what we are trying to prevent. The fewer synagogues, the fewer opportunities to congregate and to keep Jewish separateness.[1]

Towards the end of the 1950s, Jewish anti-religious propaganda became more intensive and more vitriolic. It also differed in tenor from the propaganda directed against other religious cults. In addition to the classical arguments used against all religious faiths, the following arguments were used against the Jewish religion above all others:

1. The tenets of the Jewish religion are of a particularly immoral character; money is the god of the Jewish faith.

2. The Jewish religion promulgates the idea that the Jewish people is a chosen people, a notion that breeds Jewish hatred of other peoples.

3. The Jewish religion promotes allegiance to another state, the State of Israel, and to a reactionary, pro-imperialist movement—namely, Zionism.[2]

---

[1] Schechtman, op. cit., p. 146.

[2] Characteristic of the calibre of anti-Jewish Soviet propaganda of that period was the highly critical attitude taken even by the pro-Soviet communist parties of the west. For instance, the official organ of the Italian communist party, *L'Unita*, criticized on 15 December 1964, the booklet *Contemporary Judaism and Zionism*, by F. Mayatsky under the unequivocal heading 'An antisemitic libel'; the article rebukes the author for asserting that 'Judaism is the worst of all religions: pessimistic, nationalistic, anti-feminine and anti-popular . . . Born from

In accordance with these views, two Jewish rituals came again under vehement attack: The rite of circumcision, allegedly denoting the concept of a chosen people, and the observance of Passover, with its Jewish-national content (symbolized by the phrase 'next year in Jerusalem', as pronounced at the *Seder* meal).

Accordingly, information on the medical value of circumcision and its growing acceptance by non-Jews abroad was rigidly suppressed, and the preparation of unleavened bread for the Passover, permitted even during the worst of times under Stalin's oppressive rule, was rendered all but impossible under Stalin's successors. Jewish anti-religious propaganda, conducted before the war almost exclusively in Yiddish, was now conducted in Russian, and extensively also in the Ukrainian and Moldavian languages read by only a very small number of Jews.[1] The inescapable conclusion must be, therefore, that the anti-religious Jewish propaganda conducted in languages other than Yiddish and Russian, was aimed not at Jews but at their non-Jewish neighbours. Characteristically, Jewish anti-religious items which sometimes appeared in the Yiddish-language journals *Sovietish Heymland* and *Biro-Bidzhaner Shtern*, were much milder in form and devoid of the specific charges raised exclusively against the Jewish religion.

The character and calibre of Soviet anti-Jewish propaganda have become familiar to the west through the book *Yudaism bez prikras* (Judaism without Embellishment) by Trofim Kichko, published in Kiev in 1963. Yet Kichko's book was but a compilation of the arguments and charges against Judaism to which previous Soviet publications had given repeated expression. The furore aroused by the book outside Russia was probably due to the concentration in one volume of so many groundless accusations and falsifications, to the inclusion of Nazi-type caricatures, and to the publication of the book by as scholarly an institution as the Ukrainian Academy of Science. Contrary to popular belief; the book was, in its essence, not repudiated by the communist party, which only pointed out some 'mistakes' in presentation. Following the barrage of protests from abroad, however, including petitions from most communist parties of the west, the book was silently withdrawn from circulation.

In the same period (1959–62), a substantial number of the remaining

such principles, the State of Israel could only become the worst of all States' (*Jews in Eastern Europe*, May 1965, p. 16).

[1] According to the census of 1959, only 3 per cent of the Jewish population in the Ukraine declared Ukrainian to be their native language, and only 1 per cent in the Moldavian republic claimed the Moldavian language as their native tongue. The overwhelming majority of Jews in the Soviet Union speak and read Russian and/or Yiddish.

synagogues was closed, among them the large synagogues of Lvov and Chernovtsi (Ukrainian S.S.R.). The closure of these synagogues followed the classical, long-established pattern, with some modifications in policy geared to a new stage of 'historical development' and to the existence of the State of Israel. First stage: letters and articles in the press, citing illegal, criminal activities, and/or pro-Israel propaganda in the synagogue. Next stage: requests from readers, including 'religious believers', to liquidate the 'nest of corruption' and/or terminate 'pro-Israel and anti-Soviet propaganda'. The final stage consisted of a decision by the local authorities to close the synagogues 'in compliance with the wishes of the community'.

Two simultaneous campaigns were conducted during this period which influenced, to a substantial degree, the overall situation of the Jewish population in the country.

The first was a campaign directed against the State of Israel, which was portrayed as a puppet of the imperialist states and designated as their agent in the Near East. The second was a vehement campaign waged against black-market dealings, widely publicizing the cases in which Jews were involved, creating thereby the impression among the general populace that these illegal activities were fostered mainly by Jews.

It was, of course, inevitable that strong antisemitic sentiments should be stirred up anew by the two campaigns. Religious Jewry was, naturally, affected by these campaigns no less than non-religious Jews.

Soviet law recognizes two types of religious organizations, which are referred to collectively as 'religious associations'. The first designation is that of the religious societies which are administered by 'groups of twenty' (*dvatsatka*), and the second consists of groups of believers, 'not numerous enough to organize a religious society'.[1]

Information about the first type of religious associations is scarce; information about the second type is almost non-existent. It is, however, clear that the basic Jewish religious unit is, at present at least, the religious society. The society administers a synagogue, under a lease agreement with the local soviet, and functions under the strict control and super-vision of both the local soviet and the plenipotentiary of the Council for

---

[1] The Law on Religious Associations of 8 April 1929 was published in *Sobranie Uzakonenii i Rasporiazhenii Rabochekrestianskovo Pravitelstva R.S.F.S.R*, no, 35, 1929, text no. 353; amendments: *Sobranie Uzakonenii*, etc., no. 8, 1932, text no. 41, 116, 'Instructions', following the law were issued 1 October 1929 and were published in the *Biuleten* N.K.V.D., R.S.F.S.R., no. 37, 1929. English translations of both texts can be found in *Church and State under Communism*, special study prepared by the Law Library of Congress, Washington, 1964, pp. 12–17 and 18–24.

the Affairs of Religious Cults, who often appoint and dismiss members of the governing bodies of the synagogues.[1]

In addition to these *registered* groups, we know of the existence of *unregistered* prayer groups, called *minyanim*, organized in those areas where the local authorities do not permit them to function legally. There are several kinds of unregistered *minyanim*: groups that meet regularly, groups formed *ad hoc* for the High Holiday season only (the most frequent type), and small groups organized primarily for the purpose of enabling mourners to say the Kaddish prayer for the dead.[2]

The unregistered groups are forced to function illegally, although their existence is compatible with Soviet law. A clause in the Soviet statutes on religion, perhaps little known, provides that small groups may hold *ad hoc* religious services, provided they submit information to the authorities regarding each individual service.[3]

According to existing Soviet legislation on religion, a religious society may be converted into a group of believers when it is short of the twenty members responsible to the authorities, yet such a case has never occurred, as far as we know, in respect to Jewish groups. Indeed, one of the favourite methods employed by the Soviet authorities to effect the closure of a Jewish house of prayer is to create, or to take advantage of, a situation whereby the number of members responsible for the synagogue falls below twenty. The number of open synagogues dwindles from year to year, and only a handful are left of these which existed before the great onslaught on Jewish houses of prayer began in the late 1920s.

According to Soviet sources, 1,103 synagogues were still in existence in January 1926, after almost a decade of Soviet rule and of Soviet harassment

---

[1] For instance, according to reports coming from the Soviet Union, the Commissariat of State Security (K.G.B.) dissolved the executive body of the Moscow synagogue and appointed three new members, Fishlowich, Mikhalovich, Oletsky, and then in turn ousted the three-man executive body in 1964 and appointed new replacements (*Yalkut Mogen*, Tel Aviv, August 1960, p. 7, *New York Herald Tribune*, 10 July 1964).

[2] There are also *minyanim* organized, illegally, by followers of various Chasidic movements. Testimony from a Soviet source indicates that Chasidism in the Soviet Union is not yet extinguished: 'And in the U.S.S.R. Chasidism makes known its existence. There is a section in the Choral synagogue in Moscow where the Chasidim pray. In Kishinev, Leningrad, and in some other towns of our country many believing Jews consider themselves followers of the teachings of Besht. The Beshtants disseminate myths and legends which are meant to prove the "democracy" and "originality" of Chasidism.' (*Osnovy nauchnovo ateizma, uchebnoe posobie*, Moscow, 1964, p. 153.)

[3] Paragraph 22 of the 'Instructions', op. cit., permits 'the holding of prayer meetings on premises which are not especially adopted for religious purposes' and continues: 'believers who have not formed a Religious Society or Group of Believers must notify authorities regarding each prayer meeting separately.'

of religion.[1] Now their number has decreased, according to the best of our knowledge, to only sixty-two.[2]

The geographical distribution of the existing synagogues is very significant for the appraisal of Soviet policy in respect to the Jewish religion. Thirteen of the 62 synagogues, or 20 per cent of the total, are located in the republic of Georgia, where only 2½ per cent of the Jewish population of the country resides. An additional 17 synagogues exist in the communities of oriental Jews in four central Asian republics (Kazakhstan, Uzbekistan, Kirgistan, Tadzhikistan; there is no synagogue in the fifth central Asian republic of Turkmenistan), and in parts of the Caucasus outside of Georgia. Thus almost one half (30 out of 62) of the Jewish congregations are located in the non-European parts of the Soviet Union, in an area inhabited *by less than 10 per cent* of the total Jewish population of the country.

The uneven geographical distribution of synagogues is, as we have indicated, basically attributable to two factors: the fact that the religious affiliation of western Jews is opposed by the regime more doggedly than the same affiliation on the part of oriental Jews, and the fact that oriental Jews are ready to defend their religious institutions and observances more defiantly than the more secularized western Jews.

The absence of a central Jewish religious organization renders each synagogue a separate unit, forced to wage its battle for survival all alone, isolated from all other synagogues in the country (in contrast to other religious cults, and in contrast to the Jewish condition in other countries of the socialist bloc). The central synagogue in Moscow does not have a status different from any other synagogue in the country, neither does the Moscow rabbi enjoy a special status. Only because the Moscow synagogue is located in the capital, and the Soviet Government finds it sometimes necessary to produce a Jewish religious spokesman, does the Moscow synagogue acquire, at times, something resembling the *de facto* status of a representative body.

No Jewish religious bulletin is published currently in the Soviet Union (again in contrast to other religious cults and to the situation in other socialist countries, such as Rumania and Czechoslovakia, where similar bulletins do appear). No Jewish literature of a religious nature has been published since 1928, with the exception of the prayer book in 1957 and

---

[1] *Di alfarbandishe komunistishe partei un di yiddishe masn*, p. 58, quoted in *Razsviet*, no. 2, 1929, and in Gershuni, op. cit., p. 117.
[2] *Synagogues in the Soviet Union*, a study prepared by Joshua Rothenberg, Institute of East European Jewish Affairs, Brandeis University, Waltham, Mass., March 1966, pp. 6–8.

several tiny Jewish calendars, published sporadically by the Moscow and Leningrad synagogues.

Promises—reiterated every year during the last five years—to print a new edition of the prayer book have not been fulfilled; the information disseminated in 1965 that the prayer book was already on the printing presses, has by now been proved false.[1]

The religious education of children is not tolerated, in spite of the expressed right granted to all Soviet citizens to teach their children religious doctrines 'in a private manner'. Rarely nowadays will a father venture to teach his children the Hebrew alphabet (an act which would be characterized as 'poisoning his soul'), and rarely does a Jewish clergyman dare to teach religion to a Jewish child—with the exception of the oriental Jewish communities where the attitude of the authorities is much more lenient. When the first higher institution of Jewish religious learning was established in 1957 at the Moscow synagogue, the entire Jewish religious community of the country responded enthusiastically. Many synagogues granted subsidies and were prepared to send students to the Yeshivah. Rabbi Schlieffer announced at the inauguration of the school that he had enough students to fill three large schools.[2] But a war of attrition followed. Students from outside Moscow were refused the right to return to Moscow after their summer vacations; the leaders of the Yeshivah were harassed by the Soviet authorities. Today, the Yeshivah is in fact no longer in operation.

The average age of Jewish clergymen (rabbis, ritual slaughterers, ritual circumcisers) is above 70. The average age of cantors is somewhat lower. Cantors with good voices are paid relatively well and are much sought after; some of them are former professional singers. There is little likelihood that the older generation of clergymen will be succeeded by the younger generation, as there are no institutions for the training of religious functionaries. The problem of the supply of clergymen is one of the most acute problems confronting Judaism in the Soviet Union.

Foreign contacts have recently been extended. In 1968 Rabbi Levin of Moscow and D. M. Stitskin, the cantor at Leningrad, visited America.

[1] A comparison with the Baptist church (about 600,000 followers) which is certainly not the most favoured religious denomination in the Soviet Union, clearly shows the inferior treatment accorded to Jewish religion. Baptists are permitted to appoint a central administration, to train ministers and preachers, to maintain 500 ordained preachers, send young ministers abroad to further their study, and to publish an illustrated bi-monthly, the *Fraternal Herald*. The Baptists hold conferences of their own and have attended many international congresses of the Baptists and other Protestant groups. Delegations of Baptist churchmen have visited foreign countries. All these activities were denied to the Jews. (See *Jews in Eastern Europe*, September 1963, p. 36; Schechtman, op. cit., p. 139.)   [2] Ibid., p. 122.

In 1970 Rabbi Levin headed a delegation to Belgrade. No Jewish student has ever been sent abroad for study, in sharp contrast to the treatment accorded to other religions. Nor were Soviet Jews allowed to produce religious objects, or to accept them from abroad. In 1968 this ban was partially lifted.[1]

Ritual slaughterhouses exist and ritual slaughterers still function in some communities of Ashkenazic Jews, and in most communities of oriental Jews. In these places the kosher slaughtering of *fowl* is permitted; kosher slaughtering of cattle is rarely allowed, however, especially in the European areas of the country.

The ban on *matzo*-baking has been extended geographically each year; by 1964 it was enforced almost throughout the country. Sustained protests from abroad have induced the Soviet leaders to lift the ban partially, and in 1965 Jewish communities in a number of larger Soviet towns were again allowed to bake *matzos*.

Although the shipment of individual *matzo* parcels was never *officially* prohibited, a vocal campaign against receiving parcels from abroad (an 'ideological diversion') was waged in the Soviet press in 1964, and consequently many parcels never reached their destination. Agencies in several western countries continue to encourage the shipment of Passover parcels, including *matzos*, to the U.S.S.R.[2] The total effect of all these measures has brought about a situation where only a minority of those Soviet Jews who desire *matzos* for Passover, are allowed to obtain them.

Burial in the consecrated ground of a Jewish cemetery, conducted according to Jewish religious law, was always one of the basic and most universally observed Jewish religious rites. In the post-war Soviet era this observance has become more and more difficult. Cemeteries of various religious faiths became filled up and must eventually close for lack of space. New cemeteries are of a general, non-sectarian character.

According to Soviet law, burial grounds which are not used for twenty to thirty years (depending on the nature of the soil) can be converted into public gardens.

[1] After 1953, Jewish religious leaders were allowed on certain occasions to send messages to foreign Jewish communities. The first message, on Rosh Hashana (New Year) 1953, was sent by Rabbi Schlieffer to the Jews of Britain. On March 1955, a message was published and signed by the rabbis of eight cities to the 'Jews the world over' in which a protest against 'the preparations for nuclear war' was voiced. In November 1956, a group of rabbis protested at Britain's and France's military actions against Egypt, and censured Israel's Sinai campaign. In June 1957 a new 'appeal for peace' was published, signed by four rabbis of Moscow and the Moscow District. As can be seen, these appeals were dictated by political considerations of the Soviet Government and can hardly be classified as 'contact with Jews abroad'.

[2] At a very high cost; in 1967 a 10 lb. parcel of *matzos*, sent from the United States costs $18.50, in addition to $12.00 paid as a 'dispatch charge'.

Circumcision, not prohibited by Soviet law, is practised without hindrance by the great majority of the approximately 25 million Moslems in the country. But the same practice when performed by western Jews is scorned and subjected to heavy harassment. Very few *mohalim* (ritual circumcisers) are at present functioning legally in the Soviet Union. It is impossible to ascertain the proportion of Jewish male infants who undergo the operation of circumcision, as most operations are performed in secret, but the frequency of the rite is probably very low. An educated guess would place the proportion as not more than 10 per cent of all the newborn Jewish males in the country. Thus a basic Jewish ritual, observed almost universally by Jews throughout countless generations, has now become practically extinct in the Soviet Union.

Attendance at Soviet synagogues follows in the main those patterns prevalent in other countries, with some exceptions. As in other Jewish communities the world over, synagogue attendance is highest on the days of the New Year and the Day of Atonement and on the days when 'Yizkor', the prayer for the dead, is said.

There is hardly a Jew in the Soviet Union who did not lose a close relative either in the Holocaust, or at the front, and on the days when 'Yizkor' is recited prayer houses are crowded. Even non-religious Jews are moved to honour the memory of their departed relatives in the traditional Jewish way.

However, one Jewish holiday has changed considerably in its character and mode of celebration. This is the Rejoicing of the Law (Simchat Torah), which in the last ten years has become in the Soviet Union the holiday of youth. Thousands of Jewish youngsters, among them many non-believers and members of the Komsomol, flock to the synagogues, particularly in Moscow and Leningrad, with their musical instruments, sing Hebrew and Yiddish songs, thus converting the holiday into a festival of Jewish song and dance. These assemblies on the occasion of Simchat Torah provide an opportunity for those of the young Jewish generation who feel Jewish, to express their Jewish identity in the only way left open to them. As no secular institutions of Jewish culture are available, the synagogue remains the only focus of Jewish identification.

The number of rabbis functioning at present in the Soviet Union is believed to be no higher than ten to fifteen, mostly with the Oriental communities. In many synagogues religious functions are performed by lay members.

In the Soviet Union today, *organized* Jewish religion represents only the tiny visible part of the total entity, and Jewish religious observances are but the visible trickle from a powerful wellspring of Jewish consciousness erupting in one form or another, sometimes unexpectedly, from beneath the frozen surface of Soviet reality. In addition to the large numbers of religious, observant Jews (it is impossible to estimate how large), there are thousands of *non-observant* Jews for whom Jewish religious literature, and Jewish tradition remain an integral part of their Jewish identity.

Conclusions

1. The fate of Judaism in the Soviet Union during the first fifty years of Soviet rule—1917–67 is in many respects dissimilar from the fate of other religions in the country.

2. In the early 1950s the Soviet Government concluded that the disintegration of Jewish identity in the Soviet Union had progressed to such a degree that with a suitable policy and a little effort the highly objectionable 'Jewish separateness', in both the religious and national sense, would completely disappear.

3. The fact that the Jewish group in the Soviet Union constitutes both a 'nationality' and a religious group, creates a situation where any action or policy concerning either of these groups affects all Soviet Jews. The mutual interdependence is augmented by the characteristic feature that all followers of the Jewish religious cult belong also to the Jewish nationality, *and to no other*, and that membership in the religious group is not made public. Rarely will a Soviet citizen reading attacks on 'Judaists' make an effort, nor is it at all possible, to distinguish between 'Judaists' and 'Jews'.

4. The present underprivileged status of the Jewish religion is no longer a matter of conjecture. Many facilities and avenues of religious expression available to other religious cults, are not available to Jewish religious believers. The Soviet contention that this is due to a lack of demand is untenable. (Soviet charges of an existing black market in Jewish religious articles provide one example that visibly contradicts this contention.)

5. A decline in the position and influence of Jewish religion would undoubtedly have taken place in the Soviet Union, even if repressive measures against religion had not been implemented. A certain decline in religious practice is noticeable in the last fifty years in most Jewish communities throughout the world. However, the sharp decrease of religious practices in the Soviet Union, the drastic contraction in the number of prayer houses, and the cessation of religious education, are for the most part, a result of administrative measures and official pressure, and only in some smaller degree due to the historical process of secularization and to the influence of communist ideology.

6. A sublimation of Jewish 'national' feelings into religious channels and symbols is apparent—as is evidenced in the participation of non-religious young Jews in the Simchat Torah celebrations. This development is a result of the total suppression of secular Jewish channels for the expression of Jewish identity. The self-defeating features of the Soviet 'nationality policy' have been nowhere more clearly demonstrated than in this case; this policy has produced precisely those effects which the regime had laboured to prevent.

7. If the present Soviet policy continues unabated for a protracted period of time, a gradual process of attrition of Jewish religious life in the Soviet Union may be anticipated. A change in Soviet policy towards Jewish religion will depend on several factors and the scope of their efficacy: the expected liberal trend in the development of internal Soviet policies, the fortitude of Soviet Jewry in upholding their faith, and the extent and influence of public opinion abroad.

8. The events and processes of the last decade have demonstrated the fallacy of the Soviet appraisal. Jewish religion is more tenacious than might have been expected, and secular Jewish endeavour has been infused with unexpected vitality and creativity. (One Yiddish periodical which was allowed to appear solely for the purpose of placating public opinion abroad (*Sovetish Heymland*) has become an important rallying point for many talented and creative Yiddish writers and their numerous readers.)

Instead of the expected decrease, a notable *increase* in Jewish awareness, and in pro-Israel sentiments, has become manifest. Only the elimination of restrictions and pressures will allow a confrontation and a fair play of ideas and beliefs in the Soviet Union. Without it, no credence can be given to Soviet assertions that compulsion and force are not the prime cause of the present sorry state of the Jewish religion in the Soviet Union.

SELECTED BIBLIOGRAPHY
(In addition to the references in the footnotes)

Ben Ami, *Bein Hapatish Vehamagal* (Between the hammer and the sickle, a personal experience among Jews in the Soviet Union), Am Oved, Tel Aviv, 1965.

Decter, Moshe, 'The status of the Jews in the Soviet Union', *Foreign Affairs*, New York, January, 1963.

Chanin, N., *Soviet Rusland vi ihk hob yir gezen* (Soviet Russia as I saw her), New York, 1929.

Church and State under Communism; special study prepared by the Library of Congress, Washington, 1946.

Even Shushan, Shlomo, *Sipuro shel masa, esrim yom be-Brit Hamoatzot* (The story of a voyage, twenty days in the Soviet Union), Tel Aviv, 1964.

Gershuni, A. A., *Yahadut be-Russia ha-Sovietit* (Judaism in Soviet Russia), Jerusalem, 1961.

Gidulianov, D. V. (ed.), *Otdelenie tserkvi ot gosudarstva* (The separation of church and state), Moscow, 1926.

Gilboa, Yehoshua, *The Black Years of Soviet Jewry 1939–1953*, Boston, 1971.

Goldberg, B. Z., *The Jewish Problem in the Soviet Union*, New York, 1961.

Instructions of the R.S.F.S.R. People's Commissariat for the Interior, 1 October 1929 on Rights and Obligations of Religious Associations, in *Biuleten N.K.V.D., R.S.F.S.R.*, no. 37, 1929.

Kolarz, Walter, *Religion in the Soviet Union*, New York, 1961.

Law on Religious Associations of 8 April 1929, in *Sobranie Uzakonenii i Rasporiazhenii Rabochekrestianskovo Pravitelstva R.S.F.S.R.*, no. 35, 1929, text 353.

Lestshchinsky, Jacob, *Dos Sovetische Yidntum* (Soviet Jewry), New York, 1941.

Marshall, Richard H., Jr., ed., *Aspects of Religion in the Soviet Union 1917–1967*, University of Chicago Press, 1971.

Orleanskii, N., *Zakon o Religioznykh Obyedineniakh* (The Law on Religious Associations), Moscow, 1930.

O Religii i Tserkvii, sbornik dokumentov (On religion and Church, a collection of documents), Moscow, 1965.

Rothenberg, Joshua, *The Jewish Religion in the Soviet Union*, New York, 1971.

Schechtman, Joseph, *Star in Eclipse: Russian Jewry revisited*, New York, 1961.

Sobranie Uzakonenii i Rasporazhenii Rabochevo i Krestianskovo Pravitelstva (Collection of legislative acts and orders of the Workers and Peasants Government), respective issues.

Struve, Nikita, *Les Chrétiens en U.R.S.S.*, Paris, 1963.

Study of discrimination in the matter of religious rights and practices, Summary of information relating to the U.S.S.R., United Nations Commission on Human Rights, Sub-Commission on prevention of discrimination and protection of minorities, Conference Room paper no. 35, 30 January 1959.

Schwarz, Solomon M., *The Jews in the Soviet Union*, Syracuse University Press, New York, 1951.

Schwarz, Solomon M., *Evrei v Sovetskom Soiuze s nachala vtoroi mirovoi voiny* (Jews in the Soviet Union, from the beginning of the Second World War), New York, 1966.

Shashar, Michael, *Israeli be-Moskva* (An Israeli in Moscow), Jerusalem, 1961.

Yehudi Soveti Almoni, El akhai biMdinat Israel, mikhtovim ivrim miBrit Hamoatzot bli tsenzura (To my brothers in the State of Israel, Hebrew letters from the Soviet Union without censorship), Kiryat Sefer, Jerusalem, 1957.

9
Jewish Themes in Soviet Russian Literature

MAURICE FRIEDBERG

The word 'themes' or 'problems' appeared necessary in the title in order to avoid a number of possible misunderstandings. The proposed study will not deal with the contributions by individual Jews to Soviet Russian literature—although the number of Jews writing in Russian in the U.S.S.R. has been and remains very large, and runs into several hundreds, with additional scores writing in a number of other languages. We shall also not be concerned exclusively with the overall portrayal of recognizably Jewish characters in modern Russian fiction, poetry, and drama. The present essay will discuss only those works of Soviet literature that tackle specifically 'Jewish' themes, i.e. those in which the protagonists face problems and dilemmas that are, in one way or another, clearly 'Jewish', as distinct from those in which their Jewishness is in itself of little importance. We trust that an examination of this subject may shed some light on the changing status of Russia's Jews in the half-century of Soviet rule.

This writer is clearly aware of the pitfalls of this approach. A similar sociological analysis would brand the England of Dickens a land of rampant antisemitism, while Mickiewicz's Poland would emerge as a land of exemplary tolerance if not, indeed, of sentimental philo-semitism. Two considerations spoke in favour of the possible value of the proposed investigation: the generally stringent controls exercised over Soviet literature, which minimize the likelihood of unduly subjective and personal treatments of the subject by individual authors (i.e. those clearly at variance with the prevalent official views), and the simple fact that the extreme scarcity of objective information on the social, economic, and psychological position of Russia's Jews inevitably makes an undertaking such as the present one more worth while and more reliable as historical evidence than a similar study of western European or American literature. Let us hope that the time will come soon in the U.S.S.R. when a greater degree of freedom for both the creative artist and the social scientist will make the work of the former more 'subjective' and of the latter more objective, and thus render investigations such as this superfluous.

Pre-revolutionary Russia was the world's largest centre of Jewish population, particularly since the final partition of Poland in 1795. Yet, in spite of this, comparatively few Jews appear in the pages of nineteenth-century Russian literature, and the rare portraits of Jews created by Russia's great writers are, with very few exceptions, either crude and malicious caricatures or, more rarely, idealized unreal romantic figures. In this respect there is no appreciable difference between the aristocratic Byronic poet Lermontov and the plebeian and earthy novelist Gogol. The Jew emerges as an equally despicable creature in the prose of the reactionary Dostoyevsky and of Dostoyevsky's personal and literary foe, the otherwise liberal and enlightened Turgenev. Most Russian writers simply preferred to shun Jewish themes altogether. It was not until nearly the turn of the century that major writers such as Nikolai Leskov (1831–95), Vladimir Korolenko (1853–1921), Maxim Gorky (1868–1936), Alexander Kuprin (1870–1938), and Leonid Andreyev (1871–1919) attempted to 'understand' the Jews as human beings. Yet even these authors failed to penetrate beneath the outward manifestations of anti-Jewish persecutions and prejudice and, while expressing sympathy for the Jew's plight, made no serious attempt to explore the complex problem of the Russian Jew's tragic predicament.[1]

Lenin's famous dictum dubbing tsarist Russia a 'prison-house of nations' led, from the first years of the Soviet regime, to numerous works of fiction, poetry, and drama which described the various forms of antisemitism under tsarism as well as the persecution of the Jews by the anti-Soviet forces during the civil war. At the same time Soviet literature has, from the very outset, conformed to the spirit and letter of another of Lenin's pronouncements, whereby every ethnic group is divided into two 'nations', the exploiters and the exploited. The poor, exploited Jews who —again, according to Lenin—constituted the majority of the Jewish people, could thus be depicted as victims of two simultaneous forms of oppression, the economic and the ethnic. By the same token, however, it was advisable for Soviet authors to point out that tsarist Russia's rich Jews, far from suffering from antisemitism, were, in reality, members of the empire's ruling clique. The fact that antisemitism was aimed at *all* Jews, and that the rich Jews were protected from it only to the extent to which the wealthy sick enjoy some advantages over the poor who are afflicted with similar ailments, could not openly be stated in any work of Soviet literature, for this would blatantly contradict a major article of the

[1] The most important, though far from satisfactory, study of the subject is Joshua Kunitz, *Russian Literature and the Jew*, New York, 1929.

Leninist faith. Thus, from the very outset, rigid adherence to a dogma imposed serious limitations on those Soviet writers who would describe tsarist antisemitism and resulted in a number of curious distortions—distortions that would, in a malignantly consistent way, result some thirty years later in a stubborn Soviet refusal to acknowledge that the Nazis, while admittedly inhuman in their treatment of millions of Russians, Ukrainians, etc., were incomparably more merciless in their treatment of the Jews—*all* Jews, communists and rabbis, workers and merchants, and that even the members of the *Judenräte* were ultimately not to be exempted from Hitler's 'final solution'.[1]

Similarly, Soviet writers were given to understand that antisemitism in pre-revolutionary Russia was to be attributed in their works only to the 'ruling circles' and their hirelings, and in no case to old Russia's working class.[2] Given, however, the facts that most of tsarist Russia's Jews were, if

[1] Thus, e.g. Nikita Khrushchev emphasized in his speech of 8 March 1963 that 'the Russian working class was a relentless enemy of any national oppression, including antisemitism, before the Revolution as well' and that 'Jewish pogroms were inspired by the tsarist government, capitalists, landlords and the bourgeoisie'. In the same speech, in his eagerness to illustrate the correctness of the Leninist doctrine of 'two nations in each nation', Khrushchev related the story of a Jew named Kogan who, he claimed, had been an interpreter to a Nazi general at Stalingrad: 'So it seems that one Jew served as an interpreter with von Paulus's staff, while another, serving in the ranks of our army, took part in the capture of von Paulus and his interpreter. People's conduct is assessed not from the national but from the class point of view.' (Cited in *Khrushchev and the Arts: the Politics of Soviet Culture, 1962–4*, Priscilla Johnson and Leopold Labedz (eds)., Cambridge, Mass., 1965, pp. 184, 185).

The factual basis for Khrushchev's story was challenged, albeit indirectly, by Ariadna Gromova in a letter which appeared in the Moscow *Literaturnaya gazeta* on 9 August 1966, i.e. after Khrushchev's downfall. The letter criticized P. Gavrutto's novel *Clouds Over the City* for claiming that one A. G. Kogan had betrayed an underground anti-Nazi organization to the Germans and had also served as Marshal von Paulus's interpreter. This, Gromova asserted, was not true, since the identity of the Nazi marshal's interpreter and of those who had betrayed the underground was well known, and Kogan was not implicated in either case. Gromova deplored the fact that Kogan was thus an innocent victim of a myth. But on 19 November 1966 E. Fediai, the editor of a small newspaper in the town of Brovary, near Kiev, published a letter in *Literaturnaya gazeta* defending the novelist Gavrutto—though, again, there was no direct reference to Khrushchev. While not mentioning the interpreter to von Paulus at all (and hence, tacitly admitting that both Gavrutto and Khrushchev had invented the story), Fediai insisted that one A. G. Kogan, presently a resident of Brovary, had been a Nazi collaborator and had served a ten-year sentence for his crimes.

[2] This did not, of course, correspond to historical truth. Not only were significant segments of tsarist Russia's workers and peasants virulently antisemitic, but on a number of occasions revolutionary parties had displayed a highly conciliatory attitude toward the anti-Jewish pogroms, welcoming them as manifestations of belated political activism among the hitherto inert masses which would, hopefully, eventually assume a more 'positive' direction. See P. B. Axelrod, 'Socialist Jews Confront the Pogroms', *The Golden Tradition: Jewish Life and Thought in Eastern Europe*, edited with an historical introduction by Lucy S. Dawidowicz, New York, 1967, pp. 405–10. The editor's brief foreword to the article includes the complete text of an inflammatory antisemitic proclamation published by the Russian revolutionary

not exactly proletarians in the Marxist sense of the term, then certainly members of the pauperized stratum of town-dwellers, and that the old antisemitism had, indeed, most often been inspired and abetted by the authorities, many Soviet writers at various times turned to this theme in their works. Thus, the 'gentler' types of Jew-baiting in pre-revolutionary schools were described by Lev Kassil (b. 1905) in his *Shvambraniia* (1933), one of the best works of Soviet juvenile literature, and in a 1926 auto-biographical sketch by Ilya Ehrenburg.[1] Scenes of pogroms appear in numerous novels; they range from the comparatively little known, such as *The Story of My Life* (1935) by Aleksei Svirskii (1865–1942), to the widely read but relatively apolitical *A Lonely White Sail Gleams* (1936) by Valentin Katayev (b. 1897), and even include a classic of socialist realism, *How the Steel Was Tempered* (1934–6) by Nikolai Ostrovskii (1904–36). The fullest portrayal of Jewish travail during the last years of tsarist Russia and at the time of the civil war, and the only one wrought by the pen of a major artist, is to be found in *Red Cavalry* (1926) and *Odessa Tales* (1927), the two collections of stories by Isaac Babel (1894–1941). Babel was an Odessa Jew who, until his death in a Soviet prison, wrestled with the problem of reconciling within himself the partly sentimental and partly cynical Jew, only recently emancipated from the commandments of orthodox Judaism, with the stringent requirements of his newly acquired communist orthodoxy.

Among the central figures of the new Soviet republic there were many men of Jewish origin—Trotsky, Zinoviev, Sverdlov, Kamenev, Radek, and others. Without actually concealing their origins—which, in any case, would have been quite useless—they tried, as a rule, to sever all links with their Jewish backgrounds.[2] This phenomenon found its reflection in Russian literature dealing with the civil war, which abounds in portraits of

---

party *Narodnaya Volya* (People's Will) in 1881. Pavel Borisovich Axelrod, one of the founders of the Russian social democratic movement, was dismayed by this and other manifestations of the revolutionaries' indifference to and even encouragement of 'popular' antisemitism.

[1] The passage in question described Ehrenburg's first day in a Russian school: 'Then the First Moscow Gymnasium. The boys around me said: "The little kike sits on a bench, we'll sit the little kike on a fence".' However, as Edward J. Brown points out, some thirty years later, in his 1960 autobiography, Ehrenburg was eager to impress on his readers that the situation was not all that tragic. In the new version of the same experience Ehrenburg faces not many tormentors, but only one, and the incident has a happy ending that was lacking in the 1926 account, i.e. the fresher one: 'When I first entered the gymnasium one of the pre-paratory students began teasing: "The little kike sat on a bench, let's sit the little kike on a fence." Without a moment's hesitation I hit him in the face. But soon we became friends. And no one insulted me again.' See Edward J. Brown, *Russian Literature Since the Revolution*, New York, 1963, pp. 248–9.

[2] See, e.g. Leon Trotsky, 'A Social Democrat Only', *The Golden Tradition*, op. cit., pp. 441–7.

communist fighters who were obviously born Jews but who feel no kinship with other Jews or with the Jewish culture and traditions. Suffice it to mention the upright communist leader in *The Commissars* (1926), a novel of Yurii Libedinskii (1898–1959), the heroic commissar Kogan in the famous 'Lay of Opanas' (1926) by Eduard Bagritskii (1895–1934), and probably the most important of them all, the chief of an embattled Bolshevik guerrilla detachment in the far east, Levinson in *The Rout* (1927), a novel by Alexander Fadeyev (1901–56). This is one of the most important works in the entire body of Soviet writing. Aside from their names and occasional references to their recognizably Jewish parents, there is nothing specifically Jewish about these positive heroes of Soviet literature—although, it may be noted, they never quite merge with their non-Jewish environments and, though respected, they remain at least partly outsiders. In fact, not infrequently these Bolshevik protagonists display a curious reticence about divulging their Jewish antecedents, and their non-Jewish comrades must reassure them that their Jewish backgrounds will not be held against them. Thus, in *Silent Don* (1928–40), almost certainly the finest novel in Soviet literature to date, a Jewish girl who has joined a machine-gun unit is shown being interrogated by the group's leader:

'Now it is my turn to question you. Are you Ukrainian?'
She hesitated for a second, and then replied firmly:
'No.'
'Jewish?'
'Yes. Why do you ask? Do I sound it?'
'No.'
'Then how did you guess that I am Jewish?'
Trying to walk in step with her, shortening his steps, he replied:
'It's your ear, the shape of your ears and your eyes. Otherwise, there's little of your nation in you.' And then, as an afterthought, he added:
'It's good that you are with us.'
'Why?' she inquired.
'Well, it's like this. The Jews have a reputation, and I know that many workers think so, you see, I am a worker myself'—he added in passing—'that the Jews only like to order everybody around but never go under fire themselves. That is incorrect, and you are the best proof that this view is unfounded.'[1]

That the novel's Nobel Prize winning author, Mikhail Sholokhov (b. 1905), is known for his communist fundamentalism, only serves to enhance the documentary value of the passage.

[1] Mikhail Sholokhov, *Sobranie sochinenii v vos'mi tomakh*, vol. iii, Moscow, Izdatel'stvo *Pravda*, 1962, p. 204.

Since Jewish participation in the right-wing anti-Soviet armies during the civil war was slight (the Jews were prominent in the liberal and social democratic opposition, but these were rarely portrayed in Soviet fiction), anti-Soviet Jewish villains are few in Soviet fiction set during that period. One of these is a Jewish bourgeois in Libedinskii's *A Week* (1922) whose pharmacy has been requisitioned by the Bolsheviks and who yearns for a return to the 'good old days'. He is aware that the Russians of similar political persuasions are, as a rule, strongly antisemitic, but, in conformity with communist theory, his class allegiances prove stronger than any possible qualms of an ethnic nature.

In their personal lives as well as in their works many Soviet men of letters of Jewish origin appear to have copied the Bolshevik leaders of Jewish descent in trying to forget or, if necessary, suppress, their Jewish identity. The communists among them escaped into an aggressive 'proletarian internationalism'. Among these were Mikhail Golodny (1903–49; real name Epstein), Isaac Goldberg (1884–1939) and, most notably, Mikhail Svetlov (1903–64), the author of 'Granada' (1926), a ballad about a Ukrainian lad's desire to liberate the peasants of far-away Spain. Others, less ideologically minded, sought to flee spiritually to western Europe— foremost among these were Veniamin Kaverin (b. 1902, pseudonym of Zil'berg), who tried to refashion Russian prose along western lines, and, until shortly before his death, Samuel Marshak (1887–1964), known chiefly for his translations of English verse and for his poetry for children. Still others, whose rejection of Jewishness was most impassioned, found refuge in Russian and western history: Osip Mandel'shtam (1892–1938), a Warsaw-born Jew and one of Russia's finest poets in this century, was the only major Soviet writer whose muse was nourished by ancient Hellas. Finally, in the case of a handful, the escape from Jewishness led to Russian Orthodox Christianity—which, under Soviet conditions, cannot possibly be discounted as a manifestation of opportunism. Foremost among them was the late Nobel Prize winner, Boris Pasternak (1890–1960).

But there were also those who attempted to portray the effects of the revolutionary upheaval not only on those Jews who seized the opportunity to escape the confines of the old ghettos, but also on the majority of the Jews who voluntarily remained in them, whether through inertia or by reasoned choice. Most of the writers tackling this theme wrote in Yiddish, but several used Russian as their medium. Perhaps the most successful politically conformist treatment of the issue is to be found in the twenty-page poem entitled '*A Tale About Motele the Redhead, Mister Inspector, Rabbi Isaiah and Commissar Bloch*' (1924–5) by Iosif Utkin (1903–44).

Written in a highly effective stylized Russo-Yiddish jargon, it depicted the impact of the new Soviet regime on the daily lives of traditionalist Kishinev Jews. One of them, the humble redheaded tailor Motele eventually becomes a Bolshevik commissar, while his erstwhile enemies, the policeman and the rabbi, symbolizing, as it were, the dual yoke of ethnic and class oppression, are now forced to bow to a man who, in the words of the 'Internationale', 'was nothing and became everything'.

There was much historical truth in the depictions of numerous *shtetl* Jews joining in the struggle for the Soviet cause, but there was also much oversimplification. For the fact is that the choice was not an easy one and that it required much soul-searching. The *shtetl*, after all, represented not only hunger and pogroms. To millions of Russia's Jews it meant also an accustomed way of life, intimately linked with warm memories of childhood, family, folkways—not to mention the security of firm religious beliefs and the sense of belonging and continuity imparted by Jewish culture and traditions. And even those of Russia's Jews whose 'modernization' and contacts, however superficial, with secular non-Jewish culture caused their attitude towards the traditional Jewish values to be detached and irreverent, were not likely to embrace a new dogma without some serious misgivings.

We do not have any autobiographical printed works of Russian literature which would illustrate the feelings of members of the former group. These would not have been allowed to appear in print, not even during the relatively permissive 1920s. The feelings of these religious, traditionalist Jews can only be appraised through their occasional portrayal in the writings of men who view them from the vantage point of the second group, the alienated and the assimilated, or, very rarely, from the works of non-Jews who could view both Jewish groups with detachment.

In Utkin's poem the tailor Motele who is said to have practised '*davenen* on Friday evenings and eating *gefilte fish* on the Sabbaths' appears, somewhat incongruously, not to have had any qualms about shedding his faith and the habits of a lifetime in order to become a Soviet official. More convincing is another Jewish tailor, Lazik, the hero of Ehrenburg's *The Stormy Life of Lazik Roitschwantz*, a novel published abroad in 1927, who is at least consistent in his scepticism. Unable to accept the traditionalist sham and pretence of the pillars of the old *shtetl* society, he demonstrates similar suspicions about the grandiloquent slogans of the *shtetl*'s new communist masters. A pariah before the Revolution, he is arrested for his disrespectful utterances by the revolutionary Soviet authorities; when he makes his way to capitalist Poland, he is promptly packed off to gaol as a likely Bolshevik spy. In western Europe, he is tossed from one tragi-comic misfortune to another, and finally dies in Palestine where he finds the local Jewish dignitaries little different from the *balebatim* in the old *shtetl* whence he began his ill-fated odyssey.

Isaac Babel, like Ehrenburg a doubter and an iconoclast, but a much more perceptive artist, could even, in spite of his communist convictions, see the real conflict that tormented the country's impoverished but tradi-tionalist Jews. By so doing, he shed a brilliant light on the ethical predica-ment of a man who is willing to accept the new—but not if he must discard the noble and the just and the beautiful in the heritage bequeathed to him by his forefathers. Thus, in Babel's *Gedali* the dilemma is effectively summarized by the old shopkeeper: 'The Revolution—we will say "yes" to it, but are we to say "no" to the sabbath?' And the simple Jew posits a real moral problem when he confronts the Bolshevik commissar with the following query:

The Poles, my dear Sir, shot because they were the counter-revolution. You shoot because you are the revolution. But surely the revolution means joy. And joy does not like orphans in the house. Good men do good deeds. The revolution is the good deed of good men. But good men do not kill. So it is bad people that are making the revolution. But the Poles are bad people too. Then how is Gedali to know which is revolution and which is counter-revolution?[1]

The painful choice is formulated with even greater clarity in another story of Babel's, *The Rabbi's Son*. Elijah Bratslavskii, the scion of a rab-binical dynasty, joins the communist party and dies fighting for the Soviet republic. The list of his belongings casts a light on his desperate attempt to reconcile the world of his Hebrew heritage with the ethos of the nascent Bolshevik state:

His things were strewn about pell-mell—mandates of the propagandist and note-books of the Jewish poet, the portraits of Lenin and Maimonides lay side by side, the knotted iron of Lenin's skull beside the dull silk of the portrait of Maimonides. A lock of woman's hair lay in a book, the resolutions of the party's sixth congress, and the margins of communist leaflets were crowded with crooked lines of ancient Hebrew verse. They fell upon me in a mean and depressing rain—pages of the *Song of Songs* and revolver cartridges.[2]

[1] Isaac Babel, *The Collected Stories*, edited and translated by Walter Morison, with an introduction by Lionel Trilling, New York, 1955, p. 71.
[2] Ibid., p. 193. A subject almost never discussed in Soviet literature of the 1920s is the fate of the numerous Jews who, before the Revolution, had been active in the Zionist movement. The only example we have come across is the short story 'Rasskaz o kliuchakh i gline' (The Tale about the Keys and the Lime) by Boris Pilniak (1894–1941). The story originally appeared in 1927 (*Rasplesnutoye vremia*); it has never been republished in the Soviet Union. In Pilniak's

Perhaps there is some significance in the fact that the rabbi's son, a communist and a poet, chose as his most cherished memento not the portrait of a poet such as Yehuda Halevi or Ibn Gabirol, but one of Maimonides, the author of *The Guide for the Perplexed*; and that the little old man whose basic moral questions on means and ends Babel wisely decides to leave, in essence, unanswered, bears the Hebrew name of Gedali—'the great', perhaps a reference to the greatness of Gedali's idea of an 'international of good men'.

The end of the civil war brought to the Soviet regime a military victory; the country's economy, however, was in a state of chaos and necessitated the introduction, in 1922, of the New Economic Policy, with its permissive attitude towards private enterprise, particularly small-scale manufacturing, crafts, and commerce. The numerous Jews who availed themselves of the opportunity to re-enter their accustomed 'Jewish' occupations were soon to be portrayed—as a rule, in a negative light—in Soviet Russian literature. Among these were the repugnant criminal businessman in *The Tale about Max the Dwarf* (1926) by Mikhail Kozakov (1897–1954), the strongly Jewish-coloured black marketeers in *Minus Six* (1930) by Matvei Roizman, and the almost antisemitic caricatures of crooks in Yulii Berzin's *Ford* (1927), to mention but three novels of the period. (All three authors were Jews.) There were also lampoons of 'cosmopolitan' Jews, such as the dissolute young communist who tries to conceal his origins and is fond of calling himself an 'internationalist' and 'little Trotsky' in *The Moon is on the Right Side* (1926) by Sergei Malashkin. Yet, in spite of the fact that during the 1920s antisemitic acts were a punishable offence in the U.S.S.R. (but then, it may be argued, the same laws were in force during Stalin's worst persecution of the Jews) and that the 1920s were a period during which a campaign against antisemitism was being waged throughout the country,[1] the most violent attacks were directed at Kozakov's *The Man Who Prostrates Himself* (1929). This was

---

tale the reader is shown a shipload of Zionists about to leave the Soviet Union for Palestine. The Zionists are presented as quixotic dreamers and are contrasted with a realistic Jewish communist who envisages a happy Jewish future in the U.S.S.R. The author of the story was arrested in the late 1930s and has disappeared in a labour camp.

[1] Trials against antisemites were given publicity in the press (e.g. the Barshai case, *Izvestiya*, 6, 16, 18–20 January 1929), and pamphlets bearing such titles as *Who Slanders the Jews and Why*, *The Truth About the Jews* and *Hatred of the Jews* were turned out in considerable quantities. There were also serious works on the subject, such as L. Radishchev's *Poison: On Contemporary Antisemitism* (*Yad: ob antisemitizme nashikh dnei*), Leningrad, 1930, and even novels and plays aimed at combating anti-Jewish prejudice. See Bernard J. Choseed, 'Jews in Soviet Literature', *Through the Glass of Soviet Literature: Views of Russian Society*, edited, with an introduction by Ernest J. Simmons, New York, 1953, p. 122.

most probably because of its implication that, in different forms and degrees, various types of antisemitism, ranging from 'well-meant' discrimination in employment to physical assaults, were to be found in the 1920s in the U.S.S.R. To aggravate the situation, Kozakov's novel demonstrated that antisemites in the U.S.S.R. are not merely survivors of the pre-revolutionary bourgeoisie, but also upright Soviet proletarians and even high Soviet government officials, and that the Soviet Jew still found it wiser to conceal his ethnic identity. Thus, Soviet literature of the 1920s suggested that the Jew, though officially emancipated (incidentally, not, as is generally believed, by the Soviet authorities, but by its predecessor, the Provisional Government), still had to contend with problems that were peculiar to him as a member of a particular ethnic group. But the official literary (and non-literary) policy had already begun to shift towards denying this problem's very existence, even if only as a passing phenomenon, as another 'survival' of the tsarist past.

From the early 1930s until the Second World War Jewish characters did, indeed, appear in numerous works of Soviet literature set in that period, but, as a rule, they were endowed with no specifically 'Jewish' traits or aspirations. They were, so to speak, Jews in origin only, and not even 'communist Jews' in the sense that the Jewish protagonists of Soviet Yiddish literature of the period had been. With no discernible memories of a Jewish past, no awareness of any characteristically Jewish problem in the present, and no desire whatever to perpetuate any Jewish cultural values (let alone religious or national ones), these protagonists of Soviet Russian literature merely served to illustrate the thesis that Russia's Jews had already become fully absorbed into the organism of a supra-ethnic Soviet society.[1] Such were the indefatigable engineer Margulis in Valentin Katayev's famous 'production' novel *Time, Forward!* (1932), and a number of secondary characters in a long list of works of Soviet fiction, drama, and poetry.[2] That this did not correspond to reality, mattered

---

[1] 'Jewish' Jews did often appear in works written in the 1930s, but set in earlier periods.

[2] Since several references have been made to the works of Valentin Katayev, perhaps it is worth pointing out that Katayev is not a Jew, but has been familiar with the Russian-Jewish *milieu* since his Odessa childhood.

Curious is the case of Mikhail Sholokhov's *Virgin Soil Upturned*, the best Soviet novel dealing with the theme of collectivization of agriculture (part I, 1931; part II, 1961). The novel's hero, the young communist Davydov, was, as Sholokhov has recently declared, modelled after a real-life communist, a Jewish engineer. Yet there is no reason to assume that he would have been drawn differently had his name in the novel been more transparently Jewish—say, Davidson. On the other hand, Jewish problems outside the U.S.S.R.—although, as a rule, these were limited to portrayals of antisemitism which, it was claimed, was but another capitalist aberration—were often discussed in writings of Western authors translated into Russian and other languages of the Soviet Union. This, too, came to a sudden halt in

little. By then, the requirements of artificially optimistic socialist realism had become of greater importance than objective facts. The Stalinist period of 'varnished' literature had already set in.

Whatever illusions may have been harboured in Russia and abroad about the successful assimilation of Soviet Jews and the disappearance of antisemitism in that country in the 1930s, were all shattered during the very first days of the Nazi–Soviet war in the summer of 1941. It came as a shock to many that the majority of non-Jews in the Nazi-occupied parts of the U.S.S.R. viewed the fate of their Jewish neighbours with indifference, while not a few actually helped the Nazis in their slaughter of Soviet Jews. The Nazi massacres of the Jews received only fleeting mention in Soviet literature published during the war (e.g. in Boris Gorbatov's novel *The Unvanquished* (1943); *For Whom the Time Bows*, a 1945 play by Lev Sheinin and the Tur brothers; and Vasilii Grossman's short story *The Old Teacher* (1942)). But the complicity of Soviet citizens in Nazi crimes was mentioned—if at all—only in rare instances and then on the condition that examples of these actions by local Nazi collaborators be outweighed by scenes depicting other, allegedly much more numerous Soviet citizens, who offered aid to the Jews. As a result, the poem 'Abraham' by Savva Holovanivs'skii (b. 1910), a Jewish author writing in Ukrainian, in which a Kiev Jew is killed by the Nazis while Russians and Ukrainians calmly observe the proceedings, was subjected to a bitter attack by the head of the Ukrainian Writers' Union who called the poem a 'terrible slander on the Soviet people' and a 'lump of mud into the face of the Soviet people'.[1] But the height of absurdity in the ideological consistency in the presentation of the wartime Jewish tragedy was reached, perhaps, in Vladimir Popov's post-war novel *Steel and Slag* (1949) in which the 'two nations in one nation' dogma led the author to depict the Nazis as combating communist sympathies among older Soviet Jews with Zionist propaganda.

Ironically, it was the Soviet Yiddish newspaper *Aynikayt* that provided, in 1946, the clearest formulation of the party's warnings against devoting excessive attention to the Nazi extermination of the Jews. The trouble, according to *Aynikayt*, was that in too many works 'the German fascist

---

1939, after the signing of the Nazi–Soviet pact. Anti-Nazi films depicting persecutions of Germany's Jews, such as *Professor Mamlock* (script by Friedrich Wolf) and *The Oppenheim Family* (script by Lion Feuchtwanger) disappeared from Soviet screens, and even Feuchtwanger's historical novels on Jewish themes were 'withdrawn' from general libraries. Feuchtwanger's works began to be published again after Stalin's death. See Paul Babitsky and John Rimberg, *The Soviet Film Industry*, New York, 1955, p. 179.

[1] Quoted in Choseed, op. cit., p. 142.

crimes against the Jewish population are shown as isolated, and are not tied in with the Hitlerite murders of the Soviet people in general.'[1] There is grim incongruity in the fact that *Aynikayt's* ideological objections, voiced before the unleashing of the 'anti-cosmopolitan' purges, have, in essence, outlived not only their authors, many of whom were shot in 1952 during the mass execution of Yiddish writers, as well as the newspaper in which they appeared (the journal was suppressed only two years later), but even the several changes in the leadership of the U.S.S.R. and its literary organizations in the twenty years that followed. Basically, the policy has remained unchanged, although there have been variations in the degree of stringency with which that policy has been enforced.

At the time of the 'anti-cosmopolitan' purges during which, as the veteran Soviet film director Mikhail Romm pointed out several years ago, the expression 'cosmopolitan without a fatherland' was used merely as a convenient synonym for '*zhid*'—'yid'—[2] Jewish themes were simply shunned by most Soviet writers.[3] Thus, Ilya Ehrenburg recalls in his memoirs how he and the late Vasilii Grossman were prevented from bringing out a book on the Nazi slaughter of Soviet Jews—although books on Nazi atrocities *in general* were frequently published and with much official encouragement.[4] Moreover, in conformity with the Soviet custom of 'updating' history to make it conform with present-day policies, many new editions of literary works were purged of passages suggesting that the Jews had faced any difficulties as a group even *before* the Revolution. Such was the case of an entire chapter entitled 'From A Good Family' in the 1935 edition of Lev Kassil''s *The Land of Shvambraniia*, in which the author described his troubles with an antisemitic governess.[5] The chapter was deleted from the 1948 edition.[6] In the same book Kassil' recalls how, as a child, he refused to read aloud in class Gogol's *Taras Bul'ba* because of its author's unsympathetic portrayal of Jews murdered

[1] Quoted in ibid., p. 143.

[2] Quoted in *Khrushchev and the Arts*, op. cit., p. 97. Romm's speech had originally appeared in the December 1963 issue of *Commentary*.

[3] Protagonists with obviously Jewish-sounding names did, from time to time, appear in Soviet Russian literature of the period (e.g. Liberman and Zalkind in Vasilii Azhayev's Stalin-Prize winning novel *Far from Moscow*, 1948), but these were, basically, survivors from the 'denationalized' protagonists of Jewish origin found in Soviet writing of the 1930s.

[4] Much useful information on this, perhaps the saddest, period of Jewish history under Soviet rule, may be found in S. Shvarts (Solomon Schwarz), *Evrei v Sovetskom Soiuze s nachala vtoroi mirovoi voiny (1939–1965)*, (Jews in the Soviet Union, from the beginning of the Second World War.) New York, 1966, pp. 198–244.

[5] Lev Kassil', *The Land of Shvambraniia*, translated by Sylvia Glass and Norbert Guterman, New York, 1935, pp. 34–6.

[6] Kassil', *Izbrannye povesti*, Moscow, Sovetskii Pisatel', 1948, p. 30.

by the Cossacks.[1] The incident is missing from the 1948 version, i.e. one printed after such Cossack figures as Bogdan Khmel'nitskii, notorious for his slaughter of the Jews of the Ukraine in the seventeenth century, had been admitted to the pantheon of illustrious predecessors of the Soviet state.[2]

The 1936 edition of Aleksei Svirskii's *The Story of My Life* gave an account of Odessa Jews shortly after a pogrom:

David speaks to himself, he speaks in the dark, and most importantly, he speaks in Yiddish, which he had never done in the past.

'To leave, we must leave this horrid Russia', he continued, 'to Palestine, to America ... do I know where? Only not here. ... Can we, Jews, live here among drunkards, savages, robbers ... No ... a thousand times no ... No!'[3]

The removal of this monologue in the 1947 version of the novel foreshadowed, as it were, the pogrom of Soviet Yiddish cultural institutions that was to take place the following year.[4]

A truly remarkable case was found in the 1940 edition of Bill'-Belotserkovskii's play *The Frontier Guards*. It related the story of a Red Army man, a Jew named Kogan, who is kidnapped by foreign agents and offered money to work as a spy in the U.S.S.R. Kogan refused and managed to throw a grenade, which killed both himself and his kidnappers. At the beginning of the play the following conversation took place between the Soviet Jewish soldier and the officer of an unnamed capitalist intelligence service.

Captain: Jewish?
Kogan: Yes. A Jew of the Soviet land.
Captain: Why this emphasis? Is the Jew of our country any worse?
Kogan: He may not be worse, but he is worse off.
Captain: How about pork, do you eat it?
Kogan: Ask my father.
Captain: Why father?
Kogan: He is the best pig-breeder in Biro-Bidzhan.[5]

This conversation, as well as all the other numerous references to Kogan's being a Jew, were carefully removed from the 1950 version of the play.[6]

[1] Kassil', *Izbrannye povesti*, Moscow, Sovetskii Pisatel', 1935 edn., p. 62.

[2] Kassil', ibid., 1948 edn., p. 46.

[3] Aleksei Svirskii, *Istoriya moyei zhizni*, Moscow, Sovetskii Pisatel', 1936, p. 214.

[4] Ibid., Moscow, OGIZ, 1947, p. 17

[5] Vladimir Bill'-Belotserkovskii, *P'ysey*, Moscow-Leningrad, Gosizdat 'Iskusstvo', 1940, p. 273.

[6] Ibid., Moscow-Leningrad, Goslitizdat 'Iskusstvo', 1950, p. 208. The play, incidentally, was not included in the post-Stalin two-volume set of Bill'-Belotserkovskii's works published in 1962, otherwise the most complete edition of his writings (*Izbrannye proizvedeniya v dvukh tomakh*, Moscow, Goslitizdat, 1926).

Of the three writers (all, incidentally, Jews), Kassil' and Bill'-Belotser-kovskii may have been 'consulted' about the proposed revisions of their works. No such consultation could have taken place in the case of Svirskii who died in 1942, i.e. some years before the anti-Jewish policies began to make themselves felt retroactively in Soviet literature. The changes were made by the Soviet censors, and it is their text, and not the author's, that is now being reprinted.[1]

It was only after Stalin's death in 1953 that the themes of wartime Jewish heroism and martyrdom and, occasionally, even that of the post-war Stalinist antisemitic purges, began to appear, if ever so rarely and timidly, in Soviet Russian writing. The latter subject usually took the form of references to the infamous 'Doctors' Plot' of 1952, in which a group of Jewish physicians, allegedly acting on orders from western Jewish philanthropic organizations, was said to have planned a 'medical murder' of Soviet leaders; the doctors were freed soon after Stalin's death.[2] We find mentions of this in A. Val'tseva's short story *Apartment No. 13* (1956), in the poem 'Whistle-Stop Winter' (1955) by Yevgenii Yevtushenko (b. 1933) as well as in the portrait of a Jewish woman doctor in Ehrenburg's novella *The Thaw* (1954). The common denomi-nator of all of these is the theme of terror and of not-so-subtle Jew-baiting in the post-war U.S.S.R.

More than twenty years have elapsed since the defeat of Nazi Germany, yet the vision of the war continues to haunt the imagination of Soviet writers and hardly a month passes without the appearance of new works dealing with this theme. On the whole, Soviet writers of Jewish origin appear to stifle within th mselves what cannot but be a powerful urge to raise an outcry of pain about an event that must have affected most of them personally; one senses that they are 'stepping on the throat of their own songs', as the great Soviet poet Mayakovsky once put it. There are, however, exceptions, and from time to time we encounter impassioned brief works, for the most part verse, inconspicuously buried in thick an-thologies of their writings. Such poems may be found in the multi-volume edition of Ehrenburg still in progress, in the works of Boris Slutskii (b. 1919) and of Ilya Sel'vinskii (1899–1968).[3] The most famous poem

---

[1] Thus, Svirskii's novel was republished in 1956, i.e. at the height of the post-Stalin 'thaw' in a provincial city in the Caucasus (Ordzhonikidze, Severo-Osetinskoye Knizhnoye Izdatel'-stvo). The deleted passage was not restored.

[2] One of the leading figures in the 'literary' antisemitic campaign of the period, the writer and journalist Nikolai Gribachev (b. 1910) is now the editor-in-chief of the new Soviet English-language propaganda journal, *Sputnik*.

[3] Thus, Sel'vinskii's poem 'The Terrible Judgement' ('Strashnyi sud', in Ilya Sel'vinskii,

to deal with the subject of the Holocaust, though no artistic masterpiece, was, beyond doubt, Yevtushenko's 'Babi Yar' (1961), inspired by the site of the mass execution of Kiev Jews by the Nazis. The fact that this politically very orthodox poem—it condemns antisemitism from a rigidly communist position and, while absolving the Russian people from the crime of antisemitism, proudly extolls 'true' 'internationalist' Russia—precipitated one of the great storms in Soviet literary history, illustrates the irrational stubbornness with which the Soviet establishment clings to the myth of the non-existence of specifically Jewish memories and hopes. The poem's defenders were few and timid, while its detractors included Khrushchev himself, who attacked it in his speech of 8 March 1963.[1] The opening line of Yevtushenko—'There are no monuments at Babi Yar'—still holds true. And Anatolii Kuznetsov's post-Khrushchev documentary novel *Babi Yar* (1966), while containing some powerful eyewitness reports of the massacre, nevertheless supports in its conclusions the stale Soviet assertion: there was no Jewish tragedy as such during the Second World War. Not even at Babi Yar. All of the peoples of the U.S.S.R. shared in the ordeal of the Nazi occupation, and there is no reason for 'separating' the Jews as a special case.[2]

Lirika, Moscow, Goslitizdat, 1964, pp. 427–30) is, in this writer's opinion, one of the more powerful creations in the Holocaust literature found in any language.

[1] Yevtushenko's poem has also inspired an unofficial polemic. It is noteworthy that while the attacks on Yevtushenko's 'Babi Yar' were printed in a major Soviet journal (the poem by Aleksei Markov in which Yevtushenko was charged with defiling the Russian people with 'pygmy's spittle' as well as the diatribe by the critic Dmitrii Starikov both appeared in *Literatura i zhizn'*, now defunct), the defenders of Yevtushenko were represented only by poems circulating in manuscript form and thus, of course, of unacknowledged authorship. The October 1965 issue of the Russian-language *Byulleten'* of the Israeli Association of Immigrants from China printed the texts of poems attributed to Konstantin Simonov, Samuel Marshak, Margarita Aliger, Ilya Ehrenburg, as well as Yevtushenko's own reply to Markov.

[2] Anatolii Kuznetsov reiterated the official Soviet position in an article written specifically for western consumption, and hence one in which he might have been expected to adopt a less dogmatic attitude towards the subject. Thus, he emphasized: 'The Germans shot countless numbers of Russians and Ukrainians, and for Kiev Babi Yar became a monstrous symbol of the occupation—and of Fascism in general.' Kuznetsov takes pains to dissociate himself from Yevtushenko's unduly 'Jewish' approach: ' . . . Yevgeny Yevtushenko wrote his well-known poem, "Babi Yar", which provoked some serious criticism, because he devoted it to only one aspect of the problem and only to the very first few days of Babi Yar, when the Germans were shooting the Jewish population of Kiev. But altogether there were 778 days. In my novel, I set myself the aim of writing about all those 778 days.' (Anatoly Kuznetsov, 'The Memories', *The New York Times Book Review*, 9 April 1967, pp. 4–5; the article was published simultaneously in the April 1967 issue of the English-language magazine *Sputnik*. Two years later, in the summer of 1969, Kuznetsov was granted political asylum in Great Britain.

Soviet authorities impose rigid limitations on the availability of translated works dealing with the Holocaust in order to avoid too marked a contrast with the restrictions

In *The Little Golden Calf*, a Soviet comic novel by Ilya Il'f and Yevgenii Petrov which was first published in 1931, there is an episode in which a visiting foreign journalist, one Mr. Berman, 'observed slyly that, being a Zionist, he was more interested in the Jewish problem in the U.S.S.R.' A conversation follows:

'There is no such problem here,' said Palamidov.
'How is that possible?' Berman asked in astonishment.
'It doesn't exist.'
Mr. Berman was upset. All his life he had written articles for his paper on the Jewish question and it would be painful for him to part with it. 'But surely there are Jews in Russia?' he asked warily.
'Yes, there are,' Palamidov replied.
'Then you have a Jewish problem.'
'No, there are Jews, but no Jewish problem.'[1]

Some thirty years after the publication of Il'f's and Petrov's book and after such events as the Nazi annihilation of millions of Russia's Jews and Stalin's strangulation of Soviet Jewish culture, the Soviet leadership persists in an attitude that might have resembled premature wishful thinking when voiced by a fictitious personage in the Soviet satirical novel but which, given the present realities of Jewish life in the U.S.S.R., has a ring of cruel mockery. Soviet Jews are not allowed to assimilate or to emigrate. They are, however, denied a Jewish present and, consequently, a Jewish future. They are also, retroactively, deprived of their Jewish past. One is, somehow, reminded of an aphorism by the contemporary Polish satirist Lec: 'They said that he was dead—and then they killed him.'

Yet the truth is that there *is* a Jewish problem in the U.S.S.R. It is merely being denied official recognition. Thus, together with other

---

imposed on its treatment in Russia. Thus, several years ago, a visiting Italian troupe, after much haggling, was allowed to give two performances of *The Diary of Anne Frank*; subsequently there was a small Soviet edition of the book. The monthly *Inostrannaya literatura* announced the publication of Arthur Miller's *Incident at Vichy*, then decided not to print it. Only after some pressure began to make itself felt both at home and abroad, did the play finally appear in print. Some Soviet critics none the less found fault with Miller's 'nationalism' (!), and in order to counteract the ideological weaknesses of *The Diary of Anne Frank*, a homegrown Soviet 'Anne Frank's' diary was published. Mariya (Masha) Rol'nikaite's *I Must Tell* (*Ya dolzhna rasskazat'*, Moscow, Izdatel'stvo Politicheskoi Literatury, 1965) conformed, not unexpectedly, to the requirements which make Holocaust literature acceptable to the Soviet authorities: the 'Jewishness' of the inmates of the Vilna ghetto is deemphasized and their travail appears to be caused mainly by the fact that they are *Soviet* people in *Nazi* captivity. See my article, 'On Reading Recent Soviet Judaica', *Survey*, London, January 1967, pp. 167–77.

[1] Il'f and Petrov, *The Complete Adventures of Ostap Bender*, translated from the Russian by John H. C. Richardson, New York, 1962, p. 294.

'unproblems'—paradoxically, the basic questions of the human condition, the probing of which preoccupied the Russian classical writers, such as the existence of God, the purpose of life and the dimensions of justice—it is now tackled only by 'underground' Soviet literature.[1] Indeed, the painful dilemma of the Soviet Jew constitutes one of the central themes of that body of Soviet literature that has recently come to public attention both in Russia and in the west as a result of the trials of the poet Brodskii and of the prose writers Siniavskii and Daniel'.

The young Leningrad poet Iosif Brodskii (b. 1940) is not particularly conscious of his Jewish heritage. The volume of his work published in the west (his original poetry has never been printed in the U.S.S.R.) contains only two 'Jewish' items, the long biblical poem 'Isaac and Abraham' and the shorter 'A Jewish Cemetery Near Leningrad'.[2] The latter is a moving evocation of the Jewish world and Jewish values buried and forgotten by Brodskii's contemporaries. Yet his trial in February 1964, during which Brodskii was not accused of anything more serious than 'parasitism' (i.e. a too frequent change of jobs) and sentenced to exile and forced labour, had distinct antisemitic overtones.

At the Moscow trial of Siniavskii and Daniel' in February 1966 the prosecution produced an unexpected witness, a *littérateur* named Andrei Remezov who was described as an accomplice in the defendants' efforts to smuggle their manuscripts abroad. Andrei Remezov, it appears, is the author of a play entitled *Is There Life on Mars?* published in Paris in the original Russian under the pseudonym 'I. Ivanov'.[3] Combining the devices of science fiction with the plot of the Biblical Book of Esther, Remezov-Ivanov created what may be the most caustic satire on Soviet antisemitism during the last years of Stalin's life, with emphasis on Soviet hypocrisy in not considering the Jews a 'nationality' and thus depriving them of whatever benefits this might entail, and yet subjecting them to 'national' discrimination—while, of course, professing all the time that the Jews are equal citizens of the Soviet state.[4]

[1] It is interesting that similar observations were made in January 1966 by the Soviet physicist and mathematician V. I. Levin (in all probability, a Jew) in a letter sent to *Izvestiya* in connection with the trial of Siniavskii and Daniel'. Wrote Mr. Levin: 'Still, many themes remain forbidden [in Soviet literature]: antisemitism, the responsibility of those guilty of criminal acts in recent years. . . . The lifting of the ban on themes such as these would only benefit our people.' The letter was never printed by the Soviet newspaper. It appeared in the *émigré* Russian literary journal *Grani*, no. 62 (1966), pp. 39–43.

[2] Iosif Brodskii, *Stikhotvoreniya i poemy*, New York, 1965, pp. 54–5, 137–55.

[3] I. Ivanov, *Yest' li zhizn' na Marse?* Paris, Instytut Literacki, 1961.

[4] A fuller treatment of the work was given in my article 'A Play from the Soviet Underground', *The Reporter*, 18 January 1962, pp. 28–30.

It is, however, in the now famous writings of Abram Tertz (pseudonym of Andrei Siniavskii, b. 1925) and Nikolai Arzhak (pseudonym of Yulii Daniel', b. 1925) that the tragic predicament of the Soviet Jew is portrayed most fully. That both authors are young, formed entirely in a Soviet environment (thus excluding the possibility of their living, so to speak, in the 'pre-revolutionary past'), and that both men, the first a non-Jew and the second a Jew, give essentially similar portrayals of the condition of the Soviet Jew since the Second World War, is in itself significant. The works of the two subsequently imprisoned young writers loudly confirm that which is only hinted at in 'legal' Soviet literature: the outwardly assimilated, Russian-speaking young Soviet Jew is painfully aware of his Jewishness. Official and 'spontaneous' antisemitism prevent him from ever forgetting it. The young Soviet Jew may not know much about his roots, but he is, if anything, obsessed with them. Consider the following portrait in Siniavskii's novel *The Makepeace Experiment*:

I once had a Jewess in my life—I won't forget her to my dying day. . . . She spoke Russian like a Russian—you couldn't tell the difference—and the only Jewish word she knew was *tsores*, which in their language means sorrow or trouble, or a kind of prickly sadness littering the heart. There was a grain of this *tsores* buried in her like a raisin you could never dig out—immured in her as it were, mixed into the very composition of her soul.[1]

The Russian characters in the works of Siniavskii have their share of sorrows and troubles, and it is to these that the writer devotes the bulk of his work. The Jews share in all of them, but they are also tormented by pains that are theirs alone, and there is grim logic in the fact that these are called by their Yiddish name *tsores*—significantly, the last Yiddish word a young Soviet Jew remembers.

There are many sad and tragi-comic Jewish protagonists scattered throughout Siniavskii's other works, Dostoyevskian buffoons and frightened intellectuals, most notable among them the physician Rabinovich (in Russian, the 'classic' Jewish name) in a Soviet labour camp, whose fate personifies the antisemitic campaigns triggered by the 'Doctors' Plot' of 1952 (*The Trial Begins*, 1961). The novel *The Makepeace Experiment* has, among its protagonists, two living Soviet writers, Anatolii Sofronov (b. 1911) and Vsevolod Kochetov (b. 1912), both unreconstructed Stalinists; they are depicted exchanging antisemitic remarks.

The insecurity and fear that plague the Soviet Jew half a century

---

[1] Abram Tertz, *The Makepeace Experiment*, translated from the Russian and with an introduction by Manya Harari, New York, 1965, p. 49. The novel's Russian title is *Lyubimov*.

after the establishment of the Soviet state, with its official abhorrence of antisemitism—Stalin's definition of antisemitism as 'the most dangerous hangover of cannibalism' was, indeed, often quoted at the height of the antisemitic purges of the late 1940s and early 1950s—is also reflected in the works of Yulii Daniel'. In his *This is Moscow Speaking*, a novella built around a fantasy of a day of 'open murders', when the announcement is heard over the radio that on a specific date murder will be permitted, a Jewish protagonist, Margulis, immediately decides that the measure is probably aimed at the Jews. Pointing to a revolver, a souvenir from his army days, Margulis warns, 'If on 10 August there will be a Jewish pogrom, I will fight. This is not Babi Yar. . . .'[1] Siniavskii's and Daniel''s preoccupation with Jewish themes was duly emphasized at their trial. It was cited as evidence of Siniavskii's antisemitism, while Daniel', who, being a Jew, could not comfortably be so labelled, was charged with 'slandering' the Soviet people as antisemitic.[2]

By an ironic coincidence, the protagonists of Katayev's much-praised novel, *Time, Forward!* and of Daniel''s *This is Moscow Speaking*, published surreptitiously abroad exactly thirty years later, share the common Jewish family name of Margulis. The Margulis of the 1930s, though he bore the very Jewish first name David, was but dimly aware of his origins and appeared secure in his status as an equal Soviet citizen. The Margulis of the 1960s, while endowed with a typical Russian name, Vladimir, a member of the Russian intelligentsia and a Soviet war veteran, feels constantly threatened and is only too painfully aware that, as a Jew, he is not accepted

---

[1] Nikolai Arzhak, *Govorit Moskva*, Washington, 1962, pp. 15, 21.

[2] Thus, the prosecutor: 'You write that the people are antisemitic and just waiting to start a pogrom. You compare its mood with what led to Babi Yar. But there the killers were Fascists. Isn't it blasphemous to compare our entire people with the Fascists?' Daniel': 'It does not follow from the passage that the entire Soviet people is antisemitic; all that follows is that a few individuals are so inclined.' (*On Trial: The Soviet State versus 'Abram Tertz' and 'Nikolai Arzhak'*, translated, edited and with an introduction by Max Hayward, New York, 1966, p. 69).

As for the absurdity of the charge that Siniavskii's writings are antisemitic in content, it should suffice to point out that the antisemitic observations in his works are voiced only by 'villains', and that Siniavskii's disapproval of these personages and their pronouncements is obvious throughout.

Siniavskii was also accused of a deliberate antisemitic provocation and of failing to uphold the national dignity of a Russian by his deliberate choice of a Jewish-sounding pseudonym—'Abram Tertz'. An interesting letter was written in this connection to *Izvestiya* by Yu. Grechuk, an art critic and historian. Alluding to Dmitrii Yeremin's article in the 12 January 1966 issue of the newspaper, Grechuk wrote: ' . . . Yeremin's insinuation that it is unworthy of one "born a Russian" to use a Jewish name is convincing evidence that antisemitism does, indeed, exist, and not just anywhere, but among *Izvestiya*'s contributors.' The letter was never published by the Soviet newspaper. It appeared in *Grani*, op. cit., p. 46.

as a fully-fledged member of the Soviet society, but is merely being tolerated—and that, too, perhaps only temporarily.

More ominous is another coincidence—one in real life. Yulii Markovich Daniel''s father was the Soviet Yiddish writer Mark Naumovich Daniel' (pseudonym of Meyerovich). Judging by the entry in the post-Stalin *Concise Literary Encyclopedia* which gives only an approximate date of his death in 1940—i.e. in peacetime—the older Daniel', a veteran of the civil war and for many years a Soviet Yiddish writer in good standing, must have died in prison. There are, however, no reasons to assume that he had been convicted on specifically 'Jewish' charges. His son Yulii Daniel', a Soviet veteran of the Second World War, discharged after being severely wounded, is now in his early forties, outwardly 'assimilated', and writes in Russian rather than Yiddish. Yet every indication suggests that the younger Daniel' is far more alienated from the allegedly supra-national Soviet society and far more aware of his Jewishness than was his Yiddish-speaking father. True, his 'Jewishness' is almost entirely 'negative'; it is an awareness formed nearly exclusively by the persecutions of the war and its aftermath. This, however, does not detract from its intensity; in fact, it proved to be a major factor in Yulii Daniel''s 'crime' and in the prison sentence he is currently serving. One may, indeed, find much evidence to support the thesis that the careers of the two Daniel's embody the different fortunes of Soviet Russia's Jewish fathers and sons.[1]

[1] No attempt has been made in this article to deal with the few virulently antisemitic novels that have appeared in the U.S.S.R. since the Six-Day War, such as Ivan Shestov's *In the Name of the Father and the Son* and *Love and Hate*, both published in 1970 (*Vo imya otsa i syna*, Moscow, 1970, 65,000 copies; *Lyubov' i nenavist'*, Moscow, 1970, 200,000 copies). Evidence currently at our disposal is too scanty to allow serious consideration of the subject.

10

Jewish Contributions to Soviet Literature

MAURICE FRIEDBERG

Literature in Russia, in the modern sense of the word, is a relatively recent phenomenon, dating back not more than 200 years, while Jewish participation in it, however modest, begins only in mid-nineteenth century. There were no counterparts in Russia of such writers of Jewish ancestry as Heinrich Heine. When secular literature finally made its appearance among the Jews of Russia during the Haskalah period, the centuries of enforced isolation of Russia's Jewish community were reflected not only in its nearly total preoccupation with narrowly Jewish subject matter, but also in the fact that most of it came to be written in Yiddish and in Hebrew. The few Jewish authors writing in Russian (for the most part, only recently learned), appeared to address themselves primarily to a Jewish audience or else to plead the cause of their oppressed co-religionists before the more liberal segment of the Russian intelligentsia. In this respect they resembled the first Russian writers of other ethnic minorities. Like them, they cannot, in retrospect, be considered a part of the mainstream of Russian writing and are generally ignored by historians of Russian literature.

It was not until the turn of the century that Jews began to take an active part in Russian literature as writers, poets, and critics. That this antedated the communist Revolution of 1917 is amply illustrated by the fact that a significant number of them left Soviet Russia and were destined, in the years to come, to play a major role in émigré Russian literature in western Europe and America. Suffice it to mention Mark Aldanov (pseudonym of Landau, 1889–1957), probably the most gifted Russian author of historical novels; the widely read chronicler of pre-revolutionary Russia's Jewry, Semyon Yushkevich (1868–1927); the mystical poet Nikolai Minskii (pseudonym of Vilenkin, 1855–1937); the satirist Sasha Cherny (pseudonym of A. M. Glückberg, 1880–1928); and the literary critic Yulii Aikhenvald (1872–1928). Even larger was the number of those who combined literary activity with journalism. Many non-Jewish Russian *émigrés*, faithful readers of Vladimir Zhabotinskii, were quite unaware of his other claim to fame as a Jewish political figure.

Furthermore, a significant number of Jews active in the literary life of the U.S.S.R. began their careers before 1917. These included the novelists Vladimir Lidin (pseudonym of Gomberg, b. 1894) and Isaac Goldberg (1884–1939); the critics and essayists Akim Volynskii (pseudonym of Flekser, 1863–1926), Mikhail Gershenzon (1869–1925) and Arkadii Gornfeld (1867–1941); and the poets Samuel Marshak (1887–1964) and Zmitrok Biadulia (pseudonym of Samuel Plavnik, 1886–1941). The latter, a former Yeshivah student, wrote in Byelorussian, then a language with almost no literary tradition.

It would be safe to assume, however, that the number of Jews who entered Soviet Russian literature in the last half a century exceeds that of any other country or historical period. Most of them, to be sure, were no better and no worse than the thousands of practitioners of socialist realism who came to constitute the membership of the Union of Soviet Writers. The great majority have produced uninspired art and pedestrian criticism; not a few have, over the years, been active in the literary bureaucracy. It may be of some interest, however, to examine the output of a number of distinguished Russian Jewish authors and attempt to determine whether, apart from having enriched Russian literature with their works, they have actually helped shape it and whether the character of these influences may, in one way or another, be traced to these writers' Jewish backgrounds. Speculation of this sort need not necessarily be dismissed as a futile parochial 'nationalist' exercise. It is, for example, an established fact that in Russian music both composers and performers have traditionally favoured the Romantic, if not, indeed the sentimental style. It is also equally well known that Russian literature has, on the whole, excelled in the realm of the novel and (a fact less familiar in the west) in poetry, but has produced very few plays of lasting merit—this, in spite of the fact that Russia's theatre is one of the world's most famous. While a serious investigation of these phenomena is yet to be undertaken, few would question the assumption that they must, in one way or another, bear some relationship to that country's ethos, its history, political institutions, and so forth. It appears reasonable to expect, therefore, that Soviet writers of Jewish origin, whose personal memories and experiences, as well as the traditions bequeathed to them by their Jewish *milieu*, set them apart from their non-Jewish contemporaries, should exhibit in their works some tendencies that are more characteristic of Soviet writers who are Jews than of those who are not.

The least unexpected and yet most striking feature of writings by Soviet Russian authors of Jewish origin is their non-nationalistic, cosmopolitan character. One senses that their creators, consciously or unconsciously, felt that a demonstratively Russian stance in their works would appear unpleasantly unnatural and, therefore, attempted to avoid exhibitionist patriotism, Slavic folksiness, or even lyrical outbursts provoked by such innocent 'national' factors as the Russian landscape. One gets the impression that the Soviet Jewish author writing in Russian wished to dissociate his 'natural' and 'honourable' joining of a Russian culture from the opportunistically motivated pre-revolutionary conversions of Jews to Eastern Orthodoxy.[1] As a result, with the notable exception of Efim Dorosh (b. 1908), Jewish writers favour, as a rule, the less ethnically coloured urban settings and avoid historical novels and drama—unless set abroad. (Occasionally, they turn to such themes apparently as a result of pressures. Thus Natan Rybak, a Jew writing in Ukrainian, is best known for his novel *The Mistake of Honoré de Balzac*, which appeared before the war; during the anti-cosmopolitan purges marked by persecutions of writers of Jewish origin Rybak published *The Council of Pereyaslavl*, which is set in the seventeenth century and glorifies Bohdan Khmelnitsky, the antisemitic Cossack leader.)

The attraction of non-Russian settings may also be attributed to the fact that these afforded their Jewish authors an opportunity of viewing them with a detachment that was both expected and approved and which was in no way different from the one that an ethnic Russian writer would adopt. It might, indeed, be said that it is only *vis-à-vis* aliens that a Soviet Jewish author could, in good conscience, regard himself as a Russian. The aliens could be foreigners, they could be non-Russians within the borders of the Soviet Union, or could even inhabit the never-never world of fantasy.

It is our contention that most of Soviet Russia's important writers of Jewish origin were attracted by such non-Russian settings, and that much of their specifically 'Jewish' contribution to Russian letters in the last half-century consisted in broadening the hitherto rather narrow historical and geographic vistas of the Russian literary imagination. The historical

---

[1] Ironically, the greatest pre-Soviet painter of 'ethnic' Russian landscape (i.e. one replete with birch trees, green pastures, etc.) was the baptized Jew, Isaak Levitan (1860–1900). The ostentatiously 'Russian' tastes of pre-revolutionary Russia's baptized Jews were masterfully ridiculed by Isaac Babel in his story 'Guy de Maupassant'. Some pre-revolutionary apostates found an ingenious way to shed their Judaism and all the disabilities it entailed while retaining their status as aliens—albeit tolerated and respected ones—by embracing a Christian creed other than the ruling Eastern Orthodoxy, e.g. Lutheranism.

novels of Mark Aldanov, the *émigré* novelist mentioned above are, beyond doubt, the most sophisticated Russian prose describing western Europe. Millions of Soviet citizens have formed their impressions of what the United States is like on the basis of the comic novel *Little Golden America* (1936) by the team of humorists of Ilya Ilf and Yevgenii Petrov, the first of them an Odessa Jew (real name Fainzilberg, 1897–1937). Another 'American' was Vladimir Bill'Belotserkovskii (b. 1885), whose seven-year stay in the United States inspired many of his short stories and plays and even earned him the nickname 'Bill', now a part of his legal name. Similarly, before the outbreak of the Spanish civil war, in Soviet literature Spain was known almost solely through 'Granada' (1926), a famous ballad by Mikhail Svetlov (1903–64), a young Jew from the old Pale of Settlement. Similarly, the far north, particularly the borderlands of Finland, is chiefly known in Soviet literature through the works of Gennadii Fish (1903–71); the Siberian tribes were portrayed by Isaac Goldberg. Most exotic settings of all—Ethiopia and Somaliland—figure in the early works of Venyamin Kaverin (pseudonym of Zilberg, b. 1902), now one of the most eminent living Soviet novelists.

The two most famous Jews in Soviet literature provide the best support for this hypothesis. Both Isaac Babel (1894–1941) and Ilya Ehrenburg (1891–1967) wrote, primarily, about non-Russian locales. It was in these that both were most successful. Their 'Russian' works are, in comparison, pale and unconvincing. It is not unlikely that among the reasons for this was the uncertainty of the two authors' 'Russian' identities—after all, both had vivid memories of pre-revolutionary Jewish ghettos and could not convincingly affect a securely Russian pose when confronting purely Russian material. They had no such qualms when facing non-Russian subject-matter. No Russian would doubt Babel's Russianness when facing the exotic Hassidic Jews of his civil war tales, just as nobody would question Ehrenburg's Russian credentials ('*Mais vous êtes russe, Monsieur Ehrenburg*') when, for decades, he served as Russia's unofficial envoy to western Europe's left-wing intellectuals.

Of the two writers, Ehrenburg was by far the more prolific. At his death in 1967 his writings filled some thirty-odd volumes. Most of these comprised his journalistic output and superficial, propagandistic fiction. His two best works were both written very early. Of these, *The Stormy Life of Lazik Roitschwantz* (1927) is discussed in my other chapter in the present volume (see pp. 194–5). Ehrenburg's unquestionable masterpiece is *The Extraordinary Adventures of Julio Jurenito and of His Disciples: Monsieur Delhaie, Karl Schmidt, Mr. Cool, Aleksei Tishin, Ercole Bambucci, Ilya*

Ehrenburg, and Aisha the Negro, in the Days of Peace, War and Revolution in Paris, Mexico, Rome, Senegal, Kineshma, Moscow and Other Places: As Well as Sundry Reflections of the Master on the Subject of Pipes, Death, Love, Freedom, the Game of Chess, the Hebrew Race, Reconstruction and Likewise Many Other Things. We have quoted the title in full because it conveys something of the cosmopolitan, iconoclastic sarcasm of the book. It speaks well for Ehrenburg's taste that shortly before his death he declared that early book (first published in 1922) his favourite: it is one of the few books in Soviet literature in which the sceptic's savage jeers at the corrupt values of the bourgeois world are not nullified by the pious believer's dutiful genuflections to the wisdom and justice of its alleged alternative, the Soviet system, a situation which, incidentally, has resulted, for all intents and purposes, in the death of satirical writing in the U.S.S.R. Ehrenburg's later novels are much inferior, yet some of these, such as *The Fall of Paris* (1941), achieved considerable fame, much of it undoubtedly due simply to its eyewitness descriptions of Paris and the French, a rare treat in the singularly ethnocentric Soviet literature. It is safe to assume that Ehrenburg's memoirs, serialized in the Soviet monthly *Novy Mir* between 1960 and 1965, owed much of their enormous popularity to similar factors: they offered Soviet readers glimpses of Spain, London, New York, and long, loving descriptions of France, particularly of her capital and its artists, poets, and bohemians.

Isaac Babel's uncontested position as one of the truly great Russian writers of this century, and probably the most sophisticated one, was achieved through two collections of short stories, *The Red Cavalry* (1926) and *The Tales of Odessa* (1927). The former, a series of episodes from Babel's career in the Red Army during the civil war, related with a polished brilliance and economy unequalled in Russian prose (significantly, Babel's masters whom he strove to emulate were both non-Russian, Flaubert and Maupassant), has a significantly double-imaged narrator. Babel, appearing here under the name of Lyutov, is secure in his position as a Russian, a communist, and a soldier of the Revolution only when facing patriarchal Jews from the old *shtetlech*, the Polish gentry, and the Roman Catholic clergy. On the other hand, whenever Lyutov remains face-to-face with *Russian* soldiers and peasants, his Russian veneer becomes thin: to them he is an alien, an outsider, one whose claim to belonging must constantly be tested, whose residence permit as a Russian is always subject to revocation. As a committed communist writer, Babel attributes his own insecurity and his Cossack companions' misgivings to class antagonisms, in this case to his intellectualism. Yet even the most casual reader of the tales cannot fail to observe that Babel conceals an important truth, that the taunts and suspicions of the Cossacks are aimed, first and foremost, at Babel as a Jew. The accusation that Babel's refusal to kill a wounded companion is proof of his lack of compassion rather than his inability to kill, the repeated jokes about his eyeglasses, the very absurdity of the presence of this bookish man among the healthy, romanticized 'noble' savages—all of these underscore the precariousness of the Jewish narrator's position as a Russian fellow-fighter for a common cause. Significantly, the tension of *The Red Cavalry* is absent from *The Tales of Odessa*, a series of predominantly picaresque tales of the physical metamorphoses and spiritual demise of the once fascinating universe of Odessa's Jewry. Babel does not feel threatened as a *Russian* intellectual when he depicts as a sympathetic outsider a series of vignettes from the lives of Odessa's Jewish tradesmen, gangsters, beggars, and plain towns-folk. He is certain that *they* have accepted his defection from their ranks. He is never equally certain that he was accepted by the Russian *milieu* he so desperately sought to join.

Among the genres in Soviet literature in which no clear-cut ethnic (or, for that matter, strictly ideological) identification is required of the author, except in the most general terms, are science fiction and juvenile literature. Unlike adults, children are only dimly aware of their ethnic affiliation and their devotion to the Soviet cause need not be stated with much ideo-logical precision. As for Soviet science fiction and social utopias, these are usually deliberately vague on both issues, emphasizing, instead, the technological marvels of the future. Many Soviet writers who preferred to retain a degree of latitude in dealing with either problem were attracted by these genres. They included an exceedingly large number of Jews, among them the playwright Yevgenii Shvarts, whose fantastic and deliberately ambiguous parables were banned from the Soviet stage for decades and reappeared only after Stalin's (and their author's) death.[1] The most famous writer of Soviet juvenile literature to date was the poet Samuel Marshak. In fact, to Marshak, children's literature was something of a 'family enterprise': both his brother Ilya (1896–1953) and his sister Liya (Leah) Preis (1901–64) wrote for juvenile readers. The first wrote popular science under the pseudonym of M. Ilyin and the latter composed

---

[1] The Soviet children's theatre, founded soon after the Revolution, was the brainchild of Nataliia Sats (b. 1903), and Jews have been active in it as playwrights and actors ever since. See Gene Sosin, 'The Children's Theater and Drama in Soviet Education', in *Through the Glass of Soviet Literature* (ed. Ernest J. Simmons), New York, 1953, pp. 159–200.

nursery rhymes under the name of Yelena Ilyina. Mention was made on page 191 of the celebrated Soviet children's writer Lev Kassil'.[1]

It would, admittedly, be futile to speculate whether the studiedly 'pure' poetry of such masters as the Nobel Prize winner Boris Pasternak (1890–1960) and Osip Mandelshtam (1892–1938) represented flight from social reality (as orthodox Marxist critics, led by Plekhanov, assure us would have to be the case), or from their ethnic and religious heritage, or perhaps from both. That the latter possibility cannot be dismissed is illustrated by several passages in Pasternak's *Doctor Zhivago* and by a few of his poems. Similarly, in Mandelshtam we find some expressions of fear at being haunted by the 'yellow and black stripes' (an allusion to the Jewish prayer shawl). This also applies to his poem written in 1931, 'Alexander Gertsevich, the Jewish Musician'.[2] A stronger awareness of the poet's Jewishness emerges from the two volumes of his widow's memoirs, *Hope Against Hope* and *Hope Abandoned*, both published only in the West. The two volumes are probably the richest and best-written literary chronicle ever to emerge from the U.S.S.R., thus earning Nadezhda Mandelshtam a distinguished place in her own right in any future history of Russian literature.

Jews participated prominently in the revolt against traditional realism in Russian literature at the beginning of our century, and it is noteworthy that nearly all of them were to be found in the ranks of the innovators. Having no stake in Russian literature of the past, they were eager to make a clear break with its heritage. The poet and painter David Burliuk (1882–1964) was among the founders of the Russian Futurism and its most vocal proponent. The poet, Ilya Selvinskii (1899–1968) was a leading Constructivist, a movement advocating, among other things, the assimilation by poetry of modern technological devices and vocabulary. Lev Lunts (1901–24), the leading spirit of the Serapion Brothers, the most important group of Russian writers of the first post-revolutionary years, condemned what he considered the static quality of traditional Russian prose and called for a 'western' type of literature, with swiftly moving plots,

[1] Curiously, many Soviet Yiddish poets—first and foremost Leyb Kvitko (1890–1952), but also including Itzik Fefer, Rokhl Baumvol, and others—wrote children's verse and the Russian translations of their works resulted, unexpectedly, in the fact that more Russians know Soviet Yiddish poetry than prose. In general, Russian children read more foreign literature than their elders. Rokhl Baumvol is now in Israel.

[2] The image of the Jewish fiddler on the background of an unreal town, now familiar to millions through the paintings of Marc Chagall, is to be found in a poem by Julian Tuwim, who was like Mandelshtam, a descendant of assimilated Jews. Tuwim's Polish poem closes with the words 'Never shall we find haven nor peace/We, the singing Jews/The Jews gone berserk'. Tuwim's possible allusion to Ophelia adds to the effectiveness of the poem.

suspense, etc. Traditional Russian socio-political evaluation of literature (which was later made obligatory in Soviet criticism), was opposed by the so-called Formalist movement, one of whose leaders, Viktor Shklovskii (b. 1893) emphasized that literature is primarily an art of dislocating reality and presenting it in an unusual perspective.

Finally, Jews have figured most prominently in the ranks of Soviet literary scholars concerned with foreign literature as well as of translators from languages ranging from Latin to Chinese. Among the academics, Viktor Zhirmunskii (1891–1971) should be noted, an outstanding scholar working in the fields of German literature and literary theory; Alexander Anikst (b. 1910), a specialist in English and American writing; Pavel Berkov (1896–1969), an authority on Russo-Western literary relations, and others too numerous to mention. The translators, in addition to Marshak and Pasternak, both of whom rendered into Russian much of English poetry, include a number of other prominent poets in their own right (e.g. Boris Slutskii, b. 1919) as well as professionals, such as Vladimir Admoni (b. 1909), who translated into Russian German and Scandinavian writers,[1] and the classical scholar Simon Markish, the son of the executed Soviet Yiddish poet Perets Markish. The younger Markish is now in Israel.

There is every indication that the wave of departures from the U.S.S.R. in the 1970s will bring about the emergence of a second émigré Russian literature, as rich perhaps as that of the 1920s. Many of its potential leaders are Jews whose literary reputations were established while they were in the Soviet Union, such as, for instance, the poet Naum Korzhavin (pen name of Mandel, b. 1925), the novelist Grigori Svirsky, and the dramatist, balladeer, and satirist Alexander Galich. Others, such as Iosif Brodskii, though unpublished in the U.S.S.R., are rapidly achieving recognition abroad.

The foregoing brief essay has no claim to completeness. It was not meant to be a list of the hundreds of Soviet writers, critics, and scholars who happen to be Jews or of Jewish descent. In the previous chapter an attempt was made to describe some *specifically* 'Jewish' themes and conflicts as they are found in Soviet Russian literature. In this chapter we have tried to point to some Soviet authors whose writings, in our opinion, bear some recognizable stamp of their Jewish origins. To present an 'all-inclusive' list of writers of Jewish descent, Soviet or otherwise, we consider worse than pointless. Suffice it to say that the Jews have not

---

[1] Admoni was subjected to ridicule because of his foreign-sounding (e.g. Jewish) name at the trial of the poet Iosif Brodskii in February 1964. Brodskii's poetry is permeated with the feeling of alienation, often attributed by the poet himself to his Jewishness.

merely 'contributed' to Soviet literatures—the Russian, the Ukrainian, Byelorussian, Georgian, and others. They have helped create them and share in the credit for their accomplishments and the responsibility for their shortcomings.

11

Hebrew Literature in the U.S.S.R.

YEHOSHUA A. GILBOA

These pages deal solely with those Hebrew writers who first emerged during the Soviet regime. They can generally be described as the 'younger generation'. We are not concerned with a number of prominent Hebrew writers who continued to live in Russia for several years after the Bolshevik seizure of power, nor with those who remained there till their last days but who were already known before the Revolution.[1]

The very fact that these writers of the younger generation chose the forbidden or ostracized Hebrew language in which to express themselves, together with their remoteness from contemporary centres of Hebrew literature (notably in Palestine), makes their emergence all the more worthy of investigation. In reviewing these writings, attention must also be given to the writers' emotional environment and to the hard struggle for existence waged by the Hebrew language in the Soviet Union.

Abraham Kariv, one of the writers involved, later depicted their specific fate:

From afar it is hard to conceive the orphanhood and affliction that comes from writing in a language uprooted from the living soil—a language that found its last refuge on the gravestones of Jewish cemeteries; being cut off from the mines of that language, deprived of an old book or a new one ... in a hostile world concealing only dangers and lacking the warmth and encouragement so acutely needed by a writer.[2]

In another testimony, of a moving personal character, Kariv described the climate surrounding those who 'exchanged confidences' with the excommunicated Hebrew muse:

The strangeness all around was boundless, and the existence of a Hebrew world somewhere far away was beyond all conception. I can say for myself that the

---

[1] A large number of Hebrew writers left Russia after the Revolution; in 1921 a group of twelve writers (and their families), headed by Ch. N. Bialik, was permitted to leave.

[2] Abraham Kariv (ed.), *Ha'anaf Ha'gadua* (The Hewn Branch), Jerusalem, 1954, preface, pp. 12–13. Kariv (Krivorutshka) was one of the Hebrew writers whose literary activities began under the Soviet regime. He left the U.S.S.R. at the end of 1934.

Bible was not in my hands all those years; it was also dangerous to keep it in the room. Time passed and I never saw a printed Hebrew line. I preserved in those years old hidden notes of mine, and took them out from time to time and read them for the sake of hearing by myself the whisper of Hebrew. Sometimes, while I was alone, writing a Hebrew poem, a strange doubt crept into my mind: am I not the man who invented this language out of his imagination?[1]

Full understanding of this extraordinary literary phenomenon requires a brief clarification of the position of Hebrew in the U.S.S.R. No formal decree outlawed Hebrew. But without a legal endorsement, the illegality of Hebrew had been firmly established in practice. However, in the first decade of the Soviet regime certain circles not only managed to keep alight Hebrew's 'glowing embers', but also made open efforts to ensure that formal recognition be given to Hebrew creative writing.

Some of the people involved in these efforts sincerely believed that the actual ban on Hebrew was merely a temporary misunderstanding, and therefore bound to disappear quite soon. Writing some twenty years later, one of them described his immediate emotional reaction to the ban: 'Forbid Hebrew? This order was so surprising by its lack of logic, so anti-October.'[2] Several sources have confirmed the loyalty of these Hebrew enthusiasts to the Soviet order. 'All of them were fervent supporters of the regime, and some also belonged to the communist party'— this was discovered by a Hebrew-American writer, who visited the Soviet Union in 1929 and came in contact with a group of young Hebrew writers.[3] Kariv asserts that several of these writers 'whole-heartedly believed in the newly emerging world and desired to secure in it a place for the Hebrew language to which they were devoted. . . . They considered Hebrew a last survivor that had to be rescued from a world allegedly doomed to disappear from the historical stage.'[4]

To boycott Hebrew also looked senseless from the purely proletarian point of view. How could you account for hostility towards a language in which the principles of social justice—i.e. revolutionary ideas—had been embodied in ancient times? The devotees of Hebrew found the revolutionary regime inconsistent in this respect. Characteristically, in various memoranda, they pointed emphatically to the progressive nature of the Hebrew language. A number of Russian personalities, mainly from the world of literature and art, shared the views of the Hebraists and also

[1] Abraham Kariv, in *Moznayim*, Tel Aviv, October 1962, p. 329.

[2] Y. Saarony, in *Mishmar*, Tel Aviv, 7 November 1943. Saarony's previous name was Matov. He also used the pen-name Yosyfon.

[3] Daniel Persky, in *Hadoar*, New York, 20 January 1961.

[4] Kariv, *Ha'anaf Ha'gadua*, preface p. 12.

tried to intervene in protest at the discrimination against Hebrew and its literature.[1]

These efforts succeeded, occasionally, in winning some concessions. But as a rule a hostile attitude, nourished by narrow-minded political calculations, prevailed. Hebrew was regarded as the language of rabbis and clerical reaction, and as a vehicle of Zionism, in itself a servant of British imperialism. By this reasoning, 'even the "Internationale" in a Hebrew translation is counter-revolutionary'.[2] In the Soviet Union, therefore, an unusual development, even for a totalitarian censorship, took place: literary works were banned, not necessarily because of their perilous contents, but because the language itself was viewed as defective and dangerous (reactionary, bourgeois, clerical). Unbelievable though it may sound, even communist and explicitly pro-Soviet publications in Hebrew, or Hebrew translations of Russian and Soviet literature, were prohibited in the U.S.S.R

The efforts made by a handful of devotees to win permission for the use of Hebrew were quite exceptional. On the one hand, the authorities denied that Hebrew was persecuted, but they stated, almost simultaneously, that 'Hebrew was a dead language, and a corpse had no rights'. The Hebraists argued 'We are Soviet writers, writing in Hebrew, and we are strangled; for 200 languages there is room in the Soviet country—should only Hebrew be disqualified?'[3] On several occasions the young writers applied for permission to arrange Hebrew literary evenings and to publish Hebrew periodicals. It seems that to some degree these efforts were stimulated by the fact that the official line in regard to Hebrew still appeared undefined. Indeed, not only had no formal ban on Hebrew been pronounced, as already mentioned, but probably the operative guidelines in this respect were also not always precisely clear. This vagueness can, partly, be explained by tactical calculation: in the face of public opinion, abroad at least, it was more convenient to suppress Hebrew in practice without actually decreeing its suppression. To some extent, however, the uncertainty stemmed from genuine hesitation on the part of the authorities: after all, doubts regarding the wisdom and justice of forbidding Hebrew might easily penetrate thinking minds. (The very different character of the twenties in the life of the Soviet Union, as

---

[1] These included Maxim Gorky who had shown a particular interest in Hebrew culture. He and others also tried to protect the Hebrew theatre, *Habimah*, which was founded in Moscow after the Revolution and left the Soviet Union in 1926.

[2] Saarony, op. cit.

[3] Y. Saarony, 'The Leningrad Group', in Chaim Lensky, *Meever Nhar Halethy* (Across the Lethe River), Tel Aviv, 1960, pp. 233–4.

compared with later years, must not be forgotten.) On the other hand, the same lack of clarity constituted an additional source of distress to the Hebrew activists. Characteristically, certain petitions requested a definite reply that would relieve the authors of anxious doubts. In the words of one such petition of 1927:

If our language, for reasons we are unable to understand, is really harmful and counter-revolutionary, then we demand its suppression by law. But if national policy permits the existence of all languages, then we demand a law forbidding its persecution.[1]

The petitions and appeals were mainly an outward expression of the stubborn struggle for Hebrew in the U.S.S.R. Of more lasting value was the continuance of Hebrew creative writing.

This first resulted in a number of 'organs', in handwritten or mimeographed form, which passed from hand to hand. One such periodical—*From the Storm*—was a bi-weekly published in Kharkov and copied by sympathizers elsewhere.[2] A number of Hebrew publications was issued by the *Hechalutz*. In 1925 the Central Committee of the illegal *Tarbut* launched a mimeographed periodical, entitled *Filling the Breach*, which reached three issues.[3]

Some endeavours failed, but some produced relatively substantial results. One was a booklet entitled *Gaash* (Storming) which contained three poems by Mili (Samuel) Novak, and was published at Kiev in 1923. The story of its publication is as curious as it is instructive. On 25 March 1923, the author asked the local printing authority to publish the booklet. He submitted three poems and emphasized that their motifs were 'social-revolutionary'. Because 'the question of publishing Hebrew literature is a matter of principle', the local authority consulted the central authority, and added the conclusions of a 'polit-editor' (Kogan). The latter's remarks were quite revealing and are worthy of being quoted in full:

The booklet, which contains three poems, is an attempt to give expression in Hebrew to the trends of our modern communist poetry. The influences of Blok and Mayakovsky are undoubtedly evident. The verse is clear-toned, acute at certain points. One of the poems sounds like a hymn to October, imbued with deep contempt for the world of yesterday and its morality. Another poem deals with one of the plagues of our reality—prostitution. The third one reflects the reverse side of the revolution—the counter-revolution. To whom are these

---

[1] A. L. Tsentsiper, *Esser Sh'not R'difot* (Ten Years of Persecution), Tel Aviv, 1930, p. 242.

[2] Saarony, *Mishmar*, op. cit.

[3] B. Zlatsin, in Benjamin West (ed.), *Naftulei Dor* (The Wrestling of a Generation), vol. 1, 2nd edn., Tel Aviv, 1947, pp. 310–11.

poems directed? Obviously, in other circumstances, in Palestine, this booklet might serve as propaganda material for the communist party there, because a considerable part of the Palestine workers speak Hebrew. But in the conditions of our life the booklet is bound to serve as literary-philological nourishment for the clerical bourgeois segment of the Jewish public. It is clear that this publication is undesirable.[1]

Fortunately, the final outcome of Novak's efforts did not correspond with Kogan's suggestions, and the booklet, as already said, was published the same year.

Two other authorized symposia must be discussed more fully: *Zilzelei Shoma* (a type of ancient musical instrument, resembling a cymbal), published by the Kharkov group in 1923, and *Bereshith* (In the Beginning), published in 1926.

The first was brought to Palestine by the delegation from Trade Union Federation (Histadruth) to an agricultural exhibition in Moscow. The sponsors of the collection referred to it as 'our cultural produce which ripened throughout the years of revolution', and which emerged like 'a solitary island in a sea of indifference and animosity towards the Hebrew language and literature'. Further, the sponsors stressed the 'spiritual nearness' between themselves and those working for the rebirth of Palestine. They asked understanding for their 'orphanhood' and hoped that the new Hebrew literature would somehow relieve their loneliness.[2]

Bereshith has a strange 'technical' story behind it. Its place of publication is given as Moscow–Leningrad, but it was printed in Berlin, as noted on the reverse side of the title page, in German: 'Druckerei Gutenberg, Berlin'. Semi-officially, this was said to be due to the lack, at that time, of Hebrew type-faces in the printing establishments of the country. But it may also be assumed that those establishments were reluctant to be involved in printing literature in a language to which the authorities were not kindly disposed. Another theory is that certain officials refused to allocate paper for a Hebrew publication. In any event, *Bereshith* was the first and last, although a second issue was prepared. Not more than 300 copies were allowed to enter the Soviet Union.

The Soviet boycott of the Hebrew language and literature becomes all the more astonishing if these three publications are examined.

[1] Novak's request, the decision of the local authority and the conclusions of the 'polit-editor' are reproduced both in the original (Russian) and in Hebrew translation in Yehoshua Gilboa (ed.), *Gehalim Lohashot* (Glowing Embers), Tel Aviv, 1954, pp. 378–80.

[2] *Kuntres*, no. 163, Tel Aviv, 1924.

Zilzelei Shoma and *Bereshith*, as well as Mili Novak's booklet of poems, presented some kind of parallel or conjoint loyalties: to the Revolution and to Hebrew. All the pieces there really assert that the young Hebrew writers—most of them poets—welcomed October with varying degrees of enthusiasm. Some of them expressed reservations as to the policy of the regime towards Jewish problems, but none was hostile to the new order. The reader is persuaded that they mainly wished to preserve the right to sing to the Revolution in their ancient tongue. Their poems have many features in common with the Russian revolutionary poetry of that time, and were greatly dominated by a declamatory tone. Influences of Maya-kovsky's marching rhythms and Yesenin's '*hooliganschina*', as well as Blok's symbolist reflections, are clearly discernible.

Zilzelei Shoma not only accepts the new political and social values; it also acclaims the literary fashion of October. The introduction rhetori-cally asks: 'Are these pages worthy to appear in public?' The editors reply: 'We do not hesitate, October also permitted the placard.' The whole collection is full of praise for the principles as well as the incidental aspects of the new regime. G. Hanovits, in a review of Blok's *The Twelve*, is excited by the poet of 'beauty in chaos'. Furthermore, Blok's hallowing of flowing blood, his dauntless confrontation with road-side corpses is fascinating: 'Blok knows that in a time of world upheaval'—Hanovits writes with approval—'there is no room for weeping mercy: petty personal ethics do not count when two giant systems measure their power against each other.' The time mirrored here is a time of rebellion against the symbols of yesterday rather than of the construction of the new order. Y. Borovits assails the world of landlords, warlords, and the property-laden bourgeoisie, and shouts: 'We yearn for battle, we are thirsty for slaughter.' Hanovits is ready to give the Revolution 'buckets of his blood, to adorn leprous walls with red-coloured placards'. Curiously enough, one of the participants of *Zilzelei Shoma* introduced himself, not only by his name (Yakov Boruchin), but also by his position: 'Red Soldier of the G.P.U.'

Bereshith was a much bigger undertaking; its 200 pages introduced a dozen writers. Its contents are more complex, and also emotionally or 'ideologically' more diversified. Unlike *Zilzelei Shoma*, which a Hebrew poetess of Russian origin complained had nothing 'from our Jewish life in upheaval',[1] *Bereshith* gave considerable space to Jewish themes. But these themes are viewed from a quite specific angle. As the title of the collection indicates, the prevailing tendency is to proclaim a new beginning,

---

[1] Elisheva, in *Hashiloah*, vol. 43, Jerusalem, 1925, pp. 471-4.

to open a fresh chapter in Hebrew cultural history. For several of the
participants at least, this meant a denial of continuity and inheritance;
a Hebrew literature, which would draw its inspiration almost exclusively
from the ideals of the Revolution. Here and there a lament for the dying
Jewish tradition, or *shtetl*, is heard but the impression left is that the
triumphant march of the Revolution would inevitably silence these
laments. 'The Revolution is the exclusive reality of life for us. . . . We
prefer death to agony amidst the decaying wreckage of the past', says
Z. Broin (another pen-name of M. Hayog). S. H. (Simon Haboneh),
reviewing the *Gaash* of M. Novak, accuses him of 'lacking the organic
Leninist devotion to October'.[1] In another review the same writer
rejoices at the elimination of the old-style Jewish town, with its ghost, the
shopkeeper, from the Soviet soil.

Many elegiac notes, too, are intermingled in *Bereshith*. A. Krivorutshka,
whose poem opens the collection, tries to silence the pain of the declining
past with the 'herald of the morrow'. But the old 'anonymous town',
that nourished his youth, comes before him—enveloped in humiliation
and longing—and he is unable to withstand its grief. The heart of Y. L.
Zfasman is similarly torn. He would like to embrace both the rising newborn child and the departing grandfather. M. Novak turns in distress to a
grandmother: 'Your grandson is putting out the sparks of light in his
soul and does not kindle fresh ones; who will lighten his depths in a
gloomy night?' Characteristically, the only translated pieces in *Bereshith*
are several short stories by the famous Russian-Jewish writer Isaac Babel
(a note states that he authorized the translations). Among them is 'Gedali':
the narrator, in the role of the Red Cavalry fighter (in the stormy days of
the civil war), finds himself in the shop of old Gedali who tells him of his
idea for a very original 'Internationale', an 'International of good people'.
He adds: 'The Revolution—we will say "yes" to, but are we to say "no"
to the sabbath?' Apparently, a great part of the *Bereshith* group was beset
with similar doubts and questions.

A few words should be said of Simon Haboneh, not because of
his artistic qualities, but because he personified—in a somewhat strange
form—a specific mood that may be termed 'Hebrew-Communism'.
He conceived the highly imaginative idea of a Bolshevism devoted to the
cultivation of the Hebrew language and literature; Hebrew as a value in
itself, or as a tool of the redemptive revolution, devoid of any affinity
with the Jewish historical heritage or with contemporary Zionist aspirations. This way of thinking was not typical of all the young Hebrew

[1] Cf. the opinion of the 'polit-editor' Kogan.

writers, but it was also not fully distinct from their legitimate line, so to speak. Another Hebraist speaking collectively, 'We are not Zionists. We don't think at all that a piece of land, small as a palm, where a small part of world Jewry lives, is an essential principle without which Hebrew expression is null and void.'[1] Also illustrative are complaints against the old, well-established Hebrew writers who 'out of fear of October abandoned the struggle, ran away, deserted'.[2] On the contrary, the young Hebrew writers in the early phases of the regime, did not think of emigration but rather of a new 'Hebrew-revolutionary' centre in the Soviet Union. From Leningrad in 1927, came the following declaration:

Despite all the people of little faith . . . we live here as citizens of the Soviet Union, who share her joys and griefs. We have grown up in the bosom of the Revolution. We do not wish to wander over alien countries, to flee from the workbench of the new life. Russia, which put its imprint on all Hebrew literature for the last 100 years, will again bring forth a new spirit and provide new foundations for the golden thread of our old-new literature.[3]

These dreams were, in general, born of a sincere faith in a fundamental harmony—only temporarily violated—between the Revolution and Hebrew culture. Such illusions were not the exclusive domain of these young Hebrew zealots. An established writer who left Russia early, wrote a kind of manifesto in 1919 entitled 'The Hebrew Communist', in which he fervently welcomed the Revolution and visualized a natural role for Hebrew culture and 'Red Jewry' in the battles of the Revolution and the new order.[4] More curious were those religious leaders who tended to believe that the Revolution embodied something of the messianic age, because 'all events are given by God', and 'the Almighty enfolded himself into materialism and light sparkled in the world'.[5] These two examples, although extraordinary, help to elucidate the emotional background which made such illusions grow more fervently among the young Hebraists. It must be added that, with all their revolutionary pathos, they did not indulge in flattery and self-abasement before the authorities.

[1] Sh. Rusi, in *K'thuvim*, Tel Aviv, March 1927.
[2] Yosyfon in *K'thuvim*, Tel Aviv, August 1926.
[3] Sh. Rusi, In *Davar Supplement*, March 1927.
[4] Eliezer Shteinman, *Ha'komunist Ha'ivri* (The Hebrew Communist), Odessa, 1919. Reproduced in *Orlogin*, no. 5, Tel Aviv, 1952, pp. 311–16.
[5] Quoted by A. A. Gershuny, *Yahadut Brusia Ha'sovyetyth* (Judaism in Soviet Russia), Jerusalem, 1961, pp. 127–8. It must be stressed that these opinions were not typical of the Jewish religious literature that was devotedly written or collected (and has partly come to light) under the Soviet regime. This literature is a remarkable chapter in the history of Jewry in the U.S.S.R.

An instructive point is, naturally, the fate of those who nurtured such dreams. Five of the participants of *Bereshith* and some others, whose confident statements about the future of Hebrew creative writing under the Soviet regime are quoted above, later left the U.S.S.R. and went to Palestine.[1] Those who remained in the Soviet Union were destined to be destroyed, or 'to disappear', in one way or another.

The limited scope of this study does not permit me to deal extensively with the works of all the young Hebrew writers in the Soviet Union. But I do wish at least to mention the following: Zvi Preigerson, Bath-Hama, Y. Alsharif, Pier Edny, Aron Olin, Gershon Frid, and Shmuel Lotesh. Three of the most remarkable figures will be singled out for more detailed review.

The first is the prose writer Abraham Freeman. He earned his reputation with a great novel entitled *1919* that was to consist of four or five volumes. Three were published in Tel Aviv in book-form.[2] It is uncertain whether the remaining one or two parts perished or whether the author succeeded in completing them. But the published parts of *1919* earned Freeman the Bialik Prize of Tel Aviv for literature.

Using a broad canvas, Freeman drew a picture of Jewish life in the Ukraine in the difficult period of the civil war. This was in general a time of chaos and confusion; for the Jews it was marked by bloody pogroms. But Freeman portrayed the dreadful year of 1919 in an unusual light. His interest was not concentrated on the miserable victims but on Jewish self-defence, with its slogan 'to raise the price of life'. Solomon, the organizer and leader of fighting units, heads the colourful cast of *1919*. He is revengeful and indifferent to danger: he does not expect to die a natural death. He is a practical leader who thinks of supplies, communications and, above all, how to link hundreds of towns in one chain of battle-ready units. His men, well disciplined, no longer hope to oppose force by spirit, but rather raise fist against fist. Their boast is not of erudition and brilliance but of sheer physical strength.

---

[1] The participants in *Bereshith* who left the Soviet Union included A. Krivorutshka (Kariv), Yocheved Bat-Miriam, D. Gur (Pines), G. Hanovits and Y. Norman. Elisheva, Y. Matov (Yosyfon, Saarony) and Sh. Rusi (Sosensky) also went to Palestine. Valuable sections are devoted to the works of the Hebrew writers in the Soviet Union, in Ch. Shmeruk (ed.): *Pirsumim Yehudiim Bivrit Hamoazot* (Jewish Publications in the Soviet Union), 'Galuyot', The Historical Society of Israel, Jerusalem, 1961, pp. 17–41 and pp. 406–9 from the bibliography, and the Introduction by Yehuda Slutski, 'Hebrew Publications in the Soviet Union during the years 1917–60', pp. 19–54. The latter also contains a list of those writings of the Hebrew writers in the Soviet Union published outside the U.S.S.R.

[2] A. Freeman, *1919*, Tel Aviv, 1930; II, 1935. *1919* (three parts), Tel Aviv, 1968.

Freeman's epic revealed great skill in observation, though the detail is occasionally exaggerated. He also has a sense of humour and a compelling irony. Here is an example: because of the frequent changes in authorities at that time, the small Jewish town had to consider which political ally to choose. At one time, the inhabitants looked hopefully to the Great Russians—'let the bear come and make order in the flock'. At another, they were tempted to believe in the Cossacks. But they soon became convinced that it was not 'soil and freedom' that the Cossacks sought. Occasionally the Jews hoped for salvation from the Bolsheviks: after all, apart from their slogans of peace and justice, were they not led by Aryeh, the son of David (Leon Davidovitch Trotsky)?[1]

Freeman makes a beautiful blend of human emotions and natural scenes. The coming of spring not only puts an end to the cold days and nights, but also, temporarily drives dreadful memories into oblivion. In words which seem to paraphrase a famous verse of Bialik (after the pogrom of Kishenev: 'God summoned the spring and the slaughter together') the Jews in *1919* wonder why 'it is spring and there is no persecutor near', and human vitality triumphs at once.

His letters[2] show Freeman to have been a sensitive man, with abundant *esprit*. 'His conversation possessed unimagined force.'[3] But this dynamic nature was doomed to a lonely life, replete with suffering. He sought for escape through his literary work, but consolation could not easily be attained when it was impossible for him even to see those parts of his novel which were printed abroad. As he himself complained: 'For years I write and send away incessantly, but get no answer . . . For years I have not seen a Hebrew book . . . There are those who take care that nothing should reach me.'[4] Against the background of such forced seclusion 'not merely is *1919* a great epic; the way it was created is a heroic epic in itself'.[5]

For a long time Freeman hoped to leave for Palestine, but in vain. He was born in a small settlement in the Ukraine in 1890. In 1934, while living in Odessa, he was gaoled and released after several months. He was imprisoned again in 1936 (the Bialik Prize was awarded to him while he was still a prisoner). Ten years later he was released. He died in December 1953.

<hr />

[1] Aryeh = Hebrew for 'lion'; Davidovitch = Russian for 'son of David'.

[2] Many letters were written to A. Kariv to whom the present writer is grateful for putting them at his disposal.

[3] Kariv, in *Moznayim*, op. cit., p. 330.

[4] Y. Opatoshu, in *Zamelbicher*, no. 8, New York, 1952, p. 211.

[5] Kariv, in *Gilionoth*, vol. I, no. 5, Tel Aviv, 1934.

The poet, Elisha Rodin, born in 1888, began his literary career as a Yiddish writer. He attached himself to Hebrew only after it had become a social and political 'outcast'.

His poetic range is not wide. Probably also his command of the language was not powerful. Sometimes he complained that editors (of the periodicals in Palestine, where his work was published) corrected him too drastically, but time and again he himself pointed to the wonder that, in his situation, he was still able to use Hebrew at all. Unparalleled pain surely emerges from a sentence such as the following: 'I begin to forget already the language in which I am writing.'[1] Even so, the reader is captivated by the truth and torment that inform Rodin's poems. He himself admits in one poem: 'No surprises I have brought with me, but heart I do bring.'

Rodin's 'heart' overflows, to the point of religious devoutness, with love of the Hebrew language, the Bible and the Jewish land. All three themes are linked, yet each has a life of its own in the poet's world. He is filled with love for the language: 'the language of languages', 'the source of all blessings', 'mother of poetry', 'solace for a man in distress', 'last remnant of our treasures'. The humiliated tongue becomes for Rodin 'a great goddess'. He even carries his affection and reverence to the Hebrew dictionary: from its pages 'generation after generation calls' to him. It has been said that Rodin's 'prayers and hymns' to Hebrew breathe a yearning similar to that of Yehuda Halevi in his songs of Zion: 'never before has our poetry so yearned for the Hebrew tongue, which became for Rodin . . . a new myth.'[2]

Where the Bible was concerned, Rodin felt himself obliged to carry 'the load of the prophets amidst scorn and derision'. And of ancient, reborn Palestine he declares 'all my longing is for her, for the single one'.

In notes entitled 'In the Land of Fire' Rodin weighs the pros and cons of the Revolution. He welcomes it but is unable to overlook 'the tears' it cost. Among his reservations: 'Those ideals are yet unborn which might morally entitle anyone to eliminate from the earth our essential image'— an image which is marked by Hebrew from times immemorial. He also cannot forgive the Revolution for profaning his Bible, which he must 'wrap in *Pravda* to protect it from a hostile eye'.

'In the Land of Fire' also mentions Rodin's son, Grisha (Gregory). This was another source of grief in the poet's life. After school, behind closed doors, he managed to read to the boy chapters from the Bible,

[1] From a letter to *Davar*, Tel Aviv, dated 10 April, 1942.
[2] Kariv, in *Ha'anaf Ha'gadua*, op. cit., p. 200.

'to air' his brain, 'stuffed all day with five-year plans . . . and the defamation of God, Judaism and humanity'. But tomorrow, in school, the boy will again listen to the slanders heaped on the Bible: 'They are many, and I am one. Who will win?'

The struggle for Grisha had also to be waged against the boy's mother. Rodin's marriage was unhappy. Apparently, his whole behaviour, and specifically his attempt to give his son a Jewish consciousness, were ridiculed by his wife. After his 'conversion' to Hebrew, the poet was expelled from the Union of Soviet Writers and deprived of important material benefits derived from his membership. He was compelled to earn his bread by casual hard labour, such as street cleaning. In addition, Rodin had at times to be treated by institutions for the mentally disturbed, and was often 'invited' to the N.K.V.D. All this reinforced the barrier between him and his wife. In her eyes, his sacrifices and sufferings were senseless. She also feared that one day she and Grisha would be imprisoned or exiled on account of sentiments that she wholly rejected. Finally, in 1941, while the Germans were approaching Moscow, she left Rodin taking the boy with her.

Grisha volunteered for the Red Army. He too, apparently, was of a sensitive character, and at that time felt a warmer affinity than ever towards his father, and in his letters to him expressed a feeling of kinship with his ideas. From army camps, Grisha sent his father some pieces of poetry in Russian, to which his father responded with verses in Hebrew. Certain of Rodin's poems dedicated to his son, clearly indicate that the boy was 'both saddened and heartened, because I understood my father a little'. Moreover, through the events that brought him to the camp, 'the truth about myself was here revealed to me'. Recalling these confessions of the son, the father later sang 'I am sure that your eyes were opened to Hebrew before they closed forever.'

The son, 17 years old, was killed in March 1942 on the Kalinin front. Rodin devoted a series of poems to him, some written before his death and some after. A curious event now occurred. The poet formally applied to the authorities for permission to forward to Palestine the Hebrew poems about his son. Here is this document in full:

Respected comrades of the military censorship!

The poems that I am sending to you are about my son, Rodin, Gregory Abramovitch, who volunteered for the battlefield and died on the Kalinin front on the 14th of March, 1942.

The poems are written in the language of the Bible which is the language of my childhood, the language of my people and which I love as my musical instrument, because only in this language am I able to express my emotions.

I request that you show these poems to a person sufficiently familiar with this language, who is also honest and without personal ties with the Jewish national cause in Palestine. I am sure that an exact and honest translation of my poems would permit you to transfer them without delay to Palestine, because my poems serve our common interest: the destruction of Hitler.

In memory of my son, who shortly before giving his life expressed satisfaction in the fact that I was writing about him, I ask you to treat these poems with respect and to forward them to Palestine, where my writings are published.

> With Greetings
> The Hebrew Poet,
> Elisha Rodin.

Rodin's request was approved and his poems 'To The Son' were published in Palestine.[1] The poet's wish for his dead son was fulfilled: 'May your soul, as mine also, be gathered in the eternal life of our language.'

Previously, as Rodin himself indicates, his writings had also been printed in Palestine,[2] but this never occurred with the official endorsement of the Soviet authorities. Permission in this instance was connected with the circumstances and interests of the war, mainly the belief in Moscow at that time that poems by a Hebrew poet in Russia about his son's heroic death in battle might also serve to mobilize the sympathies of world Jewry. But this positive occurrence was not without some bitterness. A copy of 'To The Son' was sent from Tel Aviv to Rodin at the address of the Jewish Anti-Fascist Committee in Moscow, where Rodin was employed part-time in translating Yiddish-Soviet poetry into Hebrew. But certain officials of the Committee withheld the copy from the author and even concealed its arrival from his knowledge. Devious measures had to be taken to enable Rodin to see his own work in print.[3] Rodin, who suffered to the last, died in a Moscow hospital in 1947.[4]

My last section is devoted to Chaim Lensky. The richness and virtuosity of his poetry is such that it is hard to imagine that he was cut off from centres of Hebrew culture and environment. This 'nightingale

[1] Elisha Rodin, *Laben* (To the Son), Tel Aviv, 1943. This book also reproduces a letter from the divisional commissar to Rodin, in praise of his son's heroic death, and the poet's letter to the military censorship.

[2] Apart from publications in periodicals, a collection of Rodin's writings was published before the Second World War: Elisha Rodin, *B'faathei Nechar* (On the Borders of the Alien Land), Tel Aviv, 1938.

[3] A. Sutzkever, in *Am Vasefer*, Tel Aviv, August 1963, pp. 45–6.

[4] Rachel Korn, in *Davar*, 10 March 1959.

without a nest'[1] made an outstanding individual contribution to modern Hebrew literature.

The story of his life is painful. He was born in 1905 in Slonim, Grodno district. His parents divorced when he was barely out of his cradle and he was cared for by his grandfather, a hard-working and observant Jew. At the age of 12 Lensky tried to write his first poems; about the same time he succumbed to a lust for reading. When his region was occupied during the First World War by the Germans, he managed to learn German, and Heine later became one of his favourite poets. In 1921 his grandfather died. For a time Lensky attended the Hebrew teachers' seminary in Vilno. In a moment of overwhelming despair, in 1923, he tried to take his life. Later, a letter from his father, who lived in Baku, reached him, and he smuggled himself into Soviet Russia. It is hard to determine the decisive motives which forced Lensky to take this step: a longing to see his father from whom he had not heard for years, a certain sympathy with the Soviet Union, sheer curiosity about the great experiment on the other side of the border—or a combination of them all. After some initial difficulties, (a short period of detention, disappointment when he met his father, the quest for a living) he moved from Baku to Moscow at the end of 1925 and thence to Leningrad.[2]

There his poetic powers flourished. In the poems of the Leningrad period the poet's emotional affinity to the scenes and experiences of his childhood is manifest. The long poem 'Lithuania' sounds like a song of praise, replete with nostalgic and humorous notes, for the sights and scenes of his youth. The grandfather, to whom Lensky was devoted, is depicted in this poem as an admirable blend of physical strength and Jewish traditionalism: 'strong muscles beneath the phylacteries on the arm.'

In one of the poems of the series entitled 'Petropolis', Lensky introduces himself as 'a child of the Lithuanian forest', whom Styraxes suckled with resin—and asks: 'What have I to do on the shores of the Neva?' The poet yearns to quit the all too noisy world of action for the 'azure of gentility'. This is also associated with the sparkle of the sabbath candles. To other aspects of Soviet reality, mainly of a moral nature, Lensky's poetic reactions in 'Petropolis' are markedly ambivalent.

In Leningrad—a friend of his recalls—Lensky seldom changed his clothes, but almost every day a new book was added to his crowded shelves. He worked in a metallurgical factory, where, despite physical weakness, he won recognition as a skilled metal worker. Then he

---

[1] Kariv, *Ha'anaf Ha'gadua*, op. cit., p. 17.
[2] From a letter to Kariv, ibid., pp. 182–5.

succumbed to tuberculosis and for this reason was released from military service.

At the end of 1934 Lensky was arrested. He was probably engulfed in the wave of mass arrests that followed the assassination of Kirov (1 December 1934). The opportunity was taken to remind him of his Hebrew sins. From a labour camp he sent an appeal to Gorky; his whole crime, Lensky complained, was that he wrote in the language of the Bible and Bialik (both admired by Gorky). But it is even doubtful whether this appeal ever reached Gorky.[1] Shortly after Lensky's release, the German–Soviet war broke out. He volunteered for the army, but was soon discharged because of ill health. This did not prevent him from being arrested a second time. He died in a camp in the winter of 1942–3, at the age of 38.

These biographical details illuminate the most striking feature of Lensky's poetry: the fact that in periods of imprisonment his lyricism grew stronger. He himself says in a poem written in Leningrad, in prison, on 25 December 1934: 'The wormwood enthralled me with the bitterness of its sharply-aromatic juice.'

This mood is particularly apparent in the poems that Lensky wrote in Siberia, as though the winds and snow-storms of the far north gave him new inspiration. He dug trenches but also lived a poetic life. Among his greatest worries was doubt whether his poems would ever reach the Tel Aviv journals.[2] More revealing are the poems themselves. He was excited with 'the north of the world'. From many of these poems the poet seems to emerge as a butterfly dressed in prisoner's clothes. The cruelty of his life in Siberian exile was alleviated by the primeval beauty around him, and the stirrings of understandable acrimony gave way to optimistic, life-affirming strains.

It seems unlikely that this was escapism. The poet had no illusions about his fate, but he refused 'to hang up a violin as long as one scale is joyfully singing. . . . ' Lensky could hardly repeat the proud saying of Russian revolutionaries in tsarist times: 'Siberia is also Russian soil.' Nevertheless, poetically, he sensed a kind of cosmic gratification there. Perhaps the whiteness of Siberia reminded him of the basic innocence of the human soul. Possibly, when face to face with the wonders of creation, he felt himself secure in a world of his own, or perhaps he allowed his poetry a free and independent life. In any event, he proved himself a poet to the last. His poetic image is fittingly portrayed in one short poem,

[1] Y. Ben-Mash (Pen-name of a camp-mate of Lensky), in Lensky, *Meever Nhar Halethy*, op. cit., pp. 252–4.   [2] Ibid., pp. 248–9.

in which he turns to the cold-eyed sentry, in front of his rifle, and asks him not to shed the poet's living blood: 'Let me end my hymn to the sun and the blessing of enjoyment at its beauty.'

The Hebrew language responded graciously and colourfully to the wishes of the loving poet. Yet the element of martyrdom was present in this alliance. The poet had few illusions about his destiny; so, too, he was perfectly aware of his fate as a Hebrew poet. He compared himself to a last wild bull: pain-stricken, when shot, he would remember 'the last of Hebrew poets on the alien soil of Russia'.

In 1939, while Lensky was living in a camp, a collection of his poetry was published in Tel Aviv.[1] For a long period no definite information concerning him was available or whether other works were extant. It was all the more remarkable therefore when in 1958, several yellowed notebooks of Lensky, miraculously preserved, were brought to Israel. They contained, in Lensky's miniature handwriting (famous amongst his friends), an unsuspected literary heritage: 131 new poems as well as 65 that had already appeared in print. A year or two before his death, Lensky had entrusted these notebooks to a friend, and for almost twenty years they had been preserved from destruction.[2]

In one of his poems Lensky acknowledges that his days are numbered. But as long as he breathes he will dispatch from his ark a 'little dove'. To our advantage, the poet's 'doves'—though probably not all of them—have arrived at safe shores.

But in general it can surely be assumed that many Hebrew writings in the Soviet Union have been lost. They shared the fate of their authors. Elisha Rodin said a short time before his death: 'the dense trees of Hebrew poetry were cut down one after another'.[3]

[1] *Shirei Chaim Lensky* (Poems of Chaim Lensky), Tel Aviv, 1939.
[2] These newly discovered poems, together with those previously published are contained in Chaim Lensky: *Meever Nhar Halethy*, op. cit. Shlomo Grodzensky, who prepared Lensky's work for publication, also wrote a preface to this edition in which he gives a description of the notebooks and the biographical information they provide.
[3] Rachel Korn, op. cit.

12

Yiddish Literature in the U.S.S.R.[1]

CH. SHMERUK

I

Yiddish literature occupies a central place in the limited framework of Jewish culture in the Soviet Union as it emerged after the Revolution. Jewish cultural activity had previously been highly varied, in both the religious and secular spheres, and Jewish literature had been basically trilingual (Hebrew, Yiddish, and Russian). Of all areas of Jewish culture only Yiddish and its secular literature received—in theory and practice—the seal of legitimacy and the right to exist under the new regime. The roots of this limitation are to be found in internal Jewish developments which preceded the October Revolution and laid the groundwork for the political situation into which Soviet Jewry was propelled after October 1917.

The origins of modern literature in eastern European Yiddish reach back to the end of the eighteenth century. This literature developed with vertiginous speed. A didactic literature of popular enlightenment at the beginning of the nineteenth century, it had become, as the First World War approached, a variegated modern literature. This change was accompanied by continuous attempts to define its mission, place, and purpose in the complex of contemporary ideology. Those who spread modern enlightenment (*Haskalah*) among the Jews of eastern Europe in the nineteenth century, and who themselves wrote in Yiddish, saw first and foremost their literary work in this language as a useful though temporary tool. Its exclusive purpose was to bring the writers' thoughts to the ordinary people who understood no other language. At the same time they saw Hebrew, or the languages of the country, as the ideal medium for intellectual and artistic expression, beyond immediate needs. The Jewish intelligentsia which began towards the end of the century to join the revolutionary movements in eastern Europe, inherited from the *Haskalah* the belief in the importance of Yiddish as a weapon of propaganda to spread knowledge and promote the ideology of the labour movement. But development of Yiddish literature broke through the narrow

[1] This article was translated from the Hebrew by Miriam and Alfred A. Greenbaum.

bounds that were set for it earlier. This surpassed the expectations of the *maskilim* and the early ideologists of the labour movement among the Jews, and may even have surprised them. Mendele Moykher Sforim, Sholem Aleichem, and Y. L. Perets began their Yiddish literary work from a firm *Haskalah* position. Yet by the end of the nineteenth century, in the consciousness of these writers and many of their contemporaries, Yiddish literature had become a force and value in its own right, and gained artistic stature of a specifically national kind.

This development was not accepted as obvious by the modern movements which predominated on the eastern European Jewish scene on the eve of the First World War. To the extent that the assimilated Jews had a consistent Jewish cultural ideology, they generally continued to despise and denigrate the Yiddish language and its literature, and predicted and desired its early death. The main groups comprising the Zionist movement saw the revival of Hebrew as a spoken language as an indispensable part of the programme for returning the people to its homeland in Palestine. Zionism feared that the recognition of Yiddish as the national tongue might hurt the cause of Hebrew. Zionism, therefore, not only did not recognize in Yiddish and its literature legitimate national values *per se*, but felt the need to oppose them openly. A situation was thus created in which only the non-Zionist sections of the Jewish labour movement, and particularly the Bund, gave full recognition to Yiddish and its literature. In the doctrines of this movement, as it crystallized from the beginning of the twentieth century, Yiddish and its literature occupied a highly respected place. Yiddish became the main cultural support on which national aspirations rested.

The tensions that surrounded the Yiddish language and culture in this ideological and political context reached their climax during the years preceding the First World War. At the conference for Yiddish which took place at Czernowitz in 1908 a vigorous attempt was made to proclaim Yiddish the exclusive Jewish national language. Those who fought for this extreme proposal came from the non-Zionist Jewish labour movement; the resolution itself was placed before the conference by Esther Frumkina, a Bund leader who joined the Bolsheviks after the Revolution.

Even before the Revolution, the demand that Yiddish be exclusive in the cultural sphere had wide-ranging effects. The Jewish labour movement, which was basically atheistic, repudiated the Jewish religion on principle. Its adherents included in this concept the entire Jewish cultural heritage, which was mainly in Hebrew. They identified Hebrew with clericalism on the one hand and with 'nationalistic' and 'chauvinistic' Zionism on the other; thus even modern secular Hebrew literature was, in the eyes of the extreme Yiddishists, illigitimate in principle. Because of fundamental opposition to Russification the labour movement also repudiated in practice Jewish literary expression in Russian.[1] The intolerance of the ideologists in the non-Zionist labour movement towards the various facets of their people's culture and literary activity had fundamental significance for the position of Yiddish literature, as well as for the demands made on this literature during the decisive years of its growth and development in the years before 1914.

The newpapers and periodicals affiliated with or friendly to the labour parties in eastern Europe, the United States and England, were controlled in practice by these ideological leaders. It was they who generally decided which works of contemporary authors were worth publishing. A not insignificant number of the critics writing for the extensive Yiddish periodical literature saw it as their task to determine how the literature would fit in with the ideology which they themselves represented. They also made the ability of the 'popular masses' to understand a literary work a basic criterion of its value; to them the 'masses' were the only legitimate audience. After 1905 the symbolist trend took hold among young Yiddish writers in eastern Europe and in the United States (the group '*Di Yunge*'— 'The Young Ones'—in New York). These writers encountered the most energetic opposition and the most violent criticism from these very guardians of Yiddish literature who proclaimed the exclusive position of Yiddish in Jewish cultural life. The modernistic elements which predominated in Yiddish literature in those years: ideological weariness, scepticism with regard to the accepted solutions of social and national problems, individualism and confusion, mysticism, arts for art's sake, refinement of expression, manifest disinterest in the ability of 'mass readers' to comprehend— all this aroused a very hostile reaction from leading critics. The sharpest criticisms of the new currents in Yiddish literature were published in the party or semi-party periodicals in eastern Europe and in the United States.[2]

---

[1] I have written at greater length on these problems in my article 'Hatarbut hayehudit be Verit hamo'atsot' (Jewish Culture in the Soviet Union), *Haumah*, no. 13, Jerusalem, 1965; *Gesher*, nos. 2–3, Tel Aviv, 1966, and in Italian translation in the collection *Gli ebrei nell' U.R.S.S.*, Milan, 1966.

[2] No summary of the history of Yiddish literary criticism exists. The attitude of the critics to symbolism and related tendencies comes to the fore, e.g. in the article by B. Brokhes (B. Vladek), 'Blayshtift Notitsn', *Di naye tsayt*, vol. 3, Vilna, 1908. *Di naye tsayt* was the organ of the Bund. For the group '*Di yunge*' in the United States, see e.g. the negative criticism by S. K. Shneyfal in his article 'Di yiddishe literatur' (Jewish literature) and by Sh. Epshteyn on the collection *Literatur*, both of them in *Di tsukunft*, New York, 1910, pp. 71–4, 662–4. Both these critics returned to the Soviet Union. The critical essays on Der Nister's work are very instructive, Der Nister being the outstanding representative of symbolism. Cf. Sh. N.

Conditions during these years are perhaps typified by the story of the relationship between Y. L. Perets—recognized as the central personality in Yiddish literature, the respected teacher and leader of the younger writers—and those who tried even before 1914 to define Yiddish literature in an over-simplified manner, according to their political and social views. Perets greatly feared possible rigidity and intolerance in literature, art, and intellectual life generally, after the victory of the revolutionaries, whom he knew at close range. This fear had already found sharp and prophetic expression at the beginning of 1906 in his article 'Hofenung un shrek' (Hope and Terror). Perets had been friendly to the Jewish labour movement, and had given it considerable encouragement among Yiddish readers both in his own writings and in the collections which he edited during the 1890s. But now he felt the time had come to express his fear for the future of intellectual life after the Revolution. Such a state had matters reached by 1912 that Perets now complained it was impossible for him to publish the final version of the play *At Night in the Old Market*, in which he tried to sum up the path he had taken in literature and life, and to which he gave most of his attention in his last ten years. In one of the fragments of the play Perets exclaimed: '*In shul arayn!*' (Into the synagogue!'). An over-simplified interpretation of this cry added to the anger of many 'progressive' ideologists, who in any case could not bear Perets's symbolistic manner of expression in the drama. As a result Perets was doomed to loneliness in Warsaw, the most important centre of Yiddish literature before the First World War. Those who opposed him and his views on literature turned their backs on him and, in effect, ostracized him. Perets openly complained about this in an article entitled 'A vikuah' (A debate). In this imaginary debate he tried once more to convince his critics of the need to base Jewish culture and its revival on the fundamentals of Jewish tradition in the widest sense, while absolutely rejecting cheap and superficial atheism. Perets severely criticized the lack of vision and the exaggerated self-assurance of those who adhered to the accepted 'progressive' ideology.[1]

(Shmuel Niger) in the bibliographical section of *Di yiddishe velt*, Book 1 Vilna, 1913 and Sh. Rosenfeld, 'On a bodn' (Without Firm Ground), *Di tsukunft*, 1914, pp. 662–3. Soviet criticism later made the same complaints against Der Nister.

[1] 'Hofenung un shrek' (Hope and Terror), *Der veg*, no. 5, Warsaw, 18 January 1906; 'A vikuah' (A Debate), *Der haynt*, no. 206, Warsaw, 18 September 1912. The two articles are included in Perets's collected works in Yiddish and Hebrew. Perets complained to Elisha Rodin of the impossibility of publishing the drama in its entirety. Cf. the memoirs of the latter in *Di royte velt*, no. 4 (19), Kharkov, p. 99. For the attitude of Soviet criticism to this period in Perets's literary work see Litvakov's articles on Perets in his *In umru*, vol. 1 (1919?), especially pp. 100–3; *In umru*, vol. 2, Moscow, 1926, pp. 34–49.

The modernists in Yiddish literature were sceptics and felt the whole complexity of their people's national and social problems deeply. Arranged against them, arrogant and sure of themselves, stood the *litterateurs* and critics from the camp of Jewish labour—at a time when the labour movement was the mainstay of Yiddish and its literature. Tension between the two groups was unavoidable. It existed even before October 1917. But political and social conditions before the Revolution were still of such a character that those who were interested in controlling Yiddish literature and directing its development according to their own ideas had no real power to do so. The Revolution and the regime which afterwards arose made the time ripe to realize these ideological ambitions in respect of Jewish culture and Yiddish literary work. The one-time leaders of the Jewish labour movement who had split their parties and joined the Bolsheviks now controlled the institutions which the new regime sponsored for the Jewish population. They brought to these institutions their pre-revolutionary views on the right way to develop Jewish culture. Now that they had power they were able to limit Jewish culture exclusively to the sphere of Yiddish and its secular literature. The new authorities readily believed these Jewish leaders when they claimed that only by means of Yiddish was it possible to bring about the sovietization of the 'popular masses'. Hebrew culture was, so they said, identified with 'reactionary clericalism' and Zionism; and in any case propaganda in Hebrew would have no significant influence. This argument was accepted by the ruling elements in the new regime as early as the first years after the Revolution, and the foundations were thus laid for the development or Yiddish culture in the Soviet Union. Schools with Yiddish as the language of instruction were established, theatres which presented plays in Yiddish, a Yiddish press, and publishing houses for Yiddish books. All this was done amidst the deliberate and merciless suppression of all other manifestations of Jewish education and culture, and especially of religious and Hebrew education. Yiddish literature was expected to integrate itself into the general cultural framework and thus justify the claims made for its usefulness and influence. The earlier demands which critics friendly to the Jewish labour movement had advanced, now received authoritative sanction when the Bolshevik party proclaimed as its goal the sovietization of the literatures of Soviet nationalities. Literature was seen as a means of educating the masses and spreading Bolshevik ideology. In this manner the goals proclaimed by some Jewish social movements before the Revolution encountered, and merged with, the Soviet regime's own aims.

It is only fair to add—even to emphasize—that in the light of the prevailing doctrine of the rights of Soviet nationalities the Jews were treated with generosity. Theoretically, the Bolsheviks recognized only national territorial autonomy, and the Jews lacked a national territory within the Soviet Union. But for practical reasons necessitated by the times as well as for propaganda purposes the authorities deviated from their declared principle after the Revolution. The Jewish cultural functionaries were conscious of this contradiction, and this must account in part for the interest of many of them in furthering the cause of Jewish land settlement within the country; the success of this programme, it was thought, would base Jewish culture on the foundations of the ruling ideology and place it beyond the tactical considerations and needs of the moment. This is not the place to outline the reasons for the failure of the land settlement plans;[1] but because of this failure Soviet Jewish culture even in its limited framework was not equal in rank and scope to the cultural base established for those Soviet nationalities who had a territory in the Union. The very existence of this Jewish culture rested on a weak foundation. Its existence was assured only as long as the government had some use for it in terms of internal and—at times—foreign policy. But new political and social conditions could easily change the minds of the authorities and disturb their faith in the influence or loyalty of Jewish culture. Consequently the danger of further constriction, gradual liquidation and even total extinction hovered over this culture, which lacked a defined national territorial backbone. The weak foundations of Soviet Yiddish culture were always a disadvantage, and this made itself felt with special force during the political upheavals in the Soviet Union. The right of Yiddish culture to exist could be guaranteed only by its adaptation to every change in the general policy and to the changing demands of the party as formulated by those who proclaimed the goals of Soviet literature. But the unceasing efforts to bring about this adjustment did not help; they also did not avert the destruction of Yiddish culture in the Soviet Union at the end of 1948 and the killing of the most important Yiddish writers on 12 August 1952.

II

It might seem that there is no difficulty in determining the beginnings of Yiddish literature in the Soviet Union. The borders of the state as fixed

---

[1] Ch. Shmeruk, *The Jewish Community and Jewish Agricultural Settlement in Soviet Byelorussia, 1918–1932* (in Hebrew, with English summary), Jerusalem, 1961; J. Lvavi, *The Jewish Colonization in Birobidjan* (in Hebrew), Jerusalem, 1965.

after the Revolution served and still serve to mark the periodization of this literature.[1] The truth of the matter is that such formal periodization must ignore certain essential problems and contradictions. These problems become clear enough even on a superficial bibliographic examination of the Yiddish works published within the Soviet Union after October 1917 and during the first years after the Revolution.

At the outset of the new regime there were writers in the Soviet Union whose style had matured before the Revolution. Much of their work was completed before 1917 but found its way into print only afterwards. Not a few writers who published their works within Soviet Russia by the beginning of the 1920s later emigrated, some permanently, some to return in the second half of the 1920s and the beginning of the 1930s. The twisted road taken by most Yiddish writers during the former decade and their ideological and artistic struggles pose a basic question over and above the formal problem, concerning the very possibility of periodization, which seems to preclude true solutions because it must often ignore essential difficulties.

The contributors and the contents of the collection *Eygns*, which appeared in Kiev in 1918 and 1920, may epitomize both the formal fluctuation and the essential ambivalence of Yiddish literature in the Soviet Union in its beginnings. It is generally agreed that these collections were the outstanding literary phenomenon in the first years after the Revolution, and perhaps even until the middle of the 1920s. They can be seen as the truest and most characteristic expression of the 'Kiev group'; many of the writers in this group would in time have important achievements in Soviet Yiddish literature to their credit. It was unfortunate that the same writers would, in the future, also become the main victims of the purges and murders affecting Yiddish literature at the end of the 1940s and the beginning of the 1950s.

In prose, the writers represented in *Eygns* were Dovid Bergelson, Der Nister, and A. Katsizne. Katsizne left the Soviet Union after a short time, and between the two world wars, lived and worked in Poland. Dovid Bergelson published two of his longer stories in *Eygns*; one, on his own admission, was written between 1911 and 1913, and the other was finished in 1919.[2] Neither from an ideological and thematic standpoint nor from

---

[1] See also the recent articles: H. Remenik, 'Tsu der frage vegn di onheybn fun der yiddisher sovietisher literatur' (Concerning the Problem of the Beginning of Soviet Yiddish Literature); Y. Serebryani, 'Khronik fun der yiddisher sovietisher literatur' (Chronicle of Soviet Yiddish Literature), both in *Sovietish Heymland*, no. 11, Moscow, 1966.

[2] 'Materialn tsu Bergelsons bio-bibliographye' (Materials for Bergelson's Bio-bibliography), *Visnshaft un revolutsye*, nos. 1–2, Kiev, 1934, p. 67.

the standpoint of Bergelson's impressionistic style—which matured before the First World War—do these stories represent any significant turning-point for Soviet literature in Yiddish, even though his style had considerable influence on later Soviet Yiddish prose. Nobody bothered to reprint his stories from *Eygns* even when Bergelson was already recognized as a Soviet writer, and when many of his books were published in the Soviet Union. The same is true of Der Nister, who also continued writing symbolist stories in *Eygns* in his original style which had matured in his stories by 1913 at the latest. Both Bergelson and Der Nister left the Soviet Union at the beginning of the 1920s, after which they wrote and published abroad. The former came back to stay in 1933, and the second in 1926. Their contributions to *Eygns* and many of their works that were written and published before their return cannot readily be attributed, even in the formal sense, to Soviet literature.

Drama is represented in *Eygns* by a surviving play of Beynush Shteyman, a most talented young writer who was killed by a stray bullet in the streets of Kiev in 1919. He was then only 24 years old. The few modernistic dramas which were left by Shteyman are very instructive examples of the fusion of Jewish traditional apocalyptic elements with present-day revolutionary insight. It seems that because of these Jewish elements Shteyman's name was completely forgotten in the Soviet Union and remained, until our day, a 'blank page' in the history of Yiddish literature in the Soviet Union.[1]

The status of poetry in the collections of *Eygns* is more complex. The increased importance of poetry as compared to prose is quite obvious in these collections. This was a feature which contemporary Yiddish literature in Russia had in common with the foreign centres of Yiddish literature. In poetry the following writers were represented in *Eygns*: Dovid Hofshteyn, Lipe Reznik, Osher Shvartsman, Kadye Molodovski, Leyb Kvitko, Perets Markish, and Yehezkel Dobrushin. Kadye Molodovski had already left the Soviet Union at the beginning of the 1920s. Dobrushin was active in Soviet Yiddish literature until the purge of the 1940s, but as time went on he left the field of poetry, in which he did not particularly excel, and devoted himself to criticism and literary research.

The lyric poetry of Hofshteyn and Shvartsman, although marked by their individual tone, is a direct continuation of the modernistic lyrics written in Yiddish before the First World War. We know that the

[1] His surviving manuscripts were only collected in Warsaw where they were published in his book *Dramen*, Warsaw, 1922. For the attitude to Shteyman in the Soviet Union see Remenik's article, loc. cit., pp. 138–9.

greater part of Hofshteyn's poems, which were published in the Soviet Union after 1917, were in his possession in manuscript before 1912. Osher Shvartsman did not earn his place of honour as the founder of Soviet Yiddish literature for his poems, but because in 1919 he fell in battle defending the Revolution. In his surviving work (mostly from the years 1908–17) and even in the few poems from the years 1918–19 it is almost impossible to find clear ideological justification for the leading position in Soviet Yiddish literature Soviet critics and scholars later attributed to him. We must assume their reason for doing so was largely biographical.[1]

Lipe Reznik, in his poems in *Eygns*, writes in a completely symbolistic mood. Soviet criticism ceaselessly exposed and condemned the symbolism even in his later poetry as a basic fault which was inconsonant with Soviet literature.

The main innovations of Yiddish poetry in the collections *Eygns* were represented by Perets Markish, Leyb Kvitko and, to a certain extent, also by Dovid Hofshteyn in his new poems. Each in his own way produced expressionistic poetry parallel with the simultaneous breakthrough of the new trend in the other centres of Yiddish literature—in Warsaw, New York, and Lodz. This was understandable and natural in the post-symbolistic mood in Yiddish literature which was also the dominant trend in European poetry after the First World War. All the young Yiddish poets shared these feelings at that time. With eyes wide open these poets put into words the horror, the suffering, and the brutality to which the people of their generation had been exposed as human beings and as Jews. Despair, the desire to belong somewhere, and the search for solutions to national and social problems made some poets both inside and outside Soviet Russia accept the Revolution; among these were Markish, Kvitko, and Hofshteyn. But this acceptance was basically ambivalent. And it is quite impossible to equate the confused acceptance of the Revolution in their poetry of the early 1920s with the declarative poetry which later translated into verse the political announcements of the party. Markish, Kvitko, and Hofshteyn, who in time became the outstanding representatives of Yiddish literature in the Soviet Union, left the country in the early 1920s and returned only in the second half of the decade. After their return they gradually abandoned the earlier manner as expressed in *Eygns* and in their poetry published abroad, which was never fully and faithfully collected in their later Soviet publications. Of the

---

[1] The most complete edition of O. Shvartsman's literary legacy is *Lider un briv*, Kiev, 1935; see also his *Ale lider un briv*, Moscow, 1961.

Eygns group Dovid Bergelson, Der Nister, Hofshteyn, Markish, and Kvitko were victims of the murders during the last years of the reign of Stalin.

We can now see how problematic it would be, both in form and essence, to include *Eygns*, the first serious post-revolutionary literary achievement, in the general conceptual scheme of Soviet Yiddish literature as it appeared after its writers were integrated into the ideological and artistic framework of conformism.

One of the main problems we must consider is the fact that Yiddish literature at the beginning of the Soviet regime remained loyal to the literary trends and national ideologies which had dominated it before the Revolution. Even where it opposed them by innovations, the logical continuum was clearly to be seen. This literature thus aroused disappointment and hostility among the very writers and critics who took pride in prescribing its post-revolutionary purpose and duties. Whereas they expected Yiddish literature to express its loyalty to the government and to help in the sovietization of its potential readers, it was clear that the works actually published in Yiddish during that time were in practice meant for persons with a highly developed and refined literary taste—in other words the small élite among Yiddish readership, and not the 'masses' of the former Pale of Settlement. This fundamental contradiction between the artistic achievements of Yiddish literature—even if we ignore its ideological direction—and its purpose as proclaimed by the functionaries came to the fore in Moyshe Litvakov's critical article on the first *Eygns* and in Bergelson's reasoned and crushing reply.[1] The differences of opinion between these two were not confined to theoretical discussion. As early as 1922 their controversy reached the stage of open threats on the part of Litvakov. The latter, by virtue of his position in the central bureau of the Jewish Sections of the Bolshevik party, was the chief spokesman in Soviet Yiddish criticism. His threats heralded the various pressures which Soviet Yiddish literature would soon have to endure for many years.

In 1921 a group of writers came together in Moscow. They established literary evenings, published pamphlets by young poets, and planned to bring out the literary monthly *Shtrom* (five issues appeared between 1922 and 1924). Among the active members of the group were the Kiev writers D. Hofshteyn and Y. Dobrushin. They were joined, among others, by the young poets Arn Kushnirov and Ezre Fininberg, who were in

[1] M. Lit (vakov) in *Bikher velt*, no. 1, Kiev, 1919, pp. 19–25. Bergelson's answer in 'Dikhtung un gezelshaftlekhkeyt' (Literature and Society), ibid., nos. 4–5, 1919, pp. 5–16.

agreement with the Kiev men, and whose writings in *Shtrom* showed a tendency towards moderate expressionism. We must add—indeed emphasize—that this group recognized the Soviet regime as a matter of principle. We cannot find in their published works or in other writings of this group during that period any sign of opposition to the government and its political theories. But there were two things which set the men of *Shtrom* apart from M. Litvakov, who was then already the editor-in-chief of the daily newspaper *Der emes* (The Truth), central organ of the Jewish Sections attached to the department of propaganda of the Bolshevik party's Central Committee. The writers openly favoured artistic autonomy; their declarations and writings suggest a deep concern for the present and future of the Jews in the new political situation. They tried to give appropriate artistic expression to this concern even if they overstepped the dominant party line. Litvakov, on the other hand, expected from the writers, first and foremost, real help and active participation in strengthening *Der emes* with its declared mass propaganda purpose. When the writers stubbornly ignored Litvakov's demands, he attacked them in a sharply aggressive article. He was not content merely to reprove them for shutting 'themselves up in their own world and in their artistic problems'. He ended his statement with an unambiguous threat: 'When *Emes* becomes established and has more time to remember "old" accounts, it will do so with all the fiery spirit it can muster.' It seems that threats of this kind had already a real meaning. Nevertheless the writers rejected Litvakov's demands in an open letter, and insisted upon the distinction between literature and publicistic writing 'even in a central outlet such as *Emes* . . .'. They also reaffirmed this stand in the literary declaration which was shortly afterwards published in the second issue of the monthly *Shtrom*.[1]

Whereas the *Eygns* and *Shtrom* writers gave clear support to the notion of literary autonomy, other writers appeared at the same time who completely identified themselves with the ideology of the new regime. This soon led to long battles—open as well as concealed—with the men of Kiev and those holding similar views. This group of young writers, outstanding among whom were Itzik Fefer in the Ukraine and Izi Kharik in Byelorussia, represented a new stratum in Yiddish literature whose appearance was already tied directly to the Revolution. When they began, their poetry did not go beyond fiery and unreserved support for the

---

[1] Litvakov's article '*Der emes*' un di literatn' (*Der emes* and the writers), *Der emes*, Moscow, 9 January 1922, and in his *In umru*, vol. 2, pp. 74–9; the answer of the men of *Shtrom* was published as an open letter in *Der emes*, 13 January 1922.

Revolution. Their various forms of proclamations and primitive poetic outcries turned Yiddish poetry back to the 1890s, when the revolutionary 'proletarian' poetry of Winchevsky, Edelstadt, Bovshover, and Rosenfeld had dominated the American branch. The complex developments in Yiddish poetry since the beginning of the century did not seem to exist for the young writers. But soon some of these writers, who had barely left the small towns remote from literary centres, began to take heed of contemporary Yiddish and Russian poetry. The more talented among them adopted the modern poetic manner under the obvious influence of the *Eygns* and *Shtrom* poets. The metamorphosis of form in their poetry also paralleled a greater depth and sharper insight into the subjects of their poetry. In Fefer's case, for example, this found expression in the romantic attitude to the Revolution and the civil war. He used methods which are similar, in part, to Russian futuristic poetry, and in part to the poetry of Hofshteyn. Kharik showed nostalgia for the *shtetl* (small town) and mourned its decline and sad fate. In his poetry we hear echoes of Yesenin's Russian poetry and also of the *shtetl* idyll in pre-war Yiddish poetry. But in spite of this development in the poetry of the young writers, they felt themselves to be the only legitimate representatives of the new regime in Yiddish literature; they based this on their unbounded loyalty to Bolshevik ideology and on their much emphasized 'proletarian' origins. In Soviet political conditions such 'privileges' had great importance even in the area of literature. Together with the young critics who had similar views and 'privileges', these poets had decisive influence in the internal personal and group battles a few years later, when demands for hegemony in literature were based on origin and ideological identification. The struggle was conducted amidst loud and insulting rejection of any literary expression in which 'foreign aims' and 'remnants of the past' could be felt. In most cases the young poets supported this cause with revolutionary fervour; they were joined in the struggle by the young critics and Jewish cultural functionaries who based the mission of Soviet Yiddish literature on clearly political foundations. Most of their hostility was turned against the men of *Eygns*, who began to return from emigration from the middle 1920s onwards.

Here, too, we must point out the fact that Moyshe Litvakov and Izi Kharik perished during the purges of the 1930s; yet Izik Fefer was shot as well as the men of *Eygns* on 12 August 1952. The differences of opinion and approach which characterize Soviet Yiddish literature from its inception found their cruel and unexpected resolution in the violence which indiscriminately befell all camps.

III

We can see the period from the 1920s until 1941, the year of the German invasion of Soviet Russia, as the period when Soviet Yiddish literature flourished. The Yiddish language and literature remained, in the last analysis, the only Jewish elements in the network of Soviet schools which had Yiddish as the language of instruction. A notable part of the work of the Jewish scholarly institutes in Kiev, Minsk, Moscow, and Odessa was devoted to research into the Yiddish language, folklore, and literature. Numerous theatrical troupes, both permanent and improvised, presented plays, in Yiddish, from a repertory based mainly on Yiddish literature. Daily newspapers and different types of periodicals in Yiddish appeared in the main centres of Jewish cultural activity: Kiev, Kharkov, Odessa, Minsk, and Moscow, and from the 1930s, also in Biro-Bidzhan. Government publishing houses in the Ukraine, Byelorussia and Moscow published hundreds of books in Yiddish each year.[1] All these created for Yiddish literature and its writers unprecedented possibilities. Neither in scope nor in effort could parallels be found in the centres of Yiddish literature outside the Soviet Union. Indeed, the flourishing of Yiddish cultural activity in the Soviet Union attracted some highly competent men from abroad and also brought back a large part of the *Eygns* writers. In the 1920s the following immigrated and became Soviet citizens: the writer Moyshe Kulbak, the linguist and literary scholar Nokhem Shtif, the literary critic and scholar Max Erik, and the literary historian and belle-lettrist Meir Wiener. During the same period Der Nister, Leyb Kvitko, Dovid Hofshteyn, Perets Markish, and, lastly, Dovid Bergelson returned. We could not even begin to assess Yiddish literature in the Soviet Union without the contributions of these men.

It would be wrong to assume that these writers and scholars were attracted to the Soviet Union because they fully identified themselves with the ideology and government of the Soviets. Some of them, to be sure, did so. But the most effective appeal during this time was the range of opportunities which they thought lay open to Yiddish culture in the Soviet Union. They believed that only a government which ensured the growth of Yiddish culture and literature by financial support could guarantee its future. The conditions in which the Yiddish writers worked before they came to the Soviet Union could only strengthen their optimism about

[1] Details of this cultural activity are found in the following works: J. Lestschinsky, *Dos sovietishe idntum*, New York, 1941; S. M. Schwarz, *The Jews in the Soviet Union*, 1951; N. Mayzel, *Dos yiddishe shafn un der yiddisher shrayber in Sovetnfarband*, New York, 1959; *Jewish Publications in the Soviet Union, 1917–60*; bibliographies...(ed. by Ch. Shmeruk), Jerusalem, 1961.

working under the Soviet regime.[1] In addition, certain of the general developments in the cultural and social sphere could convince even the sceptics that the price asked for government support of culture and literature was not too high, and even from the writers' point of view might be worth it in the long run. These decisions must be seen in the context of Soviet encouragement for the periodical *Smena vekh* (New Directions) among those Russians who had opposed the Revolution and emigrated to western Europe. Some of the Russian writers who had left a few years earlier were thus induced to return to the homeland. This encouragement was accompanied by the relaxation of ideological pressure in the years of the N.E.P.; by giving special status to various kinds of specialists, among whom veteran and experienced writers were generally included; by recognizing the rights of writer 'fellow-travellers' to exist, and not expecting full ideological commitment from them but only basic acceptance of the regime.

But while Soviet Yiddish literature reaped benefits from these political conditions, the Jewish application of every general trend and the continuous attempt to adjust to all the passing political and ideological fluctuations limited possibilities and accomplishments. Parallels between developments in the literature of other Soviet nationalities—especially Russian literature—and developments in Soviet literature in Yiddish can be readily observed in many areas. Like Russian literature, Yiddish literature quickly underwent 'differentiation', and with it came bitter battles between the 'proletarian' writers organized in their associations and those writers who for various understandable reasons were outside these associations, and who were tolerated only thanks to the vague official support of the 'fellow-travellers'.

We cannot observe parallels among Yiddish writers for the period of Russian 'Proletcult' activity; but around the periodical *Shtrom* there already broke out a severe quarrel between those who were loyal to 'proletarian' fundamentals in literature and those writers who argued in favour of specific autonomy for literature. Some of the latter writers, among them Aaron Kushnirov, quickly left the battlefield and joined the 'proletarian' group, whose assumption of control can already be observed in the final issues of *Shtrom*.[2]

[1] A very important and characteristic article assessing the future of Yiddish literature in the Soviet Union was published by Bergelson as early as 1926. Cf. D. B. (Dovid Bergelson), 'Dray tsentren' (Three Centres), *In shpan*, no. 1, Vilna-Berlin, April 1926, pp. 84–96.

[2] The only publication I have been able to find sponsored in the field of Yiddish literature by the 'All-Russian Proletcult' is a pamphlet of poems by Khayim Gildin: *Hamer klangen*, Moscow, 1922.

In 1925 a Jewish Section was organized as part of the Association of Proletarian Writers in Moscow. This organization published the monthly *Oktyabr* in Russian at the beginning of 1924; the Jewish Section likewise published a literary collection under this name in Yiddish in 1925. It, too, appeared in Moscow, and it, too, had the same aim. Just as the 'fellow-travellers' in Russian literature concentrated around the Russian monthly *Krasnaya nov* (Virgin Soil), so too did a literary collection in Yiddish appear in Moscow in 1925 with a similar name, *Nayerd*. In these two Yiddish collections we still cannot distinguish clearly that extreme differentiation which the proletarian writers advocated. Nevertheless, the description of the two collections by one of the writers and critics of the 'proletarian' camp had precise significance even then: '*Oktyabr* is ours, *Nayerd* is with us.'[1] When the struggle for the hegemony of the 'proletarians' intensified, this distinction assumed a very practical meaning. The 'proletarians' were not satisfied with those who already walked the straight and narrow path but were not yet 'ours'. After a short time some of the participants in *Nayerd* became loyal to the 'proletarian' line, either for reasons of 'opportunism' or because of sincere belief in its justice.

The dividing line between the 'proletarian' writers and undefined writers or 'fellow-travellers' in Yiddish literature became clear enough during the second half of the 1920s in those literary monthlies which began to appear regularly in the Soviet Union at that time. *Di royte velt* (The Red World), which appeared in Kharkov from the end of 1924 until 1933, was a refuge for 'fellow-travellers' during the second half of the 1920s. The writers who returned from emigration here found the opportunity to publish. The monthly *Der shtern* (The Star) which began in Minsk (May 1925) and appeared there continuously until the middle of 1941, became the fortress of the 'proletarian' Yiddish writers in Byelorussia during the second part of the 1920s until 1932. From there Kh. Dunets, Y. Bronshteyn, and B. Orshanski, the most extreme 'proletarian' critics, guarded ideological purity in Soviet Yiddish works. In April 1928 a third literary monthly, *Prolit* (Proletarian Literature) began to appear in Kharkov. This fighting monthly was the official organ of the Yiddish members of the All-Ukrainian Association of Proletarian Writers[2] until

---

[1] Quoted from an article by B. Orshanski, 'Der "birger krig" in der literatur' (The Civil War in Literature), *Der shtern*, no. 1, Minsk, 1925, pp. 59–62.

[2] In 1933–7 the literary monthly *Farmest* appeared in Kiev in place of *Prolit* and *Di royte velt* which had been liquidated following the decision of the Central Committee of the party in April 1932. The monthly *Sovietishe literatur*, which appeared in Kiev in 1938–41, is the continuation of *Farmest*. In 1934–41 the almanac *Sovietish* appeared in Moscow, with nine volumes in all. A literary quarterly named *Forpost* appeared in Biro-Bidzhan, 1936–40.

1932, when the writers' organizations were liquidated by decision of the Central Committee of the communist party.

True, in 1927 another attempt was made to establish the writers' group 'Boy' (Construction or Building) which unified the Yiddish writers in the Ukraine who did not identify themselves with the 'proletarian' line. But this attempt had no practical importance and no prospect of success at a time when the Jewish sections of the 'proletarian' writers' organizations were active in Moscow, the Ukraine, and Byelorussia. These made strong demands for complete authority in Yiddish literature. At the end of the 1920s they became even more aggressive, and because of their incessant demands and unrestrained actions they more or less received what they wanted. The 'proletarians' acquired nation-wide status through the acquiescence of the Central Committee of the party; so, too, did the Jewish 'proletarian' writers receive perhaps even more explicit support from the Jewish Sections, who decided party policy in the Jewish area with special reference to Yiddish literature.[1]

The significance of organizational and political battles in the literary arena is always open to doubt. Marginal though it may be, however, we still cannot escape an ideological confrontation between Soviet literary politics and Soviet Yiddish literature. The main reason is that the short period of the 'proletarian' domination of literature had long-lasting effects on the very nature of Yiddish literature in the Soviet Union—effects which stretched well beyond 1932, when the 'proletarian' organizations were abolished. Authors then fell into the habit of anticipating possible criticism by the editors and critics of the 'proletarian' camp, and this led to very unfortunate results in all fields of literary endeavour. We should not underestimate what happened at that time merely because the threat of physical destruction during the 1930s was so much worse. From the viewpoint of preparing the writers' minds and 'educating' them for the coming years the fateful significance of the later 1920s is beyond doubt.

We must emphasize here that many works judged unfit for publication have not come down to us; nor do we have the original text of works which were 'corrected' by various censors. Censorship in the Soviet Union is one of the central problems in the development of its literature. It has a number of levels. The first level is the writer's own: he examines his work lest something be found which might harm him even if his words were never printed. This self-censorship became significant only at

---

[1] The resolution of the Jewish Sections of April 1927 on literary matters was published in *Di royte velt*, nos. 5–6, Kharkov, 1927, pp. 151–3; a later resolution of 30–31 May 1929, proposed by M. Litvakov, was published in *Der emes*, 2 July 1929.

the time of increased pressure when the 'proletarian' groups were in charge. The other levels are imposed by the editors of periodicals and publishing houses, where the responsibility for the printed word rests. Only at the end does the work receive the approval of the political censor. One has reason to assume that this final level has no great importance, since the authors only submit their work for publication after self-censorship plus sifting by conscientious editors, who themselves are concerned for their employment and status.

Although we do not have the actual manuscripts before us, we do have clear and authoritative testimony about the stage of ideological revision prior to publication. M. Levitan, a leader of the Jewish Sections in the Ukraine and one of the responsible editors of the monthly *Di royte velt*, wrote about this openly. When the agitation against the 'evil-doers' in Yiddish literature began, he also joined the campaign of 'serious accusations', though he tried to tone them down by referring to the special condition of the Jews. One of the main 'faults', in his own words, was 'nationalism' or 'deviation to the right'—accepted terms in Soviet terminology of the period. In addition, Levitan argued: 'I do not base my conclusions only on published works but include writings which could not be published because they were suffused with alien class tendencies; or which at the outset contained dangerous ideological elements but whose writers removed them, thanks to instructions and with the aid of suitable editors.'[1]

The conclusion is inescapable that, at the latest, from the end of the 1920s, the period of Levitan's frank words, the works published in Yiddish in the Soviet Union do not reflect what went on in the inner world of this literature. At best we know works which were combed by stages with a fine ideological comb. It is very doubtful if the day will ever come when we will know the true face of Yiddish literature before the triple sifting. It is well known that many Soviet writers also write for the 'desk drawer'. Even works of this type have not reached us from Yiddish writers in the Soviet Union, except in a few insignificant cases which are of no real use for general evaluation.

IV

What faults did the 'proletarian' critics find in Yiddish literature of the second half of the 1920s? Quite a detailed answer is given in the following

[1] M. Levitan, 'Der ideologisher veg fun undzer literatur' (Our literature's ideological road), *Prolit*, no. 4, 1929, p. 64.

short summary from an article by A. Abtshuk, one of the active writers
and critics of the 'proletarian' camp:

1. The writers are cutting themselves off from real life and moving towards
   individualism and symbolism—Der Nister, L. Reznik.
2. Idealization of the gradually disappearing classes, with emotional participation
   in their fate—N. Lurye.
3. A passive attitude towards our reality—Y. Kipnis.
4. Epicureanism, glorifying the passing moment—Z. Akselrod.
5. Lack of self-definition, neutralism, going along at a distance—a general evil.[1]

To these 'sins' we may add the continuing stigmatization of Jewish
'chauvinism' and 'nationalism', and to the list of 'sinners'—the names of
Perets Markish, Shmuel Halkin, Ezre Fininberg, S. Rosin, L. Kvitko, A.
Kahan, and others who merited direct attacks by the 'proletarian' critics.
We need not fear that the accusations were exaggerated. A reading of the
works of the writers under attack confirms the truth of all the accusations,
if we take the 'proletarian' view. Indeed, from that viewpoint, almost all
Yiddish literature from the second half of the 1920s lay outside the con-
formist trend in Soviet literature when it first became a decisive force.
A few 'affairs' which were publicized in the Soviet Union may clarify the
matter and incidentally bring us closer to some of the writers.

In 1929 Perets Markish published two new books. One, *Dor oys, dor
eyn* (A Generation Goes, a Generation Comes), is the first volume of a
wide-ranging and very tense epic. The author describes in rich and flowing
prose the growth of revolutionary heroism in the Pale of Settlement. His
second book, *Brider* (Brothers), is a long poem with strong emotional
impact which depicts the period of the Revolution and the pogroms. In
these two books Markish displayed his great ability both as poet and prose-
writer. There is no doubt that they are among the outstanding achievements of Yiddish literature in the Soviet Union. There is no doubting
the honest identification of the author with the revolutionary movement
and the Revolution itself. Yet the two works evoked a very strong critical
reaction from Litvakov. He accused Markish of making only Jews his
heroes; 'it follows that the Revolution was made by Jewish revolutionaries'. In Litvakov's opinion the books are suffused with 'moods of martyrdom', and they show Markish to be 'restricted to a national point of
view'. These words were spoken at a public meeting on 27 May 1929, held
in honour of Markish's new books. Markish was forced to admit 'a few
errors', but he nevertheless rejected Litvakov's demand that he must show

[1] Quoted from A. Abtshuk, 'Af fremde vegn' (On alien paths), *Prolit*, nos. 8–9, 1928, p. 78.

non-Jewish revolutionaries in his books: 'This is not particularly necessary,' he claimed, 'because a Russian novel in which only Russian revolutionaries are described is not subjected to any such demands.' The words are quoted from a report in *Der emes*.[1] Its writer, or the newspaper's editor himself, saw fit to add that Markish's declaration 'produced consternation in the hall'. While we may doubt this reaction, we need not suspect the truth of the quotations themselves. Here stands revealed one of the constants in Yiddish criticism: it tried, almost pathologically, to cast out from Yiddish literature anything which was likely to be interpreted as 'restricted' to a Jewish national point of view. The writers who wrote for Jews and in a Jewish language, and did so out of complete *Jewish* identification with the Revolution and with deep insight into the Jewish aspects of revolutionary change, were now asked to adapt themselves to simplistic internationalist slogans. For writers such as Markish it may even have been beyond their ability. Markish's epic works even in his later years reveal his exclusive interest precisely in Jewish heroism. The origins and growth of this heroism—during the generations before the Revolution—occupied him exclusively. The sources of Markish's pathos lay in his extraordinary ability to express it by way of contrasting metaphors in which Jewish tradition and the new world clash and yet form a strong and convincing unity. Markish, and surely other Jewish writers as well, lacked the proper artistic tools and background to create non-Jewish heroes. These would have been forced to be mere shadows compared with Jewish figures of undiluted vitality and tragic realism. One cannot imagine that a perspicacious critic such as Litvakov did not understand this problem when reading the new books of Markish, whom he had already 'indulged' in the criticism of *Eygns*, mentioned earlier. But the atmosphere among the 'proletarian' critics was what caused Litvakov—perhaps even against his own will and sentiment—to make his ridiculous demand on Markish. Litvakov, it seems, already felt that the young 'proletarian' critics had no faith in him.

The same year a storm raged around his other 'indulged child', the poet S. Halkin. Here Litvakov was on the defensive and—even more ironically—found himself charged with supporting 'nationalist' elements in literature. In 1929 a collection by Halkin, *Vey un mut* (Sorrow and Courage) appeared in Moscow. It contained his poems from the 1920s which vacillated between deep pessimism about the condition of Soviet Jewry and faith in general social solutions. But there is no doubt that the note of sorrow had the greater weight of the two motifs. In addition, motifs

[1] In the issue of 30 May 1929.

reminiscent of Jewish traditional literature are an important element in Halkin's verse. The 'proletarian' critics in Minsk now revealed that this same Halkin had enjoyed Litvakov's support for a long time, which would make Litvakov nothing but a hidden 'lover of Hebrew'. The group of fanatical critics in Minsk—Dunets, Bronshteyn, and others—directed their complaints about Halkin's poems against the central bureau of the Jewish Sections in Moscow, and accused its members, and especially Litvakov, of masked Jewish nationalism.[1]

The sharp competition among the 'proletarian' critics themselves reveals a little of the personal relationships in this camp. There necessarily resulted a fanatical pursuit of faults and deviations amidst the constant fear of being accused by colleagues of liberal attitudes to literature. Yet this entire faction, split though it was, closed ranks when faced by outside attack. The Kvitko 'affair' is evidence of this. At the beginning of 1929 L. Kvitko published a series of poems in *Di royte velt* satirizing various negative phenomena in the Soviet Union. He naïvely thought that the slogan 'self-criticism' also allowed him to make known his views of Litvakov. One of these satiric poems bore the title of '*Der shtinkfoygl Moyli*' (The Stinking Bird Moy(she) Li(tvakov)). Here Kvitko sharply assails the position of the all-powerful critic, who is like a millstone around the neck of literature. This poem also appeared in the collection of Kvitko's poetry *Gerangl* (Kharkov, 1929). This took place at the time of ferocious agitation against Boris Pilniak, the Russian writer who dared to publish in Berlin a story which was rejected by Soviet journals because it criticized the life of a Russian country town ('Mahogany'). Pilniak's story served as a pretext for an 'educational' campaign among Soviet writers in the whole country. Kvitko's attack on Litvakov was found suitable for the Jewish version of the general campaign. In Moscow, Minsk, Kharkov, and Kiev meetings of Jewish writers were called in protest at Kvitko's 'counter-revolutionary act' and a call went out for 'ethical conduct' in Soviet Yiddish literature. We need hardly add that they connected Kvitko's deed with the 'crime' of Pilniak. In this 'affair' the quarrelling 'proletarian' critics appeared as a single unified group.[2]

'Proletarian' critics, particularly the younger ones, assumed far ranging authority and boldly legislated on matters of aesthetics for literature as a whole. Literature was henceforth judged by the enthusiasm that—in the critics' view—the author expressed for the construction of cities and

---

[1] Bibliographical details of this episode in: *A shpigl oyf a shteyn* (ed. Ch. Shmeruk), Tel Aviv, 1964, p. 761. (For details on this work see bibliography at end of article.)

[2] Bibliographical details on the Kvitko affair, ibid., p. 751.

countryside. Positive heroes, party members, and class-conscious builders of socialism received special attention. But where 'negative' characters were concerned the critics demanded the removal of any emotional participation and of any real depiction of human feelings and struggles. As an example we may cite Moyshe Kulbak's excellent book *Zelmenyaner* (Zelmenian), published serially in the monthly *Der shtern* in 1929–30, and in 1931 in Minsk. Kulbak's book is one of the few works in Soviet Yiddish literature which depicted with irony and yet understanding the changes undergone by a large traditional Jewish family during the period of Soviet rule. The author's attitude to his heroes was ironic, grotesque, but in the main, forgiving. This applies both to 'positive' characters and to those considered 'negative', by the accepted standards of 'proletarian' criticism. This forgiveness, and even more the open sarcasm in the portraying of the 'positive' heroes (communists and Soviet youth) aroused the particular opposition of the critics Dunets and Bronshteyn. They could not accept the character of one member of the family who fought for the Revolution, became a party member, and after returning from the front joined the police. Kulbak showed him as a coarse ignoramus, unfit to understand anything in depth, who excelled only in gluttony. The only possible standard recognized by 'proletarian' criticism was here severely violated.[1]

Writers found different ways to express opposition to the increasing pressure of 'proletarian' criticism. Markish admitted some of his 'errors' but also rejected ridiculous charges. Not all the writers who were present at the meetings to protest against Kvitko accepted the resolutions of condemnation. Dovid Hofshteyn showed unusual courage in this affair. He sent out a personal letter to dozens of writers and cultural functionaries entitled 'Against the degradation', in which he cited Litvakov's deeds as the justification of Kvitko's poem. A copy of the letter reached Litvakov, who published the entire text in a strong attack on Hofshteyn.[2]

Different and more complex was Der Nister's reaction in a story 'Unter a ployt' (Under a Fence), first published in *Di royte velt* in 1929, and reprinted in his book *Gedakht* (Kiev, 1929). P. Kaganovitch, known by his pen name Der Nister (The hidden one), began his career in Yiddish literature in 1907, and from the very outset was noted for his trend towards symbolism. He tried to unite symbolism, then at its peak in Russian

[1] Critical articles on Kulbak's book can be found in the following works: Kh. Dunets, *Kritishe etyudn*, Minsk, 1933, pp. 25–39; Y. Bronshteyn, *Farfestikte pozitsyes*, Moscow, 1934. For the 'positive' characters see pp. 175–9. The two articles were published previously in literary monthlies.

[2] The article together with Hofshteyn's letter appeared in *Der emes*, 22 October 1929.

literature, with a style and thought rooted in Jewish tradition. He achieved an original and successful fusion of Jewish mystical and folk elements within the framework of current literary modernism. Der Nister created a new form of the Jewish short story. Its perfection of style is unique in Yiddish literature. 'Under a Fence' is one of his most significant stories in this genre.

Two worlds wrestle with each other in this story: the closed and contemplative world of a hermit shutting himself up in his tower. This is a world based on tradition, i.e. the heritage of teachers, self-discipline, and the consciousness of a mission. Facing it is a circus with its empty games which attracts and seduces by stimulating desires. The circus is supported by the taste of its mass visitors and by its managers' ability in catering to this taste. The circus is deliberately frivolous, unstable, and essentially treacherous—characteristics which are embodied in the circus rider 'Lili', who has some elements of the popular demonic figure 'Lilith', the queen of the demons. Between the two poles stands a fellow of questionable origins, ally of the circus director. He succeeds by magic and trickery in causing the hermit to hate his own world and enter the circus as an 'attraction' for the masses. The story is presented in the form of a confession by an anonymous scholar. In a 'realistic' framework, as it were, the serious scholar, a devoted father to his daughter, tells of his failure as Lili's lover. In his visions, while drunk, this scholar becomes a hermit and, in a court of hermits, confesses to leaving the tower and to what he is doing in the circus. The feeling of guilt due to the betrayal of high principles is common to the central character in his 'realistic' state and to his delusions when changed into a hermit. He is given a triple punishment for his disloyalty: stoning and burning in the fantastic part, but in the 'realistic' frame the scholar finds himself rolling in mud out of doors *under a fence*, outside the camp. From beginning to end the narrator emphasizes the great sorrow of the scholar-recluse but accepts the punishment meted out to him.

This work of Der Nister, like other works of his, seeks to show the split in man's soul. In German and Russian letters this theme has a respectable tradition. The hermit-teacher who presides over the court of hermits in the story is named Medardus—recalling Medardus and his doubles in E.T.A. Hoffmann's *The Devil's Elixir*. It is well known that the Serapion Brothers, the writers' group active in Leningrad at the beginning of the 1920s, derived its inspiration from the fantastic elements in Hoffmann's writings and it is named after another hermit who appears in Hoffman's stories. Through the use of Medardus's name in Der Nister's story it is possible to identify the literary tradition he drew on in constructing his tale, which is nothing less than a grotesque protrayal of a Soviet writer's struggles and hardships. When Der Nister's story was published the Serapion Brothers were considered a negative phenomenon of the past, which Soviet literature had already overcome. But Der Nister now re-examined the fate of the 'hermits'. His two main symbols, which are obvious enough, also testify to the programmatic nature of the story. The tower and the lonely hermit are permanent motifs in symbolist metaphor; and it is not hard to see the noisy and superficial circus as the utter negation of all art which penetrates to the depths and is meant only for the few. The treacherous finale to the struggle between the opposed elements, a result of self-deception, was presented by Der Nister in the unfortunate figure of the scholar-recluse who receives the punishment which he deserves. It is almost certain that this story contains the author's own confession predicting what was coming to him and to his kind. During this period it is hard to find the likes of Der Nister's story in Soviet literature. It is no wonder that a 'proletarian' critic ruled it 'the most reactionary in all his questionable work'.[1]

'Fully conscious of what they were doing, Yiddish writers in the Soviet Union yielded to the inevitable and began to adjust themselves to it. The results were not long in coming. In 1929 and the beginning of the 1930s Markish, in collecting his earlier poems, was already cautious in the selection he made. He also introduced textual changes intended to eradicate whatever might displease Soviet criticism and arouse ire. The second volume of his *A Generation Goes, a Generation Comes* did not appear until 1941. We need hardly add that this volume made room for non-Jewish revolutionary heroes. But it is doubtful whether it has the impact of the first (1929). In 1932 Halkin published a collection of new poems called *Far dem nayem fundament* (For the New Foundation). It is hard to recognize the lyrical, sensitive poet of old in the declarative and flat poetry in this collection; nor do we find even a remnant of his former doubts and painful reflections. Kvitko was dismissed from the editorial board of *Di royte velt* in 1929. His bitter experience made him concentrate on children's poems in his later years. These were largely Soviet patriotic poems, and brought him fame throughout the country. He gave up his expressionistic style of writing completely and also stopped writing satiri-

[1] This is based on Ch. Shmeruk, 'Der Nister's "Unter a ployt" ', *Di go dene keyt*, no. 43, Tel Aviv, 1962, pp. 47–68. An expanded and revised English-language version of this article, 'Der Nister's "Under a Fence": Tribulations of a Soviet Yiddish Symbolist', was published in *The Field of Yiddish*, second collection (ed. U. Weinreich), The Hague, 1965, pp. 263–87.

cal poems. No 'deviations' can be found in any of his later works; they are in fact characterized by extreme political caution. When Kulbak was about to publish the second volume of *Zelmenyaner* (in *Der shtern* serially in 1933–5 and afterwards in book form in 1935), he found it necessary to add a special chapter at the beginning in which he rewrote the entire biography of the 'positive' character, already known from the first volume. This desperate attempt to correct himself, required by his critics, proved unsuccessful. Because of this 'correction' and many similar examples the second volume suffered both artistically and also in mode of expression. Kulbak was now careful not to go too far in the forbidden satire of 'positive' Soviet characters, and he limited as much as possible any attitude of forgiveness and empathy where his 'negative' heroes were concerned.

'Under a Fence' was Der Nister's last symbolic story. Until the middle of 1931 he did not publish anything. In 1931–3 he tried to justify his existence as a Soviet writer by writing reportage (*Ocherki*), while searching for new ways suitable to his character as a writer. During those years he had difficulty earning his livelihood. When, in 1934, he found what he wanted, he was forced to turn to his brother in Paris for financial help in order to fulfil his plan. The paragraph below, quoted from Der Nister's letter to his brother, is one of the very rare documents of its kind which have come down to us. It clearly reflects the condition of a Soviet writer forced to abandon completely his manner of writing and to look for new possibilities acceptable both to himself and to the overlords of Soviet literature:

If you ask why have I done only technical work and not original independent writing, I answer you that what I have written up to now aroused strong opposition in our country. This is merchandise in very little demand. Symbolism has no place in Soviet Russia, and as you know, I am and always have been a symbolist. It is very difficult for a person like myself who has worked hard to perfect his method and his manner of writing, to pass from symbolism to realism. This is not a question of technique. Here it is necessary, as it were, to be reborn. Here one has to turn one's soul upside down. I have made many experiments. At first nothing succeeded at all. Now, it seems, I have found a way. I have begun to write a book which I and my close acquaintances think important. I want to give my all to this book. It includes my whole generation—what I saw, lived, and imagined. Up to now it was hard to write at all because all my time was spent earning money for my expenses. From my previous writings I could not get one kopek. Now, because the publishing houses were transferred from Kharkov to Kiev, my technical work is also over with. But I am forced to write my book, because if I do not, the man within me is destroyed. If I do not I am erased from literature and from life, because, I do not have to tell you, the meaning of a writer who does not write means that he is not living, that he does not exist in the world. . . .[1]

V

Developments at the end of the 1920s and the early 1930s were such that a general evaluation of Soviet Yiddish literature from the 1930s until 1941 presents less complexities than the earlier period; and this in spite of the fact that this decade saw more Yiddish books published in the Soviet Union than in the 1920s. Generalizations are now easier to make because the works published during this period are generally in accord with the unchallenged principle of 'socialist realism', though it was not always sufficiently clear. These works remain within the changing limits of the prevailing ideological policy. *Inter alia*, we can note a trend not to interpret too freely the literary aspect of the slogan 'national in form and socialist in content'. The slogan's plain interpretation and practical application made Yiddish literature for the most part national only in its language medium. Even then, authors were careful not to over-use 'Hebraisms', which were suspect because of their 'clerical' origin. The principle was a barrier against 'non-realistic' tendencies, while the slogan inhibited elements which could be interpreted as 'nationalist' and 'chauvinist'. This conformism came to the fore most clearly in those works—in poetry, prose, and drama—whose 'realistic' subject-matter was directly connected with post-revolutionary Soviet life.

Yiddish verse abounds at this time in hymns and paeans to such subjects as the party and its leaders—especially Stalin; socialist construction in city and country, and its heroes; the Red Army; and the celebrations on the anniversary of the Revolution and the first of May. The poems often relate directly to internal and external events publicized in the Soviet press. All this was done amidst unbounded loyalty to the frequently changing official line. In the long poems, in narrative prose, and in realistic drama the plots are repetitive; and the tension is generally based on conflicts, stereotyped 'positive' characters representing the party and their real or imagined political or class enemies: the 'kulaks', clericals', and other 'remnants of the past' of some sort. Everything is presented in black and white, in the dogmatic and uncompromising spirit of the party's appraisal. We must remember that this 'current-events' literature served as an accompaniment to the cruelty of collectivization, hardship in city

---

[1] For the original text and photostat of the letter of Ch. Shmeruk, 'Der Nister, Hayav viytsirato' (Der Nister, his Life and Work), in Der Nister, *Hanazir vehagedayah*: stories, poems, articles, Jerusalem, 1963, pp. 13–15 (Hebrew).

and country, a continuous struggle with all kinds of deviationist and 'enemies of the people', and a growing fear of liquidations and arbitrary arrests. Neither in Yiddish nor other Soviet literature can we now find a true confrontation with the realities of Soviet life.

From the Jewish point of view the signs of gradual liquidation were already clear on the horizon. The accomplishments in education and in colonization upon which cultural functionaries and writers based the national future of Soviet Jews in the 1920s, were threatened. Pessimism and despair took hold of the Jewish writers. We have clear proof of this in a frank—though fragmentary and tendentious—article by I. Fefer. He attacked the writers for the atmosphere he found at a Yiddish writers' meeting of 1933, from which he quoted the following outbursts:

Mikhoels complained that the party pays little attention to Jewish culture. . . . Godiner hurled the dangerous word 'denationalization', and Markish began to shout that the reader is going away, that Yiddish literature is ill, that Jewish writers sit in local stations while the express trains pass without stopping. With all the differences in manner of appearance and mood of the speakers at the conference, one basic note was struck by all: the lack of a perspective for Yiddish culture and literature. . . . Let us take the harps and sit down to mourn the fate of the Jewish people! Notes of nationalistic hysteria were heard ('We are the last poets'), of nationalistic pride ('We have almost the best literature'), of national panic ('We have no literature'), of nationalistic maximalism ('We do not want to be a minority!'). Some comrades did not give sufficient weight to the harmful nature of such basically nationalistic utterances. And strange indeed was the conduct of those comrades who for many years had themselves been affected by the disease of nationalism, and who now kept their peace and expressed no opposition to the prevailing mood.[1]

Yiddish literature may be searched in vain for the direct reflection of the problems and opinions expressed at that meeting. But probably the most painful example of the forbidden topics was the persecution of European Jewry—especially Polish Jewry. Silence was forcibly imposed on Yiddish literature at the beginning of the Second World War. This was in effect from 1939 to the summer of 1941, while the Ribbentrop-Molotov agreement was in force. And this at a time when Yiddish writers had direct contact with the Polish refugees, and were greatly shocked by the stories they told! But this found no mention in the works approved for publication in the Soviet Union.[2] This tendentious literature, oriented

---

[1] Itsik Fefer, 'Tseshmetern dem Yiddishn natsyonalizm!' (Smash Jewish Nationalism!), no. 1, *Farmest*, 1934, pp. 196-7.

[2] On this problem cf. Ch. Shmeruk, 'Yiddish Publications in the U.S.S.R. from the Late Thirties to 1948', in *Yad Washem Studies on the European Catastrophe and Resistance*, vol. 4,

to contemporary life, has not for the most part withstood the test of time. Yet it has documentary value in clarifying the path of Soviet Yiddish literature, and it has importance as historical though one-sided evidence.

This applies to that part of Yiddish literature which accepted the demands of 'socio-realistic' portrayal and served as a conscious or unconscious propaganda weapon. It is immaterial in this context whether this was done enthusiastically or because there was no alternative. Fortunately, however, several areas remained to Yiddish literature in the Soviet Union where the writer could express himself with relative freedom. Lyrics about the author's self or about nature served in part this purpose. These were inconspicuous in the collections of verse published at the time, but were not entirely absent. In the lyrics of those years it is indeed hard to find a refreshing novelty of form or surprises in style and imagery. Still, they served as an escape and a vital channel for untrammelled intimate human emotion over and beyond the dominant trend of political declarative poetry.

In the 1930s Yiddish writers began increasingly to translate from the world classics and especially poets in which they found an escape from the need to depend on Soviet reality. Russian poetry from Pushkin and Lermontov to Mayakovsky is particularly well represented. Halkin translated Shakespeare's *King Lear* which was performed with great success at the Jewish State Theatre in Moscow. Dovid Hofshteyn and Ezre Fininberg independently of each other translated Goethe's *Faust*. The translations of Lipe Reznik show great variety. In those years he translated Pushkin's *Boris Godunov*, the Finnish epic *Kalevala*, and a series of Hebrew poems by Judah Halevi, Solomon Ibn Gabirol, Moses Ibn Ezra, and Emmanuel Haromi.[1] Hebrew medieval poetry was the only branch of Hebrew literature to be translated. Modern Hebrew literature was utterly taboo—and was in fact not even mentioned except by way of negative reference as 'reactionary' and 'Zionist' literature.

In the 1930s an increasing number of collections of poetry and prose appeared, which included works published before the end of the previous decade. A writer such as Der Nister had nothing to offer for a collection of his writings, because at that time it was already impossible to republish his symbolist stories. Those writers who did prepare retrospective collections of their writings re-edited them carefully on the basis of whatever

1960, pp. 114–17 (pp. 20–3 in the reprint cited at the end of article); and see their footnote 35 on Markish's 'Tsu a yiddisher tenserin' (To a Jewish Danseuse).

[1] The translations of L. Reznik from medieval Hebrew poetry were printed in *Der shtern*, nos. 11–12, Minsk, 1940, pp. 99–107.

criticism they might have encountered at one time or another, and in the light of current demands at the time of republication. Writings which could not be 'corrected' were not allowed to be published afresh. The new collections lacked any independent thought, ambiguous images, and even a Hebrew word which would make their authors suspect in the eyes of Soviet critics. The results of this new screening are obvious by a comparison of the versions which were printed before the end of the 1920s with the later Soviet editions. Those who evaluate the works of these writers by their publications of the 1930s are doing great injustice to the men whose work underwent this unfortunate treatment.[1]

The noteworthy achievements of Yiddish literature for this period were fiction and drama with a background in the past. The further the subject was removed in time from the Soviet present, the easier it was to avoid obstacles and to skirt problems which had ready-made dogmatic solutions. Even when dealing with historical themes it was, to be sure, not possible to omit evaluations in the spirit of historical materialism; the class struggle had to be exposed even in remote times. Nevertheless, freedom of expression was much greater here than for contemporary topics, and the dividing line between the opposing camps was not so sharp.

Typical in this respect is Bergelson's novel *Bam Dnyeper* (At the Dnieper; vol. 1, 1932, vol. 2, 1940). It is a partly autobiographical work which gives a broad description of the life of the Jews in the Ukraine, and especially Kiev, at the end of the nineteenth and the beginning of the twentieth century. Bergelson does succeed in painting plastic, lively portraits of his heroes. But the more closely the story approaches 1905 (the year when revolutionary forces made themselves felt) the more we note the surrender of artistic and historical truth. The author did this in order to adapt the events to the historical appraisal of the communist party, which retrospectively diminished the contribution made by other parties, and especially the Jewish revolutionary parties, in order to show the Revolution as an exclusively Bolshevik accomplishment. Those who knew Bergelson and his family identify the author with Penek, the main character. According to them it is reasonable to assume that in this novel Bergelson settled his class account with his 'bourgeois' family, detaching himself from it in his desperate desire to free himself from the 'stigma' which his origins placed on him. There are nevertheless many chapters in the novel which justify its appraisal as an achievement of which Soviet Yiddish literature may be rightly proud.

[1] On this 'treatment' see the introduction to *A shpigl oyf a shteyn*, pp. 23–9; much material on the textual variations in Soviet editions is collected there in the notes, pp. 773–804.

Even greater is the achievement of Der Nister, the friend and contemporary of Bergelson, in the two first volumes of his novel *Di mishpokhe Mashber* (The Mashber Family; vol. 1, Moscow, 1939; vol. 2, New York, 1948). A third volume was scheduled to appear in Moscow in 1948, but so far only one chapter has been published. *Di mishpokhe Mashber* is the work for which Der Nister turned to his brother in Paris in the letter we quoted previously. This story is of wide scope and stands out as one of the peaks of all Yiddish fiction. *Di mishpokhe Mashber* has a broad epic canvas which unfolds the story of the generations at the end of the nineteenth century. For them the spiritual crises of a Judaism rooted in tradition, confronting the destructive currents of the new era, had already begun. This book, which superficially fits the model of 'the principles of realism', absorbs uch of the experience and manner of expression of the author's symbolist period. The Hasidim of Bratslav in their inner struggle and their search for God are one of the focal points of the narrative. The split in the soul of man and Jew, so characteristic of Der Nister's work, now became embodied in the characters of the three brothers of the Mashber family and of Sruli Gol, a fascinating blend of the Elijah image of folklore with demonic elements. The author intended to make this work a kind of family saga on the European model. In the two extant volumes the narrative takes place in the 1870s. This made it unnecessary to come directly to grips with 'dangerous' problems such as the labour movement, and it was possible to avoid the harm done to Bergelson's novel. Yet Der Nister's ability in using different viewpoints from which to narrate the story made it possible for him to fulfil his duty towards Soviet criticism, to hold the scale between his own purpose and the demands of ideology without being false to himself. Against this background of contemporary Soviet literature there is special significance in those pages of *Di mishpokhe Mashber* which make the reader compare sombre Soviet reaility with the spiritual greatness and inner freedom of figures from the not too distant past—and this despite the fact that such figures should have been portrayed in a completely negative light because of their class origin and their deep attachment to religion.[1]

Halkin wrote two verse dramas during these years: *Bar Kokhba* (1939)

[1] See, e.g. the Hasidic tale about a captive bird and a slave who (as in Exodus 21:5f.) refuses to leave his master, in Der Nister's *Mishpokhe Mashber*, vol. 2, pp. 327–8 (a Hebrew translation is given in the introduction cited in note 25, pp. 40–1). The real-life application of this paragraph is perfectly transparent. I do not know whether this chapter of the book was published previously in the Soviet Union. One chapter from the continuation of *Di mishphokhe Mashber* was recently published in *Sovietish Heymland* (1967, no. 2), but without any explanatory note about the whole manuscript and its contents.

and *Shulamis* (1940). These were at that time the only literary works in Soviet Yiddish literature where the plot went back to ancient times and was set in Palestine. Both dramas won great success on the Soviet Jewish stage.

To compare the 'literature of the present' with works dealing with the recent or more distant past is to be made aware of a basic and instructive contradiction. The 'literature of the present' was forced to fight against all the 'remnants of the past' which still existed in Soviet life. In doing so, it tended to split away broad layers of Jewish cultural tradition and to undermine the feeling of national and historical continuity among its readers. Those writers, however, who turned to historical topics stressed this very continuity. The further the historical background was removed in time, the more varied and positive could the attitude towards the past become. In certain cases it is even possible to attribute to the authors a conscious desire to confront national disintegration in the Soviet Union with the social and national solidarity of the traditional Jewish *milieu*. It was a bold expression of romantic nostalgia, a longing for a past more exalted than the present and thus worthy of the reader's appreciation.

In the 1920s the number of new young faces in Yiddish literature was an encouraging and irrefutable fact and seemed to presage a promising future. In the next decade, however, new names in Soviet Yiddish literature became increasingly rare. Even the few new Yiddish writers had nothing really fresh and meaningful to say in their works.[1] Yiddish literature was already suffering from a dearth of new blood and young talent when the liquidations of the 1930s removed writers who had not yet come to the end of their road. In these years Moyshe Kulbak and Izi Kharik 'disappeared'; imprisonment and death was the fate of the poet Zelik Akselrod as the German invasion neared. The historian of Jewish literature, Yisroel Zinberg, the scholar and critic Max Erik, the short-story writer and critic A. Abtshuk, and the critics M. Litvakov, Y. Bronshteyn, and C. Dunets were also liquidated. It is a strange paradox that this was the fate of the most loyal of the critics, whose aggressiveness had helped to bring Yiddish literature to its turning point in that decade.

VI

The summer of 1941 was tragic and decisive for Soviet Yiddish literature. After a short period of helplessness and confusion during the retreat

[1] In 1939–41 dozens of Yiddish writers from the newly annexed areas—Poland, Rumania, and the Baltic states—associated themselves with Soviet Yiddish literature. They included refugee writers from the part of Poland conquered by the Germans. Most of these writers left the Soviet Union after the war. Their publications in the Soviet Union were basically no different from the works of veteran Soviet writers.

of the Red Army the authorities began to exploit all forces able to help the war effort. Thus the Jewish Anti-Fascist Committee was established, whose most active members were Yiddish writers. Solomon Mikhoels, the dramatic artist, was its leader. Yiddish publishing had been destroyed by the capture of Kiev and Minsk and the evacuation of Moscow; it was now restored under the sponsorship of this committee by dint of much effort and hard work. [1]

Yiddish literature in the Soviet Union during the war and the three years following underwent the most dramatic chapter in its history. The tie between this literature and the deepest emotions of the entire people—not only in the Soviet Union—became stronger again during these seven years with the effort to explore the meaning of the war and of the catastrophe for the Jews. Almost no political fears or prognostications impeded this harmony. The patriotic feeling of the Russian writers quickly became a sincere expression of Russian national sentiment in the war against the invader, and received the ideological encouragement of the authorities. In consequence the Yiddish writers, too, whose loyalty was then beyond all doubt, were given the right to express their national feelings with almost complete freedom. The contribution of Russia's allies could be described in a positive light; similarly, there was nothing wrong in mentioning the unity between the Jews of the Soviet Union, the Jews persecuted under the Nazi regime, and the Jews in the capitalistic countries fighting side by side with the Soviet Union. Yiddish literature during the war and afterwards was full of national Jewish feeling the like of which had hardly been seen in this literature in earlier years. Sorrow and mourning for the destruction were added to the natural pathos of wartime, as well as vague hopes for a better future after victory.

In many ways, a rapprochement took place between Soviet Yiddish literature and Yiddish literature in other countries, from which Soviet literature had shut itself off before the war. This rapprochement was most felt in themes common to all the Yiddish literature of the time—themes which caused Soviet literature in Yiddish to utilize more traditional and biblical images and more Hebrew elements in the vocabulary as compared with the earlier period.

Most prose and poetry was basically orientated to the present and a strong desire to emphasize the heroism of the Jews and their part in

---

[1] The following are the periodical publications in Yiddish which appeared in the Soviet Union at the time of the war and in the next few years: *Aynikayt*, 1942–8 (Kuibyshev-Moscow); *Heymland*, 1947–8 (Moscow, 7 numbers in all); *Der shtern*, 1947–8 (Kiev, 7 numbers in all); *Biro-Bidzhan*, 1946–8 (3 numbers in all).

achieving victory came to the fore. Here and there apologetic notes intruded and the response to the slogan of the Soviet 'brotherhood of peoples' aroused occasional suspicion. There was frequent stress on the heroism of individuals integrated into armies of various nationalities; here only the hero's Jewish name acted as a catalyst for seeing the war in its meaning for the Jews as a group. Jewish life in Soviet Russia no longer provided a convenient background for an epic work in its people's group life. Yet at this very time a strong desire impelled the Jewish writers to see the war and the Holocaust in terms of the Jewish collective's national solidarity. Hence we find the rise of a highly suggestive phenomenon, which is a help to the understanding both of the twisting course of Soviet Yiddish literature and of the changes in a Jewish society where writers were forced to find a specific way out of their dilemma: a clear and deliberate tendency to transfer the scene of events to a geographic and political location which allowed the writer to describe the longed-for Jewish wholeness. This traditional wholeness had already been destroyed in Soviet reality; the proclaimed standards and principles of Soviet literature in any case only allowed its *mis-en-scène* outside the borders of the Soviet Union.

It seems that the first writer to draw the expected conclusion from this situation was Der Nister, who chose Poland as the locale of his stories—*Korbones* (Victims, 1943)—describing the fate, reactions, and manifestations of traditional Jewishness of the Holocaust victims. Not without good reason also did Perets Markish, in his wide-ranging epic *Milkhome* (War, 1948) integrate the most important chapters dealing with the Jewish aspects of the war into a plot sequence which took them beyond the Soviet Union's borders. In his last prose work *Trot fun doyres* (The March of the Generations)—which he did not live to see published [1]—Markish also turned to the Jews in Warsaw and to the Polish Jews in the Soviet Union in order to express a Jewish wholeness and continuity which had disappeared in his time, and indeed before his eyes, in Soviet Russia. Even writers like Itzik Fefer (*Shotns fun varshever geto*—Shadows from the Warsaw Ghetto),[2] and Yehiel Falikman (*Di shayn kumt fun mizrekh*—The Light

---

[1] The book was found among Markish's surviving manuscripts. Separate chapters were printed in 1956 and 1958 in *Yiddishe shriftn* and *Folkshtimme* in Warsaw, and in *Sovietish Heymland*, 1963. After many delays the book appeared at the beginning of 1967; the date on the title page is 1966.

[2] The book was sent for publication to New York before its appearance in Moscow. It appeared in 1945 in New York. In the version of the poem included in Fefer's *Shayn un opshayn* (Moscow, 1946) many corrections were made, the purpose of which was to weaken the poem's national elements.

Comes from the East, 1948), found themselves impelled to describe the ghetto in Poland. Halkin's dramatic poem 'Af toyt un af lebn' (A Matter of Life and Death),[1] which deals with the revolt in the Warsaw ghetto, is most enlightening from this viewpoint. In this play he is daring enough to rehabilitate the men of the *Judenrat* and even the Jewish police, who united with the communists, Zionists and Hasidim in preparing for the revolt. Zionists and Hasidim could no longer exist on the Soviet scene and the very conception of such total Jewish unity could not be depicted there. Such a play could only be created out of a burning desire to see integral Jewish life in its multi-coloured variety, encompassing the totality of Jewry, even including those who no longer could be seen or described in the officially established Soviet reality.

As a continuation of the earlier trends we may see renewed interest in historical topics that embodied great national tension. The writers fused a more distant perspective with a clear hint at the contemporary outlook. Thus, during the war, Bergelson wrote the drama *Prints Reuveni*[2] in which he projected the ambivalence of modern Jewish existence against a medieval historical background. In the papers of Ezre Fininberg, who died in 1947, we find evidence that he worked on a play called *The Jew from Portugal* and on a long poem about the 'eternal Jew'. In these very topics one can readily see a similarity with the problems that occupied Bergelson in his play.

Barely a year after victory was achieved the retreat from the liberal outlook in Soviet wartime literature began. A speech of Zhdanov in August 1946 and a decision of the Central Committee of the party attacked those monthlies which published writers who 'have no place in Soviet society and its literature'. Soon afterwards wild incitement was directed against 'cosmopolitans' and 'cosmopolitanism' accompanied by overtones of the lowest kind of Russian nationalism and antisemitism. Many Jews who wrote in Russian were among the targets of this campaign. For the first time an open and dangerous discrepancy appeared between the attitude to nationalism in Soviet Russian literature, now encouraged on the highest levels, and a negative attitude to such tendencies in the literature of other Soviet peoples. It was a tragic mistake on the part of Soviet Yiddish

[1] Halkin's drama was included in his book *Der boym fun lebn*, Moscow, 1948. This book is extremely rare. It was one of the last Yiddish books published before the liquidation of Yiddish culture and only a few copies found their way abroad.

[2] This drama (New York, 1946) appeared only outside the Soviet Union. During the war and afterwards the Jewish Anti-Fascist Committee used to send works of Yiddish writers abroad for publication. As a result, quite a few works were saved which did not appear in the Soviet Union itself.

writers that they forgot the lessons of the late 1920s and the purges of
the 1930s and supposed that the favourable atmosphere of the war years
would continue into the post-war period. Unfortunately they failed to pay
attention to what happened in Russian literature after Zhdanov's speech.
It is also possible that in 1946 it was in any case already too late to turn
back and deny their true feelings.

A fictionalized piece of reportage by Itsik Kipnis could still be published
in the Warsaw newspaper *Dos naye leben* (The New Life) on 19 May
1947. This Kipnis became the scapegoat in the Jewish version of the events
taking place in Soviet literature. The name of the story was *On khokhmes,
on kheshboynes* (No joking and no reflection). It tells of two Jewish children and a country woman who saved them during the war. The children
were destined to stay in a non-Jewish environment, but they were not
willing to separate from the woman who saved them. They would
assimilate without knowing anything about their Jewishness. This fact
casts a shadow over the author's joy in the saving of Jewish lives, and
brings Kipnis to 'dangerous' reflections:

In the last few years I have become very fanatical. I am very anxious for whatever
survived. When I see a Jewish student, a young, pretty girl, a brave strong soldier,
an academician, or an ordinary Jew, I long for them to speak to me in Yiddish.
I want all the Jews now walking the streets of Berlin with the assurance of victors
also to wear on their chests a small, beautiful Jewish star together with their
medals. . . . I very much want the two children who were saved to speak to me in
my language. . . .

Kipnis's burning desire to demonstrate Jewish identity and pride
immediately became the subject of a leading article in the Moscow
Aynikayt that denounced 'nationalism' in Soviet Yiddish literature. At the
beginning of January 1948 a meeting of writers was called in Kiev, in
which a speech was given on the 'manifestations of nationalism and
national segregation in Yiddish literature'. The old familiar indictments
from previous years were repeated; *inter alia*, a point was made of the
exaggerated use of Hebrew words in the writings of Hofshteyn, Oshero-
vitsh, Platner, Grubyan, and Dobin. At that meeting Kipnis was also
forced to 'confess' his errors.

The revelations of 'nationalism' in literature were followed by other
and more dangerous revelations of Jewish 'nationalism'. The establishment of the Jewish State in Israel, the War of Independence, the ambassa-
dorship of Golda Meir and subsequent demonstration at the Moscow
synagogue, the renewed social solidarity of Soviet Jews after the Holocaust, the nebulous Crimea affair—all this and more pointed to Yiddish

writers as the main 'culprits' in keeping alive Jewish feelings among the citizens of the Soviet Union. From the 1920s onwards these writers had been presumed to be responsible for Jewish nationalism. At the end of 1948 the standard-bearers of Soviet Yiddish culture, the Yiddish writers of the Soviet Union, fell victim to a tragic fusion of Jewish internal circumstances with external considerations in the minds of the Soviet rulers. The latter found no other solution than to arrest and execute writers, and totally liquidate the remnants of Jewish culture in the Soviet Union.

VII

In the final years of Stalin's rule most of the Yiddish writers in the Soviet Union were imprisoned. Der Nister died in prison. Dovid Hofshteyn, Dovid Bergelson, Perets Markish, Leyb Kvitko, Itzik Fefer and Shmuel Persov were executed on 12 August 1952. At the same time most of the Yiddish writers were scattered in remote prison camps in the northern part of the country. In the years 1955–6 a start was made with releasing those writers still alive. Shmuel Halkin, greatest of the surviving poets, died in 1960 as a result of his experiences in prison.

Information concerning the liquidation of Yiddish culture and the killing of Yiddish writers penetrated to the west. Complete credence and publicity were not at first given to these reports; this was due, among other reasons, to false denials by various Soviet spokesmen. Hitherto no official or semi-official Soviet description has revealed all this tragic affair. Yet even in Soviet publications it is already possible to find complete confirmation by piecing together reports about individual authors. These are contained in articles in Soviet encyclopaedias, in introductions to translations of these writers' works into Russian and other languages, and in incidental notes and hints in *Sovietish Heymland*. Jewish communists in Poland and the west have played an important part in revealing the details of this complete liquidation. Strong pressure by world public opinion, which was brought to bear on the leaders of the Soviet Union, including demands by loyal communists, brought about the resumption of publication in Yiddish in the Soviet Union after repeated promises and much delay on the part of the authorities.

In 1959 after an interruption of eleven years, three books in Yiddish appeared in the Soviet Union. These were selected works of Mendele Moykher Sforim, Y. L. Perets, and Sholem Aleichem. In 1960 another book appeared, this time a publicistic collection devoted to Biro-Bidzhan. In 1961 two further books appeared: the selected works of Bergelson and a collection of the poetry of O. Shvartsman. In the middle of 1961 the bi-monthly *Sovietish Heymland* began to appear; in January 1965 it became a monthly. In 1964–5 five more books in Yiddish appeared, all by the surviving Yiddish writers who publish in *Sovietish Heymland*. In the Soviet weekly *Novye knigi S.S.S.R.* six more books in Yiddish were announced. They were to appear in 1965 and 1966, but by February 1967 only two of them had done so: a book of poems by Halkin, and the above-mentioned *Trot fun doyres* by Markish.

We may conclude from these few books, and from the literary works published in *Sovietish Heymland*, that the remaining writers have for the most part continued to work in a tradition established for Soviet Yiddish literature by their comrades who had been in the centre of this literature before falling victim to the great blood-purge. At present these works are neither innovating nor searching nor combatant. They do not seek new stylistic or artistic expression; nor have they anything new to say in the realm of ideas. Their thematic scope and the manner of their presentation are well known, both positively and negatively, from the years before 1948. The Second World War and the Holocaust remain a chief interest for many writers. But because these subjects became commonplace even outside Soviet Yiddish literature it is also hard to find in them anything really new that transcends what have become clichés. Lyric verse is found again but it largely uses themes and forms which have become trite in modern Yiddish poetry. It is now possible, however, to discern a conscious desire to extend the limited cultural horizons of Soviet Yiddish literature into such areas as Hebrew literature, which were previously taboo on principle. But these tendencies have not yet borne any real fruit.

Apart from some young writers in *Sovietish Heymland* whose writings do not in any case change the general picture, most Yiddish writers belong to the generation which arose in the 1920s. There are also a few authors who joined Soviet literature when the Baltic countries and parts of Rumania were annexed at the beginning of the Second World War. They too are now already nearly fifty, if not older. While one is even now impressed on occasion by writers with real talent, it would be hard to single out any of them able to bear comparison with those who previously stood at the centre of Soviet Yiddish literature.

Nevertheless it is still too early to pass judgement on the revival and future of Yiddish literature in the Soviet Union on the basis of the works before us. It is obvious that the limitations and caveats pertaining to other Soviet literatures apply here too. In such conditions the ability of the writers cannot show itself fully. It might even be assumed that those writers who are still alive after the tribulations of Yiddish literature have learned from bitter experience to be more careful than others; they are less likely to write about matters whose 'ideological purity' is doubtful from any point of view or which might cast doubt on their loyalty at any time in the future. The past fate of Yiddish literature means that such fears confront both writers and editors. We may perhaps now understand why an open and incisive treatment of topics and problems which should by right be central is almost completely absent from Yiddish writing. These problems are: the writers' own suffering during the last years of Stalin, antisemitism, and the whole complex question of present-day Jewish national existence in the Soviet Union. Even authors very sympathetic to Soviet Yiddish literature have recently complained publicly on this score.[1] Time will tell whether this literature will overcome the obstacles which stood and stand in its path. But it is well to remember that this does not solely depend on the desires and aspirations of the writers.

POSTSCRIPT

The monthly *Sovietish Heymland* continues to appear regularly in Moscow. The poet A. Vergelis, who has edited the journal from its beginnings and continues to do so, has introduced no substantial changes into its layout or political objectives. But it is possible to discern in the journal a perceptible increase in the anti-Israel attitude since the Six-Day War and the beginning of the 1970s with the emergence of emigration from the Soviet Union to Israel.

Between 1967 and 1975 *Sovietskii Pisatel* continued to publish, at fairly regular intervals, further volumes in Yiddish, all in the realm of belles-lettres. A total of thirty-seven such titles appeared, of which most were the work of authors connected with *Sovietish Heymland*, and a minority the posthumous work of those writers who died in the purges of the 1930s and the beginning of the 1950s.

In these new literary works, and in the publications that have appeared recently in Moscow, there is in general no essential shift as far as concerns content, and no innovations in style or form. None the less, Soviet-Yiddish literature does display a number of achievements that are undoubtedly worthy of note. They include *S'iz nokh groys der tog* by Nathan Zabara, published by instalments in *Sovietish Heymland*. This is a historical novel in which, for the first time in Yiddish literature, the author dealt *in extenso* with the life of the Jews in Southern Europe (Provence,

Italy, Spain) in the thirteenth century. The novel is written with great descriptive skill and with a broad knowledge of the historical sources and the many-hued Hebrew literature of the period. It aims to suggest thought-provoking analogies between circumstances of the distant past and problems of Jewish society and culture in present-day Soviet-Jewish life.

To all appearances Zabara intended to make his story into a novel of the encounter between the Jews in Western Europe and the Jewish settlement in Eastern Europe in its formative period. From the manuscript of the early chapters which reached Israel, it is clear that the author's text, as published in *Sovietish Heymland*, underwent a fundamental revision which weakened its national-Jewish foundations. Zabara died at the beginning of 1975 and, it appears, was unfortunately unable to complete his work.

Erev, a novel by Eli Shekhtman, was also published first in *Sovietish Heymland*. The first part appeared in Moscow as early as 1965 in book form. It is a saga of the many-branched Boyer family in the Ukraine, and its tempestuous history from the beginning of the twentieth century. In rich prose, stamped with an individual style, Shekhtman describes the turbulence of the period through a series of unforgettable images. In 1972 Shekhtman emigrated to Israel, where he is continuing to work on the novel, in which his characters are to play their part in the Soviet period. The first two volumes of the book appeared in 1974 in Tel Aviv.

From 1971 onwards a considerable number of Yiddish writers reached Israel from the Soviet Union: R. Boymvol, M. Kharats, Y. Kerler, Y. Latsman, Y. Lerner, Kh. Maltinski, H. Osherovitch, E. Roytman, Sh. Roytman, M. Saktsier, Kh. Seltser, E. Shekhtman, Z. Telesin, Y. Yakir, M. Yelin, and the critics and historians of literature B. Makhlin and L. Podryatchik. The widows and families of David Hofshteyn and Perets Markish, who were killed on 12 August 1952, arrived in Israel at the same time. Israel became an important centre for the survivors of Soviet-Yiddish writing. Most of the writers had been among the regular contributors to *Sovietish Heymland* and some had published their works in the Soviet Union from the beginning of the 1960s. They collaborate now in the quarterly *Die Goldene Keyt*, which has appeared in Tel Aviv since 1948. They are active in the establishment and editing of new media for Yiddish writing—*Bey Zich* (from 1972), *Yerushalaymer Almanakh* (from 1973)—in which they also publish their books. In Tel Aviv there have hitherto appeared about fifteen works by writers from the Soviet Union. The publications of these *émigré* writers in Israel were first and foremost the expression of free Soviet-Yiddish literature. Israel saw the first publication of many works in Yiddish, written in the Soviet Union but without any prospect of appearing there. These works complement essentially the distorted image of the Soviet-Yiddish writers as gathered from their publications in the Soviet Union. Their works indeed witness to that penetrating grappling with tormenting themes and problems that is sought in vain in Yiddish writing in the Soviet Union since the establishment of *Sovietish Heymland*. The comprehensive confrontation between Soviet writing in Yiddish, published in Moscow, and the publications of these writers who have emigrated to Israel, will certainly become an instructive theme even for those future research workers whose interests extend beyond the sphere of Yiddish literature alone.

The emigration of a significant group of Yiddish writers from the Soviet Union has perceptibly weakened the activity of the Soviet-Yiddish centre. In the absence of the possibility of replenishment through new forces, it seems without prospects over a prolonged period.

October 1975

SELECTED BIBLIOGRAPHY

(In addition to the references in the footnotes)

Reyzen, Z., *Leksikon fun der yiddisher literatur, prese, un filologye*, 4 vols., Wilno, 1928–9.

Leksikon fun der nayer yiddisher literatur. In progress (7 vols. to date), New York 1956.

Abtshuk, A., *Etyudn un materialn tsu der geshikhte fun der yiddisher literaturbavegung*, *in F.S.S.R.*, Kharkov, 1934.

Shmeruk, Ch., and Ben-Yosef, A., *Jewish Literature in the Soviet Union During and Following the Holocaust Period*, Jerusalem, 1960, reprinted from *Yad Washem Studies on the European Catastrophe and Resistance* (ed. Shaul Esh), vol. 4, 1960.

A shpigl oyf a shteyn; an Anthology of Poetry and Prose by Twelve Soviet Yiddish Writers. Selected by B. Hrushovski, Ch. Shmeruk, and A. Sutskever; biographies and bibliographical assistance by M. Pyekazh (ed. with an introduction and notes by Ch. Shmeruk), Tel Aviv, 1964.

---

[1] Kh. Sloves, 'Oysruf-tseykhhs, freg-tseykhs un klamern: finf yor *Sovietish Heymland*' (Exclamation points, question marks and parentheses: five years of *Sovietish Heymland*), *Yiddishe kultur*, no. 8, New York, 1966, pp. 4–17. Earlier detailed assessments of *Sovietish Heymland*: M. Abramovits, 'Ketav-ha'et hasovyeti hehadash beyiddish' (The New Soviet Yiddish Periodical), *Molad*, no. 163, Jerusalem, Tel Aviv, 1962, pp. 11–17; Joseph and Abraham Brumberg, '*Sovietish Heymland*'—*An Analysis*, New York, 1966.

13

Soviet Jewry in the Second World War

REUBEN AINSZTEIN

In the middle of the 1930s, Soviet Jewry's progress as a nationality reached its zenith. But the effects of two combined forces arrested its further advance. The first force was generated by the revival of Russian national imperialism or, as Lenin had once called it, Great Russian chauvinism. When the hope in world revolution had passed away and when Stalin had proclaimed the possibility of building socialism in the Soviet Union alone, the rising generation of Russian communists once again saw their people not as a backward member of the western world, but as the bearer of a unique role in human history. In practical terms, for example, the reassertion of Russian cultural imperialism found its almost symbolic expression in the years 1937–40 in the replacement of the Latin alphabet, which had been imposed in place of the Arabic script on the Moslem peoples and used to provide a written language for the primitive tribes of Siberia, by the Cyrillic alphabet.

The Jews, of course, were by no means the only people to suffer in their national rights from the various administrative and cultural effects of the reassertion of the Russian national ego.[1] They were also not the only nationality whose communist leaders and intellectual élite were decimated in the purges on trumped-up charges of bourgeois nationalism. But, unlike those other nationalities which suffered during this period, the rights of Soviet Jews were further undermined by Stalin's use of traditional

[1] For instance, the Abkhazian writer Georgy Gulya, made famous by his book *Spring in Saken*, has revealed that in 1937 almost all Abkhazians were removed from leading positions in the Abkhazian autonomous republic as part of a process described as 'the correct regulation of cadres'. In 1946 all Abkhazian schools were closed and the 350,000 Abkhazians were told to become Georgians or Russians. His father, the poet Dmitry Gulya, who laid the foundations of Abkhazian literature, and created his people's first alphabet in 1891, and whose *History of Abkhazia* has shaped his ancient people's national consciousness, was ordered from Moscow to write a critique of his history to prove that 'there is no such thing as an Abkhazian people' and that 'assimilation is the key to paradise for small nationalities'. When he refused to do so, Mikhail Delba, the Abkhazian Prime Minister, wrote a pamphlet proving the need for Abkhazians to disappear as a nationality and published it under Dmitry Gulya's name. After Stalin's death he justified his action by claiming that he had committed the forgery to save the life of Abkhazia's national poet (see Georgy Gulya, *Dmitry Gulya*, Moscow, 1963).

antisemitic prejudices and emotions. These he manipulated first to win his battle against Trotsky and his adherents inside the party, and then to consolidate his position as absolute dictator by conciliating the nationalist complexes and ambitions of the Russian people.

The Russo–German pact thus came at a most critical moment in the history of Soviet Jewry. There is no doubt that the majority of Russians, Ukrainians and Byelorussians agreed with Stalin's policy of keeping their country out of a European war and regarded the pact as fully justified in view of the policies pursued by the governments of Britain and France. For apart from their personal memories of the horrors of war, they were also moved by an almost subconscious feeling that in all such wars in Russian history they had served as cannon fodder for a scheming and selfish west. The Russo–German pact offended the consciences of an idealistic Marxist minority, but not those of the mass of party members and the nation as a whole. As for the feelings and reactions of Soviet Jews, we still do not know enough about them. But it is obvious that many more Jews than non-Jews were critical of the pact itself and its effects on Soviet life. They could not help but be alarmed when reading, for example, in the issue of *Bezbozhnik* of 5 May 1940 an article by a correspondent who had recently visited Germany. This argued that the Nazi attack on the Jewish religion was the principal achievement of the Third Reich; it was therefore the duty of Soviet atheists to assist their new political allies in their fight against religion.[1]

Perhaps the best assessment of that period was made by the Jew Mark Gallai, who was regarded by many Russians a few years ago as the leading Soviet test pilot.[2] 'For my generation the twenty-two months between the signing of our Non-Aggression Pact with Hitler and the outbreak of the war were strange and incomprehensible', he recalls.

Much appeared to us inexplicable, incredible, unnatural. Our doubts were not caused so much by the fact that such a treaty had been signed, for it was clear to us that in the existing situation nothing else could have been done. Most of us accepted the treaty as one takes a dose of medicine: it was horrible but necessary. But the signing of the treaty was followed by happenings that were no longer understandable. The fascists were no longer called fascists—it became impossible to find the word in the press and even in semi-official lectures and speeches. What we had been taught to abhor as hostile, evil and menacing from our Komsomol—nay, Pioneer—days, suddenly became, as it were, neutral. This was not stated in so

[1] B. Z. Goldberg, *The Jewish Problem in the Soviet Union*, New York, 1961, p. 306.

[2] M. Gallai, *Pervyi boi my vyigrali*, *Novy Mir*, Moscow, September (no. 9), 1966; Mark Lazarovich Gallai, Hero of the Soviet Union, *Notitsn fun an oisshpir-flier*, *Sovietish Heymland*, Moscow, November (no. 11), 1965.

many words, but the feeling stole into our souls as we looked at photographs of Molotov standing next to Hitler, or read reports of Soviet grain and oil flowing into fascist Germany, or watched the Prussian goose-step being introduced at that very time into our armed forces. Yes, it was very difficult to understand what was what!

Grigory Baklanov (real name: Fridman) in his novel *July 1941*[1] has provided a dramatic illustration of what it was to be a devoted Jewish communist during those twenty-two months. The novel, which appeared in 1965, dealt more boldly than anything hitherto published in Russian literature with the causes of the catastrophic Soviet defeats of 1941. One of its central figures is Regimental Commissar (i.e. Colonel) Brovalsky, whose faith in Stalin was not even shaken by the revelations of his brother, a high-ranking Red Army officer arrested during the purges, but later released. In the critical months of 1941 he is political commissar of an infantry corps stationed on the Russo–German border. A few days before the Nazi attack, he goes on leave to Moscow aware of the German military preparations and the refusal of his army commander, following orders from the Kremlin, to take even the most essential precautionary measures. On the last night of his leave he entertains a girl friend in a restaurant, when the following incident occurs:

Two German air force officers entered the restaurant and made for his table, which was near the entrance. One smiled gallantly at Brovalsky's companion and reserved some of his smile for Brovalsky before asking his permission to sit at his table. Their presence at his table would have meant a spoilt evening; for obvious reasons Brovalsky wanted to be alone with his companion. Nevertheless, when the German smiled, Brovalsky felt his own face grin back. For they were guests and, in the spirit of the treaty, friends. Moreover, he was their host and, in a way, represented his country. It was his readiness to smile back and to get up and offer them seats at his table that Brovalsky could not forgive himself. The Germans stopped and the one who had smiled said quite loudly in German: 'Don't, Kurt! There's a Jew sitting there. Let's find another table.'

   And they walked off. In his struggle to stop himself from following them and using his fists on their mugs, Brovalsky bit his lips until they bled. A few years earlier he would not have hesitated. But since then he had acquired the habit of making his actions accord with a certain Person's implicit, all-regulating views, which, even if they had not been made quite clear in relation to the present situation, nevertheless existed like some invisible code. The habit of seeing events through that Person's eyes had now become part of himself. He had to consider what would happen if he, a regimental commissar, beat up an air force officer of a friendly power. And so Brovalsky, a Red Army regimental commissar, a strong

[1] Grigory Baklanov, *Iyul 1941 goda*, Moscow, 1965.

man and no coward, remained seated, covered with ignominy. They, the fascists, behaved in a foreign country as though they were at home, whilst he, who was at home, had to think of the possible consequences of his actions. . . .

The unnatural twenty-two months ended in the early hours of 22 June 1941, and, in the words of the official Soviet history of the war, 'Soviet people cannot and will not forget the tragedy of the first day of the war. They will not forget it not only because at dawn of that day an unprecedented act of treachery was committed against our peace-loving country, but also because the consequences of the surprise attack were much too severe.'[1] The consequences, according to official Soviet statements, were the loss of over 20 million Soviet lives as a result of Stalin's purges and miscalculations.

Under the impact of the terrible defeats suffered in the opening stages of the war, Stalin allowed Soviet Jewry to raise its voice as a people again. On 24 August 1941, Solomon Mikhoels, Perets Markish, Dovid Bergelson, Red Army man Jerome Kuznetsov, Academician Peter Kapitza, Sergey Eisenstein, Academician Boris Yapan, Samuel Marshak, Ilya Ehrenburg, and Shakhno Epshteyn spoke in Moscow, and proclaimed their pride in belonging to the Jewish people whom the Nazis had chosen as the chief target of their hatred. For the first time since 1918, the voice of all Russian Jewry resounded in the appeal adopted by the meeting, 'To Our Jewish Brothers All Over the World':

In the countries seized and enslaved by murderous fascism, our unfortunate brothers have become the first victims. . . . Their blood does not call for fasts and prayers but for retribution! It does not call for annual remembrance candles, but for a conflagration to devour the destroyers of mankind. It calls not for tears but for hatred and resistance. It calls not for words but for deeds. The time to act is now or never! On our long road of martyrdom stretching from the time of Roman domination to the Middle Ages, our long-suffering people never experienced a calamity comparable to the present one, which fascism has inflicted upon the whole of mankind, and whose main ferocity is directed against the Jewish people.

The appeal continued:

The brown plague, which has brought to all mankind tears and misery, suffering and despair, will find its eternal grave on the blood-soaked plains of the Soviet Union. In its battles against Nazism, the executioner of entire peoples, our Red Army is breeding heroes whose peers are unknown in the history of the human race. And among the names of the glorious warriors we see with pride the names

---

[1] *Istoriya Velikoi Otechestvennoi Voiny Sovetskovo Soyuza 1941–1945,* 6 vols., Moscow, 1961–5. Referred to henceforth as *IVOVSS.*

of Jews, who, animated by Soviet dignity, defend human culture against the fascist barbarians. And, fighting shoulder to shoulder with our men, we find the finest daughters of our people.

Not until the October Revolution could Russian Jews prove to the world and to themselves that despite their unmilitary background and the absence of a continuous warlike tradition, they lacked neither physical courage nor military skills. Not only did they give the Russian Revolution its Carnot in the person of Leon Trotsky, but in Yakir, Shtern, Eydeman, Feldman and Gamarnik, Russian Jewry produced military leaders whose role in the civil war put them alongside such legendary figures as Blucher, Gai, Kotovsky, Timoshenko, Primakov, Putna, Chapayev or Shchors. Moreover, unlike so many famous civil war heroes who never outgrew their limitations as partisan leaders, the Jewish commanders proved themselves able to grow both intellectually and in military knowledge. It was these qualities that created a bond of personal friendship between Marshal Tukhachevsky, the intellectual nobleman, and the Jewish generals. Together they can be said to have belonged to the relatively small group of Red Army leaders who laid the foundations for the present Soviet war machine. In the Ukraine summer manœuvres of 1935, for example, when the Red Army astounded western military observers by parachuting and landing 3,000 airborne troops, the man in command of the operation was Yona Emmanuilovich Yakir, the Jew from Kishinev.

In June 1937 Stalin had Tukhachevsky executed. The same fate was shared by Yakir, Feldman, Eydeman, Gamarnik, the Lithuanian Putna, the Pole Uborevich, and the Russian Primakov. Only Grigory Shtern remained alive of the group of Jewish military leaders. On his return from Spain, where, as General Kleber, he had been chief adviser to the Republican Army in 1936-7, Shtern was posted to the Soviet far east as Marshal Vasily Blucher's chief-of-staff. When the Japanese in 1938 decided to test the Kremlin's determination to resist aggression against their own territory, and occupied important heights on the Soviet side of Lake Khasan, Blucher delegated Shtern to take command of the Red Army forces facing the enemy. Fully aware of the importance of the operation, Stalin sent Lazar Mekhlis, his Jewish deputy Commissar of Defence, to act as Shtern's supervisor. In August 1938 Shtern brilliantly routed the Japanese and was awarded the Order of the Red Banner and promoted to the rank of junior army commander.

Determined to wipe out the disgrace of their defeat, the Japanese crossed the Khalkhin Gol River in the summer of 1939 and invaded

Mongolian territory. Shtern was now Commander-in-Chief of the Soviet far eastern forces after Blucher's execution on Stalin's orders, in November 1938. Together with Corps Commander Grigory Zhukov as his second-in-command, he inflicted on the Japanese a decisive defeat of such dimensions that it was probably responsible for Japan's decision to remain neutral after Hitler's attack on the Soviet Union.[1] An important part in the battle was played by the Red Air Force led by Corps Commander Yakov Smushkevich, a Lithuanian Jew. As General Douglas he had commanded the Republican Air Force in Spain in 1936–7. His personal bravery and leadership in the battle of Guadalajara earned him the title of Hero of the Soviet Union. Shtern and Zhukov were made Heroes of the Soviet Union for their Khalkhin Gol victory. Smushkevich won the title a second time—an unprecedented occurrence at the time. Shtern died in mysterious circumstances in 1940 while commanding an army group in the Finnish campaign. Smushkevich, however, was appointed Commander-in-Chief of the Red Air Force in 1940 and promoted to the rank of lieutenant-general, when Stalin re-introduced general ranks and epaulettes, which for so long had been the very symbol of tsarist Russia.

Such, in brief, were the most important military achievements of Soviet Jewry from the October Revolution to the German attack on Russia. When war came, they made a contribution to ultimate victory that was 'great and important both quantitatively and qualitatively', to quote the Soviet-Jewish historian, Yakov Kantor.[2]

In order to ascertain the extent of Jewish participation in the Soviet armed forces, let us follow Kantor's deductions, for no official Soviet statistics have so far been published. According to the Soviet 1939 population census, the 3 million Soviet Jews came numerically after the Russians (99,619,900), the Ukrainians (26,670,400), the Byelorussians (5,267,400), the Uzbeks (4,844,000), the Tatars (4,300,000), and the Kazakhs (3,020,100). But almost a million Soviet Jews fell into the hands of the Nazis in the first six months of the war; thus there were in actual fact only 2 million Jews left to provide manpower for the Soviet armed forces. According to the same census, 63 per cent of all Soviet Jews were of working age in 1939. If we assume that 65 per cent of the 2 million Jews surviving outside the Nazi-occupied territories were also of working age, then the whole manpower reserve of Soviet Jewry a few months after the outbreak of war amounted to 1,300,000 men and women. Even

---

[1] G. N. Sevostoyanov, *Voyennoe i diplomaticheskoe porazhenie Yaponii v period sobytii u reki Khalkhin-Gol, Voprosy Istorii*, Moscow, August 1957; *IVOVSS*, vol. i.

[2] Y. Kantor, *Yidn oif dem grestn un vikhtikstn front, Folkshtimme*, Warsaw, 18 April 1963.

if half of this total figure were men, there were only 650,000 of them. Yet, from information gathered by the Jewish Anti-Fascist Committee and from documents in the Moscow Museum of the Soviet Army it is possible to conclude that almost half a million Jews served in the Soviet armed forces in the war against Nazi Germany. That many of them must have been volunteers is obvious.

No less impressive is their record in battle. Kantor has the names of 121 men and women who were awarded the highest Soviet military decoration, the title of Hero of the Soviet Union, but he is certain that the total must be even higher. With 121 holders of this decoration, the Jews ranked fifth as a nationality after the Russians, Ukrainians, Byelorussians, and Tatars, and ahead of the more numerous Uzbeks and Kazakhs.[1] As regards other military orders and medals, the Jews again ranked fifth after the Russians, Ukrainians, Byelorussians and Tatars. Moreover, an analysis of the total number of decorations earned by the major Soviet nationalities in relation to their size shows that the Jews had an even more impressive record. With 160,772 orders and medals or 5,369 per every 100,000 Jewish men, women and children, the Jews came fourth after the Russians, Ukrainians and Byelorussians, and ahead of the Tatars.

Impressive as these figures are, they still do not tell the whole story of Jewish valour. They certainly fail to reveal the special part played by Jews in some of the crucial operations of the war. Thus, according to Kantor, of a group of 900 Red Army officers and men awarded the title of Hero of the Soviet Union for the part they played in September 1943 in forcing the Dnieper and establishing bridgeheads on its western bank, 607 were Russians, 181 were Ukrainians, 27 were Jews, 9 were Tatars, 8 were Kazakhs, and 68 were members of the many other Soviet nationalities. In this operation Lieutenant-Colonel Serdyuk's Special Operations Brigade played a critical part. Major A. A. Bloishteyn, who commanded one of the battalions of Serdyuk's force, was awarded the title of Hero of the Soviet Union for his part in the battle. Another Jew, Sergeant Nahum Zheludov, the son of a Gomel artisan, crossed the Dnieper with his unit under enemy fire. He held out for seven days and nights on the western

---

[1] On 6 May 1965, for the first time since the 1940s, *Pravda* enumerated Jewish Heroes of the Soviet Union when describing the part played by the various Soviet nationalities in the victory over Nazi Germany. In an article headed '*Druzhba narodov S.S.S.R., a nasha velikaya pobeda*' (The Friendship of the Peoples of the U.S.S.R. and Our Great Victory), *Pravda* said: 'The titles of Heroes of the Soviet Union were earned by 7,998 Russians, 2,201 Ukrainians, 299 Byelorussians, 161 Tatars, 107 Jews, 96 Kazakhs, 90 Georgians, 89 Armenians, 67 Uzbeks, 63 Mordvinians, 45 Chuvashes. . . .' Kantor's figures were 8,124 Russians, 2,031 Ukrainians, 299 Byelorussians, 157 Tatars, 121 Jews, 96 Kazakhs, 91 Georgians, 81 Armenians, 68 Uzbeks.

bank before reinforcements could reach his bridgehead. He too was made a Hero of the Soviet Union.[1]

The contribution of Soviet Jews to their country's victory was particularly weighty because of the high proportion of officers among serving Jews. This was mostly due to the fact that the percentage of people with a secondary or university education was much higher among Jews than among other Soviet nationalities. No official data are available on the number of Jewish officers, but it is known that there were several hundred Jewish colonels and lieutenant-colonels. The number of Jewish generals amounted to some two hundred.[2]

[1] Y. Kantor, *Zey zainen der shtolts fun undzer folk*, Folkshtimme, Warsaw, 5 May 1965.

[2] The following list records, where available, the highest rank they reached during the war or since and the first name and patronymic:

Army General Lev Zakharovich Mekhlis.
Army General Yakov G. Kreyzer.
Colonel-General L. Z. Kotlyar.
Colonel-General Alexander Tsirlin.
Colonel-General Viktor Tovyevich Volsky.
Lieutenant-General I. S. Beskin, Hero of the Soviet Union.
Lieutenant-General Breydo.
Lieutenant-General Y. A. Chernikhovsky.
Lieutenant-General David Dragunsky, twice Hero of the Soviet Union.
Lieutenant-General Academician Boris Golyakov.
Lieutenant-General Academician Aaron Gershevitz Karpanosov.
Lieutenant-General Arkady Khasin.
Lieutenant-General Simon M. Krivoshein, Hero of the Soviet Union.
Lieutenant-General Yuri Abramovich Laskin.
Lieutenant-General Mikhail Lev.
Lieutenant-General G. B. Mekhlin.
Lieutenant-General Hirsh Davidovich Plaskov.
Lieutenant-General G. Presman.
Lieutenant-General S. S. Raikin.
Lieutenant-General A. B. Ravin.
Lieutenant-General M. A. Reyter.
Lieutenant-General Grigory Davidovich Stelmakh
Lieutenant-General Matvey G. Vainrub, Hero of the Soviet Union.
Major-General M. Belkin.
Major-General S. Berezinsky.
Major-General A. M. Botvinnik.
Major-General Y. M. Braun.
Major-General G. Davidzon.
Major-General Lev Mikhailovich Dovator.
Major-General A. Feyros.
Major-General Moisei Genzik.
Major-General Aaron Katz.
Major-General S. D. Kremer.
Major-General Alexander Kronik.
Major-General G. N. Levin.
Major-General Alexander Lipshitz.

Jewish generals and colonels played an impressive part as field commanders and especially as leaders of mechanized formations, as well as engineers and tank and artillery experts. General Reyter, for example, commanded the Bryansk Front Army Group for a time. Major-General Kreyzer commanded the 1st Moscow Motorized Rifle Division in the summer battles of 1941. Early in July he repelled units of Field-Marshal von Kluege's 4th Tank Army which had crossed the Berezina river near Borisov, and held up their advance for forty-eight hours. In the decisive battles for Moscow, Kreyzer led the 3rd Army. In December, he went over to the offensive against German forces endeavouring to encircle the Soviet capital from the south, and won an important victory at Yelets. In 1943, after the battle of Stalingrad, he commanded the 51st Army in the liberation of the Donets Basin. In April 1944 his 51st Army stormed the main German defence line across the Perekop isthmus and played a decisive part in the recapture of Sevastopol. A few months later Kreyzer's army, now part of the 1st Baltic Front Army Group, advanced into Lithuania and helped to block the Northern Group of Hitler's forces in Latvia and Estonia.[1]

Major-General Yuri Rabiner.
Major-General Rogochevsky.
Major-General Z. Rogozin.
Major-General Yosif Davidovich Rubinsky.
Major-General D. Shnaider.
Major-General A. Solovey.
Major-General V. A. Tseytlin.
Major-General Volkenshteyn.
Major-General D. Yoffe.

Red Air Force
Air Force Marshal Yakov Smushkevich, twice Hero of the Soviet Union.

Red Navy
Rear Admiral Pavel Treynin.
Rear Admiral Yuravsky.

Medical Services
Major-General Vovsy, Chief Therapeutics Officer of the Red Army.
Major-General Levit, Chief Surgeon of the Red Army.
Major-General Entin, Chief Stomatologist of the Red Army.
Major-General Reyngold, Deputy Chief of the Red Army Medical Services.
Major-General Gurvich, Chief Medical Officer of the Western Front Army Group.
Major-General Slavin, Chief Medical Officer of the Moscow Military Region.

Joseph B. Schechtman quotes an anonymous Jewish officer he met in Odessa who told him that between 1948 and 1953 a total of 63 Jewish generals, 111 colonels and 159 lieutenant-colonels were pensioned off. Joseph B. Schechtman: *Star in Eclipse*, New York, 1961, p. 53.
[1] *IVOVSS*, vol. ii, pp. 39, 281; vol. iii, p. 318; vol. iv, pp. 89, 191, 358.

Major-General Lev Mikhailovich Dovator, whose Cossack regiment was one of the main attractions of the peacetime military parades in Red Square, led his 2nd Guards Cavalry Corps on raids deep into the enemy's rear at a time when the fear of falling into a German 'bag' unnerved all too many Red Army commanders and men. He died commanding his corps in the first successful Soviet offensive following the German defeat at the approaches to Moscow.[1] Dovator was not the only Jew to command a Cossack force. Colonel Yefim Popov, despite his typical Russian name, was also a Jew; the Cossack regiment under his command struck terror into many a German heart.[2]

Plaskov, who received his first schooling in a Minsk *kheder* and *yeshivah*, ended the war as artillery commander of Colonel-General (now Marshal) Bogdanov's 2nd Guards Army, which stormed Berlin from the west.[3] Beskin was artillery commander of the 65th Army. On 10 January 1943 the 7,000 guns and mortars under his command opened the bombardment that led to the collapse of von Paulus's defences outside Stalingrad and to his ultimate surrender on 31 January.[4]

Krivoshein, the son of a Jewish watchmaker of Voronezh, began his military career in Budyonny's 1st Cavalry Army. In October 1936 he arrived in Spain with twenty-nine other Soviet tank officers and fifty tanks, and in the Guadalajara battle of March 1937 he and several other Soviet tank commanders, a number of them also Jews, did a great deal to arrest the advance of Franco's forces on Madrid. He commanded a mechanized corps at the outbreak of the Russo–German war and almost took Guderian prisoner in July 1941. His units destroyed the German tank commander's staff near the town of Propoisk and captured Guderian's motor-car containing his personal effects. In the final operations which led to the capture of Berlin, Krivoshein's corps formed part of Marshal Zhukov's 1st Byelorussian Front Army Group and was the first to break into the German capital.[5]

The highest ranking Jewish officer in the Red Air Force was Air Marshal Yakov Smushkevich. Born into a poor Jewish family in Lithuania, he earned his living as a porter until he joined the Red Army in 1918 at the age of sixteen. In the war against Germany he distinguished himself as

---

[1] *IVOVSS*, vol. ii, pp. 133, 260, 286, 291, 322. Pavel Fyodorov, *General Dovator*, Moscow, 1958.

[2] Y. Kantor, *Yidn oif dem grestn un vikhtikstn front*, Folkshtimme, 18 April 1963.

[3] Hirsh Plaskov, *Undzer alemens troim*, Sovietish Heymland, Moscow, May (no. 3), 1963.

[4] *IVOVSS*, vol. iii, p. 57.

[5] Shlomo Rabinovich, *Vegn dem General Shimon, dem zun fun Moishe dem zeygermakher*, Folkshtimme, Warsaw, 8 May 1965.

commander of the Red Air Force on the Leningrad front and elsewhere, but he fell foul of Stalin and disappeared before the end of the war. He was not rehabilitated until 1963—too late for the authors of the six-volume Soviet official history of the war to mention his name.

The number of Jews in the Red Air Force must have been high in relation to the total figure of Jews in the Soviet armed forces, if the number of Jewish aircrew who won the highest Soviet decoration for valour is any criterion. The Jewish recipients of the title of Hero of the Soviet Union also included several women: Polina Gelman, Zina Hofman, Lila Litvak, Rachel Zlotina. They belonged to an all-woman air regiment formed in 1941 by Hero of the Soviet Union Marina Raskina. The women flew small wooden P-2 aircraft as night bombers or carried supplies to isolated Red Army units, bridgeheads, and partisans in the enemy's rear. Nicknamed affectionately *Kukuruzniki* (maize-pickers) by the Red Army, the highly manœuvrable aircraft were feared by German infantry because of their low-level night raids with anti-personnel fragmentation bombs. Polina Gelman, the daughter of a poor Jewish family of Gomel, flew 860 bombing missions in these 'maize-pickers'.[1]

Amongst Jewish airmen, perhaps the best known holders of the title of Hero of the Soviet Union are Mikhail Plotkin and Genrikh Hofman. Captain Plotkin, the son of a Jewish cobbler in a Byelorussian townlet, was one of five air force officers awarded this decoration after successfully raiding Berlin on 7 August 1941. Plotkin's bomber stood for years in the Defenders of the Homeland Museum in Leningrad. It bore the description: 'This is the aircraft flown by Hero of the Soviet Union Mikhail Plotkin, who was the first Soviet airman to bomb Berlin as early as 1941.'[2] Hofman won his decoration for leading a squadron of Il-2 assault (*shturmovik*) bombers in 160 operations.[3]

The smallest number of Jews was found in the Red Navy. Even so, over 3,000 Jewish sailors and marines won decorations for valour, and three submarine commanders, Israel Fisanovich, Isaac Kaba, and Abraham Sverdlov, were awarded the title of Heroes of the Soviet Union.[4]

Yet it is in vain that one seeks the names of these and many other heroes in the six volumes of the *History of the Great Patriotic War of the Soviet Union 1941–1945*. The line followed by the authors of this monumental work has been to select men and women with good Slav

[1] M. D. Khayet, *Dos heldishe yidishe meydl Poline Gelman*, *Folks Shtime*, 21 July 1965.

[2] *IVOVSS*, vol. ii, p. 92; Pyotr Khokhlov, Hero of the Soviet Union: *Berlin zgaisil ognie, Czerwony Sztandar*, Vilnius, 30 April 1965.

[3] *Der ershter yidisher flier iber der grenets fun Dritn Reich, Folkshtimme*, 8 May 1965.

[4] Y. Kantor, *Zey zainen der shtolts fun undzer folk, Folkshtimme*, 6 May 1965.

names as examples of individual heroism. All other nationalities have suffered accordingly, the Jews perhaps a little more than others. But in fairness to the authors it must be said that they have included the names of four Jews: Yefim Moiseyevich Fomin, Arseny Moiseyevich Rasskin, Matvey Vainrub, and Caesar Lvovich Kunikov.[1]

Lieutenant-Colonel Vainrub, as he then was, took a sufficiently prominent part in the defence of Stalingrad to be mentioned several times by Marshal Chuikov in his memoirs and in A. M. Samsonov's *Stalingradskaya Bitva* (The Stalingrad Battle), the standard history of the operation. Chuikov appointed Vainrub commander of the virtually non-existent armoured forces of his 62nd Army after dismissing Vainrub's superior, Colonel Volkonsky. In September 1942 Vainrub and his few tanks stopped the Germans in their drive towards the Volga in the area of the central ferry landing stage. This allowed Rodimtsev's division to reinforce the decimated defenders of the city. In October he again thwarted von Paulus's final blow at the Red October Works. Later that month the intervention of his three tanks and fifty riflemen arrested the German advance between the Barricade Works and the Red October Works 400 yards short of the Volga.[2]

After the Stalingrad victory, Chuikov's 62nd Army was re-named the 8th Guards Army to mark its character as an élite force. Vainrub, now a major-general, commanded its armour in the reconquest of the Donets coalfields, the storming of Zaporozhe and the liberation of Odessa. In July 1944 the 8th Guards Army, reinforced by the 1st Polish Army, overcame the German defences on the river Bug and reached the Vistula. Vainrub's tanks led the advance of Chuikov's forces, which covered 160 miles in twelve days.

When the next Soviet offensive opened on 14 January 1945, Chuikov's army again led the advance along the shortest route to Berlin. Vainrub was wounded whilst leading his tanks in the capture of Lodz—for the third time since the outbreak of war—but he again commanded Chuikov's armour in the next and final offensive on Berlin. In its opening phase he was wounded a fourth time outside the fortress of Küstrin on the Oder.[3]

The most legendary of the four Jewish commanders is Major Caesar Lvovich Kunikov. The official Soviet history of the war, which often deals with operations involving whole armies in a few lines, devotes three

[1] Belated recognition of Jewish heroism was made in the sixth volume published in 1965 (pp. 155, 158).

[2] Marshal Sovetskovo Soyuza V. I. Chuikov, *Nachalo Puti*, Moscow, 1959; A. M. Samsonov, *Stalingradskaya Bitva*, Moscow, 1960.

[3] Marshal Sovetskovo Soyuza V. I. Chuikov, *Konets Tretevo Reicha*, Moscow, 1964.

pages in volume III to Kunikov and his bridgehead at Malaya Zemlya.

To cut off the retreat of the German and Rumanian forces from the North Caucasus to the Crimea, the Soviet High Command determined to capture Novorossiysk by landing troops from the sea. The operation took place in the night of 4 February 1943. The main assault force of 1,500 men and sixteen tanks landed at Yuzhnaya Ozereyka, but was thrown back. A supporting force of 800 men commanded by Kunikov was landed at the same time south of the fishing village of Stanichka, a suburb of Novorossiysk. By daylight it had established a bridgehead two and a half miles wide and a mile and a half deep. It resisted repeated German assaults for seven months. Kunikov was wounded whilst commanding his bridgehead and died after being evacuated to a field hospital. He was made a Hero of the Soviet Union and Stanichka was renamed Kunikovo at the request of its inhabitants.

No history of the military record of Soviet Jewry in the war against Nazi Germany can be complete without noting the contribution made by Jews to Soviet partisan warfare. According to the official Soviet history of the war, the total number of Soviet partisans was about 860,000.[1] It is, of course, not known what percentage of this total figure were Jews, but a conservative estimate of the number of Jews who fought in the second half of 1943 in Soviet, Polish, and independent Jewish partisan detachments operating in the Polish–Soviet borderlands is some 20,000. Naturally, it is impossible to state how many were Soviet Jews and how many were Polish.[2] As only some 250,000 Jews remained alive in this vast area in 1943, the percentage of Jewish partisans was very high indeed. Their numbers would have been much higher had Soviet partisan warfare in 1942 been as extensive as it later became in 1943. A year earlier, many more Jews had still been alive in the ghettos and labour camps of Byelorussia, the Ukraine, Lithuania, and Latvia.

But numbers are not everything. The contribution of Jews to the spread of partisan warfare was often of a pioneer nature. In many units they formed an iron core of fighters, from whom brigades and even divisions later emerged. It is sufficient to read the memoirs of such Soviet partisan commanders as G. M. Linkov, P. Vershigora, A. F. Fyodorov, or the Pole Jozef Sobiesiak to perceive that Soviet and Polish Jews participated in

[1] This total was made up as follows: occupied areas of the Russian Federation over 260,000 partisans; the Ukraine, 220,000; Byelorussia, 374,000; Lithuania, 5,000; Latvia, 4,940; and Estonia, 1,500.

[2] There were also Jews of other nationalities. Thus Major-General Andreyev reported to the Jewish Anti-Fascist Committee that in his unit there was a detachment of forty Hungarian Jews (Y. Kantor, *Yidishe Partizaner*, *Folkshtimme*, 8 May 1965).

most partisan units and took distinguished roles as fighters, scouts, and leaders.[1] Even the authors of the official Soviet history of the war, to whom Jews simply do not exist as a nationality, cannot avoid mentioning Jewish names when dealing with the spread of partisan activities. Thus in volume II we read that on 20 December 1941, when the Red Army liberated Volokolamsk, after pushing the Germans back from the approaches to Moscow, the first Soviet soldiers to enter the town found in the central square seven youths and one girl hanging from gallows. They were a group of Moscow Komsomols on a special mission behind the German lines, and had fallen into an enemy ambush. One of them was called N. S. Kagan. And in volume IV we twice find the name of L. E. Berenshteyn, commander of the Pozharsky unit, which he led from Byelorussia across southern Poland into Slovakia to help the Slovaks who had risen against the Germans. But perhaps the spirit of the Soviet-Jewish partisans is best epitomized in the person of Vladimir Epshteyn, a Red Army man, who together with Alexander Sharov of Krasnodar and Dmitry Volkov of Zaporozhe escaped from Auschwitz on 7 June 1944, marched east for twenty-four nights, and then formed a 70-man partisan detachment of Russians, Ukrainians, Poles, and Jews, called the People's Avenger. Under Epshteyn's command the detachment fought in Poland until 15 January 1945, when the Red Army reached its area. Among the trophies presented by Epshteyn to the Red Army command were the paybooks of 120 dead S.S. men.[2]

In the middle of August 1941 Henryk Erlich and Wiktor Alter, the Polish Bund leaders who had sought refuge in Soviet territory, were sentenced to death by a Soviet court. They were accused of 'sabotage activities directed against the Soviet Union'. The death penalty was, however, commuted to ten years in a labour camp, so that the two men were able to benefit from the Polish–Soviet Treaty signed on 30 July 1941 in London. They were released with a group of Polish politicians, intellectuals, and officers, brought to Moscow and installed in the Metropole Hotel. Some days later they were visited by Colonel Arkady Volkovysky, one of Beria's close subordinates and a Jew if his name is any indication. He asked the two social democratic leaders to forget their imprisonment and death sentences and to help the Soviet Union in the common fight

---

[1] G. M. Linkov, *Voina v tylu vraga*, Moscow, 1947; P. Vershigora, *Lyudi s chistoi sovestyu*, Moscow, 1946; A. F. Fyodorov, *Podpolny obkom deistvuet*, Moscow, 1947; Jozef Sobiesiak, *Ziemia plonie*, and *Burzany*, Warsaw, 1963 and 1964: *Sefer ha-Partizaniam ha-Yehudim*, 2 vols., Jerusalem, 1958.

[2] *Bohaterowie zywej legendy. Czerwony Sztandar*, Vilnius, 28 January 1966.

against Nazi Germany. It was the view of the Soviet Government, Volkovysky told them, that the Jews abroad, especially those in the neutral United States, could make a great contribution to the Soviet war effort. For this purpose a Jewish World Committee should be formed, to be headed by Erlich and Alter.

The two men accepted Volkovysky's proposals and a few days later presented him with a list of Jewish personalities who, they thought, should be appointed to the Committee. Thereupon they were invited to meet Beria, who received them warmly, expressed his agreement with their proposals, and asked them to write to Stalin and explain the aims and functions of the proposed Jewish World Committee. That same day the two Bund leaders wrote to Stalin. There was no immediate answer. In October they were evacuated to Kuibyshev, where another representative of Beria, by the name of Khazanovich, visited them on several occasions to discuss details of the projected Committee. But in December they were suddenly arrested and shot at Stalin's personal order. He had, in the meantime, read their letter, and remembered them as two Menshevik leaders who had opposed the Bolshevik Revolution in 1917. He had determined their fate while the outcome of the Moscow battle was still uncertain. [1]

The execution of Erlich and Alter did not lead Stalin and Beria to abandon the project of a Jewish agency able to influence Jews in the United States and Britain in favour of the Soviet Union. However, instead of the Jewish World Committee, a Jewish Anti-Fascist Committee was officially established on 6 April 1942, with Solomon Mikhoels as its chairman. After a conference attended by delegates said to represent the entire Jewish population of the Soviet Union, the Committee held its first plenary meeting and began to publish *Aynikayt*.

At home, the Committee concentrated its efforts on mobilizing and inspiring Soviet Jews in the war against Nazi Germany. Abroad, the Committee used the example of Soviet Jewry's heroism and self-sacrifice to demand from American, British, and other Jews a similar readiness to fight and die in the common war against Hitler's New Order. Soon after its creation, Solomon Mikhoels and Itzik Fefer travelled to Britain and the United States, where they were instrumental in helping to collect millions of pounds' worth of aid for the Red Army and Soviet civilians.

The very existence of the Jewish Anti-Fascist Committee was the most important concession made by the Kremlin to Soviet Jewry. For here was a body that represented all Soviet Jews, irrespective of their political and religious beliefs. Under the tsars, Russian Jewry had never been allowed

[1] Léon Lénéman, *La tragédie des Juifs en U.R.S.S.*, Paris, 1959, p. 108.

to possess a central organization of this type, though it had almost been achieved in the form of the Central Committee of Russian Kehillot between July 1918 and April 1919, when it was dissolved at the joint instigation of Stalin, then People's Commissar for Nationalities, and Samuel Agursky of the Jewish Commissariat (Yevkom). Moreover, as the war progressed and victory became certain, the Committee gradually ceased to be predominantly an instrument of the Kremlin's policies and became a body endeavouring to deal with the specific problems of war-time Soviet Jewry, including manifestations of antisemitism, and the future of Soviet Jewry in the post-war period.

In the three years of its post-war existence, the Jewish Anti-Fascist Committee played a unique part in restoring and encouraging Jewish cultural life. Furthermore, whenever and wherever it was possible, it helped Jewish survivors and evacuees returning to their native towns and townlets to deal with their appalling human problems. But it soon became clear to the leaders of the Committee that in order to survive in the cold war atmosphere, it must justify its existence to the Kremlin by becoming a rallying point for left-wing Jews all over the world. Fefer therefore proposed that a world Jewish conference be convened to discuss the need for a continued fight against fascism and world-wide measures against antisemitism, and to deal with the problem of Palestine. Only a few weeks before the suppression of the Jewish Anti-Fascist Committee, he wrote in *Aynikayt* that the State of Israel was not the concern of Zionists alone, but of the 'entire Jewish people'. He thus claimed for Soviet Jewry a part in the shaping of the future character of Israel.[1] But for proclaiming the existence of a world-wide Jewish people as late as the autumn of 1948, Fefer was to forfeit his life in August 1952.

By then, Stalin had made up his mind as to the utility of the Jewish Anti-Fascist Committee. To himself and the Russian leaders in the Krem-lin its very existence had all along been an anomaly that only wartime exigencies could justify. Moreover, even before the establishment of Israel it became clear to him and other Soviet leaders that the share of the Committee in influencing Jews outside the Soviet Union was very small. Contrary to the slogans and propaganda of the Jewish Anti-Fascist Com-mittee and local Jewish communists, the surviving Jews of Poland and other East European countries refused to trust the new socialist order and fled west. Most of them were determined to live in Israel. Furthermore, the proclamation of a Jewish state in Israel signified that Jewish commu-nists in the Soviet Union could no longer hope to provide an alternative

[1] Goldberg, op. cit., p. 99.

territorial solution, which in the 1920s and 1930s had exerted such an influence on left-wing Jews in Europe and the Americas. Any further proof needed to convince Stalin that the Committee had outlived its usefulness was provided by the unprecedented mass demonstration of Jews outside the central Moscow synagogue on 16 October 1948, to welcome Mrs. Golda Meyerson, Israel's first ambassador to the Soviet Union.

The full extent of the losses suffered by Soviet Jewry in the war against Nazi Germany are still unknown. Gerald Reitlinger in his *The Final Solution* estimated the number of Soviet Jews murdered by the Germans at 700,000 to 750,000, and included in this figure the massacred Jews of Lithuania, Latvia, and Estonia. The Anglo-American Committee's report, on the other hand, estimated the losses at 1,050,000. Joseph Schechtman, writing at the end of 1943, calculated the number of Soviet Jews who had fallen into Nazi hands at between 650,000 and 850,000. An estimate made by Yakov Kantor throws more light on the problem, but does not settle it.[1]

After analysing the data provided by the Soviet 1959 population census, Kantor drew the following conclusions: the total Jewish population of the U.S.S.R. as revealed by the 1959 census was 2,268,000, whereas the 1939 census gave a total of 3,020,000. Hence there was an apparent decrease of 752,000 between 1939 and 1959. But the 1939 census dealt with the Jewish population as it was before the incorporation of western Byelorussia, the western Ukraine, Moldavia, and the three Baltic states in the Soviet Union. 'According to a number of calculations, the Jewish population of these territories amounted to 800,000 on 1 January 1940', Kantor tells us and concludes:

That means that the actual decrease of the Jewish population amounted not to 752,000 but to 1,552,000 souls. But that is not all. If we wish to ascertain the real decrease of the Jewish population during the same period, we must also take into account the natural rate of increase during the years 1939–59 . . . Assuming that the natural increase of the Jewish population had followed the general trend of the Soviet population, the rise during the 20 years should have been about 6·6 per cent. In other words, the Jewish population should have risen by 150,000. It therefore follows that the real decrease of the Jewish population during the 1939–59 period (1,552,000 plus 150,000) is of the order of some 1,700,000 people. In other words, if the Jewish population had suffered from the war to the same extent as the rest of the population, it would have numbered about 4,000,000 souls on 15 January 1959. But there were only 2,268,000 Jews on that date. Consequently,

[1] Y. Kantor, *Certain Remarks and Conclusions Concerning the Published Results of the Nationwide Census Carried Out in the Soviet Union on 15 January 1959* (in Yiddish). *Bleter far Geshikhte*, Warsaw, xvi, 1964.

some 1,700,000 are missing. . . . If we deduct from this figure of 1,700,000 missing Jews those Jews who denied their origins during the 1959 census (children of mixed marriages and Jews who declared themselves as non-Jews), as well as a certain number of Jews awaiting repatriation to Poland but still in the Soviet Union at the time of the census, we reach a figure of 1,500,000–1,600,000 Jews murdered by the Nazis. More detailed figures cannot, unfortunately, be obtained, for nobody is engaged in compiling these statistics.

Unfortunately, even Kantor's approximate figure of murdered Jews within the 1941 frontiers of the Soviet Union cannot be accepted. For it is calculated on the assumption that there were only 800,000 Jews in the annexed territories. However, there were at least 1,300,000 Polish Jews in western Byelorussia and the western Ukraine alone, and another 600,000 lived in Moldavia, Lithuania, Latvia, and Estonia. There was also a large number of Jewish refugees from the occupied part of Poland, who swelled the Jewish population of western Byelorussia, the Wilno area, and the western Ukraine. I, personally, am therefore inclined to accept the figure of over a million given in the Anglo-American Committee's report; and even this figure, I believe, is too small to include those Soviet Jews who lost their lives in the ranks of the Red Army.

The effect of the physical losses and spiritual experiences undergone during the war was not, of course, to make all Soviet Jews see the world with the same eyes. It was to make them shed a number of illusions about their Jewish fate in a communist Russia—illusions which only the religious and the Zionists in their midst had not shared. The poetess Margarita Aliger gave public expression to the reawakening of Jewish awareness in Russified Jews when she made her mother tell her sternly, in a poem published in 1946: 'We are Jews. How dare you forget?' And even in Ehrenburg's memoirs we find several admissions that he was not justified in his facile optimism and faith in the ability of communism to eradicate the heritage of centuries of antisemitism in a few decades. As for the mass of Soviet Jews, whether religious or atheist, Russian-speaking or Yiddish-speaking, their reactions were expressed by an anonymous poet, who answered Margarita Aliger's pathetic questions: 'Mama, Mama . . . who is after us? Who are we, you and I?'

The anonymous poet replied:

> Our only crime is that we are Jews.
> Our crime is also that our children
> Strive to achieve the wisdom of the world,
> And that we are scattered over the earth
> And have no homeland.

Did not thousands of us, unsparing of our lives,
Fight battles worthy to become a legend
Only to be told: 'Where were the Jews?
They fought their battles in Tashkent!'

We are not loved because we are Jews,
Because our faith is the source of many faiths.
And yet despite it all—yes, despite it all—
We shall live on, Comrade Poetess!

Our people is immortal. It will bring forth
New Maccabees, who will inspire future heirs.
Yes, I am proud. I am proud and unwilling to forget
That I am a Jew, Comrade Poetess!

SELECTED BIBLIOGRAPHY

(In addition to the references in the footnotes)

Kantor, Yakov, *Natsionalnoe stroitelstvo sredi yevreyev*, Moscow, 1934.
Zinger, L. K., *Yevrei proletarii v S.S.S.R.*, Moscow, 1933.
Zinger L. K., *Dos banaite folk*, Moscow, 1941.
Zinger L. K., *Dos oifgekumene folk*, Moscow, 1949.
Dos yidishe folk in kamf kegn fashizm, Moscow, 1945.
Lénéman, Léon, *La tragédie des Juifs en U.R.S.S.*, Paris, 1959.
Schwarz, Solomon, *The Jews in the Soviet Union*, New York, 1951.
Schechtman, Joseph B., *Star in Eclipse*, New York, 1961.
Goldman, Guido G., *Zionism under Soviet Rule*, New York, 1960.
West, Benjamin, *Struggles of a Generation*, Tel Aviv, 1959.

14

Antisemitism in Soviet Russia

BERNARD D. WEINRYB

Definitions, Manifestations, and Forms

The term antisemitism was apparently coined by Wilhelm Marr in Germany about 1879 or earlier. It was meant to denote the racial character of 'Jew-hatred'.[1] The concept was an offshoot of the developing race theories, mainly in the middle of the nineteenth century with the emergence of Count Gobineau's ideas on the superior 'Aryan' race (to which the Germans were considered most closely related) and with the spreading practice of differentiating between Aryan (Indo-Germanic) and Semitic (Oriental) languages.[2] The term antisemitism was intended to emphasize the biologically inferior status of the Jewish race. This concept further developed after the end of the nineteenth century (influenced in part by H. S. Chamberlain's *The Foundations of the Nineteenth Century*, 1898).

But this concept of antisemitism did not remain limited to the above meaning or time: it came to denote 'Jew-hatred' generally and throughout all ages[3] (though there are writers who oppose its use for the period prior to the 1870s). As such, antisemitism had a long history over centuries and millennia of dissemination through many lands always incorporating new appeals to the particular prejudices of the given age. Thus its meaning changes from country to country and epoch to epoch. Again, the import of the concept is to some extent determined also by the ideology and attitude (as well as environment) of the individual using the term. Thus, in a country in which only mild forms prevail, such as 'polite' social exclusion or antilocution (the tendency to use unfavourable terms to characterize Jews), these will be regarded as the embodiment of antisemitism, whereas

[1] Alex Bein, 'Modern Anti-Semitism and its place in the History of the Jewish Question', *Between East and West* (ed. A. Altman), London, 1958, pp. 164–5ff. Other writers have suggested Wilhelm Scherer or Ernest Renan as coiners of the term.

[2] Count Gobineau, *Essai Sur l'Inégalité des Races Humaines*, Paris, 1853–5; Ernest Renan, *Histoire Générale et Système Comparé des Langues semitiques*, Paris, 1855; Marr, in his book of 1873 (*The Victory of Judaism over Germanism*) occasionally uses 'Semitism' to denote 'Judaism'.

[3] See also B. Netanyahu in *Haentsiklopedia Haivrit* (*The Hebrew Encyclopaedia*), vol. iv, 1954, p. 493.

in countries in which large-scale persecutions and pogroms are the rule, the covert forms may tend to be overlooked.[1]

Antisemitism may also mean different things to different people. 'It often appears to be profitable to identify antisemitism with one of its manifestations which happens not to occur in the country of which one is speaking. It then becomes easy to dismiss the other forms as not anti-semitic.' To this one should add the selective character of human perception.

'Gentiles usually insist there is much less antisemitism than the Jews claim. . . . Jews insist there is much more than the Gentiles admit.' And Jews themselves do both: 'disclaim . . . a clear case of antisemitism' as such or characterize cases which have little or nothing to do with it as antisemitic in order to explain [them] as prejudiced.[2]

The same or similar beliefs and facts may at one time be regarded as antisemitic and at another time not. For instance, in connection with beliefs about Jews it has recently been pointed out that only those which 'provide a reasonable basis for negative sentiments and perhaps hostile actions towards Jews' could be classified as antisemitic. And more or less the same criterion applies to facts. The closing of synagogues, and other actions taken against Jewish religion during the first two decades of Soviet rule are, for the most part, considered to be a part of the general anti-religious policy of the country or are attributed to the Yevsektsia (Jewish Section of the communist party) and not usually classified as anti-semitic.[3] On the other hand, similar action taken during the last two decades in Russia is often deemed antisemitic (outside the U.S.S.R.).

Hence the multiplicity of definitions becomes understandable, some of

---

[1] In the Polish-Yiddish bi-weekly *Folkshtimme* (5 February 1964), the definitions of anti-semitism in a western European dictionary are compared with one in the Polish *Mala Encyclopedia* of 1959. In the former antisemitism is defined as 'opposition to Jewish influence in politics' and in the Polish *Encyclopedia* as 'enmity of Jews, persecution, denying them full equality . . . manifests itself during various epochs since antiquity . . . persecution of Jews is generally connected with religious, racial, national, political, and social discrimination against various suppressed classes and peoples . . . it is not only an anti-Jewish movement but a movement against freedom, an anti-progressive, anti-democratic and anti-socialist movement, this being its main essence.'

The writer of the foregoing tries to prove that the west, despite the extermination of millions of Jews by the Nazis, takes antisemitism lightly as an opposition to Jewish political influence only, whereas it is defined in Poland in more concrete and acute terms.

[2] P. Bernstein, *Jew-Hate as a Sociological Problem*, New York, 1951, pp. 3, 26, 35, 39–40; M. Tumin, *An Inventory and Appraisal of Research on American Anti-Semitism*, New York, 1961, p. 2.

[3] C. Glock and R. Stark, *Christian Beliefs and Anti-Semitism*, New York and London, 1966, pp. 107–9; S. Dubnow, *Divrei Yemei Am Olam* (Hebrew), xi, Tel Aviv, 1940, pp. 45–7; J. Lestchinsky, *Dos Sovetische Identum* (Yiddish), New York, 1941, *passim*.

them contradict and others supplement each other. One author may even be offering many varied definitions of antisemitism.[1]

List of Definitions of Antisemitism[2]

1. The classic prejudice.
2. Anti-Jewish prejudice, feeling of suspicion, contempt and hatred towards Jews.
3. Group enmity.
4. Ethnic discrimination and aggression.
5. A form of social intolerance.
6. Any expression of hostility, verbal or behavioural, mild or violent, against the Jews as a group or against an individual Jew, because of his belonging to this group.
7. Expression of hostility towards Jews felt by a government or subjects of a state.
8. An inevitable effect of Jewish existence in the Diaspora (Zionist and, in part, Jewish orthodox view).
9. Above all else a political technique.
10. Religious fanaticism (Heinrich Coudenhove-Kalergi).
11. Essentially a Christophobia (Jacques Maritain).
12. A symptom of xenophobia.

[1] Scapegoating; group hostility to the Jews; prejudice, an individual evil; an example of a general human weakness; projection of unpleasant attitudes; displacement of a pent-up emotion on to a different object from the original target; 'racialism' and 'modern antisemitism is a by-product of the vast electorates created by nineteenth-century democracy'. (J. Parkes, *Antisemitism*, Chicago, 1963, pp. xi, xii, 10–12, 88.)

[2] Sources: no. 1, G. E. Simpson and J. M. Yinger, *Racial and Cultural Minorities: An Analysis of Prejudice and Discrimination*, New York, 1958, p. 288. However, Ackerman and Jahoda, *Anti-Semitism and Emotional Disorder*, New York, 1950, distinguish between dislike of Jews as a prejudice and antisemitism as an emotional disorder; no. 2, Jules Isaac, *The Teaching of Contempt*, New York, 1964, p. 21; no. 3, Bernstein, p. 44; no. 5, Oliver C. Cox, 'Race Prejudice and Intolerance', *Social Forces*, vol. 24, no. 2 (1945), pp. 216–19; nos. 10, 27, H. Valentine, *Antisemitism Historically and Critically Examined*, New York, 1936, pp. 13, 111; nos. 11, 15, 16, 17, 18, 29, 30, quoted N. Zuckerman, *The Wine of Violence: An Anthology on Antisemitism*, New York, 1947, pp. 4, 12, 14, 15, 17, 53; no. 12, P. Pulzer, *The Rise of Political Antisemitism in Germany and Austria*, New York, 1964, p. 61; no. 13, M. R. Cohen, *A Dreamer's Journey*, 1949, p. 246; no. 14, Talcott Parsons in Graber and Britt, *Jews in a Gentile World*, New York, 1942, p. 114; no. 20, Gustav Ichheiser, 'The Jews and Anti-Semitism', *Sociometry*, ix, 1, February 1946, pp. 92–108; no. 21, T. Adorno and others, *The Authoritarian Personality*, New York, 1950, pp. 604, 627; no. 22, Bruno Bettelheim, 'Dynamism of Anti-Semitism in Gentile and Jew', *Journal of Abnormal and Social Psychology*, vol. 42, April 1947, pp. 153–68; nos. 23–4, E. Simmel (ed.), *Anti-Semitism a Social Disease*, New York, 1946, pp. 20, 25, 34; nos. 25, 28, K. Pinson (ed.), *Essays on Anti-semitism*, 2nd edn., New York, 1946, pp. 40, 49, 61; no. 26, Albert Einstein, 'Why do they Hate the Jews?' *Colliers*, vol. 102, 26 November 1936, pp. 3–10, 38. *Der Grosse Brockhaus* additional volume (1935) lists under A. the '25 points' of the Nazi programme concerning Jews.

13. Expression of generalized xenophobia.
14. Manifestation of social disorganization.
15. Individual and group neurosis (I. S. Wechsler).
16. A psychic aberration; a form of demonopathy (Leo Pinsker).
17. Symptom of a widespread social disease (Karl Menninger).
18. A search for a scapegoat (Nicholas A. Berdyaev).
19. An emotional disorder based on unconscious hostilities.
20. A typical form of socio-psychological irritation.
21. A symptom resulting from a conflict (part of a syndrome of ethno-centrism).
22. A psychological defence against dangers originating either in the person or in the outside world.
23. A malignant growth on the body of civilization.
24. A form of regression . . . mass psychosis.
25. An atavistic malady, a reversion to primitive, emotional ways of thinking and acting.
26. A diversion which enables a small group to retain power over the mass of the people.
27. Means of diverting the fury of the impoverished classes from their real enemies (Marxists).
28. Belief that Jews are a pernicious influence in . . . modern life and hence must be effectively removed.
29. An extreme form of race chauvinism . . . most dangerous survival of cannibalism (Stalin).
30. Attempt to divert the hatred of the workers and peasants for the exploiters towards the Jews (Lenin).

Dictionaries and encyclopaedias, too, are somewhat ambivalent, and offer a variety of definitions. These include: 'Prejudice against Jews, dislike or fear of Jews and Jewish things. Discrimination against or persecution of Jews'; 'Anti-Judaism . . . social and political agitation, sentiments, acts directed against the Jews'; 'hostile expressions and actions against the Jews'; 'hostile opinions and actions against Jews and Judaism'; 'movement to degrade Jews to an inferior position' . . . 'term applied generally to incitement . . . and action aiming to circumscribe the civil, religious and political rights of the Jews. . . .'[1]
If the definitions vary so widely so, too, do the formulations of which

---

[1] *Webster's International Dictionary*; *The Encyclopaedia of the Social Sciences*; *Encyclopaedia Britannica*, vol. 2, 1963; *Encyclopaedia Judaica*, vol. 2, 1928; *The Universal Jewish Encyclopaedia*, vol. 1, 1941.

manifestations and forms should be considered antisemitic. Here, too, the divergencies may be virtually contradictory. One writer may find that manifestations of 'a political policy . . . [involving] the imposition of civil and juridical disabilities on Jews as individuals and sometimes the physical persecution of individual Jews'[1] are to be classified as antisemitism. Another may go so far as to state: 'those who do not advocate educating people to live and to respect the right of others to live in free competition with each other are . . . *ipso facto* Nazis, guilty not only of *de facto* anti-semitism . . .'.[2]

Between these the literature mentions such features as: 'aversion to Jewish religion', 'antisemitic utterances', 'verbal expression of hostility', being 'mild or more overt', 'repressed or outspoken', intolerance, rejection, defamation, antipathy, aversion, 'ideational aggression', denigration of Jews or accusations of various, often contradictory, traits (backwardness and fostering revolution; clannishness and easy assimilation, poverty and wealth; also materialism, abstractness, conspiracy, unproductiveness, dishonesty, etc., etc.); stereotyping, social exclusion, restrictions.

On the other hand, more violent forms are also depicted: exclusion from citizenship, discrimination, aggression, persecution, physical attacks, pogroms and during the last quarter of the century also extermination ('exterminatory antisemitism').

In fact, most studies of antisemitism—the long articles on the subject in the various encyclopaedias (the *Encyclopaedia Judaica* article, for instance, contains 148 columns), and some general and specific books—usually survey many facets of Jewish trials and tribulations or general historical events in the Jewish groups in many countries throughout the ages, ranging from real and imagined slights to serious discrimination and pogroms. These numerous contrasting features and varied views and

[1] Stephen P. Dunn, 'Letter to the Editor', *The Slavic Review*, xxvi, no. 1, 1967, p. 155. Dr. Dunn's emphasis on 'individuals' ('civil disabilities of individuals' and 'persecution of individuals') is a mistaken approach. German and Austrian antisemitism have been racial in character since the 1870s. The Russian pogroms of the 1880s and 1890s and 1905–6 were not organized against specific Jewish individuals any more than the introduction of the quota system in the schools in 1887 was intended to exclude specific Jewish individuals. The cry 'Death to the Jews' which swept France at the time of the Dreyfus Affair was not turned against Dreyfus alone. All of these were aimed at the Jewish group (incidentally, following the mentioned approach of 'individualism' one could 'logically' maintain that Negroes in the U.S. never suffered from racialism, segregation, or civil disabilities since these concerned only certain individuals).

[2] A private letter from X, Rotterdam, Netherlands (15 January 1967). See also the classifications of Glock and Stark (pp. 103ff.) into three components: beliefs, feelings, actions. But these authors deal solely with responses to questionnaires in the U.S.A. where hypothetical actions and even feelings have to be gauged from verbal answers.

definitions might be categorized into ten main forms of antisemitism (as seen in the west) as follows:[1]

1. Anti-Jewish beliefs, attitudes and sentiments.
2. Defamation of Jews and things Jewish.
3. Personal withdrawal from and resentment of members of the Jewish group (avoidance).
4. Denunciation in speech or writing of Jewish religion, culture, traditions and attitudes as being inimical to a nation's welfare.
5. Opposition by word and deed to the equal participation of Jewish people in the social and legal rights which a nation affords its people generally.
6. Exclusion from citizenship; economic boycotts.
7. Political antisemitism (as part of a broader political ideology or policy).
8. Persecution.
9. Physical attacks, pogroms.
10. Exterminatory antisemitism.

It should be added that each and every one of these is regarded as antisemitism 'when it is assumed that the Jewishness of the victim influences the enmity'. At the same time, as Bernstein remarks, 'it became common to qualify every and any unfriendly act toward Jews as antisemitic.'[2]

Russia

No matter how ambiguous the attitude of socialists towards antisemitism may have been in nineteenth-century Europe, by the beginning of the twentieth century, it had become definitely negative. The two groups into which the Russian Social Democrats split at the second conference in 1903 (Bolsheviks and Mensheviks) both vigorously condemned tsarist anti-Jewish policies and the pogroms (Kishinev, Gomel and others) and to some extent called upon the workers to defend the Jews.[3]

The negative approach to antisemitism became still stronger after the October Revolution of 1917 and during the civil war when the various anti-Soviet forces used the Jewish angle to discredit communism. By identifying communism with 'Jewish rulers' these groups attempted both to debase communism and to encourage large-scale pogroms in cities and villages.

---

[1] This categorization utilized the definitions of Henry Pratt Fairchild's *Dictionary of Sociology* (1957) and Gordon W. Alport's 'five types of rejective behaviour' or prejudice.

[2] Bernstein, pp. 42, 33.

[3] *Iskra*, 1903, nos. 39. 50, 54; ibid., no. 49, G. Plekhanov, 1904, nos. 64, 67; *Komercheskaya Rossia* (Odessa), 4 November 1905 (quoted), Y. Maor, *The Jewish Question in the Liberal and Revolutionary Movement in Russia* (Hebrew), Jerusalem, 1964, pp. 154–65.

The communist government could not help noting the connection between antisemitism and counter-revolution, and gave similar treatment to both at least for a time. The Council of People's Commissars (i.e. Soviet Government) issued a decree on 27 July 1918 which pointed out that

the antisemitic movement and anti-Jewish pogroms are fatal to the cause of the workers' and peasants' revolution ... and directs all Sovdeps [soviets of workers', peasants' and soldiers' delegates] to take such steps as will effectively destroy the antisemitic movement at its roots. It is herewith ordered that pogromists and persons inciting to pogroms be outlawed.

In one of Lenin's speeches that same year, of which phonograph records were made and used for propaganda against antisemitism, the latter is defined as 'spreading hostility toward Jews', and is characterized as a diversionary tactic of capitalists and landlords in Russia and abroad to divide the workers and divert their ire away from the real enemy, capitalism.[1]

In the decree of the Council of Commissars antisemitism is again characterized as the method of the tsar and the counter-revolutionaries 'to divert national wrath upon the Jews'. Lenin also expressed this idea in other ways.

The Soviet Russian encyclopaedias define antisemitism as follows:

Hostile attitude towards Jews ... A social-economic phenomenon whose content changes from one epoch to another. It arose as a result of competition in the market. At the same time it became an instrument of government policies. Intolerance serves as a cover-up in the struggle against Jewish competitors. Lack of rights made the Jews an object for exploitation, while pogroms became a favoured means of antisemitic policy.[2]

A quarter of a century later (after the Nazi defeat), the chauvinistic racial nature of antisemitism is emphasized:

One of the extreme forms of racial chauvinism, emerging from the class exploitation system, finding expression in hostile attitudes towards Jews, spreading hostility towards them and also in legal limitations, expulsions, massacres, and extermination.

At the end, Stalin's definition (of 1931) is quoted which regards antisemitism as an extreme form of racial chauvinism and a survival of cannibalism.[3]

The article goes on to say that in Soviet Russia 'the victory of socialism

[1] *Izvestiya*, 27 July 1918, reprinted M. Gorev, *Protiv Antisemitov*, Moscow–Leningrad, 1928, pp. 102–3; English translation Schwarz, *The Jews in the Soviet Union*, New York, 1951, pp. 274–5; The speech quoted Yu. Larin, *Yevrei i Antisemitism v S.S.S.R.*, Moscow–Leningrad, 1929, pp. 7–8.

[2] *Bolshaya Sovietskaya Entsiklopaediya*, vol. III, 1926, p. 68.

[3] Ibid., 2nd edn., vol. II, 1950, p. 512.

destroyed the ground under antisemitism'. Jews, together with all nations and races, enjoy full equality. Only in such capitalist states as the U.S.A. and Great Britain did antisemitism remain a factor, and find its expression after the Second World War in pogroms, agitation in the press, exclusion from civil service, and discrimination in schools. In another volume (vol. 15 (1952), p. 378) it was also pointed out that no Jewish problem exists in Russia and that Jews are rapidly assimilating themselves. A similar definition of antisemitism was repeated at the end of the 1950s; it added that in the U.S.S.R. and other socialist (communist) countries the basis for antisemitism had been abolished.[1]

Beside these Soviet definitions varied formulations of the manifestations of antisemitism may also be noted which are not unlike those found in the west. There is, however, a somewhat stronger emphasis on persecution, physical attack, pogroms, and extermination. We have here, too, some of the milder forms such as 'hostile attitudes', 'spreading hostility', legal limitations, and political antisemitism. Moreover, the writings on the spread of antisemitism which appeared in Soviet Russia in the second half of the 1920s (with the intent to fight it) were not greatly concerned with the violent forms (which had by then become rarer) but dealt mostly with anti-Jewish attitudes, propaganda, denunciation, opposition to Jews sharing in what opportunities the country offered, and with discrimination, etc.[2] In short, there was little basic difference between Soviet Russia and the west with respect to the definition of phenomena to be regarded as antisemitic or of the forms taken by antisemitism. This is also true of more recent statements and writings. Although, true to communist 'tradition', Lenin's definition (that antisemitism distracts attention from the real enemy, etc.) is often mentioned, anti-Jewish attitudes and ideas (dealing with Russia itself or with antisemitism in capitalist countries) are classified as antisemitic.[3]

The 'New Antisemitism'—Ambivalence and Need for Redefinition

The birth of the State of Israel in 1948 created a novel situation. It by

[1] *Malaya Sovietskaya Entsiklopaediya*, 3rd edn., vol. 1, 1958, pp. 441–2.

[2] See, for instance, the cases mentioned by Gorev, pp. 9–32, partially translated by Schwarz, *The Jews*, pp. 244ff.; see also ibid., pp. 246ff.; Larin, pp. 241ff.

[3] *Novy Mir*, no. 9, September 1966, carried a longer article by I. Kon on 'The Psychology of Prejudice'. Although this deals mostly with American research on prejudice, examples presented by the author and his remarks on some aspects of the problem indicate that he classifies as prejudice phenomena similar to the ones so classified in the west. See detailed summary in *Patterns of Prejudice*, vol. i, no. 2 (1967), pp. 15–17. In 'Reports' on antisemitism in the U.S.A. both violent and non-violent forms, discrimination and anti-Jewish propaganda and attitudes are mentioned (*Izvestiya*, 10 August 1964; *Novoye Vremya*, no. 49, 1966).

no means contributed to the disappearance of antisemitism as Zionist theory had predicted it would (that antisemitism, being a result of Jewish homelessness, would disappear with the establishment of a home and state). Remarkably enough, antisemitism continues to exist and to some extent even to grow. In fact, 'a new antisemitism' arose in connection with the state.

The political and military Arab–Israel conflicts show no signs of abating. Emotionally, Arabs outside the country and in part those inside Israel, too, are cultivating an 'Arab Zionism', a yearning for 'return' to the Holy Land ('Land of Yihad'), to the 'Lost Paradise', or are 'protesting' against being 'hewers of wood and drawers of water' for the Jews in Israel.[1] Anti-Israel propaganda as disseminated by Arabs both in their own and in other countries is for the most part of a generally anti-Jewish nature. Arab papers publish Nazi-type anti-Jewish caricatures and the Protocols of the Elders of Zion—the classic antisemitic book—has been published by the government of the United Arab Republic (three editions). Even the more liberal groups (or those who wish to appear as 'progressive') which might be prepared to combat antisemitism are also hostile to the State of Israel and Zionism and this, in fact, means spreading hatred (antisemitism) against most of the Jews.

In Soviet Russia, too, this Israel–Zionism syndrome exists and has led to a sort of 'new antisemitism' culminating in distrust of Jews, and in a variety of accusations, as well as agitation against them. Though in some ways the situation in Russia may be different—Russia, unlike the Arab countries, had official diplomatic relations with Israel and even programmes of cultural exchange—there is also a resemblance to the Arab countries in that the U.S.S.R. supports the extreme anti-Israeli Arab states (Syria, U.A.R.) and also strives to realize Russia's age-old dream of gaining a 'foothold' in the Mediterranean. In addition, Zionism is taboo for the Soviets. Lenin, in 1903 and later, strongly opposed Zionism as a 'reactionary' movement. Stalin (1912–13) and the Bolsheviks generally followed in his footsteps. After the communist revolution of 1917, anti-Zionism became—with the exception of a short period in 1947–8—a principle of communism. The motives are varied and include the fact that Zionism is nationalistic and advocates 'Jewish peoplehood', deprecates class division among Jews, and favours close relations between Russian

[1] See A. L. Tibarri, 'The Palestine Arab Refugees in Arabic Poetry and Art', *The Middle East Journal*, vol. 17, 1963, pp. 507–26; Abraham Yinnon, 'Social Themes in Arabic Literature in Israel' (Hebrew), *Hamizrach Hehadash*, xvi, 1966, pp. 349–73; 'Antisemitism and Anti-Zionism', *New Outlook*, vol. 9, no. 6, 1966, pp. 21–35.

Jews and the Jews of other countries including Israel, all of which contradicts Soviet dogma about Jews and Judaism.[1]

From the theoretical viewpoint[2] the problem arises as to the classification of these and similar anti-Jewish acts or propaganda. The anti-Jewish angle is here only a corollary or by-product of other factors—Middle Eastern and possibly world policies and general communist dogma.

Other Elements

What we have said of the Israel–Zionism syndrome also holds for the other elements of Jewish ethnic culture (Jewish literature and education, religion and tradition, bonds between different sectors of the Jewish people in various countries) and even for discrimination. Where the Jews are concerned these may all be part of general trends (i.e. discrimination connected with 'equivalent balance' and nationality quotas; the elements of ethnic culture—communist nationality concepts, communist view of religion, Soviet ethnocentrism and suspicion of those who have contacts with foreigners). But the elements of antisemitism—the special Jewish angle—in all these attitudes may lie in two phenomena:

1. The Soviet method of denouncing in sharply militant language the adversary or the given trend and the interpolation of all manner of mostly imagined 'sins' and defamation, is likely to reduce a small minority to terror. (This, apparently, is the root of the silence and dread that so many travellers have found among Soviet Jews.)

2. This becomes magnified locally or individually if and when popular or individual antisemitic feelings and prejudices exist. The attacks become more violent and defaming, more antisemitic stereotypes are employed, which in turn are likely to nourish further antisemitic tendencies. In other words, at certain times, general trends applied to Jews may take antisemitic forms and direction if and when such conditions exist.[3]

[1] Recently the U.S. Government complained to the U.N. about the 'antisemitic aspersions' of a Soviet delegate to the Human Rights Commission of the U.N. who accused a member of the American delegation (Morris B. Abram, president of the American Jewish Committee) of 'obeying the orders of the Zionists and the Jews of America' and 'of serving two masters', *The New York Times*, 7 May 1967.

[2] For the actual facts of this 'new antisemitism' and the opposition to it, the theoretical problem of definition may have little meaning.

[3] Weinryb, *Slavic Review*, xxv (1966), p. 524; E. Wiesel, *The Jews of Silence*, New York, 1965, *passim*; Svetlana Alliluyeva (Stalin's daughter) told. while she was still in India, how her friends in Russia had to conceal the fact that they saw foreigners because the regime did not

Antisemitism Under the Soviets

Russia has a long history of discrimination against Jews and of anti-semitism, going back to the eighteenth century. After 1870 violence (pogroms) became a factor in this trend. By the beginning of the 1880s pogroms became endemic, involving both the population and governmental policies. During the First World War, the Jewish population was tormented by charges of spying for the enemy, by the expulsion of Jews from regions near the western front lines whence they were transported eastward, and persecution by various Russian military detachments. Again, during the years of civil war 1919–21, the Jews suffered waves of pogroms and slaughter. In some cases these involved virtually whole communities; they were perpetrated by Ukrainians, General Denikin's army, various 'white' armies, 'independent' detachments, and occasionally also by 'red' detachments which changed from 'red' to 'white' and vice versa. It is generally estimated that some 1,300 pogroms and anti-Jewish attacks took place in the Ukraine in about 700 localities as well as in several hundred localities in white Russia where some 60–70,000 Jews were killed. Soviet sources place the number of Jews killed in pogroms during those years at 180,000–200,000.[1]

When most of the anti-Soviet forces had been defeated and Soviet authority established throughout the country, the anti-Jewish trends did not disappear overnight, despite the measures taken by the Soviets to end them.[2] Not only would it have been remarkable for an old and firmly established prejudice to vanish in so short a time, but the background of life in the U.S.S.R. was scarcely of a nature to encourage such a miracle. Whichever of the main hypotheses of the causes of antisemitism one would choose—or which combination of them—it would seem that conditions in Soviet Russia—despite propaganda to the contrary—included many

---

allow them to do so (*Life*, 24 March 1967, p. 66).

[1] Wishniak, in K. Pinson (ed.) *Essays on Antisemitism*, 2nd edn., New York, 1946, pp. 121–44; N. Gergel, 'Di Idishe pogromen in Ukraine' (Yiddish), *Yivo Schriften für Wirtschaft und Statistik*, I, Berlin, 1928, pp. 106–13; E. Tscherikover, *The Pogroms in the Ukraine in 1919* (Yiddish), New York, 1965, *passim*; Gorev, p. 112; Larin, p. 39.

[2] The idea held by some Russian-Jewish intellectuals, including Solomon Schwarz (*The Jews*, p. 241), that prior to the civil war no popular antisemitism existed in Russia, is no more than over-idealization of 'the masses', it has no basis in fact. Similarly faulty is the usual 'periodization' of antisemitism (1919–21 pogroms; 1922–5 disappearance of antisemitism; 1926–ca. 1930 rise of antisemitism and again disappearance until the end of the 1930s). This 'periodization' merely indicates the periods in which the Soviets 'wanted' the world to know about antisemitism.

social circumstances favouring the continuation and even the growth of ethnic prejudice.

Religion played a vital role in Soviet Russia during the first few decades of the regime,[1] and still plays some role today. Then, too, religious stereotypes are also usually observable among secularized people.

Socio-economic competition (another cause of antisemitism) surely existed in Soviet Russia during the years of N.E.P. and its liquidation, industrialization and the movement of the village population to the cities (during the 1920s and 1930s). This may not always have been competition in terms of class struggle but rather on an individual basis, and often had some sort of ethnic or other group basis. Some of this competition still exists in the U.S.S.R.—the effort to rise from blue-collar to white-collar employment, from worker to manager, to engineer, from clerk to the 'specialist' status, and then again from the lower rungs to the higher. Not only do the 'higher' rungs carry greater prestige; they also earn much higher wages or salaries and afford greater amenities, since the spread between 'low' and 'high' is much broader in the U.S.S.R. than in capitalist countries.

A similar situation exists with regard to the various psychological and psychoanalytical theories of prejudice and antisemitism. If ethnic hostility is caused by anxiety resulting from past or anticipated deprivations, or by aggression arising out of frustration, or is connected with the 'authoritarian personality' in which certain neuroses[2] cluster together with ethnocentrism, inflexibility, etc., the social realities of the U.S.S.R. with its totalitarianism, purges, and labour camps certainly did not serve to minimize hostility.

The repetition of the 'standard' stereotypes about Jews which intermittently appear in Soviet documents, as well as other facts which have come to light, may indicate these trends. The only communist party archives to come into the hands of western researchers—those from Smolensk for the period 1917–38—tell of peasants in the region who grumbled (1922) about the communist regime because it supposedly made them dependent on the Jewish bourgeoisie. When, in the same year, a government commission arrived to collect the gold from the churches, people threatened that if the gold were taken by force 'not one Jew will survive, we'll kill them all during the night'. Women and boys roamed the streets of the town, attacked Jews and beat them, shouting 'beat the Jews, save

---

[1] M. Fainsod, *Smolensk under Soviet Rule*, Cambridge, Mass., 1958, p. 437.

[2] The Smolensk archives tell of professors (1929–31) who attributed neurasthenia to the squeeze by taxes, nervous illness to the fight against religion, and the rise of psychoses among peasants to collectivization. Fainsod, pp. 352–3.

Russia!'. From information published some time later we hear of oppression of the Mountain Jews of Daghestan and the Jews of Uzbekistan since 1920. The Jews were accused, amongst other things, of ritual murder (and endured a pogrom in 1926).[1] We learn also of anti-Jewish propaganda (after 1922) disseminated by the authorities of the Greek Orthodox Church; of workers in a sugar refinery where new Jewish workers were tortured by the Russian workers or were discriminated against in the distribution of work-clothes. A number of press dispatches from the U.S.S.R. during 1925 tell of antisemitism in the Soviet administration of small towns in different regions or of Jewish invalids exposed to discrimination in government invalid homes or terrorization of the Jewish population, mistreatment by members of the militia, and similar complaints.[2] A 1925 report (found in the Smolensk archives) from the town of Lubavichi that 'the Jews fear the government ... [and] the militiaman is feared as was the tsarist gendarme'[3] may indicate some mistreatment by the authorities. The individual facts mentioned certainly suffice to indicate the existence of antisemitism.

The facts which came to light in subsequent years (1926–30) during the efforts of the state and the party to combat antisemitism show that the latter remained strong and invaded party and Komsomol circles. Books, pamphlets, and newspaper reports published in Russia during these years describe deep hostility to the Jews in different regions, on the part of various groups in the population.

Mikhail I. Kalinin, titular head of the Soviet state, asserted in 1926 that 'the Russian intelligentsia [is] ... perhaps more antisemitic today than it was under tsarism'. Other writers confirm the existence of antisemitism within official circles of *apparatchikis* and among students, and find it widespread also among merchants, workers, and party members. This antisemitism found expression in different ways.

In factories some Jews were heckled by non-Jewish workers; they were baited, abused, beaten, and insulted; in some instances a Jewish worker was even killed; and the management persecuted Jews. From universities and educational institutes incidents were reported in which Jewish students were abused by being beaten or contemptuously called *Zhid*. From

[1] Fainsod, pp. 43, 157; Larin, pp. 127–32. It may well be that Karl Kautsky, opposing the Soviet regime in the 1920s and advocating some action against it, but expressing his fear (1925) that 'spontaneous uprising ... might ... be diverted ... to a "slaughter of Jews"', had in mind actual information about antisemitism there (*see* Abraham Ascher, *Slavic Review*, xxvi, (1967), p. 110).

[2] Gorev, pp. 10, 169; *The Jewish Daily Bulletin*, 22 June, 1925; 5 September 1925; 20 October 1925 (quoted Schwarz, *The Jews*, p. 252).   [3] Fainsod, p. 442.

Kharkov and Moscow we hear that students demanded the introduction of a *numerus clausus* for Jews. In some (Moscow) schools Jewish children were humiliated by teachers and other pupils, some of whom threatened to kill them. Demands were voiced for the reintroduction of tsarist limitations on Jews, and the curtailment of their rights in many walks of life. A tendency developed to differentiate between 'we'—Russians—and 'they'—Jews.[1]

The Smolensk archives, too, contain information on antisemitism and antisemitic trends. These range from many complaints of anti-Jewish acts—'there is a whole folder which contains nothing else' but such complaints—to statements that a worker was elected to office after he had declared 'give me three days and I will liquidate all communists and Jews and establish order'; and information about students (1928, 1929) who were expelled from the university partly because they were anti-semitic. It is also reported that a professor remarked that 'the Jewish race was degenerate'.[2]

Some picture of the trends prevalent among the population and party members may be drawn from questions asked by the participants (party members and candidates) in seminars held in Moscow in 1928:[3]

Why do Jews live in their own exclusive environment, keep their own beliefs and customs . . . which leads to alienation from others?

Why does the Russian worker disdain the Jewish nationality more than he does the Georgian, German, and other nationalities?

Should not the cause of antisemitism be sought in the (Jewish) people itself, in its ethical and psychological background?

Why is it that Jews don't want to do heavy work?

How is it that Jews always manage to get good positions?

Why are there so many Jews at the universities. Isn't it because they forge their papers?

Won't the Jews be traitors in a war? Aren't they dodging military service?

Why were Jews in the Crimea given good land while the land the Russians received is not so good?

(This last question has to do with the plan approved in 1926 for the settlement of Jews in the northern Crimea. The local Crimean authorities opposed this policy by trying to spread propaganda in the form of all sorts of rumours about Jews.) The fiction of the period also shows traces of

---

[1] Larin, pp. 34–5, 43–5, 124ff., 148, 238ff., 241ff., 277, 281; Gorev, pp. 5ff., 9, 11–16, 25; Schwarz, *The Jews*, pp. 241–73.

[2] Fainsod, pp. 44–5, 51, 346, 361.

[3] Larin, pp. 241–4 quotes sixty-six questions of which we present eight here; Schwarz, p. 251, gives some in English translation.

anti-Jewish motifs. A Jew is denied a leading post 'because it may arouse antisemitism'. A peasant and a worker respectively maintain: Jews are getting the best land, or that they are taking over the factories, the government.[1]

In summary, the antisemitic trends which were brought to light during these years show the usual anti-Jewish bias: some violence, a pogrom, and many of the standard stereotypes and accusations remained very much alive. These latter stretch from one extreme to the other—from the statement that 'Jews are degenerate' or 'using blood in *matza*' to statements about 'Jewish domination', Jewish wealth, unfair practices, that they shirk hard work, manual labour or military service, monopolize administrative and public services and the universities; or they blame Jews for being clannish, and voice the suspicion that Jews falsify documents and are spies.

Limited Effect of Combating Antisemitism

The disclosure of antisemitic ills and the attempts to cure them during the second half of the 1920s was the second (and last) such effort in this direction[2] made by that communist generation which believed antisemitism tantamount to counter-revolution. But most of the propaganda and the counter-measures suggested or taken were none too effective. The courts were apparently lenient and the educational material and propaganda seem to have fallen on deaf ears; party-members and Komsomol people were themselves involved in the anti-Jewish trends. The elimination of antisemitic materials from libraries together with other 'heretic' books (religious, pro-tsarist and pro-capitalistic) could not have been of significant factual help.[3]

The growth of the autocratic form of state in the early 1930s, Stalin's iron-handed rule, the many purges and the movement to foster national

---

[1] Larin, pp. 150–2; B. Chosed, 'The Soviet Jew in Literature', *Jewish Social Studies*, vol. ii, p. 264.

[2] The first took place during the pogroms of the civil war years when the above-mentioned decree (1918) outlawing antisemitism was issued. The Red Army generally rescued Jews from the pogromists and was ready to (or did) organize special Jewish self-defence detachments. (They existed in Byelorussia. In the Ukraine, although their organization was supported by L. Trotsky and the Politburo in Moscow and the Ukrainian communist leadership, the opposition of the Jewish parties prevented their formation—Tscherikover, pp. 294–7.)

[3] S. Schwarz, *Yevrei V Sovetskom Soyuze*, New York, 1966, p. 274; idem., *Antisemitism v Sovetskom Soyuze*, New York, 1952, pp. 80–96; Fainsod, p. 350. It should, however, be mentioned that some non-Jewish refugees from the U.S.S.R. (left during the war or a little later) claim that the law against antisemitism was effective.

pride and Russian and Soviet patriotism did not create a climate in which such ills as hatred of the Jews would be revealed. (The Yevsektsia which, according to the Smolensk archives, took a major part in tracking down and exposing antisemitic incidents, was closed in 1930.) It may also be that in the 1930s when many millions of people moved to the cities with a consequent rapid growth in urban employment (wage and salary earners: 1930, 14·5 millions; 1931, 18·9 millions; 1932, 22·9 millions) the few hundred thousand Jews who obtained jobs in factories and offices during these years did not appear to the others as too great a threat.

But this does not mean that antisemitism disappeared, rather that it was less discussed or written about. Or it was generalized in the guise of 'great power chauvinism' of which people were being accused from about 1930 onwards.[1]

Stalin himself made a strong statement against antisemitism at the beginning of 1931 in reply to a question from the Jewish Telegraphic Agency. He pointed out that:

National and racial chauvinism is a survival of the barbarous practices of the cannibalistic period ... serves the exploiters ... to protect capitalism from the attack of the working people ... antisemitism, a phenomenon profoundly hostile to the Soviet regime, is sternly repressed in the U.S.S.R.

This statement was printed (or reprinted) in 1936 (30 November) in *Pravda*.

Some information on discrimination against Jews in jobs, as well as of antisemitic outbreaks, was noted in the Soviet Jewish press. In 1930 and 1932 we hear of discrimination in the employment of Jews on the railroads; in 1934, 1935, of incidents when non-Jewish workers beat up their Jewish colleagues or otherwise persecuted them, shouting anti-Jewish threats ('all Jews should be drowned'). In the Smolensk archives antisemitic students are also mentioned (1935). In fiction, too (1933, 1935), non-Jewish workers are depicted as unwilling to work with Jews.[2]

In the subsequent period of the great purges when thousands were executed and hundreds of thousands deported, the Jewish communist élite was also decimated—both Jewish communists and communistic Jews (e.g. the communist Jewish intelligentsia who were interested and active in Jewish life) were involved. Some of them were liquidated;

---

[1] Some writings on the 'chauvinism' accusations are listed in Schwarz, *Antisemitism*, pp. 106–7.

[2] *Der shtern*, 1930; *Tribuna*, 1932, no. 3, quoted Schwarz, *Antisemitism*, pp. 117–18; *Der emes*, 2 July 1934; 9 July 1935, quoted J. Lestchinsky, *Dos Sovietsche Identum* (Yiddish), New York, 1941, p. 263; Fainsod, p. 224; Chosed, p. 266.

others died in gaol or exile. It is impossible to ascertain if, or to what extent, overt antisemitic tendencies among the *apparatchiki* contributed to the trumped-up accusations of 'nationalism' against Jewish communists at that time. It seems, however, that the liquidation of this Jewish élite made those who survived apprehensive and fearful of appearing to defend Jewish culture or Jewish cultural institutions and schools, which were closed down at the end of the 1930s.[1]

War and Post-War

Antisemitism, like other racial and ethnic prejudices, tends to gain vigour in times of crisis. This is especially true for the period of the Second World War in Soviet Russia. This was all the more so when Nazi racial propaganda penetrated into Soviet Russia. At first it came indirectly (until June 1941) but subsequently, during the German–Russian war, it was directly disseminated by the Nazis during their occupation of large parts of the country.

Before the outbreak of the German–Soviet war on 21 June 1941, the Jews in eastern Poland (later also in Lithuania and Bessarabia) were confronted with Soviet rule. On 17 September 1939 Russian troops crossed the Polish borders and occupied eastern Poland in accordance with the Soviet–Nazi pact of 23 August 1939. These provinces, now called western Ukraine and western White Russia, were soon united with the Ukrainian and White Russian Soviet Socialist republics respectively.

The attitude of the Russian forces to Jewish refugees fleeing from Nazi-occupied western Poland could be described as vacillating. From the unclear and contradictory information it would appear that for a time the refugees were almost indiscriminately admitted; later the border was closed, and then again opened for a while. In either of these periods each commander may have acted individually. In some instances, the Jews were admitted and treated well, in others they were sent back or arrested and accused of being spies.

Later on the policy of Ukrainization and White-Russianization gave local and other Ukrainians and White Russians, who often had nationalistic and even antisemitic backgrounds, a monopoly of public offices with detrimental results for Jews. Soon also, Jewish schools began to be changed into Ukrainian or Russian ones.[2]

---

[1] Weinryb, 'Polish Jews Under Soviet Rule', p. 330. Zelik Akselrod, a poet from Minsk who visited Wilneus and Kaunas at the beginning of 1941 and who, at meetings with Jewish writers, warned that the Yiddish schools in the U.S.S.R. had been closed, was arrested and, information has it, shot in June 1941 for propagation of 'Jewish nationalism', *Yad Vashem Studies*, iv (1960), pp. 111–12.   [2] Weinryb, 'Polish Jews', pp. 333–42.

The occupation of these and other Russian lands by the Nazis (on and after 21 June 1941) involved, as we know, suffering and death for hundreds of thousands of Jews. Many inhabitants of the occupied regions—Ukraine, Lithuania, Crimea—co-operated either actively or passively in the extermination of the Jews. Extreme nationalist groups and organizations (such as the Ukrainian O.U.N. and others) adopted the Nazi attitude towards Jews. Some of them even staged pogroms before the entry of the German forces (Lithuania); others assisted the Nazis (Lithuanian and Ukrainian police) in exterminating the Jews, even beyond the borders of their respective countries. (On the other hand some Ukrainians, Lithuanians, and others were known to have helped save a Jew.) Many shared in plundering the Jewish victims thus becoming personally interested in destroying any possible witnesses to the atrocities they had committed or to their aid to the Germans.

Also, in the non-occupied parts of Soviet Russia, and among soldiers in the army, antisemitism was on the rise. Antisemitic utterances against the 'Abrams' (used instead of *Zhid*) were voiced in many places, for example, hospitals where wounded Russian soldiers were recuperating, and also gaols and labour camps. The 'usual' stereotypes and accusations were heard: Jews shirk hard work, are draft-dodgers, don't fight in the front lines, are wealthy, etc. Even the charge that they killed Christ was heard (in a *kolkhoz*.) Similar anti-Jewish sentiments were also revealed at the front lines. Some Jews in the Red Army said they took on Russian names because of antisemitism in the army. Some displaced persons are even supposed to have maintained that commissioned officers of known Jewish origin were in danger of being shot in the back by privates under their command.[1]

Certain of the anti-Jewish trends were somewhat magnified in the forests of western Russia where various partisan groups and guerrillas were roaming around and fighting the invader or each other. The nationalist anti-Soviet groups—Ukrainian (Bandera group), Polish 'Whites', Lithuanians, and others—were ready to, and did, murder Jews in the forests. In addition, the Jewish partisan, 'fulfilling' his 'usual duty' to live off the village population, and, occasionally also, to use the peasant as a scout, was often forced to be harsher than his non-Jewish counterpart who felt more akin to the peasant. This caused a stronger reaction against the Jewish partisan. Then, too, the partisan groups comprised, among others, Soviet soldiers who had been left behind, Soviet officials who had not succeeded in fleeing the German invader, escaped Soviet prisoners-of-war,

[1] Quoted Schwarz, *The Jews*, pp. 346–7.

all of whom were subject to the influence of German propaganda or to that of the local populace and thus more strongly biased against Jews. The anti-Jewish attitudes and acts observable among the non-Jewish partisans were expressed in mistrust of the Jew, in creating obstacles to his acceptance into a unit, in accusations of misbehaviour, and sometimes even of spying for the Nazis. Occasionally, too, he was the victim of a treacherous shot in the back, manhandling and robbery. On the other hand, in the second period of the war when the partisan movement was organized by commanders and leaders parachuted from Russia, most of the anti-Jewish actions disappeared, and occasionally special help was arranged for Jews,[1] so that the security of the Jewish partisan was greatly increased. Nevertheless some 'accidents' did occur. Also, the organization of the Soviet-controlled detachments tended to be on a 'territorial' basis which meant that some purely Jewish detachments had to lose their independence[2] and merge with the others.

After the war the accumulated anti-Jewish attitudes and feelings did not disappear over night. To a certain degree the bottled-up hostility and suspicion may often have been intensified by the injection of, so to say, a personal element. In the regions occupied by the Nazis, Jewish repatriates became somewhat of a menace to many collaborators. There was a real risk that some of them might be recognized by a former victim. The question of returning a formerly Jewish-owned apartment or furniture also sometimes cropped up. A Ukrainian Jew who left Kharkov and the U.S.S.R. in 1944 reports:

The Ukrainians received the returning Jews with open animosity. During the first weeks after the liberation of Kharkov no Jews ventured about alone in the streets at night.

The report goes on to tell of

. . . many cases [when] Jews were beaten on the market place and one was killed. . . . In Kiev 16 Jews were killed in the course of a pogrom. . . . Returning Jews receive no more than a small proportion of their property. . . . The Ukrainian authorities are greatly antisemitic.

The same writer lists a number of cases of discrimination against Jews:

[1] Schwarz, *The Jews*, pp. 325ff., attempts to discredit some information about the transfer of Jewish children across the lines and the freeing of Jews from some Nazi ghettos (Skalat). He was apparently unaware of the authentic information contained in Hebrew sources.

[2] Zwi Bar-on, 'The Jews in the Soviet Partisan Movement', *Yad Vashem Studies*, iv, Jerusalem, 1960, pp. 167–89. Moshe Kahanovich, *The Fighting of the Jewish Partisans in Eastern Europe* (Hebrew), Tel Aviv, 1954; *The Jewish Partisans* (Hebrew), vols. 1–2, Merchavia, 1958–9; Samuel Bernstein, *Plugath Hadoktor Atlas*, Tel Aviv, 1965.

The official answer to all Jewish representations is that the antisemitism with which the population has been infected by the Germans can only be uprooted gradually.

Some Jews from displaced persons' camps in Europe who had returned to their homes in the Ukraine in 1943–5, and later left Russia, made sweeping charges of antisemitism. A former army captain asserted: 'antisemitism in the Soviet Union is rampant to an extent that it is impossible for anyone never having lived in that accursed country to imagine'.[1] These trends are generally confirmed by non-Jewish refugees from the U.S.S.R.

The Harvard Project on the Soviet Social System[2] disclosed that a majority of those interviewed spoke of Jews in stereotypes somewhat similar to those mentioned earlier for the 1920s: Jews are money-minded, aggressive, 'pushy', occupy a privileged position. They are clannish, avoid work, are sly, dishonest, do not fight, and the like. Some simply expressed the opinion 'I do not like these people (Jews).' Another interview with a few Ukrainians who left Russia in the 1950s shows that they made similar charges (dodging the army or 'I just felt antipathy', etc.)[3]

Towards Official Antisemitism

In the Ukraine, where the authorities took cognizance of popular hostility against Jews, this trend became observable before the end of the war. The awareness of anti-Jewish feelings among the people (and Nazi propaganda labelling the war 'a Jewish war') may have contributed (in combination with the 'internationalism' inherent in communist theory) to the government's tendency to 'denationalize' the Jewish victims of Nazi aggression. Government announcements, with some exceptions, employed general categories such as Soviet or Ukrainian or Lithuanian citizens rather than identify the victims as Jews. Also, even before the end of the war, some offices—principally the Foreign Office and those departments which dealt with foreign countries—were to a great extent emptied of their Jewish officials and Jews were rarely accepted as trainees for such jobs.[4]

[1] *Bulletin of the Joint Rescue Committee of the Jewish Agency for Palestine*, March 1945, pp. 2ff.; A. R. L. Gurland, *Glimpses of Soviet Jewry: 1000 Letters from the U.S.S.R. and DP Camps* (mimeogr.), New York, 1948; Schwarz, *The Jews*, pp. 345–8.

[2] i.e. interviews conducted in 1950–1 with a sample of 329 persons who had left the U.S.S.R. either during the war or in 1946–50.

[3] *Survey* Report no. 2, 23 November 1960. Y. Bilinsky, *The Second Soviet Republic: The Ukraine after World War II*, New Brunswick, New Jersey, 1964, pp. 408–9.

[4] According to Ehrenburg, M. M. Litvinov, dismissed in May 1939 from his post as Minister of Foreign Affairs, remained officially connected with the Ministry as a deputy Minister until 1947 when he was pensioned. He and Ya. Suritz died of natural causes in 1951.

Now, returning to the western parts after the war, the Soviets were eager to avoid appearing to 'bring back the Jews'. Khrushchev, the first secretary of the communist party in the Ukraine at that time, is quoted clearly to this effect.[1] This apparently meant that Jews were supposed to play only a small role, if any, in party and government and that Jewish (Yiddish) institutions (schools, publications) would not be tolerated.

A similar situation was created in Lithuania (and possibly in other 'new territories' to which the Soviets returned after the war). In Wilno (Vilnius) the Lithuanian Soviet authorities either opposed or hampered Jewish institutions, Yiddish theatrical performances, schools, publication of a newspaper, and the organization of a Jewish museum. But they supported a Karaite museum which supposedly still exists. Moreover, it was made difficult, if not impossible, for Jews to play any considerable role in the hierarchy of state and party.[2]

Stalin had a number of Jews around him. A sister-in-law (the wife of his brother-in-law by his first marriage), a daughter-in-law (wife of his oldest son Yakov), a son-in-law for three years (Morozov, married to his daughter Svetlana), and a few half-Jewish grandchildren. At different periods some Jews were part of his household in the *dachas* (his daughter's memoirs mention Jan Gamarniks's daughters, Solomon Lozowsky a high foreign ministry official arrested 1949 and executed 1952, Molotov's Jewish wife who was a good friend of Stalin's second wife, and others). His personal attitudes may to some extent be gauged from the following: according to Svetlana, when the oldest son Yakov married a Jewish girl 'that displeased my father too. He never liked Jews, though in those days he wasn't yet as blatant about expressing his hatred for them as he was after the war'. His latent suspicion was aroused during the war. When his son Yakov was taken prisoner by the Nazis, Stalin conceived the idea that someone had betrayed him, claiming 'it seems that his wife is dishonest'.

When his seventeen-year-old daughter fell in love with a Jewish script-writer twice her age, Stalin was strongly opposed to it and had him deported. Her subsequent marriage to Gregory Morozov also displeased him. Svetlana writes 'he was Jewish and my father did not like that'. Stalin repeated the standard antisemitic stereotype accusing his Jewish son-in-law of shirking military service ('People are getting shot [at the

[1] 'It is not in our interest that the Ukrainians should associate the return of Soviet power with the return of Jews,' cited by Joseph B. Schechtman, *Star in Eclipse—Russian Jewry Revisited*, New York, 1961, p. 80. The quotation of Khrushchev is mentioned with a slight change, Schwarz, *Yevrei*, p. 257.

[2] Katcherginski, pp. 46, 56, 95, 108–9, and *passim*.

front] and look at him. He's sitting it out at home.'). About two years after their divorce, at a time when intellectuals were being arrested (1948–9) and accused among other things of Zionism, Stalin remarked to his daughter, 'that first husband of yours was thrown your way by the Zionists'. When Svetlana told him that the younger generation cared nothing about Zionism he asserted that 'the entire older generation is contaminated with Zionism and now they are teaching the young people too'. On the other hand, at the time of the 'Doctors' Plot' (1953), when his personal physician was among those arrested, Stalin was supposedly very distressed (he refused to use another physician) and remarked that he did not believe the doctors were 'dishonest'.[1]

If the information set forth by Svetlana Alliluyeva about the rise of Stalin's antisemitism at the end (and in the post-war years) is correct this may tally with other accounts. He is supposed to have noted privately at the time of one of the meetings with the other heads of the allied states held during the last war years that he was displeased with the Jews who had failed to build up their own territory—Biro-Bidzhan. (Khrushchev, too, referred to the same topic some years later.) The idea of Great Russian patriotism which Stalin fostered during the 1940s also had some edge against 'Jewish nationalism'.

On the other hand, during the war years, nationalist and religious feelings among various ethnic and other groups were encouraged by the Soviet authorities. Their aim was to promote unity and bolster resistance to the enemy. Thus, in April 1942, a Jewish Anti-Fascist Committee was organized to cultivate pro-Russian sentiments among Jews at home and abroad. The Committee published a Yiddish periodical, *Aynikayt* (Unity), and Jewish writers soon began to use Jewish images and themes in their writings. Contact with Jews all over the world was encouraged; and the leaders of the Committee made trips to the United States and other countries. Although the Jewish Anti-Fascist Committee was principally a tool for Soviet propaganda, it served to a certain extent as a rallying point for Jewish intellectuals and for contacts with Jews abroad. This continued in the early post-war years. During this period the Russian attitude towards Zionism also changed. It moved from hostility to neutrality and later to support of Jewish demands at the United Nations for the partition of Palestine (1947) and to official recognition of Israel after its founding on 14 May 1948. During these years a few Yiddish schools were also opened in the western regions acquired by the U.S.S.R. But later in 1948, with

[1] Svetlana Alliluyeva, *Twenty Letters to a Friend*, London, 1967, pp. 76, 82, 171, 193, 197–8, 206, 217.

the looming cold war, the sharpening division between east and west, the Tito 'heresy', and the *Zhdanovshchina*, there came a change.

This was heralded in an article by Ilya Ehrenburg published in *Pravda*[1] and *Aynikayt* on 21 and 23 September 1948. Ehrenburg denied that a Jewish 'people' existed, condemned Jewish 'nationalism', dubbed Israel a bourgeois state and a tool of Anglo-American capitalism that was powerless to solve the Jewish problem (which was only possible within the communist order of the Soviet Union). Soon afterwards the Jewish Anti-Fascist Committee was dissolved, *Aynikayt* closed, Yiddish schools liquidated, and Jewish writers and intellectuals arrested and deported. Thenceforth, and until Stalin's death on 5 March 1953, a number of anti-Jewish acts were perpetrated—a purge in Biro-Bidzhan, execution of top Yiddish writers (1952), discrimination against Jews, and antisemitic overtones in the campaign against 'cosmopolitans'.[2] Finally, there came the 'Doctors' Plot' (January 1953), but this miscarried because of Stalin's death. During the months in which the 'plot' lasted the Soviet press attacked many individual Jews. It charged them with divulging top secrets, embezzlement, fraud, irregularities in their university careers, Zionism and bourgeois nationalism (a group at Odessa University), falsification of records, dissipation of state funds, and similar crimes. All this seems to have been a forerunner of the campaign against the 'economic' crimes of Jews in the 1960s.[3]

The official image of Jews as a group in the U.S.S.R. which the Soviets wished to display in those years is apparently reflected in the article

[1] According to Ehrenburg's memoirs the editor of *Pravda* asked him to write the article. Some, however, accused him of 'collaborating' in the 'frame-up' of Jewish writers. Only a few days before *Aynikayt* was closed the paper published (18 November 1948) an article defending Ehrenburg's ideas against criticism from abroad. It should be mentioned that earlier Ehrenburg had apparently been dissatisfied with the lack of Jewishness of the Jewish Anti-Fascist Committee (he is quoted as saying: '*eto nye Yevreiski Komitet, eto Anti-Yevreiski Komitet*', S. Katcherginski *Zwischen Hamer un Serp*, 2nd edn., Buenos Aires, 1950, p. 70).

[2] Ehrenburg informs us that the agitation began against theatrical critics in January 1949 at the initiative of Stalin. The editors, however, were divulging the Jewish names of those who wrote under pseudonyms and reviling them as Jews. After about two months Stalin is supposed to have called in the editors and told them to stop divulging the Jewish names since 'it smacks of antisemitism': I. Ehrenburg, 'Ludi, Gody, Zhizn', *Novy Mir*, 1965, no. 1, pp. 106–7, 116, 118–21, 123; no. 2, pp. 15–16, 21–4, 34, 43–4, 50–8; no. 4, pp. 29, 35–6, 47–9, 57–62, 70 (parts reprinted in *Evrei i Evreiski Narod*, no. 19 (1966), pp. 117, 120; no. 20, pp. 97–102).

[3] For the whole affair of the 'Doctors' Plot' see Isaac London, 'Days of Anxiety', *Jewish Social Studies*, vol. 15 (1953), pp. 275–92; *Pravda*, 31 January; 1, 9–11, 14 February; *Izvestiya*, 20, 28, 30 January; 4, 7, 10, 11, 18 February; 29, 31 March; *Sovietskaya Latvia*, 16 January; *Trud*, 25, 28 January; 5 February; *Pravda Ukrainy*, 17, 23, 28 January; 11, 12 February; *Literaturnaya Gazeta*, 21 February; 26 March; *Moskovskaya Pravda*, 29 January; 7, 20 February; *Vechernaya Moskva*, 13 February; *Sovetskaya Moldavia*, 25 February.

Yevrei (Jews), published in the second edition of the *Large Soviet Encyclopaedia* (vol. 15, 1952).

'Jews' is the name of various nationalities which originated from the ancient Jews. They are not a nation since [quoting Stalin] they do not have any common language, territory, economic life, or culture. Yiddish is spoken by Polish, German and, in part, English and American Jews. In the past it was spoken by Russian Jews. In Russia hard-working Jews have the possibility of engaging in all occupations and professions and take an active part in building communism. Thus there is no Jewish problem in the U.S.S.R. Jews are being assimilated in the general population.[1]

Post Stalin Era

A month after Stalin's death the 'Doctors' Plot' was officially debunked and the accused released from gaol. The whole affair was presented as a frame-up by certain officials who were duly punished. Some two years later those surviving Jewish writers and intellectuals, arrested at the end of 1948, were released from gaols and labour camps and began to return to Moscow and other places. The names of those who had been shot in 1952 were individually rehabilitated. But no official rehabilitation came in connection with Khrushchev's destalinization speech in 1956 at the twentieth congress of the C.P.S.U. or later. Nor were any of the Jewish institutions or publications rehabilitated. Until almost the end of the 1950s official Russia pretended that there was no Jewish problem in the U.S.S.R., and no Jewish nationality, and of necessity fell back on Lenin's principle—who quoted Karl Kautsky—that Jews ceased to be a nationality since they have no territory. Nor, claimed the Soviets, is there a Jewish culture since Jews have been assimilated.

Meanwhile, discrimination and bias against the Jews apparently did increase both as a part of the general system and as a result of individual acts by people in power.

Discrimination both against individual Jews and the group in the U.S.S.R. was known before the Second World War. But after the war, with the change in policy, Jews were largely excluded from employment in sensitive security jobs, and the foreign service and high army posts were partially or wholly closed to them. Hence an abnormally low percentage of Jews entered the party hierarchy or the state administration and 'elected' offices. In higher education the prevailing principle of

[1] This second edition of the Encylcopaedia (1950–8) devotes only six columns to Jewish themes, omitting mention of many Jewish writers, whereas the first edition (1926ff.) had contained 160 columns over and above numerous individual articles on Jewish writers, thinkers, etc.

'equivalent balance' as a guide to fixing nationality quotas in the various republics came, as DeWitt points out, to be discriminatory. (Khrushchev is said to have told the French socialist delegation in 1956 that Ukrainian and other cadres were being created in order to supplant Jews.) According to DeWitt's computations the enrolment of Jewish students in universities declined in the years 1935 to 1958 from 74,000 to 53,000, whereas general enrolment doubled. (However, the data for 1960–1 show 77,177 Jewish students.)

A comparison of the percentage of Jews in the urban population and in the student body may give a good idea of the situation:

	Jews in urban pop. 1959 (per cent)	Jewish students in higher educ. instit. 1960–1 (per cent)
U.S.S.R.	2·16	3·22
R.S.F.S.R.	1·35	3·11
Ukrainian S.S.R.	4·23	4·47
Byelorussian S.S.R.	5·83	5·09
Moldavian S.S.R.	13·75	6·37
Lithuanian S.S.R.	2·33	1·54

Whereas the percentage of Jewish students in Russia as a whole and in the R.S.F.S.R. was higher than their share in the urban population, in the western republics, where the nationals compete with the Jews, the latter's share was either more or less the same as their percentage in the urban population (Ukraine, Byelorussia) or much smaller (Moldavia, Lithuania), because of the controls (or discrimination). This explains the anxiety found among Jewish parents in the U.S.S.R. in connection with their children's admission to the universities. This quota system was indirectly confirmed by Svetlana Alliluyeva at her news conference on 26 April 1967. When she was asked about Jews in Russia she replied that she did not know much about them but, having Jewish friends, she knew of 'restrictions in universities and institutes'. Very talented Jewish youngsters were sometimes refused admission whereas less talented members of other nationalities were admitted instead.[1]

Group discrimination is present when Jews are denied the practical possibility of fostering their own culture, guaranteed to every nationality by law in the U.S.S.R. (These rights are usually accorded on a territorial

[1] N. DeWitt, *Education and Professional Employment in the U.S.S.R.*, Washington, D.C., 1961, pp. 359–60. M. Altschuler, *The Jews in the Soviet Union Census, 1959*, Jerusalem, 1963, *passim*; *New York Times*, 27 April 1967.

or regional basis.) The Jews had been recognized as a national group in the 1920s and in the post-Stalin era this official recognition was apparently re-asserted when they were classified as *Yevrei* in their internal passports (fifth paragraph). In various publications of the 1959 census (*itogi*) they are registered as a nationality together with other nationalities who either do or do not use their mother tongue (*rodnoi iazyk*), and possess a (symbolic) autonomous Jewish region (Biro-Bidzhan). This is reiterated elsewhere. In a recent description of the 'nations' (*narody*) of European Russia, Jews are listed as one of the *narody* (under the rubric of *osnovniye narody*), and their language (*narodnyi iazyk*) as 'idish', and their own autonomous region, etc., is emphasized.[1]

Religion in Soviet Russia is generally viewed with contempt or animosity. Despite the Soviet constitution which guarantees the right of religious worship (as well as of anti-religious propaganda) Soviet universities (Kiev, for instance) have departments of 'atheism' but none of religion.

The assault on religion is not aimed exclusively at Jews; Catholicism, for instance, is characterized as the 'most bitter enemy of the October [Bolshevik] Revolution. Its Church participates in the conspiracies of American imperialists aginst the U.S.S.R.'[2] In the post-war years the Catholic and Uniate Churches in western Ukraine and Byelorussia have been largely liquidated and their priests deported to Siberia. (Metropolitan Joseph Slipy of Lwow was arrested in 1945 and exiled. He was released after eighteen years but did not return to Lwow.) Nor did the renewed attack on religion at the end of the 1950s concern the Jews alone. The press in Turkmen, Kirgiz, and Azerbaijan S.S.R. simultaneously assailed the Moslem religion (20–30 million believers). The local newspapers criticized the Koran and Moslem institutions and, as in the case of the attacks on Jewish religion, also the clergy and religious leaders. The themes of their 'depravities' closely resemble the ones used of the synagogue: improper conduct, robbing the people, living in luxury on the latter's account, drunkenness.[3] The main difference is that in the Jewish case these denunciations afforded all sorts of local antisemites the opportunity grossly to defile Jews as well as Judaism. The tactic which Professor Feuer has called 'protivism' (from *protiv* = against) which is used in Soviet Russia to denounce an adversary in militant, embattled language,

---

[1] *Narody Evropeiskoi chasti S.S.S.R.*, vol. i, pp. 23, 25; vol. ii, pp. 832–3, Moscow, 1964; B. Weinryb, *Slavic Review*, xxvi, no. 1 (1967), pp. 158–9.

[2] *Bolshaya Sovetskaya Entsiklopaediya*, vol. 20, 1953.

[3] Jehovah's Witnesses in Kazakhstan were also denounced at that time. I. Levine, *Main Street, U.S.S.R.*, New York, 1959, p. 393.

and name-calling, encourages the spread of antisemitic defamation and even the use of Nazi tactics and lies or scurrilous cartoons.[1] This is facilitated both by (ironically) the greater literary freedom allowed since the 1950s and by the usual tactic employed in Soviet Russia of softening up and attacking the synagogue and its congregants, accusing them of all manner of crimes so that they would close it 'of their own free will'.[2] The closing of many synagogues during the last six to eight years (reducing their number from an estimated 450 in 1956 to an estimated 60 by 1965) means so many hundreds of anti-Jewish defamations, false accusations, stereotyping, and spreading of hatred against the Jews. This may sometimes be carried out at individual or local initiative, sometimes by prearrangement or at the initiative of a higher authority.

Economic Crimes

With the reduction of terror in the post-Stalin years, the amnestying of prisoners and some normalization of everyday life, social ills—parasitism, and bribery—became more widespread or came nearer the surface. The regime, unwilling to revive Stalin's harsh measures, sought relief in new laws and campaigns against parasitism (1956–7) and against 'economic crimes' (1960s) for which the death penalty was introduced. (Despite all the assertions of high idealism in communist society, black marketeering in foreign exchange, thievery and bribery, as well as officially 'illegal' transactions, committed by managers in order to fulfil quotas and other bureaucratic demands, are not rare. They are nicknamed *tsepochka*— 'chain', i.e. that in each case there are many 'links', many individuals of different status being involved and each paying rebates to the next one.)

In 1961 there were (or the press carried information on) nine trials in which eleven people were sentenced to death, five or six of them having Jewish names. During the next few years came more trials in which over one hundred people were condemned to death. To judge by the names, more than 40 per cent were Jews. According to available information it would appear that there were many more trials throughout the country and that the *percentage* of the Jews involved was in fact small.[3] This would mean that the 'Jewish cases' were singled out—by editors or the authorities—for publication either in order to make Jews the scapegoat for the 'sins' of society, or for the purpose of spreading anti-Jewish ideas.

---

[1] Thus K. Kichko, *Yudaism bez prykras*, Kiev, 1963, and various articles in the press in Moldavia, Ukraine, Lithuania, etc.

[2] See also Ben-Ami, *Between Hammer and Sickle*, Philadelphia, 1967, pp. 61ff.

[3] Schwarz, *Yevrei*, pp. 325–46; *Sovietish Heymland*, November–December 1963, p. 83.

Antisemitic Incidents

The anti-Jewish propaganda and the designation of people with Jewish names as culprits was bound to have influenced predisposed individuals in their attitude towards Jews, even though we may assume with Professor Feuer that the militant language, the oratory and accusations are becoming in the long run a meaningless ritual.[1]

These incidents cover a varied range: arson in a synagogue in Malakhovka near Moscow on the Jewish New Year's Eve in 1959 when a Jewish woman perished. Antisemitic sheets signed by a 'Committee *Bey Zhidov*' were found nearby. A synagogue was also set on fire in Georgia (1962). In Uzbekistan (1961, 1962) Moslems accused Jews of using blood for ritual purposes. These cases supposedly led to riots (Russian official sources deny the whole matter). There is information about ganging up on Jewish children in schools in which they are attacked or abused as 'dirty Jews', etc.[2]

Admitting the Existence of Antisemitism?

In general it is consistently denied in the U.S.S.R. both officially and privately that anything resembling antisemitism or prejudice exists there. Stress is given to the fact that the Soviet constitution guarantees complete equality to all. There are signs, however, which may indicate the beginning of a change. An editorial in *Pravda* (5 September 1965) attacked manifestations of antisemitism in the country and separateness in the training of personnel (or quotas).

The article by I. Kon 'The Psychology of Prejudice', published in *Novy Mir* (1966), ends on a note indicating some admission of the continuing existence of prejudice.

Communists must bear in mind that the party . . . must not follow the modes and mistakes of the masses such as chauvinism, antisemitism. . . . It would seem that they [racial and ethnic prejudices] have entirely disappeared and been forgotten—but quite the contrary, when particular difficulties arise, they again make themselves felt, influencing backward sections of the population.

Aaron Vergelis, the editor of the Yiddish monthly, *Sovietish Heymland*, often serves as a mouthpiece for the Soviet rulers in matters concerning Jews and as a propagandist for the regime. At a meeting held during his

[1] A. Simirenko (ed.), *Soviet Sociology*, Chicago, 1966, p. 268.
[2] *N. Y. Times*, 13 October 1959; Schwarz, *Yevrei*, pp. 350ff.; *Jews in Eastern Europe*, II, no. 2 (May 1963), pp. 34–9; Ben-Ami, p. 165; Sh. Ben-Israel, *Russian Sketches. A visit to Jews without Hope*, New York, n.d., p. 33.

visit to London at the end of 1966 he is reported[1] to have admitted that antisemitism was alive among certain strata of society and that it would be necessary to combat it for a long time.

If this information is based on facts, it would be indicative of a change taking place in the attitude towards antisemitism in the U.S.S.R. This may possibly not be contradicted by Premier A. N. Kosygin's denial of the existence of prejudice at a press conference in New York on 25 June 1967. He emphasized equality of rights for the Jews, but he did not mention anything about manifestations of antisemitism.[2]

Inconsistencies in the Pattern

Whether or not the existence of antisemitism is officially acknowledged, it does exist in the U.S.S.R. as a popular strain finding an outlet in crucial areas.

In the Marxist world a dogmatic philosophic system masks reality, changing the facts to fit the dogma (this is the role of 'socialist realism' in literature). Lenin, whose tenets are not to be questioned,[3] believed (as many liberals since the French Revolution had done before him) that full equal rights for Jews would solve the 'Jewish problem', and that anti-semitism was connected with capitalistic society so that 'it is clear' no antisemitism can exist in the U.S.S.R. Similarly, Jews can continue to be officially classified as a nationality (in the passport, census reports, etc.) but denied their group existence and deprived of any possibility to cultivate their culture. The constitution may provide punishment for discrimination against a citizen or the 'establishment of direct or indirect privileges for citizens on account of their race or nationality', but nationality quotas for the purpose of an 'equivalent balance' in the republics are acceptable (failing to recognize them as the 'establishment of privileges'). The constitution may promise freedom of religion (and of anti-religious propaganda) but the party and party organs may harass religious institutions, bring about the closing of synagogues (and some churches), or cause discriminatory practices in the matter of jobs and promotions of

[1] *Haaretz*, 21 December 1966.

[2] *The New York Times*, 27 June 1967. Let us mention in passing that his statement 'there has *never been* (our emphasis, B.W.) and there is no antisemitism in the Soviet Union' certainly contradicts many Soviet authorities including Lenin himself in so far as the past is concerned.

[3] In our connection it should be mentioned that during the last few years a scholarly discussion has been going on in the U.S.S.R. of the concept of 'nation' and 'nationality' (which has some relevance to the problem of classification of Jews as a nationality). While Stalin's ideas on the problem are sometimes criticized, Lenin's are mostly taken for granted or defended (*Voprosy Istorii*, 1966, nos. 1, 2, 4, 6; 1967, nos., 1, 2, 3, 4, 6, 7, 8; *Voprosy Filosofii*, 1964, no. 11; *Narody Azii i Afriki*, 1966, no. 4 and others).

worshippers at church or synagogue. All these inconsistencies disappear if one 'changes the facts to fit the dogma'.

Other factors also leading to contradictions are:

1. Anti-Jewish phenomena are often an 'extension' of (or parallel to) general trends (the 3 million Ukrainians, for instance, living in the R.S.F.S.R. have no Ukrainian schools for their children just as the Jews have no Jewish schools).

2. Parallel with discriminatory and other anti-Jewish phenomena one finds also frequent fairer treatment: Jews receive various prizes, medals, honours, and are appointed members of the Russian Academy (in 1964: Jews received Lenin prizes; 16 out of 103 or about 16 per cent were elected to full membership in the Academy, and 58 out of 438 or 7·5 per cent to corresponding membership).[1]

3. The press, as well as attacking Jews, exposing Jewish economic crimes, and striking out against Israel and Zionism, also sometimes points out Jewish contributions to Soviet Russia, voices sympathy for their sufferings during the Nazi period, and occasionally defends individual Jews (most items, good and bad, concern individuals with Jewish names).

The volumes 19–22 of *Evrei i Evreiski Narod* (1966) contain excerpts about Jews published during 1965 in 42 newspapers and 127 periodicals appearing in different parts of the U.S.S.R. A simple count of items will show that there are as many—if not more—positive items about Jews than negative ones (of course the balance may be different in other years).

Both the fact that anti-Jewish attitudes come into play to a great extent as a by-product of general situations and crises (and the inconsistent features) may prove or explain two things:

(*a*) that some people in Russia, including some Jews, may believe there is no antisemitism in Soviet Russia (or find rationale for its existence);[2]

(*b*) that anti-Jewish attitudes and denunciation (or defence) of Jews are not necessarily always dictated by a central authority but may be of local origin, arising from the initiative of writers, editors, intermediate officials, and local party bosses—varying with the degree of leeway permitted them in the Soviet context. The character of antisemitism in the U.S.S.R. today can be regarded as being of a popular nature that uses new appeals to bolster old prejudices but takes its cues and main themes from state and party.

---

[1] L. Shapiro, in *American Jewish Yearbook*, vol. 66, 1965, p. 429.

[2] In an interview in the summer of 1966 new immigrants from the U.S.S.R. maintained that Jews were not discriminated against—facilities for minority culture generally are non-existent in big cities where most Jews live—and that pressure on synagogue and synagogue attendance comes from 'Jewish atheists' rather than from the government (G. A. David, in *Hadoar*, vol. 45, no. 31, 1966, pp. 510–11).

Fear has been reported rife among Jews in Soviet Russia by many tourists, journalists, and other writers, one of whom recently dubbed Russian Jewry the 'Jews of Silence'. Some found it among the old and middle-aged, and amongst those who remember the last years of Stalin's rule; others indicate that the younger generation, too, feels threatened. Again, the forms and content of anxiety vary. There are those who worry about their jobs and residence permits, others are concerned lest their children be refused admittance to universities; some fear arrest or a 'revival of the Stalin black years'.

Forms of fear and reactions to it also cover a wide range: fear of talking to a foreign Jew or of receiving one at home. Stories are told of brothers arriving to visit sisters who refused to allow them to enter their apartments or even denied their identity. Others would meet relatives from abroad only at such public places as railway stations, hotels, or park benches. Still others would find a foreign Jew highly suspect and would ensure that no one saw them in such company. Thus, an American Jewish professor of bacteriology who went to the U.S.S.R. to participate in an international congress talked with many Jews from different walks of life (he mentions conversations with 150 persons). He felt 'a state of palpably strong fear' amongst Jews he met in synagogues. Those Soviet Russian scientists he met were also anxious that their contacts with a foreign Jew should remain unnoticed.[1]

There are, however, two days in the year—the Day of Atonement and, more particularly, Simchat Torah—on which Jews, especially the young, are not fearful of being seen in the proximity of synagogues (Moscow, Leningrad, and elsewhere). It seems that a few years ago Jewish youngsters began celebrating the 'Simchat Torah Festival'. The police did not like it, but the authorities not only tolerated the 'disturbance' but arranged, after all, for the street to be lit during Simchat Torah night.

Some Jewish intellectuals either feel no fear or have courage enough to overcome their 'Jewish' anxiety. Professor Evsei Lieberman (professor of Economics at the University of Kharkov) appears to have been such a one when he began years ago to make suggestions for changing the organization of production in Soviet Russia. At that time his ideas were pure heresy from the viewpoint of communist theory and Soviet practice and were not accepted until years later. This also applies to the younger generation of freedom-minded Soviet intellectuals among whom the ratio of Jews seems to be considerable. Of the four defendants in the trial of

---

[1] David M. Weiss, 'The Plight of the Jews in the Soviet Union', *Dissent*, July–August 1966 (reprint).

January 1968 who were charged with anti-Soviet activities, at least one was a Jew (Alexander Ginsberg). And of the group which protested against this trial and sent a protest letter to the conference of the communist parties in Budapest (end of February 1968) at least half were Jews (Paul M. Litvinov, grandson of the late Maxim M. Litvinov; Piotr Yakir, son of the late General Yakir and nephew of the famous Hebrew poet Ch. N. Bialik; Ilya Gabai; Boris Shragin(?); Anatoly Levitin; Mrs. Larissa Daniel).[1]

SELECTED BIBLIOGRAPHY[2]
(In addition to the references in the footnotes)

Ackerman, Nathan W. and Marie Jahoda, *Anti-Semitism and Emotional Disorder*, New York, 1950.

Adorno, T. W. and others, *The Authoritarian Personality*, New York, 1950.

Allport, Gordon W., *The Nature of Predjudice*, Boston, 1954.

Altschuler, Mordechai, *The Jews in the Soviet Union Census 1959* (Hebrew), Jerusalem, 1963.

Ben-Ami, *Between Hammer and Sickle*, Philadelphia, 1967.

Bein, Alex., 'Modern Antisemitism and its Place in the History of the Jewish Question' in A. Altman (ed.), *Between East and West*, London, 1958, pp. 164–93.

Ben-Israel, Shlomo, *Russian Sketches. A Visit to Jews Without Hope*, New York, n.d.

Bernstein, Perez, *Jew-Hate as a Sociological Problem*, New York, 1951.

Bettelheim, Bruno and Morris Janowitz, *Dynamics of Prejudice*, New York, 1950.

Bilinsky, Yaroslav, *The Second Soviet Republic. The Ukraine After World War II*, New Brunswick, N.J., 1964.

Conquest, Robert (ed.), *Soviet Nationalities Policy in Practice*, New York, 1967.

Der Kampf gegen Religion und Geistlichkeit in den Sovietisierten baltischen Länder, Estland, Lettland, und Lithuanen. Reprint from *Acta Baltica V*, Königstein im Taunus, 1966.

DeWitt, Nicholas, *Education and Professional Employment in the U.S.S.R.*, Washington, D.C., 1961.

Dubnow, Simon, *Divrey Yemey Am Olam* (Hebrew), vol. ii., Tel Aviv, 1940.

Emiot, Israel, *Der Birobidzhaner Inyen*, Rochester, New York, 1960.

Ehrenburg, I., 'Ludi, Gody, Zhizn', *Novy Mir*, nos. 1, 2, 4, 1965.

Fainsod, Merle, *Smolensk under Soviet Rule*, Cambridge, Mass., 1958.

Freid, Jacob (ed.), *Jews in the Modern World*, vol. 1., New York, 1962, pp. 91–138 (Chap. 7, 'The Jews in the Soviet Union').

---

[1] *The New York Times*, 28 February 1968. The above may also indicate that people of Jewish origin fare no worse (or not much worse) than others when opposing the regime. Otherwise perhaps the non-Jewish 'liberals' would not have wanted their cause to suffer through the former's participation, or be tainted 'a Jewish opposition'.

[2] See also chapters 16 and 17.

Glock, Charles Y. and Rodney Stark, *Christian Beliefs and Anti-Semitism*, New York and London, 1966.

Goldberg, B. Z., *The Jewish Problem in the Soviet Union*, New York, 1961.

Gorev, M., *Protiv Antisemitov*, Moscow–Leningrad, 1928.

Graeber, Isacque and Stenar Henderson Britt (ed.), *Jews in a Gentile World*, New York, 1942.

Isaac, Julius, *The Teaching of Contempt: Christian Roots of Anti-Semitism*, New York, 1964.

Larin, Yu., *Evrei i Antisemitism v S.S.S.R.*, Moscow–Leningrad, 1929.

Lestschinsky, Jacob, *Dos Sovetische Yidntum* (Yiddish), New York, 1941.

Levine, Irving R., *Main Street, U.S.S.R.*, New York, 1959.

Maor, Yitzhak, *The Jewish Question in the Liberal and Revolutionary Movement in Russia* (Hebrew), Jerusalem, 1964.

Narody Evropeiskoi Chasti S.S.S.R., vol. i–ii, Moscow, 1964.

Novak, Joseph, *The Future is Ours, Comrade*, London, 1960.

Parkes, James, *Antisemitism*, Chicago, 1963.

Patterns of Prejudice, bi-monthly, vol. 1, London, 1967.

Pinson, Koppel S. (ed.), *Essays on Antisemitism*, 2nd edn., New York, 1946.

Pulzer, P. G. J., *The Rise of Political Anti-Semitism in Germany and Austria*, New York, 1964.

Sartre, Jean-Paul, *Antisemite and Jew*, New York, 1965.

Schwarz, Solomon M., *Antisemitism v Sovetskom Soyuze*, New York, 1952.

Schwartz, Solomon M., *Evrei v Sovetskom Soyuze*, New York, 1966.

Schwarz, Solomon M., *The Jews in the Soviet Union*, New York, 1951.

Simirenko, Alex (ed.), *Soviet Sociology*, Chicago, 1966.

Simmel, Ernst (ed.), *Antisemitism a Social Disease*, New York, 1946.

Stember, Charles Herbert and others, *Jews in the Mind of America*, New York and London, 1966.

Tscherikover, Elias, *The Pogroms in the Ukraine in 1919* (Yiddish), New York, 1965.

Tumin, Melvin M., *An Inventory and Appraisal of Research on American Anti-semitism*, New York, 1961.

Valentin, Hugo, *Antisemitism Historically and Critically Examined*, New York, 1936.

Weinryb, B. D., 'East European Jewry', in *The Jews, Their Culture and Religion*, (ed. L. Finkelstein), 3rd edn., vol. I, New York, 1960.

Weinryb, B. D., 'A Note on Anti-Semitism in Soviet Russia', *Slavic Review*, vol. xxv, 1966.

Weinryb, B. D., 'Polish Jews Under Soviet Rule', in Peter Meyer, Bernard D. Weinryb, and others, *The Jews in the Soviet Satellites*, Syracuse, 1953.

Weinryb, B. D. 'Solving the "Khazar Problem", A Study in Soviet Historio-graphy', *Judaism*, vol. 13, no. 4, 1964, pp. 431–43.

Wiesel, Elie, *The Jews of Silence*, New York, 1965.

Zuckerman, Nathan, *The Wine of Violence. An Anthology on Anti-Semitism*, New York, 1947.

15

After the Six-Day War

ZEV KATZ

I

The war of June 1967 between Israel and the Arab countries had a deep influence on the relationship between the Soviet Government, Soviet Jewry, and Israel. This complex of circumstances, together with the associated problem of the Soviet attitude to world Jewry and world public opinion, including that of the communist parties, forms the context of our discussion.

There can be hardly any doubt that in their great majority the Soviet Jews reacted to the results of the war with feelings very different from those of the Kremlin leadership. A clear piece of evidence is provided by Ilya Ehrenburg, as recorded by Alexander Werth:

Well, it's just as well they didn't allow themselves to be exterminated by the Arabs, as they were in the Hitler days. Although there were plenty of excellent Jewish soldiers in the Red Army, and many of them were even made Heroes of the Soviet Union, there is still this unpleasant feeling that it's 'natural' for Jews to be massacred. If, following in Hitler's footsteps, the Arabs had started massacring all the Jews in Israel, the infection would have spread: *we would have had here a wave of antisemitism.*[1] Now, for once, the Jews have shown that they can also kick you hard in the teeth; so there is now a certain respect for the Jews as soldiers. . . . And, in Russia, we always have a great respect for highly efficient soldiers and airmen, which the Jews—sorry, I mean the Israelis—certainly proved to be. . . .[2]

If this was the attitude of a communist, a man close to Stalin and an advocate of assimilation as a solution to the Jewish problem, can there be any doubt about the feelings of other Soviet Jews? Moreover, reports by foreign students in Russia, western correspondents and tourists in the U.S.S.R., Soviet expatriates and Soviet tourists abroad—all seem to indicate that the non-Jewish population had considerable sympathy for Israel, was impressed by its military victory, and disillusioned with the Arabs and the errors of Soviet diplomacy.

[1] In all quotations in this chapter, the emphasis has been added unless otherwise stated.
[2] A. Werth, *Russia: Hopes and Fears*, Cresset Press, London, 1962, p. 242.

But these sources also noted a serious aggravation in the position of Soviet Jewry.[1] An Asian student, formerly in Moscow, told the present writer:

It is only natural that some of the Jewish students were secretly celebrating the victory of the Israelis. . . . They were greatly concerned that if the Jews lost the war they would be finished off by the Arabs. . . . When the authorities learned about the celebrations, they made a large-scale search for the participants. . . . In Moscow, there were rumours of pressure brought on Jewish personalities to sign a public condemnation of Israel, backed-up by threats and arrests; but some well-known Soviet Jews were reported to have refused to sign it. . . .[2]

Reports confirm that a number of Soviet citizens and students were arrested and charged with 'Zionism', but there is as yet no evidence of the arrest of any well-known Soviet Jewish personality or of their dismissal. Even so the new Soviet propaganda offensive after the war reached a level of unprecedented vituperation against Israel, Zionism, and world Jewry which has weakened the position of Soviet Jewry. Most of its themes merely continue those already in existence but certain new features have been added. These may be summarized as follows:

(a) Jewish and Israeli leaders (ruling circles) were often presented as Nazi collaborators and friends of Western Germany even before the Six-Day War; now the Israelis in general are depicted as 'Nazis'. Jewish and Israeli leaders are described as allies of the neo-Nazis.

(b) Before 1967 Soviet sources argued that the 'policies of the ruling circles of Tel Aviv are threatening the vital interests of the people and the fate of their country'; now they often stress that they 'jeopardize the very existence of Israel as a state'—thus referring to a possibility of the total liquidation of Israel.

(c) Israel is said to be intent on establishing an 'empire from the Nile to the Euphrates', in which the Israelis will be a kind of 'Herren-volk'. Israel is an integral part of 'world imperialism', the goal of which is 'to establish imperialist rule over the whole world'.

(d) Israel is no longer merely trying to 'poison the minds' of Soviet citizens but is endeavouring to establish a 'fifth column' inside the socialist countries. Zionism and Israel are 'anti-communist by their very nature', 'implacable enemies of the socialist camp', etc.

[1] 'Soviet Reactions to the Middle East Crisis' (18 August 1967), pp. 9–10. A copy of this internal survey and analysis carried out by an organization in western Europe is deposited in the archives of the Institute of Jewish Affairs, London.

[2] Zev Katz, 'The Aftermath of the June War—Soviet Propaganda Offensive against Israel and World Jewry', in *Bulletin on Soviet Jewish Affairs*, No. 1, 1969, p. 27.

(e) Almost without exception Jewish organizations, world Jewish bodies, and Jewish communities of many countries *in toto* are described as 'the most reactionary Jewish bourgeoisie'; images such as 'a world Jewish conspiracy', 'rich Jewish millionaires', who control the great powers of the west, have become frequent in the Soviet press and radio. There is little difference between these accusations and similar pages in the Protocols of the Elders of Zion and Streicher's *Stürmer*.

(f) Finally Judaism, which for long had been depicted as a 'reactionary religion', has now become 'a religion that calls for genocide and enslavement of all other peoples by the Jews'.[1]

The most notorious examples of this campaign were provided by Trofim Kichko and Yury Ivanov. The former published his *Judaism and Zionism* (Kiev, 1968) and the latter his *Beware: Zionism!* (Moscow, 1969). The latter was described by *Komsomolskaya Pravda* as 'the first Soviet scientific and fundamental work on this subject' (6 February 1969). Both books were the object of extensive serialization and review in the Soviet mass media and thus became the main focus of the propaganda campaign. They also gave it a new intensity and directness. Their main feature is that in practice they come to attack Judaism and world Jewry *as such*, although they are officially and ostensibly directed against Zionism. Kichko does not merely attack certain aspects of Judaism while regarding other aspects as 'progressive'. He describes Judaism *in toto* as a religion and ideology akin to Nazism. The same applies to Ivanov. In writing about Israel some Soviet media still make the point that 'the ruling circles' should not be identified with 'the people' and refer to 'progressive and peace-loving forces in Israel'. (Even Kichko admits this.) But when writing of world Jewry neither Kichko and Ivanov nor the Soviet media at large present any 'positive forces'. In Kichko's book Jewry as such is represented by the image of 'the Jewish bourgeoisie', motivated primarily by

the chauvinistic idea of the god-chosenness of the Jewish people, the propaganda of messianism and the idea of *ruling over the peoples of the world*. . . . Such ideas of Judaism were inculcated into the Jews first by the priests and later by the Rabbis for centuries and are inculcated today by Zionists, educating the Jews in *the spirit of contempt and hatred towards other peoples* . . . the ideologists of Judaism, through the 'Holy Scriptures' *teach the observant Jews to hate people of another faith and even destroy them*. . . . Judaism teaches that Jews should force the subjugated peoples in the invaded lands to work for them as for a people of priests. . . . If, however, the subjugated should not want to submit, the Torah solves the problem shortly,

[1] See Appendix, pp. 334–6.

clearly and in a particularly inhuman way: 'For the nation and kingdom that will not serve thee shall perish' (Isaiah, 60:12).

Ivanov, for his part, defines Zionism as

the ideology, the ramified system of organization and the political practice of the *big Jewish bourgeoisie* that has merged with the monopolistic circles of the U.S.A. and of other imperialist powers. Its basic content is militant chauvinism and anti-communism. . . . The *international Zionist alliance* serves as a connecting link, playing the role of *a secret channel between the most reactionary forces in the Imperialist states*, primarily the U.S.A., German Federal Republic and Britain and the Israeli militarists. . . .[1]

There can hardly be any doubt that such propaganda may have a serious impact in arousing anti-Jewish prejudice, and reviving dormant anti-semitism.

II

The fate of Soviet Jewry also became linked with the spreading dissidence in eastern Europe. In March 1968 student demonstrations and clashes with police in Poland greatly intensified an overt antisemitic campaign in Poland, which had begun immediately after the Six-Day War. From the second half of 1967 onwards events took place in Czechoslovakia which resulted in the Soviet intervention of August 1968 and the consequent defeat of the 'liberal communists'. Parallel developments in the Soviet Union were a wave of intellectual protest and demands for a liberalization of the system.

At first glance these events may not appear connected, but they have certain implications in relation to their Jewish aspect. One obvious point is the prominence of citizens of Jewish origin. The other is the conscious use of anti-Jewish prejudice and even open antisemitism. In Poland a number of the student leaders were Jewish, some of them offspring of prominent Polish-Jewish communists. Here the authorities, especially the Moczar faction, openly used antisemitism as a political weapon. The Jews, many of them life-long Polish communists and prominent personages in Polish culture and science, were made a scapegoat in order to divert the frustration of the Polish masses and make place for nominees of Moczar and of others for senior positions. The Soviets were not the instigators of these policies, but supported the antisemitic tendencies without a word of criticism. Soviet media reprinted some of the antisemitic Polish publica-

[1] For fuller extracts from the works of Kichko and Ivanov see the *Bulletin on Soviet and East European Jewish Affairs* (London), No. 3, January 1969, pp. 45–7, 50–2.

tions, e.g. the writings of Walichnowski. They also repeated faithfully Polish allegations that the March events represented a conspiracy on the part of 'International Zionism'.[1]

The leadership of the 'liberal communists' in Czechoslovakia included Professor E. Goldstuecker who was elected chairman of the radical Writers' Union, and Mr. F. Kriegel, then chairman of the National Front and the only Jewish member of the Politburo. Mr. Ota Sik, then Deputy Prime Minister and father of the plan for economic reform was often presented as of Jewish origin, though he himself denied this. A number of well-known liberal broadcasters, writers, and journalists were also Jewish or pro-Israeli.

Only very few local pro-Soviet conservatives (e.g. the Jodas group) made an attempt to use antisemitism. The party leadership as such refrained from this, whereas the liberals fought against antisemitism and even against extremist anti-Israeli policies. In this case it was the Soviet leadership which made premeditated use of antisemitic appeals in order to break the unity of the Czechoslovak liberal leadership, weaken it by removing the talented Jewish personalities, and exploit the nationalist and racialist prejudice of the masses to turn them against their government. Though the liberal leaders resisted, the final result was a success for the Soviet-conservatives alliance, at least in one aspect: the Czechoslovak leadership became *judenrein*.[2]

In the movement of intellectual and liberal dissent in the U.S.S.R., much as in the revolutionary movement in tsarist Russia, persons of Jewish origin are taking a prominent part. Boris Pasternak was the first intellectual 'rebel' in the post-Stalin period. Likewise Ilya Ehrenburg in his last years may be regarded in the same light. Yuli Daniel, the dissenting writer, is a son of the Yiddish writer, Meyerovich. He was sentenced to a period of detention in a labour camp in the political trial together with Siniavskii who, though non-Jewish, wrote under the Jewish-sounding name of Abram Tertz. Daniel's wife, Larissa, who became the focus of the 'movement' and was then exiled to Siberia, is also the daughter of a Jewish writer; Paul Litvinov, the author of many 'open letters' to the Soviet leaders protesting against re-Stalinization and political trials, is the grandson of Maxim Litvinov, the Soviet Foreign Minister in the thirties.

---

[1] For a detailed description see: 'The Anti-Jewish Campaign in Present-Day Poland', prepared by L. Blit, I.J.A., London, 1968; and Z. Bauman, 'The End of Polish Jewry', *Bulletin*, No. 3, January 1969, pp. 3–8.

[2] See, e.g.: M. Decter, 'Soviet Antisemitism—An Instrument of Policy in Eastern Europe', Academic Committee on Soviet Jewry, New York, 1968; 'The Use of Antisemitism Against Czechoslovakia', I.J.A., London, 1968.

Though only 'a quarter Jew' (M. Litvinov's wife was non-Jewish) he actually received antisemitic letters full of abuse and threats. Others active in this dissent included Alexander Ginsberg (sentenced in the trial together with Galanskov), Yevgenia Ginsburg (author of *Into the Whirlwind*); her son by a mixed marriage, Vasily Aksinov (a young, talented, dissenting writer); Benjamin Kaverin (Benjamin Zilberg), the veteran deceased writer who boldly defended Solzhenitzyn; Iosif Brodskii, the young rebellious poet, who was exiled as a 'parasite' and later released after much outcry among Soviet intellectuals and in the world press; Piotr Yakir, the son of the Jewish general Yona Yakir and hero of the civil war; and many others.

Moreover, the position of Jews has become prominent in the writings of many non-Jews in the Soviet Union. Jewish themes and Jewish names are well to the fore in the stream of dissenting documents emanating from the Soviet Union and published in the west. Academician A. Sakharov in his well-known Memorandum refers to the existence of official antisemitism in the Soviet Union, and equates Stalin with Hitler. He warns against racism as 'an extreme reflection of the dangers of confronting modern social developments'. An

unenlightened zoological kind of antisemitism was characteristic of Stalinist bureaucracy and the N.K.V.D. (and Stalin personally). . . . Is it not disgraceful to allow another backsliding into antisemitism in our appointments policies (incidentally, in the highest bureaucratic élite of our government, the spirit of antisemitism was never fully dispelled after the nineteen-thirties).[1]

Jewish themes appear often in the works of Yevtushenko, Voznesensky, A. Kuznetsov, etc. Finally, a trial analysis of the names of the signatories of the many protest petitions and appeals circulating 'privately' in the U.S.S.R. shows that about one-third are Jewish: there were thirty-six Jews amongst the ninety-five signatories of a petition by Leningrad mathematicians; fifteen amongst forty-six Novosibirsk signatories; and six out of twelve who addressed an appeal to the Budapest World Communist Preparatory Meeting in spring 1968 requesting an amnesty for 'thousands of political prisoners' and protesting at 'discrimination against small nations'.[2]

In dealing with the dissent inside the U.S.S.R. the Soviet leadership has

[1] A. Sakharov, *Progress, Co-Existence and Intellectual Freedom*, London, 1968; and, 'Jewish Aspects of the Sakharov Memorandum', I.J.A., Research Report, U.S.S.R./3, December 1968.
[2] See the collections of documents in 'Problems of Communism, July–August and September–October, 1968'; I.J.A. Research Report, U.S S.R./2, December 1968.

not so far reverted to a conscious use of antisemitism as was the case in Poland and Czechoslovakia. Even so, there is considerable evidence of antisemitic overtones in connection with these events. Thus both Pasternak and Ehrenburg were regarded as 'not of our own' by conservative Russian-nationalist writers and were often attacked as 'internal émigrés' (e.g. Sholokhov questioned whether Ehrenburg was a *Russian* writer'). In the writings of both Daniel and Siniavskii the theme of antisemitism in the U.S.S.R. made its appearance. During the trial the prosecution attempted to present the non-Jew Siniavskii as an antisemite; this was emphatically rejected by Daniel.[1] In some way Soviet security had here tried to use antisemitism the other way round—by accusing the liberals of it. In his book on the political labour camps in Russia today, Yuli Marchenko describes antisemitic hostility to Daniel both on the part of other prisoners and some members of the security administration.[2] The same attitude was manifest when police agents broke up the demonstration in Red Square against the intervention in Czechoslovakia on 25 August 1968. Of the six demonstrators two were Jewish (Larissa Daniel and V. Feinberg) and one 'of Jewish origin' (Paul Litvinov). The agents attacked them, shouting: 'These are all dirty Jews (*Zhidy*)', and took special care to beat up the Jews among them.[3]

One further development shapes the situation of Soviet Jewry: the continuation (and even some intensification) of serious concern within the international communist movement regarding Soviet Jewry and Soviet extremist policies *vis-à-vis* Israel. This was pronounced after the Six-Day War in the communist parties of Sweden, Finland, Australia, the U.S.A., Holland, Denmark, Austria, Canada and even in sections of the large and influential French and Italian parties. A critical attitude towards Soviet pro-Arab policies has become dominant in most Jewish-communist publications in the west. These attitudes even found expression at the World Conference of Communist Parties in Moscow, in June 1969. Most prominent was the stand of the Australian communist delegation which refused to sign the Moscow document, on the ground, *inter alia* of disagreement with the passage that dealt with the Middle East conflict. The Australians demanded that it include a passage emphasizing the right of all states in the area to a secure existence. It also formally moved that a

---

[1] *The Jewish Chronicle*, 4 February and 4 March 1966; *Jews in Eastern Europe*, June 1966, pp. 41–4; L. Labedz and M. Hayward (eds.), *On Trial*, London, 1967.

[2] *Moi Pokazaniya*, London, 1969; see excerpts in *Observer*, 29 June 1969 and 6 July 1969.

[3] Letter by N. Gorbanevskaya, *The Times*, London, 29 August 1968; *Jewish Chronicle*, 30 August 1968.

condemnation of antisemitism be included in the Common Document and
protested when this was rejected.[1]

III

Amongst part, at least, of Soviet Jewry a new mood is discernible
following the Six-Day War: that of staunch resistance to pressures
demanding public support for Soviet policies hostile to Israel (see above,
p. 326) and of active protest at these policies. It is coupled in a number of
cases with the open renunciation of Soviet citizenship and with insistent
demands for the right to emigrate to Israel. A number of appeals, protests,
and other documents to this effect has emanated from the Soviet Union
signed by individuals and groups of Jewish citizens. But perhaps the most
significant manifestation of the reported new Jewish mood is the courageous attitude to emigration to Israel. After the stoppage of emigration
following the outbreak of the Six-Day War, the first exit visas were again
issued in autumn 1968 at the initiative of the authorities, who suddenly
revived earlier applications. But once the renewed possibility of emigration became known, thousands of Jews applied for exit visas. This in
itself was not a new phenomenon. What was new were the circumstances surrounding such a step, the atmosphere of an incessant campaign
of hate against Israel and Zionism, which make the application a serious risk.
Should the exit permit be refused, the applicant must continue to live in
the Soviet Union after having in practice revealed himself 'a Zionist'.
New also is the manner in which large numbers of Russian Jews are said
to attend railway stations or airports to bid farewell to those in possession
of an exit visa. These occasions are sometimes transformed into miniature
public demonstrations. Relations and friends sing Hebrew songs and talk
openly of their own hope to follow later.[2] If these reports are correct, they
would indicate that the 'Jews of Silence' have begun to regain their voice.

The Soviet authorities have shown themselves sensitive to the pressures
brought to bear upon them on behalf of Soviet Jewry and Israel. They
have in fact taken certain steps to appease Jewish public opinion. The
renewal of emigration of Jews from Russia albeit in very small numbers,
and, interestingly enough, the publicity given to this in communist
journals outside Russia, may be regarded as such a step. Other such

[1] Communist Party of Australia Press Release, 16 June 1969; International Meeting of
Communist and Workers Parties, Moscow, June 1969, official speeches by L. Aarons, and B.
Taft; 'World Communist Disunity over Jews and the Middle East', *Jews in Eastern Europe*,
May 1968.

[2] The present writer has this at first hand from people who were allowed to join relatives
abroad and from others who talked to them.

moves include a series of talks that the Soviet commentator on the Middle East, Belyaev, had with Jewish leaders in the United States, and a special declaration by a Tass representative in London made to the correspondent of the Israeli journal *Davar*. A small printing of the Jewish prayer book, said to be prepared in 1965, finally reached the Moscow community in 1968. And in the spring of 1969, when Rabbi Levin of Moscow celebrated his seventy-fifth birthday, invitations were sent to a dozen rabbinical leaders in the west and in Israel. But the majority of those who accepted were refused visas. In the end only two foreign rabbis attended the celebrations.[1] In the spring of 1969 even the small trickle of Soviet Jews permitted to emigrate came to a halt.

To sum up: these developments seem greatly to aggravate the future prospects of Soviet Jewry. The post-Khrushchev Soviet leadership has shown itself ready to use anti-Jewish prejudice in order to suppress a revolutionary and intellectual ferment questioning its position, in Poland, Czechoslovakia and in the U.S.S.R. itself. In some aspects the present situation is similar to that in Russia at the beginning of the century. Should the movement of dissent become sufficiently strong to endanger the present rulers and should this be coupled with a growth in Jewish national awareness and activism, the Soviet leadership may decide that the Jews constitute a convenient scapegoat and use antisemitism as a useful diversion for the masses. They may also follow Gomulka in attempting at the same time to rid themselves of the nationally conscious Jews and those active in the dissent movement by opening the gates. It is obviously impossible to predict which will be the case. Both consequences are likely at different times—and even at one and the same time. There always remains the third possibility—of a democratization in the Soviet Union itself, which can alone bring a positive solution to the Jewish problem in the U.S.S.R.

IV

The situation of Soviet Jewry clearly presents a striking paradox. On the one hand, analysis of official Soviet declarations and of the output of the Soviet media clearly shows that anti-Zionism is practically anti-semitism by proxy. At one time it was 'rootless cosmopolitans', then the 'Doctors' Plot'—now it is the 'Zionists'. Names change, the content remains the same. The sources show an almost total condemnation and hatred of Judaism, world Jewry, and Israel, in terms that often resemble

---

[1] *Morning Star* (London), 28 April 1969; for the circumstances surrounding Rabbi Levin's birthday see *Jewish Chronicle*, 14 February 1969.

and even are identical with the attacks of classical antisemitism. Thus there is a natural tendency to identify Soviet anti-Zionism with the antisemitism of Hitler or of the Black Hundreds.

But many other facts are by no means compatible with such a conclusion. Whereas discrimination is marked, cultural-national rights almost totally denied, and the Jewish religion even more oppressed than any other, certain positive aspects also characterize the situation of Soviet Jewry. Not only is there no evidence that any Jews in prominent positions have been arrested or dismissed but the latest data available in the educational field (see table A) show an interesting picture. The percentage of Jews among scientists, among the total of educated specialists in the country, and among pupils at secondary technical schools, continues to fall. On the other hand, the percentage of Jewish students in higher education has actually risen slightly in the last two years (from 2·45 per cent in 1965–6 to 2·57 per cent in 1966–7 and 2·55 per cent in 1967–8). This may be partly a result of the diminution of special preferences for applicants from factories and farms where the percentage of Jews is not high; and partly the result of a further shift of young Jews from specialized secondary to higher education. The percentage of Jews who are working specialists or studying to become specialists (item 6 in the table) has also fallen from 3·5 to 3·0 per cent between 1963–4 and 1967–8.

Despite everything, the Jews in the U.S.S.R. remain unique among all the Soviet nationalities. In their socio-cultural structure they tend to resemble Jewish communities in the developed west rather than any other Soviet nationality or even Israeli Jewry. The figure of 110,000 students in higher education in the U.S.S.R., though commensurately not as high as for the young Jewish generation in the United States, appears favourable when compared with a figure of 35,000 in Israel. The Jewish populations in the U.S.S.R. and Israel are roughly of the same size, though their totally different socio-occupational pattern must obviously be taken into account. Almost 60,000 Jews in the U.S.S.R. are 'scientific and academic workers', which still amounts to more than 7·5 per cent of the total, despite a continuous decline. At the highest level of Soviet science, Jewish participation is much higher. In 1966–7, fifty-seven Jews were members of the U.S.S.R. Academy of Sciences; twenty were members and corresponding members of the U.S.S.R. Academy of Medical Sciences. In the 1968 list of Soviet State prizes awarded for science, art, and technology there are thirty-two Jewish names out of a total of 185 (17 per cent).[1]

[1] Solomon Rabinovich, *Jews in the Soviet Union*, Novosti, Moscow, 1967, pp. 55–7; *Bulletin of News and Recent Developments in Soviet Jewish Affairs*, January 1969.

TABLE A
Latest Data on Jews in the U.S.S.R. in the Post-Khrushchev period

	1963–4	1967–8
1. Students in higher education (including evening and external)	82,600	110,000
Jews as percentage of total	2·5*	2·55
2. Students at specialized secondary schools	51,300	46,700
Jews as percentage of total	1·72	1·12
3. Working specialists with higher education	322,700†	327,800‡
Jews as percentage of total	7·1	6·27
4. Working specialists with specialized secondary education	159,700†	169,300‡
Jews as percentage of total	2·4	2·2
5. Scientific and academic workers	50,915†	58,952
Jews as percentage of total	8·3	7·65
6. Total Jewish specialists and students in the U.S.S.R. (1–4 above, including most of 5 as well)	616,300	653,800
Jews as percentage of total	3·5	3·0

* 1965–6: 2·45 per cent
† 1964: (Nov.)
‡ 1966: (Nov.)

Sources: *Soviet Union—50 Years* (Progress Publishers, Moscow, 1968), pp. 237–8. *Narodnoe Khozyaistvo S.S.S.R.* (Statistika, Moscow), 1967, pp. 803, 811. See also: J. A. Newth, 'Jews in the Soviet Intelligentsia', *Bulletin on Soviet Jewish Affairs*, no. 2, July 1968, pp. vii, 1–12.

Altogether, of an estimated Jewish population of about 2·6 million for 1967–8—including women, children, and old people—about two-thirds of a million, i.e. one in four, are specialists or are preparing to become specialists.[1] Though they lack a republic of their own, the Jews, who are in eleventh place by number, occupy on many counts the third or fourth place in the U.S.S.R.—after the Russians and the Ukrainians (and the Byelorussians).

The meaning of this seems to be that though the Soviet establishment does not wish to see Jews in politically influential positions, it cannot do without Jews in science, education, health, the arts, and economics. This applies especially in recent years, when Russia seems to have slipped behind in the strenuous technological race. It also means that despite discrimination, and the closure of many important educational institutions to Jews

[1] For an estimate that about 40 per cent of the *adult* Jewish population are in this category see J. Newth in *Bulletin on Soviet Jewish Affairs*, no. 2, 1968, pp. vii, 2–3. However, this figure is too high due to double-counting of scientific workers, who are included also in the total of 'working specialists' (see the evidence for this in *Soviet Union—50 Years*, pp. 235–6).

(e.g. the higher party schools, military academies and diplomatic schools, certain essential faculties at the best universities, etc.)—young Jews succeed in acquiring high educational standards. The work of the Jews is such that their promotion becomes indispensable and irresistible. The present writer is convinced, moreover, that were it not for anti-Jewish discrimination the number of Jewish students and scientists would be considerably higher. Many would also be prominent in the political and security field from which they are almost totally absent today. In any case, Jews today remain an integral and apparently indispensable part of the Soviet 'technological-scientific powerhouse'.

For further illumination let us consider Russian Jewry in relation to party membership. Figures available in the latest published research on the C.P.S.U. show that at the beginning of the 1960s, Jews had a membership density that is, probably, the highest among Soviet nationalities. In 1962 10 per cent of all Jews in Byelorussia and 5 per cent of all Jews in Uzbekistan and Moldavia were party members. As table B shows, the estimate for the whole U.S.S.R. is that in 1961 2·8 per cent of all party members were Jews. Another estimate puts it at about 1·5–1·7 per cent in 1965. However, even this is much higher than their proportion in the total population—though lower than their proportion in the urban population (2·2 per cent). According to the 1961 estimate, the number of Jewish communists was 260,000. If we take the *minimum* of 1·5 per cent for 1969, the number of Jewish communists would be about 210,000 (out of 14 million). This would amount to approximately 8 per cent of the total Jewish population (estimated 2·6 million) or one of every six adults. A western authority estimates that 'the proportion of communists among the Jewish population of the U.S.S.R. . . . is 80 per 1,000 (average for U.S.S.R. was 51 per 1,000 in 1965). This would make the Jews easily the most party-saturated nationality in the country, and, in terms of absolute numbers, the largest non-Slavic group of communists, with the possible exception of Tatars.'[1] The same authority adds that despite this 'the party saturation of the Soviet Jewish community fell from about 300 per cent of the national average (for the U.S.S.R.) in 1940 to about 140–180 per cent of the national average in 1965'. He indicates that this may be 'due to official discrimination', as well as to the great expansion of membership in recent years and the emphasis laid upon recruitment of workers and farmers. Since these factors are still operative in the post-Khrushchev period, Jewish membership in the party is apparently declining further.

[1] T. H. Rigby, *Communist Party Membership in the U.S.S.R., 1917–1967*, Princeton, 1968, pp. 383–8.

TABLE B
Jews in the Communist Party by Republic, 1959–1963

	Jews as percentage of party members	Jewish party members ('000)	Jewish population (1959)
Byelorussia	6·4 (1962)	14·432	150,000
Moldavia	6·3 (1963)	3·773	95,000
Uzbekistan	2·9 (1959)	6·510	94,000
Ukraine (est.)*	4·5	61·695	840,000
R.S.F.S.R. (est.)*	2·5	158·450	875,000
average	3·0 total	244·860	2,054,000
U.S.S.R. average (est.)†	2·8 total	260·000†	2,268,000

* Estimates based on: J. Newth and Z. Katz, 'Percentage of Jews in the C.P.S.U.', Research Report, U.S.S.R./7, Institute of Jewish Affairs, London, June 1969.

† My estimate based on above.

TABLE C
Percentage of Jews in the C.P.S.U.: 1922–1965

1922*	1927*	1940†	1961‡	1965†	1969‡
5·2	4·3	4·3–4·9	2·8	1·5–1·7	1·5

* **Official data.**

† Estimate by T. H. Rigby, op. cit. (see footnote 1, p. 332).

‡ My estimates from table above and based on Rigby, op. cit.

What is, in brief, the explanation of this position? The Soviet official anti-Jewish attitude, although often fed by traditional antisemitism and in turn promoting it, is by no means identical with the latter. This anti-semitism is *sui generis*: it is political and ideological rather than racialist, nationalist, or religious. It may be better understood with the help of an analogy. The traditional, non-racialist, Russian-Christian antisemite reserved his hatred, contempt, and violence for the Jew who stubbornly stuck to his Jewishness. He was, however, prepared to reconcile himself to a Jew who gave up his Jewishness totally, and accepted Christianity with all the consequences that resulted from this in tsarist Russia.

The attitude of the Soviet communist leader today is somewhat similar. To him a nationally (and religiously) conscious Jew—whether he is an extreme rightist or a Marxist—must be a 'Zionist' (it is enough if he does not wholly agree with Soviet policies on this issue). Therefore, he is also inevitably anti-Soviet, 'anti-communist', 'an ally of imperialism'. Since this is also the position of almost all Jews (including many communists) in the world—apart from those who have been forcibly deprived of self-expression and those who have become totally assimilated—Soviet antisemitism attacks world Jewry with hatred and contempt.[1] In so doing, it often uses very much the same images and methods as traditional and racial antisemitism. However, if a Jew is prepared to renounce totally his Jewishness, enter 'the communist church of the Soviet persuasion'— and, what is crucial, accept Soviet policies and work for them—then he can be accepted. He may even be entrusted with some non-political responsible position. A 'baptized' Jew would be accepted—but not as an equal. A totally 'Sovietized' Jew, who has completely withdrawn himself from anything Jewish and remains only '*Evrei po-passportu a ne po dushe*'—'a Jew by passport and not by soul', may be accepted, but not as an equal. He could not qualify as General Secretary or President. To the Kremlin leadership, Russian Jewry is in the process of becoming a totally Sovietized and Russianized group, which will totally lose all Jewish content and be prepared to put its talents at Soviet service. This may be why the Kremlin sees in every flickering of a true and independent Jewish consciousness among its citizens, in every attempt at contact with Israel and world Jewry—a kind of heresy. They may see it as a Spanish inquisitor would see a *marrano*, adhering in secret to Jewish customs.

This may be one of the reasons for the violent Soviet campaign against 'Zionism'—which in fact denounces 'Jewishness' of any kind. It is first and foremost directed at the 2·5–3 million Jewish Soviet citizens. So long as the young Jew shows no symptoms of Jewish consciousness, so long as he is prepared to become Sovietized and Russianized, a number of limited career possibilities are open to him. This is how Soviet Jewry has achieved whatever it has achieved. But the Soviet Jew, even if he accepts total renunciation of his faith and people must always remain a second-class citizen.

APPENDIX

SPECIMENS OF SOVIET PROPAGANDA AFTER THE SIX-DAY WAR

The first to accuse the Israelis of 'behaving like the Nazis' was the Soviet representative at the United Nations, Mr. Fedorenko. Moscow Radio repeated the charge on 11 June 1967. 'Radio Peace and Progress' explained: 'Israel's military plans are not Israel's military plans at all. They are imported from Washington by Haim Laskov, former Israeli Chief of

[1] See Moshe Sneh, 'Theses of the Communist Party of Israel on Communism, Nationality and the Jewish People', *Bulletin on Soviet and East European Jewish Affairs*, no. 3, January 1969, pp. 54–9.

Staff . . . the Israeli Judases are doing their utmost—with savage brutality they have rained napalm bombs on the peaceful cities and towns of their Arab neighbours.' It was stated in *Izvestia* on 15 June that 'The invaders are killing prisoners of war and defenceless peasants, driving the inhabitants from their homes and publicly executing men, women, and children. Even the western correspondents compare these crimes with those the Nazis perpetrated in the occupied countries during World War Two.' On 5 July 1967, speaking to the graduates of the military academies gathered in the Kremlin, Brezhnev said: 'The Israeli aggressors are behaving like the worst of bandits. In their atrocities against the Arab population it seems they want to copy the crimes of the Hitler invaders' (*Pravda*, 6 July). A frequent tactic in the Soviet media is to present a Soviet Jew delivering an extremist attack upon Israel and World Jewry. One such article entitled 'Whom do the "Prophets" of Zionism Serve?' was signed by V. Rabinovich (*Sovetskaya Rossiya*, 24 January 1969):

The Jewish people was never like other peoples; it was always unique. We are something more than a people, a religion or a civilization; we are all this together and therefore there is no other people like ours. If one replaces the words 'Aryan race' then, instead of the title of the President of the World Zionist Organization, N. Goldmann, one could easily write Führer Adolf Hitler. And there is nothing surprising about this. Both Zionism and Fascism are based on shameless nationalism, a bourgeois chauvinism which in its own interests affirms the special 'rights' of one nation by means of the violation of the rights of other nations—their economic exploitation, political persecution and sometimes even their physical extermination (genocide).

Soviet propaganda puts Jews in all countries under suspicion of spying and treason:

The U.S. Zionist big-shot, M. Nussbaum, said it does not matter whether you resided in Israel or not, the main thing is to serve the Jewish people. This summons, contrary to international norms, finds its apotheosis in the activities of the Israel Secret Service. Even the bourgeois (London) *Sunday Telegraph* admitted that 'the power of the Israel Secret Service lies in its ties with international Zionism'.

Attacks on Jewish personalities and organizations include the following: 'The headquarters of the International Zionist Agency (The Jewish Agency) and of the closely related World Jewish Congress are both in New York. These two organizations are headed by the same man, an American citizen, Nahum Goldmann, whose life story reeks of his other links with imperialist circles of the West' (Moscow Radio in Arabic, 24 September 1967). The American Jewish Committee is, for instance, 'the source of most unbridled anti-Soviet and anti-communist propaganda'; the American Jewish War Veterans—'an evil smelling source of anti-Soviet propaganda'; B'nai B'rith—'a most substantial American reactionary Zionist Organization', a representative of which 'welcomed the activities of American racists', etc. Obviously, one of the crimes of the Jewish organizations is 'protest in defence of the "rights" of Soviet Jews'. As a Moscow daily charges: 'The American Conference on the Status of Soviet Jews unites 24 main Jewish nationalist bodies of the U.S.A.' (*Komsomolskaya Pravda*, 4 October 1967; Moscow Radio in Arabic, 6 October 1967).

In the true tradition of antisemitism, Jews ('Zionists') are depicted as the invisible power which controls the great western powers, the international press, and business, etc. Here is one example:

The adherents of Zionism in the U.S.A. alone number from 20 to 25 million people . . . Jews and non-Jews. They belong to associations, organizations and societies which play the greatest role in American economy, politics, culture, science. Zionist lawyers comprise about 70 per cent of all American lawyers; 60 per cent of the physicists (including *those engaged in secret work on weapons of mass destruction*) and over 43 per cent of industrialists. Adherents of Zionism amongst American Jews own 80 per cent of local and international news agencies. In addition, about 56 per cent of the big publications serve Zionist purposes (*Komsomolskaya Pravda*, 4 October 1967; emphasis added).

And once more:

Zionism in our days is the ideology, organizational system and practice of the *pro-imperialist Jewish bourgeoisie*. Their basic creed is anti-communism. Indeed, the anti-Communism of the *international Zionist corporation* of those *operators in politics, finance, religion and trade* helped Zionism to grow and become the political and strategic helpmate and tool of the U.S.A. (*Za Rubezhom*, no. 32, August, 4 October 1967; emphasis added).

16

The 'Jewish Question' in the Open: 1968–1971

PHILIPPA LEWIS

The years 1968–71 saw the growth of an independent Jewish movement within the Soviet Union: Jews began to act for themselves, to break out of the vicious circle to which they were condemned—allowed neither full assimilation nor satisfaction of their national needs—by demanding the most straightforward solution to the 'Jewish question' in the Soviet Union—emigration to Israel. The few voices which raised this demand in 1968 had been taken up and echoed by a mass movement by 1971, and the West was startled by the new spectacle of a large number of people within the Soviet Union asserting their right to determine their own fate.

At a first glance the desire to emigrate seems non-political, i.e. to pose no threat to the internal structure of Soviet society. It seems a negative desire to opt out of the future of that society, if the latter is unwilling or unable to satisfy national aspirations. In this respect the Jews have an advantage over other national groups, such as the Ukrainians or Crimean Tatars, whose demands directly involve changes inside the Soviet Union. However, the demand for emigration is potentially as great a threat to the authorities as the demand for full national rights within the country: not only would large-scale emigration spoil the image of the Soviet 'fraternal union of peoples' and so lead to embarrassment *vis-à-vis* the rest of the world (not to mention complications in Soviet–Arab relations), but, perhaps more important, it would mean a loss of authority inside the Soviet Union through yielding to the demands of individual citizens for the freedom to choose how and where to live. Academician Andrei Sakharov, a founder member of the unofficial Committee for Human Rights, pointed out the implications of free emigration (as a right of all Soviet citizens) in an open letter of 20 September 1971 to members of the Presidium of the U.S.S.R. Supreme Soviet: 'The freedom to emigrate . . . is an essential condition of spiritual freedom for all.'[1]

The Jewish struggle for emigration is closely bound up with the

[1] This letter is translated in the *New York Times*, 7 October 1971.

internal developments of Soviet society, and the emergence of a Jewish movement as such was largely prompted by the general dissent movement which includes liberal, nationalist, and religious trends. These are reported in the *samizdat* journal *Khronika* (A Chronicle of Current Events), which has appeared bi-monthly since April 1968. It chronicles various aspects of the dissent movement, but itself represents what has become known as the 'Democratic Movement'—the defence of legality and human rights through open, legal struggle, a defence of the Soviet constitution itself. The Democratic Movement has become more vocal since 1968, with the protests and trials surrounding the Soviet invasion of Czechoslovakia.

Khronika provides an accurate mirror for tracing the growth of a clearly defined Jewish movement. Jews had always been prominent in the general dissent movement (see preceding chapter), and at first Jewish protest about specifically Jewish matters was a rare event, reported in *Khronika* among other instances of the individual's assertion of his rights against the authorities. Thus, nos. 8 and 9 (dated June and August 1969 respectively) report on the trial of Boris Kochubievsky; protest letters from Jews appear in no. 10 (October 1969) onwards. Detailed accounts of the arrests of Jews in mid-1970 in connection with the Leningrad hijack attempt are to be found in nos. 14 and 15 (June and August 1970), while the trial itself is described in no. 17 (December 1970). *Khronika* (nos. 14 and 15) duly noted the appearance of *Iskhod*[1] (Exodus) nos. 1 and 2, a Zionist version of itself, which is devoted to individual and collective protests and appeals by Jews, the publication of which was a sign of the crystallization of the Jewish movement. *Khronika* eventually acknowledged the fact of a distinctive Jewish movement, with its own identity and self-consciousness, in no. 18 (March 1971) which contained a new section entitled 'The Jewish Movement for Emigration to Israel'. This has remained a large section ever since (the twenty-fourth issue of *Khronika* appeared in March 1972), detailing the increasing number of protest letters and demonstrations by Jews and the authorities' reaction of harassment and trials.

Turning from *Khronika*'s reflection of the Jewish Movement to Jewish activity itself, we see the bravery of a few individuals leading to the growing self-confidence of a large number of people. Written appeals and protests multiply and tactics of direct confrontation with the authorities are adopted more and more boldly: demonstrations, sit-ins, and hunger strikes. The first letter that became known in the West was from twenty-six Jewish intellectuals of Vilnius, Lithuania, to the First Secretary of the

[1] *Iskhod* nos. 2 and 4 are available in English from the Institute of Jewish Affairs, London.

Central Committee of the Lithuanian Communist Party.[1] Dated 15 February 1968, it was reported in the American press at the end of that year. It refers to discrimination against Jews, suppression of Jewish cultural life, anti-Israeli propaganda which 'has created conditions in which anti-semitism can flourish'—and the result of these factors:

It is known that if the borders were opened up for emigration today, some 80 per cent of the entire Jewish population would leave Soviet Lithuania and go to Israel. They would leave everything behind, despite the unsettled conditions in the Near East, despite the fact that our people here are used to a damp climate, find it difficult to adjust to the climate there, in the main have no knowledge of Hebrew and do not observe religious traditions, and, being mainly employed in services, would not find it easy to become economically integrated into Israeli society.

We face a paradoxical attitude. We are not wanted here, we are forcibly de-nationalised, oppressed and even publicly insulted in the press—and at the same time we are forcibly detained. As the Lithuanian proverb goes: 'He beats and cries with pain at the same time.'

The authors of the letter explain that they are not revealing their names for fear of reprisals, but this was the first and last anonymous protest letter of which we have knowledge. The stream of letters that followed gave both names and addresses of the signatories; maybe these were taking their cue from the Democratic Movement's insistence on openness, on the legality of its protests. The Jewish protesters, too, constantly refer to the fact that they are only criticizing violations of legality and only demanding what is theirs by legal right. Article 13, clause 2, of the Universal Declaration on Human Rights is repeatedly cited: 'Everyone has the right to leave any country, including his own, and return to his country.' This appears on the front cover of *Iskhod* (*Khronika* always quotes on its front page Article 19 of the same Declaration—on the right to freedom of opinion and expression). Frequent reference is also made to Soviet Premier Alexei Kosygin's statement at a press conference in Paris on 3 December 1966, in which he upheld the principle of reunion of families through emigration.

Since the end of 1968 letters from Soviet Jews have appeared regularly in the West. The *Washington Post* on 19 December 1968 publicized a letter by Yakov Kazakov, written on 20 May 1968, in which he reiterates his renunciation of Soviet citizenship (originally made on 13 June 1967) and his demand to leave for Israel. Other instances of renunciation of citizen-ship appeared in early 1969, while the publicity given by the Israeli Government to the letter of '18 religious Jewish families of Georgia' to

[1] Extracts from this letter are given in *Jews in Eastern Europe*, London, July 1969, pp. 52–5.

the U.N. Commission on Human Rights (6 August 1969) probably encouraged more and more Jews to address their appeals abroad. Their
demands and criticisms are repetitive and insistent: the lack of national,
cultural, and religious life for Jews in the Soviet Union, the desire to join
relatives in Israel, declarations of Jewish national self-awareness and of
their right to be 'repatriated' to their own state. But protests were not
restricted to demanding emigration for themselves. Throughout 1970
and 1971 Jews began to defend themselves, to come out publicly against
the arrests of their friends, against the harassment of those who apply for
exit visas to Israel, against the virulent anti-Zionist campaigns in the
press, attacking the notion that the 'official Jews' who participated in these
campaigns represent the feelings or real situation of Soviet Jews. Noteworthy among the latter letters are two replies to a press conference of
prominent Jews held in Moscow on 4 March 1970 to condemn 'Israeli
aggression' and Zionism. A group of forty Moscow Jews in a letter of
8 March[1] disputed the right of the participants to represent all Soviet
Jews and demanded to be allowed to hold their own press conference to
put forward the other point of view; while Ilya Zilberberg, in an open
letter of 12 March voiced the anger and disgust aroused by the spectacle
at the press conference of Jews denouncing Jews.[2]

William Korey, writing in the *New York Times* on 22 January 1971,
notes that between February 1968 and October 1970, 220 appeals from
Jews had reached the West, coming from Moscow, Leningrad, Kiev,
Minsk, Riga, Vilnius, and Tbilisi. Of these, 10 per cent were from Georgia,
34 per cent from Riga, and 26 per cent from Moscow. Since then hundreds
more letters have become known, along with other forms of protest.
In February 1971 there were sit-ins at the U.S.S.R. Supreme Soviet
headquarters in Moscow,[3] which resulted in many of the participants
being given exit visas to Israel. In March of that year there were hunger-
strikes and demonstrations at the C.P.S.U. Central Committee headquarters in Moscow (see the *Daily Telegraph*, 12 March 1971) and later
that year outside the Moscow Central Post Office (see the *Guardian*,
24 June 1971). In July three hundred Georgian Jews demonstrated outside
the Party headquarters in Tbilisi (see *Daily Telegraph*, 6 July 1971) and
on 20 September a delegation of five Moscow Jews was received at the

[1] For the press conference and extracts from the letter of the forty (called in the West
'letter of the 39') see *Bulletin on Soviet and East European Jewish Affairs*, no. 5, May 1970,
pp. 14–35 (published by the Institute of Jewish Affairs, London).

[2] For his open letter see *Soviet Jewish Affairs*, no. 3, May 1972.

[3] A report of one of the most widely publicized of these sit-ins appears in the *Jerusalem
Post*, 25 February, 1972, written by one of the participants, Ephraim Sevela, now in Israel.

Ministry of Internal Affairs to discuss the question of emigration.[1] Other demonstrations marked International Human Rights Day (10 December) and the anniversary of the First Leningrad Trial (15–24 December).

The increasing militancy of Soviet Jews had two most disturbing results as far as the authorities were concerned. Firstly, the Jews succeeded in opening up the borders of the U.S.S.R. in an unprecedented way. By using the simplest methods of modern communication—the postal and telephone systems—they let the outside world know their demands, and the latter could respond—by telephoning its sympathy and support and by relaying back to the Soviet Union, on radio, information on Jewish activity inside that country, which the Soviet media did not report. Therefore, although the Soviet authorities may have been able to suppress the Jewish Movement without fear of *internal* opposition on a large scale, they now found themselves answerable to public opinion abroad, with the uncomfortable necessity of justifying their treatment of the Jews before a world opinion that was increasingly aware. Secondly, as the Jewish Movement became more widespread, vocal, and daring, it provided an example to other aggrieved sections of Soviet society—that instead of waiting for favours 'from above' it may be more profitable to challenge the authorities with insistent demands 'from below'. A noisy demonstration in Moscow, although not reported officially, is not likely to pass off without being noticed and becoming widely known unofficially. *Khronika* no. 19 had yet another new section: 'The Movement of the Meskhetians for a Return to their Homeland'. Like the Crimean Tatars, the Meskhi Turks were deported from their native Georgia in 1944 and they are now demanding their return and the emigration to Turkey of all who so desire, using tactics very reminiscent of Jewish ones.

The Soviet authorities are therefore faced with a clamant popular movement which threatens to infect other sections of the population. One may suppose that, given Jewish discontent, the authorities have two main aims: to silence and contain it—that is, somehow to isolate it from the rest of society and solve the problem discreetly while attracting the least possible attention from outside. In pursuing these aims, the authorities are handicapped by various factors. It is clear that they cannot simply crush the Jewish Movement as was possible under Stalin. And this is not only because they are now acting before the eyes of the outside world (though this is undoubtedly an important consideration). Here we are faced with the complex question of the evolution of the Soviet regime,

[1] See the account by one of the delegates now in Israel, Pavel Goldstein, in the *Jerusalem Post*, 20 December 1971.

its attempts to regulate the process of de-Stalinization declared by Khrushchev in 1956, to renounce Stalinist methods of terror and yet to prevent
any change in the power structure of society which may result from yielding to the demands of the liberal intelligentsia, economic reformists, or
national groups. Andrei Amalrik in his 1969 essay 'Will the Soviet Union
Survive until 1984?' defines the regime's inertia: 'It only wants everything
to be as before: the authorities were recognized, the intelligentsia kept
quiet, the system was not shaken by dangerous and unaccustomed reforms.
The regime does not attack but defends itself. Its motto: if you don't
touch us, we won't touch you. Its aim: let everything stay the same.'

The regime's relative humaneness since Stalin is its Achilles heel, and
its dilemma as regards internal opposition as a whole is thrown into sharp
relief by its reactions to the Jewish Movement. On the one hand, it cannot round up all the Jews and send them to Siberia (or Biro-Bidzhan); on
the other, it cannot allow free emigration and full national rights and *remain
itself*. The Jews' demands raise the question of the general lack of freedom
within the Soviet Union and their satisfaction depends, ultimately on the liberalization of the whole society. Meanwhile, they pose a threat to the *status
quo* and impel the authorities to apply a variety of measures to contain this
threat. Steering a course between the two extremes of absolute relaxation and
all-out repression, the authorities have of necessity been inconsistent, using
various means, between the limits outlined above, to control Jewish activity.

Their most dramatic reaction has been to ease emigration to Israel.
Since Kosygin's statement of 3 December 1966 there have been other
official statements on the question of Jewish emigration. Their main
feature is reticence: the fact of Jewish emigration is rarely mentioned in
the Soviet press, and then only to deny rumours of large-scale emigration
and to assert that only a few people wish to leave to rejoin their families
and that no obstacles are placed in their way (as remarked, for example, in
Izvestiya, 20 February 1971). Any more detailed policy statement is
provoked by external pressure. Thus, at the press conference of 4 March
1970, M. S. Strogovich, an eminent jurist, when questioned about the
right of Jews to go to Israel, said:

Every citizen has obviously the right to choose freely his citizenship, to live in this
or another state. This principle is written down in the Declaration of Human
Rights, which was adopted by the General Assembly of the United Nations. This
is a democratic, a progressive principle. But nobody is allowed to use it in [further-
ing] the aims of a racialist and aggressive policy, a policy of hatred, as Zionist
circles are trying to do now.[1]

[1] *Bulletin on Soviet and East European Jewish Affairs*, no. 5, May 1970, p. 28.

A similar statement was made by General D. Dragunsky, one of the most travelled of Soviet 'official Jews', at a press conference in Brussels on 19 February 1971: 'Whoever wants to emigrate to Israel has a juridical right to do so. As soon as peace has returned to the region, the emigration procedure will be speeded up.' Kosygin, on an official visit to Canada in October 1971, was besieged with questions about Jewish emigration and obliged to make some sort of a reply: '. . . you know that we are now increasing the number of people who are allowed to emigrate from the Soviet Union. In the past eight months alone 4,450 Jews were allowed to emigrate from the Soviet Union to Israel.'[1] At a press conference in Denmark (5 December 1971, reported in the *Morning Star* on 7 December) he again stressed that many Jewish applications to emigrate 'are being very actively considered and many visas are being issued to enable Jews to go to Israel'. The Washington correspondent of the *Jewish Chronicle* (14 January 1972) was told by a Soviet diplomat: 'We are going to let all Jews go who wish to except for those who might increase Israel's military potential and those who are in sensitive positions in the government.' The most recent official statement (up to April 1972) came from Boris T. Shumilin, U.S.S.R. Deputy Minister of Internal Affairs, in an interview with *Novosti* press agency which was broadcast in Arabic on 24 March 1972.[2] This was obviously designed to play down reports of mass Jewish emigration and attribute them to 'Zionists and imperialist propaganda organs in the West', who exploit 'the fact that small numbers of persons of Jewish nationality do apply to the appropriate Soviet organs requesting permission to leave for Israel.'

The main reasons for these applications . . . are: religious views, the desire to join relatives, sentiments which have survived from the past and private enterprise ambitions. Zionist propaganda also plays a part, influencing some unstable elements.

In 1971 about 10,000 people, of whom approximately two-thirds were old people and women, left the U.S.S.R. for Israel for these reasons.[3]

The actual picture of Jewish emigration is mirrored to a certain extent in these official statements: when Kosygin said in Canada that the number

---

[1] Quoted from a Canadian broadcast of a press conference on 20 October 1971. *Izvestiya* reported on the conference on 24 October, but omitted the figures that Kosygin had cited: 'So far as emigration is concerned, A. N. Kosygin further said that all these questions are considered in due procedure as established by law. He gave specific examples on this score.'

[2] Quotations here taken from *Soviet News*, 11 April 1972.

[3] The usual figure cited for 1971 (in the West) is just under 14,000. According to a report from 'informed sources' in the *Jewish Chronicle*, 11 February 1972, nearly 80 per cent of Soviet Jewish immigrants to Israel in 1971 were under 48 years and only 7½ per cent over 65.

of exit visas issued had been increased he was merely acknowledging a known fact. After the embargo on Jewish emigration following the Six-Day War, a trickle was resumed in 1968. About 3,000 Soviet Jews went to Israel in 1969 and just under a thousand in 1970. At first it seemed as though 1971 would be little different: in January there were about 50 Soviet immigrants to Israel, in February about 130. It was in March that the upsurge came, unexpectedly and dramatically, with over 1,000 Jews leaving for Israel. A relatively high, though fluctuating, rate of emigration has been maintained to date (April 1972).[1]

Naturally there has been widespread speculation concerning the reasons for this sudden increase and subsequent fluctuations. Rumours of a major Soviet policy decision on Jewish emigration abounded in the Western press in mid-March (see, for example, the *Jerusalem Post*, 19 March 1971), and certainly it is likely that the authorities were anxious to get rid of a large number of Jewish activists before the Twenty-fourth C.P.S.U. Congress (24 March–19 April 1971), which would be attended by foreign Communist Parties, some of which have been critical of the Soviet Union's treatment of its Jews. Another factor may have been the World Conference of Jewish Communities on Soviet Jewry, held in Brussels from 23 to 25 February 1971. There were reports that a special commission under the chairmanship of I. M. Shutov, Deputy Police Chief of Moscow, had been set up on 1 March to speed up the issuing of exit visas to Israel before the Party Congress. In May sixty Jews wrote to President N. Podgorny (see the *New York Times*, 6 May 1971) expressing the fear that this commission would be closed, and, certainly, there was a drop in the number of Jews who were allowed to emigrate, from May until September. But in general it may be safely stated that the monthly variations in numbers indicate the authorities' behind-the-scenes vacillation and uncertainty of how to deal with the problem. Other speculation tends to be as real as Victor Louis's theory (quoted in the *Jerusalem Post*, 14 December 1971) that the rise in Jewish emigration towards the end of that

[1] The monthly figures from January 1971 to March 1972 are estimated as follows:

1971							1972	
January	50	April	1,300	July	650	Oct.	1,300	Jan.	3,000
February	130	May	850	August	500	Nov.	3,000	Feb.	1,800
March	1,100	June	700	Sept.	1,200	Dec.	3,000	March	2,000

No official figures of Jewish emigration from the Soviet Union are available either from Soviet or Israeli sources. The figures cited here are based on a 'consensus of opinion' found in Western newspaper reports and provide at least a guide to the relative monthly increase or decrease in the flow of emigration. Estimates of the number of Jews who left the Soviet Union in 1971 vary between 13,000 and 15,000 mostly settling around just under 14,000.

year was a result of pressure from Aeroflot and the Transport Ministry in their eagerness to fulfil their yearly quotas!

However, certain principles concerning Jewish emigration do emerge. It has been estimated that half the Soviet Jews who went to Israel in 1971 were from the territories annexed by the Soviet Union during the Second World War, such as Lithuania and Latvia, 30 per cent were from Georgia, where Jewish traditions have remained strong and Jews are least assimilated, and only 10 per cent from main cities such as Moscow and Leningrad.[1] This pattern seems likely to be repeated in 1972: the Soviet diplomat whose remarks on Jewish emigration were reported in the *Jewish Chronicle* on 14 January 1972 said that: 'Most of the Jews leaving Russia this year would be from rural and outlying areas, not Moscow, Leningrad or Kiev'.[2] So far, his words have been borne out by the facts: there has been an increasing number of instances of harassment of Jews in the main cities and the difficulty of obtaining exit visas in Moscow is notorious. Zeev Ben-Shlomo, writing in the *Jewish Chronicle* on 14 April 1972, suggests that the Soviet authorities still hope to solve the Jewish question through forcible assimilation and are therefore letting out mainly those Jews who are most difficult to assimilate—the intensely religious Georgians and the relatively recent Soviet citizens of Lithuania and Latvia. However, against this, it seems that Jewish national self-awareness is on the increase in Moscow and other major Russian cities. Requests for emigration permits have been made by leading scientists whom one would have thought least likely to meet discrimination or other obstacles to assimilation. The authorities, in making it difficult for Moscow Jews to emigrate, may simply be showing reluctance to lose valuable specialists.

A second feature of Jewish emigration from the Soviet Union is the relative ease with which activists receive exit permits. The *Sunday Times* reported on 24 January 1971 that of the forty Jews who signed the protest against the press conference in March 1970, twenty-six had already received visas; and *Khronika* no. 19 (April 1971) reports that most of the participants in a hunger-strike at the Presidium of the U.S.S.R. Supreme Soviet from 10 to 11 March 1971 had received permission to emigrate by the end of that month. This policy is evidently designed to 'take the steam' out of the Jewish protest movement, although, of course, it could also rebound on the authorities and encourage activism. Jews active in the general dissent movement as well as the Jewish Movement are given exit

[1] *Jewish Chronicle*, 11 February 1972.
[2] *Yedioth Chadashot* (Tel-Aviv), 13 April 1972, reports that three-quarters of Soviet immigrants in March 1972 were from Georgia.

visas particularly quickly, and this may be seen as an attempt to prevent the two movements from acting together: if the Zionists can be isolated and made to concentrate on the limited aim of emigration, so much the better for the regime. That some 'Democrats' with Jewish connections are being encouraged to leave for Israel, as an alternative to constant harassment or worse if they remain in the Soviet Union, was suggested by a moving letter to *The Times* (9 March 1972) from five active Soviet dissidents.[1] They reproach 'educated people' in the U.S.S.R. for keeping silent during the latest attacks on the dissident community: 'And this at a time when some people are being imprisoned, others are being dishonoured and pacified, and yet others are *actually being shown the door from this country*.' (Emphasis added.)

Limited emigration is one of the Soviet authorities' reactions to the Jewish struggle: a certain number of Jews is being allowed to leave, thus preventing the pressure from building up too greatly. Moreover, Jews whose applications to emigrate are being considered may prefer to 'lie low' and wait for an answer and may even exert pressure on those around them to do the same, rather than risk arousing the wrath of the authorities. But the latter apply other methods to counteract the encouragement given to Jews, by seeing others receive permission to emigrate and realizing that leaving the U.S.S.R. is no dream but a real possibility. There are three methods of discouragement, all aimed at preventing the movement from growing to mass proportions and escaping control 'from above': anti-Israeli and anti-Zionist propaganda, harassment of those applying for emigration visas, and repression in the form of arrests and trials.

The propaganda is aimed at two levels: ideological (Israel is a Fascist state and Zionism is the quintessence of International Imperialism) and pragmatic (tales of woe from Soviet Jews who have been disillusioned with Israel, stressing the low standard of living, difficulty of finding employment, and the horrors of a military state). There have been three major anti-Zionist campaigns in the period under discussion.[2] On 30 November 1969 *Pravda* published an article entitled 'Disaster for the Simple Man Here', describing the alleged fate of Georgian Jews in Israel. Very probably this was an indirect reply to the letter of the eighteen Georgian Jews to the U.N. which had received wide publicity. Virulent

[1] Three are Jewish, one is half-Jewish, and one has a Jewish wife. In the letter they state that they are all in the process of emigrating.

[2] An excellent analysis of the function of these campaigns is to be found in an article by Jonathan Frankel: 'The Anti-Zionist Press Campaigns in the U.S.S.R. 1969–1971: An Internal Dialogue?' in *Soviet Jewish Affairs*, no. 3, May 1972.

anti-Zionist articles continued to appear in early 1970, and the campaign culminated in March.[1] March 2nd was designated a 'world day for condemnation of Israeli aggression' and Soviet Jews were induced to join in the chorus of denunciation: the press conference on 4 March was televised and reported at length in *Pravda* on 5 and 6 March. Eleven Jewish religious leaders signed a protest against Israel in *Izvestiya* on 10 March and 102 members of the Kiev Jewish religious community did so on 12 March, also in *Izvestiya*.[2] Increasing publicity was given to Jews allegedly clamouring to return to the Soviet Union from Israel. Thus, *Soviet News* claimed on 21 April 1970:

Hundreds of letters have been received from former Soviet citizens expressing disillusionment with what they have found in Israel and expressing their desire to return to the U.S.S.R.

Many are trying to repay their debts to the Sohnut agency, which is concerned with immigration in Israel, in order to be able to return.

Many letters declare that after living in the Soviet Union it is impossible to accept the ruthless system of class exploitation in Israel.

Others express disillusionment with the Histadrut organization, which they describe as a big financial-industrial monopoly operating under the guise of a trade union.

Still others complain about the inhumanity of the attitude of official Israeli circles towards Jewish immigrants, who are wanted only as cheap manpower or to serve in the armed forces against the Arab peoples.

A second round of the campaign was fired in early 1971, maybe as a counter-blast to the Brussels Conference in February of that year. *Novosti* press agency produced a new booklet: 'Soviet Jews Reject Zionist "Protection" ' which recorded a discussion held on 5 February, and V. Bolshakov wrote a long ideological attack on Zionism in *Pravda*, 18 and 19 February, under the heading 'Anti-Sovietism—the Zionists' Profession' which contained ominous words: 'A person who has turned to the Zionist faith automatically becomes an agent of the International

[1] Documents of this campaign were published by *Novosti* press agency in two booklets, both entitled 'Zionism: Instrument of Imperialist Reaction. Soviet Opinion on Events in the Middle East and the Adventures of International Zionism.' One is dated Feb.–March 1970, the other March–May 1970. The campaign is also documented in *Bulletin on Soviet and East European Jewish Affairs*, no. 5, May 1970.

[2] There is a subtle but unmistakable display of anti-Jewish wit at the expense of these 'loyal' Jews, in the significant arrangement of the signatures beneath the letter. The names are not printed alphabetically: the first name given is Zhidovetsky and the last Ovetsky. *Zhid* is the Russian for 'yid'. The echo of the first and last names, bringing out this hidden insult, implies a deliberate sneer against Jews (nothing is accidental in the Soviet press) which, especially in the Government newspaper *Izvestiya*, amounts to official encouragement to treat Jews accordingly.

Zionist Concern and consequently an enemy of the Soviet people.' Several trials of Zionists took place in mid-1971 and this statement may well have provided their Ideological motivation. In December 1971 an international conference on 'Racism—the Ideology of Imperialism and the Enemy of Social Progress' was held in Moscow, concentrating on racism in its 'Zionist version'. Reports on the conference heralded a new spate of anti-Zionist articles attacking the twenty-eighth World Zionist Congress (Jerusalem, 18–28 January 1972), with particular emphasis on attempts by Zionists to infiltrate the Socialist States and lure their citizens to Israel. Jonathan Frankel, in the article referred to above, convincingly argues that these campaigns are a form of 'internal dialogue' of the regime with its Jewish citizens, an indirect response to their demand for national rights which is otherwise officially passed over in silence. The myth of the harmonious family of peoples within the Soviet Union must be maintained and the dissatisfaction of some put down to subversive influences from outside the country.

If propaganda fails to deter would-be emigrants, the emigration procedure itself is designed to discourage all but the toughest or the most desperate. As Ilya Zilberberg describes it:[1] 'When the Soviet authorities came to the conclusion that they could no longer keep the Jews back and were forced to let them go, they decided to surround the departure procedure with such psychological and bureaucratic obstacles as would make it either completely impossible for most people or as humiliating as possible for the rest.' At the end of 1970 the cost of an exit visa was raised from 40 to 400 rubles and a charge of 500 rubles levied for withdrawal from Soviet citizenship which automatically follows receipt of permission to emigrate (900 rubles is about seven to eight months' average wages). An application for a character reference from one's place of work, which is one of the many requirements when submitting an application for an exit visa, very frequently results in dismissal from work after humiliating public discussion and condemnation of the applicant. An application for a visa may drag on for months or years, with the applicant in serious financial difficulties or even threatened with imprisonment for 'parasitism' if he does not find some menial work.[2] Zilberberg characterizes the

---

[1] 'From Russia to Israel: a Personal Case-history', in *Soviet Jewish Affairs*, no. 3, May 1972. This is a detailed and extremely illuminating account of the growth of Jewish national identity and the process of emigrating from the Soviet Union.

[2] Edward Crankshaw in the *Observer*, 22 August 1971, describes some of the more well-known cases of harassment. Leonard Schroeter in the *Jerusalem Post*, 12 January 1972, describes the predicament of Moscow Jewish scientists who cannot get exit visas. For threats of imprisonment see the *Daily Telegraph*, 28 February 1972.

emigration procedure as a steeplechase in which the authorities 'place hurdles before us which we, like lathery horses, have to clear for their pleasure or amusement.' But all these bureaucratic obstacles are means for the authorities to ensure that emigration remains a privilege, to be strenuously sought after at great personal risk and granted from above, and not a right demanded and asserted by self-respecting individuals who challenge the state's power.

Harassment is a serious deterrent to Jews desiring to emigrate. Sporadic trials of Zionists are designed to intimidate more thoroughly by making an example of leading activists. The first trial to become widely known in the West was that of Boris Kochubievsky in Kiev. He had been open in his Zionist beliefs on several occasions, had written in May 1968 a credo 'Why I am a Zionist' and applied to emigrate to Israel in November. He was arrested at the beginnning of December when permission to leave had already been granted. Charged under Article 187/1 of the Ukrainian S.S.R. Criminal Code ('Dissemination of knowingly slanderous fabrications, defaming the state and social system of the U.S.S.R.'), he was tried (13–16 May 1969) and sentenced to three years in a labour camp.[1] His conviction set the pattern for subsequent trials, when possession of material concerning Jewish history and Israel was classified as 'anti-Soviet agitation and propaganda', although there was never any attempt to demonstrate in what way these materials could be termed anti-Soviet. During the trial of six Jewish students in Ryazan (10–19 February 1970), the 'anti-Soviet' literature cited by the prosecution included Leon Uris's novel *Exodus*, a book on the Six-Day War by Randolph and Winston Churchill Jr., and articles by Zionist leader and theorist Vladimir Jabotinsky. Similar literature was quoted in the indictment of the Jewish trials of mid-1971, along with copies of *Iskhod*, *Iton Aleph* and *Bet* and documents such as 'Your Mother Tongue', an appeal to Jews to register Yiddish as their mother tongue in the 1970 Soviet census.[2] Four of the accused in the Ryazan Trial received sentences varying from three to seven years in strict regime labour camps. Information concerning this trial did not reach the West until the following year. And by then there had been a series of Jewish trials, intended to be a more drastic form of discouragement to Jews seeking to emigrate to Israel.

[1] An account of the trial of Boris Kochubievsky is given in *A Hero for Our Time*, ed. Moshe Decter, published jointly by the Conference on Status of Soviet Jews and the Academic Committee on Soviet Jewry, New York, April 1970.

[2] Extracts from the magazines *Iton Aleph* and *Iton Bet* and the document 'Your Mother Tongue' are translated in *Jews in Eastern Europe*, November 1971, which is devoted to accounts of the 1971 'anti-Zionist' trials.

Given this aim, the trials may be seen as a failure. The world-wide outcry at two death-sentences in the First Leningrad Trial (15–24 December 1970) including criticism from the French, Italian, and British Communist Parties, obliged the Soviet authorities to yield visibly to public opinion. The sentences were commuted, albeit to harsh terms in labour camps, but the damage, in the sense of spotlighting the predicament of Soviet Jews, had been done. Officially, the main charge in this trial was under Article 64-a of the R.S.F.S.R. Criminal Code, which classifies flight abroad as treason. Article 15 of the Code makes an attempted crime equal to a committed one, and thus an attempted hijack of a plane became a capital offence.[1] However, as more information concerning the closed trial reached the West, its purpose became clearer: the defendants had been arrested on 15 June 1970, the day after thirty-seven Leningrad Jews had signed an appeal to U Thant requesting him to intercede with the Soviet authorities on the question of emigration to Israel during his impending visit to Moscow: 'Our motives are not social or political, our motives are deeply national and spiritual'. Among those arrested were six signatories to this letter, who had also signed numerous other letters insisting on their right to emigrate. These facts were pointed out in the *Guardian* on 29 December 1970, while *The Times* on the previous day commented: 'Whereas many people would accept that an attempted hijacking may be punished by death, regardless of the defendants' race, the secrecy surrounding the trial has focused attention on the whole issue of Soviet Jewry.'

The year of increased emigration, 1971, was also the year of trials: the Second Leningrad and Riga Trials in May, the Odessa, Kishinev, and Sverdlovsk Trials in June, the trials of Yemilia Trakhtenberg of Samarkand in September and of Boris Azernikov of Leningrad in October. By the end of the year there were known to be forty-four Jewish prisoners in the Soviet Union serving sentences ranging from one to fifteen years in labour camps, for specifically Jewish activity. At the same time, thousands of their fellow-Jews were emigrating to Israel as the result of similar activity. Their fate had not discouraged the growth of the Jewish Movement: on the contrary, it might even have stimulated it, for their martyrdom could become an example of courage to others, a symbol of the plight of Soviet Jews, and the focal point for increased protest both inside and outside the U.S.S.R.

[1] For the First Leningrad Trial see *Jews in Eastern Europe*, April 1971 and *Iskhod*, no. 4, translated by the Institute of Jewish Affairs, London. See also 'The 1970–71 Soviet Trials of Zionists: Some Legal Aspects' by René Beermann in *Soviet Jewish Affairs*, no. 2, November 1971.

Thus the authorities' attempts at containing and silencing the Jewish Movement have failed. Protests and demonstrations continue: four times in February and March 1972 police clashed with young Jews in Kiev who were trying to attend the Sabbath synagogue service; there were violent clashes with the police at Passover outside the Moscow Synagogue (see the *Jewish Chronicle*, 11 April 1972). Yet emigration figures for 1972 are forecast at 30,000. If harassment of Jews in general grows along with emigration, then the Jews who cannot or do not want to emigrate will be in an increasingly difficult position. These may very well be the vast majority of Soviet Jews, previously only too willing to be assimilated in so far as they are allowed. But the new open assertion of Jewish national consciousness by the active minority does affect them: emigration creates a dynamism of its own and, in areas where it is high, Jews who formerly had no Zionist motivation may be swept along with the current, either fearful of remaining in relative isolation when many of their acquaintances have left, or curious about this new opportunity to leave the country. Dissatisfaction with life in the Soviet Union may be channelled into a discovery, or rediscovery, of national identity, into a refusal to play any longer the official charade that a 'Jewish question' does not exist in the U.S.S.R. On the other hand, those who demand the right to emigrate make the situation more difficult for those left behind. A national group, a section of whose members openly announces its rejection of Soviet citizenship and its affiliation to another state, is not the first candidate for the authorities' trust, no matter how much that may be sought. Given these various factors, the position of the two million or more Jews who are likely to stay in the Soviet Union is fluid, and its evolution is extremely uncertain. Meanwhile, the concrete success of emigration is a serious threat to the regime's image of omnipotence, and possibly the only way to deflate the issue of Jewish emigration would be to grant Jews national rights on a par with those of other national minorities (however limited these may be) and give those who so desire the possibility of becoming more securely assimilated.

But today we are witnessing a *de facto* reactivation of Jewish life within the Soviet Union, at a time when more and more Jews are leaving the country. We know, especially from reports of the Jewish trials, that information on Jewish history and Israel circulates in *samizdat* and that groups have formed in many towns to study Hebrew; no Jewish festival passes without letters or telegrams of greeting being sent to Israeli leaders from Soviet Jews and there have been recent reports that the Moscow *yeshiva* (seminary) has been permitted to reopen (*Jewish Chronicle*,

24 March and 7 April 1972). Although the Jewish Movement tends to concentrate on emigration to Israel, it of necessity involves raising Jewish consciousness within the Soviet Union. As this process continues, the confrontation between Jews and the authorities will grow sharper, and the outcome cannot be predicted. For essentially the Soviet Jewish struggle to emigrate is about the possibility of living as a Jew inside the Soviet Union—and ultimately, about the possibility of living there as a human being.

Chronology of Main Events, February 1968–March 1972

1968

15 February	Letter of twenty-six Lithuanian Jews
20 May	Y. Kazakov's letter renouncing Soviet Citizenship
May	B. Kochubievsky's essay 'Why I am a Zionist'
7 December	Arrest of Kochubievsky

1969

13–16 May	Trial of Kochubievsky in Kiev
6 August	Letter of eighteen religious Georgian Jewish families to U.N. Human Rights Commission
30 November	Beginning of intensive anti-Zionist campaign: *Pravda* article 'Disaster for the Simple Man Here'

1970

January–March	Anti-Zionist campaign further intensifies
10–19 February	Ryazan Trial (four sentenced)
2 March	Declared a 'world day for condemnation of Zionist aggression'
4 March	Press conference of prominent Jews
8 March	'Letter of the forty'—Moscow Jews reply to the press conference
12 March	Ilya Zilberberg's open letter
April	*Iskhod* begins to circulate
10 June	Letter of seventy-five Moscow Jews to U Thant
14 June	Letter of thirty-seven Leningrad Jews to U Thant
15 June	First arrests of Jews in connection with the 'Leningrad Hijack Affair'

| 15–24 December | First Leningrad Trial (eleven sentenced) |
| 31 December | Death sentences in first Leningrad Trial commuted |

1971

January	Anti-Zionist campaign again intensifies
5–7 January	Court Martial of Vulf Zalmanson (in connection with first Leningrad Trial)
February	Sit-ins at the Supreme Soviet
23–25 February	Brussels Conference
1 March	Formation by Soviet Government of Special Commission to expedite issuance of exit visas
5 March	*Khronika*, no. 18, includes separate section on the Jewish Movement
24 March–19 April	Twenty-fourth C.P.S.U. Congress
March	Sharp rise in number of Jews allowed to emigrate
11–20 May	Second Leningrad Trial (nine sentenced)
24–27 May	Riga Trial (four sentenced)
17 June	Trial of Valeriy Kukuy in Sverdlovsk
22–24 June	Trial of Raiza Palatnik in Odessa
21–30 June	Kishinev Trial (nine sentenced)
20 September	Academician A. Sakharov's plea for freedom to emigrate
September	Trial of Yemilia Trakhtenberg in Samarkand
6–8 October	Trial of Boris Azernikov in Leningrad
20 October	Kosygin's statement in Canada on Jewish emigration
November	Another increase in number of Jews emigrating
10 December	Human Rights Day protests

1972

18–28 January	Twenty-eighth World Zionist Congress; renewed anti-Zionist campaign
7 February	Arrest of Ilya Glezer in Moscow
24 March	B. Shumilin's statement on Jewish emigration
mid-March	Reopening of Moscow Yeshiva
29 March	First night of Passover—incidents at Moscow Synagogue

17

The Soviet-Jewish Problem:
Internal and International Developments,
1972–1976[1]

LUKASZ HIRSZOWICZ

There seems to be a link between developments on Soviet-Jewish matters during the last decade, and events of Soviet and global significance. The Six-Day War of June 1967 contributed greatly to a renaissance of national sentiment among the Jews of the U.S.S.R. Increased Soviet involvement in the Middle East brought about a systematic and virulent propaganda campaign against Israel, Zionism and Jewry at large. This campaign, directed at audiences both inside and outside the U.S.S.R., was intensified after the 1968 events, first in Poland and then in Czechoslovakia. The political ferment in these countries had its counterpart in the development of the general Soviet movement of dissent, which presented itself in some strength during the trial of the four[2] in early 1968. All this, in turn, created an atmosphere in which Soviet Jews also felt free to bring into the open their urge to emigrate. The orientation of Soviet foreign policy towards *détente*—a policy which suffered a temporary setback after the Czech invasion—inhibited the Russian authorities from bringing to bear the full weight of repression against the dissidents; this inhibition might have partly disappeared in 1973, when the *Ostpolitik*, Soviet–US exchanges, and the Helsinki Conference) were already safely on their way. In the meantime, however, the broad movement of Jewish emigration to Israel which had developed received wide support in the West.

The Emigration Movement

In an interview with Novosti, which was widely publicized abroad, Boris Shumilin, Deputy Minister of Internal Affairs, claimed that between 1945 and 31 December 1975, 122,000 Soviet Jews had emigrated to Israel

[1] I would like to thank Professor Ch. Abramsky, Dr. M. Agursky, Dr. S. J. Roth, Professor L. B. Schapiro and Professor M. Zand for their comments.

[2] Pavel Litvinov (ed.), *The Trial of the Four. A collection of materials on the case of Calanskov, Ginzburg, Dobrovolsky and Lashkova*, London, 1972.

or Palestine.[1] Although a small number of Soviet Jews were granted exit permits in the years 1945–68, and 4,300 in 1968–70, substantial emigration began only in March 1971. In 1971 a total of 14,300 Jews left the U.S.S.R. for Israel; in 1972, 31,500; in 1973, 35,300. In 1974 the total of visas granted was approximately 21,000 and in 1975 11,700, according to Shumilin, and well over 13,000 according to other sources. In 1976 the figure of Jewish emigration exceeded 14,000. (These figures do not include the small number of Jews who were granted visas for countries other than Israel.) Thus, out of Shumilin's figure of 122,000 approximately 90 per cent left the Soviet Union in 1971–5. In the period 1968–76, 132,500 Jews emigrated from the U.S.S.R. on Israeli visas, of whom 114,800 went to Israel.

This is a considerable number if compared with the figure of over 2 million Jews in the U.S.S.R. according to the 1970 census. On the basis that one out of every sixteen Soviet Jews has emigrated, it may be assumed that the number of those with relatives and close friends in Israel, and abroad in general, has increased enormously, and that a physical link of substantial strength between Soviet Jewry and Israel as well as the rest of the Jewish diaspora has been re-established in recent years.

From a legal-political standpoint Soviet-Jewish emigration is an unusual phenomenon. It neither proceeds in the framework of a repatriation agreement, nor is it simply an immigration of unrelated individuals. On the one hand, the legal-administrative framework[2] of individual emigration is preserved—a framework of rules and regulations which make emigration a privilege to be granted or refused arbitrarily, and which, in fact, virtually forbid emigration save in very special circumstances. On the other hand, to all intents and purposes a general exception has been made for the Jews, as remarked by many observers of the Soviet scene[3]—although the Soviets have never publicly admitted this.

The principle of reunification of families is used as the basis for granting Jews emigration permits. In theory, this principle applies to every Soviet citizen; in fact, only a few have benefited from it. Significantly, in the case of the Jews, the place of family reunion was to be almost exclusively Israel. Thus, whatever the legal construction, *politically* Soviet-Jewish emigra-

---

[1] Novosti Information Service Bulletin No. 36660, 23 January 1976.

[2] 'Rules of exit from the U.S.S.R. and entry into the U.S.S.R.', U.S.S.R. Council of Ministers, Decree No. 801 of 22 September 1971.

[3] See Susan Jacoby, *The Friendship Barrier: Ten Russian Encounters*, London 1972, p. 137; Hedrick Smith, *The Russians*, London, 1976, p. 500. To some extent an exception was also made for the Germans, of whom 3,900 left the U.S.S.R. in 1972, 4,400 in 1973, and 6,300 in 1974. According to the 1970 census, there were 1·8 million Germans in the U.S.S.R

tion is of a distinct ethnic character, proceeding within the framework of individual emigration.

The size of permitted Jewish emigration to a large extent reflects the Soviet state interests of the day. It has been emphasized by Soviet and pro-Soviet spokesmen that Soviet pro-Arab policies dictate the restriction on Jewish emigration. The relation between Soviet emigration policy and Soviet moves in the Middle Eastern arena is a complex subject which requires special research; *prima facie*, however, it would appear that Soviet interests in the Middle East have not been the decisive factor in determining their Jewish emigration policy.[1]

At any rate, this policy cannot be fully understood without taking into account that the habitual and deeply-ingrained opposition to emigration, and the inclination to decide the fate of individuals as well as of whole groups of people in accordance with what is regarded as being in the best interests of the state, continues to influence strongly official (and, for that matter, unofficial) attitudes.

Administrative practices are geared accordingly. In some cases, permits have been granted relatively easily, for example in the case of the Georgian and Bukharan Jews, or in the Baltic countries and Moldavia, although in these areas too it was not always so. In other instances, when persons with higher skills were involved, in particular from the main cities of Russia, permits were either refused or granted only after long delays and much harassment—a practice facilitated by the tedious emigration procedures and by the heavy fees exacted both for the visa and for release from Soviet citizenship. In August 1972 the Soviets introduced an education tax varying from 4,500 roubles for a graduate of economics, law, pedagogic and historico-archival institutes to 24,800 roubles for a doctor of sciences trained at Moscow University.[2] However, this regulation ceased to be implemented after a loud outcry in the West, although it was not removed from the statute book.

The unspecified period of waiting and the harassment of prospective emigrants has played the role of deterrent in Soviet emigration policy. The point is therefore made that the number of applications for emigration does not properly reflect the number of Jews actually wishing to leave.[3]

---

[1] It can be argued, however, that the easing of Soviet emigration policies in 1971 coincided with developments in Egypt after Nasser's death which were unwelcome to the Soviet government.

[2] *Sobranie postanovleniy Pravitelstva Soyuza SSR*, 1973, no. 1, pp. 11–12.

[3] See for example the *Daily Telegraph*, 22 June 1973; see also H. Smith, op. cit., p. 475, who calls the number of those wishing to leave 'one of the imponderable mysteries of Soviet life'.

Recently figures have been published which give a rough idea of the numbers of Jews who expressed an active interest in leaving the U.S.S.R.[1] The first step a Jew has to take if he intends to submit an application for emigration is to obtain a *vyzov*—an invitation from a relative in Israel. The Israeli authorities who keep a record of these invitations gave the number of first-time affidavits (i.e. excluding requests for renewal of affidavits) sent out to Soviet Jews in the years 1968–76 as 318,914. But many affidavits were not delivered to the addressees by the Soviet post, and not every person in possession of the affidavit feels able to go through the whole tedious emigration procedure and to withstand all the harassment and obstacles put in his or her way. Thus the quoted figure probably exceeds the number of applications submitted. Be that as it may, the number of people to whom affidavits were sent exceeds by over 180,000 the number of Jewish emigrants. In the peak years of Jewish emigration—1972 and 1973—52·6 per cent of those who were sent affidavits succeeded in emigrating, while in 1975 and 1976 only 38·9 per cent did so.

The majority of Soviet Jews live in the R.S.F.S.R., Eastern Ukraine, and Byelorussia (i.e. the parts of those republics which were included in the U.S.S.R. before the Second World War). Yet, among the Soviet Jews who have arrived in Israel up to the end of 1975, they constitute only one-seventh. About half of the new arrivals come from the Baltic countries, Bukovina (which is part of the Ukrainian republic), and Moldavia, which were annexed by the U.S.S.R. in 1940; over a quarter come from Georgia; and Bukharan (about one-twelfth) and Mountain Jews (about one-thirtieth) make up the remainder. These figures are not only the result of Soviet practices; they also reflect the composition of Soviet Jewry in terms of its national and cultural consciousness. The Jews in the Slavonic republics of the U.S.S.R., east of the 1939 Soviet-Polish borders, are culturally much more assimilated[2] than those in the territories acquired since 1939, or the Georgian, Bukharan, and Mountain Jews (the latter come from Dagestan, which is an autonomous republic within the R.S.F.S.R., and Azerbaydzhan). The fact that about 20,000 Jews arrived in Israel from the pre-1939 U.S.S.R. Slavonic areas, the majority of them from Moscow, Leningrad, Kiev, Odessa, and Minsk, seems also to justify the hypothesis that Jewish national

[1] *Insight*, vol. 3, no. 5 (May 1977).

[2] The Jews of Byelorussia are less assimilated than those of the R.S.F.S.R. and Ukraine. In 1970, 36 per cent of the Jews in the Minsk *oblast* declared Yiddish as their mother tongue, whereas only 17 per cent in the Moscow and Kiev *oblast* and 19 per cent in the Leningrad and Odessa *oblast* did so.

consciousness has increased among this group of Soviet Jewry;[1] indeed, this hypothesis is corroborated by further symptoms discussed below. But at the same time, the lack of positive links with Jewishness, which accounts for their weak Jewish identity, explains in part why many more Jews from these areas left the U.S.S.R. (well over 30,000) in 1968–76 than arrived in Israel.

The table on pages 372–3 gives approximate data for Jewish emigration from the U.S.S.R. according to places of origin.

The decline in the number of Jewish emigrants since 1974 is explained by the Soviet authorities as the result of '[their] lack of stability and security and the absence of vital privileges they were used to as Soviet citizens . . .'.[2] However, this seems at best to explain only partly the fall in the numbers of emigrants, since the formal and practical obstacles to emigration are very far from having been removed. It is clear, if only from the number of affidavits requested, that Soviet Jewry's drive for emigration is far from being satisfied.

Nevertheless, several serious problems with regard to Soviet-Jewish emigration have emerged in the past few years. One of these is the problem of the so-called 'drop-outs'. From the second half of 1973 onwards emigrants arriving in Vienna with visas for Israel proceeded to other destinations. In particular, the number of those going to the United States increased when, in August 1973, the relevant immigration restrictions were eased there. The percentage of Soviet Jewish émigrés who arrived in Vienna and chose to go to the U.S.A. and other Western countries was 4·2 per cent in 1973, 18·8 per cent in 1974, 37·2 per cent in 1975, and 49·1 per cent in 1976.[3]

There are also several thousand Soviet émigrés who left Israel for other countries in the West, mainly the United States. There were also some who opted to return to the U.S.S.R.,[4] though only an insignificant number was re-admitted. Another development, numerically insignificant but probably of some political importance, has been observed in recent years. The Soviet government forced prominent persons involved in the democratic movement, both Jewish (for instance, the poet Iosif Brodsky

[1] See Voronel, 'The Search for Jewish Identity in Russia', *Soviet Jewish Affairs*, vol. 5, no. 2, p. 74. In 1976 more than 7,000 Jews emigrated from the following large cities of the Soviet heartland: Moscow (about 1,300), Leningrad (1,200), Kiev (1,000), Odessa (1,900), Kharkov (500), and Minsk (200). See *Insight*, vol. 3, no. 5.

[2] Shumilin's interview of 22 January 1976; see above, p. 367, n. 1.

[3] Cf. *Insight*, vol. 1, no. 2.

[4] According to *Soviet Weekly*, 12 June 1976, there were about 200 applications to return in 1972, 350 in 1973, and 808 in 1974.

in 1973) and non-Jewish (e.g. Andrey Amalrik in 1976) to seek visas for Israel, although they explicitly wished to settle elsewhere. Two purposes seem to be served by such a device: the authorities, while ridding themselves of unwanted dissidents, simultaneously tar them with a Jewish brush, thus exploiting antisemitic prejudice in the struggle against the democratic movement.

The problem of the absorption of Soviet-Jewish emigrants emerged parallel with the growth of the emigration wave. A great effort was made in Israel to facilitate the integration of the new arrivals: absorption centres were created with a net of *ulpanim* offering intensive instruction in the Hebrew language, assistance was provided in finding suitable employment and retraining courses for those immigrants who needed it, subsidized housing was allotted, and significant exemptions from direct and indirect taxation were granted as a privilege to the new *olim*. The Soviet Jews who turned to other destinations also received substantial help through agencies established by the Jewish communities and, sometimes, in addition, governmental assistance.

Since absorption has its long-term aspects, as well as the important element of the emigrant's immediate settlement, it is, perhaps, too early to pass conclusive judgement on the whole process of the absorption and integration of Soviet Jews. Naturally many difficulties have already emerged in its first stages. These are on the one hand the result of factors inherent in the *émigrés'* Soviet background, such as education, working experience, expectations from life and society, etc.;[1] and on the other hand they are the result of institutional factors, such as the duplication of the functions of the absorption authorities, and bureaucratic attitudes—in particular, the lack of understanding of the psychological peculiarities and cultural varieties among the *émigrés*. Israel's particular difficulties and the general economic recession in the West complicated the problem of absorption in recent years.

It is too early to assess the full impact of the phenomenon of emigration on the national consciousness of the Jews in the Soviet Union. But it can be safely assumed that the links of Soviet Jews with their brethren in Israel and the West, deliberately restricted, weakened and cut off during

[1] See Betsy Gidwitz, 'Problems of Adjustment of Soviet Jewish Emigrés', *Soviet Jewish Affairs*, vol. 6, no. 1; G. E. Johnson, 'Which Promised Land? The Realities of American Absorption of Soviet Jews', *Analysis*, no. 47 (November 1974); J. T. Shuval, E. J. Markus and J. Dotan, 'Age Patterns in the Integration of Soviet Immigrants in Israel', *Jewish Journal of Sociology*, vol. 17, no. 2 (December 1975), pp. 151–63. Problems of absorption are constantly and sometimes bitterly discussed in the Russian press in Israel, particularly in the weekly *Nedelya*. See also *Jerusalem Post*, 18 August 1976.

Jewish Emigration from the U.S.S.R., 1968–76, by Place of Origin (see p. 370)

	No. of Jews according to 1970 census	Total no. of visas issued 1968–1976	No. of Jews in main cities according to 1970 census		No. of emigrants* from main cities 1968–1976	Percentage of visas issued in relation to Jewish population
U.S.S.R. total	2,150,700					6·2
R.S.F.S.R.	807,900	132,500			7,200	1·9
		15,500	Moscow	251,200	4,100	
			Leningrad	162,600	2,200	
			Derbent			
Ukraine	777,100	42,100	Kiev	152,000	6,000	5·4
			Odessa†	117,000	9,500	
			Chernovtsy†	37,000	12,400	
			Lviv†	28,000	3,800	
Byelorussia	148,000	2,300	Minsk	47,000	1,700	1·6
Uzbekistan	102,800	8,450	Tashkent	55,800	2,900	8·2
			Samarkand†	15,000	3,600	
Moldavia	98,100	12,300	Kishinev	49,900	6,500	12·5

Georgia	55,400	28,700	Tbilisi	19,600	6,500	51·8
			Kutaisi		5,000	
			Sukhumi		3,000	
Azerbaydzhan	41,300	3,000				7·2
Latvia	36,700	8,100	Riga	30,600	7,000	22·0
Kazakhstan	27,700	190				0·7
Lithuania	23,600	9,600	Vilnius	16,500	7,200	40·7
			Kaunas	4,300	1,700	
Tadzhikistan	14,600	1,600	Dushanbe	11,400	1,500	11·2
Kirghizia	7,700	200				2·6
Estonia	5,300	240				4·5
Turkmenia	3,500	110				3·1
Armenia	1,000	40				4·0
Others	130					

★ Arrivals in Vienna.

† The number of Jews in the given *oblast* according to the 1970 census.

the greater part of the Soviet period, have, to a certain extent, been restored.

Détente, *Human Rights and Soviet Jewry*

It was not unexpected that the plight of Soviet Jewry should have aroused first and foremost the interest of Jewish communities in Israel and the West. Indeed, no other cause—with the exception of the commitment to Israel—evoked such enthusiasm (even if it sometimes led to misguided expression), or united world Jewry to such an extent.

The issue of Soviet Jewry became an item constantly on the agenda of the existing Jewish national and international organizations, a great amount of activism and militancy was generated, and all kinds of Jewish actions with the aim of expressing solidarity, obtaining public support and media coverage, and exerting pressure on the Soviet authorities, became an integral part of the Jewish scene. Two world conferences of Jewish communities in Brussels in 1971 and 1976 provided a visible expression of this world-wide sympathy.[1] The Soviets' attempt to counteract the impact of these conferences by initiating campaigns in the U.S.S.R. against them and dispatching special delegations to Brussels demonstrated their sensitivity to international public opinion.

The position occupied by the Soviet-Jewish question in the coverage by Western media of internal Soviet developments gave striking evidence of the general significance of the Jewish issue and of the world-wide interest it commanded. This interest was not exclusively passive. Influential organizations concerned with the struggle for human rights, e.g. Amnesty International, devoted no small amount of their energy and resources to the cases of individual Jews persecuted for their desire to leave the U.S.S.R. Special concern was manifested by professional groups who protested against the misbehaviour of their Soviet colleagues. Notable examples were the protests against abuses committed by Soviet psychiatrists (there were several Jews among the dissidents incarcerated in psychiatric prisons),[2] against the trial and incarceration of Mikhail Shtern of the Vinnitsa Endocrinological Centre,[3] against the withholding of emigration permits and harassment suffered by the Corresponding Member of the Soviet Academy of Sciences, Venyamin Levich, and his

[1] On the first Brussels Conference (23 February 1971) see *Soviet Jewish Affairs*, 1, pp. 108–9; *Congress Bi-Weekly*, vol. 38, no. 4 (19 March 1971); *Les Juifs en Union Soviétique*, no. 12 (1971). On the second Brussels Conference (17–19 February 1976) see *Soviet Jewish Affairs*, vol. 6, no. 1, pp. 71–6; *Insight*, vol. 2, no. 2.
[2] See H. Merskey, 'Abuses of psychiatry in the U.S.S.R.', *Soviet Jewish Affairs*, vol. 6, no. 1.
[3] See below, p. 396.

family,[1] and the wide support for the Leningrad ballet dancers Valery Panov and his wife Galina Rogozina.[2] Demonstrations of disapproval of official Soviet behaviour by Western professionals, scientists, artists and writers have usually made a strong impact on the Soviet organizations which are desirous of maintaining contacts with their Western counterparts and with the relevant international bodies. Distinguished non-Jewish Western figures, e.g. the then mayor of New York, John Lindsay, and Senator Edward Kennedy, on a visit to the U.S.S.R., made contact with Jewish activists, thus bolstering the spirit of the latter by demonstrating that the Soviet-Jewish issue had become a recognized feature of the world political scene.

Western involvement did not cease at the level of public opinion, but entered the realm of foreign policy, as in the case of the so-called Jackson-Vanik Amendment. This Amendment to the U.S. Trade Reform Act,[3] introduced by Henry Jackson in the Senate on 4 October 1972 and by Charles Vanik in the House of Representatives on 7 February 1973, stipulated that 'no non-market economy country [i.e. the U.S.S.R. and other socialist countries] shall be eligible to receive most-favoured-nation treatment or to participate in any program of the Government of the United States which extends credits or credit guarantees or investment guarantees, directly or indirectly' as long as it 'denies its citizens the right or opportunity to emigrate', or impedes emigration by imposing taxes, fines and other charges. A political struggle developed around the Amendment in which the American-Jewish community was naturally an important participant. The amendment had, probably, the support of the majority of the U.S. public, irrespective of whether they were doves or hawks in foreign policy, and, in any case, the support of both Houses of Congress: the vote in the House of Representatives on 11 December 1973 was 319 to 8 in favour, and in the Senate the Amendment received the support of 77 sponsors.

[1] The Levichs, i.e. Venyamin, his wife Tanya, his sons Evgeny (an astrophysicist) and Alexander (an engineer), and their wives, first applied to emigrate in March 1972. All were dismissed from their jobs, and Evgeny, despite ill-health, was drafted into the army and sent to camp at Tiksi Bay beyond the Arctic Circle. After his release in 1974, the brothers received visas in April 1975 and left, but at the time of writing (July 1977) Professor Levich has not been permitted to emigrate.

[2] The Panovs, members of the Kirov ballet company, first applied to emigrate in March 1972, and were subsequently dismissed from their jobs. Galina, who is not Jewish, was encouraged by the authorities to leave her husband, while Valery was offered a visa on condition that he emigrated without his wife. Both were eventually granted exit visas in June 1974.

[3] See *Congressional Record*, 4 October 1972, S 16835–6.

The Jackson–Vanik Amendment was also enthusiastically supported by many of the Soviet dissidents, notably Academician A. Sakharov, and by Soviet-Jewish activists themselves, who repeatedly intervened in its support against those who opposed it or doubted its effectiveness.[1]

Opposition to the Amendment came from President Nixon[2] and Henry Kissinger,[3] who were alarmed at the possible effects on their policy of *détente*, of which trade relations formed an important part, and stressed the advantages of silent diplomacy; from Senator Fulbright, then Chairman of the Senate Foreign Relations Committee, who considered the Amendment to be 'meddling in internal affairs of the U.S.S.R.'[4] and from the dissident 'liberal Marxist' Roy Medvedev, in whose view restrictions on Soviet–American trade would harm freer emigration from the U.S.S.R.[5] Not unnaturally, the Soviet government repeatedly expressed its displeasure at the introduction of the emigration issue into negotiations with the U.S.A.[6]

Nevertheless, the Soviet government, increasingly aware of the link between their attitude to Jewish emigration and the benefits they expected from the U.S.A., attempted to assuage opinion in the United States by concessions (for example, the suspension of the 'diploma tax' on 21 March 1973) and by conciliatory statements. Informal assurances by Brezhnev, Gromyko and Dobrynin[7] to the Ford–Kissinger administration concerning criteria and practices to be applied with regard to emigration from the U.S.S.R. were made public on 18 October 1974, in an exchange of letters between the Secretary of State, Dr. Kissinger, and Senator Jackson. In return, Jackson and his associates agreed to include in the Trade Bill a provision allowing the President to decide whether the conditions stipulated in the Amendment have been fulfilled, and accordingly to extend most-favoured-nation status to the U.S.S.R. year by year.[8]

However, such a face-saving formula proved unacceptable to the Soviet leaders. On 18 December 1974 the official news agency Tass declared that

---

[1] Cf. Sakharov's statements of 7 November 1973 and 28 April 1974, and his letter to the U.S. Congress of 14 September 1974 reproduced in *Congressional Record*, 13 December 1974, pp. 3–4; cf. statement by 80 Jewish activists of 1 September 1974 and by four Jewish scientists reported on 18 September 1974, and many other public statements.

[2] Nixon's statement of 15 March 1974.

[3] Kissinger's testimony before U.S. Senate Committee on 7 August 1974.

[4] See his statement on 11 July 1975.

[5] See his statements of 7 November 1973 and 28 April 1974.

[6] See, for instance, *Pravda*, 24 March 1974.

[7] According to Dr. H. Kissinger's statement, *International Herald Tribune*, 4 December 1974; see W. Korey, 'Rescuing Russian Jewry: Two Episodes Compared', *Soviet Jewish Affairs*, vol. 5, no. 1, p. 15.

[8] See text in *Congressional Record*, 13 December 1974, pp. 3–4.

'leading circles' in the U.S.S.R. flatly rejected any attempt to attach political conditions to trade or to interfere otherwise in the internal affairs of the U.S.S.R.; the Tass communiqué denied that the Kremlin had given any specific assurances on emigration in return for trade concessions and credits. A letter from Foreign Minister Gromyko to Kissinger dated 26 October 1974 accusing the Kissinger–Jackson exchange of letters of giving 'a distorted image of our position' was released together with the Tass communiqué in order to prove that this was the consistently held position of the U.S.S.R. government.[1] It is probably not without significance that on 18 December 1974 a major Soviet hope of receiving substantial American credits was frustrated because of a bill adopted by the U.S. Senate on that day which, among other things, placed a very low ceiling on U.S. credits to the U.S.S.R. (300 million dollars over a four-year period). On 10 January 1975 the Russians informed the U.S. authorities of their decision to revoke the October 1972 trade agreement.

Whatever the explanation of these developments—whether opportunism on the part of those directly involved in the Soviet–American negotiations, Soviet pride and jealousy in guarding their sovereignty, or their disillusionment over the low ceiling of credits allowed by American legislators—the adoption of the Amendment did not produce the desired effects. In 1974, Jewish emigration from the U.S.S.R. declined. This coincided with the debates in the U.S. and between the U.S.A. and U.S.S.R. governments about the Amendment, but was not necessarily the result of these discussions.

The Jackson Amendment was limited to the problems of emigration from the U.S.S.R., Jewish and non-Jewish. Another document emerged in 1975 with a much broader scope, more deeply rooted in the network of international legal provisions on human rights, although devoid of the specific and direct sanctions for non-compliance built into the American Trade Reform Act. The document in question was the 'Final Act' or Declaration of the Conference on Security and Cooperation in Europe,[2] signed in Helsinki on 1 August 1975, after more than two years of negotiations. The 'Final Act' contained in particular a confirmation of the territorial *status quo* in Europe (Basket I), provisions for economic co-operation (Basket II), and provisions dealing with matters of humanitarian and cultural import (Basket III).

With regard to the problem of emigration, the following elements were introduced into the 'Final Act': (*a*) pledges to 'facilitate freer movement' in general; (*b*) specific provisions on 'reunifications of

---

[1] See *Izvestia*, 20 December 1974.   [2] Cmnd. 6198, H.M.S.O., London, 1975.

families'; and (c) reaffirmation of other international instruments, such as the 1948 Universal Declaration of Human Rights and the 1955 International Convention on the Elimination of All Forms of Racial Discrimination, which—whether as a guide or as a legally binding commitment—proclaim the general freedom to leave one's country. The 'Final Act' also contains provisions on the freer and wider dissemination of information, on co-operation and exchange in the various fields of culture, on freedom of worship, including contacts and meetings and exchange of information between religious institutions and organizations, and on the right of national minorities to equality before the law and to various linguistic, cultural, and educational activities. To a certain extent the 'Final Act' is relevant to the basic disabilities which Soviet Jewry suffers: individual discrimination in various fields of Soviet life, absence of adequate rights and facilities for Jewish life as a religious and/or national community, and curtailment or denial of the right to emigrate.[1] Although the provisions of the 'Final Act' cover the Jewish needs only to a limited degree (for instance, in the realm of culture, only respect and assistance of minorities within the state borders is postulated, while freedom of cultural intercourse with members of the same ethnic community in other states is not explicitly indicated), they create a framework for efforts in the fields of equal rights, culture, religion, and emigration, and also include provisions for follow-up machinery which may play a supervisory role in the implementation of these clauses.

Discrimination

Among the disabilities which Soviet Jewry suffers, individual discrimination is, probably, the one which most affects Soviet Jews in their everyday life. Although the available evidence points to a growth in discrimination, there is a lack of published statistical information which might make it possible to assess the extent and character of this phenomenon. There is, however, one important exception, for figures are available that illustrate the place of Jews in higher education, which is a most important avenue of social advancement in the U.S.S.R.

A decline in the Jewish proportion of the Soviet student population and scientific workers was to be expected, as a result of the general growth of higher education in the country. But shortly after the Second World War a system of quotas for Jews was introduced in many Soviet institutions of

[1] See S. J. Roth, 'The Conference on Security and Cooperation in Europe and Soviet Jewry', *Soviet Jewish Affairs*, vol. 4, no. 1, and the same author's *The Helsinki 'Final Act' and Soviet Jewry*, Institute of Jewish Affairs, London, 1976.

higher learning; in particular, admission to the better central universities and institutions was made difficult, and in some cases even impossible. While the percentage of Jewish students in the U.S.S.R.'s total student population was 15·4 in 1927 and 13·4 in 1935, it declined to 3·2 in 1960–1 and 2·5 in 1970–1,[1] although the proportion among the total number of Jews is still the highest of all the country's nationalities. From 1969–70 a numerical decline is evident, as shown in the table on page 380, which is compiled mainly from the Soviet yearly statistical publication *Narodnoe khozyaystvo SSSR* (the figures for students refer to the academic year beginning in the calendar year given in the table).

More recent information is available about the number of Jewish students in Moscow higher education establishments. This number declined by 23·2 per cent between 1970–1 and 1974–5, from 19,508 (3·16 per cent of the student body) to 14,985 (2·39 per cent).[2] An even steeper fall may be observed in the numbers of Jewish postgraduate students, of whom there were 4,945 in 1970 and 3,456 in 1973, a decline of about 30 per cent during a period when the general fall in the number of postgraduates was 567—0·56 per cent.[3]

The figures show that this decline is occurring in a period of relative stabilization of the numbers of those receiving higher education, and may therefore reflect not only the tarnished political image of the Jew in Soviet society, but also a more basic rivalry for the available places. Given such a rivalry, in Soviet conditions ethnic issues are bound to play a part, and Soviet Jews are likely to be among its foremost victims on account of their political weakness in the Soviet *apparat* and institutions.

The fact of discrimination against Jews in the allocation of jobs is now reflected in publications by members of the Jewish movement and Soviet dissidents. According to A. Voronel,[4] anti-Jewish discrimination is decisively linked to social and occupational mobility, i.e. any advance for Jews is very difficult. Sakharov in his *Progress, Coexistence and Intellectual Freedom*[5] and R. Medvedev in his 'The Middle East Crisis and the Jewish Question'[6] concentrated on discrimination in scientific institutions. Medvedev published in the *samizdat* journal *Politichesky dnevnik* (Political Diary), no. 75 (December 1970) 'A Document from M. V. Keldysh's

---

[1] See M. Checinski, 'Soviet Jews and Higher Education', *Soviet Jewish Affairs*, vol. 3, no. 2, and Zvi Halevy, 'Jewish Students in Soviet Universities in the 1920s', *Soviet Jewish Affairs*, vol. 6, no. 1.

[2] Data compiled from *Moskva v tsifrakh, 1966–1970 gg* (Moscow in Figures, 1966–70), Moscow, 1972, p. 132 and *Moskva v tsifrakh, 1971–1975 gg*, p. 160.

[3] *Vestnik statistiki*, 1974, no. 4, p. 95.   [4] A. Voronel, op. cit., p. 71.

[5] London, 1968, pp. 65–6.   [6] *Evrei v SSSR*, no. 7 (July–November 1974).

Jewish Students and Scientific Workers in the U.S.S.R.

	1950	1960	1962	1965	1968	1969	1970	1971	1972	1973
Number of all students ('000)	1,247	2,396	2,944	3,861	4,470	4,550	4,581	4,597	4,630	4,671
Number of Jewish students ('000)	n.d.	77·2	79·3	n.d.	111·9	110·1	105·8	n.d.	88·5	n.d.
Number of all scientific workers	162,508	354,158	n.d.	664,600	822,910	883,420	927,709	1,002,930	n.d.	1,108,268†
Number of Jewish scientific workers	25,125	33,529	n.d.	56,070*	60,995	63,661	64,392	66,793	n.d.	67,698†

* In 1966, out of 712,400. † *Vestnik statistiki*, 1974, no. 4, p. 92.

Office',[1] which demonstrates that a person's Jewishness is a strong argument against his being elected to the Academy of Sciences. R. Medvedev and M. Zand disclosed the existence of a secret circular which stipulated that Jews should not be given any responsible work in institutions connected with problems of defence, of missiles, nuclear weapons, or any other secret work.[2]

It follows from the above-mentioned *samizdat* publications and from many individual testimonies that a particular effort is made to hold down the number of Jews in various jobs and, at best, to keep a delicate balance between the number of Jews and non-Jews. This information relates to the late 1960s and early 1970s. There are indications that the situation has since deteriorated.

Anti-Zionism/Antisemitism

A disproportionately large number of publications on Israel, Zionism and Jewry have appeared in the U.S.S.R. in recent years: reports, cartoons and articles in the daily press and periodicals, pamphlets and books, published in editions of many thousands of copies, some of them purporting to be serious journalistic and scholarly works.[3]

Radio and television are also involved in this propaganda campaign. It may be safely assumed that the printed output is matched by propaganda lectures and meetings as well as individual agitation in institutions, enterprises, factories and clubs, since this is the normal way in which Soviet propaganda is conducted.[4]

It would appear that a special propaganda effort is made in the Ukraine, an area of acute national tensions. The phrase 'Ukrainian bourgeois nationalists and Zionists' has now become an official cliché, recurring in official speeches, statements and articles.[5]

This sustained campaign poses in the U.S.S.R. and elsewhere as anti-Zionist propaganda. However, it is more and more evident that it involves the use of traditional antisemitic devices and that it is directed against

---

[1] *Politichesky dnevnik II 1965–1970*, Amsterdam, 1975.

[2] Mentioned by W. Korey, 'The Soviet Jewish Future', *Midstream*, November 1974, p. 49.

[3] On Soviet antisemitism see chapter 14 above; W. Korey, *The Soviet Cage: Antisemitism in Russia*, New York, 1973.

[4] The Israeli Russian-language newspaper *Nasha strana* (28 May 1976) carried a transcript of a lecture on Judaism and Zionism given in 19 February 1974 in the Scientific Research Institute of the Moscow rubber industry by candidate of economic sciences V. Emelyanov, member of the *Znanie* (Knowledge) Society. The amount of crude nonsense it contains is amazing. See also *Insight*, vol. 2, no. 6.

[5] See J. Klejner, 'The Soviet Ukrainian Press on Zionism and Israel', *Soviet Jewish Affairs*, vol. 4, no. 2, p. 47.

Jewry in general. In the published anti-Zionist material the difference between a Jew and a Zionist is blurred, and often non-existent. Thus, for example, the renowned Jewish historian S. Dubnow, who outspokenly praised the phenomenon of the Diaspora in Jewish history, is designated as a Zionist, and so is, usually, the Bund, an anti-Zionist Jewish socialist party; the non-Zionist and even anti-Zionist Jews who participated in the reform movement in Poland and Czechoslovakia in 1968 are also labelled Zionists, having supposedly acted on orders from 'international Zionism', and so on.

The principal arguments of Soviet antisemitic propaganda are borrowed from nineteenth-century populist antisemitism and from the traditional criticism and distortion of the Jewish religion which was an integral part of religious antisemitism. The first can be easily detected in the arguments drawn from the 'rapacious' nature of the Jewish people. According to this view, exploitation transformed the Jews into big capitalists and gave them a decisive influence in the countries of the West, and particularly in the United States, where—some Soviet authorities claim—'35 per cent of the owners and managers of the private capital firms is made up of Jews'.[1] A world-wide plot was organized by these rich Jews with the aim of world-domination. These Jews allegedly hate the U.S.S.R. and the Soviet bloc, which they see as the main obstacle in their way.[2]

The second set of arguments was borrowed from antisemitic tracts published in tsarist Russia which abused the Christian religion.[3] These arguments include a distortion of the doctrine of the God-chosenness of

[1] Answer to a letter by assistant editor-in-chief V. Chernyavsky, *New Times*, no. 21 (1976); see also V. Bolshakov, *Sionizm na sluzhbe antikommunizma* (Zionism in the Service of Anti-Communism), Moscow, 1972, pp. 46–89; V. Ya. Begun, *Polzuchaya kontrrevolyutsiya* (Creeping Counter-revolution), Minsk, 1974, pp. 76, 117, etc.

[2] See V. Petrov, *US-Soviet Détente: Past and Future*, Washington, 1975, pp. 49–50. The author maintains that American-Jewish anti-Soviet attitudes are regarded in Moscow 'not merely as a result of the U.S.S.R.'s pro-Arab stand in the Middle East . . . but also, and perhaps primarily, as a reaction to the decline of Jewish influence in the Soviet Union'.

[3] In this respect an article from the Novosti Press Agency published in the Bulletin of the U.S.S.R. embassy in Paris, *U.R.S.S.*, on 22 September 1972, under the title 'School of Obscurantism', and the following court proceedings in a Paris court instituted by the International League against Antisemitism (L.I.C.A.), are of interest. It was shown by G. Svirsky that whole passages of this article were taken from a 1906 Russian antisemitic pamphlet by a Black-Hundred propagandist S. Rossov, *Evreysky vopros: O nevozmozhnosti predostevleniya polnopraviya evreyam* (The Jewish Question: The Impossibility of Granting Equal Rights to Jews), St. Petersburg, 1906. The court's verdict rejected the plea of the defendant that allegations 'discrediting those who belong by virtue of their origin to the Jewish race and the Jewish religion' were confined to the Zionist state and found him guilty of public racial defamation. See *Soviet Anti-Semitism: The Paris Trial*, edited and with an Introduction by Emanuel Litvinoff, London, 1974.

the Jewish people, accusations of double standards of morality for Jews and Gentiles allegedly prescribed by the Jewish religion, of bloodthirstiness and treachery inculcated by Jewish religious teachings, etc., etc. Thus, Soviet writers allege that Zionist theory and practice have deep roots in the historical and spiritual heritage of the Jews.

In their anti-Zionist/antisemitic propaganda the Soviets resort to inculcation of hatred against the Jews, including their own Jewish citizens, in many direct and indirect forms. Slanted reporting of events connected with Israel, in particular the recurring theme of 'atrocities', Soviet fiction in which Jewish personages appear almost exclusively as negative and criminal types,[1] and the association of Judaism and Zionism with all sorts of arch-enemies of the U.S.S.R. and of mankind are the principal tactics used. In the latter field the study of Soviet cartoons yields interesting and significant conclusions. Jews and Zionists are associated not only with Nazis and U.S. imperialists, with blood, the swastika, and the dollar sign, but also with the devil, the swine, the snake, the poisonous mushroom, the octopus, the spider, etc.—all symbols which were extensively used in antisemitic propaganda from the Middle Ages to the period of Nazi rule.[2]

The equation of Zionism with Nazism and racism and accusations of co-operation between the Zionists and the Hitlerites, and with antisemites in general, is a recurrent theme in many Soviet publications on Jews, Zionism, and Israel. The stubborn repetition of this subject in Soviet broadcasts, cartoons, articles, and books is a typical device of totalitarian propaganda. The obscenity of these accusations is reinforced by their use in works by Jewish authors.[3]

There are now several authors who specialize in anti-Zionist/antisemitic propaganda: V. Begun, V. Bolshakov, L. Berenshteyn, T. Kichko, Yu. Ivanov, E. Evseev, R. Brodsky, and others. It should also be pointed out

[1] See A. Sergin, 'Jews and the October Revolution in Recent Soviet Literature', *Soviet Jewish Affairs*, 2, pp. 75–8; G. Manevich, *O evreyskom voprose i blizhnevostochnom konflikte* (On the Jewish Question and the Middle Eastern Conflict), samizdat, Moscow-Riga, 1971—partly reproduced in *Jewish samizdat*, vol. 8, Jerusalem, 1975, in particular pp. 51 ff.; R. Boymvol, 'Jewish Themes in Russian Works as a Factor in the Life of Soviet Jewry', *Jewish Culture in the USSR*, Jerusalem, 1973, pp. 91–100.

[2] See J. Vogt, 'Old Images in Soviet Anti-Zionist Cartoons', *Soviet Jewish Affairs*, vol. 5, no. 1; M. Decter (ed.), *Israel and the Jews in the Soviet Mirror: Soviet Cartoons on the Middle East Crisis*, New York, 1967.

[3] See, for instance, A. Vergelis's novel *Di tsayt* (Time) printed in *Sovetish Heymland*, 1974, nos. 4, 8, 12, and 1975, no. 12; L. Yu. Berenshteyn, 'Zionism—the Tool of Imperialist Reaction' (in Russian), *Kommunist Ukrainy*, 1973, no. 3; a pamphlet in Ukrainian under the same title by Ya. M. Valakh, published in Kiev in 1972; M. D. Gaysinovich, *U zmovi z katami* (In Collusion with the Executioners), Lviv, 1975, etc., etc.

that some of their works are disseminated abroad. Yury Ivanov's *Beware Zionism*; E. Evseev's *Fascism under the Blue Star*; *Zionism—Theory and Practice*, a collective work by influential Soviet scholars and journalists; R. Brodsky's *The Truth about Zionism*—these are published in translation in Western languages, and also in the languages of the Soviet bloc countries.

The intensity of the anti-Jewish propaganda in the U.S.S.R. arouses much apprehension among Soviet Jews, who have protested against it in various *samizdat* publications.[1] Moreover, the anti-Zionist books *Fascism under the Blue Star* and *Zionism—Theory and Practice*, which were unanimously praised in the Soviet press, were the subject of criticism even by Aron Vergelis in the Yiddish journal *Sovetish Heymland*, of which he is the editor. Vergelis may have thus carried out the task assigned to him by his superiors and/or pursued his own specific aims, but he nevertheless condemned these works for their insults to the national feelings of Soviet Jews;[2] and he also identified V. Begun, T. Kichko, and E. Evseev as authors who showed themselves oblivious to Lenin's views about the Jews and Jewish culture.[3]

A characteristic feature of present-day Soviet anti-Zionist/antisemitic propaganda is the loud protest by its authors as well as those who organize and finance it against allegations of antisemitism, and their insistence on the difference between anti-Zionism and antisemitism. In support of their case they frequently include remarks or passages about Jews who struggled against, or were harmed by, Zionism. This attempt to disguise clear-cut antisemitism is the result of the ambiguities and internal contradictions of Soviet ideology, which tries to combine lip-service to values of a past revolutionary age—i.e. internationalism and belief in the equality of nations and peoples—with the contemporary policies of the Soviet state. The Soviet authorities make use of the work and services of Soviet Jews, while at the same time discriminating against them. They would like to have the benefit of exploiting traditional prejudices, but are afraid of the uncontrollable tensions which open antisemitism may create. Another factor which inhibits Soviet antisemitism is the unwillingness of the Soviet leadership to antagonize public opinion in the free world.

[1] For example Colonel Davidovich's open letter to Brezhnev of 25 April 1975.
[2] See A. Vergelis, 'Nit bloyz ameratses' (Not Sheer Ignorance), *Sovetish Heymland*, 1973, no. 6, p. 170; id., 'Farvos di fayl dergreykht nit dem tsil' (Why does the arrow fail to reach the target?), ibid., 1973, no. 12, pp. 148–9.
[3] See A. Vergelis, 'Leyenendik Leninen' (Reading Lenin), ibid., 1974, no. 1, pp. 154–6.

The Jews as a Soviet Minority

A probably inadvertent result of Soviet anti-Zionist/antisemitic propaganda is that it puts into focus the strange position of the Jewish nationality in the U.S.S.R. On the one hand, the official agitprop alleges that the Jews outside the borders of the U.S.S.R. are almost omnipotent; on the other hand, within the Soviet Union their rights are incomparably more limited than those of most other Soviet ethnic and religious minorities. Moreover, the unquestionable role they have played in the Russian Revolution and in Soviet society in the past and in the present is almost a taboo subject in Soviet literature.[1]

Some superficial and slight changes have taken place in the last few years which were, probably, prompted by the exigencies of Soviet internal and foreign policy.

In the late 1920s and in the 1930s Biro-Bidzhan, the Jewish Autonomous Region, was presented as the crown of Soviet-Jewish achievements. Since the Second World War, the Region has increasingly lost its Jewish character, both in the ethnic composition of its inhabitants, and in its cultural life.[2] It was, therefore, regarded as an innovation when on 24 July 1970 Lev Borisovich Shapiro was made First Secretary of the C.P.S.U. Oblast Committee of the Jewish Autonomous Region, the first Jew to hold this position since 1948. Further, instead of only one Jew, as in previous years, two Jews have, since 1970, been included among the five deputies in the Soviet of Nationalities to which Biro-Bidzhan, as a national autonomous region, is entitled. Also some publicity was given to Biro-Bidzhan by the Soviet authorities, in connection, *inter alia*, with the 1971 anti-Zionist campaign, and on the fortieth anniversary of the proclamation of the Region (1974).[3]

Soviet propagandists sometimes mention the allegedly high number of

[1] In a 1971 samizdat 'On the Jewish Question and the Middle Eastern Conflict', G. Manevich wrote in connection with the anti-Zionist conference of 4 March 1970 in which a group of prominent and meritorious Jews participated: 'Thus it means that not all Soviet Jews are rogues, rascals and scoundrels. Apparently among them as among other Soviet nationalities there are worthy people. Why, then, does a lively, clear, real image of a Jew appear so rarely, so extremely rarely, in present-day Soviet literature?'

[2] See L. Hirszowicz, 'Birobidzhan After 40 Years', *Soviet Jewish Affairs*, vol. 4, no. 2.

[3] See *Soviet Weekly*, 9 and 16 January 1971, *Pravda* (reported by *Christian Science Monitor*, 29 April 1971), the G.D.R. *Horizont*, 1 and 4 July 1971, etc., *Pravda*, 22 February 1974, *Sovetskaya Rossiya*, 8 May 1974, Novosti Information Service Bulletin No. 15060, 8 May 1974, Tass for abroad, 6 May 1974 (in *Summary of World Broadcasts*, 11 May 1974), etc. A group of foreign Communist journalists visited Biro-Bidzhan in October 1974, according to Radio Khabarovsk, 21 October 1974 (*Summary of World Broadcasts*, 24 October 1974).

Jews in local soviets.[1] In fact their number rose from 7,624 in all local soviets in 1959 to 8,124 in 1965, but then fell to 6,619 in 1969 and 5,173 in 1973. The Jews are thus more under-represented than any other Soviet nationality, including such scattered groups as the Poles and Germans.[2] There were six Jews in the U.S.S.R. Supreme Soviet in 1970, and the same number in 1974; two (V. E. Dymshits and Academician Yuli Khariton) sat in the Soviet of the Union and four in the Soviet of Nationalities. Of the latter, two are representatives of Biro-Bidzhan, A. B. Chakovsky represents the Mordovian A.S.S.R., and H. Zimanas (Kostas Glikas in 1970) the Lithuanian S.S.R.

In 1971, at the twenty-fourth C.P.S.U. Congress, the number of Jews elected to the supreme party bodies was increased: V. E. Dymshits, the only Jewish member of the C.C. since 1961, was re-elected; A. B. Chakovsky was elected candidate C.C. member, and two persons of Jewish nationality, the Biro-Bidzhan secretary L. B. Shapiro and Col.-Gen. D. A. Dragunsky, were elected to the Central Auditing Commission. At the twenty-fifth C.P.S.U. Congress in 1976 the number of Jewish candidate members of the C.C. increased to two, with the election of Lev M. Volodarsky.[3]

There seem also to be some developments in the field of officially permitted Jewish cultural activities in the U.S.S.R. In the 1960s an average of two Yiddish books appeared annually. It often happened that Yiddish books were announced but did not appear, or appeared only after a long delay. This situation improved marginally in the 1970s. To our knowledge, nineteen Yiddish books were published in 1971–5 apart from the literary works printed in *Sovetish Heymland*, which include also a few full-length novels. Some of these books are slim volumes of poetry, and some are collections of works written over many years.

As the number of readers of Yiddish literature in the U.S.S.R. is steadily decreasing, of presumably greater impact on the Jewish (and, for that

---

[1] R. Groyer, 'Soviet Jews As They Are', *Soviet Life*, December 1973, p. 54; [S. Rabinovich,] *Jews in the USSR*, Moscow (after 1970), p. 51.

[2] The index of representation, i.e. the quotient of the nationality's share of total deputies elected in a given year by that nationality's share of total population, was, in 1973, 27 for the Jews, 47 for the Koreans, 77 for the Poles, and 84 for the Germans: see Everett M. Jacobs, 'Jewish Representation in Local Soviets, 1959–1973', *Soviet Jewish Affairs*, vol. 6, no. 1, pp. 20–1.

[3] V. E. Dymshits is Deputy Chairman of the U.S.S.R. Council of Ministers. It is perhaps not without significance that he was elected to the Union chamber of the Supreme Soviet, both in 1970 and 1974, for the Khabarovsk *kray*, which incorporates the Jewish Autonomous Region. He is, probably, the most important Jew in the ruling circles of the U.S.S.R. A. B. Chakovsky is editor-in-chief of the weekly *Literaturnaya gazeta*. Lev M. Volodarsky is the First Deputy Director of the Central Statistical Directorate (Ts.S.U.).

matter, non-Jewish) reading public are works translated into Russian and other languages, in book form and in literary periodicals. Some of these Russian translations are issued in comparatively large numbers. For instance, I. Rabin's 'On the Niemen', published first in Yiddish, was printed in 50,000 copies in Russian in 1973 and sold out in a very short time. A relatively large number of the translations are poetic works, and some were translated by outstanding Russian, Ukrainian and Byelorussian poets.

As in the 1960s, the Jewish theatre remains the most conspicuous and widely enjoyed expression of Jewish culture in the U.S.S.R. There exist several Jewish drama, song, and music companies, the oldest being the Vilnius Jewish People's (i.e. amateur) Theatre, established in 1957. Most of its members emigrated to Israel in the 1970s. In 1962 a theatrical group under the actor Venyamin Shvartser (b. 1892) began to function in Moscow, and is now the Moscow Dramatic Ensemble under Feliks Berman. Many of its actors are the old surviving members of the famous Goset (Jewish State Theatre), which was closed down in 1948, but there are apparently also younger ones, among whom the Estonian Jewish girl, Polina Aynbinder, has acquired fame.[1]

The Biro-Bidzhan Yiddish People's Theatre started as a Jewish Drama Group in 1965 under Mikhail Bengelsdorf (1900–71), an ex-student of Mikhoels's Jewish stage studio; the theatre director is now Berta L. Shilman, also said to be a pupil of Mikhoels.

The Kishinev Jewish People's Theatre was mentioned in *Sovetish Heymland* until 1972. The artistic director of this theatre was also a student of the Goset studio, but he died tragically at the age of 47.[2]

A Jewish music-hall company under Ana Guzik, who emigrated to Israel in 1973, operated in Leningrad, and another, of which Sidi Tal is the leading player, is based in Moldavia. In the last year or two, activities by amateur artistes in Kaunas have been reported. There are also a few individual performers who include Jewish items in their programme.

None of these groups is a fully-fledged theatrical company with its own premises and stage. With the exception of the Moscow Ensemble, the

---

[1] For the Moscow Dramatic Ensemble see Yasha Chernis, 'Mit dem yidishn teater in di shtet fun Ural un Bayvolge' (With the Jewish Theatre in the Towns on the Urals and Trans-volga), *Sovetish Heymland*, 1976, no. 4; Feliks Kandel, 'Zakoldovanny teatr; razmyshleniya posle spektaklya evreyskogo ansamblya "Zakoldovannyy portnoy" ' (The Bewitched Theatre: Thoughts after the Performance of the Jewish Ensemble 'The Bewitched Tailor'), samizdat, in *Jewish Samizdat*, vol. 8 (Jerusalem, 1975), pp. 255–70.

[2] *Sovetish Heymland*, 1972, no. 3, pp. 172 and 190. An amateur Jewish performers' group reappeared in Kishinev in 1974. It presented a programme in Hebrew and Russian, and the authorities made clear their intention to suppress it.

theatres have amateur status, though there are normally some professionals on their staff. When they play in their home cities, they make use of the stages of the Palaces of Culture, sometimes of other theatres, or concert halls of large hotels that accommodate a few hundred spectators. The Biro-Bidzhan Theatre performs locally, but the Moscow Jewish Dramatic Ensemble and the Vilnius Jewish People's Theatre travel around the country.

In recent years the Moscow Dramatic Ensemble has visited Siberia and the Far East, the Ukraine and Moldavia, Byelorussia, North Caucasus, Kuban, Dagestan, the Urals, the Volga cities, and the Baltic countries. It has performed in towns with very small Jewish populations, such as Bryansk and Klintsy (1972), and Kaliningrad (1974). But cities with large Jewish populations, such as Minsk and Kiev—the capitals of Byelorussia and the Ukraine—are apparently out of bounds. The Vilnius Jewish People's Theatre, which performed in Vilnius, in the Lithuanian resorts of Druskinikai and Palenga and in the former Lithuanian capital Kaunas, as well as in the Byelorussian towns Bobruysk, Borisov (1974), and Homel (1975), did not visit nearby Minsk.

The repertoire of these Yiddish companies consists to a considerable extent of classical Yiddish plays. Music, song, and dance seem to play a most important part in the programme. New titles to appear in the programme are Buzi Miller's play of manners *Funem himl falt gomit arop* (Nothing Comes as a Godsend), which was taken up by the Biro-Bidzhan, Vilnius, and Moscow theatres, Leonov's *Nashestvie* (Invasion), dealing with the Second World War, specially translated into Yiddish and staged by the Biro-Bidzhan theatre, and Hirsh Kanovich's *Di politsey-sho* (Curfew)—dealing with the German occupation—performed by the Vilnius theatre.

According to many reports the Jewish performances enjoy great popularity,[1] thus giving the lie to the official thesis that no demand for Jewish culture exists in the U.S.S.R. To be sure, it is a very specific Jewish culture, based to a considerable degree on nostalgia on the one hand, and on the spoken word, as opposed to the written word, on the other.

The existence of the Jewish companies seems to be closely connected with Soviet nationalities' policy, which apparently prescribes that Jewish culture is treated differently in different republics, although the reasons

---

[1] The number of half a million viewers yearly is sometimes mentioned in the Soviet media. See S. Rabinovich, *Jews in USSR*, Novosti Press Agency Publishing House, p. 37; V. P. Ruben, 'Soyuz ravnykh' (Union of Equals), in *Literaturnaya gazeta*, 1 December 1976.

behind the differences are not always clear. That the Jews are officially given some place among Lithuania's nationalities—probably to balance the Poles—is borne out not only by the existence of the Jewish People's Theatre in Vilnius, but also by the fact that a Jew has been among the republic's representatives in the 1970 and 1974 Soviet of Nationalities. Jewish artistic activity has been prohibited in Latvia since 1963 in spite of efforts by numerous local Jews.[1] No Jewish artistic activity is permitted, apparently, in Byelorussia or in the Ukraine, though there is no ban in Moldavia. In the R.S.F.S.R. alone the Jews are counted as one of the republic's nationalities because Biro-Bidzhan is part of this republic. It is also of paramount importance that Moscow be seen as the U.S.S.R.'s shop window. This may explain why Jewish theatres are tolerated in Biro-Bidzhan and in Moscow. The Jewish Dramatic Ensemble performs only rarely in Moscow, has no premises of its own, and Leningrad, with its great Jewish population, was not mentioned in the chronicle notes of *Sovetish Heymland* as having been visited by a Jewish theatrical company.

Among other Jewish cultural activities in the U.S.S.R., it seems worthwhile to mention the few exhibitions of Jewish painters and sculptors whose works include Jewish themes. In the offices of *Sovetish Heymland* there is a permanent exhibition of works by Jewish painters and sculptors, and reproductions of some of them are published in the journal. It would seem that there exists in the U.S.S.R. not only a small and mostly ageing group of Yiddish writers, but also a group of Jewish painters and sculptors which includes some younger people. Moreover, many of the young Jews who are creative in the visual arts belong to the artistic underground, and their works find response mainly among non-conformists and foreigners.

It is clear that none of these cultural activities could take place without the permission of the authorities. The pressure on the U.S.S.R. authorities to permit such activities has been considerable.[2] On the other hand, neither these activities nor the comparatively wide response they evoke in the Soviet Jewish public were mentioned in the Soviet media (with the exception of *Sovetish Heymland*), since this would contradict the basic Soviet thesis about the assimilated nature of the Jewish minority. They were put to somewhat wider use in Soviet foreign propaganda. But at the end of 1976 the Soviet media, both those directed to the outside world and those directed to the Soviet public, paid considerable attention to the

---

[1] See D. Garber, 'Choir and Drama in Riga', *Soviet Jewish Affairs*, vol. 4, no. 1.

[2] Some of them are described in a letter by Boris Polevoy published in the samizdat journal *Politichesky dnevnik*, no. 9 (July 1965) (*Politichesky dnevnik, 1964–1970*, Amsterdam, 1972, pp. 102–5).

subject of Jewish culture, in response to the symposium on that theme called by activists for 21 December 1976, and the protests against its suppression by the Soviet authorities.[1]

The Yiddish monthly *Sovetish Heymland* serves as a kind of centre for these Yiddish cultural activities. Since its inception as a publication in alternate months in 1961 the journal and its editor-in-chief, A. Vergelis, have played a certain role in Soviet propaganda abroad. Before the Six-Day War Vergelis made efforts to establish contacts with Jewish writers and journalists in the West, and even the publication of a special issue of *Sovetish Heymland* devoted to Hebrew literature was envisaged.[2] These efforts, which were successful only to a very limited extent, were later curtailed, when the U.S.S.R. embarked on its anti-Zionist campaign, in which the Yiddish monthly participated. But the existence of *Sovetish Heymland* continues to be of some importance to the Soviet authorities, if only as an 'alibi', a response to the criticism of the treatment of the Jewish nationality in the U.S.S.R.[3]

The number of synagogues in the U.S.S.R. is very small, but there do not appear to have been any indiscriminate closures since Khrushchev's anti-religious campaign. While the scope of synagogal activities has remained very limited, their role in Soviet-Jewish life has undergone some changes reflecting the Jewish national revival. The synagogue has begun to attract people outside the limited circle of worshippers, viz. those young people who see in synagogue attendance the only means of expressing their Jewish identity. Feliks Kandel-Kamov, a Jewish cinematography worker who applied for emigration, wrote in the Jewish samizdat *Evrei v SSSR*, no. 7:

On Saturdays we go to the synagogue. The synagogue is a onlyclub, the place you can hear news, hear unlikely rumours, find consolation, get distressed and hearten

---

[1] See, for instance, V. P. Ruben, op. cit.; I. Gordon, 'V sem'e edinoy. O evreyskoy literature v SSSR' (In a United Family. On Jewish Literature in the U.S.S.R.), *Literaturnaya gazeta*, 8 December 1976; K. Orlovsky and S. Polin, 'Nerazrushimaya sila sovetskoy kultury' (The Unbreakable Power of Soviet Culture), *Izvestia*, 24 December 1976; E. Beider, 'Jewish arts are flourishing in Soviet Union', *British-Soviet Friendship Bulletin*, November–December 1976; Tass broadcasts by M. Evgenev, 8, 9, and 10 December 1976; etc.

[2] I owe this information to Professor M. Zand. See also *Jewish Telegraphic Agency Daily News Bulletin*, 19 January 1967.

[3] The significance of the Yiddish monthly was stressed in an article by A. Vergelis in *Druzhba narodov* (June 1975, pp. 284–6), a journal devoted to the literature of the U.S.S.R. nationalities, in which he enumerated the internal functions of his journal as the only Jewish periodical in the U.S.S.R.; Vergelis also drew attention to his foreign responsibilities, i.e. as a spokesman for the U.S.S.R. among the foreign Jewish public and as an observer of developments in World Jewry.

up. Cars go past, chance passers-by stare in amazement: who ever permitted anything like this? . . . We stand, those of us who were refused and those who have only just recently applied for a visa, those who hesitate and those who have made up their minds, and discuss problems under the vigilant eyes of the [K.G.B.] agents who do not even attempt to conceal themselves . . .[1]

The synagogue's new role in Soviet–Jewish life is confirmed in the sustained efforts made by the authorities in Kiev to prevent the local synagogue from becoming a meeting place on the Moscow pattern.[2] Clashes with the police in the vicinity of the Moscow synagogue were repeatedly reported in the Western press.[3]

The authorities attempted to use the synagogues, in particular that of Moscow, as an illustration of the freedom of religion in the Soviet Union. Indeed, the synagogue's leaders were occasionally assigned the role of claiming abroad this freedom and the well-being of Soviet Jews in general. They were also called upon to participate in the (Soviet) anti-Zionist campaign.[4] But in the age of *détente* and intensified international contacts the Moscow synagogue, and, perhaps, other Jewish religious centres also, are bound to play a somewhat bigger role. Many tourists, including rabbis, from Western countries have been able to raise questions and demand improvements at a time when—within the framework of the State's anti-religious policy—the Russian Orthodox Church and the Islamic religious communities have gained in the U.S.S.R. a somewhat better standing and some facilities.

One result of the new conditions was the sending in 1973 of two Soviet Jewish students, one from Moscow (Hayim Levitas) and one from Biro-Bidzhan (Adolf Shayevich),[5] to the Budapest Rabbinical Seminary;

[1] See *Jewish Samizdat*, vol. 10 (Jerusalem, 1976), p. 124; *The Times*, 3 December 1976, p. 16.

[2] See Leonard Schroeter, 'How they Left: Varieties of Soviet Jewish Exit Experience', *Soviet Jewish Affairs*, vol. 2, no. 2, p. 21.

[3] For instance, reports on the interruption of the 1975 Passover service.

[4] Such participation was particularly pronounced in the course of the anti-Zionist campaigns of 1970 (see Moscow rabbi L. Levin's statement, *Vechernyaya Moskva*, 28 February 1970; statement by religious leaders, *Izvestia*, 12 March 1970) and 1971 (see Odessa rabbi I. B. Shvartsblat in *Literaturnaya gazeta*, 3 March 1971; statement of a conference of representatives of Jewish communities held in Moscow Choral Synagogue 23 March 1971, *Soviet News*, 31 March 1971). See also statements of parishioners of Moscow synagogue and others about the 28th Zionist Congress, Novosti Information Bulletin No. 12182 of 20 January 1972 and *Soviet News*, 25 January 1972; see also the statement by Moscow rabbi Yaacov Fishman about the Brussels Conference broadcast on 9 February 1976.

[5] Adolf Shayevich accompanied Moscow rabbi Ya. Fishman on his U.S. visit in May 1976 and claimed that 'about ten Jews are studying at the Moscow Jewish Seminary and seven in Budapest' (Jewish Telegraphic Agency, 12 May 1967).

and others went there in 1976. Promises were given that more Soviet rabbis would be trained in Budapest and even in non-Communist states' seminaries, and that the Pentateuch would be published with a Russian translation.[1] International contacts were broadened at the initiative of the Moscow synagogue leaders, certainly with the approval and in all likelihood at the behest of the Soviet authorities.

In June 1974 a celebration of the eightieth birthday of E. C. Kaplun, chairman of the Moscow synagogue, was arranged with the participation of guests from Hungary, the U.S.A., and Canada. M. E. Tandeytnik, the chairman of the Moscow synagogue in 1974–6, travelled to a number of East European countries and acted as host to the Romanian Chief Rabbi, M. D. Rosen and the British Chief Rabbi, I. Jakobovits. Rabbi Ya. Fishman visited the U.S.A. in May 1976, apparently in connection with the preparations for the International Conference of Religious Figures for a Lasting Peace, Disarmament, and Just Relations among Peoples, held in Moscow in June 1977.[2] The Soviet authorities themselves have also been more ready to receive some visiting Jewish religious personalities, and to discuss problems relating to Jewish religious life in the U.S.S.R.

In point of fact, the Soviet leadership is in a dilemma about its Jewish policies. On the one hand the positive moves on their part with regard to their Jewish subjects may be useful in their propaganda and foreign policy in the free world, and produce beneficial effects on the mood and attitudes of Soviet Jews. On the other hand they fear that such moves might, on balance, further the growth of Jewish national consciousness and annoy those elements within the country and abroad who are satisfied with the official anti-Jewish attitudes.

Changes in the Character of the Jewish Movement

The first Soviet Jews to be affected by the new mood of national revival and to sense the new opportunities of emigration were Zionist and religious people. They came to a considerable extent from the fringe elements of Soviet Jewry—i.e. the annexed territories and the older generation who had had connections with Jewish nationalism in earlier days. In the initial struggle for emigration Georgian Jewry played an important role and, as mentioned above, together with Jews from the Baltic states, Moldavia, and Bukovina, they comprised three-quarters of the 1971–5 total of emigrants. Small Zionist circles existed also in Moscow

---

[1] See *New York Times*, 22 January 1976; *New York Post*, 19 June 1976.
[2] *Soviet News*, 29 June 1976. See E. E. Eppler, 'The Moscow "World Conference of Religious Workers"', I.J.A. Research Report USSR/77/5.

and Leningrad. In the movement's early days the activist core came mainly from among these elements and the first *Jewish Samizdat—Iton Alef* and *Iton Bet* (Newspaper A and Newspaper B)—were published in Riga in 1970, although Moscow and Leningrad activists took a considerable part in their preparation. The principal aim of the movement was emigration and no hopes were entertained of a Jewish cultural revival and of national survival in the U.S.S.R.[1] However, the majority of the initial activists departed when emigration gathered speed, and Jews from a different background took over.

The national revival among Soviet Jewry was a phenomenon closely related to ideological and spiritual developments within the U.S.S.R. Not only had the selfless struggle of the dissidents prepared the socio-political atmosphere in which the Jewish activists could count on a response among the Jews, but ideological developments in the U.S.S.R. constituted a continuous challenge to the Jewish minority. The renaissance of national feeling among many of the Soviet nationalities stimulated the Jewish national renaissance. The search of the Russian intelligentsia—among whom the greater part of the Soviet-Jewish intelligentsia had assimilated—for roots in the native soil and national traditions made some Jews take an even deeper plunge into 'Russianness', but influenced others to turn to their own roots and Jewish identity. The situation among the dissidents had a considerable impact. Ideologically, a great part of the dissidents evolved in the direction of nationalism, not excluding extremist tendencies strongly tinged with antisemitism.[2] Simultaneously, the increased pressure of the authorities on the democratic dissidents, and disillusion with the possibility of liberalizing the Soviet regime, were also important reasons why many Jews active among the democrats joined the Zionist movement.

The new Jewish activists and leaders belonged to that part of the intelligentsia which felt the drive for self-affirmation after decades of self-denial and adherence to an ideology now regarded as a delusion. Their drive for self-affirmation was expressed by their nationalism, and their pride in Jewish achievements, particularly in Israel's achievements. 'For them Jewishness'—as one keen observer of the Soviet scene in 1971–4

---

[1] The impossibility of maintaining Jewish culture in the U.S.S.R. was emphasized in the papers and speeches by recent Soviet *émigrés* at a symposium on Jewish Culture in the U.S.S.R. held by the Cultural Department of the World Jewish Congress in Jerusalem in January 1972—see *Jewish Culture in the Soviet Union*, Jerusalem, 1973. See also R. Rutman, 'Jews and Dissenters: Connections and Divergencies', *Soviet Jewish Affairs*, vol. 3, no. 2, pp. 28–9.

[2] See D. V. Pospielovsky, 'Russian Nationalist Thought and the Jewish Question', *Soviet Jewish Affairs*, vol. 6, no. 1, pp. 3–17.

observed—'was a genetic fact of life, a matter of inheritance reinforced by negative forces of Russian life, rather than a function of religious attraction and identity.'[1] It was a feeling of this kind which induced them to acquaint themselves with Jewish culture and religion and sometimes to become devout observers of the latter. Their language and culture were Russian; the ideologies they abandoned covered a whole spectrum of assimilationist attitudes, from Marxist-Leninist internationalism to conversion to Russian Orthodoxy. It was their Jewish nationalism that led them to Jewish culture and religion, and not the reverse.

A few individuals belonging to this stratum actively participated in the *aliya* movement in its earlier stages. As more of them joined, they became the activists and leaders, because so many of them belonged to the technical and scientific élite of the Soviet Union. The Soviet authorities frequently refused their application to emigrate, for a shorter or longer period of time, very often dismissed them from their posts, deprived them of the possibility of using their skills, and sometimes denied them virtually any employment. As a rule such people started struggling openly for permission to emigrate. Thus highly skilled professionals and scholars, a great part of them in their thirties and forties, who had been forcibly detained in the U.S.S.R. for many months or even years, emerged as the main group of activists. Moscow, where there are many foreign correspondents and visitors from abroad, naturally became the focal point of the movement.

Persons such as Professor Venyamin Levich, a physical chemist and corresponding member of the prestigious Soviet Academy of Sciences; Professor Alexander Lerner, cyberneticist and head of the department of large scale systems in the Institute of Control Problems of the Soviet Academy of Sciences; Mark Azbel, a senior fellow in the Moscow Institute of Theoretical Physics; Alexander Voronel, a nuclear physicist who headed a laboratory at a well-known research institute; Viktor Polsky, physicist and head of an X-ray laboratory; Vladimir Slepak, an electronics engineer and head of an electronics laboratory; Alexander Lunts, a mathematician who headed a department in the Institute of Electronic On-Line Control Computers; his co-worker Viktor Brailovsky; another cyberneticist from the military industry, Mikhail (Malik) Agursky; Vitaly Rubin, a specialist in ancient Chinese philosophy, senior fellow of the Institute of the Peoples of Asia of the Soviet Academy of Sciences—all these emerged as leading activists of the Jewish movement. They were assisted by their membership of the Soviet academic establish-

[1] Hedrick Smith, *The Russians*, London, 1976, p. 476.

ment, and by the vigilance of the international academic community, which made it difficult for the Soviet authorities to harass or prosecute them beyond a certain limit.

Thus, the leadership of the Jewish movement is, to a considerable degree, composed of members of the Soviet intelligentsia who, before applying for emigration, had been well-established in Soviet society. However, the position is different with respect to the activists of the movement, and, naturally, with respect to the mass of the Jewish emigrants. Fairly representative of the activists are the signatories of appeals and petitions to the Soviet authorities and to various organizations and individuals abroad. Scientists and artists comprised 12·1 per cent of the signatories of Jewish petitions in 1968–70 and 18·5 per cent in 1971–2, engineers and technicians constituted 40 per cent of the signatories in 1968–72, while doctors, teachers, clerks, students, workers, and housewives accounted for 47·6 per cent in 1968–70 and 41·5 per cent in 1971–2. The occupational profile of the signatories of the general democratic appeals and petitions in 1968 differed considerably: scientists and artists— 67 per cent; engineers and technicians—13 per cent; others—20 per cent.[1]

Furthermore, the wide base of the Jewish movement is reflected in the fact that it also operates outside the central cities of the U.S.S.R. It is difficult to assess the actual level of the movement's intensity in the provincial towns: in Moscow many protests, appeals, and demonstrations were reported because of the close connection of the Soviet capital with the outside world, whereas the provincial centres are clearly in a more difficult situation.

Harassment and Trials

Political conditions in the U.S.S.R. have changed considerably since Stalin's time, but to seek emigration and to involve oneself in dissident activities, including Jewish activism, remains a very risky undertaking. The way through all the formalities of emigration is often blocked by various obstacles, harassment by colleagues at work, neighbours and authorities, and the penalties for activism are sometimes heavy. These vary from 'ordinary' harassment and short (10–15 days) sentences to heavy terms of imprisonment. Sometimes harassment may prove fatal as it actually did in the case of the veteran of the Second World War, Colonel Yefim Davidovich, whose death on 24 April 1976 was widely ascribed to his continuous persecution at the hands of the authorities. The

[1] See S. Redlich, 'Jewish Appeals in the U.S.S.R.: An Expression of National Revival', *Soviet Jewish Affairs*, vol. 4, no. 2, pp. 34–6.

notorious trials of 1970–1 in Leningrad, Kishinev, and Riga were followed by many others. The charges ranged from hooliganism, malicious hooliganism, evasion of military duty, and parasitism to speculation, bribe-taking, anti-Soviet activity, and treason. No independent observers were permitted at the trials. Some of the proceedings, irrespective of the precise paragraphs of the criminal code cited, were explicitly linked with applications for emigration or with Jewish activism. Most of the short sentences for hooliganism were imposed on participants in demonstrations and 'sit-ins'; charges of evasion of military duty were made against Jews, young and old, who, after applying for emigration or after their intention to apply became known, were called up, but refused conscription on the basis that service in the armed forces in any capacity implies several years of waiting for an exit visa after discharge. Parasitism was alleged with regard to applicants and/or activists who had been sacked from their jobs but took or were given no other. Some of the seemingly non-political cases aroused a strong suspicion of trumped-up charges. Three examples out of many are the cases of I. Shkolnik, Dr. M. Shtern and A. Feldman. I. Shkolnik (tried in April 1972) was first accused of spying for Great Britain, but after a British protest this charge was replaced by one of spying for Israel by memorizing information available at Shkolnik's place of work;[1] Dr. Mikhail Shtern (tried in December 1974) was accused of accepting bribes from his patients, but most of the prosecution witnesses testified in his favour;[2] Alexander Feldman of Kiev (tried in November 1973) was accused of assaulting a woman.[3] Shkolnik was sentenced to ten years in labour camp, reduced later to seven years, Shtern to eight years in labour camp, and Feldman to three and a half years' imprisonment.

The trials aroused wide protests in the U.S.S.R. and in the West, as did some cases of harassment. The view is strongly held by Soviet activists that only publicity abroad and the Soviet fear of protests and consequent alienation of Western public opinion protects them from the full blast of Soviet repression.

Activities of the Jewish Movement

The activities of the Jewish movement may be characterized as mainly

[1] Shkolnik's case and trial was widely reported in the Western press; see, for instance, *The Times*, 12 February, 13 February, 26 March, 13 April, 4 July 1973. For a Soviet presentation see *Soviet News*, 17 April 1973.

[2] M. Sherbourne, 'The Trial of Mikhail Shtern', *Soviet Jewish Affairs*, vol. 5, no. 1; A. Stern (ed.), *Un procès 'ordinaire' en U.R.S.S. Le Dr Stern devant ses juges*, Paris, 1976. Dr. Shtern was released on 14 March 1977.   [3] See *Jerusalem Post*, 10 January 1974.

those of a protest movement on the one hand and a movement of cultural self-assertion on the other.

The protests centred, in essence, on the problem of emigration and on repression against activists and prospective emigrants. Memoranda, petitions, and appeals on emigration were submitted to Soviet institutions,[1] to international organizations,[2] and to other foreign establishments.[3] Some of the statements and appeals came from individuals, but others were signed by dozens and even hundreds of people.[4] The activists also benefited from the presence of foreign correspondents in Moscow with whom press conferences were held.[5]

Numerous demonstrations in support of emigration were staged, e.g. in front of such institutions as the Supreme Soviet, the Ministry of Internal Affairs, the Tass building, the *Izvestia* editorial premises, or in well-frequented places such as the Intourist Hotel, Moscow underground stations, or the Moscow Synagogue.[6] Demonstrations in 1973 and 1974 were also reported from Kishinev, Leningrad, and Minsk. The majority of the demonstrations were staged by a few individuals, but some had more participants; e.g., in the reception hall of the Supreme Soviet on 19 September 1972, 30 demonstrators were arrested. Up to 52 people took part in a similar sit-in and in accompanying demonstrations during the period 18–25 October 1976.[7]

[1] Mainly to the Supreme Soviet (for instance, 3 September 1972; 12 November 1973; 4 January 1974) and the C.C. of the C.P.S.U. (e.g. 20 September 1973).

[2] For instance, the United Nations (12 December 1972) and the U.N. Human Rights Commission (30 November 1973; 18 January 1974).

[3] Many appeals were directed to U.S. institutions and to the U.S. public at large, supporting the Jackson Amendment, for instance an appeal to the U.S. Congress, 15 September 1973, to President Nixon, 28 June 1974, and a statement by Professor V. Levich published in the *New York Times*, 17 December 1973.

[4] A memorandum to the Supreme Soviet containing proposals on emigration regulations (2 September 1972) was signed by 200 Moscow Jews. The petition to the U.N. which called for setting up an international commission to investigate Soviet violations of the Universal Declaration of Human Rights in refusing Jewish emigration to Israel was signed by 239 Jews. An appeal to Jewish organizations abroad (12 April 1975), demanding the setting up of a special international commission to investigate violations of human rights in the U.S.S.R. over Jewish emigration, was signed by 280 Jews from 19 Soviet cities.

[5] A few press conferences were reported in the Western press, e.g. in *International Herald Tribune*, 28 December 1972.

[6] A photograph of the demonstration in front of the *Izvestia* building on 4 May 1973 was published in the *New York Times*, 7 May 1973, and photographs of the demonstrations in front of the Ministry of Internal Affairs on 28 September 1973 were published in *The Times* and the *International Herald Tribune* on 2 November 1973.

[7] The events of October 1976 were widely reported in the Western press, in particular the manhandling of 12 Jewish activists by the *druzhinniki*, and the short prison sentences many of them received. Also, Tass reported these events on 22 October 1976.

'Sit-ins' were held in Soviet institutions, some of which, e.g. those at the Moscow Central Telegraph Office (22 November 1972) and at K.G.B. headquarters (13 March 1973), were accompanied by hunger strikes.

Hunger strikes were also held in private homes in Moscow, Kishinev, and Leningrad by single individuals or couples, for example, Miron Dorfman in Kishinev and the Panovs in Leningrad, as well as by groups of people, as in the case of the long hunger strikes by Moscow scientists who were refused visas, in June 1973 and February 1974.

Other forms of protest included renunciation of Soviet citizenship, for instance, by the Minsk retired colonel Naum Alshansky, 21 March 1974; E. Felzenshteyn of Kharkov renounced on 29 April 1974 his title of Hero of the Soviet Union.

Demonstrations and protests were also staged against repressive measures such as the march of 25 October 1973 to the U.S.S.R. Supreme Court and the demonstration of 24 February 1975 outside the Lenin Library; protests were dispatched to Soviet institutions, international gatherings (e.g. to the World Congress of Peace-Loving Forces, 26 October 1973, and the Conference on Security and Cooperation in Europe, 30 August 1974), international organizations, etc. A particular role in the struggle against repression was played by the Jewish prisoners in the camps who staged hunger strikes every year on Silva Zalmanson's birthday (25 October) and on the successive anniversaries of the Leningrad trial. Several actions were taken jointly by the Jewish and dissident democratic political prisoners, such as, for instance, the 14-day (15–28 April 1974) hunger strike in the Perm labour camps nos. 35 and 36, and the above-mentioned message to the C.S.C.E. which was sent by over 100 prisoners—Zionists, Democrats, and Ukrainian nationalists.

There were also other expressions of solidarity: in defence of Sakharov and Solzhenitsyn during the vicious Soviet press campaign against them, in August–September 1973; of Solzhenitsyn in January–February 1974; and of Tverdokhlebov, secretary of the Moscow group of Amnesty International, after his arrest on 19 April 1975. Following a tradition which dates back to the late 1960s, in 1973, on Soviet Constitution Day, twenty-five Russian and Jewish dissidents, including A. Sakharov, demonstrated in Pushkin Square against imprisonment of the regime's critics.

However, in general the problem of co-operation between the Jewish movement, which is oriented toward emigration, and the dissidents, whose aim is to stay in the U.S.S.R., but to influence the authorities to behave with greater respect for human rights, is a thorny one. A strong tendency among the Jewish activists questions the practical value of such co-operation[1]—an attitude which is paralleled by analogous doubts as to co-operation between the Jewish movement on behalf of Soviet Jewry and organizations in the free world involved in various other struggles against the Soviet authorities. But whatever the doubts, both the Jewish and non-Jewish dissidents would like to see a liberalization in the U.S.S.R., which is essential for the future of Soviet society and Soviet Jewry in particular.

From time to time the general unease of the Jews at the antisemitic indoctrination in which the authorities officially and openly engage, was reflected in open demonstrations. As mentioned above, even *Sovetish Heymland* saw fit to condemn some of the anti-Zionist/antisemitic publications produced in the U.S.S.R. The democratic dissidents, too, recorded their criticism in samizdat publications.[2] Although many Jewish activists adhere to the view that the only escape from Soviet antisemitism is emigration, Jewish protests against this ugly feature of Soviet reality have been reported from time to time. In 1974 and 1975 protests against antisemitism were reported from Minsk, where it appears that life for the Jews became rather difficult.[3] Jewish Second World War veterans were active in these protests, in particular the late Colonel Davidovich and his Minsk colleagues, Alshansky and Ovsishcher. There were also protests throughout the U.S.S.R. in the autumn of 1975 against the U.N. resolution equating Zionism and racism.[4]

The open assertion of Jewish identity and the search for Jewish companionship at times of Jewish holidays and anniversaries became an important feature of Jewish activities. Some of these started years before the Six-Day War, and were intensified in the new mood.

As mentioned above, some of Russia's few remaining synagogues became a centre of meetings on holidays. Places of Jewish martyrdom in Riga, Kiev, Kaunas, Vilnius, and recently Minsk, became destinations of Jewish pilgrimages at appropriate dates: Rumbuli (near Riga) was visited in November, Babi Yar (near Kiev) at the end of September, the Ninth Fort in Kaunas in October. Gatherings at these places have taken place

---

[1] See Leonard Schroeter, *The Last Exodus*, New York, 1974, pp. 93–4.

[2] See V. Meniker, 'The Jewish Issue in Unofficial Publications (*Samizdat*)', *Jewish Culture in the Soviet Union*, Jerusalem, 1973, pp. 101–13.

[3] For example, Colonel Davidovich's speech at the site of the former Minsk Ghetto in May 1975 (*Jewish Telegraphic Agency Bulletin*, 13 May 1975). The *Jewish Telegraphic Agency* reported antisemitic attacks in Minsk (for instance, on 19 September 1972, 16 May 1973, and 22 April 1975).

[4] E.g., letters of 24 October 1975 by 14 Moscow activists and 109 Minsk Jews. See also *Jewish Telegraphic Agency Bulletin* of 13 November 1975.

also on other occasions, such as the commemoration of the Warsaw Ghetto uprising in April, the general commemoration of the Holocaust in May, etc. As a rule, the Soviet authorities took exception to these meetings, and often acted to prevent them or to break them up. Sometimes the authorities tried to thwart Jewish meetings by arranging commemorations of their own. In one case the persistence of the Jews and the sympathy shown by some sections of the general population produced results: after long deliberations, the authorities decided in May 1975 to erect a fifty-foot monument at the site of the Kiev massacre, the obliterated ravine of Babi Yar, but without specifically mentioning the Jewish victims. The monument was unveiled on 2 July 1976.

Jewish meetings were also held occasionally in many other places: on 11 August 1972 at Mikhoels's grave in Moscow to commemorate the 20th anniversary of the execution of Soviet Jewish writers; on 29 April 1973 at the Kishinev cemetery to commemorate the 70th anniversary of the 1903 pogrom; on Jewish holidays and the anniversary of Israel's independence.

The manifestation of solidarity with Israel was the object of many demonstrations and meetings. The massacre of Israeli Olympic athletes in Munich was followed by a demonstration outside the Lebanese embassy in Moscow, by a memorial service on the eve of Yom Kippur (17 September 1972) at the Kishinev cemetery, and meetings in other towns on that day. The Kiryat Shmona and Maalot massacres were commemorated at Babi Yar in April and May 1974 respectively. Jews demonstrated against the slanted presentation of news concerning Israel in the Soviet media and biased treatment of the emigration issue, in particular during the October War.[1] At that time, there were many messages and demonstrations of solidarity. Over 100 Soviet Jews offered their blood to wounded Israelis and appealed to the International Red Cross when the Soviet branch refused to accept it. Many messages of solidarity were dispatched and the number of applications for visas increased. Widely reported in the West were pro-Israeli demonstrations outside Soviet institutions, including a demonstration by three Jews outside the C.P.S.U. Central Committee building, which ended in the arrest of the demonstrators and the detention of five Western correspondents who were present.[2]

---

[1] See M. Altshuler, 'Soviet Union: Overview', in M. Davis (ed.), *The Yom Kippur War, Israel and the Jewish People*, New York, 1974, pp. 219–41.

[2] See *International Herald Tribune*, 15 October 1973, and *Sunday Times* and *Observer*, 14 October 1973.

An important element reflecting Soviet Jewry's urge for cultural and political self-expression is the Jewish samizdat journals. *Iton Alef* and *Iton Bet*, which appeared in Riga in 1970, contained information, short articles on Jewish subjects, translations of Israeli authors, etc. Four issues of another journal, *Iskhod* (Exodus), appeared in 1970 and 1971 bearing the subtitle 'Collection of Documents' and including messages, statements, and texts of laws and decrees—documents connected with repressive measures taken by the Soviet government. Issue no. 4 was devoted entirely to the December 1970 Leningrad trial. The same pattern was followed by *Vestnik Iskhoda* (Herald of the Exodus), of which three issues appeared in 1971–2. In accordance with the development of the movement, the *Herald* contained information on demonstrations, hunger strikes, and the experiences of the applicants for emigration. The two issues of *Belaya kniga Iskhoda* (The White Book of the Exodus) appeared in 1972 in Moscow. The first issue described the *via dolorosa* of the prospective emigrant and offered practical advice to everybody who chose to embark on such an undertaking; the second was devoted mainly to Nixon's Moscow visit in spring 1972.

The growing influence of the intellectuals in the Jewish movement was reflected in *Evrei v S.S.S.R.* (Jews in the U.S.S.R.), which, modelled on the Russian traditional 'fat periodicals', began in December 1972 and differed from the publications listed above. Eleven issues had reached the West up to the spring of 1976. Its editors and authors are no longer anonymous. Its subtitle 'Collection of materials devoted to the history, culture, and problems of the Jews in the U.S.S.R.' reflects the wide range of subjects it tackles: problems of Jewish identity, analysed at the social and personal level, occupy an important place in the journal, and the variety of views and answers to pertinent questions are a fair reflection of the dilemmas of the Russified Jewish intelligentsia.

Material on history, including the history of the Jews in Russia, the U.S.S.R., and other countries relevant to the Soviet-Jewish situation (for instance, a piece from T. Mommsen on the Jews in the Hellenistic world in no. 5), on antisemitism and the Jewish question in the past and present (a piece by Roy Medvedev, 'The Near East Conflict and the Jewish Question', in no. 7 and the polemics with him are of considerable interest), prose and poetry, recollections, thoughts on Judaism and on science, show the wide range of interest and the depth of enquiry into their personal and national destinies by a high-powered group of Jewish members of the Soviet intelligentsia.

Another journal, *Tarbut* (Culture), was started in Moscow in 1975 as a supplement to *Jews in the U.S.S.R.* It was smaller in size than *Jews in the U.S.S.R.*, and more of an informative-educational character. It contained mainly reprints and translations of items concerning the national language, history, religion, and culture. Five issues reached the West up to September 1976.[1]

A number of non-periodical samizdat publications appeared in recent years devoted to recent Jewish history, and in particular to the role of the Jews in the Second World War, to Jewishness and present-day Jewish life in the U.S.S.R. (for instance, the essay by Feliks Kandel-Kamov on the Moscow Jewish Dramatic Ensemble quoted above), to problems of emigration and absorption (e.g. an interesting essay by E. Finkelshteyn published in 1974, 'Aliya and Klita: Ethics and Politics', and a 1975 appeal by G. Rozenshteyn and V. Fayn to Jews leaving the U.S.S.R. for destinations other than Israel).[2]

A significant occurrence in the development of the Jewish movement in the U.S.S.R. was the seminar in Moscow, begun in 1973 as a measure of professional self-preservation by Jewish scientists deprived of work, i.e. access to literature, apparatus, and the possibility of intellectual interchange. The scientists' discussions and their contacts with prominent Western scholars and its debates have been of considerable scholarly as well as political and cultural importance. The Moscow example was followed by scientists and activists in Tbilisi, Kiev, Leningrad, Riga, Odessa, Kishinev, Tiraspol, and Bendery. The character of the seminars was not uniform: the seminar in Tbilisi dealt with Jewish affairs, including topics relating to Georgian Jewry, while the fortnightly seminar in Kiev with the participation of fifteen scientists was similar to that in Moscow.

The Jewish meetings and seminars, the samizdat literature and the widespread teaching of Hebrew[3] constitute a kind of unofficial Jewish national-cultural activity in the U.S.S.R., which once again belies the

[1] See 'The Case of Feliks Dekter', *Nasha strana*, 23 February 1976.

[2] The publication *Jewish Samizdat* of which ten volumes appeared in Jerusalem in 1974–6 reproduces Soviet-Jewish samizdat materials. The contents page of *Exodus* no. 1 and the entire *Exodus* no. 2 was published in an English translation in *Bulletin on Soviet and East European Jewish Affairs*, no. 6, pp. 51–70. *Exodus* no. 4 appeared in English as a supplement to *Soviet Jewish Affairs*, 1; an English translation of *Jews in the U.S.S.R.* no. 1 appeared under the title *I am a Jew: Essays on Jewish Identity in the Soviet Union*, New York, 1973; and *Jews in the U.S.S.R.* no. 2 under the title *Jewishness Rediscovered—Jewish Identity in the Soviet Union*, New York, 1974.

[3] On the eve of Nixon's Moscow visit in June 1974 the number of those studying Hebrew in Moscow was estimated at about 2,000. *Sovetish Heymland* (1976, no. 5, p. 130) maliciously reports about one Goldblat who conducted five *ulpanim* (*sic*!) of five pupils each. Contrary to the journal's insinuation ('he had already forgotten about his own longing to emigrate'), Goldblat arrived in Israel.

official Soviet thesis of lack of interest in such activities among Soviet Jews.

There is little doubt that the development of unofficial Jewish cultural activity and, perhaps, also the slight shifts in official Soviet policies towards Jewish culture and religion, as well as the token changes in Jewish representation in official posts, have been a by-product of the emigration movement. It shows that the debate which has taken place in Jewish circles outside and increasingly also inside the U.S.S.R. as to whether emigration is the only acceptable and realistic solution for Soviet Jews, or whether there also exists the possibility of Jewish culture and religious life in the U.S.S.R., is to a certain extent artificial. The demand for one inevitably creates a demand for the other; and the success of one is bound to lead to the success of the other. In fact, in recent years there has been a departure from the above-mentioned negative position with regard to the feasibility and advisability of Jewish cultural work in the U.S.S.R. In particular, in 1976 several statements by Soviet-Jewish activists emphasized that alongside the struggle for emigration urgent steps are necessary in the field of culture to keep Jewish consciousness alive.[1]

On 25 May 1976 a group of Soviet-Jewish scholars issued an invitation for a Symposium on Jewish Culture to be held in Moscow on 21–3 December 1976. Many Jewish participants from several Soviet towns and a few dozen Jewish scholars from abroad were expected.

The Soviet authorities reacted by raiding the organizers' homes, detaining several of the participants, and by refusing visas to foreign guests invited to attend. These actions met with widespread criticism in the West which, in turn, evoked a concentration of pronouncements on Jewish culture in the Soviet press and radio of a clearly defensive nature.[2] The symposium and the struggle around it highlighted the issue of Jewish culture in the U.S.S.R., demonstrating that the basic Soviet assumptions in this field, the existing facilities, and the prevailing atmosphere are not conducive to the normal development of Jewish culture in the U.S.S.R.

There seems to be a substantial number of Soviet Jews who have lost faith in assimilation as the ultimate solution to the Jewish problem and

[1] A message by 112 Soviet Jews from 11 towns to the Second World Conference on Soviet Jewry in Brussels—*News Bulletin of the Scientists Committee of the Israel Public Council for Soviet Jewry*, no. 81 (15 March 1976); open letter of Jewish activists to the 25th Congress of the C.P.S.U.—*Jews in the U.S.S.R.*, London, vol. v, no. 11 (12 March 1976); policy statement by 75 Jewish activists from 13 towns—ibid., vol. v, no. 17 (30 April 1976); policy statement by 13 activists—ibid., vol. v, no. 29 (23 July 1976); similar statements by the organizers of the Symposium on Jewish Culture—*Insight*, vol. 2, no. 10.

[2] See 'The Moscow "Cultural Symposium" in Perspective', I.J.A. Research Report USSR/77/2, and L. Hirszowicz, 'Jewish Culture in the U.S.S.R', USSR/77/3.

who hold the Jewish heritage in deep respect, but who, for a variety of reasons, would prefer not to leave the U.S.S.R., or in any case not in the foreseeable future. The Soviet authorities will have to decide whether to accept the realities of life in the multinational and ethnocentric Soviet society and keep open for the Jews the option of either leaving the U.S.S.R. or of living there as equal citizens, with their own national identity.

As far as the movement on behalf of Soviet Jewry is concerned, it is abundantly clear that, within the above framework, the Soviet-Jewish problem will remain with us for the foreseeable future.

Chronology of Main Events, May 1972–March 1977

1972

22–30 May	President Nixon visits Moscow for summit talks; Jewish activists detained for the duration of the visit; press conferences during visit dominated by subject of Soviet Jewry
3 July	U.S.S.R. Supreme Soviet Presidium introduces higher education levy on emigrants
16 September	200 Jews submit 16-point memorandum on emigration procedure to U.S.S.R. Supreme Soviet Presidium
19 September	Opening of Supreme Soviet session; demonstration in reception hall against education tax: about 30 Jewish activists arrested
4 October	U.S. Senator Henry Jackson submits amendment, demanding easing of Soviet restrictions on emigration, to Trade Reform Bill; U.S. House of Representatives joins Senate in support of amendment, 7 February 1973
22–3 November	Hunger strike of Jews at Moscow Central Telegraph Office ends in many arrests and short-term imprisonment sentences; demonstration of 5 scientists against the arrests, 27 November

1973

11–14 March	Visit to Moscow of U.S. Treasury Secretary,

	George Schultz; reports that education tax was dropped after his meeting with Brezhnev, 14 March
25 March–11 April	I. Shkolnik, arrested 5 February 1972, tried in Vinnitsa on charges of spying for Israel; his sentence of 10 years in labour camp cut, after appeal, to 7 years, 3 July
27 March–25 April	L.I.C.A. trial in Paris; director of *U.R.S.S.* found guilty of racial defamation and incitement
2–9 May	New York Mayor John Lindsay visits Moscow; discusses Jewish emigration with Kissinger and Shumilin
4–8 May	Dr. Kissinger, on a visit to Moscow, transmits list of 738 Jews repeatedly refused exit visas
10–24 June	Hunger strike of Jewish scientists in protest against refusal of emigration
27 August–1 September	Trial of Petr Yakir and Viktor Krasin; after having confessed, each receives sentence of 3 years' imprisonment and 2 years' exile (reduced on appeal to 16 and 13 months respectively, 29 September)
29 August–7 September	Bitter campaign against Academician Sakharov in the Soviet media
31 August	2 Soviet students leave for course of study at Budapest Rabbinical seminary
27 September	U.S.S.R. ratifies both U.N. covenants on Human Rights without optional clause on complaints about violations
29 September	Austrian government agrees to close Schönau transit camp (for Soviet Jews) after Arab terrorists seize 3 Soviet-Jewish emigrants and an Austrian customs official
6–22 October	Yom Kippur War; U.S.S.R. blames hostilities on Israel and supports Arab States; Soviet Jews express solidarity with Israel
13 November	P. Pinkhasov, a Derbent carpenter, sentenced to 5 years' imprisonment
19 November	Alexander Feldman of Kiev sentenced to $3\frac{1}{2}$ years' imprisonment on charges of malicious

| | hooliganism; sentence evokes widespread protests in U.S.S.R. |
| 21 December | Geneva peace conference opens; foreign ministers of Israel and U.S.S.R., Eban and Gromyko, meet |

1974

14–26 February	Hunger strikes by V. Rubin, V. Galatsky, D. Azbel, and I. Nudel; Azbel and Nudel continue hunger strike until 2 March
27–8 March	Kissinger in Moscow; 24 March, *Pravda* warns U.S. to avoid emigration issue and accuses 'international Zionism' of attempts to disrupt *détente*
15–18 April	50 political prisoners in Perm camps, including 11 Jews, go on hunger strike for improved conditions
18–25 April	Senator Edward Kennedy visits U.S.S.R.; meets leading Jewish activists
16 May	Demonstration outside Lebanon embassy in Moscow to protest at Maalot massacre; protests by Jews from Moscow, Minsk, Tbilisi, and other Soviet cities sent to Brezhnev and Waldheim
16 June	Elections to U.S.S.R. Supreme Soviet: 2 Jews elected to the Chamber of the Union, 4 to the Chamber of Nationalities
25–7 June	Trial in Novosibirsk of Anna and Yury Berkovsky, who applied for emigration; both sentenced to 2 years' imprisonment on charges of speculation
27 June–3 July	Nixon–Brezhnev summit in Moscow; many Jewish activists detained
1 July	Moscow Scientific Seminar, convened by International Committee of Academics for 1–5 July, thwarted by authorities; some Soviet Jewish participants arrested, others, including foreign scientists and correspondents, removed from flat where it was due to take place

22 August	Sylva Zalmanson released from prison camp after serving 4 years of a 10-year sentence for her part in the Leningrad 'hijacking plot'
30 August	Over 100 prisoners in Soviet labour-camps—Zionists, Democrats, and Ukrainian nationalists—appeal to C.S.C.E. in Geneva: respect for human rights ought to be prior condition to understanding with U.S.S.R.
18 October	Publication of exchange of letters between Secretary of State Kissinger and Senator Jackson concerning Soviet assurances on emigration in return for U.S. trade concessions (see 4 October 1972)
11–13 December	Trial in Vinnitsa of Dr. Mikhail Shtern, who is sentenced to 8 years in labour camp for alleged professional misconduct and corruption; arrest and trial arouse world-wide condemnation
18 December	Tass publishes 26 October 1974 letter from Gromyko to Kissinger, and a statement denying Soviet concessions on emigration
20 December	U.S. Trade Reform Bill with Jackson Amendment passed by both Houses of Congress

1975

14 January	U.S.S.R. repudiates 1973 trade agreement with U.S.A.
15 January	Mikhail Tandeytnik appointed president of Moscow Choral Synagogue
24 February	Demonstration in Moscow outside Lenin Library for release of Jewish prisoners; demonstrators M. Nashpits and B. Tsitlionok sentenced to 5 years' internal exile, 31 March
20 March	Report by Telford Taylor and group of prominent American lawyers on failure of secret negotiations to secure release of 'prisoners of Zion'
14 May	Several hundred Jews gather at site of Minsk ghetto; Col. Efim Davidovich denounces antisemitic writers in Byelorussia; 16 May,

	Davidovich stripped of rank and deprived of officer's pension
9 July	U.S.S.R. Supreme Soviet ratifies decree of 23 May which imposes 30 per cent tax on monies sent from abroad, with effect from 1 January 1976; would-be emigrants, and dissidents, are not included among the numerous exemptions from the tax
1 August	C.S.C.E. Final Act adopted in Helsinki; full text published in *Pravda* and *Izvestia*, 13 September; first section on European security published also in other newspapers
25 August	20-year-old Moscow student, Anatoly Malkin, sentenced to 3 years' imprisonment for evading military service
5 September	Jews clash with militia outside Moscow synagogue during New Year's Eve service
21 September	Non-conformist art exhibition held in Moscow; paintings with alleged 'Zionist' content banned by authorities
10 October	Parliamentarians from 12 West European countries form a committee in support of Soviet-Jewish emigration
1 December	Felix Dekter, a translator and co-editor of the samizdat journals *Jews in the U.S.S.R.* and *Tarbut*, expelled from Writers' Union
15–24 December	British Chief Rabbi, Dr. Immanuel Jakobovits, and Executive Director of his office, M. Davis, visit U.S.S.R. at invitation of Soviet authorities
1976	
29 January	Council of Europe approves unanimously recommendation that member states intercede with Soviet government on behalf of Soviet Jews
17–19 February	Second World Conference of Jewish Communities on Soviet Jewry meets in Brussels
24 February–5 March	25th C.P.S.U. Congress; one Jew is elected to the C.C., two as candidate members of C.C., and two to the Central Auditing Commission

24 April	Second World War veteran, Colonel Efim Davidovich, 54, dies of heart failure in Minsk; death ascribed to harassment by authorities
1 May	Moscow Rabbi Fishman and Adolf Shayevich, a Soviet-Jewish student at the Budapest Rabbinical Seminary, arrive in New York with a delegation of Soviet clergymen for 10-day visit
12 May	Public Group to Promote Soviet implementation of Helsinki Final Act formed in Moscow, with participation of Jewish activists
15 June	Regulations go into effect substantially raising duty on parcels sent from abroad to Soviet citizens
8 July	A memorial unveiled at Babi Yar near Kiev does not specifically mention Jewish victims of Nazi massacre
18–25 October	Protest sit-ins and demonstrations by Jewish activists in Moscow; authorities seek recourse to physical violence and arrests
17 December	Vilnius Jewish People's Theatre celebrates 20th anniversary in the Great Hall of the local Trade Unions' Palace of Culture
21–3 December	Scheduled Moscow symposium on Jewish culture thwarted by authorities; only small number of planned meetings take place

1977

22 January	Anti-Zionist 'documentary' 'Traders in Souls' shown on Soviet T.V. central programme; repeated 11 March
15 March	Anatoly Shcharansky arrested following publication in *Izvestia* (4 March) of S. Lipavsky 'letter' accusing leading Jewish activists of espionage

Epilogue

LIONEL KOCHAN

Though the intent of this book has been historical, it must inevitably conclude with the question of the future. It is all too clear that a 'Jewish question' remains in the Soviet Union. It is indeed not difficult to reconstruct the image of Soviet Jewry as it appears to the Soviet leadership. Here is a body of only some two and one-half to three million people. Yet, through family ties, certain national and religious affiliations, and some remaining common ethnic bonds it has a focus of sympathy located not only outside the Soviet Union but also among communities and organizations perhaps unsympathetic or even hostile to Soviet interests. The very existence of this body produces tension within the Soviet Union and offers opportunities of exploitation for propagandist purposes in the world outside. Moreover, since attempts at enforced assimilation, repression and the creation, in Biro-Bidzhan, of an autonomous Jewish area, have all failed, there seems to be no readily available solution feasible within the Soviet Union.

The fact is that Soviet treatment of the nationality question has been bedevilled by an inner conflict: is it to create opportunities for nations and national minorities to express themselves in condition of cultural freedom; or is it to suppress national differences as obsolete remnants of a reactionary past in the interests of a unified and homogeneous communist society? The effect of this contradictory policy has been more deleterious in the case of the Jews than in that of other nationalities within the Soviet Union. It has revealed an altogether anomalous position in that a Russian Jew, acknowledged as such in his passport, lacks the territory and the means of cultural self-expression available to his fellow citizens.

From the point of view of the Soviet Government, no less than that of the Soviet Jew, this is an inherently unhealthy and unstable situation. How long may it be expected to continue? What of the future? Clearly, the Russo-Jewish future will be determined by the two factors involved—the Jews and the government. Moreover, the fate of Soviet Jewry has also become a matter of concern to world Jewry and to Western public opinion as a problem in human rights. The Jews have 'failed' to become a nation; they have also 'failed' to assimilate. Indeed, the experience of the war, the period of Stalinist antisemitism, and the increased ethnic tensions of the post-war period have all sharpened the consciousness of Jewish identity, as was predictable. To this must be added the spiritual influence and national pride arising from the establishment of the State of Israel—to say nothing of the Six-Day War. Continuing anti-Israel propaganda must also sharpen the sense of Jewish identity. This betokens no lack of loyalty to the Soviet Union but it does testify to an enduring self-identification as Jews, all the more remarkable in a body of people denied virtually all contact with the world of Jewry.

Does this perhaps suggest that the Soviet regime might consider itself better advised to abandon its support for assimilation and strike out on some alternative course? The regime wavers between suppression and recognition of the Jewish nationality. Can this uncertainty be maintained in the long run? Assuming that no recrudescence of virulent repression takes place, it is possible to discern two choices before the Soviet Government. It may decide to offer the Jews the facilities enjoyed by a nation that lacks a territory; or it may contrive to treat them as a special case and offer the possibility of mass emigration which has hitherto only been able to proceed amidst uncertainty, harassment and worse. What will eventually happen is of course so dependent on variable and unforseeable factors that no prognosis is possible. But it should be possible to suggest some likely consequences. If the government were to follow the first approach and allow Russian Jewry freedom of self-expression in an officially encouraged climate of tolerance, it would certainly enjoy the gratitude of Soviet Jewry and reinforce its allegiance. Such a policy would also enable the Soviet Union to offer a far more successful resistance to its foreign critics, both inside and outside the Communist movement. It would benefit both internally and externally, for there is also a liberal intelligentsia inside the Soviet Union that has in some degree made the treatment of Soviet Jewry a criterion of its sympathy for the Soviet regime.

If the Soviet regime continues to exercise a policy of discrimination in relation to Russian Jewry, then it cannot but perpetuate the vicious circle that characterizes the present situation. That internal contradiction whereby, on the one hand, the Jews are recognized as a nationality, and their internal passport marked as such, whereas they continue to lack the appurtenances of a nationality, both stimulates and represses the sense of

Jewish identity; and this latter must also stimulate the quest for the meaning of that identity. But any positive 'nationalist' content given to that identity must, in the present context of the Jewish problem, exacerbate in its turn Soviet measures of discrimination. In these circumstances might the Soviet Government not be better advised to offer increased opportunities for emigration to those Jews so inclined? This would meet the needs of those Jews who are anxious to maintain their Jewish identity. The demand for opportunity to maintain a Jewish differentiation in Russia would thus diminish and perhaps, in time, completely disappear. Such a policy need not necessarily wait on the solution of the Middle East conflict, though such a solution would immeasurably improve the atmosphere surrounding emigration, and, by the same token, also make a significant contribution to the alleviation of the overall problem.

Index